The Victorian City

Images and Realities

Edited by

H. J. Dyos and Michael Wolff

Routledge & Kegan Paul   London and Boston

Victorian City

Images and Realities

Volume 2

First published 1973
by Routledge & Kegan Paul Ltd
Broadway House, 68-74 Carter Lane,
London EC4V 5EL and
9 Park Street, Boston, Mass. 02108, U.S.A.
Made and printed in Great Britain by
William Clowes & Sons, Limited
London, Beccles and Colchester
Set in Monotype Modern Extended Series No. 7
with Gloucester Extra Condensed
Designed by Joseph J. Hart

ISBN 0 7100 7374 7 (Vol. 1)
ISBN 0 7100 7383 6 (Vol. 2)
ISBN 0 7100 7384 4 (The set)
Library of Congress Catalog Card No. 73–76088

Contents

Volume Two

V Ideas in the Air

Contents

Illustrations

Volume Two

Illustrations

Maps

V Ideas in the Air

18   The Awful Sublimity of the Victorian City

Its aesthetic and architectural origins

Nicholas Taylor

The eighteenth century was perhaps not wholly an Age of Reason. It was pre-eminently an age of rationalization, of attempts to define in words those things in human perception which by the very nature of their subjectivity are virtually indefinable. In architecture and landscape, as much as in philosophy or literature, it was the age which established the vocabulary of categories within which academic and critical argument could henceforth be conducted—the images through which men sought to discern common themes in uncertain reality. Thus the ways in which the Victorians argued about the environment of their cities, even about such distinctively nineteenth-century inventions as railways and gas-works and philanthropic tenements, were rooted in the categories defined by eighteenth-century authors such as Winckelmann, Walpole, Pope, and Burke. These authors remained so influential that there is some danger of over-stressing their true role. They were not themselves inventors, architects on the ground, like Soufflot or Vanbrugh or Kent. They were, to repeat, rationalizers, filing into critical pigeon-holes the actual works of art which these architects had already built. And it is those works of art, the reality, which have sometimes tended to be forgotten when the literary images have become colloquial clichés.

There were three prime categories which the eighteenth-century rationalizers discerned in the environment: the Beautiful, the Picturesque, and the Sublime.[1]

The Beautiful had been the overriding ideal of architecture since Brunelleschi. It was simply that of creating buildings which express us, not as we are, but as we could be: an architecture of perfect proportions, an anthropometric hierarchy of

431

measurements based on those of an ideal man. The major countries of the Continent developed a richer, more emotional style, the Baroque, in which the Beautiful was distorted spatially and supercharged ornamentally. England preferred chastity. Her architects, although adopting the principles of the Renaissance very late, were paradoxically fertile in constantly refreshing those principles in their pure form. The Palladianism of Inigo Jones was followed by the crisp Dutch boxes of Hugh May and Wren, and the Neo-Palladianism of Colen Campbell and Lord Burlington was followed by the Neo-Classicism of Robert Adam and James Wyatt. The Beautiful made an unexpected return to supremacy in the Italianate palazzi of Sir Charles Barry, beginning with the Neo-Quattrocento of the Travellers' Club in 1829. This style was favoured in Victorian cities up to 1870, especially for the 'aristocracy of commerce', the banks and insurance companies (recalling the Medici), where it was possible to conform to strict classical proportions without sacrificing much convenience. The National Provincial Bank's architect, John Gibson, a Barry pupil, was fished out of retirement in 1892 to receive the R.I.B.A. Royal Gold Medal just at the time when classical Beauty was being rediscovered yet again in the Neo-Georgian of Sir Reginald Blomfield and Ernest Newton, which in turn led quickly to the Edwardian Neo-Grec of Sir Charles Reilly and S. D. Adshead.[2]

Amidst the haranguing of Gothic propagandists, it is easy to forget that the vast majority of the buildings in the business centres of the great Victorian cities (except perhaps in Birmingham) remained predominantly Renaissance in inspiration, often quietly and precisely so. The particular image this conveyed was brought out very clearly by Lord Palmerston in his objections to Scott's Gothic design for the Foreign Office, in which he referred constantly to Italianate architecture as being 'modern' and letting in sufficient light. The Renaissance symbolized efficiency, clarity, economy, civic administration, and secular probity—the 'confidence' which in a quiet way was the basis of London's mercantile pre-eminence. Furthermore, the central suburbs of London, Glasgow, Edinburgh, and Newcastle continued to use the ideas of the Beautiful, first expressed by Inigo Jones in his 'piazza' at Covent Garden in 1630, right down to the 1880s. The squares of Bayswater (Sancton Wood's Lancaster Gate, for example) date from the 1850s; Smith's Charity Estate in Kensington dates mainly from the early 1860s (Sir Charles Freake's Onslow Square is the centre-piece); and the big terraces around Earls Court went on into the eighties. The westernmost classical crescent, Philbeach Gardens, was just going up in 1884 when the contrasting red-brick late-Victorian Gothic church of St Cuthbert was being planted in its midst. The ideas of the aristocratic town-house remained remarkably constant from the 1630s right through to 1886, when Soames Forsyte made the decision to abandon Bayswater.

The Picturesque was by contrast a new image for the eighteenth century, posing in direct opposition to the cerebral precision of Beauty the emotional pleasures of evocative association. Surprisingly, the first stirrings seem to have come from the scientifically-trained Wren. That most scientific of his buildings, the Royal Observatory at Greenwich, was built in 1670—'a little for pompe'—as a turreted hilltop pavilion, totally disregarding the symmetry of the new royal palace and its park below, and revelling in its accidental irregularity. When requested, Wren had no hesitation in adopting Gothic for his City churches and he delighted in such pretty silhouettes as St Dunstan-in-the-East's flying 'crown' which recalled the medieval skyline. The beginning of mainstream Picturesque can be fixed, as Pevsner has shown, precisely at 1709, when Wren's colleague at Greenwich, Sir John Vanbrugh, pleaded for the preservation of the old Woodstock Manor as a ruin in Blenheim Park. Buildings of distant times, he said, 'move more lively and pleasing Reactions on the Persons who have Inhabited them; or the Remarkable things which have been transacted in them; or the extraordinary Occasions of Erecting them.' The Picturesque was, in fact, largely an appeal to the landed aristocracy's sense of heredity and of ownership, particularly now that it was found pleasing actually to *possess* one's park by riding or promenading through it, like Mr and Mrs Andrews in Gainsborough's picture.

By the time of Nash's partnership with Humphry Repton in 1796–1803, the Picturesque had become highly developed as an art of suburban illusion, visually merging the copses close to the house with other wooded land lying beyond, as at Horace Walpole's Gothick castle of Strawberry Hill. In Nash's and Repton's jointly-designed villas at Southgate, Dulwich, Kingston, and Bromley, and in Nash's at Surbiton, it was possible for the city merchant to look from his drawing-room window onto a landscape which at least appeared to be all his. Meanwhile, the composing of landscape pictures with pleasing associations had spread to estate buildings. Nash designed some delicious thatched evocations of rusticity for the gamekeepers and gardeners of country estates; and eventually at Blaise Hamlet, near Bristol, in 1811, he sited nine of these medievalizing moppets to form a miniature village, the grandmother of the garden city. He carried the idea much further in Park Villages East and West at Regent's Park, where irregular Italianate villas of the kind he had invented at Cronkhill, Salop (1802), were disposed along leafy winding lanes. Cronkhill was the agent's house for the Attingham estate, and it is significant that agents' houses and vicarages, built for the two middle-class officials of the country house, became the principal means for translating the feudal cottages of Blaise Hamlet into the middle-class suburbs of the Victorian city.

The Picturesque was *par excellence* the image of the Victorian suburb, of Edgbaston and Jesmond, of Sefton Park and St John's Wood. Sir John Summerson discovered that the first plans for the Eyre estate at St John's Wood in 1795 contained the earliest examples yet known of that quintessentially Picturesque compromise, the semi-detached house. The Picturesque was thus an anti-civic aesthetic, a rejection of a collectivized palace front, in which ten and twenty houses had been treated as a single unit around a central pediment (as in John Wood's Queen Square, Bath, or Thomas Leverton's Bedford Square, Bloomsbury). It preached instead the gospel of individuality, of Whig freedoms in a picturesque landscape and was extended in the era of Reform to broad suburban acres, too. *Rus in urbe* meant every man possessing his own distinctively composed villa amidst his own shrubbery. Such progressive individualism eventually attacked the heart of the urban fabric in the terracotta mansions by Sir Ernest George & Peto in Harrington and Collingham Gardens, Kensington, from 1881. In Bedford Park, begun in 1875 by E. W. Godwin and continued from 1876 by Norman Shaw, such freedoms were extended to a complete garden suburb community.

These lines of descent in the Beautiful and the Picturesque are well enough known: the Beautiful through Geoffrey Scott's cleverly destructive book *The Architecture of Humanism: A study in the history of taste*, published in 1914; the Picturesque through Christopher Hussey's well-documented and semi-autobiographical essay of that name of 1927. Not so the Sublime: it has had a raw deal.[3] The visual expression of the Sublime, particularly in architecture and landscape, has tended to be treated merely as an isolated phenomenon of certain eighteenth-century artists; whereas I believe it to be as fundamental to the nineteenth-century city as the Beautiful and the Picturesque, and of increasing importance as industrial growth quickened.

In fact, the Sublime was functionally the aesthetic of just those vast new purposes which upset the proportions of Beauty and the prettiness of Picturesque: warehouses, factories, viaducts, gas-works, lunatic asylums, country gaols, railway termini, dark tunnels. Furthermore, it became emotionally the aesthetic of those vast new passions which upset no less the nicely proportioned and the pretty: the haranguing of the Evangelical preacher; the ecstasy of the Anglo-Catholic Mass; the scientific wonder of panoramas and exhibition halls; the traveller's thrill in catching trains and climbing mountains; the capitalist's pride in the hum of mass production and the hubbub of the market. Historians have tended to neglect these dominant emotional forces of mid-century, concentrating instead on the minority of critics (Dickens, Arnold, Ruskin, Morris), whose influence turned the younger generation after 1870 away from the city—away from all those things which had once seemed Sublime but now seemed merely ugly.

Yet if we are to get to grips with Victorian 'ugliness', with those lunatic asylums and yawning tunnels, we must be prepared to accept that the vast majority of intelligent men did not regard them at the time as being expressions of ugliness, but as being exciting and 'awful' in the true sense of the word. It is my contention that this amounted, consciously or unconsciously, to an expression of the Sublime in the very fabric of the Victorian city. I propose to list briefly the visual qualities of the Sublime as defined by its chief rationalizer, Edmund Burke, in that brilliant book of his youth, *A Philosophical Enquiry into the Origin of our Ideas of the Sublime and Beautiful* (1757), and then to illustrate these qualities in terms of the architecture and landscape he was trying to explain, and of the kind of descendants they had in the Victorian city.

'Whatever is fitted in any sort to excite the ideas of pain, and danger, that is to say, whatever is in any sort terrible, or is conversant about terrible objects, or operates in a manner analogous to terror, is a source of the *sublime*; that is, it is productive of the strongest emotion which the mind is capable of feeling.' Thus Burke defined the causes of Sublimity in the first part of his book, which deals with the emotional background to aesthetic experience. In the second part he deals solely with the qualities of the Sublime, and in twenty-two sections lists and describes them.

Astonishment: '. . . that state of the soul, in which all its motions are suspended, with some degree of horror. In this case the mind is so entirely filled with its object, that it cannot entertain any other, nor by consequence reason on that object which employs it. Hence arises the great power of the sublime, that far from being produced by them, it anticipates our reasonings, and hurries us on by an irresistible force.'

Terror: 'Whatever therefore is terrible, with regard to sight, is sublime, too, whether this cause of terror be endued with greatness of dimensions or not . . . And to things of great dimensions, if we annex an adventitious idea of terror, they become without comparison greater.'

Obscurity: 'To make anything very terrible, obscurity seems in general to be necessary. When we know the full extent of any danger, when we can accustom our eyes to it, a great deal of the apprehension vanishes . . . Almost all the heathen temples were dark . . .'

Power: '. . . strength, violence, pain and terror, are ideas that rush in upon the mind together . . . power derives all its sublimity from the terror with which it is generally accompanied . . .'

Privation: 'All *general* privations are great, because they are all terrible; *Vacuity, Darkness, Solitude* and *Silence* . . .'

Vastness: 'Greatness of dimension, is a powerful cause of the sublime . . . either in length, height or depth. Of these the length strikes least . . . I am apt to imagine likewise, that height is less grand than depth . . . A perpendicular has more force in forming the sublime, than an inclined plane; and the effects of a rugged and broken surface seem stronger than where it is smooth and polished . . . the last extreme of littleness is in some measure sublime likewise . . .'

Infinity: 'But the eye not being able to perceive the bounds of many things, they seem to be infinite, and they produce the same effects as if they were really so . . .'

Succession and Uniformity: '. . . that uninterrupted progression, which alone can stamp on bounded objects the character of infinity. It is in this kind of artificial infinity, I believe, we ought to look for the cause why a rotund has such a noble effect . . . On the same principles of succession and uniformity, the grand appearance of the ancient heathen temples, which were generally oblong forms, with a range of uniform pillars on every side, will be easily accounted for. From the same cause also may be derived the grand effect of the aisles in many of our old cathedrals.'

Magnitude in Building: 'To the sublime in building, greatness of dimension seems requisite . . . [but] no greatness in the manner can effectually compensate for the want of proper dimensions . . . Designs that are vast only by their dimensions are always a sign of a common and low imagination.'

Difficulty: 'When any work seems to have required immense force and labour to effect it, the idea is grand. Stonehenge, neither for disposition nor comment, has any thing admirable; but those huge rude masses of stone, set on end, and piled each on other, turn the mind on the immense force necessary for such a work.'

Magnificence: 'A great profusion of things which are splendid or valuable in themselves, is *magnificent*. The starry heaven . . . never fails to excite an idea of grandeur . . . The apparent disorder augments the grandeur, for the appearance of care is highly contrary to our ideas of magnificence . . .'

Light: 'Mere light is too common . . . But such a light as that of the sun, immediately exerted on the eye, as it overpowers the sense, is a very great idea . . . A quick transition from light to darkness, or from darkness to light, has yet a greater effect . . .'

Colour: 'An immense mountain covered with a shining green turf, is nothing in this respect, to one dark and gloomy; the cloudy sky is more grand than the blue; and night more sublime and solemn than day. Therefore . . . in buildings, when the highest degree of the sublime is intended, the materials and ornaments ought . . . to be . . . of sad and fuscous colours, as black, or brown, or deep purple, and the like.'

Burke is seen here filing into appropriate categories for criticism the raw materials of a new sensibility which had already appeared among artists. The key figure had been Sir John Vanbrugh. He started life, it must be remembered, as a soldier who had spent part of his sixteen years' active service (1686–1702) shut up in French prisons, principally the Bastille. We can only guess at what his European travels must have been, at the knowledge of Baroque palaces which he poured out instantaneously in his first architectural work, Castle Howard (1702–14)—the epitome of Burke's 'Magnificence'. What we recognize above all is his romantic enjoyment of fortification, inspired perhaps by Vauban, expressed at Castle Howard in a towered and battlemented bailey wall, pierced by yawning gates ('Terror'). At Seaton Delaval (1718–29), for a bluff admiral on the Northumberland cliffs, he re-interpreted the castle keep in terms of Baroque 'Power'. Even an apparently Palladian house of 1711–14 at King's Weston, Bristol, he topped off with an utterly unexpected arcade of top-heavy chimneystacks ('Astonishment'). For his own home at Greenwich in 1719 he secured the hilltop next to Wren's Observatory and there created an entirely original villa-castle in a deep purplish brick ('Gloomy Colour'). Meanwhile his previous villa of 1708 at Claremont, Surrey, he vastly enlarged from 1719 for its new owner, the Duke of Newcastle, as a 'rectangular Colosseum', with endless round arches as sublimely repetitive as those of a Norman cathedral nave ('Succession and Uniformity'). Similar round-arched repetition marked his short-lived palace for 'Bubb' Dodington at Eastbury Park, Dorset (*c.* 1718–23). From 1717 he superintended the buildings of the Woolwich Arsenal, notably the gun factory, known as Dial Square, which has as its centrepiece a cavernous archway with radiating voussoirs which provides an astonishing foretaste of the Victorian railway tunnel. Almost certainly he also designed the barracks at Berwick-on-Tweed and the Great Store at Chatham, which established stylistic paradigms for barracks, gaols, hospitals, and warehouses.

Such events in 1710 and 1720 may seem remote from the Victorian city, but the influence of Vanbrugh, so unwelcome to his immediate successors, the Palladians, was not felt again until the late eighteenth century. Sir Uvedale Price, author of the famous *Essay on the Picturesque as compared with the Sublime and the Beautiful* (1794–8), wrote another entitled *On Architecture and Buildings*, which was published in 1810. In this, as Boulton says, he 'thoroughly analysed Vanbrugh's art—and it was Burke who provided Price with his standards and key-terms.' Price appreciated the overtly Gothic elements in Vanbrugh and suggested that Gothic ornament too might be sublime. Vanbrugh, he said, had at Blenheim combined Grecian 'beauty and magnificence', Gothic 'picturesqueness', and 'the massive grandeur of a castle'—the Beautiful, the Picturesque, and the Sublime, no less.

The rich variety of Vanbrugh's work was not fully appreciated until after 1800, when architects had to grapple with the new demands of industry and commerce. In his Royal Academy lectures for 1809, Sir John Soane called Vanbrugh 'the Shakespeare of Architects', an interesting phrase in view of the central importance of Shakespeare (with Milton and the Bible) in introducing the idea of the Sublime into literary criticism. In particular Soane referred to Vanbrugh's 'Boldness of Fancy, unlimited Variety and Discrimination of Character' ('character' being a crucial problem when it came to interpreting architecturally the novelty of industrial structures).[4] As Sir John Summerson first suggested, Vanbrugh's 'variety in heights as well as in projections' must have inspired Soane's personal style which reached its climax at Dulwich Art Gallery (1811–14)[5]—the exemplification of 'Obscurity' externally and 'Light' internally—but he adopted similar spatial principles from 1788 at the Bank of England. There the Beauty of the Grecian detailing in the banking-halls was virtually omitted in the central Rotunda (1796), where the few incised lines on the dome merely exaggerated its womb-like immensity and foreshadowed the spider's web of ironwork similarly stressing immensity, of such Victorian rotundas as the City of London Coal Exchange by J. B. Bunning (1844–9), the oval Leeds Corn Exchange by Cuthbert Brodrick (1860), or that academic market-place, the British Museum Reading Room by Sydney Smirke (1852–7). Vanbrugh's 'Succession and Uniformity' of round arches at Claremont was revived by Soane in the Infirmary at Chelsea Hospital (1809) and in Bank Buildings, opposite the Bank of England (1801–10).

The other Sublime influence on Soane was not native English, but international: the neo-classicist fascination with the ruins of primitive antiquity, particularly of Greek Doric temples (as at Paestum) and Roman baths (such as Caracalla's). Here the crucial inspiration was that of G. B. Piranesi, stage designer and architectural engraver, who for the benefit of those on the Grand Tour produced souvenirs of Imperial ruin in which 'Power', 'Vastness', 'Light and Darkness', and at times 'Terror' are paramount. The nightmare images of his *Carceri d'Invenzione* (c. 1745)—a series of imaginary dungeons—were reflected in reality remarkably quickly, in that most terrifying of civic amenities, the prison. Newgate Gaol, rebuilt in 1770–82 by Soane's master, George Dance the Younger, had a Governor's House with row upon row of round arches in a kind of Vanbrugh revival ('Succession and Uniformity' again), instead of the Palladian hierarchy of basement, piano nobile, and attic. In his Council Chamber at London's Guildhall (1777) Dance domesticated Piranesi's

Roman rotundas to make a toplit room foreshadowing Soane's at the Bank.

But the Sublime of Vanbrugh and of Piranesi was never easily accommodated to the straight frontages of city streets. Its wholesale adoption came in those explosive new uses which initially stood outside, in the country.[6] Burke was clearly aware of the Sublime in nature, and in patronizing James Barry he encouraged the kind of epic canvases which had their climax (via Fuseli and Blake) in the megalomaniac fantasies of John Martin, of which Ruskin remarked in *Modern Painters*, 'If black and red were not productive of the sublime, what would become of the pictures of Martin?'[7] What is significant for the environment of the Victorian city is that this kind of Sublimity was very quickly discerned also in those strange new crops which industry harvested from nature in hitherto remote valleys. John Martin's painting *Pande-monium* (1841) was first bought by a railway engineer, Benjamin Hick of Bolton: but nearly forty years earlier, Philip James de Loutherbourg had exhibited paintings of Abraham Darby's ironworks at Coalbrookdale, in which the rip-snorting fury of the blast furnace was depicted with no less Sublimity than de Loutherbourg had previously lavished on Rhineland fortresses and the temples at Tivoli.

About 1789 that remarkable painter of the Sublime, Joseph Wright of Derby, thought it worth while to paint the brick mill, with its solid mass punctuated by repetitive windows, of Sir Richard Arkwright's Cromford Mill in Derbyshire. Arkwright himself had just had built, on the hillside above the mill, a castle for himself, Willersley (1782–8), designed by a London architect, William Thomas, in a manner clearly derived from the castles in Scotland of Robert Adam, himself influenced greatly by Vanbrugh. This Sublime unity of mill and castle was repeated at Merthyr Tydfil in the Crawshay family's Cyfarthfa Ironworks and in their overlooking castle of *c.* 1825, designed by Robert Lugar. The Douglas-Pennant family's Bethesda slate quarries are also associated with their powerful Neo-Norman castle at Penrhyn by Thomas Hopper (*c.* 1827–47), where the extravagant, almost Moorish interior includes a bed set on a single slab of slate intended to arouse 'Astonishment' at such a technical achievement, but also perhaps a feeling of 'Privation', as Queen Victoria is said to have refused to sleep on it. At this stage industry was still seen largely as just a specially fruitful rural crop, its sublime enormities of machinery, such as the Great Laxey Wheel on the Isle of Man, appearing merely as outsize follies on their owners' estates.

It was the rapid speed-up of communication and the great build-up of the volume of traffic which brought the Sublime to the cities. Speed was first sensed not on the steam railway but on the horse-powered stage-coach: John Nash's Archway at Highgate built in 1813 to span the road to the North, anticipated the railway viaducts by thirty or forty years. In this Nash was in turn indebted to the aqueducts of Thomas Telford, which carried the other weighty new arm of communication, the canal. At Chirk in Flintshire, Telford's stone aqueduct of 1792 was soon perfectly counterpointed by the much higher railway viaduct of 1857 by John Robertson, the two great sequences setting up a colossal Roman rhythm ('Succession and Uniformity', the hallmarks of mass production and mass consumption) across a quiet valley. As John Britton, the antiquary, remarked in his descriptive account of the engineering triumphs displayed in J. C. Bourne's *Drawings of the London and Birmingham Railway* (1838–9), 'These are in many instances so astounding as to equal, or even surpass, the fabled relations of the works of the Cyclops and Giants of romance.' The Euston Arch's Doric grandeur Britton justified as giving 'evidence of belonging to . . . a vast and gigantic work'. Bourne followed up with a second series of lithographs giving *The History and Description of the Great Western Railway* (1846), including Brunel's grand Wharncliffe Viaduct.

The most remarkable of Bourne's pictures in the two series are those of the two great tunnels, Kilsby on the London & Birmingham and Box on the Great Western, which, in their dramatic contrast of 'Light and Darkness', superbly exemplify Burke's spatial principles. The huge working shafts at Kilsby have an astonishingly close relationship aesthetically to Piranesi and particularly to the great toplit halls by Soane and Bunning and Brodrick. What also made these tunnels overwhelmingly Sublime was Burke's principle of 'Difficulty'—the evidence they gave of immense labour and danger in building them. Another striking example of this was the floating and raising of the iron tubes for the two great railway bridges across the Menai Straits (1845–50) and at Conway (1845–9); and here the constructional genius of Robert Stephenson was complemented by the visual genius of the architect Francis Thompson.

Thompson was perhaps the first to realize how the symbolism of Speed in the endless arches of the viaducts could be brought, in line with Burke's idea of 'Infinity', into the station buildings themselves. His first attempt at this on the largest scale was the Trijunct Station at Derby (1840); his finest was the still surviving General Station at Chester (1844–8), where Thompson adopted a formula of round-headed Italianate arcades which he had no doubt derived from the work of Percier & Fontaine in Paris—not just that paragon of 'Infinity', the Rue de Rivoli (1802–55), but also their various designs for markets, which Charles Fowler had in turn imitated in his markets in London (Covent Garden and Hungerford Markets, 1831–3) and Exeter (Lower Market, 1835–6).[8] Fowler and Thompson between them established the Sublime style of the railway-station shed, which was further developed at Newcastle (1846–50) by John Dobson, at King's Cross (1851–2) by Lewis Cubitt, and at Paddington (1852–4) by Brunel (with Matthew Digby Wyatt and Owen Jones). It was the sheer length of these sheds that was totally novel. The endless pillars of Newcastle's triple spans disappeared into 'Infinity' round a steep bend (as Thomas Prosser's York of 1873–7 was to do even more Sublimely a generation later). The York Road flank of King's Cross had a façade of two-storey offices and stores over thirty-five bays long, without a break. Paddington's two 'transepts' (originally for turning the engines) actually accentuated the endless arcading of the rest—for these are 'internal' transepts, spatially transparent, unlike the angular barriers of the external transepts which Burke criticized in churches. Digby Wyatt and Owen Jones also assisted Sir Joseph Paxton in creating the Sublime aesthetic of vast uniform iron-framed glasshouses in the Crystal Palace. Eventually, in the train-shed at St Pancras of 1865–8, designed by W. H. Barlow and detailed by R. M. Ordish (who also did Albert Bridge over the Thames in 1873), the logical finale was reached of the single vast cavern. Barlow justified this on somewhat specious functional grounds of flexibility, but the real aim of St Pancras was to impress London with the new-found might of the Midlands; and this Scott wonderfully achieved in his hotel, with its endless succession of Derbyshire granite columns and Nottingham bricks—with the entrance arch, spanned by the cast-iron bridge of the main hotel corridor, giving a supreme opportunity of sublime 'Astonishment' to the traveller discovering the vast train-shed beyond.

In 1826 the Prussian court architect, Karl Friedrich von Schinkel, paid a visit to England to collect ideas for designing the Altes Museum in Berlin.[9] Schinkel was no doubt influenced by Smirke's British Museum colonnade (not built until 1842–7 but already designed in 1823), but he looked principally not at museums but at industry. His strict Prussian mind, which found Bath 'dull and steeped in English triviality', was thrilled by the Sublimity of Northern machinery. In particular he was thrilled by the sheer immensity of industrial objects in the landscape—not just the viaducts of Telford, but the actual factory chimneys. Sheffield had 'hundreds of high obelisks' and at Dudley 'The thousands of smoking obelisks are a grandiose sight.' At Birmingham his hotel rooms 'offered a good view over the town. You may call this view "Egyptian" because of the many obelisks and pyramids of the factory chimneys.' This reference to Egypt, and its rather terrifying architecture, was actually made explicit, twelve years after Schinkel's visit, in a large-scale factory, Marshall's Mills at Leeds (1838–40), by Ignatius Bonomi—sublimely repetitive in its brick-arched bays within and awfully obscure in its giant Egyptian portals without. About the only industrial building which Schinkel did admire for its 'great refinement of construction', was the newly opened gas-works beside the Waters of Leith at Edinburgh, over which he was conducted by its architect, William Burn, Scotland's leading country-house designer of the generation 1825–50. And a very remarkable group of buildings they were: contemporaries called the conical roofs of the gas-holders 'Moorish', though they were more like giant dovecotes. Sir Walter Scott himself was the gas-company's principal promoter. It was a wonderfully explicit example of the way in which new functions demanded new architectural responses, neither beautifully Palladian nor picturesquely Gothick but Sublimely abstract.

The other things which excited Schinkel were warehouses. Those for Manchester cotton he liked simply for their barbaric and unselfconscious hugeness—'seven to eight storeys high and as big as the Royal Palace in Berlin'; those for London Dock (1800–5) because they were 'tremendous warehouses and vaults with stone stairs and double iron doors, iron railways for transporting the goods, and iron cranes . . .' The London Dock architect, Daniel Asher Alexander, had devised a logical rhythm for storage in the endless repetition down the quayside of recessed bays containing hoists; and it was these hoists in their recesses which were consciously dramatized

440

by Gustave Doré in his picture of 'Warehousing in London', published in *London: A Pilgrimage* in 1872. Alexander's ideas were developed superbly by Thomas Telford and Philip Hardwick at St Katharine Dock (1825–8), next to the Tower of London, and by Jesse Hartley in his Stanley and Albert Docks in Liverpool (1825–6 and 1841–5). Hartley's vast stretches of bare brickwork, supported by stocky Doric columns of iron and surrounded by quayside furniture of granite, are the epitome of the classical Sublime. Not surprisingly such buildings provoked a revival of the Baroque of Vanbrugh, on a palatial scale, by Sir John Rennie in the King William Victualling Yard at Stonehouse, Plymouth (1825–36), and in miniature in the astonishing substructure of J. M. Clark's Customs House at Ipswich (1844).

By the 1840s these dockland refinements began to penetrate the inarticulate cliffs of Manchester, and local architects, led by Edward Walters and J. E. Gregan, began to develop appropriate grandiose rhythms for cotton, expressing the highly flexible layout internally of salerooms, stores, and counting-houses and admitting floods of even light by which raw cotton could be inspected.[10] Walters had studied the mannerist palaces of Alessi at Genoa, and he appreciated the bold profiling needed to survive in a sooty atmosphere. At the Schwabe warehouse in Mosley Street (1845), he established a slow-quick-quick-slow rhythm of windows and hoists, all in exposed red brick; and at the Brown warehouse in Portland Street (1851–2), he powerfully framed his large-scale repetition by means of giant rusticated pilasters at each corner, double-height arches to ground floor and basement, and an enormous cornice concealing the toplit attic. Gregan, at his warehouse of 1850 on the corner of Portland and Parker Streets, dispensed entirely with the palazzo hierarchy, merely picking out alternate windows under pediments to give a flickering surface relief to uniformity. Similar qualities can be seen in Lockwood & Mawson's buildings at Saltaire, not merely in the alpaca and mohair mill of 1851–3, for which Sir William Fairbairn was engineer, but also in the tall houses of the famous model village, where these Bradford architects devised a highly effective stripped-down Sublime in sheer brick and round arches. Pevsner criticizes Saltaire for 'monotony', but that is the natural reaction of those who prefer the cosier Picturesque to this noble severity. The woollen warehouses of Bradford itself, many of them designed by Lockwood & Mawson, were often commissioned by German families (Behrens, Delius, Kassapian) who had settled in the town and must have specially appreciated the disciplined qualities of the Sublime. These qualities have stamped the Victorian cities of the North with that peculiarly tough grandeur which Southerners are woefully prone to despise as murk. Brodrick's buildings at Leeds are its apogee.

One of the Southerners who did appreciate these qualities was Walters' first cousin, Edward I'Anson Jnr, the leading City of London architect of the fifties and sixties. His Sublime purification of Barry's palazzo manner can still be appreciated in the British and Foreign Bible Society's warehouse in Queen Victoria Street (1866–7) and in the library wing of St Bartholomew's Hospital (1878–9). In a paper to the R.I.B.A. in 1864, *Some Notice of Office Buildings in the City of London*, I'Anson specially drew attention to the unusual size of the cotton warehouses, immigrants from Manchester, around St Paul's Cathedral. But the main part of his paper was devoted to the underlying reason for the breakdown elsewhere in London of the traditional Palladian proprieties: the emergence of a new building type, the lettable office block. The first of these was designed in 1823 by Voysey (probably the grandfather of the great Arts and Crafts architect). Others followed in the late thirties in Moorgate, following a strict façade pattern by Smirke. Finally, I'Anson himself, as his father's partner, succeeded at Royal Exchange Buildings (1842–5) in finding an appropriate expression for an 'endless' sequence of uniform office floors, with a round-arched ground floor derived from Percier & Fontaine's Rue de Rivoli via Charles Fowler's markets. However, the more strictly Sublime classicists took their cue from Schinkel's Prussia, by adopting a rectilinear grid of pilasters and trabeated beams. The most spectacular example in London was not an office building but, improbably, a square of fashionable suburban houses: Milner Square in Islington, by R. L. Roumieu & A. D. Gough (c. 1840), which Sir John Summerson says 'It is possible to visit . . . many times and still not be absolutely certain that you have seen it anywhere but in an unhappy dream'—yet it is Sublimely awful, in the true sense. But the real heirs to Schinkel's Berlin are the buildings by Alexander 'Greek' Thomson and his followers in Glasgow. These have been splendidly illustrated by Gomme and Walker,[11] so that we need to focus here only on the climactic achievement of the Egyptian Halls (1871–3): bands of identical pilasters, some of them directly glazed (with no window frame) and others brought forward as an 'eaves gallery' in front of continuous glazing—effects of a Sublimity remarkably similar to the German-financed (and often German-designed) buildings of Chicago a generation later, which also drew on the inspiration of Schinkel.[12]

But the real climax of the Sublime in the Victorian city—and of direct influence on the most important American architects of the late nineteenth century, from H. H. Richardson to Sullivan to Frank Lloyd Wright—was the Venetian Gothic style associated with John Ruskin's three thrilling volumes on *The Stones of Venice* (1851–3).[13] Once again, however, the theoretical book followed the practical work: just as Horace Walpole had been preceded by Kent, and Burke by Vanbrugh, so Ruskin was preceded by the little-known J. W. Wild in recreating medieval Italy. Wild's Sicilian-influenced Christ Church, Streatham (1842), its brick campanile an extraordinary foretaste of the 1930s, followed the recent German fashion (Persius and Hübsch) of the Italian basilica; but his Northern Schools of St Martin's-in-the-Fields (1849) went much further, in that there he evolved a repetitive method of arcading the street front of a secular building. In 1852, in fact, the young G. E. Street recommended Wild's façade, with its ground-floor blind arcade, its continuous strip of first-floor windows and its multi-columned playground loggia on the roof, as an exemplar for future commercial streets. This was in fact a secular and Continental version of the Anglo-Catholic 'functional Gothic' style which had been employed by Pugin in his convents and his Bishop's House at Birmingham (1841). The style demonstrated the *Ecclesiologist*'s dictum, in April 1851, that 'the true picturesque follows upon the sternest utility', and in effect it appealed to the emotions of the

Sublime rather than those of the Picturesque. Pugin himself had shown its secular possibilities in the 'grocer's shop' illustrated in his *Apology for the Revival of Christian Architecture in England* (1843). Its first appearance in London commerce was in the Crown Life Assurance Office at Blackfriars (1855–7) designed by Ruskin's protégé from Dublin, Benjamin Woodward. Its finest expressions were George Aitchison's lettable offices at Nos 59–61 Mark Lane (1864–5), with their tiers of round-headed arches, and George Somers Clarke's more literally Venetian office block for the Auction Mart Company in Lothbury (1866–7). Sir George Gilbert Scott's St Pancras Hotel (1865–76) and Waterhouse's Manchester Town Hall (1867–77) made the repetitive 'Infinity' of their exteriors only a prelude to the yawning 'Obscurity' of their grand staircase—and in Scott's case, as we have seen, to the 'Astonishment' of the vast single-span train-shed.

It is only in terms of the Sublime that the thrill of these buildings, so inexplicable to those who merely find them 'ugly', can be understood—the thrill, for example, of the crazily spiked vinegar warehouse at Nos 33–35 Eastcheap by R. L. Roumieu (1868), with its sliding diagonal glacis in place of the usual straight walling, or of the basilisk glare across Glasgow Green of Templeton's carpet factory (as late as 1889) by William Leiper (a pupil of J. L. Pearson).

The ecclesiastical origin of this commercial medievalism emphasizes the close connection that existed in the Victorian city between Sublimity in architecture and rhetoric in religion. The big exhibition halls, such as James Wyatt's Pantheon in Oxford Street, and the 'panoramas' such as Decimus Burton's at Regent's Park, were the natural ancestors of the Sublime preaching-houses. Joseph Bonomi's Doric cavern at Great Packington parish church, Warwickshire (1789–90) and Spiller's stock-brick colossus of St John's, Hackney (1792–7) were Anglican pioneers of a trend towards the architectural thunderclap of a wrathful Jehovah. Not surprisingly, the Freemasons were particularly fond of simulated terror as in G. A. Underwood's Egyptian temple at Cheltenham (1820–3); and the cemetery companies, an innovation of the 1830s, exploited similar frissons, as in J. B. Bunning's equally Egyptian catacombs at Highgate (1839). Admittedly, puritanism kept chapels as plain boxes until quite late, but from the time of J. A. Hansom's gasholder-like Baptist Chapel at Leicester of 1845 (known locally as the 'pork pie chapel'), the floodgates of Sublimity were opened in every Northern town. At Cleckheaton near Bradford, for example, there was until recently a particularly grandiose trio of classical chapels, designed for spectacular feats of preaching and the singing of massed choirs. Such giant auditoria continued to be built in the eighties and nineties, particularly in Scotland, where 'Greek' Thomson had achieved between 1856 and 1869 a trio of Egyptian triumphs for Free Presbyterian churches in Glasgow: Caledonia Road, St Vincent Street, and the stunning Queen's Park. The Frees regarded themselves as much more 'committed' than the other Presbyterians; the passionate rhetoric that followed the schism of 1849 found its expression not only in Thomson's terrific Egyptian, but also in F. T. Pilkington's savage Gothic—at the Barclay Church in Edinburgh, St John's at Kelso, and the unforgettable Trinity Church at Irvine. The Irvine church, built in 1864–5 for an unusually ritualistic minister (a German-educated poet),[14] has an emotional temperature surprisingly similar to the peaks of High Victorian Gothic for Anglo-Catholic ritualists in England.

Even before the Oxford Movement, there were strongly Sublime tendencies amongst Anglicans disappointed with the tepid Picturesque Perpendicular of the Commissioners' churches. They tended to adopt the sterner and purer Early English of Salisbury Cathedral, as in the two remarkable churches at Trowbridge (Holy Trinity, 1838) and Andover (St Mary's, 1840–6) by the Portsmouth architect Augustus Livesay. Pugin himself went boldly for the Sublime in his first big church, St Marie's, Derby (1838–9), exaggerating its mystical immensity by eliminating horizontal breaks and carrying the thin mouldings of each arch non-stop from base to base. Street, William White, and Butterfield similarly cut mouldings to the bone and exploited the rawness of real materials.[15] It is typical that Gilbert Scott, with his genial weakness for Beauty and the Picturesque, should have concentrated so much on mouldings and that his pupil and brother-in-law, G. F. Bodley, should have confessed himself 'tired of mouldings' before launching himself independently into the Sublime roughness of St Michael's, Brighton (1858–61) and St Martin's, Scarborough (1861–2). Meanwhile the Evangelical Goths, such as Bassett Keeling (at St George's, Campden Hill of 1868) and R. L. Roumieu (at St Mark's, Tunbridge Wells of 1864–6) were going for similar rocky glen effects to Pilkington's.

This catalogue of the High Victorian Sublime could be prolonged to include very many of the most important and impressive buildings of the period. At least we have seen how close the Sublime image lay to the functional reality: the 'Infinity' of repetitive lettable offices where each floor was of equal importance; the 'Astonishment' of the new industrial shapes—consider the vast circular water tanks at Everton (by the engineer, Thomas Duncan, 1853) and at Perth (by the Professor of Logic at St Andrews, Robert Anderson, 1839–40); the 'Privation' of the post-Benthamite prisons—from the circular towers of the Millbank Penitentiary (by John Harvey succeeded by Smirke, 1813–16) to the village-Vanbrugh of Folkingham House of Correction, Lincolnshire (by Bryan Browning, 1825), and the now thrillingly ruined fortifications of Bodmin Gaol (architect unknown, *c.* 1840). Such bold, even brutal functional expressiveness is what a French pioneer of Sublimity, Claude-Nicholas Ledoux, called *l'architecture parlante*—in his case going so far as to design for his ideal city at Chaux a state brothel (or rather, place of sexual education) on the plan-form of a phallus. It is, to repeat, the architecture of rhetoric—and it cannot be emphasized too strongly how central a place in High Victorian culture was occupied by rhetoric. And it has partly been our recoil from rhetoric, except at times of national emergency, which has made the High Victorian language of Sublimity so impenetrable to us. Much of the emotional appeal embedded in the Sublime image is of the kind which today would be kept up minute-by-minute by snippets on the mass media— but in those days had to be built into bricks and mortar for posterity: rich, glowing materials encrusted with symbolic statuary as a permanent harangue to the public.

Such permanence had a direct relationship to the permanence of the social hierarchy. It is, I believe, central to Sublimity, with its hugeness and massiveness and unashamed arrogance, that it was the aristocratic taste of the time. The Victorian taste for the *tour-de-force*, which was so spectacularly apparent in the exhibits of the Exhibition of 1851, has been interpreted by Pevsner[16] as evidence of middle-class vulgarity. In fact, it was the aristocracy who still called the tune culturally, at least until 1870. The desire of the first-generation industrial magnate to create great castles with huge furnishings was simply the age-old desire to ape the aristocracy and to have one's children absorbed into them. Sometime in the late sixties a fundamental change gathered pace. It may have had something to do with the coming of limited liability companies with professional managers; it may have had to do with the coming of prairie wheat and the slide of the landed classes from 1873 onwards; it may simply have had to do with the growing discontent of middle-class wives in putting up with domestic inconvenience of the sub-aristocratic surroundings of the stately Bayswater town houses from which Soames Forsyte tried to escape. Whatever the reason, the middle classes from 1870 onwards took to the railways more and more and moved out to Reading and Woking and Godalming and Haywards Heath and Chislehurst and Harpenden. There they built villas designed by Norman Shaw and his followers which were the very opposite of Sublime, exploiting enthusiastically the Picturesque cottage. Within five years of 1870 the great mass of fashionable opinion had shifted towards the intimate 'Aesthetic' and began to regard the vast monuments of the previous generation as 'ugly'.

Henceforth, the Sublime became appropriate only for the occasional monument —not, as had seemed possible in the mid-sixties, for the norm of the city street. All the same, the best late-Victorian architects had learnt lessons in geometry and materials which they did not forget. Architects, unlike the public, continued to admire such older colleagues as Butterfield. Shaw and Philip Webb both valued Butterfield above all other Victorian architects. Shaw's pupil, Halsey Ricardo, made explicit reference to this in his boldly polychromatic house for Sir Ernest Debenham at No. 8 Addison Road (1906–7); E. S. Prior and Randall Wells exploited High Victorian Gothic motifs in their churches at Roker (1906–7) and Kempley (1903); and J. F. Bentley actually discovered a new source for the Sublime in the Byzantine style of his Westminster Cathedral (1895–1903). This same style, which Lethaby and Swainson had made available to students in their book on Santa Sophia in 1894, was adopted by Sir Edwin Lutyens in his churches at Pixham (1903) and Hampstead Garden Suburb (1908–13). Lutyens in fact to some extent staged a Sublime Revival, coinciding with the Indian summer of opulence in Edwardian country houses: such houses as Heathcote (1905–9) and Whalton Manor (1908–9) can only be understood in terms of a Sublime which culminated in the 'Astonishment', 'Power', and 'Vastness' of the superb Viceroy's House at New Delhi (1913–30).

But the Sublime had by then become, even in Delhi, an isolated incident in suburbia, rather than a means of expressing the rhetoric of a whole city. It is ironically appropriate that Lutyens's ultimate achievement in the Sublime should have been for what Kipling called 'the silent cities'—the superb Memorial to the Missing of the Somme at Thiepval (1927–30). On the piers of this awesome pyramid of arches in perfect ratios, on the open downland above the Ancre, are incised the names of 73,357 men who were blown to bits. The appalled compassion aroused by this disaster was expressed by Lutyens in forms which, in Burke's words, are 'productive of the strongest emotion which the mind is capable of feeling'—and, one might add, are the strongest kind of architecture which an architect is capable of designing.

Notes

1 This paper is a much revised and concentrated version of the H. H. Peach Memorial Lecture for 1969 at the University of Leicester. I am most grateful to the Vice-Chancellor for his invitation, to the audience for their endurance, and to Professor Dyos for his encouragement and patience then and since. The argument is a theoretical development from my short book *Monuments of Commerce* (1968).

2 Nicholas Taylor, 'A Classic Case of Edwardianism', *Architectural Review*, cxl (1966), 199–205.

3 The comprehensive reinterpretations of it are by Professors of English Literature: S. H. Monk, *The Sublime: A Study of Critical Theories in Eighteenth Century England* (New York, 1935); J. T. Boulton in an excellent introduction to a new edition of Burke's *Philosophical Enquiry* published in 1958.

4 *Lectures in Architecture by Sir John Soane*, ed. A. T. Bolton, Soane Museum Publications, No. 14 (1929), pp. 90, 175.

5 Sir John Summerson, *Sir John Soane* (1952), p. 36.

6 See [Elizabeth Johnston], ed., *Art and the Industrial Revolution* (exhibition catalogue, Manchester, 1968).

7 *Modern Painters* (1903 edn), II, p. 366.

8 Jeremy Taylor, 'Charles Fowler: master of markets', *Architectural Review*, cxxxv (1964), 174–82.

9 L. D. Ettlinger, 'A German Architect's Visit to England in 1826', *Architectural Review*, xcvii (May 1945).

10 Henry-Russell Hitchcock, *Early Victorian Architecture in Britain* (1954); 'Victorian Monuments of Commerce', *Architectural Review*, cv (1949), 61–74.

11 Andor Gomme and David Walker, *Architecture of Glasgow* (1968).

12 Classicists who could not stomach Puritanism of the Thomson kind could revel in the sublimity of 'Magnificence' provided by French Second Empire (the Francis brothers' National Discount Company in Cornhill of 1857) or the short-lived Venetian High Renaissance (Sydney Smirke's Carlton Club of 1846–54 and David Rhind's Life Association of Scotland building of 1855 in Princes Street, Edinburgh).

13 Stefan Muthesius has traced this development in great depth in his doctoral thesis, published as *The High Victorian Movement in Architecture 1850–1870* (1972).

14 W. B. Robertson, known as 'the poet preacher': A. L. Drummond, *The Church Architecture of Protestantism. An historical and constructive study* (Edinburgh, 1934).

15 Paul Thompson, in his *William Butterfield* (1971), curiously avoids the use of the word 'Sublime' in his rather perplexed discussion of those aspects of Butterfield's 'ugliness' which are decidedly not picturesque—in such town churches, for example, as All Saints', Margaret Street (1849–59) and St Thomas's, Leeds (1849–52), with their solidly compacted masses and sheer wall surfaces. Butterfield and William White in the later fifties both used varied materials with a more picturesque sense of irregularity but Street stayed adamantly Sublime, in town churches such as St James the Less, Westminster (1858–61) and All Saints', Clifton (1864–8), and in village churches such as Westcott in Buckinghamshire and Howsham in Yorkshire. In particular, there was the fashion for Early French Gothic, which followed upon Clutton & Burges's victory in the Lille Cathedral competition of 1856: Clutton's own town churches for the Duke of Bedford at Woburn and Tavistock are splendid examples, and his pupil J. F. Bentley did remarkable furnishings in this style at Clutton's St Francis, Notting Hill (1860). But the noblest and most consistent sublimity in the Tractarian tradition was to be seen in the series of East End churches in soaring brickwork, a cross between Early French and Later German, designed by James Brooks: St Michael, Shoreditch; St Columba, Haggerston; St Chad and St Saviour, Hoxton.

16 Sir Nikolaus Pevsner, *High Victorian Design* (1951), republished in Vol. II of *Studies in Art, Architecture and Design* (1968).

296 Newgate Gaol, exercise yard: George Dance
II, 1770–82 (engraving by Gustave Doré, 1872).

In the light of present-day penal reform, this
Georgian dungeon must at first seem an abyss
of unthinking brutishness; yet every stone of
it was consciously designed by one of the most
meticulous intellects of the Age of Taste. Each
mortar joint of the polygonal enclosure was
drawn to its exact proportion by George
Dance. It was he who subtly thickened up the
window arches in order to intensify the painful narrowness of the openings, and he who
plunged the foot of the light well into gloom
providing for the visitor the Sublime thrill
which Burke called 'a quick transition from
light into darkness'. 'Terror' and 'Privation'
were essential elements of Burke's theory of
the Sublime; and a generation which finds
delight in the Theatre of Cruelty should not
find it too difficult to recapture these sensations.

297 *above left*   Leicester, County Gaol: William Parsons, 1825.
Photo: Kenneth Garfield

298 *left*   Newgate Gaol, entrance: George Dance II, 1770–82.
B. T. Batsford Ltd

299 *right*   Woolwich Arsenal, entrance to Dial Square: Sir John Vanbrugh, 1717.
National Monuments Record

300 *far right*   Lambeth, former police station at Gipsy Hill: Charles Reeves, 1854.
Greater London Council

Although Vanbrugh's appointment as Surveyor to the Board of Ordnance (and hence architect of the Arsenal) came late in life, his attitudes had always been those of a soldier, his full-time career before he turned to drama or to architecture. In his European travels in the 1690s he must have been thrilled by the solid geometry of the fortifications of Vauban. He set a style of 'Power' for architectural engineering which survived in Britain for more than two centuries, the gun factory of Dial Square uncannily foreshadowing in its yawning 'Obscurity' the Victorian railway tunnel. Dance at Newgate echoed Vanbrugh in the round-arched window bands of the superintendent's house, but having travelled in Italy, he mixed in on either side of it the rusticated Mannerism of Giulio Romano's house at Mantua and the overt romanticizing of violence in

Piranesi's *Carceri* engravings. In the swags over the doors he replaced the expected fruit and flowers by chains and shackles, making what the contemporary French neoclassicists called *architecture parlante*, the explicit expression of a building's function in its form. Vanbrugian ruggedness in stock brick, championed by the engineers of Victorian dockyards and barracks, and by sapper architects such as Captain Fowke of the Albert Hall (see no. 279), was also quietly perpetuated as an architecture of 'Privation' by the Metropolitan Police surveyor, Charles Reeves. But punishment could also mean 'Astonishment', another of Burke's categories: Leicester Gaol's cyclopic walls sport drainpipe-thin minarets of red brick, apparently evoking old Castile (but how did Parsons, as a provincial county surveyor, come to know about Spanish castles?).

301 *above left*   Arkwright's Cotton Mill,
Cromford: from a picture by Joseph Wright
of Derby, 1789.
James M. Oakes

302 *above middle*   Cox's Stack, Dundee: James
Maclaren, 1865–6.
Photo: Dundee Courier

303 *above right*   Edinburgh Gas Works: William
Burn, 1825–6.
Photo: Crown Copyright
Royal Commission on Ancient Monuments,
Scotland

304 *below right*   Marshall's Mills, Leeds: Ignatius
Bonomi, 1838–40.
Photo: de Burgh Galwey
Architectural Review

Although Wright's technique with paint was pre-
romantically precise and dry, he appreciated the
awesomeness of Arkwright's mill, its productivity
erupting in the landscape in a blaze of candle-
power. It was this kind of novelty in industries
that were still mostly exurban that thrilled the
Prussian architect Karl Friedrich von Schinkel
when he visited England in 1826. 'You may call
this view "Egyptian" because of the many
obelisks and pyramids of the factory chimneys',
he wrote at Birmingham. Semi-oriental forms in
fact were often adopted for industrial functions—
the language of the Juggernaut—as for example
in the 280-foot minaret of Cox's jute mill at
Dundee. Edinburgh Gas Works, which Schinkel
specially praised for its 'great refinement of
construction', was described by contemporaries
as 'Moorish', although Burn as a country-house
architect probably had in mind the rural
silhouettes of Italian farmhouses and Scottish
'doocots' when he designed the 'Succession and
Uniformity' of the strange conical-roofed gas-
holders. Schinkel's reference to Egypt was made
explicit at Marshall's Mills, which, in spite of the
suggestion of the 'Terror' of human sacrifice in
their awesome portals, were renowned for their
enlightened working conditions, including a roof
garden.

305 *below* Euston Station, the arch: Philip Hardwick, 1836–8. *David Francis*

306 *right* Highgate, the Archway: John Nash, 1812–13. From R. Ackermann, *Repository of Arts*, from John Summerson, *John Nash* (1949 edn), plate viii.

307 *middle right* Hungerford Market: Charles Fowler, 1831–3. From *Illustrated London News*, xli (1862), 160.

308 *below right* Chester General Station: Francis Thompson, 1844–8. From *Illustrated London News*, xiii (1848), 100.

The Sublime sensation of 'Power in the speed of communications was first experienced in stage-coaches on improved roads, a generation before the railways. John Nash's Highgate Archway across the A1 was thus a precursor of the railway viaduct, the triumphal but static gate of Mughal origin (the brothers Daniell's Indian engravings were a prolific source of Sublime imagery) being brilliantly contrasted with the dancing sequence of Palladian lunettes hurrying overhead with the traffic of Hornsey Lane. The same dramatic contrast between static entrance and rapid transport was made by Philip Hardwick for the London & Birmingham Railway when it opened in 1838, the rather slender and elegant portico to the booking hall at Curzon Street, Birmingham, being answered at the London end by the awesome propylaeum of the so-called Euston Arch. The primitive order of Greek Doric suggested the 'Power' of the Unknown and also, in its big chunks of masonry, the quality which Burke called 'Difficulty': 'When any work seems to have required immense force and labour to effect it, the idea is grand.' But for most station buildings a more integrated architecture of mass transit was evolved, in which the speed of movement was portrayed by the Sublime rhythms of 'Infinity' in arcading. Such ideas came from the Parisian architects Percier & Fontaine (in the Rue de Rivoli and in several markets), as translated into English in the ill-fated Hungerford Market of Charles Fowler, itself demolished in 1862 for Charing Cross Station. The Hungerford fish market had a freestanding iron canopy which was taken as the prototype for thousands of station platforms; while the round-headed arcades and Italianate turrets of the main building were soon turned into a railway vernacular by the brilliant Francis Thompson, whose long façade for Chester General lay *en route* to his Britannia Bridge over the Menai Straits.

One of the special challenges to Victorian architects was the enclosure of people *en masse*, not according to the specific ritual of cathedrals or theatres but in such a way as to give the greatest freedom to the greatest number. Free trade itself was given glorious expression in the Great Exhibition of the Industrial Products of All Nations in 1851. Derived by Paxton as a duke's gardener from the aristocratic conservatory, the Crystal Palace set international standards for the glazed arcade, a building type also originally French and also Anglicized by Charles Fowler, at Syon House conservatory and Exeter Lower Market. Such transparent 'Infinity' was developed most fully by provincial architects expressing the enthusiasms of provincial commerce: by John Dobson and Thomas Prosser, for example, in the two mysteriously curving station sheds at Newcastle and York, and by Cuthbert Brodrick in the billowing Baroque net of the elliptical Corn Exchange at his home town of Leeds. The shopping arcade was a spectacular democratic place of assembly, the most Sublimely vertiginous perhaps being Barton's Arcade at Manchester with its twin domes and triple tiers of balconies leading to offices at the upper levels. Birmingham still has a large part of its shopping centre under cover,

and the Great Western Arcade in its original state must have been as compellingly processional as any such *galeries* in Europe—the most impressive in its 'Vastness', Mengoni's Galleria Vittorio Emanuele in Milan, being erected by a British company. The same kinetic excitement in defying gravity ('Astonishment') was displayed just as internationally in the fun fairs, particularly the Great Wheels of Vienna or Earls Court.

313 *above* Elephant & Castle, Metropolitan Tabernacle: C. G. Searle, 1863, rebuilt Searle & Hayes, 1896–9.
Photo: G. W. Wilson
Aberdeen University Library

314 *above right* Leicester, Particular Baptist Chapel: J. A. Hansom, 1844–5.
Photo: Kenneth Garfield

315 *right* Brixton, St Matthew's: C. F. Porden, 1822–4.
National Monuments Record

316 *far right* Leeds, St Thomas's: William Butterfield, 1850–2.
Photo: Sir John Summerson

The Sublime was essentially an architecture of rhetoric, of vast crowds held spellbound by oratory, and hence was specially appropriate for the preaching house. Brixton parish church has a breathtaking 'Infinity' in its galleries, focused on an awesome pair of Doric columns behind the altar; beneath are Egyptian porches to the vaults, fore-shadowing in their 'Terror' the circular catacombs by Bunning at Highgate Cemetery. It was the same Greco-Egyptian style, rationalized by Schinkel, which Thomson adopted for his Presbyterian churches at Glasgow and which Hansom, inventor of the cab and later a Roman Catholic Gothicist, exploited in the 'pork pie chapel' at Leicester. There the gas-holder shape of the auditorium, with its giant columns strangely embossed with moulded bands, was flanked by the Choragic monuments of the gallery entrances and topped by a domed clerestory of Schinkelesque pilastrading. It shows what Burke called the 'noble effect' of the 'artificial infinity' of a 'rotund'. Inside Spurgeon's Metropolitan Tabernacle, the preacher could harangue a congregation revelling in its own 'Vastness', enclosed by a diaphanous skeleton of cast iron. Not that rhetoric was confined to the Evangelicals: surely the Sublime lies also at the root of the Tractarian ruggedness of Butterfield, with his painful insistence on truth to materials and sense of ecstasy around the altar. Butterfield's buttresses at Leeds are a defiant gesture challenging the artificiality of the industrial suburb. In terms of 'Succession and Uniformity' the High Churchmen were just as proud of their endless rows of 'free and open' pews as the Evangelicals were of their galleries.

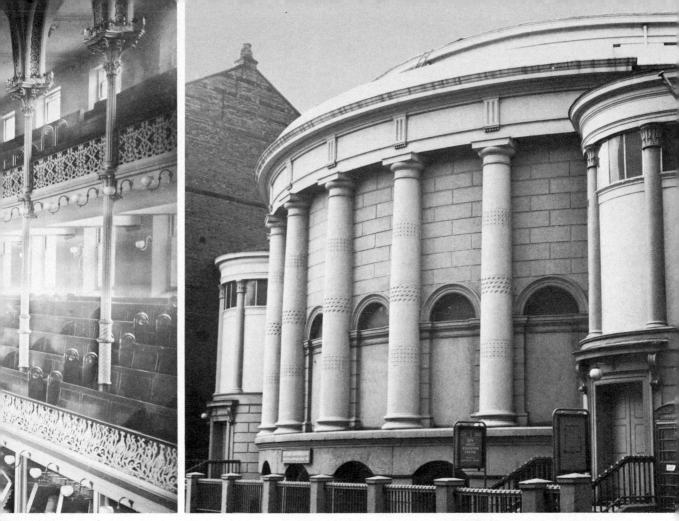

317 *above left* Islington, Milner Square: R. L. Roumieu & A. D. Gough, 1841–3.
Photo: Gareth Rees

318 *middle left* Scarborough, Grand Hotel: Cuthbert Brodrick, 1863–7. From a photograph about 1890.
Photo: G. W. Wilson
Aberdeen University Library

319 *below left* Westminster, Nos 129–169 Victoria Street: Henry Ashton, 1852–4. From *Illustrated London News*, xxv (1854), 504.

320 *above* Saltaire, lodging houses: Lockwood & Mawson, 1850–63.
Photo: Gareth Rees

321 *above right* Brixton, No. 107 Tulse Hill: Charles Hambridge, 1865.
Greater London Council

The Prussian discipline of Schinkel, with its reduction of the Doric to the 'Succession and Uniformity', in fact 'Infinity', of an endlessly repetitive grid of pilasters and trabeated beams, was taken up at its extreme by Roumieu & Gough in their tall terrace houses. 'It is possible to visit Milner Square many times and still not be absolutely certain that you have seen it anywhere but in an unhappy dream' is Summerson's description, pin-pointing exactly the 'Terror' of its Sublimity. Aesthetically less ruthless but functionally a pioneer were London's first luxury flats, a long Italianate block, faintly Parisian in tone, on the south side of the *boulevard manqué*, Victoria Street. Ashton adopted for his uniform spread of windows, over a ground-floor arcade of shops, the same Percier or Fowler style which Edward I'Anson had been using for the similar 'Uniformity' of identical floors of lettable offices in the City (Royal Exchange Buildings, 1840–2). But the residential building type which most violently blasted apart the traditional Palladian hierarchy of differentiated storey heights was the grand hotel. In his Grosvenor Hotel of 1860 (see no. 276), Knowles held down visually the 'Vastness' of his stock brick barrack of repetitive bedrooms by an even vaster crowning tent of chateau roof; a similar Empire style, in seaside stucco, was exploited by Cuthbert Brodrick at the Grand Hotel, Scarborough (see no. 164). Hydraulic lifts and central heating, not to mention improvements in catering, made such hugeness convenient as well as thrilling. Naturally the repetitive lodging houses at the model industrial town of Saltaire are quieter in tone, the Bradford architects Lockwood & Mawson having ingeniously synthesized the ideal Tuscan architecture of Quattrocento painting with the dour earthiness of the local Yorkshire stone cottages. Saltaire makes few concessions to the Picturesque, Sir Titus Salt's uniformly thorough benevolence to all his workers being expressed in the uncompromising 'Succession and Uniformity' of the street grid, against the backcloth of the huge alpaca and mohair mill. Knowles used his Grosvenor Hotel manner on terrace houses at Battersea and Clapham; and Hambridge took up the same style in a more Gothic vein at his Tulse Hill villa (as well as in a whole estate at Highbury New Park in North London).

322 *left* Bristol General Hospital: W. B. Gingell, 1852–7. From *Building News*, iv (1858), 529.

323 *below left* London & Westminster Bank, Lothbury: C. R. Cockerell, 1837–8. From the *Companion to the Almanac . . . for 1839*, p. 238.

324 *right* Halifax Town Hall: Sir Charles Barry, 1859–62. From *Builder*, xviii (1860), 41.

The most inventive Victorian classicist, Cockerell, evolved an appropriate style for corporate bodies by combining the Sublime 'Uniformity' of Schinkel's trabeated beams with fruitier reminiscences of 'Power' taken from the all-over rustication of the English Baroque. At Bristol General Hospital (for a photograph see no. 79) the local architect Gingell also went for an effect of 'Power' by adopting the Vanbrugh tradition of architectural engineering for the plinth along the quayside, with dark water gates to give 'Obscurity'; while for the main building he overlaid the rusticated dressings of the Baroque with high roofs and an angle tower of obviously French derivation, recalling the younger Hardwick's much less authoritative Great Western Hotel at Paddington the previous year. This sense of 'Power' in the over-scaled detail of massive plinths and channelled walls eventually laid hold even of the designer of the most smoothly beautiful Italianate villas and palazzi, Sir Charles Barry: his last work, Halifax Town Hall, moves on a century from his usual Quattrocento to the Venice of Sansovino, with big arched windows lurking in 'Obscurity' in the shadows of deep reveals. To this is tacked on the amazing tower in which the Venetian elements are given the 'Magnificence' of exaggerated vertical emphasis and dished up with elements of the English Baroque and the French style of Fontainebleau. The whole structure sits firmly on its sloping site on an awe-inspiring plinth, raised high above the narrow side street.

325 *left* London, warehouses
at the docks (engraving by Gustave
Doré, 1872).

326 *above right* Liverpool, Stanley
Dock: Jesse Hartley, 1844–8.
Photo: Paul Laxton

327 *below right* Manchester,
Watts's warehouse: Travis &
Mangnall, 1851.
Manchester Public Libraries

Sheer 'Magnitude of Building' in
Burke's sense can best be appreciated in the docks, where the style
for warehouses was set (at the
London Dock of 1801) by Daniel
Asher Alexander, architect of
Dartmoor Gaol; it was he who first
established the 'Succession and
Uniformity' of the vertical clefts
for the hoists as the dominant
rhythm, as portrayed by Doré in
his picture of War Department
stores on the move. At Liverpool
the dock surveyor, Jesse Hartley,
preferred instead to stress the
'Magnitude' of absolutely plain
brickwork supported on the
superbly confident 'Obscurity' of
Venetian arches on Doric columns.
For the less disciplined architects
whose clients desired 'Magnificence' even in their warehouses, it
was still possible to stress
'Magnitude' by means of a uniform
spread of small-scale arcading,
playing up the general bulk, as in
Travis & Mangnall's Watts's warehouse, where Italian Gothic rose
windows act as exclamation marks
along the roof-line of the tremendous cliff of stone.

328 *above*   Glasgow, Egyptian Halls: Alexander Thomson, 1871–3.
Photo: Crown Copyright
Royal Commission on Ancient Monuments, Scotland

329 *right*   (and plan) Manchester, warehouse in Portland Street: J. E. Gregan, 1850. From *Builder*, viii (1850), 414.

330 *far right*   Wallington Hall, Northumberland, mural painting in Central Hall: 'In the NINE-TEENTH CENTURY the Northumbrians show the World what can be done with Iron and Coal', William Bell Scott, 1856–60.
Photo: Philipson Studios Ltd
National Trust

The introduction of the lettable office block forced a radical rethinking of the traditional classical hierarchy of basement, piano nobile, and attic; each floor had to be of equal importance, so that the building owner could let it flexibly in portions. In a cotton warehouse an exceptionally full and even light was required for buyers inspecting samples. Gregan's solution was a 'Succession and Uniformity' of alternating windows picked out in Mannerist frames, making a flickering rhythm of taut proportions. Such uniform treatment of the façades implied visually that they bore no relation to any structural system inside; and that was indeed the case, for, as the plan shows, Gregan's building had a typical ironframed interior, with movable partition walls between offices and warehousing. At Glasgow, where owners and

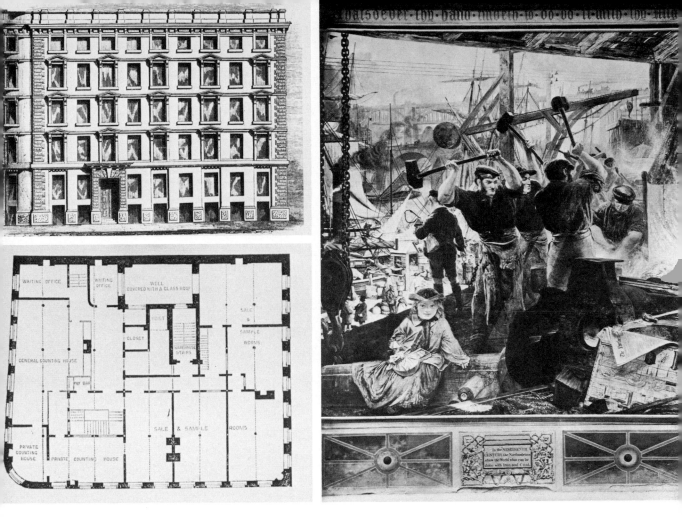

architects generally preferred greater solidity in the local Giffnock stone, 'Greek' Thomson layered his façades in depth, so that on the top floor of the Egyptian Halls there is a continuous run of glazing behind a freestanding Egyptian colonnade—the shadows enforcing the Sublime effect of 'Light' contrasted with darkness. The Victorian rich had an heroic view of their labours in the light of history so that even a country squire, Sir Walter Trevelyan, and his wife Pauline, close friends of Ruskin, could commission a local pre-Raphaelite from Newcastle, William Bell Scott, to celebrate 'Iron and Coal on Tyneside in the nineteenth century' as the last in a series of murals which ranged from the Roman Wall and the Venerable Bede to Grace Darling. The scene is the Newcastle quayside, with Robert Mylne's Low Level Bridge of 1772–9 and Robert Stephenson's dual road-and-rail High Level Bridge of 1845–9 in the background. The man with the sledge-hammer is a portrait of Sir Walter's cousin and heir, Sir Charles Trevelyan, Indian civil servant and brother-in-law of Macaulay—an interesting sidelight on the romantic egalitarianism of Ruskin's philosophy: 'Whatsoever thy hand findeth to do, do it with thy Might' is the inscription overhead. Bell Scott scores heavily in industrial realism compared with the much better known picture of 'Work' by Ford Madox Brown (see no. 345)—compare also its strident and minutely relished clangour of masts and casks, anvils and plane with the dreamy mistiness of Turner's earlier view of the same gorge (no. 356).

331 *left* Bristol, carriage factory in Stokes Croft: E. W. Godwin, 1862. From a contemporary photograph.
Reece Winstone

332 *below left* Westminster, St Martin's Northern Schools: J. W. Wild, 1849–50. From *Builder*, vii (1849), 451.

333 *right* St Pancras station, flank to Pancras Way: Sir Gilbert Scott, 1865–76.
National Monuments Record

In 1851, with the publication of the first volume of *The Stones of Venice*, Ruskin revealed to proud provincial cities how the merchant princes of the lagoon had lived, behind façades of richly repetitive arcading. But authors' theories have so often been preceded by architects' practice, and in this case Ruskin's principal disciple, George Edmund Street, was able, in a lecture of 1853, to point to a modest school in Covent Garden as an exemplar of the appropriateness of Italian Gothic to commercial purposes, particularly after the removal of the brick tax in 1850. Street pointed out the suitability of the broad ground floor arches (derived by Wild from a bridge at Pavia) for rows of shops; while the more closely set first floor windows and the open loggia to the rooftop playground led him to remark that, in urban Gothic of this kind, 'in the upper storeys the continuous lines of arcades would be very grand if prolonged to any length'—Burke's 'Infinity' in fact! In spite of Street's enthusiasm, the London church architects had little part in such work (except for William White at Audley and St Columb Major); the main Ruskinian revival was the work of provincial business architects, such as J. H. Chamberlain in Birmingham, T. N. Deane in Dublin, and the young E. W. Godwin in Bristol. Godwin's carriage and harness manufactory for Perry & Sons, with its even rows of round-headed windows over larger segment-headed openings for the carriage drive-ins, perfectly exemplifies the 'Succession and Uniformity' of High Victorian commercial buildings, which Hitchcock suggests was the major influence on the American architect H. H. Richardson (his Cheney Block at Hartford of 1875 and his Marshall Field Wholesale Store at Chicago of 1885) and hence on Richardson's pupil Louis Sullivan. An excellent example of the style in London is George Aitchison's Nos 59–61 Mark Lane (see no. 261); while Peddie & Kinnear's municipal buildings at Aberdeen (see no. 139) are superior in detail to Waterhouse's at Manchester. At St Pancras station, Scott's magnificently consistent side elevations, prolonged for several hundred yards under the railway bridges at the back, were symbolic of the Midland Railway's determination to use a Midlands style built of Midlands materials (principally Messrs Gripper's pressed bricks from Nottingham); the consistency of the rhythm was the result of the storage of beer barrels from Burton under the station, within a standard bay width. But by the time St Pancras was completed, it was already being bitterly attacked by the younger generation for its 'ugliness'.

334 *left*   Brixton, Christ Church: A. Beresford
Pite, 1897–1902.
Greater London Council

335 *middle*   Islington, tram transformer station:
E. Vincent Harris (L.C.C. architect's depart-
ment), *c.*1906.
Greater London Council

336 *right*   London County Hall, competition
design: Lanchester & Rickards, 1907.

After its period of unfashionableness in the
Queen Anne domestic revival of the seventies,
the Sublime came back for churches in the
nineties in the huge Byzantine domes of Bentley's
Westminster Cathedral, inspired partly by
Lethaby and Swainson's book on Santa Sophia
(1894). Beresford Pite, a close associate of
Lethaby's, was himself a fundamentalist
Evangelical, who used to stop suddenly in the
street, gazing heavenwards, so as to attract a
crowd to whom he could preach. His strange
Brixton church, though officially Anglican, was

for a congregation which was originally
Independent, and the preacher to this day wears
Genevan bands. The apse with its Byzantine
columns breathes an atmosphere of 'Obscurity',
if not 'Terror', although the vaulted dome is
elegantly matchboarded. The demolition of
Newgate Gaol in 1902 stimulated an increasing
interest in late-eighteenth-century classicism
amongst the younger architects. Vincent Harris
(1879–1971), later responsible for the Sublime
rotunda of Manchester Central Library, was
proud to admit sixty years later to having been
the anonymous author (under the official L.C.C.
architect, W. E. Riley) of a series of tram trans-
formers and garages in the Newgate style. But
the principal vocabulary of the Edwardian
Sublime was naturally the 'Magnificence' of the
Viennese Baroque popularized by Edwin Rickards
in the civic centre of Cardiff and in Westminster's
Central Hall. His London County Hall design,
not surprisingly rejected on grounds of cost,
would have had its tower visible from Parliament
Square as a rival to Big Ben across the river,
local government outfacing national government.

337 Thiepval, Memorial to the Missing of the Somme: Sir Edwin Lutyens, 1927–30. From A. S. G. Butler, *The Architecture of Sir Edwin Lutyens* (1950), photograph 104. *Country Life Ltd*

The 'tragic hill of Thiepval' was described by Scott Fitzgerald in *Tender is the Night* (1934): 'See that little stream—we could walk to it in two minutes. It took the British a month to walk to it—a whole empire walking very slowly, dying in front and pushing forward behind. And another empire walked very slowly backward a few inches a day, leaving the dead like a million bloody rugs.' A high ridge at a crucial point in the German positions in July 1916, Thiepval was a natural site for Lutyens's superb Memorial to the Missing, the last masterpiece of Sublime classicism by an English architect until the new library at Trinity College, Dublin, was begun over thirty years later. The ascending scale of the arches appears in black-and-white to have an element of 'Terror' about it; but in reality it is, in keeping with Lutyens's personal attitudes, suffused with compassion, in a soft pink brick —just as the helmet-shaped dome of the Viceroy's House at Delhi is unexpectedly pink-and-cream, not the 'Gloomy Colour' recommended by Burke. It is the 'Vastness' and 'Infinity' of the tragedy inscribed in the 73,357 names on the Thiepval pillars which is stupendously Sublime, a subhuman disaster transformed into superhuman 'Power' by means of the perfect proportions of the geometrical ratios and entases to which Lutyens worked.

19 Victorian Artists and the Urban Milieu

E. D. H. Johnson

Of his arrival at Bristol in 1831 the German artist-traveler, Johann David Passavant, wrote: 'The evening of the eighth of June brought us through a beautiful country to the great city of Bristol, one of the chief manufacturing *depôts* of England; whose tall pyramidal chimneys, reeking with coal fumes of countless manufactories, announce, telegraph-like, to the traveller, the useful avocations of the good people of Bristol.'[1] No aspect of the Victorian landscape would seem to have been more obtrusively evident than the manufacturing centers springing up in the wake of the Industrial Revolution. Yet the kind of scene which so impressed Passavant had strangely little impact on the imagination of English artists of the age. The Exhibition of the Art Treasures of the United Kingdom at Manchester in 1857 was intended in part to compensate for the exclusion of paintings from the Crystal Palace six years earlier. Its catalogue of more than 1,600 oils and watercolors (not including portraits) lists innumerable landscapes and views of picturesque old towns and villages, both in England and abroad, but virtually no industrial views. The same is true of the catalogue of the International Exhibition of 1862 in London, specifically organized to demonstrate that the British rivaled Continental schools of painting. The continuing reluctance of Victorian artists to paint the harsher actualities of the world about them is further reflected in the choice of plates to illustrate the pages of leading art periodicals in the latter half of the century: the *Art Journal*, the *Magazine of Art*, and the *Portfolio*.[2]

The modern metropolis is largely a product of the railway age, which dawned in 1830; and a distinction must be made between the creative responses to industry before and after this date. The great engineers and industrial architects of the late-eighteenth and early-nineteenth centuries were esteemed not only as public bene-factors, but also as true artists whose works enhanced the landscape. The mines and foundries, as well as the canals, bridges, aqueducts, and the tunnels which provided access to them, were more often than not situated in settings of conspicuous natural beauty. 'The iron industry had not yet lost its picturesque character,' wrote Francis D. Klingender. 'Still surrounded by romantic scenery, the great ironworks, with their smouldering lime kilns and coke ovens, blazing furnaces and noisy forges, had a special attraction for eighteenth-century admirers of the sublime.'[3] A notable example was the vast industrial complex at Coalbrookdale on the Severn, near the site of the first iron bridge, erected in 1779 after Thomas Farnolls Pritchard's design. Among the artists who painted views of Coalbrookdale were George Robertson, de Loutherbourg, Rooker, Farington, John Sell Cotman, Paul Sandby Munn, and J. M. W. Turner. The treatment of such scenes parallels successive phases in the technique of landscape painting. For example, the topographical backdrop against which eighteenth-century draughtsmen projected their meticulously accurate draw-ings of machinery gave way to the 'picturesque' style adopted by their more poetic-ally inclined followers.[4] A number of masterpieces illustrates the artistic appeal of each new manifestation of Britain's inventive genius. In the 1770s Joseph Wright of Derby was painting his mannerist oils of the glowing interiors of forges and smithies. J. S. Cotman's tour of western England and Wales in 1802 produced two of his finest watercolors, 'Bedlam Furnace' (Coll. Sir Edmund Bacon) and 'Chirk Aque-duct' (Victoria & Albert Museum). Another generation onwards, the railway inspired works as challengingly original as Turner's 'Rain, Steam, and Speed' (1844, National Gallery) and David Cox's 'The Night Train' (1849, City of Birmingham Museum and Art Gallery).

As a symbol of industrial progress, however, the factory town offered artists none of the romantic adjuncts of the mechanical marvels which had preceded its appear-ance. The initial optimism born of mastery over productive processes gave way to an awareness that the resulting economy had replaced hereditary ways of life with a wholly new and alien social environment. Artists tended to turn their backs on this spectacle as being incompatible with received ideals of high art. In Klingender's words: 'The alliance that had grown up in the late eighteenth century between science and art had a common foundation of humanism. When political economy abandoned the humanist standpoint for the defence of property the link between science and art was broken.'[5] At the same time there was taking place a significant shift in the complexion of the art market, occasioned by the rise of an industrial middle class bent on acquiring a semblance of culture, while devoting some part of its riches to the embellishment of its homes.[6] The two great Victorian collections of contemporary paintings were formed by John Sheepshanks, the son of a wealthy Leeds clothier, and by Robert Vernon, originally a jobmaster and army contractor. Prevailing tastes were reflected in the Manchester Exhibition of 1857, which elicited the following comment from an American visitor, Nathaniel Hawthorne: 'Pretty village-scenes of common life—pleasant domestic passages, with a touch of easy humor in them—little pathoses and fancynesses . . .'[7] Finally, painters ambitious for reputation were throughout most of the nineteenth century hindered from the realistic portrayal of their times by the absence of any tradition which would sanction and dignify such subject-matter. The hierarchies of artistic expression had been rigidly defined by the Academy, with historical (including literary) subjects at the top, followed by portraiture and landscape. The last category came into increased favor as a result of the romantic worship of nature; and, as has been said, the often sublime settings of early industrial sites made them eligible for treatment by landscapists. For the depiction of the rapidly growing industrial cities with their thronged streets and docksides, their congested tenements and slum areas, their smoking chimneys and gaunt warehouses, the readiest medium was genre, which enjoyed perennial popularity if not high academic status. According to inherited practice, however, genre painting had come to be so exclusively associated with humorous and sentimental scenes of rustic life that its adaptation to phases of industrial urban activity was a relatively late and timid development.

Hogarth's genius had, of course, raised genre to a high art, and his pictures of London life in the first half of the eighteenth century entitle him to be considered the supreme British painter of the city. But despite his continuing influence, Hogarth left no true progeny. His followers inherited his narrative emphasis and moral fervor (which Nikolaus Pevsner has identified as the dominant strains in British painting)[8] without the encompassing humanity of vision to fuse them into a matching style. In particular, Hogarth's moral satire split apart to create two schools of succession, the satire gradually relaxing to genial humor and the morality turning into sentimentality.

Under the coarsened guise of caricature, the Hogarthian vein still survived at the turn of the century in the political satire of Gillray and the social satire of Rowlandson. The latter matches Hogarth as an observer of London life; but the city which Rowlandson inhabited was still preindustrial. In the work of George Cruikshank (1792–1878) the old and the new orders are bridged. The colored aquatints which he and his brother Robert made for Pierce Egan's *Life in London* (1821) present an only slightly less boisterous version of Rowlandson's Regency world, while the temperance sermons which Cruikshank preached in such later series as 'The Bottle' (1847) and 'The Drunkard's Children' (1848) are Victorian tracts for the times. Although a bygone London survives in his illustrations for Dickens's *Sketches by Boz* (1836–7) and his own *Comic Almanack* (1835–53), Cruikshank was one of the first graphic artists to convey the impact of change. The engraving here reproduced, 'London going out of Town—or—the March of Bricks and Mortar' (1829), shows the encroachment of factories and jerry-built housing on Hampstead Heath. The companion plate, entitled 'Heaven and Earth' (1830), by Cruikshank's short-lived contemporary, Robert Seymour (1800?–36), evokes in searing detail the misery and degradation under which the lower classes of city-dwellers suffered during the early days of the industrial era.

This tone of savage mockery, traceable back through Rowlandson and Gillray to Hogarth, was uncongenial to the Victorian temper of mind, and it hardly survived beyond the 1840s. An altogether more tolerant spirit informs the London drawings of the great dynasty of *Punch* humorists, beginning with John Leech and Richard Doyle, and including Charles Keene, George du Maurier, and Phil May. Unlike their predecessors, who made carefully wrought engravings for a limited market, the *Punch* illustrators worked for a much larger audience in comparative anonymity and under editorial supervision sensitive to the pressures of public opinion. Hippolyte Taine, visiting England in the 1860s, was impressed by the blandness of *Punch* in contrast to the scathing social commentary of French periodicals. After remarking on the absence of scenes depicting prostitution or marital infidelity, he continued:[9]

> Voilà, nos gens mariés; regardons les scènes d'intérieur. Elles ne sont pas déplaisants, amèrement satiriques; point de bourgeois grimés, de vilains enfants grognons et tyrans, comme ceux que Daumier dessine si largement et avec une haine si manifeste. Presque toujours ici l'artiste juge que l'enfance est gracieuse et belle ... Ce sont les incidents, parfois les accidents, mais toujours la douceur intime et persistante de la vie domestique.

Satire implies both the inclination and the capacity for self-criticism, and the Victorian age was not much disposed to regard its unvarnished countenance in the mirror of art. The conventionality of taste exhibited by rich industrialists in the formation of their art collections fell under the ironic scrutiny of Charlotte Brontë in her description of the home of the Yorkshire manufacturer, Hiram Yorke. His visitors find 'themselves in the matted hall, lined almost to the ceiling with pictures ... A series of Italian views decked the walls; each of these was a specimen of true art; a connoisseur had selected them. They were genuine and valuable ... The subjects were all pastoral; the scenes were all sunny.'[10] The artists themselves were hardly less acquiescent to tradition. Many who had become known in the first instance as realistic chroniclers of familiar life turned for inspiration in their later careers to the heroic past or to established literary sources. David Wilkie abandoned his homely rusticity for large historical canvasses, and Holman Hunt the topical vein of 'The Hireling Shepherd' (1852, Manchester City Art Galleries) and 'The Awakening Conscience' (1854, Coll. Sir Colin and Lady Anderson) for overtly religious subjects. The social realists of the following generation, Luke Fildes, Hubert von Herkomer, and Frank Holl, were all converted into fashionable portrait-painters.

The most vigorous protest against academic authority in the early years of the Victorian period came from the Pre-Raphaelites, one of whose avowed purposes was to choose material illustrative of modern life. Writing in the group's fugitive periodical, the *Germ*, John L. Tupper asserted:[11]

> Thus it would appear from these facts (which have been collaterally evolved in the course of enquiring into the propriety of choosing the subject

from past or present time, and in the course of consequent analysis) that Art to become a more powerful engine of civilization, assuming a practically humanizing tendency (the admitted function of Art), should be more directly conversant with the things, incidents, and influences which surround and constitute the living world of those whom Art proposes to improve . . .

In actual fact, however, the revolutionary import of the Pre-Raphaelite movement was largely confined to its bold experiments with color and its precise rendering of often symbolic detail.

Among the earliest advocates of the Pre-Raphaelite school was the Liverpool Academy of the Arts, which in 1846 established a prize for painters who were not from Liverpool 'as a means of inducing artists of eminence to contribute to its annual exhibitions.'[12] The award was given twice to William Holman Hunt—for 'Valentine rescuing Sylvia from Proteus' (1851, City of Birmingham Museum and Art Gallery), and for 'Claudio and Isabella' (1853, Tate Gallery); twice to John Everett Millais— for 'A Huguenot' (1852, Coll. Huntington Hartford, New York), and for 'The Blind Girl' (1857, City of Birmingham Museum and Art Gallery); and twice to Ford Madox Brown—for 'Jesus washing Peter's Feet' (1856, Tate Gallery), and for 'Chaucer at the Court of Edward III' (1858, Art Gallery of New South Wales, Sydney). The only one of the prize-winning subjects in any sense unorthodox was Millais' 'The Blind Girl,' the choice of which was so controversial that it led to the discontinuance of the Academy's exhibitions. Even when artists used contemporary material, as in Hunt's 'The Awakening Conscience' or Brown's 'The Last of England' (1855, City of Birmingham Museum and Art Gallery), there was a general tendency to ignore the industrial or urban scene. Rossetti's 'Found' (begun in 1853, Bancroft Foundation, Wilmington, Delaware), which depicts a countryman's discovery of his former love as a London prostitute, is the artist's sole painting with a modern urban setting: and, significantly, he was never able to complete it to his satisfaction.

The original Pre-Raphaelite Brotherhood had dissolved by the end of the 1850s, and the other-worldly elements inherent in its program from the outset emerged unmistakably in the group of disciples, including Arthur Hughes (1832–1915), Edward Coley Burne-Jones (1833–98), and Simeon Solomon (1840–1905), who now gathered around Rossetti. Their practice confirmed the escapist impulse of so much English art in the latter half of the nineteenth century. They established a cult of esoteric beauty which found its apologist in Grant Allen, who wrote: 'The painter, once more like the poet, lives mainly in the storied or imagined past.'[13] The medievalism of Rossetti and his circle promoted in turn a pseudo-classical revival, led by Frederick Leighton (1830–96), Lawrence Alma-Tadema (1836–1912), and Edward John Poynter (1836–1919). Were it not for an obvious endeavor to domesticate their visions of antiquity to suit bourgeois tastes, no trace of social awareness could be discerned in the work of these artists. When Leighton painted the two frescoes, entitled 'Industrial Art as applied to War' (1880) and 'Industrial Art as applied to Peace'

(1886), which adorn the lunettes of the Victoria & Albert Museum, he characteristic-ally provided the former with a medieval and the latter with a Grecian setting.

Granted the British predilection for paintings which combine narrative interest with a moral message, genre remained the favored mode for artists concerned with representing the everyday life of their times. In this style the influence of Hogarth passed down through such painters as George Morland, Francis Wheatley, David Wilkie, and William Mulready, albeit with a progressive adulteration of the master's unflinching realism. The tradition thus firmly established continued to determine the practice of Victorian artists in their exploration of ways to come to terms with the urban environment evolving about them.

Within its limitations, however, genre offered the opportunity for considerable latitude of treatment, depending on whether the painter's interest in his material was primarily reportorial, or whether he worked rather with a didactic purpose. In the former kind, William Powell Frith (1819–1909) enjoyed unrivaled popularity. Frith declared in his autobiography: 'My desire to discover materials for my work in modern life never leaves me, and will continue its influence as long as my own life lasts; and, though I have occasionally been betrayed by my love into themes some-what trifling and commonplace, the conviction that possessed me that I was speaking —or rather painting—the truth, the whole truth, and nothing but the truth, rendered the production of real-life pictures an unmixed delight.'[14] Following his success with 'Life at the Seaside (Ramsgate Sands)' (1854, Coll. Her Majesty Queen Elizabeth II) and 'Derby Day' (1858, Tate Gallery), Frith chose for the scene of 'The Railway Station' (1862), his third large exhibition canvas, Paddington Station, which had been designed by Isambard Kingdom Brunel in 1850–2.[15] His description of the problems posed by this locale reveals much about Victorian taste in art, as well as about Frith's attitude towards his public: 'I don't think the station at Paddington can be called picturesque, nor can the clothes of the ordinary traveller be said to offer much attraction to the painter,—in short, the difficulties of the subject were very great.'[16] The work seeks to evoke the bustle accompanying the departure of a great passenger train. As in Frith's other compositions, the crowd of nearly one hundred figures is disposed about a central episode, showing the last-minute apprehension of a criminal by two detectives. Subsidiary groupings, including a newly-married couple and their attendants, a foreigner arguing with a cabby over his fare, and a mother and father sending their sons off to school, further emphasize the anecdotal content of a picture which *The Times* labeled 'natural, familiar, and *bourgeois*, as distin-guished from the ideal, epic, heroic.' Describing this work, together with 'Derby Day,' Francis Turner Palgrave perceptively remarked that they 'appeal equally to our sense of the melodramatic elements in commonplace life.'[17]

A fitting companion piece to 'The Railway Station' is 'Omnibus Life in London' (1859) by William Maw Egley (1826–1916), who, in addition to exploiting most of the other accepted styles of the day, painted this masterpiece of contemporary genre. Like his friend Frith, Egley saw in a recently developed mode of public conveyance the opportunity to assemble a heterogeneous collection of metropolitan types; and to ensure the accuracy of his representation he closely modeled his omnibus on one which he had found in the yard of a Paddington builder. Egley's attention to minute details of dress subtly discriminates the gradations in the middle-class origins of the passengers; and, although the narrative element is muted, the figures are so arranged within the cramped space as to suggest the psychological interplay among them.[18] Here reproduced are two additional paintings from about the same date which illustrate well-known centers of London life in Victorian times. George Elgar Hicks (1824–c.1892) is principally remembered for the three large canvasses which he painted in successive years, 'The Dividend Day at the Bank' (1859), 'The General Post-Office: One Minute to Six' (1860), and 'Billingsgate' (1861, all Coll. M. Bernard Esq.). Arthur Boyd Houghton (1836–75), best known as an illustrator, restrained his talent for mordant satire in portraying 'Holborn in 1861.' These pictures are recognizably after Frith in the inclusiveness and photographic fidelity of their rendering of urban milieus. Hicks and Houghton, however, were content to arrest the passing show without the adventitious intrusion of story or moral.

Wilkie's blending of humor with sentiment in a narrative context, allowing for a strong infusion of local color, supplied a pattern for much Victorian genre painting. His example is especially evident in the work of the group of artists associated with the village of Cranbrook in Kent. Along with its senior member, Thomas Webster (1800–86), the circle included John Callcott Horsley (1817–1903), Frederick Daniel Hardy (1827–1911), George Bernard O'Neill (1828–1917), and A. E. Mulready (exhibited 1863–86). While they shared the preference of Wilkie and William Mulready for rural scenes (frequently including children at play), they also invaded the city in pursuit of topical subject-matter. The obscure A. E. Mulready, possibly a brother of William, relied extensively on urban material, as in 'A London Crossing Sweeper and a Flower Girl' (1884, London Museum). Graham Reynolds has recognized him as 'one of the most original artists of his time . . . He was a sort of Mayhew in paint, acting as a pictorial journalist of the less pretty aspects of nineteenth-century life and giving his opinion on it. But the comment is restrained, and his paintings are gay and vivacious and full of the vitality of East End life.'[19]

The genre tradition was adapted to Victorian high life by the Scottish painter, William Quiller Orchardson (1835–1910) and the French *émigré* James Jacques Joseph Tissot (1836–1902), who had their graphic counterpart in the *Punch* illustrator, du Maurier. They were preeminently city artists; but they injected into their depictions of sophisticated urban settings a new psychological realism suggestive of the ambiguous relationships, especially between the sexes, existing within polite society. Although the Goncourts called Tissot an 'ingenious exploiter of English idiocy,' and although Ruskin referred to his paintings as 'mere coloured photographs of vulgar society,'[20] he was strongly influenced, notably in his Thames scenes, by Whistler, with whom he was intimate during the 1870s.

Even at its most pictorial, Victorian genre is rarely without some implicit teaching. Hogarth had spoken of his paintings as 'pictur'd morals'; and for his nineteenth-century followers the spectacle of contemporary life was no less freighted with moral significance than the world Hogarth portrayed. In some cases, though surprisingly few—and these largely confined to the earlier part of the period—art was invoked to celebrate the dignity of labor. Ford Madox Brown's 'Work' (1852–65) is the most famous example of this optimistic attitude. The artist's lengthy explanatory discussion of his painting (1865) states in part:[21]

> This picture was begun in 1852 at Hampstead. The background, which represents the main street of that suburb not far from the Heath, was painted on the spot.
>
> At that time extensive excavations were going on in the neighbourhood, and, seeing and studying daily as I did the British excavator, or *navvy*, as he designates himself, in the full swing of his activity (with his manly and picturesque costume, and with the rich glow of colour which exercise under the hot sun will impart), it appeared to me that he was at least as worthy of the powers of an English painter as the fisherman of the Adriatic, the peasant of the Campagna, or the Neapolitan lazzarone. Gradually this idea developed itself into that of *Work* as it now exists, with the British excavator for a central group, as the outward and visible type of *Work*.

In the dense iconographic detail of its treatment, a Victorian reworking of the Hogarthian theme of industry and idleness, the canvas represents all strata of Victorian society from the wealthy middle-class onlookers behind the navvies to the ragged and slightly sinister hawker of wildflowers advancing on the left. The figures in the right foreground are portraits of two 'brain-workers,' Frederick Denison Maurice, founder of the Working Men's College, Great Ormond Street (advertised on a wall poster) and Thomas Carlyle, from whose *Past and Present* Brown derived many of his themes, as well as their underlying social philosophy. That there might be no chance of the viewer missing its lesson, the frame of the picture was adorned with appropriate inscriptions. Palgrave called 'Work' 'the most truthfully pathetic, and yet the least sentimental, rendering of the dominant aspect of English life that any of our painters have given us.'[22]

Another well-known depiction of working-class activity, 'Iron and Coal—the Industry of the Tyne' by William Bell Scott (1811–90), avoids Brown's insistent didacticism. In 1856 Scott was commissioned by the Trevelyan family to paint for its residence, Wallington Hall, eight murals depicting the history of Northumberland. As the only contemporary scene in the series, 'Iron and Coal' lays claim for inclusion within the most esteemed branch of painting, that devoted to historical subjects; and Robin Ironside has called it 'one of the earliest works in which industry is taken seriously and recognized as the nineteenth century's contribution to civilization.'[23] The three central figures wielding sledge-hammers were portraits of employees in the Tyneside locomotive works of Robert Stephenson and Company; and in the background appears the Newcastle High Level Bridge designed by Stephenson in 1850. Although they are little emphasized, the scene nevertheless preserves the narrative and moralistic elements of genre, not only in such details as the newspaper in the foreground folded back to an account of Garibaldi's victory at Caserta in 1861, but also in the mural's caption: 'Whatsoever thy hand findeth to do do it with thy might.' The principal undertaking of Scott's last years was another series of twelve murals in the Town Hall at Manchester on the history of science, education, and industry, including such events as the opening of the Bridgewater Canal in 1761 and episodes from the lives of John Kay and John Dalton. Although very much in advance of their time in composition and technique, these paintings still lack the topical immediacy of Manet's similar project for adorning the Municipal Council Chamber of the Hôtel de Ville in Paris.[24]

In general, however, Victorian artists found little in the urban milieu to arouse their enthusiasm. Millais' only important incursion into this field was his tribute to London firefighters, 'The Rescue,' exhibited at the Royal Academy in 1855 (now at National Gallery of Victoria). With regard to his choice of subject he wrote: 'Soldiers and sailors have been praised on canvas a thousand times. My next picture shall be of the fireman'; and to Arthur Hughes he declared that he wanted 'to honour a set of men quietly doing a noble work—firemen.'[25] The description of the stage machinery which Millais contrived to give an air of authenticity to his canvas reads like a parody of Pre-Raphaelite practices.[26] Lower keyed, but perhaps no less artfully contrived in its evocation of the contemporary industrial scene is 'The Dinner Hour: Wigan' (1874) by Eyre Crowe (1824–1910), who devoted himself primarily to historical painting. This delineation of factory girls enjoying the luncheon hour in a setting of factories and warehouses is, indeed, almost unique in the period for its combination of idyllic atmosphere with realistically observed detail unalloyed by either anecdotal or moralistic reference.

As the century advanced and the environmental changes brought about by the Industrial Revolution became more manifest, observers of the signs of the times, like Carlyle, Dickens, and Ruskin, tended increasingly to represent man as the victim, rather than the architect of progress. This growing pessimism introduced a heightened sense of social awareness into Victorian genre painting. A favorite theme was that of the fallen woman, represented in Hunt's 'The Awakening Conscience' and Rossetti's 'Found.' For his trio of paintings, 'Past and Present' (1858, Tate Gallery), Augustus Egg (1816–63) relied on urban settings to drive home the relevance of the familiar story. The tragedy of a broken home is presented in serial form through three inter-related scenes which invite novelistic reading. The first shows the wife lying prostrate at the feet of her stricken husband, who holds the incriminating letter. The revelation of her infidelity has taken place in an elaborately studied middle-class parlor. Every detail has symbolic meaning. The couple's two daughters are building a house of cards. Half of a cut apple has fallen to the floor. On either side of the fireplace are portraits of the man and woman; above the former hangs a picture of a dismasted hulk, above the latter a depiction of the expulsion of Adam and Eve from Eden. The second and third paintings portray contrasting scenes on the same night after an intervening period of about five years during which the husband has presumably died.

457

In the first the abandoned sisters are discovered in a garret which looks out over the moonlit rooftops of the city. The companion piece reveals the disgraced mother crouched under the Adelphi Arches, clutching a shawl about her bastard child. She gazes forlornly across the Thames at the Shot Tower and Red Lion Brewery, illumined by the same waning moon. On the wall above her head are posters. One advertises pleasure excursions by steamer to Paris; another is a playbill for the Newmarket Theatre, listing two plays by Tom Taylor, *Victims* and *A Cure for Love*. Egg's series echoes Hogarth's 'A Harlot's Progress,' transferred to mid-nineteenth-century London and with a theme more suited to Victorian morality.[27] Egg's choice of setting here calls attention to the uniformity of the tendency of Victorian artists (following perhaps Hogarth's example) to choose certain districts of London, in preference to other cities, to epitomize the moral degradation associated with urban life.

Sympathy with the insufferable living conditions of impoverished city-dwellers inspired a considerable number of paintings of various types of social outcasts, made familiar by the writers of the period. Richard Redgrave (1804–88) conceived 'The Sempstress' (1844) with Hood's 'Song of the Shirt' in mind; and, during his brief period as a social realist at mid-century, George Frederic Watts (1817–1904) used the same subject. The crossing-sweepers, to whose plight Dickens drew attention in the figure of Jo in *Bleak House*, were very widely represented in Victorian genre, by Millais and A. E. Mulready among others. An especially arresting document of city life among the dispossessed is 'Shaftesbury, or Lost and Found' (1862, Coll. Mrs Viva King) by the little known William Macduff (op. 1844–66). Pictured are two urchins, one a sweep, the other a bootblack, peering through the shopwindow of Messrs Graves, the printsellers, at a number of graphic representations of children in distressed circumstances. On view as well is an engraved portrait of Lord Shaftesbury, the great befriender of the downtrodden, while on the sidewalk lies a crumpled handbill announcing a meeting at Exeter Hall of the Ragged School Union of which he was President.

A cross-section of the London populace perpetually passed over the Thames bridges and along the Embankment, and after dark these places provided a refuge of sorts for the homeless and derelict. One such night scene is hauntingly captured in the drawing here reproduced by Simeon Solomon, made when he was only seventeen. The two waifs, presumably brother and sister, illustrate the neglect of city children. The boy, barefoot and starving, begs pennies in return for feeding to his pet owl the rats which he has caught in the London sewers. The blind girl's livelihood derives from the sale of flowers and fledgling birds. Silhouetted against the night sky is a prostitute, who gazes over the parapet at the reflexion of the gas lights in the river below, while her cigar-smoking escort lolls indolently at her side.[28]

Unfortunate young women in Victorian London too often ended their lives in the waters of the Thames. Hablôt K. Browne's well-known illustration 'The River' in *David Copperfield* is contemporary with Watts's powerful 'Found Drowned,' which anticipates Egg's use of a similar setting in 'Past and Present'; and suicide by drowning also provided the theme of 'Drowned! Drowned!' (1860) by Abraham

Solomon (1824–62). Other favored locales for Victorian genre paintings dealing with the sorrows of the poor were the law-courts and prisons. Abraham Solomon painted a pair of canvasses, entitled 'Waiting for the Verdict' (1857) and 'The Acquittal' (1859, both at Tunbridge Wells Museum), which were widely circulated in engraved versions. A common subject was the hardships of the Irish, driven to seek employment in such British cities as Liverpool and Glasgow. Their lot was somberly commemorated by Watts in 'The Irish Famine' (also called 'The Irish Eviction,' 1849–50, Watts Gallery) and by Walter Howell Deverell (1827–54) in 'The Irish Vagrants' (1853, Johannesburg Art Gallery), of which Holman Hunt wrote that the artist 'had contracted the prevailing taste . . . for dwelling on the miseries of the poor, the friendless, and the fallen.' [29] In 'The Irish Emigrants waiting for the Train' (1864, Shepherd, City Art Galleries; another version at the Tate Gallery), Erskine Nicol (1825–1904) combined three recurrent motifs: the plight of the Irish, emigration,[30] and the railway.

With the appearance of the *Graphic* in December 1869 a darker hue of documentary realism becomes manifest in Victorian genre. The editor of this magazine, William Luson Thomas, invited the collaboration of a group of youthful illustrators to carry out his policy of confronting contemporary social evils with uncompromising honesty. These included Luke Fildes (1844–1927), Frank (Francis Montague) Holl (1845–88), and Hubert von Herkomer (1849–1914), all of whom, as has been said, later forsook the vein of their early work for more lucrative careers as portrait painters. Fildes' initial contribution to the *Graphic* was the engraving entitled 'Houseless and Hungry,' which he reworked into his famous canvas, 'Applicants for Admission to a Casual Ward' (1874). The setting is St Martin's-in-the-Fields on a wintry night; and in his naturalistic zeal the artist employed models from the shifting populace of the London streets. As a motto the work carried a quotation from Dickens: 'Dumb, wet, silent horrors! Sphinxes set up against that dead wall, and none likely to be at the pains of solving them until the *general overthrow*.'[31]

Like Fildes, Holl looked to the nether world of the metropolis for his subject-matter; and like Fildes he worked up his *Graphic* illustrations into such oils as 'Deserted—A Foundling' (1874) and 'Newgate: Committed for Trial' (1878, Royal Holloway College, University of London), showing figures garbed in the actual rags of East End down-and-outers. In a letter of 25 September 1876 Herkomer wrote: 'I have at last found my art master in the shape of a large Camera Obscura, which I have made. Nature is reflected and translated just as it ought to be painted.'[32] The insistence on photographic fidelity in the handling of incidental detail which characterizes the genre studies of the *Graphic* circle is observable in Herkomer's representation of 'distress amongst the labouring classes' at Coldharbour Lane, Bushey, in Hertfordshire (1885, Manchester City Art Galleries), which gained for this locality the name of 'Hard Times Lane.'[33]

The contributions of the book and magazine illustrators and of early photographers are so important as to call for separate treatment. It is worth noting in passing, however, that the two techniques are wedded in Henry Mayhew's massive

459

sociological treatise, *London Labour and the London Poor* (1861–2), in which many of the cuts purport to be taken from daguerreotypes. Even more dependent on illustrative corroboration are the three volumes which George Godwin, editor of the *Builder*, wrote 'as a record of the curious—not to say frightful—condition of London and some of its denizens in the middle of the boasted nineteenth century.'[34] The author was accompanied by graphic artists on his tours of investigation into slum conditions. Godwin believed that 'the pen is not so effective in conveying an impression of such places as the pencil,' and as evidence cited the prophetic warnings embodied in his first tract, *London Shadows: A glance at the homes of the thousands* (1854):[35]

> The statements therein made, many months before the cholera descended on the metropolis, were justified in the most remarkable manner; for it will surely be considered as something more than a coincidence when it is seen, that the first illustration in that work is taken from the neighbourhood of Berwick-street and Broad-street, Golden-square, where occurred that frightful visitation which carried nearly 700 persons to their graves in a few days; while the concluding engraving represents the condition of the houses about Ewer-street and Gravel-lane, Southwark, where the disease gave the last serious manifestation of its power in the metropolis!

No Victorian artist, however, matched the devastating candor with which two French artist-illustrators laid bare the squalor and degradation prevalent in many regions of nineteenth-century London. The earlier of these was Sulpice-Guillaume (Paul) Chevalier (1804–66), known as Gavarni, who sought asylum in England, during the period 1847–51, from the political disturbances in France. Like his friend, Eugène Lami (1800–90), Gavarni brought letters of introduction that would have assured high social patronage; but unlike Lami, he deliberately turned his back on all such opportunities in order to explore the subterranean life of the great metropolis. In the words of his biographer: 'Non content de dédaigner . . . la haute Société, il se mit avec ardeur à étudier et à rendre ce qui pouvait le plus la froisser dans son orgueil: cette mine de types étranges, de misères et d'anomalies qu'était le peuple de Londres.'[36] At different times Gavarni resided at the St Katharine Dock Hotel and in Whitechapel in the very heart of the London underworld, where, as he wrote, 'il est vraiment *possible de mourir de faim*!'[37] Previously Gavarni had been known primarily as a comic artist; but as a result of his experiences in Britain his style underwent a marked change, acquiring a caustic bite suggestive of Daumier, with whom he shared as well a tenderness for the underdog wholly devoid of sentimentality or moral revulsion. A series of eight incisive wood-engravings appeared in *L'Illustration* in 1850–1 under the title, *Curiosités de l'Angleterre, ce que l'on voit gratis à Londres*; and in 1852–3, another set of twenty lithographs, *Les Anglais chez eux*, was published in the same periodical as part of the great series, *Masques et Visages*.[38] The very titles of these drawings suggest the Dickensian range of Gavarni's familiarity with English low life: 'Ratting Sport: La Lutte et les Spectateurs,'

'Pick-pockets,' 'High Holborn,' 'Misère et ses Petits,' 'Le Gin,' 'Le Baby, dans Saint-Giles,' and 'Le Baby, dans Grosvenor Square' (a pair).

In 1872 appeared perhaps the most arresting of all graphic portrayals of the Victorian city, *London: A pilgrimage*, by Gustave Doré (1833–83), with accompanying text by William Blanchard Jerrold. Doré, like Gavarni whom he greatly admired, was struck by the extremes of wealth and poverty parading in the London streets; and like his countryman, he was drawn to the sordid Thames-side and the noisome slum districts of Bishopsgate, Whitechapel, Houndsditch, Bluegate Fields, and Seven Dials. Sensitive to the anomalies of change, he frequently drew scenes in which the old and new were violently juxtaposed. One of his most striking engravings shows the congestion in Ludgate Circus, with—in the background—a train of the London, Chatham & Dover Railway puffing across the viaduct under the shadow of St Martin Ludgate and St Paul's.[39] In all of Doré's engravings of the metropolis, however, there is an infernal, even a hallucinatory quality, reminiscent of his nightmarish illustrations for Dante. Jerrold wrote with regard to the mixed motives which inspired their prowlings about London: 'We have taken care that the happy images of the past which people the dreariest corners of London never displaced others, so as to injure the sense of public duty which they excite: but we have leant to the picturesque—the imaginative—side of the great city's life and movement.'[40] And the writer goes on to narrate a revealing anecdote of Doré's exclusively aesthetic response to one of the most heartrending of London sights:[41]

> One Sunday night (as we had been talking over a morning spent in Newgate, and of our hazardous journeys through the Dens and Kitchens of Whitechapel and Limehouse) Doré suddenly suggested a tramp to London Bridge. He had been deeply impressed with the groups of poor women and children we had seen upon the stone seats of the bridge one bright morning on our way to Shadwell. By night, it appeared to his imagination, the scene would have a mournful grandeur. We went. The wayfarers grouped and massed under the moon's light, with the ebon dome of St Paul's topping the outline of the picture, engrossed him. In the midnight stillness, there was a most impressive solemnity upon the whole, which penetrated the nature of the artist. 'And they say London is an ugly place!' was the exclamation.

Doré's rendering of urban settings was much influenced by the apocalyptic paintings of John Martin (1789–1854). Klingender was the first to propose that Martin derived from the industrial developments of the age suggestions for his architectural fantasies, and that his pictures in turn were to some degree responsible for the grandiose styles adopted by Victorian builders to dignify their designs for tunnel mouths, the portals of bridges, and the façades of railway stations.[42] This argument gains credibility from the fact that throughout a great part of his career Martin was occupied with diverse schemes for improving the ventilation of mines, for developing metropolitan rail and shipping facilities, and especially for purifying

London's water supply and disposing of its sewage. His numerous illustrated pamphlets advancing schemes for the beautification of London place him among the first of city-planners.[43]

Martin was both fascinated and appaled by visions of the megalopolis, which he conjured up in his huge canvasses, 'The Fall of Babylon' (1819), 'Belshazzar's Feast' (1820), and 'The Fall of Nineveh' (1829), as well as in such phantasmagoric illustrations for *Paradise Lost* as 'Pandemonium' and 'Satan presiding at the Infernal Council' (1824). The artist took lifelong pride in his appointment as Historical Painter to Prince Leopold of Saxe-Coburg on that prince's marriage to Princess Charlotte in 1816, and he continued to regard his work as falling within the approved mode of history painting, elevated to still loftier status by romantic theories of the sublime. The catalogue statement which he wrote to introduce 'The Fall of Nineveh' to the public declares:[44]

> The mighty cities of Nineveh and Babylon have long since passed away. The accounts of their greatness and splendour may have been exaggerated. But, where strict truth is not essential, the mind is content to find delight in the contemplation of the grand and the marvellous. Into the solemn visions of antiquity we look without demanding the clear daylight of truth. Seen through the mist of ages, the *great* becomes *gigantic*, the *wonderful* swells into the *sublime*.

The extent to which Martin's soaring imagination was stimulated by the contemporary industrial landscape is indicated by his son's assertion that one of Martin's last and most imposing 'machines,' 'The Great Day of Wrath' (1854, Tate Gallery), resulted from a night journey through the Black Country: 'The glow of the furnaces, the red blaze of light, together with the liquid fire, seemed to his mind truly sublime and awful. He could not imagine anything more terrible even in the regions of everlasting punishment. All he had done or attempted in ideal painting fell far short, very far short, of the fearful sublimity.'[45]

Related to historical painting which relies extensively on setting[46] is topography; and it is in the work of the topographers that the physical lineaments of the Victorian city most graphically emerge. Topographic art is thus the second formative influence in city painting which, like the tradition of genre, is derivative from the preceding century, but differs from it by a greater emphasis on specific locality and by the representation of scene for itself rather than as the setting for human activity. While the topographical manner in England was from the beginning associated with landscape, it showed itself equally adaptable to the features of an urban environment. The panoramic views of seventeenth-century London drawn by Wenceslas Hollar (1607–77) prepared the way for the great Thames canvasses of Canaletto (1697–1768), painted during his sojourn in England, 1746–55. The splendor of the Italian's portrayal of the eighteenth-century city was emulated by Samuel Scott (*c.* 1710–73) and his pupil William Marlow (1740–1813). Henceforth, London with its stately edifices and noble vistas became a favorite subject for many of the most skilled draughtsmen of the age, including the brothers Thomas and Paul Sandby (1721–98; 1725–1809) and the Thomas Maltons, father and son (1726–1801; 1748–1804). Their example carried over into the nineteenth century in the work of, among others, George Scharf (1788–1860), and the members of the Shepherd family, especially Thomas Hosmer (op. *c*.1824–*c*.1842), best remembered for his illustrated volumes, *Metropolitan Improvements* (1827) and *London and its Environs in the Nineteenth Century* (1829).

The early Victorian city-artists were acutely sensitive to the vanishing of familiar landmarks, and their pictures register, often nostalgically, the pulse of change.[47] The beauties of eighteenth-century London still surviving into Regency times are preserved in the 104 aquatints which Augustus Charles Pugin (1762–1832) and Thomas Rowlandson made for Ackermann's *Microcosm of London* (1808). A generation later the Victorian city has begun to emerge in *Original Views of London as it is* (1842) by Thomas Shotter Boys (1803–74). Each of the twenty-five lithographs reveals slight but telling details illustrating the accelerating pace of renovation. Excavations trench the streets where new types of equipage are in evidence, and where vans of building materials add to the congestion. Boys's prospects from Southwark and Waterloo Bridges, anticipating Whistler's favorite subject-matter, show not only the arrival of steam amidst the river traffic, but also the smokestacks breaking the skyline along the south shore. The most prominent architectural feature in the illustrated plate is St Dunstan's, John Shaw's Gothic revival church, erected in 1831–3.

The process of urban change heralded by Boys's book was the central concern of John Cooke Bourne (1814–96), who published in four parts *A Series of Litho-graphed Drawings on the London and Birmingham Railway* (1838–9). Bourne's work provides graphic corroboration of the well-known passage in *Dombey and Son*, describing how the diggings for the railway changed the face of Camden Town and disrupted the lives of its inhabitants. According to John Britton, the artist's sponsor, these drawings with their 'accompaniments of Machinery, Implements, Workmen, etc.' were designed to 'gratify both the lover of the picturesque and the man of science,' in short, 'all persons who derive pleasure in contemplating the increasing importance of the commerce, manufactures, and art of Great Britain.'[48] Bourne's success in adapting the topographical mode to his purposes as an historian of industrial progress led a writer in the *Spectator* to declare that he had made available 'new features of beauty to the English landscape painter.'[49]

Like genre, topographical painting reflects the stylistic revolution springing from the romantic sensibility. The linear quality of eighteenth-century drawings was replaced by a 'picturesque' emphasis on atmospheric effects. This shift is manifest in the poetic handling of the watercolor studies which Thomas Girtin (1775–1802) made near the end of his short life for his 'great Panorama picture of London,' the *Eidometropolis*, exhibited in 1802, but now lost. Significantly, Girtin selected for his point of vantage the roof of a warehouse belonging to the British Plate Glass Manu-facturing Company to the south-west of Blackfriars Bridge. A contemporary critic in the *Monthly Magazine* (1802) noted that 'the view towards the east appears through a sort of misty medium, arising from the fires of the forges, manufactures, etc., which gradually lessen as we survey the western extremity.'[50] Even more imaginative in their transcendence of literal fidelity were Turner's cityscapes. The burning of the Houses of Parliament on the night of 16 October 1834 'released' as Lawrence Gowing has stated, 'a fantastic force' in Turner's vision.[51] The watercolor sketches which he made on the spot and the flaming canvasses exhibited in 1835 have in the breadth and freedom of their handling an evocative power beyond any other paintings of the urban scene. The version in the Philadelphia Museum of Art, here reproduced, captures the breathless excitement of the spectacle in the scurry of boating activity on the Thames and the vast shadowy throng spilling over the bridge and along the shore.

Of special historical interest is the considerable number of pictures of nineteenth-century London inspired by ceremonial occasions. The one exclusively urban subject by John Constable (1776–1837) is his 'Waterloo Bridge from Whitehall Stairs,' which portrays the opening of John Rennie's span by the Prince Regent on 18 June 1817.[52] In the oil of this scene exhibited in 1832 (Private Collection), as well as in all the preliminary versions, the traditional pageantry on the river stands in marked contrast to the smoking chimney in the far-right distance. Many Victorian topographers served their apprenticeship as designers of stage sets, and their sensitivity to theatrical effects is evident in such works as 'The Opening of New London Bridge by William IV, 1 August 1831' by William Clarkson Stanfield (1793–1867) and 'St Paul's with a Civic Procession' (c. 1838) by David Roberts (1796–1864), both in the collection of the Corporation of London. The teeming life of the Victorian metropolis is more atmospherically embodied in Holman Hunt's gas-illuminated 'London Bridge on the Night of the Marriage of the Prince and Princess of Wales,' recording an event which took place on 10 March 1863. This was Hunt's sole excursion into a manner incorporating genre with topography, and of his labors over its composition he wrote: 'Being fascinated by the picturesque scene, I made sketches of it in my note-book, and the next day feeling how inadequate lines alone were to give the effect, I recorded them with colour on a canvas. When I had completed this, the Hogarthian humour that I had seen tempted me to introduce the crowd; but to do this at all adequately grew to be a heavy undertaking.'[53]

A rewarding field of investigation awaits the art historian who undertakes to explore the work of nineteenth-century provincial painters of the urban scene, especially those from the midlands and north, for whom the new manufacturing centers were an integral part of the English landscape. A conspicuous example is the Liverpool artist, William Gavin Herdman (1805–82), who claimed to 'have done more for Liverpool and its antiquities than any other town in England, even London, has received.'[54] Under local patronage Herdman and his sons published three series of *Pictorial Relics of Ancient Liverpool* (1843–9; 1857; 1878), which, belying the title, trace the architectural history of the city from the seventeenth century to its expansion into a great Victorian metropolis. Of higher quality is the work of Thomas Miles Richardson (1784–1848) and his family, who gained recognition for Newcastle as an

LONDON going out of Town. — or — The March of Bricks & Mortar!

HEAVEN & EARTH.
"Oh! it's very well to Live on the Taxes—but the devil to pay them."

338 *preceding page, above* George Cruikshank (1792–1878): 'London going out of Town—or—the March of Bricks and Mortar,' 1829. *British Museum*

339 *preceding page, below* Robert Seymour (1800?–36): 'Heaven and Earth,' 1830. *British Museum*

340 *above* William Maw Egley (1826–1916): 'Omnibus Life in London,' 1859. *Tate Gallery, London*

341 *above right* William Wyld (1806–89): 'View of Manchester,' 1851. *Her Majesty Queen Elizabeth II*

342 *below right* William Powell Frith (1819–1909): 'The Railway Station,' 1862. *Royal Holloway College, University of London*

343 *preceding page* George
Elgar Hicks (1824–c.1892): 'The
General Post Office: One Minute
to Six,' 1860.
M. Bernard Esq.

344 *above* Arthur Boyd Houghton
(1836–75): 'Holborn in 1861.'
Sir Colin and Lady Anderson

345 *above right* Ford Madox
Brown (1821–93): 'Work,' 1852–
1865.
Manchester City Art Galleries

346 *right* Eyre Crowe (1824–
1910): 'The Dinner Hour: Wigan,'
1874.
Manchester City Art Galleries

347 Gustave Doré (1832–83): 'Dudley Street,
Seven Dials,' from *London: A Pilgrimage* (1872).

348 Gavarni (Sulpice-Guillaume Chevalier, 1804–66): 'Le Gin,' *Les Anglais chez eux* (1852–3).

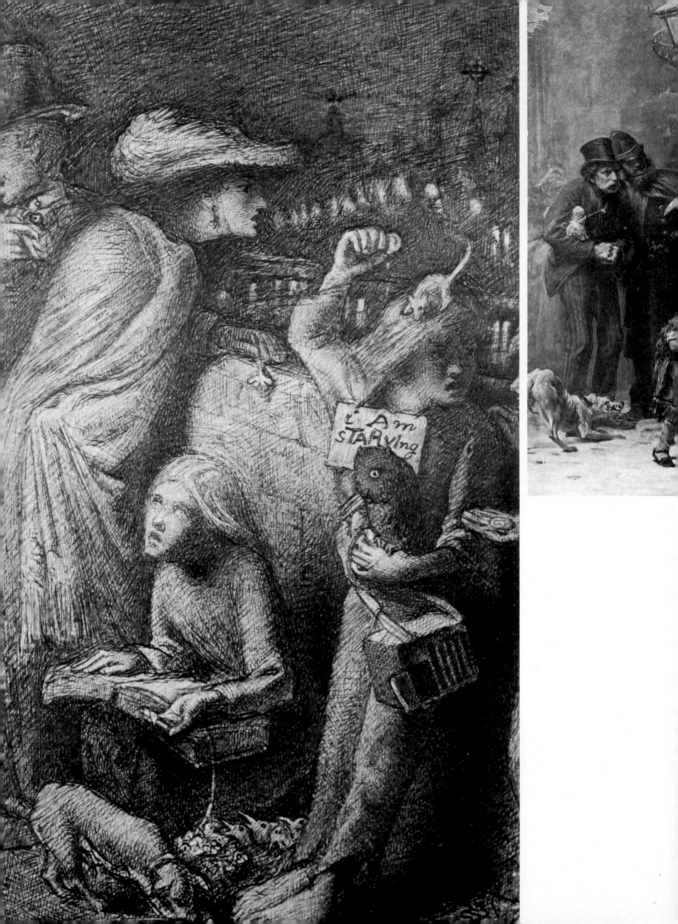

349 *left* Simeon Solomon (1840–1905): 'I am
Starving,' c.1857.
Photo: Geoffrey Clements
Davis Galleries, New York City

350 Sir Luke Fildes (1844–1927): 'Applicants for
Admission to a Casual Ward,' 1874.
See also no. 385.
Royal Holloway College, University of London

351 *below*   Frank Holl (1845–1888): 'Deserted—A Foundling,' 1874.
Formerly in Collection of Captain Henry Hill: photograph from Witt Library, Courtauld Institute of Art

352 *right*   William Holman Hunt (1827–1910): 'London Bridge on the Night of the Marriage of the Prince and Princess of Wales,' 1863.
Ashmolean Museum, Oxford

353 *below right*   George Frederic Watts (1817–1904): 'Found Drowned,' c.1850.
Photo: Donald E. F. Eldridge Watts Gallery, Compton

354 *left*　Thomas Shotter Boys (1803–74): 'St Dunstan's, Fleet Street,' from *Original Views of London as it is* (1842).

355 *above*　John Cooke Bourne (1814–96): 'Early Stages of the Excavation towards Euston,' 1836–7.
Sir Arthur Elton

356   Joseph Mallord William Turner (1775–1851): 'Newcastle on Tyne,' 1823.
British Museum

357   Joseph Mallord William Turner (1775–
1851): 'Burning of the Houses of Parliament,'
1835.
Photo: A. J. Wyatt
Philadelphia Museum of Art:
John H. McFadden Collection

358 *above* James Abbot
McNeill Whistler (1834–1903):
'Nocturne in Blue and Silver:
Cremorne Lights,' 1872.
Tate Gallery, London

359 *above right* John Atkinson
Grimshaw (1836–93): 'Hull,'
*c.*1885.
Private Collection, England

360 *right* Walter Greaves
(1846–1930): 'Chelsea Regatta,'
1871.
Manchester City Art Galleries

361 Walter Richard Sickert (1860–1942): 'The Old Bedford,' c.1890.
National Gallery of Canada, Ottawa: The Massey Collection of English Painting

important center of artistic activity.[55] Samuel Bough (1822–78) was among the earliest of a long succession of painters associated with Glasgow.[56]

Eighteenth-century topographical views of industrial localities had conventionally played down the uglier aspects of the sites by emphasizing the beauty of the surrounding scenery; and this practice was still prevalent in the Victorian period. Ford Madox Brown's diary carries the following notation of a visit to Cromwell's farm in Cornwall, July 1856: 'The river, with the picturesque old bridge . . . combine, with the church and a large factory shaft, to form a scene such as Turner has so often depicted with satisfaction to himself and others, of old England and new England combined.'[57] In his watercolor of 'Newcastle on Tyne' (1823), drawn for *The Rivers of England*, Turner gives the smoke-shrouded city a pastoral foreground. The contrast between the urban and the bucolic is even more marked in the accompanying reproduction of a watercolor view of Manchester from Kersal Moor, which William Wyld (1806–89) painted to commemorate a royal visit to the city in 1851. The upper and lower halves of the composition portray separate worlds which seem hardly to bear any relationship to each other.

By and large, Victorian painters were slow to find in the great industrial centers any aesthetic qualities equivalent to those which attracted them to the rural towns and villages of England and the unspoiled cities on the Continent. This limitation is attributable perhaps as much to their limited notions of the scope of the topographical manner[58] as to their avoidance of certain kinds of subject-matter, and might have been overcome had they been more receptive to the liberating influence of contemporary trends in French art. The exhibitions of the Impressionists which Durand-Ruel brought to London during the 1870s and 1880s failed, however, to break down insular prejudice, and the English market for French painting stopped with Millet and the Barbizon School, whose work, of course, was consonant with the native taste for landscape.[59] On the other hand, French artists from the time of Géricault's visit in 1820 had not only felt at home in England, but had devoted sympathetic study to their British *confrères*, especially Constable and Turner. Both Corot and Manet crossed the Channel during the 1860s. At the time of the Franco-Prussian War Monet, Pissarro, and Sisley lived in London; and they, along with Van Gogh and Toulouse-Lautrec, made other visits in subsequent years. Frederick Wedmore, writing on 'The Impressionists' in the *Fortnightly Review* (1883) commented on the lively interest in the life of the day shown by French painters, in contrast to the staid conventionality of native artists:[60]

> To me the study of these men is particularly interesting because it helps towards the solution of a problem always important and continually debated—the question how far modern art may reflect modern life . . . Too many of our own exponents of contemporary life express contemporary life without artistic power. In England high taste and sensitivity and the power to draw and colour are too much ranged on the side of those who hold that modern life holds no themes for art . . . In the main it is true that the

adaptibility of modern life to the purposes of art has not been fairly tried in England. Against it there has been the force of tradition in a country of tradition; the force, until lately, of academic influences in criticism—a criticism that has not perceived the artist's need of vivid and personal impression.

It was from the spectacle of late-Victorian London that the French visitors derived their most vivid impressions. Recollecting his sojourn there in 1873–5, Van Gogh wrote to his brother in 1882 that he had at that time formed a collection of engravings clipped from the pages of the *Graphic* and the *Illustrated London News* by such artists as Fildes, Herkomer, Holl, and Houghton, including one portfolio devoted to 'Sketches of London life, types of the people, from the opium-smokers, and Whitechapel and The Seven Dials, to the most elegant ladies' figures and Rotton Row or Westminster Park. To these are added similar scenes from Paris and New York, so the whole is a curious "tale of those cities."'[61] No painter viewed the British capital through more perceptive eyes than Monet, who brilliantly recorded its changing facets during his residence there in 1891 and again in 1899–1904. Long afterwards in 1918 he wrote:[62]

> I love London more than the English countryside . . . but I love it only in winter with the fog, for without the fog London would not be a beautiful city. It is the fog that gives it its magnificent amplitude . . . it is a mass, an ensemble, and it is so simple; . . . its regular and massive blocks become grandiose in that mysterious mantle . . . How could the English painters of the nineteenth century have painted bricks that they did not see—that they could not see?

In their reluctance to have their eyes opened to the fascination which the Impressionists discovered in the industrial landscape, English painters had the support, as Wedmore stated, of a body of critical opinion mobilized to support the academic cult of an ideal beauty. A leading advocate of the traditionalist position was Philip Gilbert Hamerton, editor of the *Portfolio*, who in 1892 wrote a series of articles on contemporary French art. The third of these includes the following characteristic passage:[63]

> . . . in a very great number of modern pictures art is sacrificed to mere fact. I happen to be writing this chapter in Paris, and just before coming to these lines I passed an important picture-shop on the Boulevards which afforded some interesting examples of downright modernism, and amongst others this. The picture represented one of those charming river landscapes that abound in France. On one side was a noble mass of trees, on the other a slope of land, and beyond them a hilly but not mountainous distance. Between the spectator and that distance stood a factory with its long chimney, duly emitting smoke. The artist, no doubt, was of opinion (and he was right) that the factory added the interest of life and industry to his

subject; he did not think if, or he did not care about, the artistic injury that the hideous building inflicted upon a beautiful landscape, and he appears to have been entirely destitute of that fine sense which establishes a clear distinction between the poetic and prosaic industries of men. This negligence or insensibility seems to be increasingly frequent in the new school.

Against the artificial standards which prescribed the artistic practice of the day, James McNeill Whistler (1834–1903) waged virtually single-handed warfare from the time of his arrival in England in 1859. The preceding Parisian years when he was much subject to Courbet's influence had, in Douglas Cooper's words, 'taught him to turn his eyes directly on the world around him and to paint the urban scene.'[64] Whistler first settled at Wapping, where he produced the series of sixteen etchings known as the 'Thames Set.' These river scenes carry on the topographical mode, but are drawn with a new directness and immediacy of vision. Baudelaire, who saw the Thames plates when they were exhibited in Paris (1862), at once recognized a companion spirit in the interpretation of the modern city:[65]

> Tout récemment, un jeune artiste américain, M. Whistler, exposait à la galerie Martinet une série d'eaux-fortes, subtiles, éveillées comme l'improvisation et l'inspiration, représentant les bords de la Tamise; merveilleux fouillis d'agrès, de vergues, de cordages; chaos de brumes, de fourneaux et de fumées tirebouchonnées; poésie profonde et compliquée d'une vaste capitale.

In 1863 Whistler moved to Lindsey Row, and there, intoxicated by the tonal play of the light, especially at evening, along the reaches of Chelsea and Battersea, he pursued the stylistic development which led to the 'Nocturnes' of the 1870s. To a friend, Sidney Starr, he confessed 'that only one landscape interested him, the landscape of London';[66] and in his 'Ten O'Clock' lecture (1885) he sought to conjure up in words some of the magic which the metropolis disclosed to the painter's eye:[67]

> And when the evening mist clothes the riverside with poetry, as with a veil, and the poor buildings lose themselves in the dim sky, and the tall chimneys become campanili, and the warehouses are palaces in the night, and the whole city hangs in the heavens, and fairy-land is before us— then the wayfarer hastens home; the working man and the cultured one, the wise man and the one of pleasure, cease to understand, as they have ceased to see, and Nature, who, for once, has sung in tune, sings her exquisite song to the artist alone, her son and her master—her son in that he loves her, her master in that he knows her.

Another painter who made the topographical style into a very personal medium for expressing the poetry of cities was John Atkinson Grimshaw (1836–93). This artist was associated with Whistler for a period during the 1880s; and although their techniques were so different, Whistler, according to Guy Phillips, 'confessed to

Grimshaw that he had regarded himself as the inventor of "nocturnes" until he saw Atkinson Grimshaw's moonlights.'[68] A native of Leeds who was largely self-taught, Grimshaw became preeminently the delineator of fog-enveloped docksides and city streets, seen by night in the ghostly illumination of gaslights. Better than any artist of his time he captured the feeling of loneliness and loss of identity which afflicts the modern city-dweller.

Although a pupil of Whistler, for whom he had served as a boatman, Walter Greaves (1846–1930) revealed a spontaneity of response along with an engagingly naïve style in such paintings as 'Hammersmith Bridge' (Tate Gallery) and 'Chelsea Regatta.'[69] The latter represents the waterfront as it appeared in 1871 on the eve of its destruction to make way for Sir James Bazalgette's Chelsea Embankment. His paintings of street and river scenes about Chelsea are among the freshest evocations of London at the turn of the century. The attention to atmospheric effect which characterizes Whistler's revitalization of the topographical tradition is also apparent in so masterly a city scene as 'St Pancras Hotel and Station from Pentonville Road: Sunset' (1881, London Museum) by the Irish painter, John O'Connor (1830–89), who was trained as a set-painter, as well as in the Thames pictures of William Lionel Wyllie (1851–1931).

A revolution in the methods of genre painting, similar to that for which Whistler was responsible in topography, manifested itself in the work of the French-schooled artists who in 1885 formed the New English Art Club as yet another protest against the authoritarianism of the Academy. Although such leading members of the group as Frank Bramley (1857–1915) and Stanhope Alexander Forbes (1857–1947) introduced into their subject-paintings an impressionistic handling of light, they showed little disposition to dispense with the narrative elements which typify English genre.[70] The greatest of these artists, Walter Richard Sickert (1860–1942), was also the one who devoted himself most exclusively to recreating the urban milieu. In the catalogue to an exhibition at the Goupil Gallery (1889) he wrote: 'In its [Impressionism's] search through visible nature for the elements of this same beauty, it does not admit the narrow interpretation of the word "Nature" which would stop short outside the four-mile radius. It is, on the contrary, strong in the belief that for those who live in the most wonderful and complex city in the world, the most fruitful course of study lies in a persistent effort to render the magic and the poetry which they daily see around them . . .'[71] Although a devoted follower of Degas, Sickert always maintained that his pictures subsisted by their narrative content. In the low-keyed canvasses which he produced between 1885 and 1895 he revealed the indoors night-life of London as hauntingly as Whistler had painted its outward face. His portrayal of theatrical performers and their rapt audiences in music halls like the Old Bedford revitalized the tradition of genre, distilling the beauty that lurked in the recesses of a great city. It was not until after the turn of the century in his Camden School period that there appears in Sickert's work those elements of horror and boredom which have come to be so integral an aspect of representations of city life by contemporary artists.

468

Notes

1 *Tour of a German Artist in England* (1836), I, pp. 318–19.

2 Nor would it be much easier to document Victorian city life from any of the numerous collections, exhibitions, and publications which in recent years have signalized the reawakening of interest in British art of the nineteenth century. Almost the only exception to this statement, as indicative of the wealth of available material, was the exhibition of *Art and the Industrial Revolution*, held at the Manchester City Art Galleries in the early summer of 1968. The numerous Victorian illustrated art periodicals are the best primary source for the scholar who wishes to survey the paintings of the period. Of these the longest-lived and most comprehensive in its coverage of artistic activity in Britain was the *Art Journal* which ran from 1839 to 1912 (under the title of the *Art-Union* for its first decade). For an exhaustive checklist of other publications, see Helene E. Roberts, 'British Art Periodicals of the Eighteenth and Nineteenth Centuries,' *Victorian Periodicals Newsletter*, no. 9 (July 1970). Among the illustrated volumes which in the present generation have marked the renewal of serious interest in Victorian art the following may be particularly cited: Francis D. Klingender, *Art and the Industrial Revolution*, both in its original edition (1947) and as edited and revised by Sir Arthur Elton (1968); Graham Reynolds, *Painters of the Victorian Scene* (1953), and the same author's *Victorian Painting* (1966); Raymond Lister, *Victorian Narrative Paintings* (1966); and Jeremy Maas, *Victorian Painters* (1969).

3 *Art and the Industrial Revolution*, ed. Arthur Elton (1968), p. 9. The present section of this chapter owes much to this important work.

4 Despite William Gilpin's dictum that in the picturesque mode 'the arts of industry are rejected.' See, for example, the industrial subjects in P. J. de Loutherbourg's *Picturesque Scenery of England and Wales* (1805). The vogue for incorporating realistic detail in romantic scenes is indicated by the title of a manual by W. H. Pyne, *Microcosm, or a Picturesque Delineation of the Arts, Agriculture, and Manufactures of Great Britain; in a Series of above a Thousand Groups of Small Figures for the Embellishment of Landscape* (1803–6).

5 Klingender, ed. cit., p. 115.

6 'From about 1840 it became a commonplace that the patrons of modern art had changed and that the buyers no longer belonged to the noble and landed classes but were the new prospering manufacturers.' A. P. Oppé, 'Art,' *Early Victorian England*, ed. G. M. Young (1934), II, p. 115.

7 *The English Notebooks*, ed. Randall Stewart (1941), p. 549.

8 *The Englishness of English Art* (1956), p. 25.

9 *Notes sur l'Angleterre* (Paris, 1872), p. 268.

10 *Shirley* (1849), ch. 3.

11 'The Subject in Art,' *Germ*, no. 3 (1851), 122.

12 See Mary Bennett, 'The Pre-Raphaelites and the Liverpool Prize,' *Apollo* (December 1962), 748–53.

13 *Physiological Aesthetics* (1877), p. 226. Henry James's response to the paintings of Burne-Jones at the inaugural exhibition of the Grosvenor Gallery in 1877 summarizes in Pateresque terms this aestheticism: 'It is the art of culture, of reflection, of intellectual luxury, of aesthetic refinement, of people who look at the

world and at life not directly, as it were, and in all its accidental reality, but in the reflection and ornamental portrait of it furnished by art itself in other manifestations; furnished by literature, by poetry, by history, by erudition.'
J. L. Sweeney, ed., *The Painter's Eye: Notes and essays on the pictorial arts by Henry James* (Cambridge, Mass., 1956), p. 144.

14 *My Autobiography and Reminiscences* (1887–8), II, p. 34.

15 Of the phenomena associated with the Industrial Revolution, none inspired so many artists as the railway. Treatments of the theme range all the way from Charles Rossiter's spirited rendering of a popular excursion train, 'To Brighton and Back, 3/6' (1859, City of Birmingham Museum and Art Gallery), to Augustus Egg's small picture of two elegant young ladies journeying in a first-class compartment along the Riviera, 'The Travelling Companions' (1862, City of Birmingham Museum and Art Gallery). The subject-matter lent itself especially well to pointing out class distinctions and to contrasting the lot of the rich and the poor. An example is the pair of paintings exhibited by Abraham Solomon at the Royal Academy in 1854 and now at Southampton Art Gallery, entitled 'First Class—the Return' and 'Second Class—the Parting.' Significantly the view from the carriage window in the former presents a pastoral landscape, while the latter opens on an industrial scene.

16 *My Autobiography*, I, p. 327, and see following pages for an analysis of details in the painting.

17 'The Royal Academy of 1863,' *Essays on Art* (New York, 1867), p. 17. Ruskin's comment on 'Derby Day' might with equal propriety have been extended to 'The Railway Station': 'It is a kind of cross between John Leech and Wilkie, with a dash of daguerreotype here and there, and some pretty seasoning with Dickens's sentiment.' E. T. Cook and Alexander Wedderburn, eds, *The Works of John Ruskin* (1912), XIV, p. 162. Frith not only used members of his family and friends as models, but also called in the new art of photography.

18 Egley's painting should be compared with 'The Bayswater Omnibus' (1895, London Museum) by George William Joy (1844–1925). The London General Omnibus Company supplied the original for the vehicle in Joy's work.

19 *Victorian Painting* (New York, 1966), p. 37.

20 Quoted by Henri Zerner, *James Jacques Joseph Tissot: A retrospective exhibition* (Museum of Art, Rhode Island School of Design, and The Art Gallery of Ontario, Toronto, 1968). Tissot's obeisance to convention is made amusingly apparent by a comparison of the artist's original drawing of 'Trafalgar Tavern, Greenwich' (1878, Fogg Art Museum, Cambridge, Mass.) with its etched version. To the latter Tissot added two incidental groups of figures by way of giving a cautionary dimension to the scene. A band of mud-larks has interrupted its scavenging along the Thames to gaze up at the top-hatted 'swells' on the balcony above.

21 Brown's explication is given in full in F. M. Hueffer, *Ford Madox Brown, a record of his life and work* (1896), pp. 189–95.

22 'The Pictures of Mr. Ford Madox Brown (March, 1865).' *Essays on Art*, pp. 182–3.

23 'Preraphaelite Paintings at Wallington: Note on William Bell Scott and Ruskin,' *Architectural Review*, xcii (Dec. 1942), 149. Scott's mural preceded by about fifteen years Adolph Menzel's 'Rolling Mill' (1875, Nationalgalerie, Berlin), the most celebrated of all paintings of heavy industry. Werner Hofmann perceives in

the nineteenth-century treatment of such scenes an idealizing tendency, which he accounts for as follows:

> But this heroic interpretation in some measure evaded the actual facts. It overlooked that alienation from his true personality which marked the urban worker and which was the real basis of Marx's social criticism. From Courbet right up to Van Gogh the picture of the worker as a human type was conditioned by the earnest mood and the simplicity of what was essentially an agricultural or peasant background. Nothing in it suggests the whirr of machinery or the soul-destroying mechanism of the factory process, nothing the 'new-fangled men' of the industrial age whom Marx hailed in his writings. When these painters wished to look for the real infernos of our civilisation, they did not go to the factory-worker at all, but sought out street-singers or entered railway carriages or places of nocturnal amusement.

The Earthly Paradise: Art in the nineteenth century, trans. Brian Battershaw (New York, 1961), p. 195.

24 The French artist outlined his abortive plans in a letter to the Prefect of the Seine, in which he stated his wish to 'paint a series of pictures representing "the stomach of Paris" (if I may use the expression so popular today and which illustrates my idea very well) with different guilds [*corporations*] in their own surroundings—the public and commercial life of today, I would include the Paris markets, the Paris railways, the Paris bridges, Paris tunnels, Paris race-courses and public gardens.

    'For the ceiling there would be a gallery around which would be shown, in appropriate action, all the men alive today who have contributed in a civic capacity to the grandeur and richness of Paris.' Pierre Courthion and Pierre Cailler, eds, *Portrait of Manet by himself and his contemporaries*, trans. Michael Ross (1960), p. 330.

(Manet's phrase 'le ventre de Paris' was, of course, borrowed from Zola.)

25 J. G. Millais, *The Life and Letters of Sir John Everett Millais* (New York, 1899), I, p. 248.

26 Ibid., I, pp. 249–50.

27 'A Rake's Progress' reappears in several Victorian versions, including the enormously popular 'The Last Day in the Old Home' (1862, Tate Gallery) by Robert Braithwaite Martineau (1826–69), and Frith's five serial pictures, 'The Road to Ruin' (1887), of which the artist said that it had been his purpose to show 'a kind of gambler's progress, avoiding the satirical vein of Hogarth, for which I knew myself to be unfitted.' *My Autobiography*, II, p. 121. Tissot treated a related subject in his set of four paintings, 'The Prodigal Son in Modern Life' (1882, Musée de Nantes).

28 I am indebted to Mr Lionel Lambourne for the interpretation of several details in this drawing.

29 Quoted by Robin Ironside, *Pre-Raphaelite Painters* (1948), p. 28.

30 Of the many pictorial treatments of emigration as a consequence of industrial distress and unemployment, the best-known is Ford Madox Brown's 'The Last of England' (1852–5, City of Birmingham Museum and Art Gallery).

31 Like Frith's 'The Railway Station,' this work, when exhibited at the Academy, drew such crowds that it had to be protected by a railing. The original engraving in

the *Graphic* attracted the attention of Dickens, who through Millais commissioned Fildes to illustrate *The Mystery of Edwin Drood*. In more conservative quarters, however, Fildes' painting aroused indignant protest. A writer in the *Art Journal*, xiii (1874), 201, declared: 'These deformed and wretched creatures who wait for admission to a wretched resting-place, are only admissible into art that is indifferent to beauty. But looking now, as we are bound to do, only to considerations purely artistic, there is little in a theme of such grovelling misery to recommend it to a painter whose purpose is beauty. . . . The state of things he represents to us ought rather to be removed than to be perpetuated, and its introduction into art which should be permanent is rather matter for regret.'

32 J. S. Mills, *Life and Letters of Sir Hubert von Herkomer: A study in struggle and success* (1923), p. 97.

33 Ibid., p. 153.

34 *Town Swamps and Social Bridges* (1859), p. v.

35 Ibid., p. vi. As a further vindication of his procedure, Godwin cited the testimony of Lord Ebrington (p. vii): 'I am able to corroborate from personal inspection some few, and from official knowledge most, of the reports and descriptions. May your words, and the too faithful horrors of the illustrations, help to arouse the public from that foolish and wicked apathy with which sanitary reform has been for some time viewed . . .' Any account of the contributions of book illustrators to the reporting of Victorian city life (particularly in London) would have to take into account numerous volumes which, while lacking the sociological impetus of Mayhew or Godwin, document the contemporary scene with great liveliness and fidelity. Among the artists whose graphic commentary illuminated the accompanying texts with often startling boldness were: William M'Connell, the illustrator of George Augustus Sala's *Twice around the Clock; or, The hours of the day and night in London* (1859); the anonymous illustrator of Daniel Joseph Kirwan's *Palace and Hovel: or, Phases of London life* (1870); and Alfred Concanen, who illustrated James Greenwood's journeys into the underworld, such as *The Wilds of London* (1874).

36 P.-A. Lemoisne, *Gavarni: Peintre et lithographe* (Paris, 1924), II, p. 12.

37 Ibid., II, p. 62.

38 In 1849 a volume entitled *Gavarni in London: Sketches of life and character*, edited by Albert Smith, was published in London. These examples of Gavarni's work were, however, clearly selected to avoid offending the English market, and convey an inadequate impression of the boldness and acerbity of the artist's vision.

39 A stereoscopic photograph made in 1895 almost exactly reproduces the same spectacle, and it occurs again in an oil painted about 1925 by C. R. W. Nevinson.

40 *London: A pilgrimage* (1872), p. 5.

41 Ibid., p. 6. Amelia B. Edwards recorded a statement by Doré to her 'that he thought the London poor the most picturesque figures in Europe.' See 'Gustave Doré: Personal Recollections of the Artist and his Works,' *Art Journal*, iii n.s. (1883), 365.

42 *Art and the Industrial Revolution*, ed. cit., pp. 120 ff.

43 Martin's pamphlets are listed in Thomas Balston, *John Martin, 1789–1854: His life and works* (1947), App. 5 (b), pp. 271–4.

44 Ibid., p. 107.

45 Ibid., p. 236.

46 An example is Wilkie's great canvas, 'Chelsea Pensioners reading the Gazette of the Battle of Waterloo' (1822, Apsley House). To ensure the architectural accuracy of the ambience for his groupings of figures, the artist made many preliminary sketches on the spot.

47 In the London Museum there is a watercolor by Myles Birket Foster (1825–99) of the demolition of Nash's colonnade in Regent Street, inscribed in the artist's hand: 'The last days of Pompeii.'

48 Quoted by Klingender, ed. cit., p. 155.

49 Ibid., p. 156. Among other artists skillful in assimilating industrial features into traditional landscapes was William Henry Bartlett (1809–54), engravings of whose work adorn the continuation of *Finden's Views of the Ports, Harbours, and Watering Places of Great Britain*, 2 vols (1842).

50 Quoted by W. T. Whitley, 'Girtin's Panorama,' *Connoisseur*, lxix (May 1924), 16. In 'The White House, Chelsea' (1800, Tate Gallery) Girtin, as has been often remarked, anticipated Whistler's 'Nocturnes.'

51 *Turner: Imagination and reality* (New York, 1966), p. 45.

52 With reference to Constable's many views over the city from Hampstead, Allen Staley has written that the artist 'was litle interested in the city as such but in the atmosphere and weather hanging over it.' *Romantic Art in Britain: Paintings and drawings 1760–1860* (Philadelphia 1968), p. 208.

53 W. H. Hunt, *Pre-Raphaelitism and the Pre-Raphaelite Brotherhood* (New York, 1914), II, p. 188.

54 Quoted as the epigraph to William Jackson, ed., *Herdman's Liverpool* (Liverpool, 1968).

55 Among Newcastle topographers should be listed John Wykeham Archer (1808–64), whose visit to London in mid-century was productive of a notable series of drawings of city life.

56 Bough's watercolor, 'View of a Manufacturing Town,' is the sole representation of an industrial milieu among the 285 illustrations in Martin Hardie, *Water-colour Painting in Britain: III, The Victorian Period* (1968).

57 Hueffer, op. cit., pp. 127–8.

58 The development of the art of photography tended to promote an increased literalism in the topographical rendering of city scenes. This influence may be observed in the amount of superfluous detail cluttering the canvasses of such later Victorian painters as George Vicat Cole (1833–93) and William Logsdail (1859–1944).

59 See Douglas Cooper, *The Courtauld Collection: A catalogue and introduction* (1954), to which the present section of this chapter is indebted. A series of instructive comparisons could be drawn between French and English paintings treating similar material. Whether in the realistic manner of Courbet or in the Impressionist style which ensued, the French works are characterized by a greater reliance on purely pictorial values and by a corresponding absence of all extraneous concerns, anecdotal, socio-moralistic, or documentary. Pairings illustrative of these differing emphases might include: Courbet's 'Les Casseurs de Pierre' (1849, formerly Kunstmuseum, Dresden; destroyed in 1945) and Henry Wallis's 'The Stonebreaker'

473

(1857, City of Birmingham Museum and Art Gallery), as well as John Brett's 'The Stonebreaker' (1858, Walker Art Gallery, Liverpool); Daumier's 'Le Wagon de Troisième Classe' (*c.* 1862, Metropolitan Museum of Art, New York) and Charles Rossiter's 'To Brighton and Back, 3/6' (1859); Manet's 'Le Chemin de Fer' (1873, National Gallery of Art, Washington) or Monet's 'La Gare Saint-Lazare' (1877, Fogg Art Museum, Cambridge, Mass.) and Frith's 'The Railway Station' (1862); Degas's 'La Voiture aux Courses' (1873, Museum of Fine Arts, Boston) and Frith's 'Derby Day' (1856); Manet's 'La Rue Mosnier aux Paveurs' (1878, Coll. Lord Butler), and Brown's 'Work' (1852–65).

60   Quoted by Douglas Cooper, op. cit., p. 38n. See also Frederick Wedmore, 'Modern Life in Modern Art,' *Magazine of Art*, xi (1877–8), 77–80.

61   *The Complete Letters of Vincent Van Gogh* (New York Graphic Society: Greenwich, Conn., 1958), I, p. 384. Van Gogh's correspondence is strewn with admiring references to the English school of social realists.

62   René Goupil, quoted by William Seitz, *Claude Monet: Seasons and monuments* (New York, 1960), p. 36.

63   'The Present State of the Fine Arts in France,' pp. 17–18. For evidence that Hamerton's prejudices were shared by leading painters of the day, see W. P. Frith's article, 'Crazes in Art: "Pre-Raphaelitism" and "Impressionism,"' *Magazine of Art*, xi (1887–8), 187–91.

64   Douglas Cooper, op. cit., p. 17.

65   Henri Lemaitre, ed., *Curiosités esthétiques; l'art romantique; et autres oeuvres critiques* (Paris, 1962), p. 405. To the same period of Whistler's career belongs the oil, entitled 'Wapping' (first exhibited at the Academy in 1864, now Coll. John Hay Whitney, New York). Of this 'incomparable view of the Lower Pool of London' William Michael Rossetti wrote: 'Never was that familiar scene so triumphantly well painted. . . . He realises, through Nature for the sake of art, an aim as legitimate as the more usual one of realising through art for the sake of Nature, and even more intrinsically pictorial.' E. R. and J. Pennell, *The Life of James McNeill Whistler* (1909), I, p. 127.

66   Ibid., II, p. 258.

67   James McNeill Whistler, *The Gentle Art of Making Enemies* (New York, 1927), p. 144.

68   *Exhibition of Paintings by Atkinson Grimshaw* (London, 1964). For some reproductions of this artist's paintings, see [Jane Abdy], *Atkinson Grimshaw, 1836–1893* (1970).

69   Greaves said: 'To Mr. Whistler a boat was always a tone, to us it was always a boat.' Quoted by Graham Reynolds, *Painters of the Victorian Scene* (1953), p. 102.

70   See, for example, Bramley's 'Hopeless Dawn' (1888) and Forbes' 'The Health of the Bride' (1889, both in the Tate Gallery). As members of the Newlyn School, located in Cornwall, Forbes and Bramley, as well as their associates, were primarily concerned with rural life.

71   Quoted in Robert Emmons, *The Life and Opinions of Walter Richard Sickert* (1941), p. 99.

20   The Frightened Poets

G. Robert Stange

The attitudes that English poets have taken toward the modern city offer some useful —and even surprising—data to the intellectual historian; for the literary critic, however, the interest of such a subject must be in the ways by which the poets' viewpoints shaped the conceptual form which the city assumes in their writings. But no matter how one looks at it the subject leads to unexpected confusions. We may begin by realizing that 'literary' attitudes cannot easily be distinguished from religious, mythological, or historical ones; but having accepted this fact, we must also acknowledge that all conceptions of the city—ancient or modern—seem to partake of an inherent, sometimes mystical dualism.

The elemental duality rises from the custom of building the ancient metropolis according to a mythical model of the celestial city. Jerusalem, Babylon, Sigiriya: all follow an archetype and, as Mircea Eliade has suggested, the reality and validity of urban cultures may come from their 'participation . . . in an archetypal model.'[1] St Augustine's distinction between the heavenly city of *caritas* and the earthly city of *cupiditas* may be seen as a religious application of the mythical pattern. Certainly the Augustinian antinomy is very much alive: it would seem that the most positivistic urban planners have a conception of the City of God which they pose against the Babylon of our everyday life.

Historians of the city make a distinction which, though it is strictly behavioral, seems no less rich in symbolic connotations than those of Ezekiel or Augustine. It is customary to distinguish between the village, built to shelter its inhabitants and repel the outsider, having for its end a condition of stability approaching the static, and the city, which *draws* people to it and finds its function as a crossroads of commerce, a center of government and of culture. The 'dynamism' of the city is opposed in Lewis Mumford's formulation to the 'fixed and indrawn form of the village.'[2] This city-village contrast is one that persists in the European imagination, unaffected by time or objective reality. As late as the 1840s, for example, De Quincey could envision London in two separate ways: at one point he refers nostalgically to 'London within the walls,' a term which evokes the fixed, sheltering village of an already dim but imaginable past; however, when—in his *Autobiographical Sketches*—he describes his arrival in the actual city his language approaches that of the modern sociologist; he uses figures of magnetism and suction and speaks of men and of droves of cattle, all with their heads turned toward London, flowing into it along the arterial roads:[3]

> A suction so powerful, felt along radii so vast, and a consciousness, at the same time, that upon other radii still more vast, both by land and by sea, the same suction is operating, night and day, summer and winter, and hurrying forever into one centre the infinite means needed for her infinite purposes, and the endless tributes to the skill or to the luxury of her endless population, crowds the imagination with a pomp to which there is nothing corresponding upon this planet, either amongst the things that have been or the things that are.

De Quincey, however, is unusual in being able to externalize his double vision, to hold in balance the walled London of the past—and of his imagination—and his concrete sense of the new metropolis in which he lived. For the most part the views of the city taken by nineteenth-century English writers are based on a contrast between the city and nature, a contrast that is so broadly conceived as to incorporate a set of lesser distinctions drawn from either history or imagination. As Victorian London is built, the writers—with some notable exceptions—play variations on the theme of the *naturally* good and the corrupting evil of the city; the cleanness of the ancient village is contrasted with the dingy filth of the capital; the spiritual soundness of peasant life with the decayed values of the market place. But though these attitudes may seem too familiar to require comment, it is worth pointing out that they had not always been characteristic of English literature.

Eighteenth-century writers celebrated the values of city life; Swift's 'Description of the Morning' or 'A Description of a City Shower' express both fascination with the cloacal aspects of the city and love for its immense variety. Pope's attitude is fairly suggested in the opening phrase of 'A Farewell to London': 'Dear, damn'd, distracting town'; or in his lament, the 'Epistle to Mrs. Blount: On Her Leaving the Town.' Both Pope and Gay are, as Gay put it in *Trivia*, 'Careful observers, studious of the town' (l. 285), and Dr Johnson's views on the purported pleasures of the countryside are too well known to need repeating. What is striking is the rapidity with which these attitudes are replaced by a kind of doctrinaire anti-urbanism. The radical contrast that is to be accepted by several generations of poets is succinctly put in Cowper's wonderfully commonplace lines in *The Task*, 'God made the country, and man made the town' (I, 749). 'Vast/ and boundless' London, Cowper sees as a 'crowded coop,' almost more corrupted, 'And therefore more obnoxious at this hour,/ Than Sodom in her day had power to be' (III, 834–5; 846–7).

The new ways of looking at the city come into effect very suddenly and are related both to currents of bourgeois sentimentalism and new ideas of nature. Rousseau, it is not surprising to learn, was the principal formulator of what came to be the accepted attitudes; in both *La Nouvelle Héloise* (1761) and in *Émile* (1762) he declared his aversion to 'la nouvelle Babylone.' Human beings, according to one of the letters in the *Nouvelle Héloise*, are not meant to be piled up in ant-heaps (partie iv, lettre 14), and throughout his writings he stresses his antipathy to Paris and his conviction that man's true home is in the bosom of nature.

Certainly Rousseau looms behind Wordsworth's excited passages in the seventh book of the *Prelude*:

> Rise up, thou monstrous ant-hill on the plain
> Of a too busy world! Before me flow,
> Thou endless stream of men and moving things!
> Thy every-day appearance, as it strikes—
> With wonder heightened, or sublimed by awe—
> On strangers of all ages; the quick dance
> Of colours, lights and forms; the deafening din;
> The comers and the goers face to face,
> Face after face; the string of dazzling wares,
> Shop after shop, with symbols, blazoned names,
> And all the tradesman's honours overhead.
>
> (ll. 149–59)

The poet, continuing his description of London, calls it a 'huge fermenting mass of humankind,' and speaks appalled of 'the great tide of human life' (VII, 621, 656). In 'Michael' the fate of the old shepherd's son is described with the laconicism appropriate to events that are in the order of things:

> Meantime Luke began
> To slacken in his duty; and at length,
> He in the dissolute city gave himself
> To evil courses: ignominy and shame
> Fell on him, so that he was driven at last
> To seek a hiding-place beyond the seas.
>
> (ll. 442–7)

The theme of the New Babylon was more enthusiastically developed in England than in France, and for nearly a century it dominated English poetry. Cowper's and Wordsworth's poetic successors tended either to inveigh against the city or to pretend that it didn't exist.

One might read the whole body of Tennyson's poetry, for example, without becoming conscious of modern London. The city that one feels is most real to him is the Camelot of the *Idylls of the King,* the city 'built/ To music, therefore never built at all,/ And therefore built forever' ('Gareth and Lynette,' ll. 277–9), an interesting literary recurrence of the 'archetypal model' of the celestial city. But the London which Tennyson actually experienced emerges only as part of the madman's vision in *Maud* ('I loathe the squares and streets,/ And the faces that one meets'), or as a frantic 'stream of passing feet.' The two references to London in *In Memoriam* are classic examples of the anti-urbanism of Victorian writers. In Section VII the poet-speaker visits the dark house of his dead friend in 'the long unlovely street.' In this passage the city is a symbol of desolation, but when, after a lapse of time, the poet has partly overcome his despair, he returns to Wimpole Street (Section CXIX) and finds that its metropolitan horror has been mysteriously dissolved by nature:

> not as one that weeps
> I come once more; the city sleeps;
> I smell the meadow in the street;
>
> I hear a chirp of birds.

The transformation suggested here is not unlike the one that had overtaken the sleeping city, 'Open unto the fields, and to the sky,' which Wordsworth contemplated from Westminster Bridge. Like Wordsworth, Tennyson can find beauty and value only in a city permeated by nature, one that offers itself to his imagination as something other than a busy metropolis.

There is melancholy evidence for this last statement in the fact that the only poem of Tennyson's which treats of a modern city deals with Paris, and comes close to incoherence. The work is called 'Beautiful City,' and appeared in the volume of 1889, *Demeter and Other Poems*:

> Beautiful city, the centre and crater of European confusion,
> O you with your passionate shriek for the rights of an equal humanity
> How often your Re-volution has proven but E-volution
> Rolled again back on itself in the tides of a civic insanity!

The principal emotion underlying this tiresome quatrain would seem to be fear; and, indeed, reading more widely among the Victorians, one begins to see that the writers' distrust of the city is as much a result of conservative political and conventional moral attitudes as of an acquired rural ethos. Often, one finds, 'the city' means Paris, not only the source of wicked books and loose sexual practices, but the breeding-ground of revolution. Roden Noel, a follower of Tennyson, who in the seventies and eighties wrote a number of poems about London, is a useful example. Noel was socially conscious in ways that Tennyson was not, but even with his interest in the lives of the London poor he could conceive the city only as the locale of suffering and chaos. In his long political poem, *The Red Flag* (1872), Noel, reacting to the Paris Commune, projects an apocalyptic vision of London seized by revolution: the 'towered Thames/ Rolls like the Seine, a tide of eddying flames'; and, 'Lo! surging human seas arise and fall/ Around the lurid grandeur of Saint Paul.'[4] In his *Lay of Civilisation* (1874) he evolves a set of images that were on the point of becoming clichés:[5]

> This huge black whirlpool of the city sucks,
> And swallows, and encroaches evermore
> On vernal field, pure air, and wholesome heaven—
> A vast dim province, ever under cloud,
> O'er whose immeasurable unloveliness
> His own foul breath broods sinister, like Fate.

Though Noel never rises above a pedestrian earnestness, he is an interesting representative of the explicit fusion of the endemic fear of revolution and unrestraint (the French disease) and the anti-metropolitan bias of the rural gentry, the class from which he and so many other English poets came. Noel's view of the city was both first-hand and, in its sympathies, radical; but it did not cease to be also Tory and pastoral.

With so many examples before us it might be well to pause and consider what conclusions can arise from a study of this unpromising material. In tracing the image of the modern city as it appears in Victorian poetry I am applying certain normative assumptions: I would say that the literary imagination has among its tasks that of domesticating our apprehension of the terrifying or the unknown. Literature can transform into myth, and thus make manageable to our consciousness experience we must live with, but which may appal or derange our immediate understanding. The Victorian city is one of the best examples our culture provides of such a fact; it was an inescapable milieu which seemed to have sprung into being overnight, and which produced among some of its inhabitants fear, fascination, horror, and ennui. There is a point at which quantity becomes quality; the modern city, because of its size and extension, was qualitatively different from the eighteenth-century city. The social evils which most middle-class Englishmen would have preferred not to see became more and more difficult to escape. The modern city is, in fact, a looming emblem of guilt—an emblem in which one is physically immersed. The density of urban life brought to the eyes and ears the processes of human elimination in ways that country life had not done. The modern city exposes men's physical needs; what takes place behind the hedge-row can be either overlooked or romanticized, when the same thing happens on the bricks of an urban alley it becomes an experience that must be either dealt with or repressed.

I am leading—it will be clear—toward a parallel between the facts of urban life and the facts of sex. I believe that the great penetrative imaginations of the nineteenth century—Balzac, Dickens, Baudelaire, Dostoevski—could, in varying degrees, face these experiences and release the saving powers of myth. But most of the English writers in the time of Victoria repressed their knowledge of the city, just as they repressed their knowledge of sex—and for the same reasons: Puritanism had taught them the habit of repression, and they were afraid.

The peculiarity of the English response to urban experience is made somewhat clearer by comparison with writers in the United States and France—the two other countries that had, by the mid-century, developed modern cities. In America the writers' distrust of the city has been so persistent that the intellectual historians, Morton and Lucia White, have been able to trace anti-urbanism as a dominant attitude from Jefferson, through the writers of the American Renaissance, to Louis Sullivan and Frank Lloyd Wright.[6] The Whites' marshalling of evidence for their argument is entirely convincing, but their study is disappointing in its avoidance of speculation as to the sources of the intellectual attitudes they describe, and in its virtual omission of Whitman's poetry—which is the great contradiction to the authors' thesis.

The best light that American writers cast on the treatment of the Victorian city comes—on one side and the other—from Emerson and Whitman. In a remarkable passage in his journals Emerson deploys the criteria of transcendental philosophy to reject the imaginative possibilities of the city, and at the same time suggests a psychological basis for fear and distrust:[7]

> The city delights the understanding. It is made up of finites; short, sharp, mathematical lines, all calculable. It is full of varieties, of successions, of contrivances. The country on the contrary offers an unbroken horizon, the monotony of an endless road, of vast uniform plains, of distant mountains, the melancholy of uniform and infinite vegetation; the objects on the road are few and worthless; the eye is invited ever to the horizon and the clouds. It is the School of the Reason.

Emerson's distinction between Reason and Understanding, so ingeniously applied in this context, is taken over from Carlyle's popularizations of Kant's *Vernunft* and *Verstand*. Carlyle defines Reason (*Vernunft*) as the pure, ultimate light of our nature, wherein lies the 'foundation of all Poetry, Virtue, Religion; things which are properly beyond the province of the understanding.'[8] Understanding (*Verstand*) is that lesser faculty directed to the observation of superficial things, subject to time and change. Emerson picks up traditional materials, but in his witty extension of the Kantian antinomy gives a new and sophisticated version of the town/country opposition. To locate the noumenal world in the country and to suggest that the city destroys the imagination because it is the fulfillment of the partial, phenomenal world is to translate Cowper's easy platitudes to another level. Emerson has applied the perspective of Yankee Puritanism to Romantic nature worship, and cast his reflections in the language of German Idealism. In doing so he arrives at some shrewd insights: his definition of the phenomenological aspects of the city both suggests why it seemed terrible to certain kinds of sensibility and characterizes those aspects of experience which were to stimulate the poets of the city who had not yet appeared.

For Whitman, Emerson's improbable disciple, 'Varieties . . . successions . . . contrivances' are the very substance of poetry. He blandly obliterates the distinction between the universes of Reason and of Understanding, and would consider it his bardic function to reveal the infiniteness of all the Emersonian finites. He becomes, almost incidentally, the first English-speaking writer to make city life a major theme of poetry. For him 'Superb-faced Manhattan'[9] is principally a source of *aperçus*, a reservoir of images; since every element of the city has beauty and value, its diversity and multitudinousness are to be rejoiced in and treated as emblematic of the interconnectedness of human life itself. 'See, in my poems,' he writes, 'Cities, solid, vast, inland, with paved streets, with iron and stone edifices, ceaseless vehicles, and commerce,'[10] and in 'Crossing Brooklyn Ferry,' 'Manhattan,' 'Broadway,' 'A Broadway Pageant' he imposes on the numberless, discrete items of metropolitan life the unity of his own consciousness. Whitman does not create a myth of the city, as Baudelaire was to do; he simply absorbs and registers its multiformity, gives it, somehow, an ineffable significance:[11]

> The blab of the pave, tires of carts, sluff of boot-soles, talk of the
>   promenaders,
> The heavy omnibus, the driver with his interrogating thumb, the clank
>   of the shod horses on the granite floor,
> The snow-sleighs, clinking, shouted jokes, pelts of snow-balls,
> The hurrahs for popular favorites, the fury of rous'd mobs,
> The flap of the curtain'd litter, a sick man inside borne to the hospital,
> The meeting of enemies, the sudden oath, the blows and fall,
> The excited crowd, the policeman with his star quickly working his passage
>   to the center of the crowd,
> The passive stones that receive and return so many echoes . . .

Whitman's example supports at least one explanation of the Victorian poets' neglect of the city. He was notoriously the nineteenth-century American writer who was free of a Puritan heritage and disrespectful of gentility. Both the uniqueness of his poetic achievement and his permissiveness in regard to subject matter might suggest that the city becomes available as literary material only when a writer escapes the restrictions of Anglo-Saxon, Protestant gentility.

The French experience is, in any case, profoundly different from that of the English. It is ascertainable that the Rousseauistic dualism that remained dominant in England was abandoned in France by the 1830s. It seems likely that the Revolution of 1830, an *urban* phenomenon involving the intelligentsia and a portion of the middle class, made for a liberal cosmopolitanism among writers that remained rare in nineteenth-century England. Certainly, from the early thirties on one finds in literary works what Pierre Citron has called 'la poésie de Paris.'[12] The city assumes the form of a modern myth. In *Les Mystères de Paris* (1842–3) Sue created a kind of Gothic novel in which the city, with its mysterious chambers, its glooms and labyrinthine ways, takes the place of the customary castle. In several of Balzac's novels Paris is not only the scene of action, but also a place having unique values and beauties, an ambience which gives shape to the conflicts and adventures which are most characteristic of modern life. However, it is Baudelaire who most effectively and systematically evokes the rare and frightening beauty of 'l'immonde cité,' a vast artifact which he loves and hates as a living being and finds wonderful because of its multiplicity and the bitter charm of its infernal depths. In one of the prose poems of *Le Spleen de Paris* the poet celebrates the public gardens whose shadowy retreats are haunted by grotesque figures crippled, he suggests, by life. It is, above all, he continues, 'vers ces lieux que le poëte et le philosophe aiment diriger leurs avides conjectures.'[13]

The belief that the city provides special material for the modern imagination to work upon is most eloquently stated in the epilogue to *Le Spleen de Paris*, in which the poet climbs to the height from which he can survey, with contented heart, the city in all its amplitude:[14]

> Hôpital, lupanar, purgatoire, enfer, bagne
> Où toute énormité fleurit comme une fleur.
>
> . . . .
>
> Mais comme un vieux paillard d'une vieille mâitresse,
> Je voulais m'enivrer de l'énorme catin
> Dont le charme infernal me rajeunit sans cesse.

And he concludes,

> Je t'aime, ô capitale infame! Courtisanes
> Et bandits, tels souvent vous offrez de plaisirs
> Que ne comprennent les vulgaires profanes.

In the essay called 'De l'héroisme de la vie moderne,' a section of the *Salon de 1846*, Baudelaire offers a more theoretical conception of the city as modern myth. Considering the nature of modern subjects in art, he concludes that the essential question is whether there is, for men of his time, a *particular* beauty, intrinsic with new passions ('inhérente à des passions nouvelles'); and he affirms that such a beauty, and even a new form of heroism, can be found in the thousands of beings who drift and circulate in the depths of the great city. Nineteenth-century man must not look for the heroism of Achilles or Agamemnon, but 'La vie parisienne est féconde en sujets poétiques et merveilleux. Le merveilleux nous enveloppe et nous abreuve comme l'atmosphère; mais nous ne le voyons pas.'[15] As Baudelaire sees it, the artist's function is to transmute the filth of the city into the gold of art, and it is principally his realization of the heroism of contemporary life which gives him his status as founder of the modern tradition, as himself a culture hero of a new urban society.

Many French writers followed Baudelaire as poets of the city. For Verlaine and Laforgue Paris is both scene and subject, and in the poetry of Lautréamont and Rimbaud the city becomes part of their vision, assuming the qualities of hallucination as well as of myth. While Baudelaire had conceived hell as a superbly luxurious *hôtel particulier* beneath the streets of Paris, and Satan as a talkative *boulevardier*,[16] Rimbaud's season in a distant and visionary hell ends with an accession of vigor and tenderness, so that he may—armed with an eager patience—enter, at last, the splendid cities.[17]

It is not easy to explain why Victorian poets should have been so much less interested in the city than their French contemporaries were. One cause might have been the traditional differences between the French view of their capital and the English view of London. Though France was—and still is—a much more 'rural' nation than England,[18] Paris has been, from the twelfth century on, a center of education, government, and commerce in a way that London could not be. The fact that the older universities were not in London prevented the centralization of culture that one finds in France; and—even more important—the location of Oxford and Cambridge probably reinforced their function as purveyors of the values of the landed aristocracy. This is not the place to describe in detail the differences between the social ethos which predominated among the faculty and students at the University of Paris and that which was accepted throughout the nineteenth century at Oxford and Cambridge. It is undeniable, first, that English poets tended to go to a university and, second, that the values of the gentry were more widely dispersed—and accepted —among the English intelligentsia than they were among the French. With only a few exceptions (Browning being the most notable one) the Victorian poets held to an enlightened conservatism based on attitudes associated with a tradition of rural land holding, and were not stimulated either by urban life or its political problems.

Another source of the English distrust of the city seems to have been the fear of revolution. Paris became available to the imagination of writers; London did not. France had three revolutions in the nineteenth century, in all of which artists took part; no poets and painters were to be found among the ranks of the Chartists, who were, at their climactic moment in London, dispersed with puzzling ease. In considering the Victorian attitude towards the city one tends to fall back on Halévy's famous theory which explains the absence of violent revolution in England as a result of the sublimating (and, I would add, repressing) effects of evangelical religion. If Halévy's hypothesis is sound the same set of facts would explain England's freedom from revolution, her sexual prudery, and—considering the affinity which middle-class writers felt for the values of the 'Barbarians'—the anti-urbanism of her poets.

Robert Browning, a born Londoner, spared the gentling influences of the ancient universities, and curious enough to have been interested in both the underside of the city and its unconventional politics, should have become the Baudelaire of London. That he did not do so is a sad accident of economic necessity. 'In England,' his wife once wrote, 'no one lives by verse that lives.'[19] And, indeed, after the Brownings' marriage they had to remain in Italy simply because their small incomes would not allow a reasonably comfortable life in England. Though London might have wonderfully suited Browning's interest in complexity and multitudinousness, it plays almost no part in his poetry. Mrs Browning, whose conviction was that the sole work of the poet was to represent 'this live, throbbing age' (*Aurora Leigh*, V, 202), did compose a few passages that bear on the city and on its relations to poetry. Embedded in the compound prolixities of *Aurora Leigh*, her epic of the modern age, are some almost luminous passages on London. The most notable is a reflection by Aurora on her own industrious author's life high up 'in a certain house in Kensington':

> Serene and unafraid of solitude,
> I worked the short days out,—and watched the sun
> On lurid morns or monstrous afternoons
> (Like some Druidic idol's fiery brass
> With fixed unflickering outline of dead heat,
> From which the blood of wretches pent inside
> Seems oozing forth to incarnadine the air)
> Push out through fog with his dilated disk,
> And startle the slant roofs and chimney-pots
> With splashes of fierce colour. Or I saw
> Fog only, the great tawny weltering fog
> Involve the passive city, strangle it
> Alive, and draw it off into the void,
> Spires, bridges, streets, and squares, as if a spunge
> Had wiped out London,—or as noon and night
> Had clapped together and utterly struck out
> The intermediate time, undoing themselves
> In the act. Your city poets see such things
> Not despicable. Mountains of the south,
> When drunk and mad with elemental wines
> They rend the seamless mist and stand up bare,
> Make fewer singers, haply. No one sings,
> Descending Sinai: on Parnassus-mount
> You take a mule to climb and not a muse
> Except in fable and figure: forests chant
> Their anthems to themselves, and leave you dumb.
> But sit in London at the day's decline,
> And view the city perish in the mist
> Like Pharaoh's armaments in the deep Red Sea,
> The chariots, horsemen, footmen, all the host,
> Sucked down and choked to silence—then, surprised
> By a sudden sense of vision and of tune,
> You feel as conquerors though you did not fight . . .
>   (*Aurora Leigh*, III, 169–201)

This is an interesting argument and, on the whole, good poetry. Elizabeth Barrett Browning was clearly working toward a poetics of urban life, but unfortunately no substantial work grew out of her tentative efforts.

Even, then, in the work of those English poets who believed in the city as a proper subject of poetry we find unsuccess. Arthur Hugh Clough rebuked his friend

Matthew Arnold by reviewing Arnold's first two volumes of poetry along with Alexander Smith's *A Life Drama*, and suggesting that Smith's poetry was in touch with actual life in a way that Arnold's was not. Clough demanded that poets adopt a new attitude towards the external facts of Victorian life, that they try to find a charm in images drawn from 'the busy seas of industry,' and recognize that 'the true and lawful haunts of the poetic powers' are, 'if anywhere, in the blank and desolate streets, and upon the solitary bridges of the midnight city, where Guilt is, and wild Temptation, and the dire Compulsion of what has once been done—there, with these tragic sisters around him, and with pity also, and pure Compassion, and pale Hope, that looks like despair, and Faith in the garb of doubt, there walks the discrowned Apollo, with unstrung lyre.'[20]

But Clough himself was not able to summon the Muse of the Midnight City. The London of 'In the Great Metropolis' is merely an abstractly conceived Vanity Fair, and the poem called 'To the Great Metropolis' is a lament, along conventional lines, for the fact that the stranger's fancy of London 'Is rather truly of a huge Bazaar,/ A railway terminus, a gay Hotel,/ Anything but a mighty Nation's heart.' Even Alexander Smith, though he may have been an effective stick with which to beat Arnold, never did in his poetry what Clough claimed for him. The most striking scene in *A Life Drama* takes place on a city bridge at midnight (the passage may have suggested Clough's allusion to 'solitary bridges' thronged with personifications), but Smith's poems more often fall back on the stale theme of the desirability of escape from the evils of the city to the purity of the country. Only, I think, in a few fine passages in *City Poems* (1857) does Smith effectively express his own experience of life in the Glasgow slums. In 'A Boy's Poem' he develops an impressive conceit of the slow, organic growth of the city:

> Slow the city grew,
> Like coral reef on which the builders die
> Until it stands complete in pain and death.
> Great bridges with their coronets of lamps
> Light the black stream beneath; rude ocean's flock,
> Ships from all climes are folded in its docks;
> And every heart from its great central dome
> To farthest suburb is a darkened stage
> On which grief walks alone.

There is some irony in the fact that Matthew Arnold published, in one of the very volumes that Clough attacked, what seems to me the only English poem of the time which invests the city with the symbolic depth and richness of Baudelaire's Paris. In 'A Summer Night' (1852) 'the deserted, moon-blanch'd street,' the windows which 'frown,/ Silent and white, unopening down,/ Repellent as the world,' are elements of a cramped urban landscape which becomes an image of man's limited, though possible existence. As the sky overspreads the narrow rigidities of the city streets, so the unknowable natural world surrounds man's limited being, offering its boundless freedom. It is a realization of the city which is more than just scenic or enumerative which makes this poem unique in the canon of even the most urbane of Victorian poets. Arnold's two later city poems, 'East London' and 'West London'—both in the 1867 volume—depend for their effects on stock phrases, 'the squalid streets of Bethnal Green,' or a stock situation of a poor woman in Belgravia who will beg from passing workmen, but not from the alien rich.

The Pre-Raphaelites who, like Arnold, spent their lives in London might be expected to have produced an art of the city, but they seem to have been as much inhibited as any of their contemporaries. Their theorizing was unexceptionable; in his early articles in the *Germ* F. G. Stephens spoke for the whole Brotherhood when he tried to define a new aesthetic of truth. Stephens insisted that the modern artist must 'go out into Life'; it was his task to reveal 'the poetry of the things about us; our railways, factories, mines, roaring cities, steam vessels and the endless novelties and wonders produced every day.'[21] But however committed they might be in principle to the use of contemporary materials, the Pre-Raphaelite painters could not even sympathize with—let alone attempt—the poetic studies of trains, streets, and great buildings which later gave such vitality to the Paris landscapes of the Impressionists. Ford Madox Brown's 'Work' (1852) attempts, with the help of an attendant sonnet and the artist's pamphlet of essayistic explanation, to encompass modern life by making the scene of an excavation for the laying of drains an allegory of all Victorian society. But even so ambitious and ingeniously contrived a work as Brown's seems abstracted, detached from the living materials on which the artist's imagination might be supposed to operate. The street is recognizable as Heath Street, Hampstead; Carlyle and F. D. Maurice are in evidence, along with representatives of every other class of workers and non-workers—and yet the scene has no reality: it is all symbol and no city.

The story of Rossetti's long and unsuccessful struggle to make of 'Found' a socially significant painting of urban degradation is best left to a discussion of the city in Victorian painting. It is only relevant to observe here that both the sonnet 'Found,' which serves as a program note for the painting, and the 'city' passages in 'Jenny' seem to reflect Stephens' injunction to 'go out into Life,' and to express the truth of the 'roaring cities.' They also suggest that Rossetti made a connection between the new city and sexual exploitation. But if we look in either poem for a vigorous handling of this connection or fresh treatment of urban material, we come away disappointed. The underlying moral patterns of 'Found' hark back to Cowper and Rousseau:

> 'There is a budding morrow in midnight:'—
>   So sang our Keats, our English nightingale.
>   And here, as lamps across the bridge turn pale
> In London's smokeless resurrection-light,
> Dark breaks to dawn. But o'er the deadly blight
>   Of love deflowered and sorrow of none avail

Which makes this man gasp and this woman quail,
Can day from darkness ever again take flight?

Ah! gave not these two hearts their mutual pledge,
Under one mantle sheltered 'neath the hedge
  In gloaming courtship? And O God! to-day
He only knows he holds her;—but what part
Can life now take? She cries in her locked heart,—
  'Leave me—I do not know you—go away!'

The section of 'Jenny' which most closely parallels 'Found' begins, 'Jenny,
you know the city now,' goes on to tell how love is bought and sold

When Saturday night is market-night
Everywhere, be it dry or wet,
And market-night in the Haymarket,

and ends with an image that is almost identical with one in 'Found':

      you stare
Along the streets alone, and there,
Round the long park, across the bridge,
The cold lamps at the pavement's edge
Wind on together and apart,
A fiery serpent for your heart.

Since we know that the London-bred Rossetti felt positively uneasy when he found
himself in the midst of nature, it is notable—to say the least—that he should continue to affirm the moral purity of country life and to suggest that corruption was a
consequence of metropolitan experience. The pattern of opposition in Rossetti's
poems of the city is identical with the one in Wordsworth's 'Michael.'

Whatever he might do as a political figure or social critic, William Morris did not
as a man of letters even try to face Victorian London. His first master was Ruskin,
who repeatedly opposed his sense of the cities of the past to the monotony of life in
the central streets of London. In his later writings Ruskin expressed the most
extreme anti-urbanism that is to be found anywhere. Architecture, in any true sense,
was, he felt, impossible in a city like London:[22] 'All lovely architecture was designed
for cities in cloudless air . . . .'

But our cities, built in black air which, by its accumulated foulness, first
renders all ornament invisible in distance, and then chokes its interstices
with soot; cities which are mere crowded masses of store, and warehouse,
and counter, and are therefore to the rest of the world what the larder
and cellar are to a private house; cities in which the object of men is not
life, but labour; and in which all chief magnitude of edifice is to enclose
machinery; cities in which the streets are not the avenues for the passing
and procession of a happy people, but the drains for the discharge of a

tormented mob, in which the only object in reaching any spot is to be transferred to another; in which existence becomes mere transition, and every creature is only one atom in a drift of human dust, and current of interchanging particles, circulating here by tunnels underground, and there by tubes in the air; for a city, or cities, such as this no architecture is possible—nay, no desire of it is possible to their inhabitants.

Morris translates the Ruskinian bias into verse when, in the opening lines of *The Earthly Paradise*, he urges his readers to

> Forget six counties overhung with smoke,
> Forget the snorting steam and piston stroke,
> Forget the spreading of the hideous town;
> Think rather of the pack-horse on the down,
> And dream of London, small, and white, and clean,
> The clear Thames bordered by its gardens green.

All art for Morris, the impassioned frequenter of protest meetings in Trafalgar Square, became a means of escape from the hot fermentation of the capital to 'A nameless city in a distant sea,/ White as the changing walls of faërie' (ll. 17–18).

The only English poet of the mid-century who consistently evades the traditional city-country opposition is Thomas Hood, and the nature of his achievement is merely further proof of the strength of conventional attitudes. Hood can only praise the city by assuming a comic stance which derides itself, so that though his work reveals a feeling for city life as profound as that of some of his French contemporaries, and at times as in 'Miss Kilmansegg and Her Precious Leg' (1840) an almost Dickensian pathos, he must offer his readers the opportunity to accept—or patronize—his statements as Cockney light verse. Such a poem as 'Rural Felicity' has no great literary importance, but its urbanism is genuine and refreshing. The argument of the poem can be found in the first two couplets:[23]

> Well, the country's a pleasant place, sure enough, for people that's
>   country born,
> And useful, no doubt, in a natural way, for growing our grass and our corn.
> It was kindly meant of our cousin Giles, to write and invite me down,
> Tho' as yet all I've seen of a pastoral life only makes one more partial to
>   town.

Hood's uncomfortable Londoner concludes that there are 'no fields to prefer to dear Leicester Fields up in town.'

The most substantial aspect of Hood's modest, somewhat journalistic, vision of London is his reversal of the values attached to the customary images. He depends on the familiar figures of waves and torrents, but for him the ceaseless flow of city life is a source of joy; the human movement has a power of its own, which he slyly suggests might be stronger than steam:[24]

> O, London is the place for all
> In love with loco-motion!
> Still to and fro the people go
> Like billows of the ocean.

The 'torrent of Man,' 'Gushing, rushing, crushing along,' is not menacing, but wonderful.

But Hood's light-hearted exploitation of the matter of London, and a few other survivals of jaunty Regency verse or of Lamb's mannered Cockneyism are significant merely as exceptions. It was only in the nineties that, for poets, painters, and novelists, London ceased to be regarded as a noxious drain or force of devastation (the phrases are Ruskin's). The change in viewpoint comes suddenly and is extraordinarily widespread. Though the phenomenon has not been noted by literary historians, it is one of the clearest signs of the break between the writers of the nineties and their High Victorian predecessors. Whether we look at the members of the Aesthetic Movement, at W. E. Henley, at dilettantish revivers of eighteenth-century modes such as Austin Dobson, at G. K. Chesterton, Henry James, or Gissing we find that their work embodies a new use of urban material, and that however different their attitudes and practices may be, the city has at last become for them a conceptual form—as it was for Baudelaire and Balzac. The London of these writers (and these generalizations could be reinforced by reference to the paintings of Whistler and Sickert) is still terrifying, baffling, and contradictory; but it nevertheless furnishes the artist with the materials of his imagery and, in the case of a writer like Henry James, serves as a foundation of his symbolic patterns.

Chesterton, in one of his newspaper pieces in the nineties, eloquently stated the new aesthetic of the city:[25]

> Men lived among mighty mountains and eternal forest for ages before they realised that they were poetical; it may reasonably be inferred that some of our descendants may see the chimney-pots as rich a purple as the mountain-peaks, and find the lamp-posts as old and natural as the trees. Of this realisation of a great city as something wild and obvious the detective story is certainly the *Iliad*.
>
> This realisation of the poetry of London is not a small thing. A city is, properly speaking, more poetic even than a countryside, for while nature is a chaos of unconscious forces, a city is a chaos of conscious ones. The crest of the flower or the pattern of the lichen may or may not be significant symbols. But there is no stone in the street and no brick in the wall that is not actually a deliberate symbol—a message from some man, as much as if it were a telegram or a post card. The narrowest street possesses, in every crook and twist of its intention, the soul of the man who built it, perhaps long in his grave. Every brick has as human a hieroglyph as if it were a graven brick of Babylon: every slate on the roof is as educational a document as if it were a slate covered with addition and subtraction sums.

Bringing his own special vigor to the task, Chesterton has reshaped several French motifs, joining the natural/anti-natural paradoxes of Gautier and Baudelaire to the Balzacian ennoblement of the detective as urban hero. But the value of this superior piece of journalism is in demonstrating the special place of the artificial in the work of writers at the end of the century. All the 'new' writers adopt both Baudelaire's concept of 'modernity' and his paradoxical defense of the artificial as morally superior to the natural. Following from this is a greatly increased receptivity to previously unexplored sources of inspiration. Writers of the nineties rejoice particularly in those urban features which Emerson had considered so harmful: the finites, the varieties, contrivances, rather than destroying their high visions, stimulated their imaginations and suggested new kinds of artistic experience. As Chesterton suggests, artifacts may now assume the value that was once supposed to inhere in the natural world alone: and by finding beauty in the constructions of man, the writer affirms a new kind of democratic humanism.

In poetry, then, the significant innovators become the members of what can loosely be called the Aesthetic Movement, that group whose artistic theories asserted the pre-eminence of art over nature and of aesthetic principles over ethical ones. It is only one of the paradoxes of the nineties that these artists, derided for being precious and removed from the real world, were in fact led by their theories to look at many aspects of real life that had hitherto been censored. Making dramatic use of the slogans coined in France some forty years before, they went on to invigorate the language of English poetry and to define fresh attitudes toward life and literature—attitudes which we can now see were essentially involved with the view the writer took of the city.

Arthur Symons was, in his day, the most influential, if not the most successful practitioner of Aesthetic poetry, and because he was more analytic than his colleagues he has more to say than they do about the value of the city to poetry. In an article in the *Fortnightly* for 1892 he concluded: 'I think that might be the test of poetry which professes to be modern: its capacity for dealing with London, with what one sees or might see there, indoors and out.'[26]

In the 'Prologue' to his first book of poetry, *Days and Nights* (1889), Symons attempted a kind of anti-Tennysonian 'Palace of Art' sixty years afterwards. The poet speculates as to the true dwelling place of art, which is thought to live 'withdrawn on some far peak,' 'Brooding aloft . . . Cold as the morning on her hills of snow.' However, he explains,[27] really to find Art, one should,

> Seek her not there; but go where cities pour
>   Their turbid human stream through street and mart,
> A dark stream flowing onward evermore
>   Down to an unknown ocean;—there is Art.
>
> She stands amidst the tumult, and is calm;
>   She reads the hearts self-closed against the light;
> She probes an ancient wound, yet brings no balm;
>   She is ruthless, yet she doeth all things right.

When Symons follows his precept of 'dealing with London' he tends, in his earlier volumes, merely to record impressions, though in a delicate and quite original way. A passage from 'A Winter Night' is representative:[28]

> The dim wet pavement lit irregularly
>> With shimmering streaks of gaslight, faint and frayed,
>> Shone luminous green where sheets of glass displayed
> Long breadths of faded blinds mechanically.

Symons' imagistic exercises are genuinely innovative (and indeed their effect was not lost on Pound and Eliot), but his achievement as a poet of the city involved a larger and more coherent use of his material. He becomes increasingly able to give the scattered facts of the city a metaphoric significance, and is, in fact, the first English poet who was able to write about London with something like Baudelaire's mythographic sense, to make the city a convincing milieu of spiritual adventures. The poet progresses from an assembling of the diverse images of city life to poetic situations which are modified or even created by the ambient city. *Silhouettes*, published in 1892, is largely an urban collection; the titles of its poems—'In an Omnibus,' 'In the Haymarket,' 'On the Bridge'—suggest the Baudelairean shadowy retreats where the poet was said to find his inspiration. In 'Nocturne,' to give an example that is short enough to quote, the special tonality of the lovers' relationship is communicated by the quality of place:[29]

> One little cab to hold us two,
> Night, an invisible dome of cloud,
> The rattling wheels that made our whispers loud,
> As heart-beats into whispers grew;
> And, long, the Embankment with its lights,
> The pavement glittering with fallen rain,
> The magic and mystery that is night's,
> And human love without the pain.

> The river shook with wavering gleams,
> Deep buried as the glooms that lay,
> Impenetrable as the grave of day,
> Near and as distant as our dreams.
> A bright train flashed with all its squares
> Of warm light where the bridge lay mistily.
> The night was all about us: we were free,
> Free of the day and all its cares!

> That was an hour of bliss too long,
> Too long to last where joy is brief.
> Yet one escape of souls may yield relief
> To many weary seasons' wrong.
> 'O last for ever!' my heart cried;

> It ended: heaven was done.
> I had been dreaming by her side
> That heaven was but begun.

Here the city is more than setting or subject; it embodies the emotional state which is the subject of the poem. The fragility, beauty, and impermanence of the images cast up by the London night—the reflections in the water, the passing train—are the data to which the lovers' moment of union is a corollary. The resonances of such a poem as 'Nocturne' are impressive: though the subject-matter and the approach owe something to Browning ('Two in the Campagna') and the technique to Verlaine, the ultimate issue is in the early career of Eliot, whose situation poems are often merely startling and acerb versions of a Symons-like vignette.

In *London Nights*, a book that the poet described as having been received with 'a singular unanimity of abuse'[30] the shocking and consciously 'modern' features are accounts of erotic passages with girls from the street and the stage. The subject matter, including the sympathetic treatment of soubrettes, now looks a little dated, but the poetry is important if only because the episodes which link the poems could take their origins from the conditions of metropolitan life. Symons evokes a landscape which is new to English poetry: in the series called *Décor de Théâtre*, for example, places of entertainment—the Empire Theatre, the Tivoli, Les Ambassadeurs—reflect the dissonance and pathos of lives spent in these tawdry surroundings. This poetry is close in feeling to the paintings of Sickert and the lithographs of Charles Conder; like them Symons projects a bizarre sense of the color, the harshness, the almost brutal artificiality of London and Paris at the end of the century.

Most of the poets of what Yeats called the 'Tragic Generation' wrote poems of the city, though often they merely imitated the French or reversed, *pour épater le bourgeois*, the conventional anti-urban motifs. Nevertheless, even their small works convey an excitement about city life which has its own artistic energy. In 'London Town,' for example, Lionel Johnson conscientiously inverts the accepted patterns:[31]

> Let others chaunt a country praise,
> Fair river walks and meadow ways;
> Dearer to me my sounding days
>   Is *London Town*:
> To me the tumult of the street
> Is no less music, than the sweet
> Surge of the wind among the wheat,
>   By dale or down.
>
> .   .   .   .
>
> *O gray, O gloomy skies*! What then?
> Here is a marvellous world of men:
> More wonderful than *Rome* was, when
>   The world was *Rome*!

See the great stream of life flow by!
Here thronging myriads laugh and sigh,
Here rise and fall, here live and die:
    In this vast home.

The history of nineteenth-century poetry suggests that it became possible for artists to live happily with the city at about the time that the literal Victorian city ceased to exist. If, as there is cause to think, the building of Victorian London was one of the most splendid achievements of the English spirit, it is a loss for us that the poets took so little joy in it. Their obliquity in this respect, however, tells us something about other inadequacies of their poetry. If a strange mixture of Romantic gestures, aristocratic pastoralism, and middle-class prudery blinded the poets to the grandeur and misery of their city, the same set of attitudes obviously affected their understanding of other areas of experience. But the writers of the nineties, minor as they individually were, managed to turn things around and to achieve a kind of liberation. They deserve credit for clearing the way for many new literary forms, but perhaps they did most in helping to make the twentieth-century city available to Joyce and Pound, Virginia Woolf and T. S. Eliot.

Notes

1   *The Myth of the Eternal Return*, trans. Willard R. Trask (New York, 1954), p. 10.
2   *The City in History* (New York, 1961), pp. 10–11. See also Georges Duby and Robert Mandrou, *A History of French Civilization*, trans. J. B. Atkinson (New York, 1964), pp. 130–4.
3   'The Nation of London,' *The Works of Thomas de Quincey* (Boston, 1881), II, pp. 204–5.
4   *The Collected Poems of Roden Noel* (1902), p. 114.
5   Ibid., p. 303.
6   See Morton and Lucia White, *The Intellectual versus the City* (Cambridge, Mass., 1962).
7   *The Journals and Miscellaneous Notebooks of Ralph Waldo Emerson*, ed. A. W. Plumstead and Harrison Hayford (Cambridge, Mass., 1969), VII, p. 288.
8   'Novalis,' *Collected Works of Carlyle* (1889), II, p. 278.
9   The phrase is from 'A Broadway Pageant,' Section 2 (*Leaves of Grass*).
10 'Starting from Paumanok,' Section 18.
11 'Song of Myself,' Section 8.
12 See Pierre Citron, *La Poésie de Paris dans la littérature française de Rousseau à Baudelaire* (Paris, 1961).
13 Charles Baudelaire, *Oeuvres complètes* (Edition de la Pléiade, Paris, 1961), p. 245.
14 Ibid., p. 310.
15 Ibid., p. 952.
16 Ibid., p. 275.
17 *Oeuvres de Arthur Rimbaud* (Paris, 1934), p. 309.

18 See Duby and Mandrou, op. cit., p. 488.

19 *Aurora Leigh* (1857), III, 307; *The Complete Poetical Works of Elizabeth Barrett Browning* (Boston and New York, 1900).

20 *The Poems and Prose Remains of Arthur Hugh Clough*, ed. by his wife (1888), I, p. 359. The essay originally appeared in *North American Review*, lxxvii (1853), 1–30. Mrs Clough modified it somewhat when she reprinted it.

21 'Modern Giants,' *Germ*, no. 4 (30 April 1850), p. 170.

22 'The Study of Architecture in Schools,' in *The Works of John Ruskin*, ed. E. T. Cook and Alexander Wedderburn (1903–12), XIX, p. 24.

23 *The Complete Poetical Works of Thomas Hood*, ed. Walter Jerrold (Oxford, 1906), p. 540.

24 Op. cit., p. 235.

25 'A Defence of Detective Stories,' *Defendant* (1901), 158–9.

26 'Modernity in Verse,' *Fortnightly*, lviii (1892), 184. The essay is reprinted in *Studies in Two Literatures* (1924).

27 *Days and Nights* (1889), p. 2.

28 Ibid., p. 97.

29 *Silhouettes* (1892), pp. 69–70. I have quoted the original version of the poem. Symons later revised it in minor ways.

30 Preface to *London Nights*, second edn, revised (1897), p. xiii. The book was originally published in 1895.

31 *The Complete Poems of Lionel Johnson*, ed. Iain Fletcher (1953), pp. 147–8.

21 From 'Know-not-Where' to 'Nowhere'

The city in Carlyle, Ruskin, and Morris

George Levine

One of the richest traditions of Victorian culture runs with almost paradoxical inevitability from Carlyle, through Ruskin, to William Morris, from a tough, Puritanical, radical conservatism to a joyfully explicit and proselytizing communism. All three were men of enormous energy and will, but also of profoundly divided sensibilities; each extensively influenced his contemporaries and generations following and yet felt deeply separate from the culture he wished to touch. In other times, each might have found his vocation unequivocally in art, but for each there was too much visible suffering and inequity for that.

But the sense of urgency that led Carlyle to the almost hysterical intensity of *Latter-day Pamphlets* and to his passion for Facts, that moved Ruskin to his attack on political economy and to the establishment of St George's Guild, and that turned Morris to politics, was not sufficient to keep these writers from dreaming. The fictive energy that marks the prose of Carlyle and Ruskin transforms even their most practically oriented statements into inventions; Morris's practical prose was, for good reasons, more deliberately workaday, but he too—in his imagination of the communist future, or the past—moves away from the urgency of the here and now. Perhaps the most striking evidence of the more than journalistic, non-naturalistic quality of their writings is the general absence from them of the city. These writers remained in a world imaginatively distant from the realities of a place like the East End of London, and the non-fictional city of their works looks curiously like the city of the poets and novelists—a place which exists to be denied, ignored, despised:

> In the huge world which roars hard by
> Be others happy if they can!
> But in my helpless cradle I
> Was breathed on by the rural Pan.

Like Matthew Arnold, in these 'Lines Written in Kensington Gardens,' they saw the 'real' world only in Nature.

The city is—in terms of value and human possibility—nowhere. And the absence of the city from their works—despite their own personal involvement in the life of London—is not difficult to account for. For one thing, it was too much with them, too much an accepted fact. For another, it was a symptom of the disease, not the disease itself. Eliminating the city would not necessarily eliminate those terrible aspects of modern life which produced it. Again, each of the writers tended to think of social behavior in personal ethical terms. Genuine reform depended for them all on personal reformation rather than on strictly political activity. The viciousness of the city they knew resulted from an acceptance by the community at large of the principles of greed and the 'cash nexus' underlying capitalist economy.

Another, and perhaps for these writers, even more fundamental source of their rejection of the city was the Romantic model of natural (non-human) life. The metaphor determining the way in which each of these writers valued and, indeed, saw and articulated experience tends always to be that of natural growth. Their eyes and their prose were trained by the Romantics. Carlyle and Ruskin saw the natural world as divine; Morris, without the sternness of literalist Protestantism, valued it equally and saw its organic coherence as an implicit critique of industrial, urban society.

The image of natural growth forces upon each of these writers a consciousness of the interdependence of all life, and therefore reinforces deep social consciousness; but it also embodies a profound yearning for peace. Their powerful energies, manifest in overwhelming productivity, were largely directed to the unattainable silence of natural energy, working without strain, inevitably, beautifully, to create and decay and to create again. They sought in the natural world as in the human community that 'Calm soul of all things' that Arnold saw secluded in Kensington Gardens, a 'peace' which 'Man did not make, and cannot mar.' Seeking that ultimate peace, they did not understand how deeply their personal sanity depended upon furious activity or how much they needed the unnatural comforts of the city they despised.

The city was necessarily for them the major symptom of the disease of modern life, the turbulent source of that 'storm-cloud' that blackened the skies of the nineteenth century, the shoddy mechanical construction that denied all the lessons of natural growth. Bringing to the city eyes trained on fields and hills, and perceptions trained by writers, painters, and architects living in essentially agrarian cultures, they found the ugliness almost unimaginable. And each came to attribute it to capitalist economics. It is a simple but convincing argument:[1]

> It is profit which draws men into enormous unmanageable aggregations called towns . . . profit which crowds them up when they are there into quarters without gardens or open spaces; profit which won't take the most ordinary precautions against wrapping a whole district in a cloud of sulphurous smoke; which turns beautiful rivers into filthy sewers; which condemns all but the rich to live in houses idiotically cramped and confined at the best, and at the worst in houses for whose wretchedness there is no name.

To be sure, Morris here underestimates what may be the peculiarly modern pleasure in largeness and in the cosmopolitan quality of 'unmanageable aggregations.' But it is part of the tradition of assumptions that these writers made: the 'artificial' is always, *prima facie*, inferior to the 'natural.'

Almost totally trapped by the organic metaphor, Carlyle and Ruskin never evolved social programs which could exclude certain kinds of brutality or hierarchical structures. Ruskin could not shake his old-fashioned Tory allegiances, his commitment to the Squirearchy, or his patriarchal sense of self; but he came a long way from Carlyle's stern insistence on yielding to 'fact,' on the rightness of Gurth the swineherd's servitude. Ruskin introduced to the notion of work the element of joy—of art. And this notion, in Morris, opened the way to a revolutionary vision. Untied to any metaphysic, Morris chose to take nature simply as a very beautiful model, and he focused his attention not on its tooth and claw but on its forms and textures, the curve of the leaf, the colors of the fields, the movement of the waters. The greed of profit-hunting might, in some sense, be natural, but it was not Morris's nature and it was not conducive to joy in life.

Nor was the city conducive to joy. It was the enemy of peace; and the best hope for man and nature and the inherited values of modern Western culture was to make cities disappear. A developed intelligence and sensibility might bring ordinary men back to a reverence for natural forms, opening out possibilities (especially through the joy of work) for the full expansion of their individual powers, moving them from under the control of machinery into contact with the deepest sources of their feelings. Make men recognize and value the beautiful and the ugly will disappear.

It is the beautiful, not the ugly, to which these writers devote most of their literary energies; but if the city occupies proportionately little space, it is there—implicitly, by contrast, or in allusion, or occasionally, as the object of direct antagonism. It is altogether an imagined place, though it profoundly alters the consciousness of these writers. Most often, when the city enters their prose directly, they deal with it peremptorily and angrily. But occasionally writing with their characteristic acquiescence in the nature of their subjects, Carlyle, Ruskin, and Morris reveal something of the complexity with which enemies of modern society might have to regard the city—the kind of place which, willy-nilly, was the center of their civilization. I want now, very selectively, to look at some of the ways in which the city exists in the imaginations of these writers; to watch how—despite their almost instinctive avoidance of it as a subject—the urban Inferno (as they understood it) moves them in a direction which transforms art into social action and further divides and alienates these most imaginative and creative sensibilities of the nineteenth century.

Edinburgh was the first city which Carlyle saw, and that after a one-hundred mile walk to college. He brought to it an intense sensibility, but not a highly trained visual one. His sense of life up to that point was altogether different from what Ruskin's was to be, for Carlyle knew nature as a grudging and demanding source of livelihood. He had lived with his hands far more than with his eyes, while Ruskin, sheltered from all experience but what could filter into his sparely furnished nursery, learned his asceticism by parental fiat and sought what pleasure he could find through watching, by discerning patterns in the carpet and movement outside his window in the quiet street. Both Bible-trained, both pious, both sternly moralistic, Carlyle and Ruskin differed partly because the idea of the possibility of pleasure barely entered Carlyle's consciousness. He differs from Ruskin and Morris in his politics, his social analyses, his demands for justice, because he does not allow the right to pleasure: 'Make thy claim of wages a zero, then; thou hast the world under thy feet.' [2] There is no *right* to happiness, only the duty to work. And Carlyle's vision of experience—and of the city—is determined not by a sensibility fashioned on art and on the beautiful, but on a notion of natural responsibilities and, always, on the moral significance of objects and events. He 'sees' forces, energies, rights, needs, not forms, textures, and colors.

In literary terms this difference is manifested in the fact that Carlyle is much more an allegorist than Ruskin or Morris. To be sure, they are all concerned with mythology (frequently with making it up), but Carlyle seems instinctively to have seen not events and objects, but meanings. Ruskin may see sacramentally, but it is the sensuous quality of things that puts him in touch with divine energy. In the Rue St Thomas de l'Infer, Teufelsdröckh's vision seems altogether unattached to objects. And—as it could not possibly have happened to Ruskin—it takes place in the city. Although capable in his prose of wonderfully vivid and dramatic moments, Carlyle is almost always effective because of his idiosyncratic penetration of the surface to a revelation of cosmic energies which transform (frequently belittle) the surface.

The first of his major essays to do more than recreate and mythologize the works of other writers, 'Signs of the Times' and 'Characteristics,' set the frame of his critique of contemporary culture. The former essay characterizes and condemns the age as 'mechanical.' In 'Characteristics' we get the famous attack on intellectual self-consciousness (and, implicitly, on modern science and technology) in the name of an unconscious, harmonious, and organic nature. Here he consciously adopts the metaphor of organic growth and vitality:[3]

> To figure society as endowed with life is scarcely a metaphor, but rather a
> statement of a fact by such imperfect methods as language affords. Look

at it closely, that mystic Union, Nature's highest work with man, wherein man's volition plays an indispensable yet so subordinate a part, and the small Mechanical grows so mysteriously and indissolubly out of the infinite Dynamical, like Body out of Spirit,—is truly enough vital, what we can call vital, and bears the distinguishing character of life.

Carlyle sees his metaphor as of a piece with life itself, and such high-level abstractions as these persistently inform the movement of his prose.

The first great Victorian (technically, in fact, pre-Victorian) vision of the city, Teufelsdröckh's reflections on Weissnichtwo, is created of such language. The name of the town is appropriate, in particular because very little is given about it that could distinguish it from other large towns. It exists as a provocation to large speculations. Although set in the borderland between fiction and fact that is *Sartor Resartus*, it is hardly any less 'real' than more factually named cities appearing in later prose. The passage describing Weissnichtwo is hardly the place to look to find out what the Victorian city was like, but it is important for an understanding of the conventions controlling the attitudes of many Victorian intellectuals toward the city.

The vision is, in fact, two visions. The first attempts, simply, to place the city in the aspect of eternity—and the effect is, characteristically for Carlyle, to reduce the city and its people to triviality and yet to impress us with the city's extraordinary variety and activity and with the ultimate solemnity and mystery of it all: '"I look down into all that wasp-nest or bee-hive," have we heard him [Teufelsdröckh] say, "and witness their wax-laying and honey-making, and poison-brewing, and choking by sulphur."' In all of Weissnichtwo, 'except the Schlosskirche weathercock, no biped stands so high' as Teufelsdröckh:

> Couriers arrive bestrapped and bebooted, bearing Joy and Sorrow bagged-up in pouches of leather; there, topladen, and with four swift horses rolls-in the country Baron and his household; here, on timber-leg, the lamed Soldier hops painfully along, begging alms: a thousand carriages, and wains, and cars, come tumbling in with Food, with young Rusticity, and other Raw Produce, inanimate or animate, and go tumbling out again with Produce manufactured. That living flood, pouring through these streets, of all qualities and ages, knowest Thou whence it is coming, whither it is going? *Aus der Ewigkeit, zu der Ewigkeit hin.* From Eternity, onwards to Eternity!
>
> (pp. 20–1)

The first point to be noted is Teufelsdröckh's perspective. The characteristic voice of almost all the Victorian sages comes from outside the city. Although irony and self-criticism are at work (Teufelsdröckh equates himself, by the term 'biped,' with the 'weathercock'), the view is from above the city, in a tower altogether private and isolated from the ordinary activities not only of the city but also of everyday living. The remoteness serves to provide a comprehension of the details of the city unavailable to people who participate in its life. And to deal with this special comprehension, Carlyle adopts a highly generalized and literary language. As it is visualized the scene is a series of formulae, the 'Serene Highness' as opposed to the 'aged widow,' the wooden-legged soldier, the carriage, moving in and out of town. And the peculiar richness of the passage is not in its details but in its movement to an even higher degree of generality, a degree which justifies the unoriginal generality of the details preceding—that is, that everything within the city moves not so much from city to country, but from city to Eternity and back. The vision incorporates all details into a vast cosmic movement reducing variety to a single mystical truth.

But the cosmic vision is allied to the tradition which sees all things within the limits of the organic metaphor. Teufelsdröckh watches 'the whole life circulation' of the city. Despite the conventional invocation of contrasts, what he sees essentially is ingestion, digestion, and evacuation. The latent metaphor intensifies the irony of 'Raw Produce' (including 'young Rusticity') being transformed into 'Produce manufactured.' Whatever its perversions, contrasts, variety, the city is subject to the same organic movement as individuals and as all of nature. And it shares in that mystery of life whose beginning and end are unintelligible and yet all powerful, ultimately more real than the pavement, than the city itself.

Another aspect of the passage belongs to the tradition shared by a great many Victorians: the idea of the interconnectedness of all life. The conventional contrasts developed here are actively ironic because the differences insisted on within the city are not real. Ultimately all will be gathered together (either in spirit or as the city's and life's defecation); but even within the life of the city, His Serene Highness is dependent for his solitude and comfort on the suffering aged widow, the lamed soldier, the moving wagons carrying the food which he will be eating, and, therefore, on young Rusticity and the Produce manufactured (some of which will be his and will have to be disposed of). Everything is related in the 'living flood,' and from Teufelsdröckh's perspective, one sees not only the interconnectedness at the moment but the whole panorama as 'a living link in that Tissue of History, which inweaves all being.'

The second vision, though still full of cosmic portent, and sustaining much of the generality and assertion of organic interdependence, is more specifically urban. It follows immediately upon the first, but it is a night vision, when the organism of the city is asleep under its 'smoke-counterpane.' Throughout, the pattern of contrasts and strange juxtapositions continues. But with his night eyes, Teufelsdröckh is exclusively aware of corruption and suffering. The hum of subdued traffic, 'like the stertorous, unquiet slumber of sick life, is heard in Heaven! Oh, under that hideous coverlet of vapours, and putrefactions, and unimaginable gases, what a Fermenting vat lies simmering and hid!' (p. 22). The city is diseased, and its symptoms are smoke and noise. But we also see 'Vice and Misery' prowling the streets. There is the 'proud Grandee' lingering in 'perfumed saloons,' while nearby 'Wretchedness cowers.' The diction is persistently abstract and allegorical.

Yet through the diction emerges the altogether recognizable (and almost unchanging) Romantic perception of the city in the nineteenth century. Smoke, noise, luxury, the misery of poverty, the deviousness of politicians, riot, dying children: 'all these heaped together, with nothing but a little carpentry and masonry

500

between them.' So, too, we see shabby building, cruel overcrowding, and, finally, the central moral flaw, which, in the writings of Ruskin and Morris, will occupy so much attention: greed. It is a greed which issues in competition and which shadows forth the class struggle. For the people in Weissnichtwo are 'crammed in, like salted fish in their barrel; or weltering, shall I say, like an Egyptian pitcher of tamed vipers, each struggling to get its *head above* the others; *such* work goes on under that smoke counterpane!'

Teufelsdröckh's vision is, as it were, a metaphorical outline of the attitudes of Romantic writers toward the city. Implicit in the vision of the diseased organism is the contrast with agrarian culture. To be sure, Carlyle was no sentimentalist about the life of the peasant: his own sternness and capacity to endure discomfort (though not without noisy complaining) were bred in the country; and he took his wife with him to Craigenputtock, as desolate and non-urban a place as one could deliberately find. But the passage does imply a contrast between the simplicity of natural life and the corruption of the urban. Carlyle does not so much see (no streaks of the tulip here) as see *through* to a world of reified abstractions. The city itself seems not worth detailed attention; indeed, the conventional language assumes that, in certain respects, everything that needs to be known about the city is known already. It is a nice place to be out of but lots of fun to watch and worry over: '"*Ach, mein Lieber!*" says Teufelsdröckh, "it is a true sublimity to dwell here—above the town"' (p. 22). (Carlyle, it might be remembered, locked himself up in a soundproof study above his house in Chelsea.)

Carlyle's literary interests, like those of Ruskin and Morris, were not in the city, although he found that life for him outside of it was more intolerable than life within. Though Teufelsdröckh's vision is fictional, it is as close as we can come in Carlyle to a direct experience of the city. In his later works there are, to be sure, many allusions to city life, but his preoccupation is with the moral condition of the nation, of which the city remains only a symptom.

Sartor Resartus is a book full of restrained but genuine revolutionary implications, and the life-disease of which the city is a manifestation is obviously breeding revolution such as that which burst out in Paris in 1789 and which seemed frighteningly close in England. The cure is not so much the destruction of the symptom (although, as Carlyle says in his *Latter-day Pamphlet* on Hudson's Statue, it is worth destroying the symptom too). Rather, it is the end of laissez faire, competition, and Mammonism; the acceptance of responsibility by those capable of leading, the acceptance of leadership among those destined to follow. It is the elimination of the notion of the individual right to happiness and the acceptance of the implications of the interdependence of all being. It is, finally, the willingness of man to accept his place in the natural order of things and, with it, the inevitability of change. For the natural order will reassert itself against every artificial, mechanical contrivance which disguises the continuity of all experience and the source of life and meaning in the mysterious depths of irrational but divinely just energy. The city, in such a context of moral and religious force, is barely visible.

Ruskin became a social critic by way of the late paintings of Turner, the Alps, and the stones of Venice. It was a route that Carlyle could never have imagined taking, but it brought Ruskin to a position of at least equal seriousness, and he incorporated into his criticism much that he had learned from 'Papa' Carlyle. Indeed, by the time of *Fors Clavigera*, he imagines himself and Carlyle as lonely laborers in the good cause: 'I do not pretend to tell you straightforwardly all laws of nature respecting conduct of men; but some of these laws I know and will endeavour to get obeyed . . . that it should be left to me to begin such a work, with only one man in England—Thomas Carlyle—to whom I can look for steady guidance, is alike wonderful and sorrowful to me.'[4]

Two aspects of Carlyle's vision are central to Ruskin's: first, that the slightest detail of creation is imbued with the possibilities of wonder; second, that the natural is more wonderful than the 'mechanical.' Taking literally these notions, Ruskin develops a prose style far more concerned with the notation of detail than Carlyle's. It is a style which would seem especially appropriate to a vision of the city—as it is, for example, in Dickens. It abjures generalization that has no clear foundation in particulars, distinctions, and sharp observance of relations. Yet Ruskin almost never looks closely at the city; and he does not do so—one might infer—because the city is mechanical, not natural, and therefore does not suggest the nobility and dignity, human and divine, which are the true provinces of art. Only the natural world could do that.

In the great last sections of Volume V of *Modern Painters*, Ruskin moves toward a formulation which suggests how his preoccupation with landscape could nevertheless bring him to the radical critique of his own time. In *Unto This Last* 'we find that all true landscape, whether simple or exalted, depends primarily for its interest on connection with humanity, or with spiritual powers.' Although Ruskin certainly did not begin writing *Modern Painters* with this notion consciously before him, the evolution of his career during the many years of the book's composition justifies these remarks: 'And in these books of mine, their distinctive character, as essays on art, is their bringing everything to root in human passion or human hope. . . . Every principle of painting which I have stated is traced to some vital or spiritual fact; and in my works on architecture the preference accorded finally to one school over another, is founded on a comparison of their influence on the life of the workman.'[5]

Beginning with a faith in the perfect continuity of man with nature and nature with God, Ruskin discovers that man is not only incapable of seeing nature, but also, consequently, incapable of recognizing beauty in art. 'The wild course of the present century' divides man from art, from nature, and from God; and Ruskin increasingly felt the frustration of not being able to change the conditions that would make these things available to man once more. Architecture, then, became an important link in Ruskin's progress toward social criticism, and all true architecture was, for him, based in nature.[6] 'Whatever is in architecture fair or beautiful, is imitated from natural forms,' Ruskin says. He means this quite literally, although with wonderful agility he takes into account apparent exceptions. The connection between architecture and nature is so total that, Ruskin argues, 'Architects ought not to live in our cities; there is that in their miserable walls which bricks up to death men's imaginations, as surely as ever perished foresworn nun. An architect should live as little in cities as a painter. Send him to our hills, and let him study there what nature understands by a buttress, and what by a dome' (*Seven Lamps of Architecture*, ch. 3, sec. xxiv). This motif continues throughout his career. In *Fors Clavigera*, for example, Ruskin says, 'no great arts were practicable by any people, unless they were living contented lives, in pure air, out of the way of unsightly objects, and emancipated from unnecessary mechanic occupation' (*FC*, I, Letter 9, p. 123). The very notion of the 'beautiful,' as Ruskin tries to define it, takes as its source the possibilities of nature. For example, he asserts that 'A curve of any kind is more beautiful than a right line,' largely because 'there are no lines nor surfaces of nature without curvature' (*Modern Painters*, II, p. 273).

It is, therefore, hardly a surprise that the city does not live in the forefront of Ruskin's imagination but emerges into it, on occasion, as his rage intensifies, and he cannot escape the kind of preoccupation with the sordid for which he denounced contemporary newspapers, novelists, and journalists. No wonder, too, that in the very first letter of *Fors*, he lists among the things he would like to destroy (including 'all the railroads in Wales') 'the East End of London' (to be rebuilt), 'the new town of Edinburgh, the north suburb of Geneva, and the city of New York' (never to be rebuilt) (*FC*, I, pp. 5–6). But the city remains for Ruskin a symptom of the disease, of loss of contact with art and nature. His heaviest attacks are on political economy. Carlyle saw in a possible 'Exodus from Houndsditch' a symbolic movement from the commercialism of society and the old clothes of the Old Testament. The obliteration of the East End of London might have meant the same thing to Ruskin, but—given that he did not ask for the destruction of the West End—he seems willing to live with the city. But the images of evil which increasingly preoccupy Ruskin in his last darkening years seem all to have associations with the city: that oppressive storm-cloud changing the weather of Europe (both literal and figurative); the pollution of the streams; the shabbiness of architecture; the increase of huckstering; the impossibility of communion with nature in crowded surroundings; the artificial luxuries of the wealthy; and the manufacture of unnecessary baubles. The city is a symptom of the disease gradually blighting the world of nature and erasing God's mark on the creation. With this in mind, we can look at two of the documents in which the symptom comes to the center of Ruskin's attention.

The fifth volume of *Modern Painters* begins with a sadly lyrical paean to the natural world which Ruskin has been describing in the four preceding volumes. That world is described as an old friend and teacher who has been abused and exploited and whose teachings have been ignored, who might have led us to peace but whose aid is now inaccessible: 'so long as we make sport of slaying bird and beast, so long as we choose to contend rather with our fellows than with our faults and make battlefields of our meadows instead of pasture—so long, truly, the Flaming Sword will still turn every way and the gates of Eden remain barred close enough, till we have sheathed the sharper flame of our passions, and broken down the closer gates of our hearts' (*MP*, V, p. 23). The personal failure to control the passions causes men to fail to see that nature 'ministers to them through a veil of strange intermediate being' and is 'wonderful in adaptation' to them. It is not to be fought but to be discovered and loved. Yet in their mistaken ways, men have turned the word 'rustic' into a reproach, and the city has been the only refuge for the peaceful and sensitive. The tone of painful and quiet resignation suggests how far from early Wordsworthian optimism Ruskin had moved, despite his continuing faith in the natural world. Now, unfortunately, men live within the city and:

> For the present, the movements of the world seem little likely to be influenced by botanical law; or by any other considerations respecting trees, than the probable price of timber. I shall limit myself, therefore, to my own simple woodman's work, and try to hew this book into its final shape, with the limited and humble aim that I had in beginning it, namely, to prove how far the idle and peaceable persons, who have hitherto cared about leaves and clouds, have rightly seen, or faithfully reported of them.
>
> (*MP*, V, p. 27)

Ruskin, one of those 'idle and peaceable persons, who have hitherto cared about leaves and clouds,' and who need under present circumstances to live in the city, seems ready here to allow a more complicated attitude toward the city than simple rejection. In the famous chapter, 'The Two Boyhoods,' we can watch the simpler attitude unsuccessfully trying to emerge. Of course, the contrast between Giorgione's medieval Venice and Turner's modern London is unequivocal: 'No foulness, nor tumult' in the 'tremulous streets' of Venice. 'Ethereal strength of Alps, dream-like, vanishing in high procession beyond the Torcellan shore; blue islands of Paduan hills, poised in the golden west. Above, free winds and fiery clouds ranging at their will;—brightness out of the north, and balm from the south, and the stars of the evening and morning clear in the limitless light of arched heaven and circling sea' (*MP*, V, p. 362). Here the beauty of the city is obviously seen in terms of its relation and openness to the natural world around it.

Against this city, Ruskin contrasts the London of Turner's boyhood, seen with a precision unusual for a Victorian sage looking at modern London.

> Near the southwest corner of Covent Garden, a square brick pit or wall is formed by a close-set block of houses, to the black windows of which it admits a few rays of light. Access to the bottom of it is obtained out of Maiden Lane, through a low archway and an iron gate; and if you stand long enough under the archway to accustom your eyes to the darkness, you may see on the lefthand a narrow door, which formerly gave quiet access to a respectable barber shop, of which the front window, looking into

Maiden Lane, is still extant, filled in this year (1860), with a row of bottles, connected, in some defunct manner, with a brewer's business.

(*MP*, V, p. 27)

Light is the center of the contrast. The visitor must stand a few moments under the archway to accustom his eyes to the darkness, and the black windows admit only a few rays of light. The carefully accumulated details create a kind of chiaroscuro of the sort that Ruskin so violently condemned, only a few pages before, in Rembrandt. Ironically, Dutch realism is the only style available for rendering the childhood home of his hero. For the neighborhood, though respectable, has nothing of nobility about it. The respectable barber shop had been turned into some kind of brewery, although in the haste of urban movement, even that business is gone. Nothing heroic here, nothing expansive, permanent, open to nature, but it is where the greatest of modern painters (despite Ruskin's injunctions that artists should not live in cities) learned to see.

In his treatment of the young Turner here, Ruskin is evoking an imagination much like that of Dickens—a distinctly middle-class and urban vision. We even find here the convention of the romantic transformation of the ordinary: 'enchanted oranges gleam in Covent Gardens of the Hesperides; and great ships go to pieces in order to scatter chests of them on the waves. That mist of early sunbeams in the London dawn crosses, many and many a time, the clearness of Italian air; and by Thames shore, with its stranded barges and gildings of red sail, dearer to us than Lucerne lake or Venetian lagoon,—by Thames' shore we will die' (p. 363). Through romance, the light and deep coloring of Ruskin's loved world enters to remake London. Turner's imagination recreates those sights of his childhood in the great work of his later years. And Ruskin can see and admire this.

Nor is he bothered by inconsistencies. He might have used Turner's boyhood to demonstrate the ill effect of the visions of the city on the imaginations of great artists, but he chose to do justice to the qualities in Turner's works that he imagines were most deeply influenced by early life in the city. Further on, he talks about two particular aspects of Turner's work which he sees as city bred: first, the capacity to 'endure ugliness' (p. 364), even his positive joy in 'litter' (another remarkably Dickensian quality), and, second, his 'understanding and regard for the poor, whom the Venetians . . . despised' (p. 365). Disposed, like Ruskin, for the most part to learn 'by the eyes,' Turner took what he saw as a child and treated it, affectionately, again and again, in his paintings: 'Hence, to the very close of his life, Turner could endure ugliness which no one else, of the same sensibility, would have borne with for an instant. Dead brick walls, blank square windows, old clothes, market-womanly types of humanity—anything fishy and muddy, like Billingsgate or Hungerford Market' (p. 364). The preoccupation with the effects of 'dinginess, smoke, soot, dust, and dusty textures, old sides of boats, weedy woodside vegetation, dunghills, straw-yards, and all the soilings and stains of every common labour' might have provoked in Ruskin the most serious kinds of criticism had it appeared in other writers or

505

painters. But in this chapter, at least, Ruskin is not trapped by his own morality: he recognizes Turner's capacity to transform these things into art, and his primary love of form, texture, color (and Turner) dominate.

Ruskin further admits how the early life in the city intensified Turner's love of the poor and his ability to see that peculiarly urban quality (we have seen it already in Carlyle) of enlightening juxtaposition. Turner 'got no romantic sight' of the poor, 'but an infallible one, as he prowled about the ends of his lane, watching night effects in the wintry streets, nor sight of the poor alone, but of the poor in direct relations with the rich. He knew, in good and evil, what both classes thought of, and how they dwelt with, each other' (p. 365). From his perspective at the edge of Maiden Lane (not quite Teufelsdröckh's, but created as though it were from the outside looking in), Turner was able to see the organic life of the city, the movement of commerce, from warehouse to shop, the pressure of wealth upon poverty. The great ships in that 'mysterious forest below London Bridge' are somehow connected 'with these masses of human poor and national wealth which weigh upon us, at Covent Garden here, with strange compression, and crush us into Narrow Hand Court.' Despite the powerfully vivid and aesthetic nature of the description, the visual education of Turner (as Ruskin, at least, understands it) leads inevitably to the kind of social criticism towards which Volume V of *Modern Painters* is itself moving. There is no way to look at the city carefully, without being engaged or corrupted. But Turner had the 'kind of mind' that 'did not become vulgar' (p. 367).

Although in reading these pages about what Turner learned in the city, we might feel that we already have enough evidence about the source of his greatness, Ruskin, characteristically, indicates that, whatever might have happened to Turner in the early years, he did not begin to live until after an illness that took him out of the city: 'And at last fortune wills that the lad's true life shall begin: and one summer's evening he finds himself sitting alone among the Yorkshire Hills. For the first time, the silence of Nature round him, her freedom sealed to him, her glory opened to him. Peace at last' (pp. 370–1). The prose itself opens, its rhythms intensify, as the details of the city are put behind and religion comes with the first true perception of 'Loveliness.' It is almost an aesthete's religion (and may well be more Ruskin's than Turner's), although there are here obvious connections with Wordsworthian vision. Peace comes genuinely 'not among men.' Turner discovers that 'Those pale, poverty struck, or cruel faces!—that multitudinous, marred humanity—are not the only things that God has made. Here is something He has made which no one has marred. Pride of purple rocks, and river pools of blue, and tender wilderness of glittering trees, and misty lights of evening on immeasureable hills.' It is color and shade and light and mist and the suggestion of infinitude beyond these that is Ruskin's religion. And we are back with Arnold, finding Peace and Beauty only where man's hands have not been active—that is, outside of the city.

The experience of the city—as it was countered by his experience of nature—led Turner to see men only in their 'weakness and vileness': 'They themselves, unworthy or ephemeral; their work despicable, or decayed. In [Giorgione's] eyes all beauty depended on man's presence and pride; in Turner's, on the solitude he had left, and the humiliation he had suffered' (p. 372). Obviously, there is a good deal of autobiography in this sketch of Turner. The sadness of the opening pages of the volume is echoed here, as is that terrible yearning for peace in nature. In Turner he finds a man who, in his art at least, had managed by daring and talent to record that possibility even as he allowed himself to see the great human truths of 'labour, sorrow, and death.' The closing pages of the chapter record that terrible vision of humanity and, in particular, of the horrors of his own time. It is no accident that Ruskin finds the symbolic locus for the awful death of the nineteenth century in the city, which, in this chapter, he does his best to respect. Of course, the humiliation which Turner and Ruskin suffered, the deep solitude they felt, were caused by things far more complex than the environment of the city. But the cure seemed to be in a peace that the city, with its people, its meanness, its commerce, its perpetual marring of the past, could not give. For a nineteenth-century man of sensibility, alert to the contrasts of city life, to the 'unnatural' life-circulation of its commerce, only nature could provide release. The last lines of the chapter lapse into a peculiarly Miltonic blank verse, but it is difficult not to read them as a most moving account of a sensibility at once deeply engaged with and sadly distant from its own time and from the possibilities of the urban life that it has, only a few pages before, precisely recorded: 'So taught, and prepared for his life's labour, sate the boy at last alone among his fair English hills; and began to paint, with cautious toil, the rocks, and fields, and trickling brooks, and soft, white clouds of heaven' (p. 375).

Through the sixties, the 'soft white clouds of heaven' darkened into the stormcloud. But it would be pointless here to trace in any detail the direction of Ruskin's mind as it moved toward its own ultimate darkness. Rather, I want here to look at one brief essay in which the city becomes once more an important focus—'Fiction— Fair and Foul.' Here, too, the focus does not remain on the city any longer than absolutely necessary. Beginning with a consideration of the way in which the moral disease of the city infects fiction, it moves off quickly to a consideration of Scott's novels, embodying all those ideals to which the city novel is opposed. If the prose of this essay remains rich, the antagonism to the city has stiffened. It leads him to choose, as his central example, Dickens's *Bleak House*, a novel which might be taken to embody a good many of the Ruskinian ideals, and surely much that Ruskin admired in Turner.

At the same time, the essay comes close to providing a direct explanation for the absence of the city from his works. The opening contrast between the area around his childhood home as it was when he was a child and as it had become in 1880 leads Ruskin, in one of his marvelously personal intrusions, to reflect upon his career:[7]

> Often, both in those days, and **since**, I have put myself hard to it, vainly, to find words wherewith to tell of beautiful things; but beauty has been in the world since the world was made, and human language can make a shift, to give account of it, whereas the peculiar forces of devastation

induced by modern city life have only entered the world lately; and no existing terms of language known to me are enough to describe the forms of filth, and modes of ruin, that varied themselves along the course of Croxsted Lane.

The newness of the city has outpaced the language which Ruskin commands. Everything in Ruskin's writing, the extraordinary brilliance and versatility of the language and the clear references to traditional models of beauty, suggest that, like many of his contemporaries, he found the new and growing life of the cities unintelligible. They literally had no language, and needed to invent one—as Dickens himself was doing. But for Ruskin, the invention of such a language would, in a way, sanction an abomination. The 'litter' which Turner somehow loved reappears in Dickens, but Ruskin has no tolerance for it. He struggles, himself, before he gets to the diseases which Dickens seems to have contracted from the city, to record something of the litter and horror he sees in his once loved Croxsted Lane. Perhaps surprisingly, he does very well at it, but with a Swiftian passion of revulsion. Despite some of the techniques of high rhetoric, it is self-consciously *in*organic, invoking all the qualities of fragmentation, mechanism, and waste that Ruskin despised in modern urban life:

> Half a dozen handful of new cottages, with Doric doors, are dropped about here and there among the gashed ground: the lane itself, now entirely grassless, is a deep-rutted, heavy-hillocked, cart-road, diverging gatelessly into various brickfields or pieces of waste; and bordered on each side by heaps of—Hades only knows what!—mixed dust of every unclean thing that can rot or rust in damp: ashes and rags, beer-bottles and old shoes, battered pans, smashed crockery, shreds of nameless clothes, door-sweepings, floor-sweepings, kitchen garbage, back-garden sewage, old iron, rotten timber jagged with out-torn nails, cigar-ends, pipe-bowls, cinders, bones, and ordure indescribable; and, variously kneaded into, sticking to, or fluttering foully here and there over all these,—remnants broadcast, of every manner of newspaper, advertisement or big-lettered bill, festering and flaunting out their last publicity in the pits of stinging dust and mortal slime.
>
> (*Fiction—Fair and Foul*, p. 154)

It is a prose of accumulated details corresponding to accumulating passion; but with eyes sharpened to natural curves and rhythms, Ruskin is occasionally reduced here to 'Hades only knows what' or 'ordure indescribable.' His interest is in naming, and, by choosing sufficiently contemptuous names, dismissing.

This world of decay and corruption is doomed, in Ruskin's eyes, to breed new generations preoccupied with corruption, morbidly fascinated with the grotesque and the diseased. In explaining why this should have happened, he gives his most explicit analysis of what he imagines life in the city to be. First, it is a place of 'hot fermentation and unwholesome secrecy' in which all diseases, and especially moral disease, are quickly transmitted. Second, it is a place where 'the disgrace and grief resulting from the mere trampling pressure and electric friction . . . become to the sufferers peculiarly mysterious in their unreservedness, and frightful in their inevitableness.' Third, it is a place where 'unnatural excitement' is craved because of 'the monotony of life in the central streets . . . where every emotion intended to be derived by men from the sight of nature, or the sense of art, is forbidden for ever' (p. 157). Again, the assumptions implied in the word 'natural' control the entire analysis: it is natural for man to be closely in touch with the movements of the seasons and to derive excitement from these; it is, however, 'unnatural' to derive pleasure and excitement from the variety of people and activities available in the city. Fiction, then, entertains urban man by 'varying to his fancy the modes, and defining for his dulness the horrors of Death' (pp. 158–9).

Unwilling to accept the city as a reality available to our Theoretic or Aesthetic faculties, incapable of finding a language himself which might assimilate the city to the beautiful, Ruskin condemns Dickens in *Bleak House* for catering to the diseased imagination of city-dwellers. Scott's treatment of death ennobles, but Dickens's treatment of it panders to the corruption and decay. In our own terms, we might say that Dickens constructs an imaginary vocabulary of the urban experience, an experience which Ruskin could neither understand nor tolerate. Ruskin totally refuses to see that Dickens is on his side, that his Turnerian love of the poor and of the city and of litter does not prevent him from attacking the horrors of urban life or from invoking Ruskin's own deep sense of continuity and interdependence. What Ruskin chooses to see is a catalogue of ugly deaths, which reduces the book to a parody of itself.

To use the images that were coming to obsess Ruskin's imagination, the cankerworm was in the rose, the storm-clouds darkened the skies. Ruskin was left to work futilely at his St George's Guild. The bitterness and invective intensified as the air and the water and the streets seemed increasingly more polluted and greed continued to determine power. He was left behind by his century, though we are only now beginning to catch up with him, to understand that we need to recognize some of the implications of the organic metaphor.

Ruskin's notion of 'vital beauty,' 'the appearance of felicitous fulfilment of function,'[8] served, as Raymond Williams has pointed out, not only to challenge the whole ethic of laissez faire capitalism, but, also, as it was accepted by Morris, to lead to socialism. The notion of the organic brought Ruskin and Carlyle to Medievalism, but 'acquired a distinctly future reference' for Morris—'the image of socialism' (Williams, p. 151). Morris, too, was a medievalist, and is, like Ruskin, open to the charge of sentimentalism. His socialism might seem, even more than Ruskin's critique of culture, primarily aesthetic, a revulsion from the ugliness of modern urban society, and from its technology. His 'Nowhere' is a world without machines.

But just as Ruskin's concern for nature and art led him to a concern for the working man, so Morris picks up the notion of the 'felicitous fulfilment of function' and makes it part of a program to improve the working and living conditions of the working classes. Every man, he argued, should have the opportunity to develop his latent capacities as worker and craftsman to the fullest, to become most completely a human being and to be freed from the slavery of Victorian work. Although equally without a language to cope with the modern city, Morris develops Ruskin's social thought and takes it—without Ruskin's mysticism—into direct battle with capitalism and toward revolution. Morris calls 'hatred of modern civilisation' the 'leading passion of my life.'[9] But this hatred issued in activities and ideas not merely negative or utopian, for he was willing to face—even to encourage—the antagonism of the classes, and, like Marx and many modern radicals, to foresee and attempt to hasten violent revolutionary conflict. Yet he, too, is bound by a language and a set of values unequipped for modern civilization, and there remains a curiously pastoral and idyllic quality about his program for the future.

Nevertheless, his efforts to develop ways of improving the quality of the working man's life were richly imaginative and liberating. In the lectures he gave over two decades, he elaborated with great intelligence, passion, and lucidity, the possibility of creative activity within the context of a genuinely communal society. He completes the redefinition of the term, 'Art,' begun by Ruskin, making it refer not to a special skill reserved for genius and higher sensibilities, but to the quality of life which gives it meaning and joy: 'the cause of Art is the cause of the people' ('Art and Socialism,' p. 635). Art is 'the expression by man of his pleasure in labour' ('The Art of the People,' p. 530). By insisting, as did Ruskin, in 'Traffic,' on the connection of art to the ordinary experience of men in the world, he moves from sentimentalism to a great new vision of human possibilities. And it is to this vision, as it is manifested in the lectures on art, socialism, and work, and in *News from Nowhere* that I wish now to turn.[10]

Morris found outlets for his social and sexual energies in ways that Ruskin never did. The effect, curiously, was to diminish the power of his art and to intensify the split in his activities implicit in his dual preoccupation with art and society. Morris worked out his guilt at being wealthy through political activity, while the tensions of Ruskin's guilt permeate almost everything he wrote. What was bad for Ruskin was good for his art; but Morris's radically divided career is less impressive artistically than personally. He was, much of the time, what he called himself, notoriously, in one of his poems, 'The idle singer of an empty day.' He escaped from the civilization he despised through imaginative flights in archaic language. Yet one can see in his lectures the same romantic impulses at work, but this time brought directly to bear on the problems of contemporary society in a language fresh, direct, and utterly convincing. As E. P. Thompson notes, 'Morris had lost serious hope of any widespread revival of the arts within capitalist society . . . His *own* art he thought of as a source of enjoyment and relaxation.'[11]

But in both romances and lectures, diversion or revolutionary vision, the city barely exists for Morris. The city is part of that civilization which Morris unequivocally hated, and it has no place either in the socialist future or the organic, romantic past. In the romances, the city is absent because Morris deliberately chooses subjects which do not allow the city to enter the consciousness of the narrator; in the lectures the city is absent in a more powerfully negative way; it is either dismissed violently in contemptuous asides or its elimination in a socialist society is carefully foretold. A characteristic collocation of Morris's attitudes appears in a lecture of 1888, 'The Society of the Future': In the society, 'the aggregation of the population having served *its* purpose of giving people opportunities of inter-communication and of making the workers feel their solidarity, will also come to an end . . . And of course mere cheating and flunky centres like the horrible muck-heap in which we dwell (London, to wit) could be got rid of easier still.'[12] Characteristically, there is no Ruskinian preoccupation with the power of language evident here. But there is force in that brief remark about London, deriving from Morris's utter certainty of London's insignificance, from the disparity between the size of the place and the confidence with which it is demeaned and dismissed.

Yet angry as Morris becomes in his allusion to the city, perceptive as he is about the effects of commercialism, his non-fiction shares with the romances the quality of dream. It is extraordinary, as one looks over the essays, how briefly their pre-occupation remains with the present. The titles themselves are usually sufficient to indicate their direction: 'The Society of the Future,' 'How We Live and How We Might Live,' 'A Factory as it Might Be.' All of these and many others are closely related to *News from Nowhere* in its conception of the world after the 'Great Change.' I do not mean to suggest that Morris's dreaming finally makes his socialism mere sentimental utopianism, but that his imagination failed, as did Ruskin's, to create a new and precise langue of the city. Hardheaded, even bitter, about the possibilities of contemporary culture, Morris, unlike Ruskin, imagined the inevitability of a new society growing from the ashes of the one in which he lived. The dream vision of Morris was not of worms and clouds, but of a renewed and greener England. Beyond the darkness of the moment, he worked his way through to an optimism utterly beyond Ruskin.

Morris inherits many of Carlyle's attitudes, but the sense of energy and change which we find in Carlyle, the idea that society will have to shuck off its old clothes and learn to wear new ones, becomes in Morris a more precisely directed movement: toward democracy and equality (anathema to both Ruskin and Carlyle). Although obviously much better prepared than his predecessors for violence, Morris writes of the movement in a language far less apocalyptic. Characteristically, in 'The End and the Means,' he adopts the less tense, more optimistic language of romance: 'In spite of the disappointed hopes of the early part of the century, we are forced to hope still because we are forced to move forward: the warnings of the past, the tales of bloodshed and terror and disorder and famine—they are all but tales to us and cannot scare us, because there is no turning back into the desert in which we cannot live, and no standing still on the edge of the enchanted wood; for there is nothing to keep us there, we must plunge in and through it to the promised land beyond' (May Morris, II, p. 422).

This language is appropriate because the world of 'the promised land' is one in which art and nature live quietly together and complement each other. Nature, by its insistent contrast, bears strongest witness to the failures of modern civilization, to the fact that man has—before this trip through the enchanted wood—'deliberately chosen ugliness instead of beauty, and to live where he is strongest amidst squalor or blank emptiness' (p. 501). Nature and art are seen, together, as enemies of the city which is the embodiment of that choice of ugliness over beauty (p. 514).

> Unless something or other is done to give all men some pleasure for the eyes and rest for the mind in the aspect of their own and their neighbour's houses, until the contrast is less disgraceful between the fields where beasts live and the streets where men live, I suppose that the practice of the arts must be mainly kept in the hands of a few highly cultivated men, who can go often to beautiful places, whose education enables them, in the contemplation of the past glories of the world, to shut out from their view the everyday squalors that the most of men move in.

The city, as Morris sees it, is the creation of a recklessly selfish elite middle class, a class to which Morris himself belonged. Part of the power of this passage is, surely, attributable to the split in Morris himself as he rejects his own class and yet cannot surrender those values which he can only cultivate because he belongs to it. Part of the sadness of Morris's socialism, to those who can look back and observe his career, is that it did grow out of values almost precisely like Ruskin's, and Morris was forced to struggle with the possibility of surrendering those values in order to accomplish the socialist reform. Yet he never could imagine a revolution which did not finally move naturally toward those values, and thus away from the city. Unless art were ultimately to belong to everyone, Morris, more than halfheartedly, would have seen it disappear altogether ('for a while'). But he cannot sustain the imagination of this possibility. He is confident that art, if it does disappear for a while, will return to 'make our streets as beautiful as the woods, as elevating as the mountain-sides' so that it will not be 'a weight upon the spirits to come from the open country into a town.' Again, the natural is the model of value, and art will serve to elevate the urban to the quality of the rural.

The lectures are almost univocal in their expressions of hatred for the city, and, since they are so much concerned with future possibilities, the city almost never appears in them except as casual contrast against those possibilities. There seems, thus, to be no occasion in Morris's prose writings when he stops for an extended view of the city or of its implications; yet it is clear that he incorporated and secularized many aspects of the visions of Ruskin and Carlyle. For him as for them the city violates the implications of the organic metaphor, the continuity of all experiences. Characteristically, in the following passage, there is no direct allusion to the city, but it is clear that the city is the enemy of this life-giving continuity:

> the one course which will certainly make life happy in the face of all
> accidents and troubles is to take a pleasurable interest in all the details of

life. And lest perchance you think that an assertion too universally
accepted to be worth making, let me remind you how entirely modern
civilization forbids it; with what sordid, and even terrible, details it surrounds
the life of the poor, what a mechanical and empty life she forces on the
rich; and how rare a holiday it is for any of us to feel ourselves a part of
Nature, and unhurriedly, thoughtfully, and happily to note the course of
our lives amidst all the little links of events which connect them with the
lives of others, and build up the great whole of humanity.

('Useful Work Versus Useless Toil,' pp. 612–13)

Here we have Carlyle's preoccupation with the ordinary without the accompanying
allegorizing and mysticism. We have Ruskin's insistence on the importance of joy in
human activity. And we have both writers' vision of the 'links' among events and
people. And, of course, we have the condemnation of modern civilization because of
the distance it puts between people and nature. The sage looking down on the city
can compress all of this into an allegorical vision of the city's activities, but Morris's
method is to keep his language simple, direct, and aimed at an audience with immediate practical concerns. And this stylistic difference corresponds to a major
difference in thought: for Morris, the organic metaphor leads inevitably to democracy.
Morris sees nature not as hierarchically structured, leading up to God, but as fully
democratic, all aspects of it having equal significance. The city, reflecting the commercialism which created it, implies the relation of master and slave. And thus,
finally, the city cannot seriously impinge on Morris's imagination.

Anything is justified in the extermination of capitalism and of the city which is
its manifestation. Capitalist economics is a constant state of war, and in *News from
Nowhere* Morris imagines a genuine and bloody revolution (partially modelled on
some of Morris's experiences in street meetings) which brings about The Great
Change. There is a curious mixture of very tough practicality, alertness to human
difficulty ('accidents and troubles'), and visionary ease in *News from Nowhere*. But
in that book, where free play is given to the dream quality of his socialism, where he
reconciles the two aspects of himself ('on the side of Karl Marx *contra mundum*,' and
on the side of 'Chaucer *contra mundum*'[13]), Morris builds on the contrast between the
ugly architecture, the human stewing, of London, and the world of Nowhere, in
which London disappears, with its machinery and smog, into a series of villages. A
brief look at the city in *Nowhere* will show again how Morris, like Ruskin before him,
had found no language for the modern city, and how the failure to do so seriously
damages the force of his critique of modern culture.

News from Nowhere embodies many of the details of the possibilities of life
beyond commercialism that are described in the forward-looking essays. Its center of
value can be seen in the re-creation (or, perhaps, de-creation) of the urban community.
The London in which the narrator finds himself is unrecognizable to the Victorian
eye. Even the East End, for example, though still relatively populous, has gone
through 'The Clearing of Misery'; and though, from a tradition 'that people got used

to living thicker on the ground there than in most places,' . . . 'it remains the most populous part of London,' it is architecturally handsome, and 'the crowding goes no further than a street called Aldgate.' The houses up to Aldgate are roomy and clean, and beyond them are only 'meadows and widely scattered houses' (p. 63). The great organic disease observed in Weissnichtwo is cured here by a retreat to smaller organisms. Decentralization is encouraged everywhere, each part of London being a genuine community, sufficiently small and manageable for the old bureaucratic structures of politics and police to be unnecessary. The old relation between master and servant has, moreover, disappeared: thus nobody works on anything that is not important or beautiful, and the work people do is as healthy as the place in which they live. People do not, for another example, live down by the docks, because the land is too marshy; but the area makes a good place for a Sunday walk and for the grazing of sheep. London has resolved itself into the communities out of which it emerged.

The idea of decentralization is, to the modern reader, more sensible and practical than it might have appeared until recently; but Morris's utopian city remains impossible because machinery is banished from it. In this respect, Morris continues the attack on machinery, begun metaphorically in Carlyle's 'Signs of the Times,' and continued quite literally in Ruskin's critique of the means of production in capitalist society. Morris imagines that the great change in the society of Nowhere eliminates the need for machinery. The artificially stimulated demand for shoddy produce in capitalist society has disappeared, and without it people are released to spend time making things by hand and enriching them with skilful decoration. The effect of this transformation is to make work a joy, to allow only a kind of 'natural' demand for necessary articles well made, and to return the rivers to their former purity, the country to its former greenness. Obviously, behind all this anti-mechanism the organic metaphor is operating.

Sentimental or not, Morris's vision has the salutary quality of insisting on pleasure. His language in this respect demonstrates how far he has come from Carlyle and the initial Puritan response to the difficulties of modern civilization. There is a great distance here even from Ruskin, to whom the idea of pleasure was far more important than it was to Carlyle. The second birth, which in Carlyle is seen in terms of the Phoenix or of the Apocalypse, is seen here in a more literary and sensuous way. To be sure, there is an intricate and impressive chapter describing the sequence by which the change came, and Morris does face the necessity for violence preceding change: 'Yes,' said the old man, 'the world was being brought to its second birth; how could that take place without a tragedy? Moreover, think of it. The spirit of the new days, of our days, was to be delight in the life of the world; intense and over-weening love of the very skin and surface of the earth on which man dwells, such as a lover has in the fair flesh of the woman he loves' (p. 123). The sacramental vision, which led Ruskin to a reverence for the world, here is translated into explicitly and healthily sexual terms.

By virtue of his capacity to accept the need for pleasure and a definition of pleasure that includes sexuality, Morris moves closer to a truly revolutionary way of seeing society. If he has no language to cope with the machine, he inherits and develops a satisfying one to cope with pleasure. And the new society he imagines is free not only of industrial slavery, but of sexual slavery as well. His concern with the beauty of the women in Nowhere is not merely romantic self-indulgence, or weak-kneed Victorian virginolatry. Ellen is sexually alive and intellectually and physically the equal of any man in Nowhere; she acknowledges her attractiveness to men and her pleasure in being attractive; Clare has been divorced from Dick and returns to him once more with a romantic energy not satirized by the narrator. Morris does not turn the woman into a natural object to be worshipped, but makes her a vital part of the community. To be sure, neither Morris nor his female creation is quite liberated in the modern sense; but because of his frank recognition of pleasure, he moves as close as any Victorian does to a conception of woman and society free of sexual exploitation.

Here, as in other respects, the decentralized, idealized, and sentimentally idyllic London of Nowhere is a more practical and direct invitation to change than any naturalistic report of London's condition might be. The utopia we get is not perfect, even in Morris's eyes (there are, for example, a murder, a love triangle, and a potential suicide); but the difficulties issue out of inescapable human and—we infer—natural difficulties. The socially induced evils have been eliminated. The richness and direct-ness of sexual love and commercial relationships are possible in Nowhere because of the elimination of capitalism, of the city, and of all the distorted and repressed relationships which their existence entailed.

Morris assumes that full life is only possible amidst wide spaces, in close contact with natural rhythms, and in frank recognition of the mutual responsibility of every member of the community. The modern city has no place in this imagination since it depends upon the contrast between wealth and poverty, upon commercial war, and upon the pollution of the natural world. Morris was no more capable than Ruskin or Carlyle of imagining the city in other terms, of building on the peculiar strengths of urban aggregation to develop new values or to modify the old romantic ones. Since, personally, he could live in the city with comfort, he felt a guilt, shared by Ruskin; he could indulge the pleasures of indignation and get out to the country. He shared with Carlyle an intense hatred of the injustices manifest in the city, at the per-versions of human relations implicit in the 'cash nexus' and in overcrowding, and a deep reverence for work. Unlike Carlyle, he moved to a utopian vision of what lies beyond the Phoenix burning. But there was no city in Morris's imagination, nor in the best imaginations of the great prose writers of Victorian England.

Notes

1   'How We Live and How We Might Live,' reprinted in the *Nonesuch Centenary Edition William Morris* (1946), p. 583. For convenience, all references to Morris, except where indicated, will be to this edition.

2   *Sartor Resartus*, ed. C. F. Harrold (New York, 1937), ch. 9 ('The Everlasting Yea'), p. 191. All future references will be to this edition.

3   'Characteristics,' *Centenary Edition: The works of Thomas Carlyle* (1899), XXVIII, p. 12.

4   *Fors Clavigera* (Illustrated Cabinet Edition, Boston, n.d.), II, Letter 37, p. 137. All references to Ruskin will be to the Cabinet Edition.

5   *Modern Painters* [*MP*], V, p. 233.

6   *Seven Lamps of Architecture*, ch. 3, section ii.

7   *Fiction—Fair and Foul*, p. 154.

8   *MP*, II, p. 252; see also Raymond Williams, *Culture and Society* (New York, 1960), pp. 150–1.

9   'How I Became a Socialist,' p. 657.

10 I am inclined to accept Williams's evaluation of Morris's work: 'There is more life in the lectures, where one feels that the whole man is engaged in the writing, than in any of the prose and verse romances' (p. 168).

11 E. P. Thompson, *William Morris: Romantic to revolutionary* (1955), p. 647.

12 May Morris, *William Morris: Artist, writer, socialist* (New York, 1966), II, p. 461.

13 See Philip Henderson, *William Morris: His life, work and friends* (New York, 1967), p. 303.

22   The Novel between City and Country

U. C. Knoepflmacher

Most major Victorian novelists retained and yet significantly altered the rich associations which the contrast between city and country had gathered over the centuries. After the manner of earlier writers, they regarded this opposition as an emblem for a divided existence; at the same time, however, they also felt far more deeply threatened than all those previous reconcilers who had tried to mediate between the realities represented by rural and urban life. The triumphant spread of urban civilization had resulted in unprecedented changes, in fears and uncertainties that seemed to cast grave doubts on the course of the future as well as on the guidelines of the past. Nonetheless, in their search for stability the Victorians preferred to cling to established literary conventions as a way to displace the associations evoked by the actual, physical reality of the modern city. For them, the old split between country and city thus acquired a new urgency—an intensity which at times assumed almost schizophrenic dimensions.

If the country continued to symbolize an irretrievable innocence associated with childhood and the virtues of natural growth, the city became identified with all the anxieties attributed to the rapid shifts and strains of adult civilized life. In an era marked by 'the dialogue of the mind with itself,'[1] the Inconstant City all too often stands for the confusion wrought by the bewildering changes which the writer tries to arrest or counter through his art. At first glance, the approach seems to be curiously one-sided; not only are there few spokesmen for the advantages of urban life, but urban life itself seems to be avoided by most novelists of the front rank. In an erudite essay in which he contrasts English and American representations of nineteenth-century city life, John Henry Raleigh is surprised to find that—with the important exceptions of Dickens and Gissing—most major Victorian novelists should have 'passed by' the cities of their time. He attributes the split between 'City Novel' and 'Provincial Novel' to this phenomenon.[2]

The majority of Victorian novelists did indeed by-pass the subject matter afforded to them by contemporary city life. Still, the City does very much remain an implicit 'presence' even in those novels which would seem to ignore it altogether. This essay constitutes an attempt to examine some of the metaphorical uses to which the Victorian novelist put the age-old contrast between urban and rural life. In the sections which follow, I shall examine, first, some earlier instances of the city–country dialectic and try to suggest how and why the Victorian novelist was compelled to alter this key metaphor for a divided existence. I shall next look at three important 'Provincial Novels,' *Wuthering Heights, Barchester Towers,* and *Silas Marner,* in order to show how the city acts as a presence even in those rural works of fiction which seem to shun it altogether. Finally, in the last two sections, a glance at a great variety of fictional forms and genres should reveal some of the compromises, defenses, and escapes by which Victorian novelists tried to come to terms with the Vanity Fairs and Cities of Destruction concocted by their threatened imaginations.

As a moralist in a Christian society, the Victorian novelist was the cultural heir of Protestant allegorists like Milton and Bunyan (the allusions to *The Pilgrim's Progress* in Victorian fiction, like the echoes and adaptions of *Paradise Lost,* are so plentiful that they almost call for a book-length study). As entertainers catering for a somewhat different audience, writers like Dickens, Thackeray, Trollope, George Eliot, and Meredith also remained within the comic tradition established by the English humorists of the eighteenth century, and, earlier, by the Restoration and Jacobean playwrights. Despite the differences between these two traditions, both had relied heavily on the opposition between city and country; both therefore provided the novelist with a set of metaphors distinctly understood by his readers.

For Milton and Bunyan, the Earthly City is Mammon's abode; it is the product of the pride and vanity which causes fallen men to cling to a life that remains erratic and purposeless. It is no coincidence, therefore, that the first efforts of Milton's fallen angels should be directed at the erection of a sumptuous citadel, or that, in the opening portion of *The Pilgrim's Progress,* Christian should immediately be accosted by Mr Worldly Wiseman, one who dwells in 'a very great town' near the City of Destruction 'from whence Christian came.' In *Paradise Lost,* the catalogue of opulent cities, ranging from exotic 'Cambalu' and 'Samarchand' to imperial Rome and to the mythical El Dorado vainly sought by eager explorers, is recited to remind the fallen Adam that far 'nobler sights' are in store for all those willing to rely on an inward light in order to recover God's grace (XI, 388–411). Likewise in *The Pilgrim's Progress,* Faithful and Christian must resist the allurements of the 'town of Vanity,' a cosmopolis in which the main streets are named after the richest nations of this world.

For Bunyan as for Milton, the fortuitousness of the Earthly City can be countered only by a sober introspective existence such as that led by the shepherds of the Old Testament. After their egress from Vanity Fair, Hopeful and Christian come to the well-tended gardens on top of the Delectable Mountains. In the teeming city below, Beelzebub acts as 'chief lord of the fair'; above, in the purer atmosphere of the orchards and vineyards from which the Celestial City is dimly visible, grave shepherds ready the pilgrims for the last lap in their journey. A similar juxtaposition operates in *Paradise Lost*, where Satan is pointedly contrasted to Adam, Eve, and Raphael, the trio who share a rustic meal on the 'grassy turf' of their Arcadian bower. Confronted by the yet unfallen Eve in Book IX, Satan is likened to an oppressed urbanite, one who has been 'long in populous City pent,/ Where Houses thick and Sewers annoy the Air' (IX, 445–6). By way of contrast, 'The smell of Grain, or tedded Grass, or Kine,/ Or Dairy, each rural sight, each rural sound,' seem to take on the character of the innocence which Satan is about to pollute. Eve herself is veiled in a cloud of fragrance; her 'every Air' appears like the purer emanations of 'pleasant Villages and Farms' to this presumed escapee from the stench of the city (and of sulphurous hell). Milton's simile is pregnant with irony. The bulk of Eve's descendants will emulate Satan by building the Babylons and Alcairos of the future; in a fallen world, not even the purity of rural life can ever again approximate the undefiled innocence she still enjoys. Nonetheless, by inserting his allusion to pleasant villages and farms, Milton also manages to suggest the means by which mankind can regain an Eden 'happier far' than that lost by our first parents. After the Fall, Paradise can become an internal state of mind. By cultivating this 'paradise within' and by rejecting the external shows of the Earthly City, Milton's faithful shepherds can eventually reap the fruits of the City of God and fulfill the poet's apocalyptic aspirations.

This theological formula is secularized by those seventeenth- and eighteenth-century writers who set out to combat the changeful humors of the city through the purgations of comedy and satire. In his 'Answer to Davenant's Preface to "Gondibert",' Thomas Hobbes divides human endeavors into three types of activity, each of which is associated with a particular literary genre of its own. To Hobbes, the aristocratic activities once centered around the 'celestial' court had called for the 'heroique' modes of epic and tragedy, while the 'terrestrial' activities of the countryside gave rise to the 'pastoral' modes of bucolic poetry and romance. Although Hobbes tries to justify Davenant's epic poem, it is obvious that he feels uneasy about the anachronism involved in the creation of a chivalric hero for his own day and age. Hobbes implies that the noble exemplars of tragedy and epic have become outdated relics, the 'glory of antiquity'; he makes it clear that 'rural people,' though exhibiting a desirable plainness and 'nutritive faculty,' are also notably dull. Modern life is urban. Since the 'insincereness, inconstancy, and troublesome humor' of those that dwell in populous cities are like 'the mobility, blustering, and impurity of the air,' the modern writer might prefer to make the 'aerial' city the chief target of his wit. By practising the 'scommatic' forms of satire and comedy once prevalent in Augustan Rome he can purge city-dwellers of the false humors and restore to them the virtues of true urbanity—the 'civility of Europe.'[3]

Hobbes's glossary is consistent with the practice of all those humorists who attempted to bring the city man in touch with constant values. In the urban comedies of Ben Jonson or Middleton, in Restoration drama, as in Dr Johnson's 'London' and *Rasselas*, or in *Moll Flanders*, *Tom Jones*, and *Humphry Clinker*, the city continues to act as an emblem for mutability, for values that are fitful and capricious. Yet the realism of these writers also demands that city and country be not regarded as purely symbolic entities as they were for Milton and Bunyan, and, to a much lesser extent, for a latter-day Puritan author like Richardson. Instead, city and country represent actual social activities involving 'deeds and language such as men do use.'[4] City fops and country bumpkins are exposed for their false manners rather than for their sinfulness; malodorous sewers are cited, not to epitomize the ways of Satan, but to contrast the decadence of the present with the pristine values of a golden age. The concrete realities of city and country must be fronted without reference to an other-worldly City of God. 'The man who is tired of London is tired of life': it is hardly a coincidence that the man who uttered these words should also have argued that the impossibility of visualizing Milton's shadowy Heaven remained, for him, one of the main drawbacks of *Paradise Lost*.

To the worldly writers of the eighteenth century, then, the kind of distinctions between city and country made by Milton and Bunyan had lost much of their force. Although the city man might profit from the simplicities of rustic life, to be 'rustical' meant, after all, to be 'rough, savage, boisterous, brutal, rude.'[5] Although the city's luxuries might prove to be corrupting, the polite world of the *urbs* or *civitas* also yielded the 'urbanity' and 'civility' required by enlightened nations. (Not until Coleridge and Arnold did the agrarian terms 'cultivation' and 'culture' replace 'civilization'; in Dr Johnson's *Dictionary*, the word 'civil' is defined as relating to men who live 'not in anarchy, not wild, not without rule or government.') The main task thus was to provide a synthesis between the best aspects of two modes of earthly existence, to combine sylvan constancy and urban sophistication: the editor of the *Gentleman's Magazine*, founded in 1731, accordingly took the pen-name of 'Sylvanus Urban.'

This blending is carried into a novel like *Tom Jones*. Though Tom returns to the rural life at Paradise Hall, he has benefited from his exposure to London; his and Sophia's children will presumably be able to steer a middle course by avoiding the depravity of London's Lady Bellaston as well as the brutality of the country's Squire Western. The search for a middle ground, a *via media* between rustic torpor and urban instability, also informs Smollett's *Humphry Clinker*. Suffering from anxieties that are only increased by his visits to London and Bath, Squire Bramble becomes cured in Edinburgh, a locality which combines the best features of country- and city-life. The squire's circular expedition allows Smollett to fuse the best of two anti-thetical worlds: in the course of the journey, Jery Melford, a cynical city man who is Bramble's surrogate son, becomes softened and humanized, while the boorish Humphry, Bramble's actual son, becomes civilized through his father's influence.

Bereft of the doctrinal securities inherent in Milton's and Bunyan's belief in a Heavenly City, increasingly doubtful about the social values espoused by those eighteenth-century predecessors who tried to fuse pastoral contentment with the attractions of civilized life, the Victorian novelist felt far more deeply threatened by the inconstancy of the Earthly City. In novels like *Great Expectations*, *Jude the Obscure*, and *The Mill on the Floss*, the movement from a childhood existence in the country to the adult experiences that take place in a city atmosphere leads to no synthesis. The return to Eden has become an impossibility; the Pip who has been educated in London can no longer adapt himself to the ways of Joe, the village blacksmith. On entering Joe's cottage after an eleven years' absence, Pip admits that 'that poor dream, as I once used to call it, has all gone by' (ch. 59); he can at best hope that a new Pip, the infant child of Joe and Biddy, may avoid the disappointments he has had to experience. The fates of Hardy's Jude and George Eliot's Maggie Tulliver are significantly ambiguous. Jude, who as a child, regarded the city of Christminster as an equivalent of the New Jerusalem, cannot track back to his former life at rural Marygreen, and dies, alone and abandoned, in a city room. Yet Hardy intimates that Jude is equally unfit for country life; only Arabella, who mingles with the 'hot mass' of people gathered on the streets of Christminster while Jude's corpse freezes into rigidity, can move with equal ease in country and city (VII, ch. 11). Maggie Tulliver, too, finds herself unable to bridge a rural past and a future that demands that she adjust to the motions of city life. Maggie misses her 'dear old Pilgrim's Progress' as much as the pastoral existence from which she has been debarred after the loss of Dorlcote Mill. As a child, she identified the river Floss with Bunyan's 'river over which there is no bridge.' As she grows up, the analogy proves bitterly ironic: condemned to live in St Ogg's, she drowns in the waters that have severed Dorlcote Mill from the City of Destruction. Although George Eliot wants the reader to believe that Maggie and Tom manage to relive—in death—the calm days when they had 'roamed the daisied fields,' she also makes them the victims of an irresistible turbulence which she associates with city life: brother and sister are destroyed by the 'hurrying, threatening masses' dislodged from the wharves of the industrial town (VII, ch. 5).

In a speech to the Society of Dorset Men in London, Thomas Hardy makes the predicament of the 'country beginner' who is transplanted to London stand for the alienation experienced by all those who find themselves deprived of the homogeneity belonging to a simpler state of life. Hardy hopes that 'our County Society, young as it is,' will, by bonding men together, remove the sense of loss felt, 'not only by Dorset mothers, but by those of every other county, at the time of their youthful sons' first plunge into the City alone.' Yet he adds, with characteristic gloom, that 'such anxieties—which would be intenser if all the risks were realised—can never be entirely dispelled.'[6] Hardy's words typify the horror over the disjointedness of city life felt by other country outcasts such as Thomas Carlyle (whose Teufelsdröckh moves from the village of Entepfuhl to 'that monstrous tuberosity of Civilised Life, the Capital of England'), William Cobbett (whose contempt for 'the great Wen' runs throughout his writings), or George Eliot (who declared that she could 'never love London, or believe that I am as well in the streets as in the fields').[7]

More important, Hardy's association of the city with a life devoid of the warmth of maternal care acts as a reminder of a key feature of Victorian fiction: the orphaned children and fatherless or motherless adolescents who must fend for themselves in an estranging urban world. Jo the chimney-sweep, little Nell, Hardy's Father Time, Conrad's Stevie are the city's victims; Becky Sharp, Tom Tulliver, Charley Hexam, Richard Feverel are corrupted by its values; Pendennis, Philip, Jenny Wren, Oliver Twist are scarred by its reality. To escape the city's anonymity it becomes necessary to take refuge in a Wessex, Barsetshire, or Loamshire, or to flee at least temporarily into the safety of the country as does Lizzie Hexam or Clara Middleton. Those who remain in the city must stand apart from its motions: Dobbin and his small family shy away from Becky's stall in the midst of Vanity Fair; John Harmon and his band of 'mutual friends' seek shelter in the Bower built by that infantile man, Boffin the Golden Dustman. And the eccentric Boffin can resist the adult logic that threatens to mutilate all others only by steadfastly clinging to the unreason of the child.

If the Victorian novelist could not risk immersion in the city with the confidence still possible for his eighteenth-century predecessors, neither could he derive from Nature the guarantees still extracted, only a generation before, by the Romantics. Although they, too, had discarded the social formulas by which the eighteenth century had tried to fuse the best aspects of urban and rural life, the Romantics sought to effect a higher synthesis of their own. Once again viewing the clash between country and city as a collision between internal states of being—the 'Two Contrary States of the Human Soul' of the *Songs of Innocence and of Experience*—poets like Blake, Wordsworth, and Coleridge singled out the city as the enemy of that 'fearless, lustful, happy' condition they tried to recover in their verses.[8] If for Bunyan and Milton the man-made city acted as an obstacle in the quest for the City of God, for the Romantics it also represented a deviation from a state of grace, for their belief in a transcendent Nature had merely replaced the old faith in the Celestial City.

Despite their frequent attacks on the 'dissolute city' on which they blamed the woes of modern man, the Romantics could therefore afford to be magnanimous. Blake suggests that the incomplete stages of Innocence and Experience must be superseded by a higher state—a state combining the too sanguine view of the shepherd piper whose joyous songs appeal to every child and the too bitter view of the bard who bemoans man's 'lapsed Soul.' Similarly, for Wordsworth, the 'green pastoral landscape' near Tintern Abbey allows the poet to return to the 'din of towns and cities' imbued with a new sense of direction, while the 'smokeless air' of the sleeping city beheld in the famous sonnet, 'Composed upon Westminster Bridge,' permits him to discern the same calm and freedom more clearly discerned in the country. The fixed forms of Nature can lift the city-dweller's spirits and liberate him from an oppression that may be but an illusion produced by false appearances. In Coleridge's 'This Lime-Tree Bower My Prison,' the fruition experienced by a Charles Lamb who has presumably 'hunger'd after Nature, many a year,/ In the great City pent' teaches the imprisoned poet, whose powers of imagination have allowed him to share his friend's ecstasy, that even in the narrowest plots there can be an assurance of joy. Even Shelley, perched among the Euganean Hills, looking down at Venice, is confident that a 'hundred cities . . . / Chained like thee' can be reanimated by the 'inspired soul.'

The Romantic confidence in the redemptive powers of Nature seldom operates in the world of the Victorian novel. To the Thackeray of *Vanity Fair*, life at rural Queen's Crawley exhibits the selfsame vanities found in London, Brussels, or Pumpernickel. In the chapter sarcastically entitled 'Arcadian Simplicity,' the Showman mocks the reader's sentimental expectations that the 'simplicity and sweet rural purity' of the 'honest folks at the Hall' must 'surely show the advantage of a country life over a town one' (ch. 11). Thackeray's realism is shared even by those novelists who do take refuge in the 'arcadian simplicity' of the countryside. The urban state of mind is not limited to the confines of London. In *Jane Eyre* the tentacles of civilization extend into the country itself: a beneficent Nature may guide the fate of her dear nursling Jane, but Lowood Institution, supported by 'ladies and gentlemen in this neighbourhood and in London' (ch. 5), claims the orphan Helen Burns as its martyr. Although the country frequently acts as a shelter in Dickens's novels, existence there is not necessarily free: the hulks of the prison-ship are but a stone's throw from Joe Gargery's smithy.

In a Darwinian universe, the retreat into Nature could hardly signify a complete return to pastoral innocence. The lush landscape in *Tess of the D'Urbervilles* or *Adam Bede* hides the same anxieties that growing men and women encounter in the city; a stranger beholding 'this joyous nature' would be deceived by its seeming placidity, unaware 'that hidden behind the apple-blossoms, or among the golden corn, or under the shrouding boughs of the wood, there might be a human heart beating heavily with anguish' (*Adam Bede*, ch. 35). In Conrad's *Heart of Darkness* the movement from city to jungle and back into the city reveals the universality of an even greater anguish. The motionless London which acts as a backdrop for Marlow's story, far from being touched by Wordsworth's soothing Nature, hides the same horror more clearly discerned in the virgin forests of the Congo: '"And this also," said Marlow suddenly, "has been one of the dark places of the earth".' Civilization is a sham, a grim absurdity; yet its illusion of order is necessary if life is to be sustained. The Marlow who has seen the Heart of Darkness must be 'civil' and preserve the lie which allows Kurtz's Intended to stay alive in the city that resembles a 'whited sepulchre.'

By going back to a childhood self nurtured on the emotions stimulated by daffodils, waves, and mountains, Wordsworth could find the securities that would allow him and an elect band of like-minded readers to withstand the adult uncertainties he represented by the City. In the fluid and multi-faceted world of the Victorian novel such stasis is hard to attain. It is in the country marshes, after all, that Pip's 'great expectations' first manifest themselves; his sojourn in the city merely charts the outcome of his earlier, irrevocable fall from childhood grace to the mistaken priorities of adult life. The finger-post which Pip passes at the threshold of the village points back to an innocence that cannot be recovered. He must say farewell to this 'dear friend' and move into the uncertain future that lies ahead: 'all beyond was so unknown and great' (ch. 19).

Although the country could no longer be celebrated as an impregnable Eden, it still remained a desirable refuge, a bulwark against the uncertainties of city life. Reacting to H. T. Buckle's proposition that 'the more men congregate in great cities . . . the less attention they will pay to the peculiarities of nature, which are the fertile source of superstition,' an indignant George Eliot wrote to a friend visiting the Lake Country: 'I am very far behind Mr. Buckle's millenial prospect, which is, that men will be more and more congregated in cities and occupied with human affairs, so as to be less and less under the influence of Nature, i.e. the sky, the hills, and the plains; whereby superstition will vanish and statistics will reign for ever and ever.'[9] Even if Nature had lost the immanent powers ascribed to it by the Romantics, the country continued to appeal to writers deeply perplexed by the increasingly doubtful course of their civilization. The tighter social organization of provincial towns and villages assuaged their fear of change; the country's folklore and superstitions placated the hunger for romance once satisfied by Scott. 'Human affairs' seemed less chaotic if examined in a removed rural atmosphere, apart from the disturbances of city life. The challenges of civilization could at least be obliquely met in settings such as those used by the three provincial novels discussed in the section that follows.

Whereas novels like *Great Expectations*, *The Mill on the Floss*, or *Jude the Obscure* depict the archetypal pilgrimage that takes a protagonist from country innocence to city experience, *Wuthering Heights* (1847), *Barchester Towers* (1857), and *Silas Marner* (1861) reverse this process by transplanting an urbanite into a rural enclave where, in Wordsworth's words, 'the essential passions of the heart find a better soil in which they can attain their maturity' and 'elementary feelings coexist in a state of greater simplicity, and consequently, may be more accurately contemplated.'[10]

In *Wuthering Heights* the city-intruder is the observer Lockwood, an escapee in search of a 'misanthropist's heaven' completely removed from 'the stir of society' (ch. 1). Lockwood soon meets with experiences which belie his initial identification with Heathcliff, that other city-creature transplanted into the country after he had been found in the streets of Liverpool by the old master of Wuthering Heights. Lockwood's stereotyped notions about the pleasures of rural solitude—expressed in the polite diction of eighteenth-century cultists of Nature such as Akenside or Joseph Warton—are quickly shattered. At the Heights, Lockwood is confronted with irrational instincts he has so far suppressed. His urban sense of decorum is disturbed by Heathcliff's incongruous behavior; what is more, his encounter with that other inhabitant of the Heights, the first Catherine, threatens to collapse the very forms by which he has hitherto ordered reality. The sight of the spectral 'child's face' peering through the window in his dream so terrifies Lockwood that he lapses into savagery in order to prevent the apparition from entering the room: 'Terror made me cruel; and, finding it useless to attempt shaking the creature off, I pulled its wrist on the broken pane, and rubbed it to and fro till the blood ran down and soaked the bed-clothes: still it wailed, "Let me in!"' (ch. 3). Lockwood's cruel repulsion of the child who wants to 'come home' illustrates that mixture of sadism and sexuality which, according to Freud, plagues the repressed civilized man.[11] Heathcliff's visitor awakes in a 'frenzy of fright' and asks to be conducted to the safety of Thrushcross Grange, the onetime home of the civilized Lintons.

Lockwood's initial progress from the anarchic instinctual life reigning at the Heights to the sublimations possible at the Grange epitomizes Emily Brontë's own attempts to mediate between eros and civilization, the too passionate Earnshaw blood and the too refined ways of the Lintons. At the Grange, Nelly Dean, a 'steady, reasonable kind of body' whose steadiness is as much derived from 'living among the hills' as from reading the books in the Linton library, tries to order Lockwood's excited mind. But Lockwood does not avail himself of the mode of life offered by the Grange. He prefers the safe distance of the observer. Just as he has initially fled to the country in order to resist the allurements of a 'most fascinating creature' he met at a spa, so he now resists his attraction to the second Catherine. On recovering from his illness, he decides to spend 'six months in London' (ch. 30). Upon returning to the Grange, he finds that events have passed him by. The second Catherine and Hareton have, during his absence, also left the world of the Heights. Yet their move has been constructive: by implanting Earnshaw vitality into the too-ordered gardens of the Lintons, they have carried with them the means to go beyond the self-destruction of the first Catherine and Heathcliff. They have grown. Lockwood, on the other hand, remains as stiff and wooden as ever. At the end of the novel, he beats a hasty retreat from the Grange. Unlike the other two refugees from the Heights, he is destined to remain a perpetual wanderer, a fugitive.

In the more realistic world of *Barchester Towers*, where manners rather than the irrationality of romance convey Trollope's meaning, the representatives of the city are directly involved in the plot. The clash which sets the story in motion is that between London, or what the narrator calls 'the world at large,' and the sleepy cathedral town of Barchester. London's ostensible representative in the novel is Dr Proudie, the imported Bishop who has been foisted on Barchester by the meddling powers at the capital; its actual and more dangerous representative is the hypocritical Mr Slope, the new Bishop's secretary. Dr Proudie represents London's empty pomp; Mr Slope, its deceit. Though appointed as provincial Bishop, Dr Proudie cannot part with London: 'How otherwise could he keep himself before the world? how else give the government, in matters theological, the full benefit of his weight and talents?' (ch. 3). At the end of the novel, the weak Dr Proudie, appointed to the House of Lords but ruled by his wife, gives the nation the benefit of his weighty opinions by registering an occasional vote 'in favour of the Government.' The Bishop displays the ostentatiousness of the metropolis; his secretary, however, knows how to tap its true sources of power—the shifting opinions of its unstable newspapers and political parties. Slope the city man exploits the changefulness of the 'world at large' and infects Barchester with the factionalism of the capital. Like the witty servants of Roman and Elizabethan comedy, the Bishop's chaplain accommodates himself to change, no matter how abrupt and unforeseen. None the less, Barchester, lethargic and inert, defeats this nimble intruder. Although London's anarchy soon spreads to the provincial town, whose clergymen and merchants are after all directly connected to the capital both by railroad and by the new 'Electric Telegraph,' it is in retrograde Ullathorne that Mr Slope experiences his first reversals.

Ullathorne Court, the feudal home of the Thornes, is a rural domain which screens out the inconstant world at large. At the Court and at the parish of St Ewold —taken over by the Rev. Mr Arabin, Mr Slope's diffident rival—time almost stands still. The Londoners descend on Barchester by the speedy railroad; the Barchesterians pride themselves on the horse-drawn carriages they ride even for the shortest distances. No vehicle, however, can pass Ullathorne's 'iron gate': 'If you enter Ullathorne at all, you must do so, fair reader, on foot, or at least in a bath-chair' (ch. 22). Those few privileged to be drawn past the gates profit from their experiences. It is there, in the novel's heart, that the affairs of the heart can be resolved. Ulla-thorne encourages a display of impulse and instinct: Mr Slope drops his verbal indirections and admits his sexual passion for Eleanor Bold; his advances are met, just as directly, by the little hand that boxes his ears. In the world presided over by the archaic Miss Thorne, Slope is replaced as Eleanor's suitor by the virginal Mr Arabin. Like Lockwood, that other displaced suitor, the overreaching Slope must go back to London.

In *Silas Marner*, a novel fusing the modes of romance and realism, the figure of the intruding urbanite is taken over by the protagonist himself. Silas Marner escapes from an unnamed industrial town in the North into the fertile agrarian world of Raveloe. In the city's impersonal atmosphere, Marner was forced to express his need for love and friendship through the narrow religion practised at Lantern Yard. The beliefs of this urban sect, however, have become detached from their original sources: form has been severed from feeling. Silas, whose mother had acquainted him with the powers of medicinal herbs, is warned by his religious brethren that prayer does not require the aid of such natural remedies, so 'that his inherited delight to wander through the fields in search of foxglove and dandelion and coltsfoot, began to wear to him the character of a temptation' (ch. 1). When this child-like man is pronounced guilty by the lots, his abstract religion collapses; bereft of any tangible props to buttress his broken 'trust in man,' the excommunicated linen-weaver inveighs against 'a God of lies, that bears witness against the innocent' (ch. 1). Without the protection of his religion, the entire universe has become for him as chance-ridden and as alienating as the city he now flees. Lockwood's misanthropy is a pose; Silas's is genuine. Whereas Lockwood steals away from involvement, Silas seeks permanent isolation in 'this low, wooded region, where he felt hidden even from the heavens by the screening trees and hedgerows' because his desire for communion has been so sorely thwarted. Dead to the city, not yet reborn to the country, he hovers in a state of suspension that makes him seem even more inanimate than before: 'He seemed to weave, like the spider, from pure impulse, without reflection' (ch. 2).

In *Silas Marner*, however, George Eliot attempts to reverse the fate suffered in her previous novel by Maggie Tulliver, the unwilling victim of the City of Destruction. In rustic Raveloe, Silas gradually rediscovers the natural, human foundations on which his earlier belief ought to have been based. His new roots prove to be therapeutic. By observing the growth of the child deposited at his doorstep, Silas can revert to a healthier and more elemental stage of life. On finding his fate to be inextricably interwoven with that of Godfrey Cass, Eppie's true father, he can even satisfy his primitive need to believe in the existence of inexplicable powers binding man to his fellowman.

Despite acute differences in mode and in approach, *Wuthering Heights*, *Barchester Towers*, and *Silas Marner* illustrate similar antagonisms. All three provincial novels indict the renunciation of instinct forced upon men by civilization and city-life. Each novelist acknowledges that a total liberation from the temporal reality represented by the City is impossible, yet the pastoral mode allows each to tame the wantonness of change. Change itself is unavoidable; compromise becomes a necessity. Though identifying with the uncompromising Heathcliff, Emily Brontë rewards the nurslings of the adaptable Nelly Dean for their ability to go beyond the impossible stasis desired by the first set of lovers. Likewise, the realism of both Trollope and George Eliot forces them to admit the inevitability of change into their wishful fictive worlds. In *Barchester Towers*, Trollope's endorsement of his archaic country innocents is as guarded as Fielding's endorsement of Parson Adams: a modern Barchester connected to London can hardly be expected to relapse into the feudalism still encouraged at Ullathorne. In *Silas Marner*, the idyll of Silas's rebirth is seriously qualified by an acute consciousness of history: the narrator insists that the 'unity' between 'past and present' found by Silas could be attained only among rustics who still adhere to an 'old-fashioned country life' no longer in evidence in the complex 1860s. Still, no matter how strongly they qualify their wishfulness, all three writers obviously prefer the deliberate changes of this 'country life' to the abrupt and erratic shifts they associate with the city.

In *Wuthering Heights*, the absolute freedom enjoyed by the two companions who had roamed the heath soon becomes an impossibility: on growing up, Catherine yields to the civilized attractions of the Grange, while the spurned Heathcliff reappears, no longer looking like a coarse 'ploughboy,' but rather as one whose passions are at odds with his genteel exterior: 'A half-civilized ferocity lurked yet in the depressed brows and eyes full of fire, but it was subdued' (ch. 10). To regain the freedom and oneness they possessed as children, the lovers must escape to a different reality. Just as it is no coincidence that the waif who entered Lockwood's dream should have appeared in the shape of a child, so, too, it is no less coincidental that the two ghostly figures on the moor should be seen by a little shepherd boy 'with a sheep and two lambs before him' (ch. 34). The fusion of the lovers is possible only in a realm of essences such as that discerned by Blake's shepherd piper. In the temporal world they vacate, compromises are possible. Edgar Linton's daughter educates Hindley Earnshaw's sullen and rusticated son; conversely, Hareton rekindles Cathy's powers of feeling. The second Catherine and Hareton thus manage to merge the seemingly irreconcilable realities represented by the Grange and the Heights. Whereas Cathy and her husband remain in a green and pleasant pastoral land, Lockwood, Cathy's pseudo-suitor, retreats into the anonymity of London. Fixed in his chosen role of voyeur, he remains an outsider barely affected by the rebirth he has witnessed.

In the social comedy of *Barchester Towers*, the nucleus that forms around Eleanor Bold's small child successfully resists the more capricious changes that 'the world at large' has tried to inflict on Barchester. Although the new Bishop of Barchester cannot be dislodged, the townspeople are comforted by the thought that he, too, will be forced to adhere to tradition as soon as 'the new-fangled manners of the age have discovered him to be super-annuated.' All other alterations have been minimal. There is a new Warden at Hiram's Hospital and there will be twelve old women and a matron in addition to the twelve male inmates, but this equality in numbers almost seems a male victory in an era in which, according to Trollope's narrator, women do not usually settle for such parity. There is also a new Dean, but Francis Arabin, the shy scholar who hails from the Oxford of Newman and Arnold and hence is hardly a radical, will help to perpetuate the old church music that Mr Harding loves and that Slope has so rashly attacked. Eleanor's husband is almost as unworldly as her father, who happily resumes his eccentric ways by preferring his imaginary violoncello to the instrument with 'new-fashioned arrangements' given to him by his other son-in-law. Miss Thorne, the match-maker responsible for Eleanor's union to Arabin, also persists in her eccentricities, even if she ceases to demand that her tenants tilt at the quintain in imitation of the yeomen of the past. At Ullathorne, Eleanor and Arabin confess to each other their mutual delight in 'old-fashioned mansions, built as this, and old-fashioned gardens.' When Eleanor vows that 'old-fashioned things are so much the honestest,' Mr Arabin evades the question as being one 'on which very much may be said on either side. . . Some think we are quickly progressing towards perfection, while others imagine that virtue is disappearing from the earth' (ch. 48). Trollope's own preferences, however, are quite clear. He prefers the timidities of Arabin and Mr Harding to Slope's chameleon-like adherence to whatever opinions best serve his self-interest. Slope the innovating city man depends on social change for his rise. He cannot succeed in a pastoral world where men are content to cultivate their own gardens. In the delightfully archaic chunk of 'Merry England' invented by Trollope, Slope is defeated; back in a London governed by the reality-principle, he once again can thrive. His marriage to the rich widow of a sugar-refiner and his eminence as a preacher in a church 'in the vicinity of the New Road' should sweeten the cinders that Barchester—and Trollope the fantasist—have made him swallow.

Silas Marner, too, ends with a country wedding in a pastoral atmosphere; here, too, some changes prove inevitable. Silas's cottage near the Stone Pits has been altered to accommodate Eppie's husband. The surrounding garden has also been enlarged: 'The garden was fenced with stones on two sides, but in front there was an open fence, through which the flowers shone with answering gladness' ('Conclusion').

The semi-opened garden built for Eppie symbolizes the rechannelling of Silas's blocked emotions which she has brought about. The foundling is named after Silas's dead mother and lost 'little sister.' The unlearned weaver cannot fathom the significance of this 'Bible name,' but his creator expects her readers to link it to his redemption: 'thou shalt no more be termed Forsaken; neither shall thy land be termed Desolate; but thou shalt be called Hephzibah' (Isaiah, 62:4).[12] Eppie's growth reawakens memories which Silas has stifled since his own childhood in the city: 'As the child's mind was growing into knowledge his mind was growing into memory; as her life unfolded, his soul, long stupefied in a cold narrow prison, was unfolding too, and trembling gradually into full consciousness' (ch. 14). After Eppie's identity is revealed to her and Silas, he becomes all the more eager to reconcile his own past to his present and proposes that they visit his birthplace. As they venture through the streets of 'the great manufacturing town,' Silas is bewildered 'by the changes thirty years had brought.' Looking for Lantern Yard, they light on Prison Street; the jail, at least, is unaltered. Though the shuddering Eppie declares it to be a 'dark ugly place,' worse than the Workhouse, Silas uses the building to orient himself: 'It's the third turning on the left from the jail doors—that's the way we must go.' The changeful city, however, has completely swallowed up the chapel of Lantern Yard; a 'new opening' is occupied by a 'big factory.' Even the graves of Silas's Brethren have disappeared. On his return to Raveloe, the puzzled weaver acknowledges that he has 'no home but this now' (ch. 21). The bridal procession that moves from the 'open yard' before the Rainbow tavern to the 'open fence' of the cottage marks Silas's acceptance of a future based on continuity and growth. The vegetative world in which Eppie has sprouted has finally released the self arrested and imprisoned by the wanton changefulness of the City.

If the analysis of the three Provincial Novels in the preceding section proves that Victorian fiction never completely 'passes by' the city's challenge, it is nonetheless true that this challenge is seldom met directly or literally. In the City Novel the protean reality of the city acts primarily as a setting for the struggles of characters in search of their identity. The disguises and transformations possible in a metropolis hold a peculiar fascination for the Victorian novelist. The City of Mystery informs both the horror story and the novel of sensation; it provides the background for symbolic romances such as *Daniel Deronda*; it gives rise to the genre of the detective story, which tends to remind us, in G. K. Chesterton's words, 'that we live in an armed camp making war with a chaotic world.'[13] Inherent in all these modes is the same antithesis observed by the Provincial Novel. If Lockwood must be transported to the Heights to face the sadistic self he has repressed, Stevenson's civilized Dr Jekyll can stay in the city and be protected by its sheltering anonymity as he stalks the streets, metamorphosed into the brutal Mr Hyde. The alterations in Dorian Gray's features also remain hidden from the men and women he encounters during his city prowls. His fall from the 'stainless purity of boyish life' to the 'bestial, sodden, and unclean' self recorded on the canvas painted by Basil Hallward is presented through the conventional country–city antithesis: Wilde stresses that Dorian's fall was occasioned by 'those subtle poisonous theories' which were uttered in Basil's garden by Dorian's seducer, Lord Harry, the Satanic city man (ch. 7). Conversely, in a novel like *Daniel Deronda*, Mordecai, the Jewish visionary who refuses to be deceived by the city's 'outward signs,' brings about the 'transformation of self' which restores to Deronda his childhood identity (chs 37, 41). The aimless young Gentile rowing on the Thames can now become a Moses able to lead his people back to a green Canaan.

In their essentially metaphoric treatment of the city, the Victorian novelists by and large eschewed its literal reality. With the exception of Dickens, the city-novelist *par excellence*, only second-rank writers like Mrs Gaskell, Kingsley, or Gissing address themselves to the actual conditions of those struggling 'among these foul sties, which civilisation rears—and calls them Cities' (*Alton Locke*, ch. 41). And even Dickens himself, whose work was so strongly identified with London by foreign visitors that their preconceptions about the capital were 'prë-eminently Dickensy,'[14] regards the city as a surrealistic entity, an emblem of the shackles by which civilization binds the self. Despite their accurate description of the low-life catalogued by Henry Mayhew, despite their genuine indignation over the actual squalor and actual pain documented by other reformers of the time, Dickens's novels resort to symbolical devices to express their author's mixture of fascination and horror over the mutations he associates with the city. The moat-surrounded house in Walworth in which Wemmick exorcizes his unfeeling city-self, the garden on the roof-top where Jenny Wren and Riah seek relief from the painful world that lies below, the lock which Betty Higden must cross in order to pass from one world to the other, belong to a different imaginative order from the rhetorical assaults on the masters of Coketown or the institution of the Workhouse.

In *Bleak House* Jo's plight epitomizes that of all beings arrested by the City of Destruction; the golden cross that reaches into heaven from the summit of St Paul's—the 'sacred emblem' of a religion that once allowed men to transcend their temporal captivity—has become in Jo's eyes, 'the crowning confusion of the great, confused city' (ch. 19). The boy who is asked to 'move on' must die, like Heathcliff and Catherine, in order to become free again. Jo's flight from city to country is inextricable from the movements of Esther and Lady Dedlock. The latter, detained in the country only by Sir Leicester's gout, perishes in the heart of the city by her lover's grave; the former can recover her frozen identity only by looking at the confusing city from the perspective afforded by Bleak House. Standing by the 'garden-gate,' Esther involuntarily contrasts the 'lurid glare' of distant London with the pale afterglow of the sun that has sunk in the north-west; 'the contrast between these two lights, and the fancy which the redder light engendered of an unearthly fire, gleaming on all the buildings in the city' causes Esther to regard this moment, in which she knows herself 'as being something different' from what she has been, as the turning point in her career (ch. 31).

The shimmering lights of the City of Experience may prove deceptive, but their glow beckons like alluring 'goblin eyes' which act as 'the guardians of some secret, however crude, which the writer knows and the reader does not. Every twist of the road is like a finger pointing to it; every fantastic skyline of chimney-pots seems wildly and derisively signalling the meaning of the mystery.'[15] If, in romances like *Wuthering Heights* or *Jane Eyre* the novelist tries to pierce the veil of Nature, the city-romancer can exercise his imagination by probing into mysteries of a different order: as Chesterton observes, 'while Nature is a chaos of unconscious forces, a city is a chaos of conscious ones.' The intrigues once locked in the dungeons of Gothic castles are now concealed in a city-scape where every 'brick has as human a hieroglyph as if it were a graven brick of Babylon.'

The city thus becomes the domain of men like Jaggers or Tulkinghorn who hold the key to secrets 'associated with darkening woods in the country, and vast blank shut-up houses in town' (*Bleak House*, ch. 22). It becomes the hunting ground for the sharp-eyed detective officer Bucket and for Sherlock Holmes, the sober rationalist who can pierce through the false appearances that baffle lesser men. In the opening of Wilkie Collins's *Woman in White*, Walter Hartright meets the solitary madwoman who points 'to the dark cloud of London.' About to leave for Cumberland, Hartright is as yet unaware that the mystery in which he will become involved—a mystery that originates at Limmeridge House in the North and will be complicated at Blackwater Park in Hampshire—can ultimately be resolved only in the 'house-forest of London' to which Anne Catherick has pointed. It is in the great city, the eraser of identity, that he and his female companions must hide until Laura Fairlie's identity can be restored: 'we three were as completely isolated in our place of concealment as if the house we lived in had been a desert island, and the great network of streets and the thousands of our fellow-creatures all round us the waters of an illimitable sea' (Bk III, ch. 3).

The notion of the city as an impassive yet mysterious cosmos, 'as vast as a sea,' is taken over in Conrad's *The Secret Agent*. Though written in 1907 and thus, strictly speaking, a post-Victorian work, 'This Simple Tale of the XIX Century' deliberately retreats to a Dickensian London of gas-lamps and horse-drawn carriages. In his prefatory 'Author's Note,' Conrad explains how a 'monstrous town more populous than some continents' disturbed his 'quieted-down imagination' and replaced his earlier vision of South America, 'a continent of crude sunshine and brutal revolutions, of the sea, the vast expanse of salt waters.' In *The Secret Agent* the impersonal Nature of Conrad's previous romances gives way to the wet city and its masses of faceless people; Marlow the interpreter of Nature becomes the all-seeing Assistant Commissioner of Police. Like Marlow, this detective who has lived in the tropics is aware of the absurdities of the civilization he protects; like his prototypes in the fiction of Dickens and Collins, he nonetheless tries to maintain order by thwarting those who would exploit the anarchy feared by civilization. If Bucket and Hartright track down foreign criminals, the Assistant Commissioner solves the riddle that puzzles others by identifying the urbane Vladimir as the prime agent for the terrorist act which has claimed the life of Stevie. Still, though he pieces together the jagged fragments torn asunder by the novelist, the Assistant Commissioner cannot resolve the 'impenetrable mystery' of Winnie Verloc's suicide. The young woman awakens after her seven-year sleep in a 'triangular well of asphalt and bricks, of blind houses and unfeeling stones' (ch. 12), but her awakened passions only lead to her self-destruction. Her 'madness and despair' are brought about by her belated recognition of the true anarchy that lurks beneath the forms of civilized existence.

To the city-novelist, then, London obscures, annuls, or maims the identity of characters in search of their true self. Even those writers who would seem to find positive aspects in the experiences afforded by urban life often reveal, on closer inspection, a highly ambiguous reaction to the city. In *Villette*, Lucy Snowe stops at London on her way to Belgium; the city's vitality strikes this provincial girl 'who never yet truly lived' as a token of the adult life she wants to front: '"I did well to come," I said, proceeding to dress with speed and care. "I like this spirit of London which I feel around me. Who but a coward would pass his whole life in hamlets, and forever abandon his faculties to the eating rust of obscurity?"' (ch. 6). The words are brave, but they are also a measure of Lucy's inexperience. She will never come back to London, but stay arrested in an intermediate stage in the quieter foreign town of 'Villette.' If Jane Eyre—that previous projection of Charlotte Brontë—finds happiness by returning to a rural hamlet, Lucy remains unfulfilled, vainly cultivating plants in M. Emanuel's garden, without 'the fruition of return' (ch. 42). The adult world of London is not destined to be hers.

In *The Way of All Flesh*, Butler's narrator Overton is even more emphatic in his endorsement of London life: 'The want of fresh air does not seem much to affect the happiness of children in a London alley: the greater part of them sing and play, as though they were on a moor in Scotland' (ch. 6). Indeed, in tracing Ernest Pontifex's development, Butler seems to invert the usual associations ascribed to country and city by his contemporaries: it is at rural Battersby-on-the-Hill that Ernest is most sorely repressed, and, of all places, in a London jail that he first experiences freedom. Ernest's progression thus would seem to counter the fall from pastoral grace so often depicted in other Victorian novels: shackled as a child in Battersby-on-the-Hill (Vol. I, part ii) and Roughborough (II, i), deluded by the education he receives at Cambridge (II, ii), the young man breaks with his past in the prison at Coldbath Fields (III, i), learns self-reliance as a penurious family-man living 'in the neighbourhood of the Elephant and Castle' (III, ii), and finally gains his independence as a wealthy and cultivated bachelor who resides in the most fashionable quarters of the city (III, iii).

This forward movement, however, is deceptive, for it is accompanied by a regression into a simpler state of life. In the city Ernest actually manages to recapture for himself and for his children—whom he turns over to a bargeman—the instinctual vigor once possessed in the country by his great-grandfather, the carpenter John Pontifex. Ernest's pilgrimage from country to city thus erases the dire effects of a similar movement portrayed in the opening section of the book (I, i) when George Pontifex, Ernest's grandfather, deserts Paleham village and begets the debilitated city-son who becomes Ernest's father, Theobald. In the city Ernest therefore merely builds a bridge leading his race back into a happier ancestral past. What is more, although Ernest frees himself from the strangulating shibboleths of Victorian civilization, he continues to be plagued by his self-consciousness, aware of his inferiority to the original Pontifexes. It is Ernest's son George, a sailor, and not the urban Ernest, who recovers the freedom formerly enjoyed by John Pontifex in a more primitive stage of life.

It should by now be evident that the Provincial Novel and the City Novel alike display the Victorian tendency to recoil from the massive changes that seemed so threatening to all writers of the age. The Victorian novelist who wrote for an essentially urban public could not quite retreat into a hazy Arthurian world or rebuild the stones of medieval Venice. Despite his occasional escapism, he at least tried to provide his readers and himself with the psychological means of resisting the confusing present which he equated with the City. To achieve some distance from and control over this urban present seemed imperative. *Middlemarch*, George Eliot's accepted masterpiece, probably furnishes the most complex illustration of the attempt to fabricate a fictional reality which, though removed in time and space, also might partake of the fluctuations of modern life.

Situated in the 'north-east corner of Loamshire' (ch. 1), Middlemarch is a mythical community in the Midlands; its inhabitants, who regard 'London as a centre of hostility' (ch. 58), are as retrograde as Trollope's Barchesterians. Yet whereas Trollope's quaint eccentrics defy the realities of modern life, the time-conscious narrator of *Middlemarch* uses hindsight to assess the progress of the Middlemarchers from the vantage point of 'the present.' By providing a network of allusions ranging from 'older Herodotus' down to this present, the novelist scales the fictitious history of her characters against the actual history of civilization. This wider range permits narrator and reader to tap a font of experience not available to the young provincial reformers who are still innocent about their future. In the course of the novel, Dorothea must be removed from the innocence of Tipton Grange and become exposed to the sedimentations of history visible in Rome, the City of Experience; Lydgate, on the other hand, must learn that, despite the sophistication he has acquired in modern Paris, he is not above the moral distinctions still insisted upon, in the country, by men of the caliber of Caleb Garth. The physician who moved to Middlemarch in order to keep away from the range of 'London intrigues, jealousies, and social truckling' (ch. 15) discovers to his chagrin that he has become enmeshed in the pettier intrigues of a provincial Vanity Fair.

The community of Middlemarch thus provides George Eliot with a middle ground between past and present, reaction and progress, pastoral traditionalism and urban mobility. The novelist dissects the narrow provincial life that thwarts the aspirations of Dorothea and Lydgate; at the same time, however, she grants fulfillment to Fred and Mary within the small town's confines. Re-educated by Caleb

Garth, Fred can become 'rather distinguished in his side of the country as a theoretic and practical farmer'; his marriage to Caleb's daughter proves as great a 'beginning, as it was to Adam and Eve, who kept their honeymoon in Eden' ('Finale'). But if Fred and Mary can rebuild a paradise in prosaic Middlemarch, Dorothea and Lydgate must venture into the changing world that lies beyond. In London, Dorothea adapts herself to 'an imperfect social state' by accepting the anonymity she must share with all those noble Victorian helpmeets who improve the lots of others in 'incalculably diffusive' ways. Lydgate's removal is far more bitter. His alternations, 'according to the season, between London and a Continental bathing-place' represent his abject surrender to the shifting world he has so vainly tried to set in order.

Middlemarch is not a historical novel, yet the impulses which led George Eliot to devise the temporal and spatial correlatives operating in her greatest novel are akin to those which led other Victorian novelists to explore earlier stages of civilization by ranging either historically into cities of the past or geographically into regions untouched by modern city life. Though partly attributable to the continuing popularity of Scott, the profusion of historical novels in the Victorian age owes much to this search for some fountainhead from which novelist and reader might safely observe their present. Seldom, however, do these novels exhibit anything other than the dissociations found in the present. In *Marius the Epicurean*, Pater implies that his reconstruction of second-century Rome is not to be regarded as an antiquarian undertaking, but rather as an effort to isolate the problems besetting modern men: 'That age and our own have much in common—many difficulties and hopes. Let the reader pardon me if here and there I seem to be passing from Marius to his modern representatives—from Rome, to Paris or London' (ch. 16).

This tendency of disguising the present as a historical past explains the incongruities of novels like *Hypatia* and *Romola* and accounts for the curious resemblances, noticed by Ernest Baker, which a Raphael Ben Ezra living in fifth-century Alexandria or a Tito Melema living in fifteenth-century Florence bear to a 'blasé West-Ender' living in Victorian London.[16] Marius's disappointment along the grave-studded Appian Way differs little from the anguish of the Mark Rutherford to whom modern London seems as a vast 'mausoleum.' Past and present reveal the same necropolis. The world-weariness that prompts Sidney Carton's self-sacrifice in revolutionary Paris and the consumption that extinguishes Jude Fawley's will to live in Christminster are expressions of an identical death-wish. In their imaginative reconstructions of earlier cities the Victorian novelists only met the same forms of life from which they had tried to escape: finding Renaissance Florence to be no different from the St Ogg's that alienated Maggie Tulliver, George Eliot was forced to slap on a pastoral ending to her novel by carrying Romola into an Italian Raveloe and furnishing her heroine with a foundling child like Silas Marner's Eppie.

The urge to escape into a different geographical setting was equally strong. Butler's Gulliver-like Higgs in *Erewhon* and the protagonist of Bulwer's *The Coming Race*, an American proud of his nation's industrial accomplishments, shed their civilized selves among the superior natives of the Utopian communities they discover.

In Disraeli's *Tancred*, the liberating spiritual truths of the Middle East can be carried back to an England overly concerned with the mechanics of civilization; Meredith's *Vittoria* portrays the contest between a repressive Austrian government and the natural impulses that guide Italian freedom-fighters. Kingsley's *Westward Ho!* can be regarded as a sequel to his city novel, *Alton Locke*. In the earlier work, the Cockney tailor to whom 'Italy and the Tropics, the Highlands and Devonshire are known only in dreams' cannot rid himself of his city self, but must die of the wounds inflicted by London on his passage to America, a Canaan 'flowing with milk and honey' (chs 1, 41). In the later novels, however, the Devon explorers range at will through the rainforests of America; after their vain search for 'the golden city of Manoa,' these free men return to defeat the Spanish Armada. By the end of the nineteenth century, the City is shunned altogether. Wemmick's little island in Walworth has multiplied into the tropical isles to which Conrad's isolatoes have escaped; the villages from which the distant lights of London could be seen have changed into the virgin forests where Mowgli, that curious Rousseauvian child of nature, can learn the exotic codes of the animal world; in a work like Richard Jefferies' *After London*, the city has quite literally disappeared—in its place there is a dark primeval swamp penetrated only by the most intrepid explorers.

In *Alice in Wonderland*, Alice's older sister cannot quite follow the example of the 'child of the pure unclouded brow' who had so easily retreated into a chimerical world: 'So she sat on, with closed eyes, and half believed herself in Wonderland, though she knew she had but to open them again, and all would change to dull reality' (ch. 12). The Victorian novelists, too, found themselves hovering between the alternates of regression and growth, between the temptation to shrink back into a pastoral Wonderland and the necessity to accept the uncertainties of change. They compromised, as we have seen, by attacking the 'dull reality' of the City of Experience through indirection and ellipsis. Only after gaining strength and self-confidence late in their careers as novelists, did Charlotte Brontë, Trollope, George Eliot, Hardy, and Conrad—in *Villette, The Way We Live Now, Daniel Deronda, Jude the Obscure*, and *The Secret Agent*—dare to take a direct look at contemporary city life. Earlier, a Yorkshire, Barsetshire, Loamshire, Wessex, and the tropical forests of the Malay Peninsula were needed to refract the ominous 'vision of an enormous town,' a 'cruel devourer of the world's light' ('Author's Note,' *The Secret Agent*).

In his preface to *The Secret Agent* Conrad describes the 'mental change' which led him to abandon the exotic lands of his previous fiction and substitute, in their stead, the London he had for so long avoided: 'There was room enough there to place any story, depth enough there for any passion, variety enough for any setting, darkness enough to bury five millions of lives.' The re-creation of a London of the eighties in *The Secret Agent* is both Victorian and modern in emphasis. Conrad still demands sympathy for Victorian innocents—for the seraphic Michaelis whose belief in a 'self-regenerated universe' is belied by his grim surroundings and for the child-man Stevie who dies uncomprehending, after being taken from Michaelis's country cottage to the city's slippery Greenwich Park. At the same time, however, Conrad forces himself and his readers to face the anarchy exploited by the sinister little Professor who clutches the detonator of the bomb he has invented, yet passes unnoticed, 'unsuspected and deadly, like a pest in the street full of men' (ch. 13). This true anarchist, who searches for a 'variable and yet perfectly precise mechanism' with which he can terrorize his fellow men, is both the enemy and the product of a mechanical civilization, Conrad's modern man. In a twentieth century forced to confront outrages and incongruities which the still innocent Victorians could hardly have predicted, their half-belief in Wonderland had begun to seem suspect.

Notes

1 Matthew Arnold, 'Preface to the 1853 edition of the *Poems*,' in *The Poetical Works of Matthew Arnold*, ed. C. B. Tinker and H. F. Lowry (1957), p. xvii.

2 John Henry Raleigh, 'The Novel and the City: England and America in the Nineteenth Century,' *Victorian Studies*, xi (1968), 308.

3 'Answer to Sir William Davenant's Preface before "Gondibert",' *The English Works of Thomas Hobbes*, ed. Sir William Molesworth (1840), IV, pp. 443–5.

4 Ben Jonson, *Everyman in his Humour*, Prologue, l. 21.

5 Samuel Johnson, *A Dictionary of the English Language* (4th edn, 1773).

6 'The Society of Dorset Men in London,' in *Thomas Hardy's Personal Writings*, ed. Harold Orel (1966), p. 75.

7 *The George Eliot Letters*, ed. Gordon S. Haight (New Haven, 1954–5), III, p. 369.

8 'Vision of the Daughters of Albion,' Plate 6, l. 4.

9 H. T. Buckle, *History of Civilization in England* (1857–61), I, p. 112; *The George Eliot Letters*, III, p. 417.

10 'Preface to . . . "Lyrical Ballads",' in *Wordsworth's Poetical Works*, ed. Thomas Hutchinson, rev. Ernest de Selincourt (1966), pp. 734–5.

11 Sigmund Freud, *Civilization and Its Discontents* (New York, 1961), p. 66.

12 Hephzibah is derived from the Hebrew, 'my delight is in her'; Silas's own Christian name, ostensibly that of St Paul's city-companion, is a contraction of the Latin 'Sylvanus,' the rural deity who acted as 'protector of husbandmen and their crops' (Charlotte M. Yonge, *History of Christian Names* [1884], pp. 49, 179).

13 G. K. Chesterton, *Defendant* (1907 edn), 120.

14 Mary Weatherbee, 'Europe on Nothing-Certain a Year,' *Century Illustrated Magazine*, xxxii (1886), 937.

15 Chesterton, op. cit., 120.

16 Ernest Albert Baker, *The History of the English Novel* (New York, 1937), VIII, p. 170.

23 Dickens and London

Philip Collins

'Mr. Dickens was a man who lived a lot by his nose', recalled a member of his magazine's office staff. 'He always seemed to be smelling things. When we walked down by the Thames he would sniff and sniff—"I love the very smell of this", he used to say.' By the late 1860s, just before his death, the Thames was being cleansed and improved, to Dickens's satisfaction. The Embankment was 'the finest public work yet done' he thought: by 1865, it was 'really getting on. Moreover, a great system of drainage. Another really fine work, and likewise really getting on.' But if there was much to be sniffed and sniffed at, his office-boy's recollections must belong earlier, when, as Dickens wrote in *Little Dorrit* (1855–7), 'Through the heart of the town a deadly sewer ebbed and flowed, in the place of a fine fresh river.'[1] For this curious love of the disgusting, he had a favourite expression: 'the attraction of repulsion'. It occurs for instance in an essay where he describes his 'attraction of repulsion' to a grim little city churchyard 'with a ferocious strong spiked iron gate, like a jail . . . ornamented with skulls and crossbones, larger than life, wrought in stone', and how, 'having often contemplated it in the daylight and the dark, I once felt drawn towards it in a thunderstorm at midnight.' Another occasion on which the phrase appears is in an important passage in Forster's *Life*,[2] describing his childhood years in London, and clearly based on what he himself had told Forster:

> . . . neglected and miserable as **he** was, he managed gradually to transfer to London all the dreaminess and all the romance with which he had invested Chatham. There were then at the top of Bayham-street some almshouses, and were still when he re-visited it with me nearly twenty-

seven years ago [i.e., *c.* 1844]; and to go to this spot, he told me, and look from it over the dust-heaps and dock-leaves and fields (no longer there when we saw it together) at the cupola of St. Paul's looming through the smoke, was a treat that served him for hours of vague reflection afterwards. To be taken out for a walk into the real town, especially if it were any-where about Covent-garden or the Strand, perfectly entranced him with pleasure. But, most of all, he had a profound attraction of repulsion to St. Giles's. If he could only induce whomsoever took him out to take him through Seven-dials, he was supremely happy. 'Good Heavens!' he would exclaim, 'what wild visions of prodigies of wickedness, want, and beggary, arose in my mind out of that place.'

Bayham Street, the almshouses, the dust-heaps, St Paul's, Covent Garden, the Strand, the criminal rookeries of St Giles—all these recur in the novels, and several of them in an illuminating essay, 'Where we stopped growing', about places, books, experiences associated with his childhood but never 'out-grown'. Many of the London scenes in the novels had been thus imposed on his imagination since childhood; over London, as in some other areas of his work, he did in some respects stop growing. His letters comment on those improvements such as the Embankment, but these do not figure much in his novels. There are, indeed, exceptions; sometimes the novels record the process of urban change, as buildings or whole areas are destroyed, eminently in the remarkable pages in *Dombey and Son* (1846–8) about the disappear-ance of Staggs's Gardens to make way for the new railway (a drastic alteration of the London townscape to which he reverts in an essay, 'An Unsettled Neighbour-hood'). He was fascinated by the spectacle of the countryside retreating before 'the invading army of bricks and mortar', and by the dismal temporary state of these edges of the city, 'neither of the town nor country . . . but . . . only blighted country, and not town'. But his favourite fictional locales do not change much over the middle third of the century, which comprised his writing career: the City and Westminster, the Inns of Court area, the poor areas to the East (Limehouse and Whitechapel), or on the South bank (Lambeth, Southwark, Bermondsey, and Deptford), the shabby-genteel suburbs of the 'clerk population . . . Somers and Camden Towns, Islington, and Pentonville', the more comfortable suburbs where live the honorary fairy-godfathers and the parents of desirable but unattainable young ladies (Finchley, Fulham, Norwood, Putney, Twickenham, and Richmond).[3] He never, I think, mentions the underground railways, being established in the early sixties; even the suburban commuters' train hardly appears in the novels. Most of his characters journey around London on foot or, if well-to-do or in a hurry, by cab. London, even by 1860, stopped well short of such independent towns or villages as Tottenham, Highgate, Wimbledon, Streatham, and Lewisham, but Dickens's interest (as a novelist) stopped further short of the expanding boundaries of the metropolis. His final novel, *Edwin Drood* (1870), is set mainly in his one important locale outside London—Kent, and particularly Rochester—but its London scenes are his old favourites: Furnival's Inn (where he had lived in the thirties), Staple Inn (the other side of Holborn, and next-door to Barnard's Inn where Pip in *Great Expectations* lived), Southampton Street (off Holborn, where Mrs Billikin has her establishment), and the opium-den to which John Jasper repairs (location unspecified, but Dickens was thinking of Shadwell).

It was not only personal memories, going back to childhood, that drew him constantly to these central areas. Here was conducted the business of London with which he was concerned—commercial, institutional, political, social, recreational. Moreover there were artistic advantages in concentrating most of his characters within walking-distance of one another, and in areas the names and associations of which would be familiar to non-metropolitan readers. Even the central districts contained, of course, areas, social or geographical, which he did not much use. 'He knows the dry arches of London Bridge better than Belgravia', Walter Bagehot remarked in 1858: and twenty years earlier the *Quarterly Review*, among other journals, had welcomed the vicarious exploration of unknown and unrespectable London that his readers were now enabled to make: 'Life in London, as revealed in the pages of Boz, opens a new world to thousands bred and born in the same city . . . —for . . . the regions of Saffron Hill are less known to our great world than the Oxford Tracts; the inhabitants are still less.' Dickens knew Saffron Hill better than other novelists did, but there were other areas about which—at least, *qua* novelist— he knew and cared little. The great town-houses appear more often and to greater effect in Disraeli, the clubs more often in Thackeray. Dickens is interested in the Law Courts and legal quarters and the prisons, but not in the Court or Downing Street or Whitehall: in the theatres and pleasure-gardens, but not in the art-galleries, concert-halls, or historic buildings. His true world, said the *Saturday Review* dismissively, was 'a world where the genteel people live at Pentonville and the ungenteel people frequent the bars of inns, old chambers, wharf-sides, small shops, and minor theatres'. No author, even one so prolific, so alert and knowledgeable as Dickens, can comprehend a city so vast and multitudinous as London; simply, he includes more than any other creative writer, and has a richer sense of the quiddity of urban life. Bagehot splendidly summarized an important part of his significance, then and since. 'He describes London like a special correspondent for posterity.'[4]

His genius was, as Bagehot was arguing, 'especially suited to the delineation of city life', and how remarkably dependent upon London its functioning was appears in some famous but inevitably requotable letters written when he was living abroad. In Genoa in 1844, he found great difficulty in settling down to writing *The Chimes*: 'He craved for the London streets,' Forster recalled. 'He so missed his long night-walks before beginning anything that he seemed, as he said, dumb-founded without them.' 'Put me down [he wrote] on Waterloo-bridge at eight o'clock in the evening with leave to roam about as long as I like, and I would come home . . . panting to go on.' Two years later, in Lausanne, he found similar difficulty:

I suppose this is partly the effect . . . of the absence of streets and numbers of figures. I can't express how much I want these. It seems as if they supplied something to my brain, which it cannot bear, when busy, to lose . . . [The] toil and labour of writing without that magic lantern [London] is IMMENSE!! . . . *My* figures seem disposed to stagnate without crowds about them. I wrote very little in Genoa (only the *Chimes*), and fancied myself conscious of some such influence there—but Lord! I had two miles of streets at least, lighted at night, to walk about in; and a great theatre to repair to, every night. [And a week later—] The absence of any accessible streets continues to worry me . . . I should not walk in them in the day time, if they were here, I dare say: but at night I want them beyond description. I don't seem able to get rid of my spectres unless I can lose them in crowds.

All this was, as he said, 'quite a little mental phenomenon', and there are several points worth noting.[5] First, he was not personally unhappy; his anguish related only to his art. Secondly, he was not living in the country, but in quite sizeable towns; even Genoa, however, with its two miles of lighted streets, lacked the crowds, the vastness, and the associations to nourish his imagination. Thirdly, it was the city at *night* that he needed: partly, no doubt, because he wanted, at the end of a working-day, to relax and recharge his energies, but more, it appears, because something about the city at night had a special meaning for him (recall that midnight sortie to the church-yard)—the mystery and threat, the gaiety, perhaps the sense of man's obvious presence through the conquest of Nature's darkness (note his emphasis on the lights).[6] Lastly, those letters belong to his early career; in the late fifties, after living in London for thirty-five years, he bought a country-house (Gad's Hill, near Rochester), and maybe the later Dickens was, in this respect as in others, different from the earlier, though I shall argue otherwise.

Certainly throughout his career, and even in his boyhood, he had felt that 'attraction of repulsion' to the aesthetically, socially, or morally ugly. In his earliest novels, *Pickwick* (1836–7), *Oliver Twist* (1837–9), and *Nickleby* (1838–9), though more confident than he was later that there was a way to the Better, he had given a full look at the Worst—the Fleet and Newgate prisons, the criminal underworld, the squalid Jacob's Island area of Bermondsey where Bill Sikes meets his death, Smith-field market (a reiterated topic for disgust in his fiction and journalism), the 'very dirty and dusty suburb' where Madeline Bray lives, the 'unheeding restless crowd' which Nicholas Nickleby contemplates, containing 'pale and pinched-up faces, . . . hungry eyes, half-naked shivering figures', and seen against a background of riches, for they were illuminated by 'the brilliant flood [of light] that streamed from the windows of the shops . . . emporiums of splendid dresses . . . vessels of burnished gold and silver'. This juxtaposition of rich and poor, so blatant and extreme in a big city, is important for Dickens, both to make his reiterated point that 'repletion and starvation laid them down together' in London, 'a shameful testimony to future ages, how civilization and barbarism walked this boastful island together', or for the artistic advantages he could gain from moving between these disparate environments (as Shakespeare is apt to switch, often ironically, from his courtly or lordly groups to his low-life or low-comic ones). Part of Bagehot's argument[7] about why Dickens's genius was so suited to city life was that

> London is like a newspaper. Everything is there, and everything is disconnected. There is every kind of person in some houses; but there is no more connection between the houses than between the neighbours in the lists of 'births, marriages, and deaths'. As we change from the broad leader to the squalid police-report, we pass a corner and we are in a changed world. This is advantageous to Mr. Dickens's genius. His memory is full of instances of old buildings and curious people, and he does not care to piece them together. On the contrary, each scene, to his mind, is a separate scene,—each street a separate street.

This is unjust to Dickens's art (he makes many connections, mechanical and thematic, between his various kinds of person), but certainly he needed the amplitude and variety of characters, classes, and scenes which London could best provide.

The mean and squalid and socially disgraceful had, as we have seen, been important in his work from the start, but the preponderance of the dark and disgusting increases in the later books. Book III of *Our Mutual Friend* (1864–5) begins, strikes the keynote (as Dickens puts it elsewhere):

> It was a foggy day in London, and the fog was heavy and dark. Animate London, with smarting eyes and irritated lungs, was blinking, wheezing, and choking; inanimate London was a sooty spectre, divided in purpose between being visible and invisible, and so being wholly neither. Gaslights flared in the shops with a haggard and unblest air, as knowing themselves to be night-creatures that had no business abroad under the sun; while the sun itself, when it was for a few moments dimly indicated through circling eddies of fog, showed as if it had gone out, and were collapsing flat and cold. Even in the surrounding country it was a foggy day, but there the fog was grey, whereas in London it was, at about the boundary line, dark yellow, and a little within it brown, and then browner, and then browner, until at the heart of the City—which call Saint Mary Axe—it was rusty-black. From any point of the high ridge of land northward, it might have been discerned that the loftiest buildings made an occasional struggle to get their heads above the foggy sea, and especially that the great dome of Saint Paul's seemed to die hard; but this was not perceivable in the streets at their feet, where the whole metropolis was a heap of vapour charged with muffled sound of wheels, and enfolding a gigantic catarrh.

Fog had of course always been prominent in Dickens's pictures of London; it was conspicuous then, and for years after, in every Londoner's existence, and Dickens was not alone in describing it, nor in using it as an outward and visible sign of spiritual and social disgrace. This passage lacks, however, the counterbalancing comic-grotesque of the famous opening of *Bleak House* (1852–3):

> London. Michaelmas Term lately over, and the Lord Chancellor sitting in Lincoln's Inn Hall. Implacable November weather. As much mud in the streets, as if the waters had but newly retired from the face of the earth, and it would not be wonderful to meet a Megalosaurus, forty feet long or so, waddling like an elephantine lizard up Holborn Hill.

Or, to go back nine years before that, the fog in the opening scene of *A Christmas Carol* (1843) is almost bracing:

> It was cold, bleak, biting weather: foggy withal: and [Scrooge] could hear the people in the court outside, go wheezing up and down, beating their hands upon their breasts, and stamping their feet upon the pavement stones to warm them . . . To see the dingy cloud [of fog] come drooping down, obscuring everything, one might have thought that Nature lived hard by, and was brewing on a large scale.

By the end of the *Carol*, there was 'No fog, no mist; clear, bright, jovial, stirring cold; cold, piping for the blood to dance to', but, in *Our Mutual Friend*, though there are changes in the weather, there is little to dance about:[8]

> A grey dusty withered evening in London city has not a hopeful aspect. The closed warehouses and offices have an air of death about them, and the national dread of colour has an air of mourning. The towers and steeples of the many house-encompassed churches, dark and dingy as the sky that seems descending on them, are no relief to the general gloom; a sun-dial on a church-wall has the look, in its useless black shade, of having failed in its business enterprise and stopped payment for ever; melancholy waifs and strays of housekeepers and porters sweep melancholy waifs and strays of papers and pins into the kennels, and other more melancholy waifs and strays explore them, searching and stooping and poking for anything to sell. The set of humanity outward from the City is as a set of prisoners departing from gaol, and dismal Newgate seems quite as fit a stronghold for the mighty Lord Mayor as his own state-dwelling.
>
> On such an evening, when the City grit gets into the hair and eyes and skin, and when the fallen leaves of the few unhappy City trees grind down in corners under wheels of wind . . .

Another comparison between the earlier and later Dickens—which I cannot expand upon here—might usefully be made between two well-known rooftop scenes: the view from Todgers's in *Martin Chuzzlewit* (1843–4), so brilliantly, if partially, discussed by Dorothy Van Ghent, and Jenny Wren's strange reflections from her rooftop in *Our Mutual Friend*, of which J. Hillis Miller has remarked that no passage in the novel is of greater importance: ' "We are thankful to come here for rest, sir," said Jenny . . . "It's the quiet and the air . . . you feel as if you were dead . . . Oh, so tranquil! Oh so peaceful and so thankful . . . And such a chain has fallen from you, and such a strange good sorrowful happiness comes upon you!"' This was written around the time when London was being improved by the Embankment and that drainage system, and by slum-clearances which pleased Dickens. If the London of *Our Mutual Friend* is drab, colourless, hostile, swept by a 'grating wind [that] sawed rather than blew; and as it sawed, the sawdust whirled about the sawpit', this was much less a comment on objective changes in London between the forties and the sixties than a reflection of Dickens's mood and of the special needs of this novel.[9] He could of course create what weather he wanted in his fiction. 'Sorry that you had such bad weather', as George VI is alleged to have said to John Piper, on examining his pictures of Windsor.

The obvious importance of remembering literary contexts and purposes, the danger of using fictional passages over-simply for historical-documentary ends, can be simply illustrated from *Edwin Drood*. Chapter 11 begins:

> Behind the most ancient part of Holborn, London, where certain gabled houses some centuries of age still stand looking on the public way, as if disconsolately looking for the Old Bourne that has long run dry, is a little nook composed of two irregular quadrangles, called Staple Inn. It is one of those nooks, the turning into which out of the clashing street, imparts to the relieved pedestrian the sensation of having put cotton in his ears, and velvet soles on his boots. It is one of those nooks where a few smoky sparrows twitter in smoky trees, as though they called to one another, 'Let us play at country', and where a few feet of garden-mould and a few yards of gravel enable them to do that refreshing violence to their tiny understandings. Moreover, it is one of those nooks which are legal nooks; and it contains a little Hall, with a little lantern in its roof: to what obstructive purposes devoted, and at whose expense, this history knoweth not.

Familiar Dickens country here, as I have remarked: one of the old legal Inns, let off into bachelor chambers (see the *Uncommercial Traveller* essay, 'Chambers'), enabling him to indulge his taste for the old, fusty, and quaint, and to have a dig at the archaic irrationality of everything to do with the law. The weather, in the succeeding paragraphs, is December fog. The description then moves to an interior, the rooms of the good-hearted solicitor Mr Grewgious:

> There was no luxury in his room. Even its comforts were limited to its being dry and warm, and having a snug though faded fireside. What may be called its private life was confined to the hearth, and an easy-chair, and an old-fashioned occasional round table that was brought out upon the rug after business hours, from a corner where it elsewise remained turned up like a shining mahogany shield. Behind it, when standing thus on the defensive, was a closet, usually containing something good to drink.

Six chapters later, we return to Staple Inn, where now lives another character who had appeared earlier, Neville Landless, presently under a cloud, being suspected of murdering Edwin Drood:

> An air of retreat and solitude hung about the rooms and about their inhabitant. He was much worn, and so were they. Their sloping ceilings, cumbrous rusty locks and grates, and heavy wooden bins and beams, slowly mouldering withal, had a prisonous look, and he had the haggard face of a prisoner. Yet the sunlight shone in at the ugly garret-window, which had a penthouse to itself thrust out among the tiles; and on the cracked and smoke-blackened parapet beyond, some of the deluded sparrows of the place rheumatically hopped, like little feathered cripples who had left their crutches in their nests; and there was a play of living leaves at hand that changed the air, and made an imperfect sort of music in it that would have been melody in the country.

Later, we meet one of Neville's neighbours, Mr Tartar, late of the Royal Navy:

> Mr. Tartar's chambers were the neatest, the cleanest, and the best-ordered chambers ever seen under the sun, moon, and stars. The floors were scrubbed to that extent, that you might have supposed the London blacks emancipated for ever, and gone out of the land for good. Every inch of brass-work in Mr. Tartar's possession was polished and burnished, till it shone like a brazen mirror. No speck, nor spot, nor spatter soiled the purity of any of Mr. Tartar's household gods, large, small, or middle-sized. His sitting-room was like the admiral's cabin, his bath-room was like a dairy, his sleeping-chamber, fitted all about with lockers and drawers, was like a seedsman's shop; and his nicely-balanced cot just stirred in the midst, as if it breathed.

The description continues, with everything gleaming, spick and span, redolent of paint and varnish: and it is a bright summer day.[10] Now, certainly three sets of chambers in one building will differ according to the means, morale, and domestic efficiency of their occupants, and certainly London has days both foggy and bright; but obviously these three passages reflect the exigencies of the novel rather than the visual and historical qualities of Staple Inn. Tartar's chambers, instead of Neville's, could have had those 'prisonous' locks and grates, and oppressive 'sloping ceilings', but the literary purposes would not have been served.

Dickens died with *Edwin Drood* uncompleted, and we cannot be sure how it would have developed. As I have remarked, its main locale had been Rochester (renamed Cloisterham), and, though London was the only other locale, the novel looked like being more provincial than any that Dickens had written except *Hard Times*, which had been in this as in other respects the odd-book-out in his *oeuvre*, for it had contained no scenes at all in London, being set entirely in the industrial North about which he knew relatively little. London had been overwhelmingly the most important locale of his novels, and his *Sketches by Boz* (1836), which immediately preceded his career as a novelist, had been entirely a metropolitan book. One of his colleagues remarked, 'He was a master in London; abroad he was only a workman.' Another colleague, George Augustus Sala, himself an authority on London, recalled[11] how he would encounter Dickens

> in the oddest places and most inclement weather, in Ratcliffe-highway, on Haverstock-hill, on Camberwell-green, in Gray's-inn-lane, in the Wands-worth-road, at Hammersmith Broadway, in Norton Folgate, and at Kensal New Town. 'A hansom whirled you by the Bell and Horns at Brompton, and there he was striding, as with seven-league boots, seemingly in the direction of North-end, Fulham. The Metropolitan Railway sent you forth at Lisson-grove, and you met him plodding speedily towards the Yorkshire Stingo. He was to be met rapidly skirting the grim brick wall of the prison in Coldbath-fields, or trudging along the Seven Sisters-road at Holloway, or bearing, under a steady press of sail, underneath Highgate Archway, or pursuing the even tenor of his way up the Vauxhall-bridge-road.' But [remarks John Forster] he was equally at home in the intricate byways of narrow streets as in the lengthy thoroughfares. Wherever there was 'matter to be heard and learned,' in back streets behind Holborn, in Borough courts and passages, in City wharfs or alleys, about the poorer lodging-houses, in prisons, workhouses, ragged-schools, police-courts, rag-shops, chandlers' shops, and all sorts of markets for the poor, he carried his keen observation and untiring study. 'I was among the Italian Boys from 12 to 2 this morning,' says one of his letters. 'I am going out to-night in their boat with the Thames Police,' says another ... For several consecutive years I accompanied him every Christmas Eve to see the marketings for Christmas down the road from Aldgate to Bow; and he had a surprising fondness for wandering about in poor neighbourhoods on Christmas-day, past the areas of shabby genteel houses in Somers or Kentish Towns, and watching the dinners preparing or coming in.

It had been thus since he was a boy (he came to London at the age of ten, having earlier been there as a toddler). His first employer recalled, that, at the age of fifteen, 'His knowledge of London was wonderful, for he could describe the position of every shop in any of the West End streets'; and one of his fellow clerks at that time wrote, similarly:

> He could imitate, in a manner I have never heard equalled, the low population of the streets of London in all their varieties, whether mere loafers or sellers of fruit, vegetables, or anything else. He could also excel in mimicking the popular singers of that day, whether comic or patriotic, ... and imitate all the leading actors of that time ... I thought I knew something of the town, but after a little talk with Dickens I found that I knew nothing. He knew it all from Bow to Brentford.

'I suppose myself to know this rather large city as well as anyone in it,' remarked Dickens, with justified complacency: and, on another occasion, 'I walk into all sorts of suburbs every day.' Much of this went into his novels, though, as has been mentioned, the London of his novels is smaller than the London he knew; his fictional London did not expand as the actuality did. 'There seemed to be not much to add to our knowledge of London,' wrote Forster about his early career, 'until his books came upon us, but each in this respect outstripped the other in its marvels.' Way on in 1867, *The Times* greeted one of his minor works, the Christmas story *No Thorough-fare*:

> Mr. Dickens . . . always looks out for new subjects. It is true that he confines himself very much to London life. But London is in itself a world, and Mr. Dickens has constantly something new to tell us of its inhabitants. He tells now of life at the Foundling Hospital, of life among the Swiss of Soho-square, of life in the house of a city wine-merchant . . .

—but all, one notes, central areas. Some less impressed contemporaries judged him too much caught up with time and place, damagingly local and temporary. The *Saturday Review*, for instance, never one of his warmest admirers, offered this view, in 1858:

> All the oddities of London life he has sketched with inimitable vigour; but class characteristics and local peculiarities are of a very transient nature. Fifty years hence, most of his wit will be harder to understand than the allusions in the *Dunciad*; and our grand-children will wonder what their ancestors could have meant by putting Mr. Dickens at the head of the novelists of his day.

Manifestly this has not proved so, partly because Dickens's wit, and his other imaginative qualities, have a vitality much underestimated by this reviewer, but also partly because London has remained one of the great symbols of this phase of civilization. 'This is the age of great cities,' as another reviewer wrote, 'and Dickens is the painter of great cities, . . . the novelist and poet of great cities and of civil [*sic*] life, especially of London life. We do not know of whom beside we can say this.' (And of whom in later English literature could we say it?) One of the reasons for Dickens's greatness is that, partly through the accidents of his upbringing, he was impelled into using as his dominant fictional setting—and often London becomes subject as much as setting—the central locale of mid-nineteenth-century civilization. As Emerson said in *English Traits* (1856), 'London is the epitome of our times, and the Rome of today': and Dickens, he added, 'writes London tracts'.[12] Not only in the locale, but also through the need for large numbers of characters from very various classes and occupations, Dickens's artistic temperament is as essentially metropolitan as Wordsworth's was formed by and suited to the Lake District. Great creative literature can, manifestly, be written from and about the Lake District as well as from and about London; but, certainly by the mid-century, many of the central human experiences could only be examined through the town and the metropolis. As Matthew Arnold was commenting at this time—and his remarks apply to the Wordsworthian inheritance in Victorian poetry as well as to Wordsworth himself— 'Wordsworth's eyes avert their ken / From half of human fate'; Wordsworth had, in effect, 'retired (in Middle-Age phrase) into a monastery', had 'voluntarily cut himself off from the modern spirit'.[13]

Reviewers of Dickens had, from the start, discussed the vivacity and range of his London pictures. The sequence *Sketches by Boz, Pickwick, Oliver Twist,* and *Nickleby* (1836–9) had obviously invited such comment and, though *The Old Curiosity Shop* (1840–1) represented a new direction (the movement as *away* from the city), *Barnaby Rudge* (1841) brought the action back to London, and the sequence that followed were all enormously rich in London scenes and in the feel of urban living. Boz, wrote reviewers in the 1830s, had opened up a new literary mine by his discovery, particularly of London low-life; Sam Weller was of course the archetype figure here, and Sam obviously resembled his creator in that his 'knowledge of London was extensive and peculiar'. Some cannier reviewers noted that Dickens was hardly a pioneer here; not only had the great eighteenth-century masters Defoe and Fielding and Hogarth exploited this vein before him, but also, and arguably with more relevance, so had the wags of the twenties and thirties (Pierce Egan, Theodore Hook, John Poole, Thomas Hood). Particularly in his essays, too, he resembles Charles Lamb and Leigh Hunt, markedly in their concern with the quaint odd corners of London life and topography. Much, I think, remains to be discovered about the quality and intricacy of his debt to all these predecessors, and to De Quincey, whose work he much admired. Lamb's famous letter to Wordsworth,[14] declining his invitation to the Lake District, might have been a manifesto for Dickens:

> I have passed all my days in London, until I have formed as many and intense local attachments as any of you mountaineers can have done with dead Nature. The lighted shops of the Strand and Fleet Street; the innumerable trades, tradesmen, and customers, coaches, waggons, playhouses; all the bustle and wickedness round about Covent Garden; the very women of the Town; the watchmen, drunken scenes, rattles; life awake, if you awake, at all hours of the night; the impossibility of being dull in Fleet Street; the crowds, the very dirt and mud, . . . the pantomimes—London itself a pantomime and a masquerade—all these things work themselves into my mind, and feed me, without a power of satiating me. The wonder of these sights impels me into night-walks about her crowded streets, and I often shed tears in the motley Strand from fulness of joy at so much life . . . Have I not enough, without your mountains?

Dickens, however, had a far richer, wider, and more compassionate mind than any of these predecessors. Thus, he shared all the interests and delights that Lamb lists, but also had a more intelligent curiosity about London as a social and economic organism, and a greater awareness of what Wordsworth mentioned in passing, though Wordsworth lacked the sort of talent that could fill out the phrase with particularities—

>   the fierce confederate storm
> Of sorrow, barricadoed evermore
> Within the walls of cities . . .

In that first book, *Sketches by Boz*, which contains so many hints of themes and characters and scenes to be developed more fully in the novels, he had opened his essay 'Thoughts about People': 'It is strange with how little notice, good, bad, or indifferent, a man may live and die in London. He awakens no sympathy in the breast of any single person; his existence is a matter of interest to no one save himself; he cannot be said to be forgotten when he dies, for no one remembered him when he was alive.' There is Dickens, at the age of twenty-three, opening up the theme of urban alienation, *anomie*, that was to be so important in nineteenth- and twentieth-century literature. What is less well remembered, because less in accordance with current literary-critical predilections, is his sense also of other elements in urban life, equally well handled in the *Sketches* and later works. Thus, the section 'Scenes' in *Sketches by Boz* consists of the following (the list is worth giving in full, as an indication of his interests at this time, and it is worth remembering, too, the full title of the book—*Sketches by Boz, illustrative of Every-day Life and Every-day People*): 'The Streets—Morning', 'The Streets—Night', 'Shops and their Tenants', 'Scotland Yard', 'Seven Dials', 'Meditations in Monmouth Street', 'Hackney-coach Stands', 'Doctors' Commons', 'London Recreations', 'The River', 'Astley's', 'Greenwich Fair', 'Private Theatres', 'Vauxhall Gardens by Day', 'Early Coaches', 'Omnibuses', 'The Last Cab-driver and the First Omnibus Cad', 'A Parliamentary Sketch', 'Public Dinners', 'The First of May', 'Brokers' and Marine-store Shops', 'Gin-shops', 'The Pawnbroker's Shop', 'Criminal Courts', and 'A Visit to Newgate'. The recurrent themes, as even a mere list makes clear, are streets and shops, transport, crime and the law, and popular amusements. The last of these categories is particularly important. Attending the Bloomington conference on the Victorian City, which is the inspiration of this book, I was invited to give a recital on 'The Dickensian City'. Set to suggest this in brief compass, I included in my selection the wet Sunday in London passage from *Little Dorrit* (Book I, ch. 3), the death of Bill Sikes (*Oliver Twist*, ch. 1), and Dickens's splendid letter to Miss Coutts about a squalid Bermondsey scene (7 January 1853). Having thus represented Dickens's sense of the ugly and undesirable in London Life (and given satisfaction to my distinguished academic colleagues who, city-dwellers almost to a man, nevertheless held the proper notions about the terribleness of urban living), I read some of those passages in which Dickens usefully reminds us about why, despite the noisome and violent, and the lonely, aspects of the city, so many people have still found living there far more tolerable than in the empty desolate eventless countryside: the cheeky cheap-jack in *Doctor Marigold*, 'Greenwich Fair', and the Nubbleses at Astley's circus:[15]

Dear, dear, what a place it looked, that Astley's, with all the paint, gilding, and looking-glass; the vague smell of horses, suggestive of coming wonders; the curtain that hid such gorgeous mysteries; the clean white sawdust down in the circus; the company coming in and taking their places; the fiddlers looking carelessly up at them while they tuned their instruments, as if they didn't want the play to begin, and knew it all beforehand! What a glow was that, which burst upon them all, when that long, clear, brilliant row of lights came slowly up; and what the feverish excitement when the little bell rang and the music began in good earnest, with strong parts for the drums, and sweet effects for the triangles! Well might Barbara's mother say to Kit's mother that the gallery was the place to see from, and wonder it wasn't much dearer than the boxes; well might Barbara feel doubtful whether to laugh or cry, in her flutter of delight.

Then the play itself! the horses which little Jacob believed from the first to be alive, and the ladies and gentlemen of whose reality he could be by no means persuaded, having never seen or heard anything at all like them—the firing, which made Barbara wink—the forlorn lady, who made her cry—the tyrant, who made her tremble—the man who sang the song with the lady's maid, and danced the chorus, who made her laugh—the pony who reared up on his hind legs when he saw the murderer, and wouldn't hear of walking on all fours again until he was taken into custody—the clown who ventured on such familiarities with the military man in boots—the lady who jumped over the nine-and-twenty ribbons and came down safe upon the horse's back—everything was delightful, splendid, and surprising! Little Jacob applauded till his hands were sore; Kit cried 'an-kor' at the end of everything, the three-act piece included; and Barbara's mother beat her umbrella on the floor, in her ecstasies, until it was nearly worn down to the gingham.

The vigour and animation, the delight in life and specifically in the simple pleasures of 'everyday people', apparent in such passages, are as important a part of Dickens's report on the London of his times, as the passages analogous to those 'Thoughts about People' or the letter about Bermondsey.

'There was . . . a great ball at Lady Bardolf's, in Belgrave Square,' writes Disraeli in *Tancred*, adding—'One should generally mention localities, because they very often indicate character.' Class rather than character, or character as influenced by class, one would object; but Dickens, as was noted, was not as a novelist much interested in the classes who inhabited the great Squares, though of course he had his Sir Leicester Dedlocks, his nouveau-riche Veneerings, his pretentious Wititterleys (in *Nicholas Nickleby*) who live in Cadogan Place, Sloane Street, and he often makes some pertinent comments or analyses:

Cadogan Place is the one slight bond that joins two great extremes; it is the connecting link between the aristocratic pavements of Belgrave

Square, and the barbarism of Chelsea. It is in Sloane Street, but not of it. The people in Cadogan Place look down upon Sloane Street, and think Brompton low. They affect fashion too, and wonder where the New Road is. Not that they claim to be on precisely the same footing as the high folks of Belgrave Square and Grosvenor Place, but that they stand, with reference to them, rather in the light of those illegitimate children of the great who are content to boast of their connexions, although their connexions disavow them. Wearing as much as they can of the airs and semblance of loftiest rank, the people of Cadogan Place have the realities of middle station. It is the conductor which communicates to the inhabitants of regions beyond its limit, the shock of pride of birth and rank, which it has not within itself, but derives from a fountain-head beyond; or, like the ligament which unites the Siamese twins, it contains something of the life and essence of two distinct bodies, and yet belongs to neither.

As Bagehot said, 'The amount of detail which there is in [his works] is something amazing,—to an ordinary writer something incredible. There are pages containing telling *minutiae* which other people would have thought enough for a volume.' One manifestation of this is his practice of mentioning localities—the journeys in his novels, for instance, 'every turn in which [as one reviewer sneered] is enumerated with the accuracy of a cabman':[16]

> They [Oliver Twist and the Artful Dodger] crossed from the Angel into
> St. John's Road; struck down the small street which terminates at Sadler's
> Wells Theatre; through Exmouth Street and Coppice Row; down the little
> court by the side of the workhouse; across the classic ground which once
> bore the name of Hockley-in-the-Hole; thence into Little Saffron Hill; and
> so into Saffron Hill the Great . . . [and to] a house near Field Lane.

Or take this sample of the dwellings specified in *Bleak House*.[17] The London of that novel ranges from the slum Tom-all-Alone's to the Dedlock mansion, from Astley's circus to the graveyard, from Lincoln's Inn to Bell Yard where live the humblest officers (and the victims) of the Chancery Courts. Some of the locations are unspecified: the pestilential graveyard, for instance (though in a letter Dickens gave precise instructions about where to find it). Nearly all the London scenes are pinpointed, however: Mrs Jellyby lives in Thavies Inn and later lodges in Hatton Garden; Guppy at 87 Penton Place, Pentonville, and later at Walcot Square, Lambeth; his mother at 302 Old Street Road; Harold Skimpole in The Polygon, Somers Town; Snagsby and Coavinses in Cursitor Street, Turveydrop in Newman Street near Soho Square, though later, with increased prosperity, Prince and Caddy move two miles west. Richard Carstone lodges near Queen's Square, but when another lodging is required later in his story Dickens hesitated (as his manuscript notes show) between Cursitor Street, Carey Street, Dyer's Buildings and Symond's Inn. As this hesitation shows, Dickens's locations were not arbitrary; his choice depended partly on narrative convenience, but more on the social nuances represented by particular areas: he was as much a social as a physical topographer.

'He describes London like a special correspondent for posterity.' He was, too, a special correspondent for the non-metropolitan reader at that time, and one tribute to the power of his projection of a vision of London is the way in which he formed the view of it which American and Continental, and provincial, readers held. Harriet Martineau, missing 'the pure plain daylight in the atmosphere of his scenery', might lament that foreigners must be forming a very wrong image of England from his novels, but many of them, when visiting London, were more impressed by the suggestiveness and accuracy of his renderings. Of course they often looked for what he had encouraged them to see, and observed through his eyes. As a country-cousin on her first visit to London put it: 'I saw wealth, and beauty, and power, so closely connected with crime, suffering and poverty, that I thought the enjoyment of the former must be marred by the presence of the latter. Perhaps I looked on everything with an intensity which might be attributed to my having seen it all in fancy's glass, by the aid of that masterly delineator, Charles Dickens' (Joshua Priestley, *True Womanhood*). To cite some American visitors: 'When I got to London', wrote Francis Parkman in 1843, 'I thought I had been there before. There, in flesh and blood, was the whole host of characters that figure in *Pickwick* . . . The hackney coachmen and cabmen . . . the walking advertisements . . . and a hundred others seemed so many incarnations of Dickens's characters.' In 1856 Nathaniel Hawthorne was walking in Upper Thames Street, and recalling that Arthur Clennam's house in *Little Dorrit* (then being serialized) stood thereabouts—'But many of Dickens's books have the odor and flavor of courts and localities that I stumble upon, about London.' About this time, Henry Adams arrived in London for the first time. Aristocracy, he found, was *real* here: 'So was the England of Dickens. Oliver Twist and Little Nell lurked in every churchyard shadow, not as shadow but alive.' Two decades later, Henry James, lodging in Craven Street (which runs from the Strand down to the river—authentic Dickens country, indeed), felt that 'the whole Dickens procession marched up and down, the whole Dickens world looked out of its queer, quite sinister windows—for it was the socially sinister Dickens, I am afraid, rather than the socially encouraging or confoundingly comic who still at that moment was most apt to meet me with his reasons.' Earlier in his autobiography, James had spoken for his age—and for America too, where he had spent the years he was there describing—in this testimony to Dickens's enormous popularity and imaginative potency:[18]

> How tremendously it had been laid upon young persons of our generation
> to feel Dickens, down to the soles of our shoes, no more modern instance
> that I might try to muster would give, I think, the least measure of . . .
> There has been since his extinction no corresponding case—as to the
> relation between benefactor and beneficiary, or debtor and creditor; no
> other debt in our time has been piled so high, for those carrying it, as the
> long, the purely 'Victorian' pressure of that obligation.

An author so universally read as Dickens, so imaginatively powerful, and in his genius so highly visual and sensory, could not fail to impress upon the imaginations of his readers, then and since, an overwhelmingly strong vision of the great city which was the central and recurrent scene of his novels. 'We cannot', wrote a commentator in 1858, 'look out upon the world save through his eyes. Indeed it is not our world, but his, that we gaze upon.' A final illustration of this, in a form which approaches caricature, may be taken from one of the main texts of later-nineteenth-century Decadence, Huysmans' *A Rebours* (1884). Its hero, Des Esseintes, is in an uneasy state of mind and body, when suddenly

> The works of Dickens, which he had recently read in the hope of soothing his nerves, but which had produced the opposite effect, slowly began to act upon him in an unexpected way, evoking visions of English life which he contemplated for hours on end. Then, little by little, an idea insinuated itself into his mind—the idea of turning dream into reality, of travelling to England in the flesh as well as in the spirit, of checking the accuracy of his visions; and this idea was allied with a longing to experience new sensations and thus afford some relief to a mind dizzy with hunger and drunk with fantasy.
>
> The abominably foggy and rainy weather fostered these thoughts by reinforcing the memories of what he had read, by keeping before his eyes the picture of a land of mist and mud . . .
>
> The appalling weather struck him as an instalment of English life paid to him on account in Paris; and his mind conjured up a picture of London as an immense, sprawling, rain-drenched metropolis, stinking of soot and hot iron, and wrapped in a perpetual mantle of smoke and fog. He could see in imagination a line of dockyards stretching away into the distance, full of cranes, capstans, and bales of merchandise, and swarming with men—some perched on the masts and sitting astride the yards, while hundreds of others, their heads down and bottoms up, were trundling casks along the quays and into the cellars.
>
> All this activity was going on in warehouses and on wharves washed by the dark, slimy waters of an imaginary Thames, in the midst of a forest of masts, a tangle of beams and girders piercing the pale, lowering clouds. Up above, trains raced by at full speed; and down in the underground sewers, others rumbled along, occasionally emitting ghastly screams or vomiting floods of smoke through the gaping mouths of air-shafts. And meanwhile, along every street, big or small, in an eternal twilight relieved only by the glaring infamies of modern advertising, there flowed an endless stream of traffic between two columns of earnest, silent Londoners, marching along with eyes fixed ahead and elbows glued to their sides.
>
> Des Esseintes shuddered with delight at feeling himself lost in this terrifying world of commerce, immersed in this isolating fog, involved in

this incessant activity, and caught up in this ruthless machine which ground to powder millions of poor wretches—outcasts of fortune whom philanthropists urged, by way of consolation, to sing psalms and recite verses of the Bible.

On his way to the railway-station, he stops at a tavern frequented by English people, and the sight of them reminds him of 'The Londoner's home as described by the novelist—. . . with bottles being slowly emptied by Little Dorrit, Dora Copperfield, or Tom Pinch's sister Ruth—[which] appeared to him in the guise of a cosy ark sailing snugly through a deluge of soot and mire.' He settles down comfortably in this 'London of the imagination'—and soon decides not to 'risk spoiling such unforgettable [imaginative] experience by a clumsy change of locality'.[19] Des Esseintes seems an improbable recruit to the Dickensian fraternity, and his apprehension of that 'London of the imagination' is subjective and not always accurate: but the passage provides a fascinating version of the set of stereotypes to which Dickens was made to administer.

'London is a vile place,' Dickens wrote at a period of exasperation. '. . . I have never taken kindly to it since I lived abroad. Whenever I come back from the country now and see that great heavy canopy lowering over the house-tops I wonder what on earth I do there except of obligation.' But, though he had spells of living abroad, he never became an expatriate, like Browning, nor a rural recluse, like Tennyson. It was not until the late 1850s that he bought a country house (a place, Gad's Hill near Rochester, which was encrusted with childhood memories for him, as London was), and, as his son Charley remarked,

> His personal habits underwent little change in this alteration of his life . . . he never took at all to what most people understand by a country life . . . he never acquired, or cared, I think, to acquire, the accurate knowledge of country sights and sounds, the intimate friendship, so to speak, with nature, which comes . . . very rarely to the town-bred man who takes in middle age to the woods and fields.

It is noticeable that his essays in the *Uncommercial Traveller* series, written in the 1860s, and many of them very personal, are almost all dated from 'my rooms in Covent Garden' (his apartment above his magazine's office in Wellington Street, Strand), and only three of the thirty-odd use Kentish subjects. He returns, but in a more plangent or a more indignant tone, to the topics of his first book of *Sketches*: again to quote a few titles—'Wapping Work-house', 'Two Views of a Cheap Theatre', 'City of London Churches', 'Shy Neighbourhoods', 'Night Walks', 'Chambers', 'Arcadian London', 'The City of the Absent', 'Titbull's Almshouses', 'A Small Star in the East' (i.e. the East End). Here, as in the later novels, there is a frequent sense of 'London . . . at its worst. Such a black, shrill city, combining the qualities of a smoky house and a scolding wife; such a gritty city; such a hopeless city, with no rent in the leaden canopy of its sky'—of a London indifferent or hostile to human happiness, as it seems to the newly-wed Arthur Clennam and Little Dorrit: 'They went quietly down into the roaring streets, inseparable and blessed; and as they passed along in sunshine or in shade, the noisy and the eager, and the arrogant and the froward, and the vain, fretted, and chafed, and made their usual uproar.' Take, for instance, this *Uncommercial Traveller* passage about that Waterloo Bridge he had, sixteen years earlier, so yearned for in Genoa ('Put me down [there] . . . at eight o'clock in the evening'). The essay is entitled 'Night Walks', and Dickens—and the houseless—are 'walking the street under pattering rain'. He reaches the Thames, a feature of London that appears so often in his novels and other writings:

> the bridge was dreary . . . the river had an awful look, the buildings on the banks were muffled in black shrouds, and the reflected lights seemed to originate deep in the water, as if the spectres of suicides were holding them to show them where they went down. The wild moon and clouds were as restless as an evil conscience in a tumbled bed, and the very shadow of the immensity of London seemed to lie oppressively upon the river.

Even the city lights that meant so much to him are here a further item of menace and the macabre. Nor do the *Uncommercial Traveller* essays contain such spirited essays on popular amusements as *Sketches by Boz* had provided so liberally: and the backstage theatre episode in *Little Dorrit* (Book I, ch. 20) and the fairground scene in *Our Mutual Friend* (Book IV, ch. 6) are disenchanted equivalents to the earlier Astley's and Greenwich Fair passages, though, it should be acknowledged, Mr Wopsle's performance as Hamlet in *Great Expectations* (ch. 31), written in 1861, is as straightforwardly hilarious as anything in *Sketches by Boz* or in the Crummles episodes in *Nicholas Nickleby*. Undoubtedly, Dickens's view of London, or of other elements in life, became in later years less ebullient and cheerful; sometimes 'tragic' seems the word for his mood, sometimes 'disillusioned', sometimes plain 'grumpy'. Of his country retreat in these later years, he was certainly very proud, and he enjoyed retiring to it, but probably he spent as much of his time, in his last decade, in London as in Kent, and, though Rochester moved him creatively, the woods and fields around Gad's Hill did not. He needed, as a subject for his art, the more complex life of the great city, and the higher tension of the feelings it provoked. A few weeks before his death, the son of his old friend Douglas Jerrold ran in to him at Charing Cross, 'and he spoke cheerily, in the old kind way—not in the least about himself— but about my doings, about Doré, about London as a subject (and who ever knew it half so well as he, in all its highways and byeways?)'[20]

Notes

Unless otherwise specified, Dickens's novels and other published writings are cited from the New Oxford Illustrated Edition (1947–59), and his letters from the Nonesuch edition, ed. Walter Dexter (3 vols, 1935). John Forster's *Life of Dickens* is cited from J. W. T. Ley's edition (1928). To facilitate reference to other editions, the chapter (and, where relevant, book) numbers are also given.

1 Catherine Van Dyke, 'A Talk with Charles Dickens's Office Boy', *Bookman*, lix (March 1921), 50; *Letters*, III, pp. 698, 445; *Little Dorrit*, Bk I, ch. 3, p. 28. On the Thames at a time when even 'a short whiff' of it was 'of a most head-and-stomach distending nature' (July 1858), see *Letters*, III, p. 30.

2 'The City of the Absent', *Uncommercial Traveller*, p. 234; Forster, *Life*, Bk I, ch. 1, p. 11.

3 *The Old Curiosity Shop*, ch. 15, p. 116; *Dombey and Son*, ch. 33, p. 472; 'The Streets—Morning', *Sketches by Boz*, p. 51. The essays 'Where we stopped growing' (*Household Words*, 1 January 1853) and 'An Unsettled Neighbourhood' (ibid., 11 November 1854) are reprinted in his *Miscellaneous Papers*, ed. B. W. Matz (Biographical Edition, 1908), pp. 358–64, 455–61.

4 Bagehot, 'Charles Dickens', in *Literary Essays*, ed. Norman St John-Stevas (1965), II, pp. 85, 87; [Richard Ford], *Quarterly Review*, lxiv (1839), 87–8; *Saturday Review*, 23 February 1861, 195 (probably by James Fitzjames Stephen).

5 *Life*, Bk IV, ch. 5, p. 346; Bk V, ch. 5, pp. 423–4. Dickens's discomfort while writing *The Chimes* was probably the more acute because inevitably he was reminded of the previous year when he was writing his first Christmas book, *A Christmas Carol*, and had 'excited himself in a most extraordinary manner in the composition; and thinking whereof he walked about the black streets of London, fifteen and twenty miles many a night when all sober folks had gone to bed.' (*Letters*, I, p. 553)

6 Dickens had written from Lausanne, a month before the letter quoted above, about a story he was conceiving: 'It will mature in the streets of Paris by night, as well as in London' (*Life*, Bk V, ch. 5, pp. 422–3). A few months earlier, in London, he wrote: 'Vague thoughts of a new book are rife within me just now; and I go wandering about at night into the strangest places, according to my usual propensity at such a time . . .' (*Letters*, I, p. 740).

7 *Nicholas Nickleby*, ch. 46, p. 603; ch. 32, pp. 408–9; *Bleak House*, ch. 11, p. 151; Bagehot, *Literary Essays*, II, p. 87.

8 *Our Mutual Friend*, Bk III, ch. 1, p. 420; *Bleak House*, ch. 1, p. 1; *A Christmas Carol*, stave 1 (*Christmas Books*, pp. 8–9), stave v (p. 72); *Our Mutual Friend*, Bk II, ch. 15, p. 393. For examples of *Punch* using London fog in a very 'Dickensian' way, see Janice Nadelhaft in *Studies in the Novel* (1969), I, p. 234.

9 *Martin Chuzzlewit*, ch. 9, p. 130; Dorothy Van Ghent, 'The Dickens World: a View from Todgers's', *Sewanee Review*, lviii (1950), 419–38; *Our Mutual Friend*, Bk II, ch. 5, p. 281; J. Hillis Miller, *Charles Dickens: The world of his novels* (1958), p. 314. Miller also discusses the Todgers's scene (pp. 116–18). My reservation about Miss Van Ghent's very influential essay is, briefly, that in *Martin Chuzzlewit* Dickens is deliberately stressing the quaint, queer, and picturesque, so that the Todgers's passage should not, I think, be given quite the representative status she claims for it.

10 *Edwin Drood*, ch. 11, p. 114; ch. 17, pp. 195–6; ch. 22, pp. 242–3.

11 John Hollingshead, *According to my Lights* (1900), p. 12; Forster, *Life*, Bk XI, ch. 3, pp. 836–7, quoting G. A. Sala, *Charles Dickens* [1870]. With Hollingshead's remark, one might compare Ruskin's on reading *The Old Curiosity Shop*: 'It is evident the man is a thorough cockney, from his way of talking about hedgerows, and honeysuckles, and village spires; and in London, and to his present fields of

knowledge, he ought strictly to keep for some time. There are subjects enough touched in the *Sketches* which might be worked up into something of real excellence. And when he has exhausted that particular field of London life with which he is familiar, he ought to keep quiet for a long time, and raise his mind as far as in him lies, to a far higher standard, giving up that turn for the picturesque which leads him into perpetual mannerism . . .' (letter of 6 June 1841, in *Works*, ed. E. T. Cook and Alexander Wedderburn [1903], XXXVI, pp. 25–6).

12   *Charles Dickens by Pen and Pencil*, ed. F. G. Kitton (1890), pp. 130–1; *Letters*, III, p. 210; I, p. 749; *Life*, Bk II, ch. 4, p. 123; *The Times*, 27 December 1867, 9; *Saturday Review*, 8 May 1858, 475, probably by James Fitzjames Stephen; *Eclectic Review*, new series i (1861), 460, 463; Ralph Waldo Emerson, *Works* (1889), pp. 339, 352.

13   Matthew Arnold, 'Stanzas in Memory of the Author of "Obermann"', ll. 53–4; 'Heinrich Heine', *Essays in Criticism: First Series* (1906 edn), p. 115.

14   *Pickwick Papers*, ch. 20, p. 269; letter of 30 January 1801, *Letters of Charles Lamb*, ed. Ernest Rhys (Everyman's Library, 1909), I, pp. 177–8. For some early discussions of the originality or otherwise of Dickens's presentation of London, see *Spectator*, 26 December 1836, 1234; 31 March 1838, 304; 24 November 1838, 1114–16; *Quarterly Review*, lix (1837), 500–7, lxiv (1839), 87–92; *Westminster Review*, xxix (1837), 196; *National Review*, i (1837), 445–7; *Examiner*, 27 October 1839, 677. Most of these passages are reprinted in my collection, *Dickens: The Critical Heritage* (1970).

15   Wordsworth, Preface to *The Excursion*, ll. 78–80; *Sketches by Boz*, p. 215; *The Old Curiosity Shop*, ch. 39, pp. 293–4. On this element in Dickens, see my essay 'Dickens and Popular Amusements', *Dickensian*, lxi (1965), 7–19, and Edgar and Eleanor Johnson's anthology, *The Dickens Theatrical Reader* (1964).

16   Disraeli, *Tancred*, Bk II, ch. 12; *Nicholas Nickleby*, ch. 21, p. 264; Bagehot, *Literary Essays*, II, p. 85; 'Charles Dickens and his Works', *Fraser's Magazine*, xxi (1840), 400; *Oliver Twist*, ch. 8, pp. 55–6. For an entertaining contemporary version of the social topography of London, see 'The Geology of Society', *Punch*, i (1841), 157, 178.

17   The following passage is borrowed from my study *Dickens's 'Bleak House'* (1970).

18   Harriet Martineau, *Autobiography* (1877 edn), II, pp. 377–8; Joshua Priestley, ed., *True Womanhood: Eliza Hessel* (1859), p. 32; Mason Wade, ed., *The Journals of Francis Parkman* (1947), I, p. 221; Randall Stewart, ed., *The English Notebooks of Nathaniel Hawthorne* (1941), p. 283; *The Education of Henry Adams: An autobiography* (1918 edn), p. 72; Frederick W. Dupee, ed., *Henry James: Autobiography* (1956), pp. 572, 388.

19   John Cordy Jeaffreson, *Novels and Novelists, from Elizabeth to Victoria* (1858), II, p. 326; J.-K. Huysmans, *A Rebours*, ch. 11, here cited from Robert Baldick's translation, *Against Nature* (Penguin Books, 1969), by kind permission of the publishers and translator.

20   *Letters*, II, p. 272; Charles Dickens, 'Reminiscences of my Father', *Windsor Magazine*, December 1934, 23–4; *Our Mutual Friend*, Bk I, ch. 12, p. 145; *Little Dorrit*, Bk II, ch. 34, p. 826; Blanchard Jerrold, 'Charles Dickens: In Memoriam', *Gentleman's Magazine*, new series, v (1870), 240. Dickens's relationship to Doré, and

to other artists of the urban scene, would repay further investigation; Hillis Miller (op. cit., in note 9, pp. 161–2) offers some useful hints. I might here refer the reader to some other discussions of Dickens and London, which supplement mine or adopt very different approaches: Hillis Miller in the book cited; E. B. Chancellor, *The London of Dickens* (1924); Donald Fanger, *Dostoevsky and Romantic Realism* (Cambridge, Mass., 1965), ch. 3, 'Dickens: realism, subjective and indicative'; Christopher Hibbert's 'Dickens's London' in *Charles Dickens, 1812–1870*, ed. E. W. F. Tomlin (1969), and his book *The Making of Charles Dickens* (1967); Alexander Welsh's 'Satire and History: the City of Dickens', *Victorian Studies*, xi (1968), 379–400 and his book (published since this essay was written) *The City of Dickens* (1971); for topographical details, Walter Dexter's *The London of Dickens* (1923) and 'The London Dickens knew', *Dickensian*, xxv–xxvi (1929–30), with maps; also the useful portfolio of maps in *A Dickens Atlas*, ed. A. A. Hopkins and N. F. Read (New York, 1923). I should here also acknowledge the stimulus I have received from discussions with one of my postgraduate students, Mr Roy Winstanley.

24 Pictures from the Magazines

Michael Wolff and Celina Fox

One of the most striking concomitants of the process of Victorian urbanization is the growth of the press. The relationship between the press and the city is very close for, against a background of industrial and technical development, only city-dwellers can assure a mass readership capable of escalating faster than their own numbers. The growth of the Victorian press, much more rapid even than that of the Victorian city, was perhaps the first demonstration of the potential of the mass media and the closest verbal and graphic equivalent which we have of Victorian urbanism.[1]

The city and the press depend upon each other. It is the Victorian city that brings together for the first time that 'unknown public' for whom tens of thousands of different newspapers, magazines, and reviews were printed, some, to be sure, disappearing after only one issue and very few copies, but others with circulations of hundreds of thousands surviving throughout the period and into our own day. It is journalism which, by becoming the most important vehicle in the formation of public opinion, enabled the urban population to influence events. It was largely through journalism that people, as they gathered in the cities, articulated their developing group and class consciousness.[2] In short, journalism was essential both in the creation and the revelation of a general urban culture.

The Victorian press is not only a vital part of the history of the Victorian city; it is also an important source of contemporary opinion about the city. Indeed, one can readily conceive an elaborate and careful sampling of evidence from Victorian periodicals being molded into a sort of primer of Victorian urban self-consciousness, which told the city-dweller about himself as well as telling the historian about the reader. It is hard to think of any other body of evidence that might be so used. The press is one of the most tangible products of the shift from a tradition-oriented society to one characterized by mobility and change, an immediate present dominated by speed and punctuality.[3] Journalism shares many things with the city: scale, anonymity, lack of intimacy, fragmentation, diversity, the physical juxtaposition of elements otherwise widely separated from each other, an almost deliberate formlessness. In his essay on Dickens, Bagehot described this constant all-engulfing presence and yet internal discontinuity:[4]

> London is like a newspaper. Everything is there, and everything is disconnected. There is every kind of person in some houses; but there is no more connection between the houses than between the neighbours in the lists of 'births, marriages and deaths.' As we change from the broad leader to the squalid police report, we pass a corner and we are in a changed world.

Because of these affinities, the press can offer, we believe, an unrivaled source for the understanding and appreciation of city life, especially of the dynamics of those social regroupings which accompanied urbanization and of the psychological interaction of the city and its inhabitants. It can lead us, we hope, towards some comprehension of that actual quality of urban life which it is hard to imagine in quantified demographic or economic terms.

In this essay we are concerned with evidence of attitudes towards the city disclosed by the way in which London is treated in illustrated magazines, in particular in the two which dominated the century, the pioneer and long-run examples of an illustrated paper specifically directed to a London readership, the *Illustrated London News* (which began in May 1842) and *Punch*, with its metropolitan subtitle, the *London Charivari* (which began in July 1841). It is clear enough, not only from their names but also from their contents and from their extraordinary and lasting success, that there was a substantial metropolitan readership whose interests were met by these journals. In addition we have looked at the city in some of the successors and imitators of the *Illustrated London News*, such as the *Pictorial Times* (1843–8), the *Illustrated Times* (1855–72), the *Penny Illustrated Paper* (1861–1913), and the *Graphic* (1869–1932); and also those of *Punch*, such as *Fun* (1861–1901), *Tomahawk* (1867–70), *Judy* (1867–1907), *Will o' the Wisp* (1869–70), and *Moonshine* (1879–1902).[5]

On 7 January 1843, at the end of its first half-year of publication, the *Illustrated London News* presented its readers with a large engraving of London, made from a daguerreotype taken from the top of the Duke of York's column. Other journals recognized the propriety of this gesture. *The Times* of 10 January wrote: 'There could not be a more appropriate and acceptable present in so portable a form for country friends; and we can imagine the interest with which the "young ones" to whom London is but a dream would gaze at this fine picture of its glories.' The *Morning*

362 'View of Manchester,' from *Illustrated London News*, i (1842), 225.

363 *above* 'London in 1842' [Northern prospect], from *Illustrated London News*, ii (1843).

364 *left* 'Mosley Street—St Peter's Church' [Manchester], from *Pictorial Times*, ii (1843), 29.

365 *right* 'The Fleet-street Sewer,' from *Illustrated London News*, vii (1845), 213.

366 *above* 'Fish Market, Billingsgate,' from *Illustrated Times*, new series, xiii (1868), 200.

367 *right* 'Down Whitechapel Way,' from *Penny Illustrated Paper*, xvi (1869), 285.

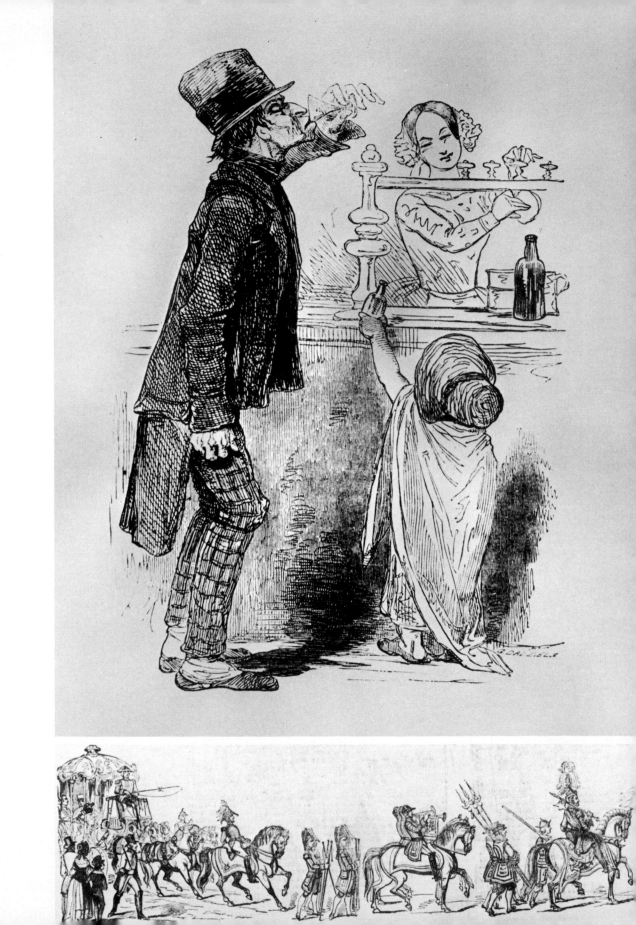

"FAMILIARITY BREEDS CONTEMPT!"

Habitual Criminal (to Swell Betting-Man). "To see the Lord Mayor! Ah! if they knowed the Lord Mayor as well as you and I, Bill, they wouldn't make such a fuss about him!"

368 *left* 'The Dram-drinker,' from *Illustrated London News*, xii (1848), 298.

369 *middle* 'The Return of the Civic Procession [of the Lord Mayor] from Westminster to Guildhall,' from *Illustrated London News*, i (1842), 424–5.

370 *above* 'Familiarity breeds Contempt,' from *Punch*, lix (1870), 222.

371 *above* 'Lord Brougham opening the Social Science Congress at Sheffield,' from *Illustrated London News*, xlvii (1865), 368.

372 *above right* 'Meeting of the Social Science Congress with working men at Sheffield,' from *Illustrated Times*, new series, vii (1865), 229.

373 *below right* 'Opening of the Thames Embankment,' from *Illustrated London News*, lvii (1870), 84–5.

Swell (anxious to explain that he is the West-End article):
"HERE, WAITAW, I WANT TO GO TO A PLACE CALLED ISLINGTON. SUPPOSE, IF I TAKE CAB, IT'LL BE ALL WIGHT—
I SHA'N'T BE WAYLAID OR WOBBED ON THE WOAD?"

376 From *Fun*, new series, x (1869–70), Almanac for 1870, 12.

SUNDAY MORNING
WORKMANS HOME
LEATHER LANE

374 *left* From *Punch*, xxxiii (1857), 114.

375 *above* 'Sunday morning. Workman's Home, Leather-lane,' from *Illustrated London News*, lxvi (1875), 253.

THE GREAT SOCIAL EVIL.

Time:—Midnight. A Sketch not a Hundred Miles from the Haymarket.

Bella. "Ah! Fanny! How long have you been *Gay*?"

THE NEAREST WAY HOME

LADY.—"Where do you live, my dear?"

CHILD (*crying*).—"Dun'now, M'm—dun'now!"

BYSTANDER.—"Ask of her where she gits the beer, Mum."

377 From *Will o' the Wisp*, iii (1870), 283.

CULTURE FOR THE MILLION; OR, SOCIETY AS IT MAY BE.

NEW CHAMBER OF HORRORS AT MADAME TUSSAUD'S. (*The Right man in the Right Place*).—"DON'T BE AFRAID, YOU LITTLE GOOSE! IT'S ONLY WAX-WORK! WHY, *I* RECOLLECT WHEN PEOPLE LIKE THAT WERE ALLOWED TO GO LOOSE ABOUT THE STREETS!"

SUBSTANCE AND SHADOW

379   From *Punch*, v (1843), 23.

NOBODY THAT KNOWS THEM COULD DOUBT THE RESPECTABILITY OF THESE TWO GENTLEMEN, YET YOU WOULD HARDLY CREDIT THE UNNECESSARY PANIC THEIR IMAGINATIONS CAUSED THEM THE OTHER NIGHT IN THE FOG!

380 *above left* From *Punch*, xix (1850), 30.

381 *below left* '"The Demonstration" in Hyde Park—Drawn by John Leech,' from *Illustrated London News*, xxvii (1855), 12.

382 *above* From *Punch*, lviii (1870), 72.

IMPORTANT. FROM THE SEAT OF WAR.—Extract from Correspondent's Letter

"*Notwithstanding their superiority of numbers, our* RIGHT *and* LEFT, *by a rapid and well-directed movement, were planted full in the face of the enemy; and the reserve coming up at a critical moment, they were put to a complete rout.*"

Advertiser added its praise: 'all combine to make this the most eligible picture of London which has ever been produced. It is in short the sole means by which foreign and country readers can form to themselves any idea of the grandeur of the British metropolis.' But in the complacency of these references to London's glory and grandeur there are clues to the view of London offered to the readers of the *Illustrated London News* and—presumably—therefore to the idea of London which they either had or wished to have. For this panorama and others like it were not preliminary to any more precise vision of London. The grand view did not foreshadow any serious effort to show the city and its inhabitants in significant detail. For, although the techniques and medium represented by the paper were urban, the message hardly drew its readers' attention to much that was new or characteristic about mid-Victorian London life. This contradiction suggests that city-dwellers of the socio-economic level of the readership were in a very limited relationship to their surroundings. Although the *Illustrated London News* was a perfectly competent transmitter of non-urban messages, it seems to have been fighting a rearguard action on behalf of its readers against any too meaningful acknowledgment of the social and cultural problems brought about by urbanization.[6] Its main effect, however unconscious, was to protect those to whom and for whom it spoke from too clear or deep an understanding of the complexities of the industrial city and their own role in it.

The *Illustrated London News* was, in fact, presenting a picture of the city so much distanced through artistic convention that the new environment of urbanization —the increasing population and the increasing diversity of that population which could not be assimilated to the old modes of organization—was not apparent. The panoramic view of London was merely magnified and broken up into architectural drawings of individual buildings, either in stark isolation or in a formal context, given perspective by the addition of a few stock figures in a way quite unrelated to the actual day-to-day urban scene. However informative the Victorian volumes of the *Illustrated London News* were about foreign and colonial parts, about battles and naval engagements, events and accounts about theatres and exhibitions, about archaeological discoveries and the doings of the Royal Family 'interesting only to the Butterflies of Society,'[7] the picture of London offered by the illustrations was of a busy capital but one that was uncluttered, calmly administered, prosperous, and socially comfortable. It is hardly the London of the 1840s and later, as we know it to have been, and as the readers of the *Illustrated London News* must themselves have in some sense known it. What characterized the paper for Charles Knight, founder of the *Penny Magazine* and himself deeply concerned with the problems arising from urbanization and mass audiences, was its 'endless repetitions':[8]

> The scenery is varied; the actors are the same. Sometimes we have incidents that could never have been seen by the artists—ships foundering—mines exploding. The staple materials for the steady-going illustrator to work most attractively upon are, Court and Fashion; Civic Processions and Banquets; Political and Religious Demonstrations in crowded halls;

561

> Theatrical Novelties; Musical Meetings; Races; Reviews; Ship Launches—
> every scene, in short, where a crowd of great people can be got together,
> but never, if possible, any exhibition of vulgar poverty.

He went on: 'This view of Society is one-sided. We must look further for its "many coloured life." We want to behold something more than the showy make-up of the characteristics of the age. We want to see the human form beneath the drapery.' Superficially, at least, the *Illustrated London News* was seeking to prolong a simplified and relaxed version of city life and thereby catering to those who preferred not to be reminded that the substance of the city was becoming, or had already become, something different.

It would seem on the face of it that news illustration would be the most revealing type of illustration. But, as it happens, whatever revelations the illustrated newspapers have to offer must be sought by the historian; they do not spring from the page. For the techniques of illustration employed and artistic conventions used reflect social values, present in both staff and reader, which collaborate towards distancing the urban reader from the urban scene.

Take, for instance, the first engraving of a city to appear in the *Illustrated London News*. It was in fact the first illustration on the front page of the first number: of a fire in the city of Hamburg. The source was, it turns out, an old print of the city copied in the British Museum to which crowds, boats and flames had been added.[9] Nor was this unusual.[10] It shows how easily the technological process involved in bringing illustrated newspapers to the readers and the conventions open to the artists increased the distance between the reader and the substance of the city.

If the basic justification for news illustration was to provide an authentic pictorial record of the events of the day, then one of the principal prerequisites was speed: it had to follow on the event as quickly as was technically possible.[11] However, even with the photo-engraving processes at the end of the century, the illustration never caught up with the 'word picture' which could be 'flashed over the telegraph wires, written out, set up in type and printed off long before an artist had made a sketch to illustrate the same fact.'[12] After the introduction of the electric telegraph in 1844, the illustration would always be stale compared with the news. The history of news illustration is in part that of a long effort to combat the time-lag inherent in the medium through as many short-cuts as possible. All of these technical short-cuts worked against the intrusion of any of the worrying 'reality' of city life.

Just as Knight had noticed the impossibility of on-the-spot illustration of ships foundering and mine explosions, so also it was often inexpedient to have an artist at large in the city at all. This was especially common in the early days of illustrated journalism when there were no precedents for authenticity beyond a certain level of topographical accuracy or circumstantial description. The stock block, the all-purpose illustration stocked in block form by jobbing printers for use as the occasion demanded, is a practice as old as printing itself.[13] These blocks headed ballad and broadsheets, illustrated chapbooks and covered executions, murders, miraculous occurrences, and news of fighting.[14] They included symbols of authority and heraldic emblems, and signs denoting trades. In the nineteenth century the main area for expansion lay in their suitability for packaging and advertising purposes, but as late as the 1890s A. S. Hartrick mentions the practice of drawing 'stock' in the *Graphic* offices, when not out sketching.[15] Vizetelly derided the *Illustrated London News*'s pretensions in its opening address to represent 'the spirit of the truth' by pointing out that not a single engraving in that number was derived from an authentic source.[16] In John Gilbert's time, the most common method used to produce engravings of current events—metropolitan as well as, more excusably, foreign and provincial—was to scan the morning papers carefully, cut out those accounts which would make good illustrations and send them with the necessary boxwood blocks to the draughtsman. Gilbert could complete one in an hour; Kenny Meadows complained that 'Nature put him out,' and William Harvey never drew from the living model. Thus, with a mixture of general 'fillers,' more specifically topical illustrations drawn in advance of a predictable annual social event or a change of season, and imaginative recreations by artists far from the scene of the news item, it is not surprising that the overall effect tended towards vagueness and generalization, so that mistakes would not be too apparent. After all, the authenticity could always be bolstered by the addition of an appropriately explanatory caption.[17] Yet perhaps the most misleading method employed was the use of old illustrations with altered captions.[18] When Herbert Ingram, in addition to the *Illustrated London News*, owned the *Illustrated Times* and the *Penny Illustrated Paper*, such interchange was quite common. On one occasion, for instance, the *Penny Illustrated Paper* reprinted in 1869 a crowd scene from the *Illustrated Times* of 1867—of a reform demonstration in Hyde Park—and used it to illustrate a Fenian Amnesty Meeting. Dickens, in *Bleak House* (1853) suggests that dishonesty of this sort was fairly common practice. He is describing the activity following Krook's death by spontaneous combustion:[19]

> Then, there comes the artist of a picture newspaper, with a foreground and figures ready drawn for anything, from a wreck on the Cornish Coast to a review in Hyde Park, or a meeting in Manchester,—and in Mrs. Perkins' own room, memorable evermore, he then and there throws in upon the block, Mr. Krook's house, as large as life; in fact considerably larger, making a very Temple of it. Similarly, being permitted to look in at the door of the fatal chamber, he depicts the apartment as three-quarters of a mile long, by fifty yards high.

Technical innovations further increased the speed of the operation, but for some time these brought no improvement in the generalized conventional quality of the illustrations: rather the reverse.[20] Not only did photography take over from the artist at a very slow rate but also the sophistication of the new processes required a greater division of labor, splitting up among various hands the different steps of the process.[21]

When Mason Jackson described the stages in 1885, first the whole design was traced or photographed on the block, sometimes by the original artist, more often by another draughtsman in the office.[22] Often, when there was a great hurry, the jointed block—limited in area by the narrow girth of the box tree—was separated piece by piece as parts of the drawing were completed, so as to enable the engraver and the draughtsman to work on the same subject at the same time. In some cases, the draughtsman never saw the whole of his drawing together: John Gilbert often operated in this way. When the drawing was completed, the engraver 'set' the lines across the joints of the block before the different parts were distributed among other engravers who followed the master's key. Finally, the master engraver would retouch the completed block to try to achieve a harmonious whole ready for the printing process.[23] The result of these exertions was often deplorable. Frequently the necessity of using a predetermined system of engraved lines, in which the engravers were trained, reduced all work to a 'flat, dull plain of reasonability.'[24] This was especially likely in the case of the large wood blocks used for news magazines, more so than in that of the small humorous cuts which could be handled by one man. Nevertheless, there still lay the main gap between the artist and the engraver. As William Ivins has explained, the lines of the engraver were laid within the requirements of a particular convention or system of linear structure, and anything that that way of seeing and that convention of drawing were not calculated to catch and bring out, failed to be brought out in the final visual statement.[25] There were complaints levelled on both sides, of which Rossetti's against the Dalziels is only the most famous.[26] But what they all underline is the enormous gap which lay between what happened on the street and what actually appeared in the newspaper.

Another force which worked to undercut whatever immediacy there might have been in the illustrations of the news magazines was the traditional treatment of subject matter which inevitably shaped the artists' work. Thus, even where the illustrated newspapers aspired to depict the most assertive new presences in the city, its new buildings and its new inhabitants, the artists made use of older, preurban conventions of illustration.

As far as buildings were concerned, the artists were in large part bound by the tradition of the topographical print, mainly used in pre-Victorian times to record 'prospects' of town or country, noteworthy residences, or public edifices. In the early years of the illustrated newspapers, series of such illustrations appeared which scarcely extended the tradition at all. In its first year, the *Illustrated London News* produced series devoted to 'Nooks and Corners of Old England' and 'Churches of London.' The *Pictorial Times* ran not only 'The Schools of England' and 'Clubs of London' but also pictorial histories of Newcastle and Manchester in the 1840s, making use principally of old prints of the cities.

But even when this tradition was modified, namely, in the recording of projected, recently completed, or otherwise prominent buildings, the inertia of the tradition prevented the artists from conveying much sense of a rapidly growing city. The Fleet Sewer became a dramatized Piranesi fretwork of the Sublime; a new water tank in St Giles resembled an ancient ruin. The pages of the *Illustrated London News* were full of detailed views of churches, town halls, charity schools, asylums, institutes, and orphanages, which appeared with monotonous regularity in every issue, almost always divorced from the life which must have surrounded them and conforming to the tradition of the topographical print by being depicted in the sort of isolation or semi-rural idyll which at once aggrandized and sterilized them.[27]

The other new phenomenon in the Victorian city that demanded attention was the vast numbers of new people, and particularly people of the laboring and poorer classes. In this case, the obligation for showing them to the readers of the illustrated newspapers was harmlessly taken care of through an extension of the tradition of prints of street criers and itinerant tradesmen. Of these, Francis Wheatley's *The Itinerant Traders of London*, issued between 1793 and 1797, was probably the most popular, but more interesting and certainly less ingratiating were Thomas Rowlandson's *Characteristic Sketches of the Lower Orders* (1820), and W. M. Craig's anonymous illustrations for *Modern London* (1805), in which the figures were placed against a recognizably distinct corner of London.[28] In 1829, *Bell's Life in London* began a series of wood-engraved character sketches from etchings by George Cruikshank, Robert Seymour, and Kenny Meadows called a 'Gallery of Comicalities,' which continued at intervals until the end of 1840 along with other sketches, for example, 'Phizogs of the Tradesmen of London,' 'Kitchen Stuff, or Cads of the Aristocracy,' 'Portraits down the Road,' and so on.[29] Meadows, who had drawn *Heads of the People* [1840], a book to which Thackeray and Jerrold had contributed, also did some similar sketches for the opening numbers of the *Illustrated London News*, including a series called 'Characters about Town.'[30] The *Illustrated Times* carried on the traditions with frequent portrayals of London street scenes and amusing series of picturesque and stereotyped characters to be found in certain corners of London.

In some ways this stereotyped treatment of the poor had the same effect as the treatment of buildings as isolated items in a topographical tradition. Both were identified as fixed and classifiable objects of primarily visual interest, available for architectural information or light human relief; both had little or nothing to do with the new industrial city.

The channeling of contemporary reality through conventions developed in less tumultuous times—the style of depiction of both people and buildings in the *Illustrated London News*—reveals the general social impulse of its readership to avoid facing anything radically new, startling, or threatening in the city.

At the point where stock characters in the city are displayed with comic intent, the news magazine overlaps considerably with the humor magazine, stemming as they do from the same caricature tradition. Blanchard Jerrold maintained that 'the taste for pictorial journalism was distinctly the creation of our caricaturists,' and the great variety of subjects treated with a vigorous, fresh, and racy humor by young artists like Meadows and the Cruikshanks gave a foretaste of *Punch*, which was to start a decade or so after *Bell's Life in London*.[31] Furthermore, the humor magazine will take over events of the week if they are either rich in comic possibilities like the arrival of the first hippopotamus at the Regent's Park Zoo in 1850, or too overwhelming to be ignored like the Franco-Prussian War of 1870. But even a cursory glance through the pages of *Punch* and its fellows shows that life in the city in the form of urban energy, complexity, and confusion seems to have found in the comic magazines a place which was denied in the news magazines. There is evidently greater freedom in the comic magazines for a sort of picturing of urban reality, and on the face of it their view of the city is at once more spontaneous and more authentic than the convention-bound or blinkered treatment which characterizes the illustrated newspapers.

This greater apparent freedom is presumably a function of comedy. The mood in which both artist and reader approach a topic differs when one moves from the news to the comic magazine. Illustrations in the news magazines are visual statements; that is, they claim, however inaccurately, the factual existence of what they depict; the contract between illustrator and viewer calls at least for the pretense of a transparent medium, an open window onto the scene. This theme of authenticity, one of the fundamental tenets of nineteenth-century news illustration, was constantly reiterated in the newspapers themselves. The 'reality' of the illustrations, the pen of of the artist 'oracular with the spirit of truth,' they saw as the fundamental advantage over the writings of the pen, which could easily be led into 'fallacious argument.'[32] A drawing was impartial, being 'able to illustrate events uncontaminated by party spirit—in a word, with truth, and without bias';[33] for the artist spoke a 'universal language' and was thus able to 'illustrate passing events truly and graphically.'[34] In illustrating a republican procession during the 1870s, the *Graphic* declared:[35]

> The only way out of this confusion, if one cares to find a way out of it at all, is, to see the International Democratic Association for oneself. This the artist has enabled us to do. He has no theory of his own, but has dealt conscientiously with his facts. He has drawn the Democratic Association and, having seen it, we are at liberty to think of it exactly as we like.

Throughout the early decades, in the descriptions attached to the illustrations, there is a constant stress on authenticity—'an accurate and most faithful sketch,' 'a spirited and authentic sketch,' 'a faithful depiction,' 'a faithful delineation.'[36] As we have tried to point out, this transparency of communication is in fact wishful thinking which was broken by the intervention of obsolete conventions and flattening techniques. Almost paradoxically, the illustrated magazines were further inhibited by their overall function and claims to truth. They could not admit disturbing material, which gave any clue to individual bias, prejudice, or argument, just as the need to meet deadlines and speed up production prevented anything but an anonymous, conventional treatment of subject matter.[37] Only by reducing the medium, in fact, to this 'flat dull plain of reasonability' could the claim of the illustrations to *news value*—both its immediacy and its accuracy—be honored.

But with the comic magazines there is a qualitative difference in approach. Traditionally, graphic humor has always been closely connected with comment, individual bias, and prejudice. It is recognized as being a distortion of reality to point an effect or achieve a purpose.[38] The strong satire of Gillray was retained, in diluted form, in the 'big cuts' of the humorous weeklies, often making use of the same vocabulary of visual conventions as did their predecessors. In the small cartoons also, the contract between illustrator and audience did not involve the concept of impartiality, and in addition the artist rarely had to meet a topical deadline. The consequent freedom of subject matter, a product of the artist's relaxation and the acceptance by the audience of his bias, is exemplified in *Punch*'s 'star system' whereby the paper's major artists indulged themselves constantly in attacking their favorite targets.[39] The saving factor in all this was, in watered form, that freedom enjoyed by the individually produced print in the eighteenth and early nineteenth centuries, compared with the libel risk run by newspapers burdened by the threat of editorial responsibility.[40] The freedom enjoyed by the caricaturist may be described in psychological terms too, in which emphasis is placed on the role of comedy as a release function. For example, Gombrich and Kris in their book on *Caricature* advance the argument that caricature fulfills the function of being a 'well guarded playground' in which forces not normally allowed full rein can be given scope without allowing them to get out of control.[41]

The effect of this argument about the comic magazines' relatively freer capacity to use potentially disconcerting material is to confirm what an examination of the volumes themselves discloses, namely, that more about the real world of the Victorian city slips through in the illustrations of the comic magazines than in those of the news magazines.

For example, the *Punch* cartoon of 1870 (by Charles Keene) contrasts with the elaborate ceremonial and fashionable depiction of the Thames Embankment opening in the *Illustrated London News* of 1870. The effect of comparison here is to puncture the pretension of the news magazine that its version of a civic procession is a valid one, that it is conveying the real news about the event. In the *Illustrated London News*, all the people and accoutrements actually in the procession are drawn in some detail, though conventionally, but the crowds watching the procession are shadowy and vague, looking like the stage backdrop which it is their role in the drawing to imitate. *Punch* permits itself a close-up of certain elements in that indistinct crowd by focusing on two of its members. Thus the viewer is placed at eye-level within that crowd and exposed to the ordinary reality that underlies the 'news' about the ceremony. Other examples of differences in treatment could be taken, say, from the Derby, where the portrayal of the event in the news magazines identifies the reader with the elite of the inner enclosures, whereas the comic magazines, with implications to be discussed later, are willing and able to render something of the sensation of being present at a densely and heterogeneously populated occasion.

There are, it seems to us, two specific though hardly separable aspects of the new urban reality which are almost entirely without visual representation in the leading news magazines, but which do appear with some regularity and frequency in the humor magazines. These aspects have to do precisely with what is not only new but also especially visible about the changing environment of the city, and they are closely related to the two traditions of character sketching and topography to which we have alluded. They involve the depiction of the poor themselves, and of their presence in the streets of the city; for just as the poor embody what was most dangerous about the city, so the street was the site of those dangers most likely to be encountered.

The respectable city-dweller, the reader of the illustrated journals, was face to face with a considerable and disproportionate increase in the numbers of cohabitants socially and economically below him, people whose ways, to say the least, were strange and unreliable. It was impossible to avoid some sort of attention to these newly visible inhabitants of the Victorian city. One sort of attention was the willed inattention characteristic of the upper-middle-class news magazines; another was the unqualified identification of the urban poor as a whole with their most objectionable social tendencies. To represent them all—however comically or good-humoredly—as lazy, drunken, or criminal was primarily a hostile attitude. Yet it was their comic treatment which made the poor palatable subject matter in ways not open to the news magazines. The implicit social hostility seemed to have lost some of its sting. The 'laughing philosophy' of Mr Punch himself by no means produced the 'broad daylight' approach to the depiction of the city, which Charles Knight seemed to believe was the main characteristic of the humorous, as distinct from the news magazines.[42]

Until the 1870s, the urban poor themselves are altogether absent from the pages of the *Illustrated London News* except as smudges in some crowded panorama or as figures safely insulated within some charitable institution. Only in 1875 did it venture into working-class districts of London and depict workmen's homes in Islington and Leather Lane, and the narrow alleys of Bloomsbury and Drury Lane. Even then the illustrations were used to further the cause of specific remedies: in this case, the proposed Artisans' Dwellings Bill; or construction companies like Sir Sidney Waterlow's Improved Industrial Dwellings Company, or working-class villages like Shaftesbury Park at Battersea, which would prove to be good investments.[43] There is little feeling of sympathy for the conditions of the poor in themselves. Furthermore, the working people shown were peculiarly 'cleaned-up' and well-fed specimens, an impression conveyed also in the much-vaunted school of 'social realism' in the *Graphic* of the 1870s.[44] Indeed, the work of artists like Luke Fildes and Hubert von Herkomer was not a new departure, but a sentimentalized painterly extension of themes anticipated—not only in subject matter but also in artistic convention—by cheaper and ultimately less successful periodicals like the *Illustrated Times* and the *Penny Illustrated Paper* earlier in the century.[45]

568

Yet poverty in all its aspects was surely the manifest problem of urban life, the image that was blazoned on every city, as other contributors to those volumes show. In the industrial cities poverty was often more concentrated and provided an increasing contrast to the lives of the well-to-do—economic facts which were often strongly accentuated as the heterogeneity of the pre-industrial city was lost and, notably in London, classes were divided off into their own areas. Dickens drew attention in *Master Humphrey's Clock* to the 'worlds' within the city and added that each 'has its own inhabitants; each is distinct from, and almost unconscious of the existence of any other.'[46] Areas inhabited by the poor were habitually thought of as strange out-the-way places into which respectable people would not lightly venture.[47]

The result was an increasing ignorance about the poor and a tendency, both factual and psychological, always to oversimplify, often to overdramatize. Similarly, the treatment of the poor in the humorous magazines can scarcely be described as straightforward. Just as the pictorial conventions used by the news magazines had little or no relevance for the contemporary reality of the city, so too in the humorous magazines, despite the seemingly greater scope, the visual conventions used were outdated and traditional, more conforming to the image and clichés directed against a preurban mob, with all its alleged drunkenness and criminality, than to a complex working-class social structure.[48]

Take, for example, the cartoon, 'The Nearest Way Home,' from *Will o' the Wisp* for 1870. Two comments seem called for. First, the characteristic joke of the period treated working people and the poor as qualitatively different from other human beings. Leech and Du Maurier headed a bevy of lesser artists who produced a stubby, large-jawed, unshaven specimen in much the same way that Mayhew assigned physiognomic characteristics to his species of street folk.[49] Caricature, like physiognomy, rests on the age-old assumption that the character of a man can be read from his external appearance, and the complex of underlying strains which contributed to this theory reached their most extreme form in nineteenth-century comic illustration with the progressive simianization of the Irish.[50] In this particular case, the heavy coarseness of the children and the poor woman is contrasted not only with the umbrella-carrying benign respectability of the lady and her companion but also with their height and the clean decency of their faces. Second, there is the assumption that, however stupid or helpless the child might be, it could be taken for granted that to mention the fetching of beer would trigger off in her some usable association. The assigned image frequently had the working man hovering round the public house as his natural habitat or having a horizon so limited by the pub—as in the picture joke from *Fun* for 1870, for example—that he could only give directions to an enquiring clergyman by naming pubs on the route.

This conviction of the poor being different to the point of their having a reduced humanity was usually represented physically, but Leech made a simple joke of the absurdity that arose if one tried to imagine 'them' acting like 'us.'[51] In *Punch* for 1850 an example of 'right words in the wrong mouths' entitled 'Gems from the Advertisements' (in this case for Amandine soap) showed a particularly grubby and stunted collier addressing a shopkeeper: 'Now, Mister, I wants my delicacy of touch restored and the seal of helegence impressed upon my bunch of fives.' At the time of the Education Act of 1870 Du Maurier intensified both the feeling separating 'us' from the lower classes and the fear of that distance being diminished in a series entitled 'Culture for the Million, or Society as it May Be' which appeared in the *Punch* almanac for that year. In one cartoon a trio of policemen drag off the street a screaming urchin who is accused of dropping an H. In others, servants below stairs sing arias from Italian opera; the butler offers his services to the duchess when she has need of a dictionary; and nursemaids compliment the paintings of their military beaux in highly technical language.[52] What is so remarkable is how little the stock had changed since the 'March of Mind' caricatures of the 1820s.[53] In one print by William Heath, two servants in fashionable liveries shake hands left-handedly on the pavement of Cavendish Square. The conversation runs: 'How do ye do Thomas'— 'Pretty well tank'ee'—'*excuse* my *Glove*, Massa William.'[54] Much the same message is implicit in others which Heath did under the pseudonym of Paul Pry: dustmen demanding three-pronged forks to eat with, street singers rendering Rossini, coachmen reading *The Times*, a butcher and dustman playing chess, an applewoman engrossed in Byron.[55] The well-worn theme ran that the main consequence of education for the masses would be the neglect of their duties. The cartoonists vacillated between this approach and assuring themselves that the poor were content with their ignorance and unwilling to be improved—as in the two cartoons reproduced here from *Punch* and *Judy*, both from 1870.

The second significant feature of urban life neglected in the leading news magazines and given some attention in the humor magazines is life in the streets. It is not that there were no streets in the news magazines, for, of course, the great ceremonial parade was one of the events that the *Illustrated London News* most delighted to record. But in these cases there is little life, certainly little of what one could call street life: the scene is arrested and static, the mood is theatrical, the primary trappings or main figures are posed as in a tableau, and the surrounding figures are fused into a role that is more scenic than human. And even when the newspapers closed in a little and pictured the street crowd for its own sake, as occurred more frequently after 1870, the Christmas shoppers or shelterers from April showers were a very neat and genteel assortment.

However, in reality the city street was not simply another setting: it was the quintessentially urban locale. It was in the streets that all the elements of the new city could be and habitually were simultaneously present. Moreover, they were present in a context at one and the same time unprotected by any tangible status barriers, and exposed to the levelling and endemically urban qualities of dirt and hurry. For the respectable city-dweller, being out of doors was a risky affair even though the risk for the most part might be nothing more than the risk of inconvenience or annoyance. One was normally safe enough if one were in a private carriage or if one were accompanied by servants, for then one could be said to be maintaining the privacy of the indoor setting in portable form. Yet no one with any social standing was putting himself at risk in going out of doors in the country. On the contrary, it was for him more often a means of confirming the stability of society and his niche in it by every encounter, more like the civilized procedures of being *indoors* in the city than of venturing out. To be alone on city streets, to have to depend on public transport, to be alone in public under novel and little understood conditions, was to allow oneself to risk being part of the whole urban uncertainty, that mixing of classes that characterized the modern city for those of its inhabitants who knew (or thought they knew) what an orderly community should be like and who cherished and largely depended on the idea of being part of such a community. In the street, the division between one's own safe familiar world and the world of the rest, the others, could never be complete. The insulation upon which it was felt that an orderly society depended was stretched to its utmost limits and could all too easily be broken down to reveal things which it would have been more comfortable to ignore. We contend that one of the things which the comic magazines did was to provide a release for the respectable city-dweller from the dilemma posed for him by the sight of poverty and the fear of chaos—things at once too persistent to be ignored yet too alarming to be faced. They created an illusion of portraying urban reality that was both plausible in its presentation and harmless in its deflationary effect. Take the cartoon of two perfectly respectable gentlemen who, in the fog, 'an urban phenomenon,' look to each other like ruffians, their umbrellas blurred into cudgels: 'Nobody that knows them could doubt the respectability of these two gentlemen, yet you could hardly credit the unnecessary panic their imaginations caused them the other night in the fog!'

On the most trivial level, it was a discomfort caused by street obstacles which came to the attention of the humorous magazines. The theme had not been ignored in prints issued during the early part of the century. Both Dighton and George Cruikshank produced series of 'Street Nuisances,' and crowded London with umbrellas, carts, and hawkers, with slops thrown from upper windows providing the worst hazard to be encountered. In 1850, *Punch* noticed that the real street obstacles were not flower-sellers and orange-girls but the solider sandwich-men and carriers of street-advertisements. There were, potentially at least, specific encounters that carried with them more frightening possibilities, however muffled those possibilities might have been. Within stock situations and using stock figures, it is surprising how frequently *Punch* makes note of these encounters. Take a *Punch* cartoon of 1870 entitled 'A Slight Mistake.' On the relatively crowded and busy pavement are paterfamilias with rather fierce whiskers and extremely proper bearing and dress and his daughter, fashionably but not ostentatiously dressed in a tam-o'shanter and a tartan skirt. She is accosted by a drunk soldier, reeling in from the gutter, rumpled and coarse featured, who says, 'Hullo, Cumrad! Wha' resgh'ment do you b'long to?'[56] The joke is, strictly speaking, a stock joke about fads in women's fashions but the incongruity of the encounter testified to by the appalled and glassy stare of the respectable father and daughter remind us—and, we suppose, the readers of *Punch*—of the unprecedented vulnerability that accompanies a stroll in the city. This particular example is mild enough, but a more serious aspect of the worry is brought out in a conversation among three women, Mrs Brown and Mrs Jones being rather over-dressed compared with the demure Mrs Robinson. Mrs Brown complains that 'a lady cannot walk by herself in London without being followed, accosted, and otherwise annoyed by men.' Mrs Jones never goes out alone but 'even then, men will stare in the most offensive manner.' Mrs Robinson, the demure one, avows that she is never so bothered.[57] Again the ostensible topic is the dateless theme of fashion and female vanity, but the notion of the city being a place where large numbers of uncontrollable ruffians are ready to take advantage of any weakness of sex or situation is present under the conventional front of the cartoon. It is the equivalent of Arnold's fear of a community inhabited largely by 'the working class . . . now issuing from its hiding-place to assert an Englishman's heaven-born privilege of doing as he likes . . . marching where it likes, meeting where it likes, bawling what it likes, breaking what it likes.'[58]

It is true that most of the victims of these 'slights' are women or that recurrent target for ridicule, the fop or swell. Indeed when a 'real' gentleman is assaulted by roughs (as in the cartoon from *Judy* for 1870) he turns out to be a rather magically successful pugilist who puts the roughs, staves and all, to flight before the policeman arrives. But to concentrate all the disturbances of being out in the streets on to the persons of what might be called natural victims, that is, people whom the reader is quite willing to see discomforted, is to allow both the reader and the artist an unpleasant situation without having to experience the unpleasant emotions which would accompany it if it happened to themselves.

By keeping within the framework of convention, both as to function and the tradition of subject matter and styles of depiction, the most successful and widely-read of the news and humorous illustrated magazines reveal the way of seeing of both artist and audience, and the constraints existing between the social experience of the city in everyday reality and its depiction on paper. The illustrated newspapers believed that their role was to depict truth without bias; the humorous magazines used bias to depict truth. For both however, despite the greater apparent freedom of the comic world, they were not free of their particular context and their 'truth' was only partial and related to their own particular view. The *Illustrated London News* and *Punch* reveal the city as they saw it, or rather as their tradition enabled them to see it.

That their views were not monolithic and unchanging is apparent even on the surface—*Punch*, for instance, was much more radical in the 1840s than it was later to become, while the *Illustrated London News* loosened its style a little in the 1870s after the *Graphic* had given new impetus to the medium. And there is a deeper inadequacy in our account, an over-simplification which is the result of concentrating mainly on the conspicuous elite of the illustrated journals. There was a much more sporadic element in the field, less ploddingly consistent, cheaper, yet lacking in technical

THE HOMELESS POOR.

"AH! WE'RE BADLY OFF—BUT JUST THINK OF THE POOR MIDDLE CLASSES, WHO ARE
OBLIGED TO EAT ROAST MUTTON AND BOILED FOWL EVERY DAY!"

385 *above left* 'Houseless and Hungry,' from *Graphic*, i (1869), 9. See also no. 350.

386 *below left* 'Distress in London. Applicants for Relief obtain tickets at a Police Station,' from *Illustrated Times*, new series, x (1867), 81.

387 *above right* 'Supper to Homeless Boys in the Refuge, Parker-street, Drury-lane,' from *Illustrated Times*, new series, vii (1866), 117.

388 *below right* '"The Young Ravens"—A Friday Dinner at Great Queen-street,' from *Graphic*, vi (1872), 585.

389 *above* 'The room in the house in Lincoln-court where the lost child was discovered' [after being abducted], from *Illustrated Times*, xiii (1861), 193.

390 *above right* 'Rent Day,' from *Punch*, xviii (1850), Almanack.

391 *right* 'The Dormitory at the House of Correction, Coldbath-Fields,' from *Illustrated Times*, xii (1861), 137.

392 *above* 'Men's Casual Ward, West London Union,' from *Illustrated Times*, iv (1857), 137.

393 *above right* 'Attic occupied by family of 10, Bethnal-Green,' from *Illustrated Times*, new series, iii (1863), 265.

394 *right* 'Dwellings of the Poor in Bethnal-Green,' from *Illustrated Times*, new series, iii (1863), 265.

THE REAL SUFFERERS BY THE MONEY PRESSURE.—A SKETCH FROM LIFE IN THE FACTORY DISTRICTS.

He was sickly, and feeble, and famished, and old
And his thin tattered garments flapped loose in the cold,
And timidly knocking, he asked with a sigh
For a pallet of straw to lie down on and die;

"WE ARE FULL," said a voice; "we have room for no more:
Thou'rt not of our parish; begone from the door!"
And the pauper scarce able to crawl from the gate,
Lay down with a groan and prepared for his fate.
— MACKAY

395 *above* From *Pictorial Times*, x (1847), 257.

396 *above right* 'Taking the census in Belgravia,' from *Illustrated Times*, xii (1861), 243.

397 *right* 'Paterfamilias filling up the census return,' from *Illustrated Times*, xii (1861), 242.

398 *above left* 'The census enumerator in a Gray's Inn-lane tenement,' from *Illustrated Times,* xii (1861), 242.

399 *left* 'Early morning—the enumerator taking the census in St James's Park,' from *Illustrated Times,* xii (1861), 246.

400 *above* 'Taking the census in the dark arches of the Adelphi,' from *Illustrated Times,* xii (1861), 246.

401 'Poor Law divorce,' from *Pictorial Times*,
viii (1846), 136–7.

402 'Poor Law exercise (Punishment of the
Able-bodied Pauper),' from *Pictorial Times*,
viii (1846), 136–7.

403 'Poor Law imprisonment—the Union windows always looking inwards, country prospects are exchanged for expansive views of the walls,' from *Pictorial Times*, viii (1846), 136–7.

404 'Transportation of the casual poor—the
halt, the lame, the blind, in search of a suburban
famine house (Punishment of the Travelling
Pauper),' from *Pictorial Times*, viii (1846), 136–7.

405 'Condition of the poor,' from *Pictorial Times*, viii (1846), 225.

know-how and reliable capital, which disappeared and reappeared throughout the century. Bibliographical difficulties alone must partially account for its neglect and the 'showy make-up' of the most obvious success stories have tended to monopolize all the attention. But an alternative way of seeing did exist which reveals more about the city than the drawing-room reflections of the *Illustrated London News* and *Punch*. These journals were catering for an audience more immediately engaged with what was going on in the city and not insulated to any extent by layers of comforting traditions. To study them is to provide a control for the upper-middle-class magazines, and to offer clinching evidence of their lack of real involvement with the problems of urbanization.

Compare for instance Luke Fildes's famous 'Houseless and Hungry,' which depicted a queue of people outside a police station waiting for tickets of admission to the workhouse casual ward, with Matt Morgan's illustration of the same scene three years previously in the *Illustrated Times*. Morgan's work is comparatively free of the painterly sentimentality which pervades the lurking shadows and picturesque, swathed stances of the figures and their garments in the *Graphic* picture. Again, compare the Friday dinner in the Great Queen Street Boys' Refuge, Lincoln's Inn Fields for 'Young Ravens'—those children who *regularly* attended one of the ragged schools of the Committee of the National Refuges for Homeless and Destitute Children—pictured in the *Graphic* for 1872, with the dirty, cheeky atmosphere of supper-time in the Refuge for Homeless Boys, Parker Street, Drury Lane, in the *Illustrated Times*. It is not simply that there is a difference in the artistic style, but there is a difference in the way of seeing, a difference in what was considered important, what was noted. When the *Illustrated London News* ventured timidly inside a workman's home, it showed the head of the family dandling a robust infant on his lap or the mother putting a bonnet on a little girl; when the *Illustrated Times* traced a lost child back to its home in Lincoln Court, Drury Lane, mother was delousing the hair of a rather more bedraggled urchin. The reporters and illustrators on the *Illustrated Times* were informed by a desire to go and look for themselves. In 1863 they went into the dwellings of the poor in Bethnal Green; they showed, by means of people queueing for a tap, the state of the water supply; they recorded an attic occupied by ten persons. In 1861 they followed the census enumerator on his round, not only into the country at large and into the more respectable areas of London, but also into a Gray's Inn Lane tenement and a workhouse casual ward, and to the bottom of the social heap—the destitute who had spent the night in St James's Park or under the dark arches of the Adelphi.

Twenty years before, at the time when the *Illustrated London News* and *Punch* were just becoming established, the *Pictorial Times* played the same role. In connection with a particularly bad slump, illustrated with the sketch of a pauper being refused entry to a work-house, the *Pictorial Times* wrote:[59]

> In periods of national prosperity, it is usual to gratify the aggregate vision with pictures of palaces, and amuse the general ear with tales of happiness.

573

> At this moment, when by the operation of wretched financial legislation, our merchant princes are sinking into parish paupers, representation of the workhouse is a subject of national interest—happily for many of the men who were but a few weeks since eminent on 'Change.'

For the *Illustrated London News* the times were always prosperous, the City always healthy. The *Pictorial Times* insisted on digging deeper and bringing to light the inadequacies and iniquities of the new Poor Law, 'peculation and fraud, selfishness and inhumanity.' It denounced the Whigs and the philosophy behind their Act was, it insisted, also a failure in practice.[60] In a series of four illustrations entitled 'The Crime of Poverty and its Punishment' it recorded these results as they affected the 'Aged,' the 'Travelling Poor,' the 'Intelligent Pauper,' and the 'Able-bodied Pauper.' A month later, on 10 October 1846, it led on its front page with a dramatic representation of a mudlark, sketched on the banks of the Thames between Lambeth Palace and Vauxhall Gardens, and accompanied this with a long article on the poverty of the city: 'London is a city of Contrast—not merely poverty, not merely filth, but it is a combination of squalid want, of utter filth and abject misery such as makes the flesh creep again with disgust and horror.' This was the city that the *Illustrated London News* never encountered and *Punch* so quickly forgot.

Even this brief glance at what lay beneath the leading illustrated papers does reveal a vast new source of visual material about the city. It also highlights the complexities related to the depiction of the city in illustrated journalism. The nuances of change attached to editors and artists are symptomatic of deeper differences of view among and between magazines. The way of seeing of both artist and audience was governed by the techniques available and by the artistic traditions which were conventional to that particular framework. Yet the framework differed from social group to social group. Perhaps by cross-comparing conventions used within particular frameworks we can learn more about the complex of attitudes towards the city present in the groups they represented, and also refine our understanding of the psychological interaction of the city and its inhabitants. The absence of threatening material in the 'Establishment' of the news magazines and their muted and neutralized presence in its comic equivalent, makes more probable, in contrast with less formal journals, what might otherwise be inferred, that there were some frightening aspects of the new city which their middle-class readers were not willing to face up to. The suppressed nervousness about the new and inescapable environment, as exhibited by certain classes of city-dweller, is a likely ingredient of Victorian social psychology which needs to be further explored, and examined for its possible effects upon the more overt behavior of its sufferers.

Notes

1 The most scrupulous recent estimate of the urban population of England and Wales shows it to have multiplied very roughly eight times in the course of the nineteenth century, from just over 3 millions to nearly 25½ millions; the population contained in the major cities of 100,000 or more grew over fourteen times, that in the smaller places proportionately less (see C. M. Law, 'The Growth of Urban Population in England and Wales, 1801–1911,' Institute of British Geographers, *Transactions and Papers*, No. 41 (1967), 130, 142). The total numbers of serial publications, on the other hand, grew very much faster, over thirty-seven times, from 129 to 4,819. Put another way, whereas there were about 68,500 persons per publication in the country as a whole at the beginning of the nineteenth century, there were only 6,750 at its end. Most of this growth occurred after the repeal of the newspaper stamp duty in 1855, when magazines and reviews rose rapidly towards the numbers of newspapers being published. The best detailed figures we can find to illustrate these trends are shown in the Table.

Table 24.1 *Numbers of serials current in England and Wales during selected years, 1781–1900*

	Magazines and Reviews	Newspapers	Total
1781			76
1791			96
1801			129
1811			171
1821		267	
1831		295	
1841		472	
1851		563	
1861	481	1,102	1,583
1871	638	1,450	2,088
1881	1,097	1,886	2,983
1891	1,778	2,234	4,012
1900	2,328	2,491	4,819

1781–1811 figures compiled from *Tercentenary Handlist of English and Welsh Newspapers, Magazines and Reviews* (1920); 1821–51 figures from *Newspaper Press Directory* for 1861; 1861–1900 figures from the annual issues of *Newspaper Press Directory*.

It is very difficult to be precise about the circulation figures themselves. Richard D. Altick tells us in his illuminating book, *The English Common Reader* (1957), that 'In Great Britain as a whole during the period 1800–30, the annual sale of newspaper stamps had virtually doubled, from sixteen million to thirty million, while the population had grown half as fast, from ten and a half million to sixteen million . . . a much greater spread of the reading habit than is suggested on the face of the stamp returns' (p. 330). The Appendix to Professor Altick's book gathers and comments on a good deal of the available evidence, and his figures dramatize vividly the growth in readership: circulations tended to be in the thousands in the 1820s, tens of thousands in the 1840s and 1850s, in the hundreds of thousands by the 1860s, and reached a million before the end of the century. When related to the growth in numbers of serials current, these figures suggest an exponential climb in periodicals of all kinds. See also A. P. Wadsworth, 'Newspaper Circulations, 1800–1954,' *Transactions of the Manchester Statistical Society*, 9 March 1955, especially Appendix B concerning the stamp returns.

2   At first only the upper and middle classes were allowed to express their views, and the severity of the laws restricting the freedom of the press after the outbreak of the French Revolution reveals how alive the authorities were to the dangers of the press if it was allowed to get into the wrong hands. In the 1820s the attack was mounted on the radical press principally by means of the libel laws; this has been studied in William H. Wickwar, *The Struggle for the Freedom of the Press* (1928). Joel H. Wiener, *The War of the Unstamped* (1969), and Patricia Hollis, *The Pauper Press* (1970), have extended research into the 1830s and have revealed the bitterness of the struggle of the predominantly working-class unstamped press against the stamp taxes. It is worth noting that the tax was only reduced, not abolished, in 1836, and was in fact more strictly enforced; the 'taxes on knowledge' were not finally repealed until the abolition in 1855 of the stamp tax and in 1861 of the excise duty on paper.

3   See Walter E. Houghton, *The Victorian Frame of Mind 1830–1870* (New Haven, 1957), pp. 6–8. This process has also been studied in the context of the early growth of industrialization in Sidney Pollard, *The Genesis of Modern Management* (1965), ch. 5. See, too, E. P. Thompson, 'Time, Work-Discipline and Industrial Capitalism,' *Past & Present*, 38 (1968) and, for a later period, E. J. Hobsbawm, *Labouring Men* (1964), ch. 17.

4   Walter Bagehot, 'Charles Dickens,' *National Review*, vii (1858), 468. Dickens's observation, he believed, paralleled this and entitled him to the role of 'special correspondent for posterity.' Certainly Dickens described the alienation of modern men 'who live solitarily in great cities as in the bucket of a human well' (*The Old Curiosity Shop* (1841), ch. 15).

5   The best available figures to illustrate the very general social level of readership of a score of leading periodicals in 1870 are as follows:

Fortnightly Review	2s. 0d. monthly	2,500 copies
Economist	8d. weekly	4,000
Spectator	6d. weekly	4,000
Westminster Review	6s. 0d. quarterly	4,000
Blackwood's Magazine	2s. 6d. monthly	7,000
Edinburgh Review	6s. 0d. quarterly	7,000
Tomahawk	2d. weekly	10,000
Athenaeum	3d. weekly	15,000
Cornhill Magazine	1s. 0d. monthly	18,000
Fun	1d. weekly	20,000
Saturday Review	6d. weekly	20,000

Punch	3d. weekly	40,000
All the Year Round	2d. weekly	50,000
Chambers' Journal	1½d. weekly	60,000
The Times	3d. daily	63,000
Illustrated London News	5d. weekly	70,000
Leisure Hour	1d. weekly	80,000
Daily Telegraph	1d. daily	190,000
Reynolds' Weekly	1d. weekly	200,000
Lloyd's Weekly	1d. weekly	500,000

Alvar Ellegård, 'The Readership of the Periodical Press in Mid-Victorian Britain,' *Göteborgs Universitets Årsskrift*, lxiii (1957).

6 Similarly, when Hazlitt described *The Times* as 'the lungs of the British Metropolis,' in the *Edinburgh Review* of 1824, he was referring solely to 'the mouthpiece, oracle and echo of the Stock Exchange; the representation of the mercantile interest . . . It takes up no fallen cause, fights no up-hill battle; advocates no great principle . . . it is ever strong upon the strong side.' *The Times* was still being referred to in the 1840s on the Paris Bourse as 'le journal de la Cité.' By the 1840s it was, however, also filling up with reports on the 'Condition of England' question; it attacked the new Poor Law; it was conscious of the evils of sweated labor; and it was altogether more liberal than it was to be after John Walter II's proprietorship (1812–47) had ended. See *The History of The Times* (1950).

7 A phrase used by the radical *Manchester Herald* in its opening number of 31 March 1792 in describing what it vowed to avoid.

8 Charles Knight, *Passages of a Working Life* (1864), III, pp. 246–7.

9 Henry Vizetelly, *Glances Back Through Seventy Years* (1893), I, pp. 233–4.

10 See E. H. Gombrich, *Art and Illusion* (1959), ch. 2, for further examples.

11 ' . . . il y a dans la vie triviale, dans la métamorphose journalière des choses extérieures, un mouvement rapide qui commande à l'artiste une égale vélocité d'exécution.' Charles Baudelaire, 'Le Peintre de la Vie Moderne,' *Figaro*, 26 November 1863. Baudelaire was referring to Constantin Guys who drew in Paris and in the Crimea for the *Illustrated London News*.

12 William Gamble, 'Pictorial Telegraphy,' *Penrose's Pictorial Annual*, iv (1898), 2.

13 Kenneth Lindley, *The Woodblock Engravers* (Newton Abbot, 1970), ch. 6.

14 See Charles Hindley, *The History of the Catnach Press* (1886). He describes the large collection of wood blocks of the 'oddest and most ludicrous character' which were stored in the Catnach premises in Seven Dials: 'Amongst the lot were several well-known places, the scenes of horrible and awful crimes, engravings of debauchery and ill-fame, together with an endless number of different kinds, suitable at the shortest possible notice, to illustrate every conceivable and inconceivable subject' (pp. 257–8).

15 A. S. Hartrick, *A Painter's Pilgrimage Through Fifty Years* (1939), p. 82.

16 Vizetelly, I, p. 237.

17 See Gombrich, op. cit., p. 59, on the relationship between pictures and labels.

18 In copperplate engraving there was a tradition of relabelling and altering the actual plates to save time and money, especially in the production of political broadsides

and lampoons which required immediate retort. The last example cited in George Soames Layard's *Catalogue Raisonné of Engraved British Portraits from Altered Plates* (1927) is a mezzotint of Queen Victoria riding in Windsor Park, in the first state with Lord Melbourne and in the second with the Prince Consort.

19 Charles Dickens, *Bleak House* (1853), ch. 33. Charles Hindley, op. cit., describes the same process with reference to a colliery disaster (p. 259).

20 The power printing press (first introduced on *The Times* in 1814), coupled with Bewick's prior innovation of boxwood blocks cut on the cross, permitted a larger output of good-quality, illustrated papers at lower unit-cost than anything previously available. They were exploited together for the first time when Charles Knight founded his weekly *Penny Magazine* in 1832. The output of two men working an eight-hour day was raised from 1,000 sheets by the old hand-operated press to 16,000 sheets printed on both sides. The culmination of numerous improvements to the printing of cheap illustrated newspapers was the Ingram Rotary Press, an adaptation made by William Ingram, son of the founder of the *Illustrated London News*, to the Walter rotary press. This printed at the rate of 6,500 sheets an hour, cutting, folding, and turning them out complete.

21 Daguerreotypes had been used as the bases for portrait engravings and the occasional topographical view since the 1840s. About 1860, Thomas Bolton, a minor wood-engraver, succeeded in sensitizing the surface of the wood block on which he had a photograph printed from a negative, after a relief by Flaxman. He made the engraving through the photograph as though it had been a drawing in tint on the block. The *Illustrated London News* printed its first application of photography on wood in the edition of 24 August 1861. Thus the original drawing of the artist was preserved and the draughtsmen in the office rendered superfluous, except for improving very sketchy designs. Until the end of the century in England and America, wood-engraving over or through a photograph printed on the face of the block remained the typical way of reproduction for illustration. On 13 September 1879 the *Graphic* printed its first line-block; on 6 September 1884 it ran its first cross-line half-tone, four years after a New York newspaper had done so. Just as new printing and artistic techniques had encouraged Knight to found his *Penny Magazine*, so the mechanization of the reproduction process prompted W. L. Thomas, the editor of the *Graphic*, to start the *Daily Graphic* in 1889. It was the first successful illustrated daily newspaper.

22 Thus Gavarni had to blow up onto the wood block for the *Illustrated London News* Guys's sketches sent from the Crimea.

23 Mason Jackson, *The Pictorial Press: Its origins and progress* (1885), pp. 315–24.

24 William M. Ivins, Jr, *Prints and Visual Communication* (1953), p. 99.

25 Ivins, op. cit., pp. 60–1.

26 Rossetti wrote in 1855 on the proof engraved by the Dalziels of his drawing for 'The Maids of Elfen-Mere': 'That wood-block! Dalziel has made such an incredible mull of it in the cutting that it cannot possibly appear.' Forrest Reid, *The Illustrators of the Sixties* (1927), p. 32. Hubert von Herkomer wrote that the original drawing was cut away, and the only satisfaction left was to 'growl' at the engraver: 'In only too many cases the creed of the latter was "cut through that shower of lines, never mind what the artist drew," with the result that we could barely

recognize our own work.' He described the 'cruel destruction' of his artistic lines for his famous picture in the *Graphic*, 'Sunday at Chelsea Hospital' (Sir Hubert von Herkomer, *The Herkomers* (1910), pp. 82–3). On the other hand, it must be said that no engraver could make a good work out of a bad drawing. After Bewick's time very few artists had a knowledge of the sort of design which could be used for drawing on wood. The principal figures had to be distinctly made out, and black and white were the only means by which a subject could be represented; few artists could manage this with originality. The Dalziels replied to Rossetti's criticisms by pointing out that the artist had used wash, pencil, coloured chalk, and pen and ink 'producing a very nice effect, but the engraved reproduction of this many tinted drawing, reduced to the stern realities of black and white by the printer's ink, failed to satisfy him.' The Brothers Dalziel, *A Record of Fifty Years' Work, 1840–1890* (1901), pp. 86–7.

27   See Francis D. Klingender, *Art and the Industrial Revolution*, edited and revised by Sir Arthur Elton (1968), chs 4–7. This practice of disguising the new industrial buildings in preurban forms was of course common in the actual architecture. Klingender cites an example of the Soho Manufactory of Boulton and Watt. In an aquatint by Francis Eginton in Shaw's *History . . . of Staffordshire* (1798–1801), the buildings are shown standing in what appears to be a splendid park with cattle grazing on the banks of an ornamental lake which is, in fact, the mill pool in disguise (pp. 79–80).

28   See Charles Hindley, *A History of the Cries of London, Ancient and Modern* (1884); Andrew W. Tuer, *Old London Street Cries and the Cries of Today* (1885); William Roberts, *The Cries of London* (1924); Frederick Bridge, *The Old Cryes of London* (1921); Stanford Rayner, *Cries of London* (1929); Mary Webster, 'Francis Wheatley's Cries of London,' *Auction*, iii (1970), 44–9.

29   According to Blanchard Jerrold, *The Life of George Cruikshank* (1882), pp. 90–2, George Cruikshank's contribution had originally appeared as etchings in *Phrenological Illustrations* (1826), *Illustrations of Time* (1827), and *Scraps & Sketches* (1828), all published by the artist himself. There is some dispute as to whether Dowling, the editor of *Bell's Life in London*, ever received full permission from the artist to reproduce them. Certainly Cruikshank received no payment for the transaction.

30   Of course the standards of artistic depiction varied and some of the finest series of character sketches were done abroad by foreign artists, like, for example, those done by Gavarni in the French Revolution of 1848 for the *Illustrated London News*. In fact they were so outstanding that they appeared again in the *Penny Illustrated Paper* for the Revolution of 1870 in Paris.

31   Jerrold, op. cit., p. 93. He even suggests that Cruikshank had an indirect hand in creating *Bell's Life in London* through his connection with its fore-runner, Pierce Egan's *Life in London* (1821). The extent of this connection is under dispute and, according to Egan's recent biographer, Jerrold greatly exaggerates Cruikshank's claims (J. C. Reid, *Bucks and Bruisers* (1971), pp. 52–5). For further examples of the connection between caricature and cheap illustrated literature, see, for example, William Hone, *Aspersions Answered* (1824), p. 49; see also M. Dorothy George, *English Political Caricature 1793–1832* (1959), pp. 257–60.

32   The opening address of the *Illustrated London News*, i (1842), 1.

33 On the installation of the new Chancellor of Cambridge University (*Illustrated London News*, i (1842), 136).

34 *The Economist* in an article entitled 'Speaking to the Eye,' reprinted in the *Illustrated London News*, xviii (1851), 451.

35 *Graphic*, iii (1871), 390.

36 See also Jackson, op. cit., p. 1. 'The child of civilized life looks with delight on his picture book long before he can make out the letters of the alphabet, and the untutored Esquimaux treasures up the stray number of an illustrated newspaper left in his hut by the crew of some whaling ship, though he cannot understand one word of the printed page. But the pictures speak a universal language, which requires no teaching to understand.' That news illustration was value-free, that the 'illusion' was perfect, seems never seriously to have been called into question in nineteenth-century England.

37 The anonymity of the news illustrators only really slipped with the advent of the 'social realist' school of artists who worked on the *Graphic* in the 1870s under W. L. Thomas's editorship. The *Graphic* was praised as much for its 'artistic merit' as for the subjects it tackled. Significantly, it was only then that one hears of complaints against the hack work done by the engravers from illustrators with artistic pretensions like Herkomer, and not before from draughtsmen whose work would lack signature anyway. Furthermore, while Gilbert and Guys worked with great speed, the artists on the humorous magazines, like Keene, went to endless trouble to get the right pens, washes, and paper for their drawings. The news illustrators simply did not have the time for these personal indulgences.

38 See E. H. Gombrich and E. Kris, *Caricature* (1940); also E. H. Gombrich, *Art and Illusion*, ch. 10, and 'The Cartoonist's Armoury,' in *Meditations on a Hobby Horse* (1963). The latter refers mainly to political caricature, the most obvious manifestation of bias. See also M. Dorothy George's introduction on this, in *English Political Caricature to 1792* (1959).

39 Take for instance Thackeray on George Cruikshank: 'For Jews, sailors, Irishmen, Hessian boots, little boys, beadles, policemen, tall Life Guardsmen, charity children, pumps, dustmen, very short pantaloons, dandies in spectacles, and ladies with aquiline noses, remarkably taper waists, and wonderfully long ringlets, Mr. Cruikshank has a special predilection' (*Westminster Review*, xxxiv (1840), 18).
For the artists of *Punch*, according to Ruskin, 'the street corner is the face of the whole earth, and the only two quarters of the heavenly horizon are the east and west—End' (*The Art of England* (1883), Lecture 5 on 'The Fireside').

40 'The caricaturists' virtual immunity from proceedings for libel or sedition which had given such freedom and licence to English caricature in its classic age was inconsistent with the responsibilities of an editor' (M. Dorothy George, *English Political Caricature 1793–1832*, p. 260).

41 Gombrich and Kris, op. cit., pp. 26–7: 'Willingly we may yield to the caricaturist's temptation to us to share his aggressive impulses, to see the world with him, distorted . . . What Freud has taught us about Wit and its relation to the unconscious applies no less to the graphic expression of Wit. For a short respite we cast off the bridles which restrain our aggressive impulses and prescribe the strict path of logic to our thought.'

42 Knight, op. cit., p. 248.

43 *Illustrated London News*, lxvi (1875), 242.

44 This 'school,' of whom the main representatives were Luke Fildes (1844–1927), Frank Holl (1845–88), and Hubert von Herkomer (1849–1914), was apparently much encouraged by the editor himself, W. L. Thomas, to go out and look for subjects. See, for instance, Herkomer's account of Thomas's role in *The Herkomers*, pp. 80–3. Van Gogh much admired their work: 'I always feel greatly attracted by the figures either of English draughtsmen or of English authors because of their Monday-morning like soberness and studied simplicity and solemnity and keen analysis which can give us strength in the days when we feel weak.' (Letter 237 to his brother Theo.) He led a chorus of praise for the 'motives of real significance and truth instead of futilities and fantasies' (Harry Quilter, 'Some "Graphic" Artists,' *Universal Review*, ii (1888), 97–8).

45 See below, p. 573.

46 Charles Dickens, *Master Humphrey's Clock* (1840), ch. 6.

47 See P. J. Keating, *The Working Classes in Victorian Fiction* (1971). Apart from a few isolated examples, such as Thomas Wright's *The Great Unwashed, by 'the Journeyman Engineer'* (1868) or Douglas Jerrold's *St. Giles and St. James* (1851), distinctions among different classes of working men were rarely made in literature until the latter part of the century.

48 Donald J. Gray, in 'The Uses of Victorian Laughter,' *Victorian Studies*, x (1966), 145–76, has advanced psychological reasons as to why comic journalism, along with literary travesty and the writing of nonsense, could afford to be 'teasingly engaged with profoundly disrupting actualities.' Like Gombrich and Kris he argues: 'Finally, however, this laughter was innocuous because it worked to deprive familiar objects of ordinary significance, to confirm rather than to challenge dominant political and social opinion, and to insulate its audience from the threat of disruptive powers which it refused to take seriously.'

49 Henry Mayhew, *London Labour and the London Poor* (1861–2) I, pp. 1–3.

50 See L. Perry Curtis, Jr, *Apes and Angels: The Irishman in Victorian caricature* (Newton Abbot, 1971).

51 See, for the opposite view-point, Richard Hoggart, *The Uses of Literacy* (1957), ch. 3.

52 George Orwell, in his essay on *Charles Dickens* (1939), takes note of the number of jokes in nineteenth-century comic papers dealing with the uppishness of servants: 'For years *Punch* ran a series of jokes called "Servant Gallisms"—turning on the then astonishing fact that a servant is a human being.' He maintains that for a sympathetic character, *Punch* produced a recognizably feudal type.

53 See M. Dorothy George, op. cit., ch. 11. The 'March of Intellect' in general and Brougham in particular, were ridiculed increasingly from 1825, often being tied in with references to new applications of steam-power. See also Dr George's *Catalogue of Political and Personal Satires, 1828–1832* (1954), XI, describing prints nos 15497–17391 in the Department of Prints and Drawings in the British Museum, and her Introduction. The references below are to prints in this volume.

54 15604, 'The March of Intellect' (W. Heath).

55 15604 and 15604†, 'The March of Intellect' (Paul Pry).

56 *Punch*, lviii (1870), 11.

57 *Punch*, lviii (1870), 182.
58 Matthew Arnold, *Culture and Anarchy*, ed. J. Dover Wilson (1960), p. 105.
59 *Pictorial Times*, x (1847), 257.
60 *Pictorial Times*, viii (1846), 136–7.

VI   A Body of Troubles

25   Fact and Fiction in the East End

P. J. Keating

In 1884, addressing a Birmingham audience on the subject of 'Art and the People',
Walter Besant began by making what at any earlier time in the nineteenth century
would have been considered an outrageous confession: 'As regards Birmingham,
Manchester, Sheffield, Glasgow, and any other place where there is a great industrial
population, I know nothing. If, therefore, exception be taken to any expressions of
mine as applied to some other city, I beg it to be remembered that East London alone
is in my mind.'[1] But at this late date his narrow approach was perfectly well understood, for by the mid-eighties the East End of London had become as potent a
symbol of urban poverty (the natural, virtually inevitable, point of reference for
anyone wishing to place the urban working classes), as Manchester had been of
industrial conditions in the 1840s. As with Manchester, novelists and journalists
played crucial roles in establishing an image of the East End which was simple
enough in outline to be grasped immediately by the general public: stark and emotive
enough to stir consciences, yet inclusive enough to contain, in essence, the central
problems already troubling late-Victorian social reformers. The part played by the
popular novelist in this process is of a special, if rather ambiguous, nature. Timing is
of the utmost importance: it is as undesirable for him to be in the vanguard of informed opinion as it is for him to be in the rearguard of public opinion. In addition,
his concern is not merely to purvey the ideas of other more informed or more perceptive men than himself, but rather to refine and simplify those ideas or perceptions
into symbolic images capable of entering the public consciousness with a minimum
of opposition or thought. It would be impossible for him to exist without the ground

already having been prepared by, for instance, the conscientious analyst or dedicated reformer, but they, in turn, can only communicate with a large uninformed public by using the special techniques and understanding of the popular novelist. By crystallizing complex issues into over-simplified yet still valid images the popular novelist becomes an invaluable middleman, skirting the rational debate, of which he is an off-shoot, and appealing, often in the name of reason, directly to the emotions. A similar function may be served by a spectacular public event (in this case, the dock strike or Whitechapel murders), in that it possesses the two essential ingredients of a successful social reform novel—immediate impact *and* lasting mythopoeic quality.

The image of the East End which first emerged during the last two decades of the nineteenth century, and which survives little changed today, was the product of a constant mingling of fact and fiction. It was the creation of Edward Denison, Samuel Barnett, Charles Booth, Walter Besant, Arthur Morrison, and Jack the Ripper.

Earlier in the Victorian period no special significance was attached to the East End. Slum priests, journalists, foreign visitors, and social reformers referred to it frequently but they did not seize upon it as epitomizing central social problems. It existed, in the terms to be used so often later in the century, as a vast neglected area which attracted public attention only at moments of crisis—a particularly severe winter or a cholera outbreak.[2] When the crisis passed the East End passed from view also. For the early- and mid-Victorians, the slum areas of St Giles's, the Seven Dials, Drury Lane, and the Borough, represented working-class London at its worst, and when Whitechapel, St George's-in-the-East, or Bethnal Green were added to the list it was in order to emphasize the wide-spread nature of the life described.[3] Mayhew usually distinguished between the East End and other working-class areas only when this was made necessary by special trade conditions (like those prevailing in the docks or the clothing industry) and it was for the same reason that Charles Kingsley chose the East End as the setting for his gruesome description of a sweater's den in *Alton Locke* (1850). For the slum climax of this novel the reader is moved to South London. Dickens, who is still often wrongly considered as a chronicler of East End life (a misunderstanding which testifies in the strongest possible way to the post-Dickensian image of the East End as *the* home of working-class Londoners), rarely deals extensively with any London district east of Aldgate Pump, the traditional entrance to the East End. In *Sketches by Boz* (1836) Dickens wrote: 'The gin-shops in and near Drury Lane, Holborn, St. Giles's, Covent-garden, and Clare-Market, are the handsomest in London. There is more of filth and squalid misery near these great thoroughfares than in any part of this mighty city.'[4] He never saw cause to revise this early opinion. If we add Southwark to Dickens's list, then these are the principal slum areas in his novels. That he was as familiar with the East End as with all other areas of London is apparent from *The Uncommercial Traveller* where he describes some of his walks in Shadwell and Wapping, but in his novels such areas appear only briefly and then usually in connection with crime or criminals. Captain Cuttle is an exception to this, though the reason for him lodging in the East India Dock Road is obvious enough. More significant are Nancy, who came originally 'from that remote but genteel suburb of Ratcliffe' and who is murdered at Bill Sikes's home in Whitechapel; the opium den of *Edwin Drood*; and, in *Our Mutual Friend*, the Six Jolly Fellowship-Porters, the favourite Limehouse haunt of Gaffer Hexam and Rogue Riderhood.

Dickens's choice of representative London slum areas is interestingly echoed, much later, by James Greenwood, a writer who was very familiar with life in the East End. Pointing out to an ignorant public the prevalence of slums in London, he gives examples from throughout the metropolis, noting that, 'in the East you might take your pick from a hundred examples . . . I should recommend a neighbourhood between Rosemary Lane and Limehouse Hole . . . But it would be fairest, perhaps, to take a slice out of the centre of the city. It is rotten to the core.'[5] If Greenwood had been writing this fifteen years later, he would have rejected the East End in favour of the city only as a conscious reaction against the excessive publicity it was receiving.

In so far as readers in the first half of the century possessed any single dominant image of the world east of Aldgate Pump, it was of Ratcliffe Highway, the notorious thoroughfare that skirted the river from the Royal Mint to Limehouse, and which Dickens described as, 'that reservoir of dirt, drunkenness, and drabs; thieves, oysters, baked potatoes, and pickled salmon'.[6] Famed for its cosmopolitanism, public-houses, and prostitutes, Ratcliffe Highway catered for sailors on shore-leave and provided refuge for the men who systematically plundered the ships as they lay out in the river waiting for their cargo to be transferred by lighters. In 1797 it was estimated that losses by theft amounted annually to half a million pounds, a statistic that prompted traders to form a company for the construction of the East London Docks; the first of which, the West India Docks, were opened in 1802, the last, Millwall Docks, in 1868.[7] Several murder cases early in the century also contributed to the Highway's notorious reputation. The most celebrated took place in 1811 when a sailor named Williams massacred two respectable Ratcliffe families and provoked a public outcry hardly less hysterical than that in Whitechapel nearly three-quarters of a century later. Williams avoided trial by committing suicide, but his body was paraded through Stepney and Wapping before being buried at an East End cross-roads with a stake through his heart.[8] The murders were sufficiently renowned for De Quincey to include them in his masterpiece of the grotesque 'On Murder considered as One of the Fine Arts' (1827).

To the image of Ratcliffe Highway as a place of highly organized plunder and violent murder, Pierce Egan added a further ingredient—the picturesque. *Life in London* (1821), an enormously popular book and play in the 1820s and 30s, and frequently reprinted throughout the century, traces the adventures of the Corinthians, Tom and Jerry, in their rambles through the metropolis. In search of 'a bit of Life at the East End of the Town', they move from ALMACKS in the West to ALL-MAX in the East where 'Lascars, blacks, jack tars, coal-heavers, dustmen, women of colour, old and young, and a sprinkling of the remnants of once fine girls, &c., were all

587

jigging together'.[9] There they drink max [gin] with the sailors, dance with the prostitutes, and swop slang with all and sundry before staggering home to the west.

Egan's contribution to the literature of the East End is two-fold. He established the contrast in the public mind between east and west London and he created an archetype of the Regency or early-Victorian slummer. In the late-Victorian period both of these features are of great importance, but only when the meanings given them by Egan have been entirely transformed. For Tom and Jerry, the young Corinthians out on the spree, the East End is a playground, but a playground normally addicted to pleasure and therefore not merely a show laid on for their benefit. In class terms, the relationship is quite harmless. As the inhabitants of the Highway are all thieves, professional beggars, prostitutes, murderers, or drunkards, the Corinthians cannot be regarded as agents of corruption, and they, in turn, are unlikely to be corrupted by their experiences in ALL-MAX because of their awareness that they are merely satisfying a temporary taste for 'low-life'. When they have had enough they can return to the West End equivalents. The relationship is best summed up by Renton Nicholson's jingle:[10]

> From East-End to West-End
> From worst end to best end.

There is no sense of social conscience involved. As Tom and Jerry discover, each half of the city is enjoying the same pleasures, albeit in entirely different trappings. When the west is bored it can go to marvel at the east, the best can look at the worst; but, in this context, it would be meaningless for the east to participate in the enjoyments of the west, or even desire to do so, for the east is never bored. It is gloriously contented with its lowness.

Real-life Corinthians continued to visit the Ratcliffe Highway for the same purposes as Tom and Jerry until well into the 1860s. Chroniclers such as Captain Donald Shaw and George R. Sims have left records of visits by groups of young bloods, now accompanied by a local detective and professional 'minders', to Paddy's Goose and the Jolly Sailors, where they gazed upon the sailors and prostitutes, and waited eagerly for a fight to break out.[11] The Highway itself was perhaps the greatest attraction: 'The Highway was a shameful sight in the daytime, but at night it was an inferno. Along it passed a continuous procession of drink-sodden sailormen of all races and all creeds and all colours, and the majority of them had brilliantly bedizened and roughly rouged roysteresses hanging on to them. All the oaths of the world rang out upon the night. It was a Babel of Blasphemy.'[12] Both Shaw and Sims see the 1860s as the Highway's final years, and certainly by the next decade it is making way for an entirely different image of the East End. Sims delighted in the irony of Paddy's Goose eventually becoming a Wesleyan mission, but Shaw, writing in 1908, viewed the changing pattern of London night-life with more of the spirit of an ex-Corinthian: 'So extensive indeed has been the transformation, that, if any night-bird of those naughty days were suddenly exhumed, and let loose in Soho, he would assuredly wander into a church in his search of a popular resort, and having come to scoff, might remain to pray, and so unwittingly fall into the goody-goody ways that make up our monotonous existence.'[13] Shaw does not here automatically think of the East End, but he might well have done, for the transformation he so deplored was connected irrevocably with the opening up and exploration of the unknown eastern half of London.

Historians usually consider that the starting point for this upsurge of interest in the East End was the publication of George Sims's newspaper articles, collectively called *How the Poor Live* (1883), and the appearance of the immensely influential *The Bitter Cry of Outcast London* in the same year. But a distinction must be made between the awakening of the public conscience to the problem of urban poverty as a whole, and the almost immediate acceptance of the East End as a symbol of that poverty; for although these two books do refer to the East End they are by no means primarily concerned with it. *The Bitter Cry* concentrates mainly on South London slums, while Sims moves from area to area (the Mint, Borough, and Drury Lane as well as the East End) in much the same way as Dickens and Greenwood had done in their sketches of London life. Furthermore, neither the tone of the books nor the information contained in them represented anything radically new. The mixture of religious emotion, dramatized characterization, graphic descriptions of poverty, and rather hazy statistics, can be found, in like proportion, in many earlier works. The enormous impact they made was largely due to their being published at just the right time. They coincided with the final stage of a process of change in Victorian England which Beatrice Webb described as: 'A new consciousness of sin among men of intellect and men of property; a consciousness at first philanthropic and practical . . . then literary and artistic . . . and finally analytic, historical and explanatory.'[14] Of much more importance than *How the Poor Live* and *The Bitter Cry* in establishing the late Victorian image of the East End was Walter Besant's novel *All Sorts and Conditions of Men* (1882), though, in the wider issue of publicizing slum conditions, the three books should be seen as reacting upon each other.

In *All Sorts and Conditions of Men*, Angela Messenger, the wealthiest heiress in England, whose money comes from a great brewery, in the East End, goes straight from Newnham to Whitechapel where she disguises her true identity and opens a model dressmaker's shop. She is helped by a young man, Harry Goslett, who has also turned his back on an upper-class life and returned to the slums disguised as a cabinet-maker with the intention of discovering his working-class ancestors. Struck by the terrible monotony of the slums, they plan a vast Palace of Delight, which is secretly built by Angela. The novel ends with a ritualistic marriage in the Palace which is attended by all the poor people with whom the two aristocrats have come in contact. It is worth concentrating on this incredible fairy story because out of it came an interpretation of the East End which may be considered as Besant's most original and influential contribution to fiction.

What Besant stresses in his portrait of working-class life is not individual poverty and hardship presented as pathetic case studies, but a generalized total impression in which the essence of East End life is defined entirely in negative terms. He concentrates exclusively on creating an atmosphere of 'meanness' and 'monotony', so much so that the East End is finally seen as one huge cultureless void:[15]

> Two millions of people, or thereabouts, live in the East End of London. That seems a good-sized population for an utterly unknown town. They have no institutions of their own to speak of, no public buildings of any importance, no municipality, no gentry, no carriages, no soldiers, no picture-galleries, no theatres, no opera—they have nothing. It is the fashion to believe that they are all paupers, which is a foolish and mischievous belief, as we shall presently see. Probably there is no such spectacle in the whole world as that of this immense, neglected, forgotten great city of East London . . . Nobody goes east, no one wants to see the place; no one is curious about the way of life in the east. Books on London pass it over; it has little or no history; great men are not buried in its churchyards, which are not even ancient, and crowded by citizens as obscure as those who now breathe the upper airs about them. If anything happens in the east, people at the other end have to stop and think before they can remember where the place may be.

In this and other novels, in his many articles and lectures, and finally in his study *East London* (1901), the message Besant presses home is that the most urgent problem of the East End is not poverty or crime but meanness. Gone entirely are the dramatic slum descriptions of earlier fiction, as are the colourful criminals of Ratcliffe Highway. Gone also is the idea that the East End was merely one slum area among many: it is now regarded not as part of London but as a complete city in its own right; a city of poverty and meanness in the east, set against a city of wealth and culture in the west.

What the East Ender needs, Besant argues, is leadership, contact with the upper classes, and an awareness of art, books, and music, and all of these things can be achieved through vocational education. In *All Sorts and Conditions* Besant captured, just as it was emerging, a dominant mood of late-Victorian England and conveyed it to a large audience in three graphic images—the East End (the urban working class as a mass force), the Palace of Delight (the university settlement) and the upper-class slum worker (consciousness of sin). In each case Besant was drawing upon ideas currently circulating among social reformers. His fundamental faith in education and cultural consciousness had its roots (as, indeed, had the whole of the settlement movement) in Christian Socialism, and in the social theories of Ruskin; while the idea of a Palace of Delight had been conceived, in a less romantic form, by John Barber Beaumont forty years earlier, and plans for its construction were being made at the very time Besant was writing *All Sorts and Conditions*.[16] And most important of all, the image of the East End publicized by Besant came from Edward Denison ('the pioneer of a great invasion')[17] whose strange and tragic life haunted the minds of many East End social workers in the eighties and nineties.

Edward Denison was born in 1840 and educated at Oxford. For four years after leaving university he toured the Continent and on his return to England took a post as Almoner of the Society for the Relief of the Distressed in Stepney. This, his first contact with the poor, deeply shocked him and in 1867 he moved to Philpot Street where he lived among the poor doing what he could to help educate them. After a period of eight months he could no longer bear the loneliness and he accepted an offer to become M.P. for Newark. He died of tuberculosis in 1870. The letters he wrote to his West End friends while living in Philpot Street were published in 1872, and these, together with his practical example, profoundly influenced Besant and many others. At times Denison directly anticipates Besant: 'I imagine that the evil condition of the population is rather owing to the total absence of residents of a better class—to the dead level of labour which prevails over that wide region, than to anything else. There is I fancy less absolute destitution and less crime than in the Newport Market region; but there is no one to give a push to struggling energy, to guide aspiring intelligence, or to break the fall of unavoidable misfortune.' Poverty and suffering were not seen by Denison as the most evil aspects of East End life; they were, rather, 'its uniform mean level, the absence of anything more civilising than a grinding organ to raise the ideas beyond the daily bread and beer, the utter want of education, the complete indifference of religion'. Open-handed charity and well-meaning philanthropy were useless because 'the lever has to be applied from a distance, and sympathy is not strong enough to bear the strain'. The answer to the problem was, as Denison demonstrated, to go and live in the East End, to work in the same manner, though he himself does not use the image, as an African missionary. Finally he saw the East End as a complete city, cut off from the rest of London: 'Stepney is on the Whitechapel Road, and the Whitechapel Road is at the east end of Leadenhall Street, and Leadenhall is east of Cornhill, so it is a good way from fashionable, and even from business London.'[18]

Twenty-five years after Denison wrote these words they reappeared in the Introduction to Arthur Morrison's *Tales of Mean Streets* (1894): 'The East End is a vast city, as famous in its way as any the hand of man has made. But who knows the East End? It is down through Cornhill and out beyond Leadenhall Street and Aldgate Pump, one will say: a shocking place, where he once went with a curate.' The line of influence that stretches from Denison (the isolated saint-like figure whose letters were widely read in the seventies), through Besant (who publicizes a new image of the East End in the eighties), to Arthur Morrison (whose short stories and novels establish the tone of slum fiction in the nineties), is an important one. Morrison belongs to the second generation of East End explorers, and is open to the influence of a whole range of social and literary influences which Denison and Besant, as pioneers, helped to formulate. The most potent of these influences was the exploration of the East End and the sociological examination of the working man.

591

'It seems incredible now', James Adderley wrote in 1910, 'that it should have been thought something very extraordinary to propose to live in the East End, if you were not obliged to do so, but it certainly was twenty five years ago when I went to live there as a layman.'[19] The approximate date chosen by Adderley, 1885, is the crucial one. In that year Toynbee Hall had been officially opened, an event which was a personal triumph for Samuel Barnett, who, when he accepted the living of St Jude's, Whitechapel, in 1873, had been warned by his Bishop that 'it is the worst parish in my diocese, inhabited mainly by a criminal population.'[20] It was also largely due to Barnett's influence that one year earlier the Universities Settlement Association had been registered and the breakaway settlement Oxford House established. In 1886 Charles Booth began work on his great survey of East End life, and the following year the Queen officially opened the People's Palace in the Mile End Road. Sir Edmund Hay Currie, with a distinguished career in philanthropic work already behind him, was placed in charge of administration and Besant became editor of the *Palace Journal*, and for a while it actually looked as though a fairy story was to come true. Also in 1887 the Salvation Army, originally founded by William Booth after a visit to the East End in 1865, announced a change of policy which emphasized social reform as an essential prerequisite to the saving of souls, a new concern with reality that culminated with Booth's *In Darkest England and the Way Out* (1890). In the wake of this invasion by settlers, salvationists, and sociologists, came religious missions, philanthropic laymen, university graduates, fashionable slummers, and journalists in such numbers that by 1896 an international survey of urban poverty concluded that, 'Awakening is not needed. Every thinking man has thoughts upon this matter. And along with this realisation has come practical experiment, in many places and on an immense scale, towards a solution.'[21]

From the early eighties onwards it became customary to talk of the East End as somewhere heathen, outcast, and totally neglected by religious leaders and social reformers, thus yoking together the different images advanced by *The Bitter Cry* and *All Sorts and Conditions of Men*. In relative terms such a view was true, but there was also a certain amount of rather empty rhetoric involved, rhetoric which was used to arouse public interest in various causes. When, for instance, Walsham How was appointed to the East London Bishopric in 1879, he declared: 'The Church is *nowhere* in East London',[22] and his cry was taken up repeatedly by other clergymen during the next twenty years, most of whom conveniently forgot about priests such as J. R. Green, Lowder, E. C. Hawkins, and Brooke Lambert, all of whom had been working in the East End long before Bishop How denied their existence. Only Denison seemed to bridge the decades and he, significantly, was both layman and martyr.

But views such as How's were not intended, of course, to be taken literally; they were merely bricks being used to construct a symbolic East End. The ambiguous mood of the eighties has been neatly captured by Henry Nevinson: 'One was carried along by a tide setting strongly towards "social reform," "social economics," and all the various forms of "Socialism" then emerging as rather startling apparitions. There was some talk of a revolution, more of "the workers' rights," most of "Outcast

London".'[23] For the late-Victorians 'Outcast London' epitomized the class conflicts they most feared. A similar situation had existed in the 1840s, when the threat of class warfare had focused attention on the industrial worker. A being distant and strange, the industrial worker, considered in the mass, had carried with him connotations of strength and power. He represented muscle, the furnace, the engine, and demanded reform actively and dramatically. The image of Manchester that obsessed early Victorians was a mixture of power and suffering. The image of East London created in the eighties was entirely different, a mixture of passivity and suffering. Until the late eighties, even Engels had given up all hope of the vast mass of workers gathered in the East End: 'Hitherto the East End was bogged down in passive poverty. Lack of resistance on the part of those broken by starvation, of those who had given up all hope was its salient feature.'[24] Yet the form taken by late-Victorian politics—an inevitable movement towards mass democracy—gave this passivity a new terrifying aspect. It was now no longer physical force that counted, but single votes, mounting one by one into millions. By the late nineteenth century it was not only the two major political parties that had learned this lesson, but also the Socialists and the Trade Unionists. In so far as violence played a part in this new class conflict, it came from the reaction of the Establishment against mass demonstrations, and from the anarchists who pursued a lonely, rather melodramatic path. The east–west contrast (two classes facing each other, *en masse*, across the capital city of the Empire), reflected all of these attitudes, though also much more besides. The London of the mid-Victorians (the London of Dickens in effect) was a mixture of all classes; the slum backed on to the mansion, so that there was always the chance that the rich individual would step round the corner and save a poor individual.[25] By the eighties one crucial aspect of this kind of paternalism had gone. The wealthy individual still had a part to play, but now he had to save a whole class in order to show his sincerity; he needed to stand before the workers and confess his sins, like Ruskin, Denison, or Arnold Toynbee: better still if the west could build permanent bridges to the east to annihilate the contrast altogether. Mass passivity was dangerous, too dangerous to be left to fester, but it possessed advantages also. It meant that awakening could still be brought about along the right West End lines.

Toynbee Hall and the People's Palace represent two contrasting attempts to solve the problem. Barnett's sincerity was unquestionable. Firm in his belief that the poor were better regarded as deprived than debased, he encouraged the expression of a variety of religious and political viewpoints at Toynbee Hall, and urged the young settlers to understand that 'they have come to settle, that is, to learn as much as to teach, to receive as much as to give'.[26] The principal aim of Toynbee Hall was to help the working classes to relieve their state of cultural monotony and to lay the foundations for a University of the East End. The natural comparison was with Oxford and Cambridge in the Middle Ages when the poor scholars had 'crowded in thousands round the feet of the great scholastic teachers',[27] and by appealing mainly to the more respectable members of the East End, Toynbee Hall did achieve some success in setting up scholarships to send its best students to university. But the most important single aspect of Barnett's leadership was his insistence that 'exact knowledge of an area must be gained before anything else can be done'.[28] Settlers were encouraged to conduct sociological research and employ the knowledge obtained to play a full part in the life of the community. The various reform movements in which Toynbee Hall residents participated make an impressive list. They helped to found Whitechapel Public Library in 1892, and conducted publicity campaigns in the 'phossy jaw', dock, and busmen strikes; they worked actively in local government reform, urban development, and the systematic analysis of the causes and extent of poverty in London. J. A. R. Pimlott's description of Toynbee Hall as 'one of the sociological laboratories on the patient work of which legislators and administrators so largely depend',[29] is by no means exaggerated.

The People's Palace was both more idealistic and less successful than Toynbee Hall. It was perhaps inevitable that Besant's fairy-tale Palace, which was to cure the ills of the East End overnight, should have ended in cultural disillusionment: 'Everything did not go on quite well. At the billiard tables, which were very popular, the young men took to betting, and it was thought best to stop billiards altogether. The literary club proved a dead failure; not a soul, while I was connected with the Palace, showed the least literary ability or ambition.'[30] Yet during its brief existence as a cultural catalyst, before it became a technical school, the Palace did attempt to bring a whole new range of experience (art shows, public debates, literary study groups, cheap holidays at home or abroad, and sport), within the reach of the working man; and, albeit radically altered, it does survive today as the only university college in East London.

In the late eighties the attempts by various religious and social reform groups to publicize the life and labour of the people in East London received unexpected help from three spectacular events. The first was the strike by Bryant and May matchgirls led by Annie Besant. In 1888, they tried to create public sympathy for their cause by personally delivering a petition to Parliament. Dressed in their ragged working-clothes they marched through the West End, indicating in the most graphic manner the gulf that separated the two areas of London. Later in the same year five White-chapel prostitutes were savagely murdered by 'Jack the Ripper' and the press of the whole world temporarily directed its attention on the East End. Among others George Bernard Shaw seized the opportunity to stir the conscience of the west: 'The riots of 1886 brought £78,000 and a People's Palace . . . it remains to be seen how much these murders may prove to be worth to the East End in *panem et circenses*. Indeed, if the habits of duchesses only admitted of their being decoyed into White-chapel backyards, a single experiment in slaughterhouse anatomy on an aristocratic victim might fetch in a round half million and save the necessity of sacrificing four women of the people.'[31] For many months the newspapers were obsessed with Jack the Ripper, suggesting bizarre methods by which he might be apprehended, giving intimate details of the lives and deaths of his victims, upbraiding society for allowing the East End to exist and the police for their incompetence. One of the more recent of the many writers who have tried to solve the mystery of Jack the Ripper has claimed that 'the case points to the use of murder as a means of social protest',[32] and further that many of the social reforms of the nineties proceeded directly from the publicity produced by the murders. So long as this type of publicity is considered only as a part of a much wider and more inclusive interest in the East End, there may be some truth in the contention. Of more revelance here is that, coming at a time when social reformers were slowly building up a less sensational picture of East End life, to stress the meanness rather than the poverty, the monotony rather than the violence, the gruesome activities of Jack the Ripper thrust into the public mind an image of East London as somewhere violent and outcast, rather than monotonous and outcast. It represented a movement away from Denison, Besant, and Barnett, and back to the Ratcliffe Highway of the early nineteenth century.

Only a few months after Jack the Ripper had claimed his fifth and final victim, the London Dock Strike showed a more progressive aspect of East End life to set against the retrograde image of the Whitechapel murders; it was an event which caused Engels joyfully to eat his words about the passivity of the East End workers: 'In brief, it is an event . . . a new section enters the movement, a new corps of workers. And the bourgeois who only five years ago would have cursed and sworn must now applaud, albeit dejectedly, while and because his heart is palpitating with fear and trepidation. Hurrah!'[33] Like the matchgirls, the dockers drew attention to their cause by daily meetings on Tower Hill and by marching on the City and West End. The dock strike also tested the faith of settlers and salvationists who responded with sympathy, enthusiasm, and practical aid. Support from institution representatives such as Canon Barnett, Stewart Headlam, William Booth, and Cardinal Manning served both to give a sense of direction to public feeling, and to consolidate the position of the institutions in the East End. But the lesson learned from events such as the strikes by matchgirls and dockers, and the Whitechapel murders was that, in spite of the opportunities offered by settlements and missions, the East End as a whole was still largely misunderstood and neglected. What was required was further detailed, objective knowledge of the East End workers as a class. Symbolic images had served their pioneering purpose and now needed to be brought more in line with reality.

The publication of *East London* (1889), the first volume of Charles Booth's *Life and Labour of the People in London*, marks a culminating point in the discovery of the East End. Whereas earlier writers had relied on emotional arguments to make their case, Booth, for the first time in the nineteenth century, set out to study not the poor but poverty, not the individual but the mass. Panaceas he rejected, his principal purpose being to determine 'the numerical relation which poverty, misery and depravity bear to regular earnings and comparative comfort, and to describe the general conditions under which each class lives'.[34] Although he eventually allowed himself to make certain suggestions for reform he did so 'with much hesitation', believing that his task was to gather, in as objective a manner as possible, the necessary information which would enable others to solve problems. He himself, however, was faced with the difficulty of combating widely held public images:[35]

> East London lay hidden from view behind a curtain on which were painted terrible pictures: Starving children, suffering women, overworked men; horrors of drunkenness and vice; monsters and demons of inhumanity; giants of disease and despair. Did these pictures truly represent what lay behind, or did they bear to the facts a relation similar to that which the pictures outside a booth at some country fair bear to the performance or show within? This curtain we have tried to lift.

Out of a total population of 908,959 Booth estimated that only 1·2 percent could be classified under section A ('the lowest class of occasional labourers, loafers and semi-criminals'), while the largest single group, E, consisting of those workers living above the line of poverty and drawing a regular wage, comprised 42·3 percent of the total. The upper-middle class, H, accounted for only 5·0 percent, and more than two-thirds of this group lived in Hackney. The most disturbing of Booth's statistics showed that 35·2 percent (groups A–D inclusive) lived in conditions of poverty. Taken as a whole, Booth concluded, the proportion of those who lived in 'comfort' to those who lived in poverty was approximately 65/35 percent.[36] Separate areas, however, showed enormous variations. Hackney stood completely apart with its 'well-to-do suburban population'; and while the poverty level fell to 24·6 percent in Mile End Old Town, it rose to 49·1 percent in Whitechapel and to a horrifying 58·7 percent in Bethnal Green.[37]

We can see from these statistics that the image of the East End set out by Denison and Besant (predominantly an area of monotonous and bleak respectability, interspersed with sections of terrible suffering, a relatively small but vicious criminal element, and virtually no upper-middle-class members to provide a lead or contrast) was, in the main, vindicated by Booth's survey, although, of course, Besant had exaggerated the lack of cultural expression in the East End and ridiculously underplayed the degree of poverty. On the other hand, Sims and the author of *The Bitter Cry* had stressed the degrading poverty virtually to the exclusion of all else. The total portrait is graphically illustrated by Booth's maps, on which the East End is represented by various shades of blue and grey, varied only by streaks of black, while the black patches of the West End are swamped by a brilliant orange.

The true importance of Booth's work was that it destroyed myths, allowing moral and emotional appeals statistical support if they were strong enough to bear it, and the possibility of refutation if they were not. In examining the 'life' as well as the 'labour' of the people (with the keen sense of observation and deep sympathy for the working classes that constantly emerge in spite of his objectivity in purely statistical matters), he was able to refrain from offering standard moral condemnations, and give some much-needed publicity to the happier features of East End life—the theatres, music-halls, public-houses, and the enthusiastically attended Sunday debates in Victoria Park. Perhaps his greatest single achievement was that once and for all he destroyed the view that the working classes were morally debased. We have already seen that his basic analysis showed that only 1·2 percent of the population could be classified as such, and his study of the causes of poverty led to a similar conclusion. In groups A and B only 4 percent were described as 'loafers', while 55 percent suffered from 'questions of employment', 27 percent from 'questions of circumstance' (e.g. illness), and 14 percent from 'questions of habit' (e.g. drunkenness). In groups C and D the loafers disappear entirely and 'questions of employment' are shown to cause the poverty of 68 percent, circumstances 19 percent, and habits 13 percent.[38] Finally, as volume after volume of the survey appeared, it became clear that the poverty level of East London was not so much greater than that of London as a whole (35·2 percent compared to 30·7 percent), while certain areas of Southwark, Greenwich, and Goswell Road were worse even than Bethnal Green.[39] As an isolated city of the working classes, the East End remained a special case, as Booth's survey had shown; but the survey had also shown that, so far as the question of poverty in London as a whole was concerned, it was misleading to give an exaggerated importance to the East End. Yet in spite of this the nineties brought more public attention to the East End than ever before.

Rudyard Kipling and Arthur Morrison were the first novelists, belonging emphatically to the 1890s, to deal with the East End. Kipling's grim picture of Gunnison Street in 'The Record of Badalia Herodsfoot' which appeared in *Harper's Weekly* (November 1890), was widely regarded as inaugurating a new, frank approach to the subject, but Kipling did not go on to write further stories of this kind and it was left to Arthur Morrison (who had already begun to publish sketches of East End life) to establish the tone of slum fiction in the nineties. Very little of a personal nature is known about Morrison's early life, but it is now clear that he was born in Poplar in 1863, the son of an engine fitter, and that almost certainly some of his childhood was spent in the East End.[40] For two years, from early 1887, Morrison worked as a clerk at the People's Palace where he met Walter Besant and acted as sub-editor of the *Palace Journal*. In an article called 'Whitechapel', published in the *Palace Journal*, 24 April 1889, Morrison mockingly rejected two common descriptions of the East End —the first, that of a criminal ghetto, 'the catacombs of London—darker, more tortuous, and more dangerous than those of Rome, and supersaturated with foul life': the second, outcast London, 'black and nasty still, a wilderness of crazy dens into which pallid wastrels crawl to die'. At this stage Morrison was more concerned with rejecting the 'graphically written descriptions of Whitechapel, by people who have never seen the place', than with advancing any original interpretation of his own. This he did in October 1890 when he published an article called 'A Street' in *Macmillan's Magazine*, which, carefully revised to make it even more austere in tone, later became the introduction to *Tales of Mean Streets* (1894):

> Of this street there are about one hundred and fifty yards—on the same pattern all. It is not pretty to look at. A dingy little brick house twenty feet high, with three square holes to carry the windows, and an oblong hole to carry the door, is not a pleasing object; and each side of this street is formed by two or three score of such houses in a row, with one front wall in common. And the effect is as of stables.

Morrison's studies of East End life combine Besant's bleak monotony, an awareness of small intimate detail that came from personal knowledge of the scene described, and Charles Booth's sociological care in distinguishing between the many contrasting ways of life to be found in the East End as a whole. The East End is now seen as a vast area of seemingly never-ending streets where the barely sufficient creates stultifying respectability, rather than squalid suffering. Poverty and violence are neither heightened nor glossed over: they are placed with care and precision. Above all else Morrison was determined to write of working-class life in terms of its own attitudes and values, with the result that the actual inhabitants of the mean streets become the centre of concern in his stories and Besant's conscience-stricken upper-class philanthropists, acting out their bizarre slum pastoral, disappear entirely. Unfortunately for the literary image of the East End, 'Lizerunt', the one really violent story in *Mean Streets*, received more than its fair share of publicity, without being read, as it should be, in relation to the other stories in the collection. In spite of Morrison's furious denial that he had 'generalised half London as a race of Yahoos',[41] the damage was done, and meanness and violence became inextricably associated in the public mind.

A Child of the Jago (1896), Morrison's second working-class novel, was intended, in part, as a reply to those who had misinterpreted *Mean Streets*. Violence is now placed at the very centre of the novel, but Morrison goes out of his way to stress that he is dealing with an exceptional, if historically explicable, aspect of East End life. The Jago (in real life the Old Nichol, situated on the boundary of Bethnal Green and Shoreditch) is a criminal ghetto, a plague spot that threatens the neighbouring districts: 'What was too vile for Kate Street, Seven Dials, and Ratcliff Highway in its worst day, what was too useless, incapable and corrupt—all that teemed in the Jago.'[42] *A Child of the Jago* represents the final rejection of the earlier Ratcliffe Highway image of the East End. In Morrison's novel the Highway has shrunk from a mile-long stretch of infamous pubs and brothels to a tiny slum area fighting a rearguard action against the moral force of Father Sturt and the physical power of the London County Council. Sturt and the L.C.C. inevitably win (as Morrison was writing the novel, blocks of working-class flats were rising on the site of the Old Nichol) but their victory is not total: most of the inhabitants of the Jago refuse to be absorbed into this new, strange way of life, and wander off to seek yet one more last stronghold, spreading their violent ways thinly through the dull monotony of the mass. In the space of eighty years they have been transformed from the norm to the exception. In *To London Town* (1899), the final novel of his East End trilogy, Morrison attempted to find a middle way between monotony and violence, but the novel is hardly a success, and merely emphasizes the originality of his earlier work, in which he became the first English novelist to explore the crucial relationship between these two aspects of working-class life. When he returned to the theme of East End violence in *The Hole in the Wall* (1902) he significantly gave the novel an historical setting.

Following the success of Morrison's early work, novels and short stories about the

East End flooded on to the market. Not all of the new authors were simply following a current fashion. Henry Nevinson was the most unlucky. His collection of short stories *Neighbours of Ours* (1895) had been ready for publication two years earlier but a delay by his publisher allowed Morrison's *Mean Streets*, 'to beat us by a week, with the result that mine was praised and his was bought'.[43] Nevinson's cynical tone is understandable: *Neighbours of Ours*, written entirely in cockney phonetics, never received the acknowledgment it deserved, and even today remains completely over-shadowed by Morrison's more dramatic work. Israel Zangwill had also begun to explore a prominent, though in literary terms neglected, aspect of East End life— the mysterious, enclosed world of the Jewish immigrant—in *Children of the Ghetto* (1892), *Ghetto Tragedies* (1893), *They That Walk in Darkness* (1899), and a host of others. And writers such as Arthur St John Adcock in *East End Idylls* (1897) and *In the Image of God* (1898), and William Pett Ridge, *A Son of the State* (1900), made serious attempts to follow Morrison in his austere studies of the relationship between monotony, respectability, and violence in East End life. James Adderley, in a preface to Adcock's *East End Idylls*, expressed what by this time had become the common point of view:[44]

> The East End remains unique in one respect. Poverty lives by herself there: she is monarch of all she surveys. Street upon street drags out its monoto- nous length quite unrelieved. For though Whitechapel Road is broad it is squalid, and cannot compare with Oxford Street or Regent Street as a brilliant set-off to the poverty close by; and Victoria Park, with all its peculiar attractiveness, cannot be mentioned in the same breath with its sister 'Hyde' or with Kensington Gardens.
>
> No: there is a dulness and a sadness in East London, peculiarly its own.

But the greater part of the fiction about the East End produced in the late nineties was the work of camp-followers, who took the basic ingredients from Morrison, added a dash of Besant's peculiar brand of philanthropic romance or a melodramatic plot, and concocted bizarre travesties of Morrison's seriously inten- tioned work: K. Douglas King, *The Scripture Reader of St. Mark's* (1895) and *Father Hilarion* (1897); Joseph Hocking, *All Men are Liars* (1895) and *The Madness of David Baring* (1900); R. O. Prowse, *A Fatal Reservation* (1895); Morley Roberts, *Maurice Quain* (1897); J. Dodsworth Brayshaw, *Slum Silhouettes* (1898); Harry Lander, *Lucky Bargee* (1898); Harley Rodney, *Hilda: A Study in Passion* (1898); John A. Steuart, *Wine on the Lees* (1899); and John Le Breton, *Unholy Matrimony* (1899), can stand as representatives. In these novels lip-service is paid to the image of the East End as a city of working men but is immediately denied by the arbitrary violence, caricatured working-class relationships and the prominence given to upper-class heroes and heroines who find love, class-responsibility, spiritual redemption, or simply long lost relatives, in the monotonous East End.[45] Informed reviewers were quick to point out that whole areas of East End life were being ignored by novelists. George Haw, in particular, noted the significant omission of the East End's 'manifold industries':

'For, after all, the East-end is the workshop of London. The East-end pulsates with industry. The East-end is for ever busy and for ever useful. It is all-enduring, full of wondrous patience. Its real people labour, they do not loaf; they toil, they do not thieve. Labour here is very laborious, and the pulse of energy knows little slackening.'[46] But the literary image had been too firmly established for this kind of perfectly just criticism to have much effect. It was left for a later generation of explorers to extol the variety and colour, the industry and activity of East End life; for the late-Victorians, monotony and meanness were its predominant characteristics.

Not all working-class fiction of the 1890s was set in the East End. Somerset Maugham's *Liza of Lambeth* (1897) is an obvious exception: and the hero of Richard Whiteing's *No. 5 John Street*, one of the best-selling novels of 1899, who wishes to live for a while in the slums, deliberately rejects an East End settlement as 'a mere peep-hole into the life I wanted to see', and chooses instead a nearby slum in Mayfair. Nor were books as variously interesting as George Moore's *Esther Waters* (1894), William Pett Ridge's *Mord Em'ly* (1898), Clarence Rook's *The Hooligan Nights* (1898), and Edwin Pugh's *Mother–Sister* (1900), set in the East End. But what is so striking is that, whether the greater part of the slum fiction of the 1890s is set in the East End or not, it is Morrison's interpretation of the East End slum environment that predominates.

There were many attempts to challenge the monopoly held by the East End. As we have seen, Charles Booth had shown that many other areas of London were equally poverty-stricken, and Arthur Sherwell, in his study *Life in West London* (1897) claimed that Soho was the 'terra incognita' of London and supported his argument with an impressive collection of statistics. But by the very nature of its frequency this kind of response merely serves to emphasize the symbolic importance of the East End in this period, too central to be easily replaced, too firmly established for denials to have much effect. As James Adderley wrote in 1897: 'People say that they are tired of hearing of the East End. Certainly there has been much written and said about that part of London during the past twelve years, but as certainly not *too* much.'[47] One year earlier, while trying to draw attention to poverty in other parts of London, Robert A. Woods had noted the essential point. In moving from the City to the East End, he wrote, 'one feels a sudden chill, as when passing out of a warm breeze into another with a touch of winter in it . . . East London will still continue to be thought of in a special way as the nether London.'[48]

Notes

Some sections of this chapter are reprinted from my book *The Working Classes in Victorian Fiction* (1971).

1   Walter Besant, *As We Are and As We May Be* (1903), p. 248.
2   There were serious cholera outbreaks in the East End in 1849, 1855, and 1866. This last was the most severe, with the death-rate in the St George's district alone rising to 37·5 per 1,000. Cholera, however, was not the only cause of premature

death in the East End during the middle years of the century. One slum priest argued that more people died of starvation, resulting from unemployment, than were killed by cholera. See R. H. Hadden, *An East-End Chronicle* (1880), pp. 88–9.

3   There are, of course, exceptions to this generalization. Among novelists the most striking is Augustus Mayhew whose *Kitty Lamere* (1855) and *Paved With Gold* (1858) are both set in East London. Of the many social explorers during this period only Hector Gavin in his remarkable house-by-house survey of Bethnal Green, *Sanitary Ramblings* (1848), regarded the East End as a special case; though many Bible-women and tract distributors also saw it as a particularly deprived area. See Mrs Mary Bayly, *Ragged Homes and How to Mend Them* (1859), *The Ministry of Women and The London Poor* (1870), and L.N.R. [Mrs Ellen Ranyard], *The Missing Link* (1859), ch. 10.

4   Ch. 22.

5   *In Strange Company* (1873), pp. 180–1.

6   *Sketches by Boz*, ch. 21.

7   Sir William Foster, *East London* (Historical Association Pamphlet, No. 100, 1935), p. 14. 'According to Patrick Colquhuon, the contemporary authority on mercantile affairs, over 10,000 persons took a nefarious living from the Pool around 1800, not to mention whatever proportion of the 120,000 persons officially employed in the port was hand-in-glove with the thieves.' H. J. Dyos and D. H. Aldcroft, *British Transport: An economic survey from the seventeenth century to the twentieth* (Leicester, 1969), p. 57.

8   Millicent Rose, *The East End of London* (1951), p. 212.

9   Ch. 12.

10   *Autobiography of a Fast Man* (1863), p. 86.

11   *London in the Sixties by One of the Old Brigade* [Captain Donald Shaw] (1908); George R. Sims, *Glances Back* (1917).

12   Sims, op. cit., p. 26.

13   Shaw, op. cit., p. 1.

14   *My Apprenticeship* (1950 edn), p. 154.

15   *All Sorts and Conditions of Men* (1882).

16   See Fred W. Boege, 'Sir Walter Besant: Novelist, Part One', *Nineteenth Century Fiction*, x (March 1956), 266–9; also the obituary notice of Sir Edmund Hay Currie, *East End News*, 13 May 1916.

17   Besant, *As We Are and As We May Be*, p. 247.

18   Sir Baldwyn Leighton, ed., *Letters and Other Writings of Edward Denison* (1872), passim.

19   *The Parson in Socialism* (Leeds, 1910), p. 173.

20   Henrietta Barnett, *Canon Barnett* (2 vols, 1918), I, p. 68.

21   *The Poor in Great Cities: Their problems and what is being done to solve them* (1896), p. viii.

22   Frederick How, *Bishop Walsham How* (1899), p. 129.

23   *Changes and Chances* (1923), p. 78.

24   Friedrich Engels in a letter to E. Bernstein, 22 August 1889, *Marx and Engels on Britain* (Moscow, 1962), pp. 566–7.

25   This kind of class relationship, so common in early- and mid-Victorian fiction, is epitomized by the popular comparison of St Giles and St James's. John Leech

employed it for his social conscience sketch, 'St. James turning St. Giles out of his Parks', *Punch*, xix (1850), 167; and Douglas Jerrold for the title of his novel, *St. Giles and St. James* (1851).

26 Henrietta Barnett, I, p. 302.

27 Ibid., II, p. 14.

28 A. F. Young and E. T. Ashton, *British Social Work in the Nineteenth Century* (1956), p. 233.

29 J. A. R. Pimlott, *Toynbee Hall: Fifty years of social progress 1884–1934* (1935), p. 95.

30 Besant, *Autobiography* (1902), p. 246.

31 Quoted in Robin Odell, *Jack the Ripper in Fact and Fiction* (1965), p. 51.

32 Tom Cullen, *Autumn of Terror* (1965), p. 243.

33 *Marx and Engels on Britain*, p. 567.

34 *East London* (1889), p. 6. The second volume of *Life and Labour* which examined East End poverty in relation to London as a whole appeared in 1891.

35 Ibid., pp. 591–2.

36 Ibid., pp. 32–62.

37 *Life and Labour*, II, p. 25.

38 *East London*, pp. 146–9.

39 *Life and Labour*, II, pp. 18–39.

40 See P. J. Keating, 'Arthur Morrison: A Biographical Study', Introduction to *A Child of the Jago* (1969).

41 In a letter to the *Spectator*, lxxiv (16 March 1895).

42 Ch. 1.

43 *Changes and Chances*, p. 117.

44 Adderley also wrote two rather feeble novels which proclaim the advent of a new phase of Christian Socialism, and in which the same view of the East End is advanced: *Stephen Remarx: The story of a venture in ethics* (1893), and *Paul Mercer: A story of repentance amongst millions* (1898).

45 Besant's view of upper-class slumworkers in *All Sorts and Conditions of Men* was essentially secular and non-intellectual. The novel which played a large part in bringing to public attention the changing attitudes of priests and intellectuals towards social-reform work was Mrs Humphry Ward's *Robert Elsmere* (1888). It is by working in the East End that the hero of this novel discovers a new purpose in life and a new meaning in religion.

46 'The Novelist in the East-End', *Weekly Sun Literary Supplement*, 6 December 1896.

47 Preface to *East End Idylls*.

48 Robert A. Woods, 'The Social Awakening in London', *The Poor in Great Cities*, pp. 1–3.

26   Unfit for Human Habitation

Anthony S. Wohl

The participation of doctors in local government is of particular significance to the urban historian, for, throughout much of the nineteenth century, medical officers of health[1] represented professional training and skills in what were otherwise predominantly amateur and part-time urban governments. The medical officers of health, with their highly specialized education and increasing competence in preventive medicine, gave local government in the second half of the nineteenth century an authority and expertise hitherto lacking, and they supplied a lead in the agitation for, and administration of, sanitary legislation which laymen were quick to follow. As a group they stood in the forefront of vigorous urban administration, and played a critical role in the development of civic government.

The place of doctors in the early public-health movement and their growing concern with urban pathology have been carefully studied, and the contribution of Simon and the reports on living conditions in London by the doctors Arnott, Kay, and Southwood-Smith for the Poor Law Commission (in which the connection between overcrowding and disease was first made in an official document) are well known.[2] The work of medical men such as Southwood-Smith, Hector Gavin, and William Guy was crucial in the development of public awareness of urban social ills, and doctors—Liddle, Aldis, Barnett, Tite, Gavin, and Guy—were prominent on the central committee of the Health of Towns Association, of which Southwood-Smith was vice-president. Yet one must agree with Southwood-Smith that during the first half of the nineteenth century medical men failed to play that 'active part in promoting sanitary reform which the obligations of knowledge, and the duties arising

603

out of their particular profession require them to take.'[3] It was not until after mid-century, with the compulsory appointment of medical officers throughout London, the skillful use of medical specialists by John Simon at the medical department of the Privy Council, and the transformation of the health section of the National Association for the Promotion of Social Science into a pressure group for sanitary reforms by various medical officers of health and by doctors Rumsey and Stewart, that doctors began to guide the development of public-health legislation and administration.[4] The influence of the medical profession as a whole upon the growth of urban sanitary regulation is too great to cover within the confines of this paper. Instead I shall concentrate on the medical officers of health and their attitude towards and influence upon the gravest problem which beset Victorian London—overcrowding.

In the past the contribution of the medical officers of health has been blotted out by the dazzling brilliance of their most prominent member, Sir John Simon, who rose to national prominence as medical officer of health for the City of London, and who advanced the cause of public health as Medical Officer to the General Board of Health, the Privy Council, and the Local Government Board. Since Simon's brilliant espousal of sanitary reform has been so well recorded, I shall focus upon the other medical officers for London, 'the men, who though now often forgotten, were the tools with which Simon forged his national armour against the unforeseen vices of exuberant industrialization.'[5] It is time they were given the center of the stage.

In the first half of the nineteenth century, although there were Poor Law medical officers (who had no powers of house visitation), and, in times of crisis like the 1831–2 cholera epidemic, local boards of health with medical officers on them, there was no general legislation empowering local bodies to establish medical officers of health. Chadwick, in his 1842 report on the sanitary condition of England, had recommended the appointment of local medical officers, although he generally placed far greater faith in sanitary engineers than in doctors. The Health of Towns Association agitated for the appointment in London of health officers, and the Royal Commission on the Health of Towns made a similar recommendation. The *Lancet* also called for the establishment of medical officers to help cure 'the insalubrity of streets and dwelling-houses.'[6]

The first local medical officer of health in England was Dr William Henry Duncan, appointed by Liverpool under a private Act, the Liverpool Sanitary Act, in 1847. The following year the City of London was granted power, under the City Sewers Act, to appoint a medical officer, and selected Simon. Simon's energetic battle against filth and high death-rates won the support of the City Corporation, and his annual reports drew the nation's attention to urban housing problems and to the value of having a local officer of health. In the same year, 1848, the Public Health Act permitted the creation of local boards of health. Leicester (1849) and Ware (1849) quickly appointed medical officers, but around London only Tottenham (1853) and Uxbridge (1854) did so. In 1855 the Metropolis Management Act made them compulsory throughout London.[7] Not until 1872 were local governments throughout England required to appoint medical officers.

The Metropolis Local Management Act required that every vestry and district board should 'appoint one or more legally qualified Medical Practitioner or Practitioners of Skill and Experience to inspect and report periodically upon the Sanitary Condition of their Parish or District.' Although an M.D. degree was not required, the Act implied that the appointee should be a man of professional competence. The 1875 Public Health Act required medical officers to be registered doctors, and, under the Local Government Act of 1888, medical officers to a county or district with a population over 50,000 had to be qualified doctors holding a Diploma of Public Health or its equivalent. The creation of these officers stimulated public-health courses in medical schools, and these in turn raised the officers' standard of professional competence. In response to agitation by the medical officers of health, St Thomas's Hospital created a Lectureship in Public Health in 1855 and appointed the authority on preventive medicine, Dr Edward Headlam Greenhow, who later filled a similar post at Middlesex Hospital.[8] The uncertain status of public health within the medical profession can be gauged by the fact that the St Thomas's Lectureship was unpaid. But as the work of the medical officer became more complex and better appreciated, the need for specialized training became increasingly urgent. In 1875 the first English Diploma in Public Health was established at Cambridge University (Trinity College, Dublin had introduced the D.P.H. in 1870), and many other institutions followed Cambridge's lead, so that in 1886 the General Medical Council (the central superintending body in British medicine) formally registered the Diploma in Public Health as a medical degree. Two years later it became a requirement for all medical officers of large districts.[9]

The examination for the Diploma in Public Health at Cambridge was exacting and its comprehensiveness reveals the broad duties of the medical officers. Part One tested candidates in physics and chemistry; methods of analysis of air and water; applications of the microscope; laws of heat; principles of pneumatics, hydraulics, and hydrostatics; ventilation; water supply; drainage; construction of dwellings; disposal of sewerage and refuse; and sanitary engineering in general. Part Two consisted of an examination in the statutes regulating public health; sanitary statistics; the origin, propagation, and prevention of epidemics and infectious diseases; effects of overcrowding, unhealthy occupations, vitiated air, and impure water and food; nuisances injurious to health; water supply and drainage; the distribution of diseases within the country; and the effects of soil, season, and climate. This training, combined with their regular medical education, gave the officers an expertise which contrasted sharply with the amateur administrations in which they served.

Since the 1855 Act did not fully define the duties of the medical officer, the General Board of Health issued the following instructions:[10]

> The officer of health is appointed in order that through him the local
> sanitary authority may be duly informed of such influences as are setting

against the healthiness of the population of his district, and of such steps as medical science can advise for their removal; secondly, to execute such special functions as may devolve upon him by the statute under which he is appointed; and, thirdly, to contribute to that general stock of knowledge with regard to the sanitary condition of the people, and to the preventible cause of sickness and mortality which, when collected, methodised, and reported, Parliament by the General Board of Health, may guide the legislature in the extension and amendment of sanitary law.

Gradually, both as a consequence of legislation and as a natural development of public health requirements, the duties of the medical officer grew, until he had under his supervision water supply and its purity; drainage; the cleanliness and healthiness of houses; overcrowding; domestic and industrial nuisances; workshop regulations; food analysis; registration of diseases, births, and deaths; control of epidemics; regulation of disinfecting machines; milk supply; vaccinations; slaughter-houses; cemeteries and mortuaries; collection of street refuse; street-cleaning; public conveniences; bake-houses; baths and wash-houses; and the issue of model by-laws. The medical officers generally divided their reports into major categories according to duties; thus the reports of the medical officer of health for Westminster were usually organized in the following manner: Part One. A. Vital Statistics. B. Communicable Diseases. Part Two. C. House Property, etc. (with a sub-section devoted to the housing of the working classes). D. Workshops, etc. E. Food Supply. F. General (smoke prevention, cemeteries, etc.). The essential function, however, was the *prevention*, as distinct from the *cure* of diseases. 'Let us never forget,' the President of the Society of Medical Officers of Health urged his colleagues in 1878, 'that, as medical officers of health, we are practitioners of *preventive medicine*, and nothing else.'[11]

The medical officer had one or more sanitary inspectors—called by contemporaries 'medical police'—under him, and it was their duty to make house-to-house visitations, either alone, or with the medical officer. The appointment of an inspector of nuisances was compulsory under the Metropolis Management Act, but no qualifications for the office were set, and neither the 1875 Public Health Act nor the Local Government Act of 1888, both of which set professional requirements for the medical officers, did likewise for the inspectors who carried out many of the daily sanitary duties. The certificate of the Sanitary Institute remained a desirable but entirely optional proof of competence, and as late as 1889 the Mansion House Council on the Dwellings of the Poor complained that, despite recent improvements in their education and training, there were still too many inspectors of the old type, 'men whose antecedents and technical knowledge are altogether inadequate for the important duties they are called upon to fulfill.'[12] The standard of the inspectors of nuisances rose towards the end of the century and by 1900 there were few rank amateurs—ex-sailors, ex-soldiers, and retired policemen—among their number, and far more professionally qualified men.[13] Great advances were also made in the number of inspectors whom the vestries provided for the medical officers. Shortly after mid-century, for example, St Pancras, with a population of 200,000, and Bethnal Green, with 100,000 inhabitants, had only one inspector each.[14] At the end of the century there was an average of one inspector for every 20,000 people (the worst vestry was Paddington, with one inspector for every 4,829 inhabited houses and every 39,282 inhabitants; the best was the City, with one inspector per 575 inhabited houses and 3,750 inhabitants): the 51 medical officers of health in London were assisted by 256 sanitary inspectors.[15] Between 1885 and 1892 every local authority with the exception of St Olave's and St Martin's-in-the-Fields had doubled, trebled, or quadrupled its staff of inspectors.[16]

The inadequacy for much of the second half of the nineteenth century of the medical officers' staff reflects the vestries' attitudes towards the novel concept of preventive medicine and their determination to obey cherished precepts of low rates and laissez faire. The Metropolis Local Management Act specifically placed the medical officers' tenure and removal at the pleasure of the vestry, which created a delicate and anomalous situation, for, as the *Pall Mall Gazette* commented, it was widely recognized that to ask the vestries to enforce sanitary legislation was akin to asking poachers to enforce the game laws.[17] Friction was bound to arise between medical officers determined to improve the slums and their political superiors who were often the owners of slum property. One medical officer was greeted on his appointment by the scarcely encouraging words of the vestry chairman, 'Now, Doctor, I wish you to understand that the less you do the better we shall like you.'[18] John Liddle, the zealous officer for Whitechapel, lamented that so many vestrymen had property interests in the slums, and declared that 'had the local Boards not been compelled to appoint medical officers of health such officers would not have been appointed, and in their opinion, such appointments were unnecessary.' The medical officer, Liddle urged, 'should be entirely free from local influence.'[19] Dr Lankester, medical officer for St James's, Westminster, argued, while serving as President of the Health section of the National Association for the Promotion of Social Science, that 'from the fact of the medical officer of health being entirely dependent on the vestries of London for his appointment, his duties have in many districts been interfered with, and his ability to act for the public good has been reduced almost to a sinecure.'[20] Ernest Hart, editor of the *British Medical Journal*, and Chairman of the National Health Society, argued that 'nothing is more anomalous in our present system of sanitary government than the position of the medical officer of health,' and William Farr at the office of the Registrar-General observed 'in certain districts in London the Medical Officer of Health is under all sorts of restraint. If he is active, they look upon him with disfavour, and he is in great danger of dismissal.'[21] The *Lancet* acknowledged in 1868 that the medical officers of health were 'in a very awkward position; if they conscientiously carry out the duties imposed, they can hardly fail to come into antagonism with the local authorities to whom they are subordinate.' The drawback to all sanitary legislation, the journal reflected, lay in the fact that 'admiration for the principle of local self-government induces the Legislature to entrust important sanitary powers to local authorities, constituted largely of a class against whom those powers ought most frequently to be exercised.'[22] Yet, despite the constant pressure for security of tenure from the medical journals and organizations such as the British Medical Association, the Metropolitan, Yorkshire, Midland, and North-West Associations of Medical Officers of Health, and the Society for the Encouragement of Arts, Manufactures, & Commerce, the government refused to take the necessary steps, and thus, in the words of a petition from medical officers' organizations throughout England to the Local Government Board, their term of office remained 'in the discretion of those who may desire to evade the obligations of the Acts they are called upon to administer.'[23]

The notoriously indolent vestries such as Clerkenwell, the complaints against their vestries by medical officers like Griffith (Clerkenwell), Lord (Hampstead), Barclay (Chelsea), Evans (Strand), Burdon-Sanderson (Paddington), and Millson (Stoke Newington), and above all the resignation of Rendle, the outspoken and volatile officer of St George's, Southwark (he was the only medical officer to resign 'in disgust that he was not allowed to carry out the duties of office') were well publicized by housing reformers.[24] Yet energetic and determined medical officers in London—unlike provincial officers—achieved considerable freedom of action and won for themselves de facto security of tenure. All but five of the appointments held in 1856 were held by the same men ten years later, and several outspoken and active medical officers had remarkably long careers—G. P. Bate was officer (Bethnal Green) for thirty-seven years, R. Dudfield (Paddington) for over thirty years, and J. Bristowe (Camberwell) for over forty years.[25]

Given the onerous duties involved and the composition of vestries in 1855, it was generally assumed that few prominent or even competent doctors, capable of earning their livelihoods as specialists or general practitioners, would offer themselves as candidates, and that even fewer would be selected. As the first elections approached there occurred a flood of special pleading on behalf of family doctors and relatives. The *Lancet*, which regarded the appointment of medical officers as 'a new era in the history of medicine' and argued that 'the honour of the profession will be largely in their keeping,' urged the vestries to ignore flashy family doctors and quacks and to shun 'men who have acquired a spurious repute by means of itinerant lecturing, crochetty and incomprehensible ideas, hobby-horse steeple-chasing, and other popular arts.'[26] The selection of a candidate to fill the experimental office of practitioner of preventive medicine presented a problem to local authorities. 'How on earth are we poor ratepayers or hardworked vestrymen, whose experience of medical men does not reach beyond the family doctor,' asked one perplexed Kensington inhabitant, 'to judge between scores of gentlemen, every one of whom bewilders us with an equal surface of close-printed assurances of his universal qualifications for the office?'[27] Sir Benjamin Hall, the President of the General Board of Health, wanted an examining body of qualified men to help the vestries select medical officers, but his plan met with general opposition on the grounds that it would lead to too much central interference and result in the appointment of academically competent but perhaps impractical or weak men. Examinations, *The Times* criticized, would merely produce 'the wrangler in vital statistics, and first-class men in meteorology,' and Simon, it observed, 'the best public health officer of our time, was not a child of the examination system.'[28]

With the defeat of Hall's plans, the appointment of medical officers was left in the hands of the vestries. Despite fears to the contrary, not only competent, but in several cases outstanding, doctors were selected. Of the forty-nine doctors first appointed after the 1855 Act, eleven were sufficiently prominent to be included in the *Dictionary of National Biography*, and of the forty-nine medical officers listed in the *Medical Directory* in 1857, seventeen were prolific authors and another ten had significant publications to their name. Only eighteen of the first group of medical officers possessed their M.D. degree, but thirty-seven were Licentiates, Members, or Fellows of the Royal College of Surgeons, and a further ten had gained admittance to the Royal College of Physicians. These honors were not, it is true, indications of professional brilliance, but both the Royal College of Physicians and the Royal College of Surgeons were influential representatives of the medical profession. They acted as spokesmen in medical matters before the government, and were useful pressure groups. As the century progressed the number of distinguished medical officers increased. Many were the foremost specialists of their day.[29] Despite the fact that only Paddington submitted the candidates for interview by a panel of doctors, in most areas excellent men were selected. The vestries cannot take full credit for this, for most of them seem to have chosen their medical officers casually—indeed, almost in a state of absent-mindedness—and, just as in Edinburgh the selection of the first medical officer, Dr Littlejohn the Police Surgeon, was meant to be a temporary appointment (he in fact remained for forty-six years), so in London the vestries seem to have had few long-term plans when they appointed their officers. Most of the vestries left it to the new appointees to interpret their duties; Wandsworth was exceptional in taking the time and interest to draw up a list of suggestions and required duties.[30]

The caliber of the medical officers was not reflected in their salaries. The advocates of low rates had not been in favor of medical officers in the first place—in Edinburgh the 'economists' in the Town Council almost succeeded in preventing the appointment of Littlejohn[31]—and the cry of economy combined with the general apathy concerning preventive medicine to produce salaries which in many cases were not much higher than wages earned by slum-dwellers. Hampstead's medical officer received only £50 per year in 1875, and in the same year Wandsworth paid its six medical officers only £50 each.[32] Several vestries paid their medical officers £100 per year in 1856, which compared favorably with the £15 per annum Lincoln, or the £30 per annum Oldbury paid.[33] By the end of the century salaries had greatly improved, reflecting the rise in prestige and importance of the officers. Most were earning between £350 and £600 per annum in 1900; Kensington paid its medical officer £800 per annum, as did the City of Westminster, while the City of London paid £1,500 per year.[34] The medical officer for Whitechapel argued in 1869 that the low salaries were part of a deliberate vestry policy to force their officers to devote more time to private practice or hospital work than to local government duties.[35] Although the General Board of Health advised local authorities to appoint full-time medical officers, few were willing to do so, and few medical officers wanted to exist on their official salaries only. When Duncan was appointed medical officer of Liverpool in 1847 he received the salary of £300 a year and the right to continue in private practice. But Duncan believed that he could not be an adequate official on a part-time basis, and when, shortly after his appointment, he became a full-time health officer, Liverpool generously advanced his salary to £750 p.a.[36] Few London vestries were prepared to make a similar financial sacrifice.

With their manifold duties occupying them fully, responsible to often unknowledgeable or openly hostile vestries, and dependent upon other means of livelihood, it would have been understandable if the medical officers had sunk into the obscurity of petty local functionaries. As individuals and collectively, however, they managed to transcend daily activities in their localities, to grasp the problems of London as a whole—a triumph of good sense and perception in an age of localism.[37] They revealed their reluctance to remain merely local figures when, a year after they were appointed, they formed themselves into the Metropolitan Association of Medical Officers of Health and invited Simon to be their president.[38] Through this Association and by frequent correspondence with similar Associations and medical officers throughout Britain, the medical officers of health developed the competence and understanding that comes with comparative analysis and frequent interchange of ideas with fellow experts. Their Association could be interpreted as a drive towards centralization, especially since they met in one of the rooms of the General Board of Health.[39] The Association's frequent meetings, published transactions, and journal, *Public Health*, gave them an *esprit de corps*, and provided a forum in which to present housing reforms.

From the annual reports, which the medical officers of health were obliged to submit, there emerges a picture of perseverance and a conviction of the power of preventive medicine to improve greatly the health of a nation in which, in Simon's words, 'physiologically speaking, . . . at least nine-tenths of the entire mortality occurs more or less prematurely.'[40] But, more important, the reports reveal a remarkable grasp of the complex problem of overcrowding, the forces making slums, and the social costs of house demolition and slum clearance. The medical officers managed to rise above the minutiae of local sanitary administration and to develop a keen understanding of the impact of an unregulated urban environment upon the working classes. This awareness was gained through a course of action new to the English experience— regular house inspection. Although they rarely undertook the night inspection legally permitted, they did enter the homes of the poor, and they thus formed an inspectorate, a word which then possessed dreadful connotations of Continental despotism. The Nuisances Removal Act of 1855 allowed medical officers to enter houses on the order of a J.P., and the Torrens Act of 1868 first permitted them to enter on their own initiative.[41] After that date they no longer had to wait until a house was sufficiently insanitary, for they could enter on suspicion of a nuisance. House-to-house inspection is now an integral part of public health, but the public-health movement in the first half of the nineteenth century had stressed *external* factors—main sewers, main water supply, refuse—and, as Dr Duncan pointed out for Liverpool, 'the benefit to be derived from an inspection of the *interior* of the dwelling has been in great measure overlooked.'[42] So convinced were medical officers that 'house-to-house inspection . . . is the life and soul of sanitary work' that they called for the extension to private houses of the system of registration and regular inspection which applied to common lodging houses.[43] The right to require the registration of houses let to more than one family and let under a certain rent (to be fixed by local by-laws) was granted in the 1866 Sanitary Act; included in the registration was the power to define and set penalties for overcrowding.[44] The great advantage of putting tenement houses on a register was that overcrowding could be treated as a finable offence which, unless abated immediately, was subject to further daily fines. The procedure was speedier and more effective than treating overcrowding as an offence under the Nuisance Removal Act of 1855.[45] Yet disappointingly few houses were placed on the register.

In 1885 the Royal Commission on the Housing of the Working Classes discovered that only Chelsea and Hackney were enforcing the regulations of 1866; four years later, under pressure from the Local Government Board and an aroused public opinion, about half the London local authorities began to implement the Act.[46] Nevertheless, the vestries moved slowly. At the end of the century only 7,713 houses were on the register throughout London, and of these over half were in four parishes, Kensington, Westminster, Hampstead, and St Giles's.[47] Lewisham, Greenwich, Battersea, Fulham, Newington, had under 150 houses each on their register, and the fast-growing working-class suburbs Willesden and Tottenham were even more lax.[48] The medical officers could only recommend registration to their vestries, and even after the Public Health (London) Act of 1891 compelled local authorities to make by-laws governing houses let in lodgings, they were helpless in the face of vestry apathy. Nothing better illustrates the medical officers' dependence, for effective sanitary administration, upon the good-will of their vestries.

Nevertheless, they pushed ahead with house inspection, and their visitations revealed overcrowding to be an evil of far greater magnitude than had hitherto been suspected.[49] Overcrowding was not recognized by politicians and the public to be the most critical aspect of the slum problem until the eighties, but it was extensive well before that decade.[50] The medical officers were among the first to recognize this, and overcrowding appeared as a problem separate from other problems of public health in their earliest reports. 'Let me urge the dismissal from your minds,' wrote the medical officer for the Strand in 1858, 'of the idea, long entertained by many, that sanitary improvements consist exclusively in works of drainage and of water supply.' Overcrowding, he argued,[51] is without doubt the most important, and at the same time the most difficult [subject], with which you are called upon to deal; and sooner or later it must be dealt with. Houses and streets may be drained most perfectly, the District may be paved and lighted in such a manner as to excite the jealous envy of other Local Authorities; new thoroughfares may be constructed and every house in the District furnished with a constant supply of pure water; the Thames may be embanked, and all entrance of sewerage into that river intercepted; but so long as twenty, thirty, or even forty individuals are permitted—it might almost be said compelled—to reside in houses originally built for the accommodation of a single family or at most of two families, so long will the evils pointed out in regard of health, of ignorance, of indecency, immorality, intemperance, prostitution, and crime continue to exist almost unchecked.

By the end of the century many medical officers would have endorsed the statement of the medical officer for Whitechapel: 'I know of nothing,' he wrote, 'which has caused me more trouble, nor over which I have spent more time in thought, than the burning question of "overcrowding".'[52] Overcrowding inspired the medical officers to write some of the most moving and forceful passages to be found in official documents. To most, overcrowding was 'a jarring discord in the civilization we boast—a worse than pagan savageness in the Christianity we profess,'[53] and they advocated its removal as the cure for crime, intemperance, prostitution, brutality, irreligion, socialism, illiteracy.[54]

The medical officers stressed that overcrowding had two main consequences, one physical, the other moral. They rightly assumed that overcrowding increased the risk of infection and fatal diseases.[55] 'There can be little doubt,' wrote George Newman, medical officer of health for Finsbury (he later became the first Medical Officer to the Ministry of Health on its creation in 1919), 'that there is a very intimate relationship between the overcrowded condition of the central district of London and the high phthisis and zymotic death rates in those districts.'[56] 'The main cause to which we must attribute the high mortality,' wrote the medical officer of health for the Strand in 1856, 'is the close packing and overcrowding which exists throughout the district . . . Overcrowding and disease,' he added, 'mutually act and react upon each other.'[57] Dr Lankester estimated before the National Association for the Promotion of Social Science that overcrowding caused five deaths in every 1,000 and cost the nation £5 million per year.[58] Dr Shirley Murphy, the first Medical Officer of the London County Council, concluded from his elaborate mortality tables for the whole of London that 'the decrease of mortality [from phthisis] as the line travels from the most to the least overcrowded districts is well marked, and the same, but in less degree, is also seen in the mortality from "all causes".'[59]

The medical officers stressed even more persistently the effects of overcrowding upon morality. The 'consequences of overcrowding are not limited to the impairment of health,' the medical officer for the Strand informed his vestry, 'but the moral life

612

is also degraded and debased.'[60] The worst effects of overcrowding, the medical officer for St Giles's stressed, were the 'moral depravation and loss of self-respect and responsibility.'[61] Few felt that their position as public health officials disqualified them from paying attention to the morality of the poor whose homes they visited. 'Though my official point of view is one exclusively physical,' wrote Simon in his Eighth Report to the Privy Council (1865),

> common humanity requires that the other aspect of this evil [of over-crowding] should not be ignored. For where overcrowding exists in its sanitary sense, almost always it exists even more perniciously in certain moral senses. In its higher degree it almost necessarily involves such negation of all delicacy, such unclean confusion of bodies and bodily functions, such mutual exposure of animal and sexual nakedness, as is rather bestial than human. To be subject to these influences is a degradation which must become deeper and deeper for those on whom it continues to work.

'To children who are born under its curse,' he concluded, 'it must often be a very baptism into infamy.'[62] The medical officers drew special attention to the sexual vices engendered by the sharing of one room, often one bed, by large families. Unfettered by those considerations which confined within the bounds of respectability popular novelists like Dickens or journalists such as George Sims, they graphically described the vices they discovered. Perhaps, as Lambert says of Simon, they were not above playing upon Victorian prudery in order to shock their readers into sympathetic support. They drew attention to the incestuous relationships which the one-roomed system could create, and when the Royal Commission on the Housing of the Working Classes (1884–5) examined the claim of the author of *The Bitter Cry of Outcast London* that 'incest is common,' the medical officers of health who were called as witnesses repeated what they had stressed in their reports—that over-crowding was corrupting the morals of the nation.[63]

The officers considered the improvement of housing to be one of their most important functions and they were technically responsible for initiating slum-improvement schemes. But under the Nuisance Removal, Sanitary, Torrens, and Cross Acts, they found themselves operating under legislation which harmed rather than helped the poor; for while the legislation enabled them to recommend and initiate the demolition of houses and the eviction of the inhabitants, or the prosecution of overcrowded tenants, they knew that the poor could not wait for, or afford, the model dwellings which were provided under the rehousing clauses of the Cross Act.[64] Thus the medical officers found themselves in an anomalous position—and many of them preferred inactivity to negative solutions of 'pull down and push out' which could only aggravate overcrowding. Dr Tripe, the medical officer for Hackney, declared that if he had carried out the overcrowding clause in the 1866 Sanitary Act, he would have forced ten thousand people to sleep in the streets, while the medical officer for Bermondsey wrote that it was useless for him to evict people for overcrowding since 'as they are all poor and cannot afford to occupy more than a single room, they would but go into some other locality equally objectionable.'[65] To one medical officer, legislation attacking overcrowding forced the evicted to choose 'between the streets, the workhouse, or some neighbouring region which they would overcrowd to a double degree,' while another, explaining his inactivity, wrote 'if the occupation of rooms throughout the district were regulated, there would not be sufficient accommodation for the inhabitants.'[66] The utterance of one old lady evicted three times by the local authority put the situation in a nutshell in the view of the perplexed medical officer for Finsbury: 'Thank 'evins,' she exclaimed, 'now I shall 'ave a little rest: the board of 'ealth ain't so strick where I am going next.'[67]

The negative approach to the housing question placed the medical officers in a dilemma. After visiting one crowded room, the medical officer for St Marylebone in 1874 wrote:[68]

> My first impulse was to declare the house unfit for human habitation, and, by means of a magistrate's order, to remove the inmates at once. A moment's reflection, however, convinced me that by adopting that course I should really accomplish no good object, inasmuch as the poor people, thus suddenly ejected, would be compelled to seek shelter in dwellings probably more crowded and in an equally bad sanitary condition.

The medical officers felt little elation at the destruction of slums for railway or street construction, or even for clearance schemes, for they could not afford to turn a blind eye, as did many of their contemporaries, to the back alleys and hidden courts into which the evicted poured. Yet in initiating proceedings under the Cross Act, and in recommending the use of the Torrens Act, many medical officers had a hand in the destruction of working-class homes and thus greatly aggravated overcrowding. Under the Metropolitan Board of Works alone there were twenty-two housing-improvement schemes, demolishing over 7,000 dwellings inhabited by over 27,000 people.[69] Yet the medical officers knew that slum clearance merely stirred overcrowding around, and they submitted demolition schemes as an evil necessity. The medical officer for St Marylebone, arguing that 'if every vestry had worked the Artisans' and Labourers' Dwellings Acts thoroughly, an appalling amount of misery, of overcrowding, and of poverty would have been the result,' was one of many calling for positive legislation granting vestries the right to build. 'Until tenements are built in proportion to those demolished at low rents,' he argued, 'it is not humane to press on large schemes.'[70] But although most medical officers agreed that more housing was essential, little consensus emerged as to who should do the building. Most were opposed to state, municipal, or local authority construction and ownership, but a surprising number argued that it was the duty of public authorities to provide houses for the very poor. Impatience with the results of laissez faire in house provision led the Royal College of Physicians, in which medical officers were active, to take the unprecedented step of presenting, in 1874, a remarkable petition to the Prime Minister.[71] It condemned philanthropy and laissez faire and attacked 'enabling powers' as useless. The petition stressed that 'private enterprise is powerless to provide the fresh air and improved house accommodation which is required for those who have been expelled from their former habitations, in addition to that which is called for by the constant increase of the population.'[72] Dr Buchanan, medical officer of health for St Giles's, like many of his colleagues, did not view municipal housing projects with enthusiasm, but, he wrote,[73]

> when I look at what the effect would be of erecting such institutions on a sufficient scale, adapted to the wants of all classes and becoming popular even among the lowest; when I am convinced that the houses might be made to pay well, and that disease and pauperism would decline with their prosperity; when I know that the law against overcrowding could then be exercised without scruple, and that from that moment several hundreds of lives would be annually preserved—with all these convictions I feel it my duty to raise the question, at whatever risk of being thought wild and Utopian.

Throughout the second half of the nineteenth century the medical officers advocated the use of the moribund Shaftesbury Act, or called vaguely for state housing, and by the end of the century statements from medical officers to the effect that: 'the difficulties of providing decent dwellings at rents commensurate with the earnings of the classes which most require such accommodation are practically insurmountable if private enterprise alone is to be relied upon,' or, 'a stage has been reached at which it is almost impossible to house working classes in inner London without direct or indirect subsidisation' were increasingly heard.[74] When in 1900 the London borough councils were given permission to erect houses for the working classes, the medical officers of health were most influential, giving advice, drawing up plans, and passing judgment on the desirability of housing schemes.[75]

Although most medical officers could contemplate municipal or vestry house building only if there were no resulting burden upon the rates, they were among the first to realize that the housing problem was but part of the greater problem of poverty.[76] Not until the 1880s did the construction costs, rents, and wages aspects of the 'housing question' command general attention, but well before that date medical officers realized that 'overcrowding . . . is a poverty problem, nothing more nor less.'[77] Dr Dudfield, the experienced and energetic medical officer of health for Kensington, asked 'what are the main causes of overcrowding?', and answered, wearily, 'Poverty and high rents. Over these conditions,' he added, 'the Local Authority have no power.'[78] Newsholme, one of the most talented medical officers, argued that since there was no way of cheapening houses (he rejected state subsidies) the only solution to overcrowding lay in 'increasing wages, so that people can pay a fair rent.'[79] The awareness that rents were too high for working-class wages drove the President of the Society of Medical Officers of Health to declare in 1884 that 'there would have to be fixity of fair rent.' He made this statement at a time when the fair rent movement had achieved success in Ireland and was making some stir in the East End.[80]

We may almost say of the metropolitan medical officers in general what has recently been said of Dr Littlejohn of Edinburgh: 'His role in the adoption or hastening towards the statute book of new sanitary legislation was practically negligible.'[81] The one great exception is the Torrens Act. Torrens drew up his bill in consultation with the Society of Medical Officers of Health. It provided for vestries erecting and owning workmen's dwellings, but Parliament mangled the bill, despite the Society's petition in its favor. As passed, the Torrens Act allowed the vestries to destroy insanitary houses. Perhaps to ease their disappointment and his, and in gratitude for his original intentions, Torrens was made an honorary member of the Society.[82] The experience of the medical officers proved invaluable when Richard Cross, Disraeli's Home Secretary, drew up his Act (it placed the demolition of whole areas in the hands of the Metropolitan Board of Works), and their experience with the Torrens and Cross Acts at the local level was of vital importance when both these Acts were amended, and new, simplified, legislation was passed in the late seventies and early eighties.[83] In one other way the medical officers had an indirect influence upon legislation. Victorian housing legislation moved from permissive to compulsory and from negative to positive powers; the medical officers, with their awareness of the short-sightedness of destructive legislation, and their distrust of permissive legislation under which vestries could remain inactive, played a large role in this transition. They constituted a pressure group at once diffused and centralized, and their plea for legislation which would commit and compel local authorities to a course of action was a direct challenge to cherished concepts of laissez faire and local autonomy. The difficulty of trying to get their vestry to prosecute a slum landlord, or set about extensive registration and control of tenements let in lodgings was enough to cause conscientious medical officers to advocate central controls and compulsory legislation. 'The duty of making these sanitary improvements should be imperative instead of permissive,' argued the medical officer for St Giles's in 1870. 'It was wise, at first, perhaps, that our sanitary legislation should be tentative and experimental,' he added, 'but experience having proved its necessity it should be made more stringent.'[84] Dr Stevenson, the President of the Association of Medical Officers of Health, argued in 1878 that 'the distrust which has been excited by the apathy of many local authorities' had 'strengthened the feeling of our profession that permissive legislation must, as regards sanitary measures, be replaced by paternal legislation.'[85]

Just as the professional interests of the medical officers led them to demand legislation which helped to break down local autonomy, so their house inspections helped to break down the concept of the sanctity of private property. Their house-to-house visitations destroyed the belief that a man's home was his castle and the illusion that in England there was no governmental bureaucracy to prevent a man doing what he liked with his own. Their inspections made the home no more sacred or private than a workshop or bakehouse, and the influence of their daily work upon the concept of the rights and duties of property cannot be exaggerated.

The medical officers assisted the development of centralization and the decline of local liberties in other ways. Their official representations initiated action under the Cross Acts, and in calling upon the Metropolitan Board of Works to employ the Cross Acts, they indirectly assisted the coming of subsidized housing, for the land purchased by the Board in their demolition schemes was sold to the model dwelling companies at well below market rates, and represented, before the coming of the council flat, a typical Victorian mixture of state aid and philanthropic endeavor. The energetic work of Simon at the head of the medical department of the Privy Council strengthened the position of the central government in public health. Though the Privy Council and the Local Government Board initiated little housing legislation, Simon's brilliant team of special medical officers and assistants enabled the central government to gather accurate information on urban conditions, and made the case for housing reform more pressing.[86] Simon's team—from part-time assistants earning £3 per day, to full-time inspectors at £100 per year—illustrated how valuable a central government Department of Health could be. Guy, Greenhow, Seaton, Edward Smith, Parkes, Hunter, Bristowe (medical officer of health, Camberwell), Burdon-Sanderson (Paddington), Buchanan (St Giles's), Hillier (St Pancras), Evans (Strand), and Barclay (Chelsea) were all men of distinction, and the reports of Greenhow, Hunter, and Smith are classics in the literature of housing conditions and urban pathology.[87]

In one aspect of their work the medical officers played a crucial part in the development of urban sociology, for they greatly helped to refine statistical techniques and develop the science of social statistics. The Board of Health in its original instructions concerning the appointment of medical officers had stressed the great importance of a knowledge of vital statistics, and it was partly under the guidance of Dr Farr, Superintendent of the Statistical Department of the Registrar-General's Office, that the medical officers developed a uniform system of tables for diseases, life-expectancy, and so forth, as well as a sophisticated expertise in comparative statistical analysis. Farr was deeply interested in matters of public health (he had hoped to establish a course of lectures in Hygieology), and he gave the medical officers every assistance. He called statistics 'an arsenal for sanitary reformers to use,' and in the eyes of Dr Newman his medical statistics 'reoriented the whole business of State Medicine.'[88] The medical officers appreciated the complexities of vital statistics, and their emphasis upon figures—comparing, for example, life expectancy in different areas, or at different ages, or between different classes—drew attention to over-crowding and poverty as factors aggravating and spreading diseases.[89] One may say of the medical officers generally what Lambert said of Simon, that they 'possessed a genuine belief in the dynamic power of mere information, in the inevitability with which accumulated knowledge would induce progress.'[90] Certainly figures such as Shirley Murphy's, showing that the death-rate was twice as high in Southwark as in Hampstead, had a telling effect upon public opinion.

The medical officers' reports constitute a hidden dimension to Victorian urban social reform, for in an age when laissez faire and free market forces had to be proved guilty before men would accept the necessity for state interference, the never-ending supply of facts, figures, and reasoned emotion which flowed from their pens was of the greatest significance. Their description of overcrowded interiors increased contemporaries' awareness at a time when writers for the public generally confined their descriptions to external scenes. Their emphasis upon the moral damage of overcrowding could not be denied in an age of critical self-appraisal, and their convinced environmentalism forced men to consider causes other than character, for the sorry plight of the urban masses. If one agrees that the 'first prerequisite of social policy was the willingness and ability to define social problems,' and if the second prerequisite is to ascertain and gather exact, preferably quantifiable facts, then the role of the medical officers must be seen as crucial.[91]

In fact how well known were the medical officers and how well read were their reports? Simon's reports achieved national fame, sold out quickly, and had to be reprinted, and were summarized or reproduced unabridged in the national papers. To a lesser extent the reports of Letheby, Liddle, Buchanan, Dudfield, Newman, and others were carried in the papers and their statistical tables often formed the factual pegs on which reformers and journalists hung their rhetoric.[92] Within the National Association for the Promotion of Social Science and the Royal Sanitary Institute they found a wider audience and formed a coherent and important group, and their connection with the Privy Council, the Royal College of Physicians, and the Royal College of Surgeons gave them contact with bodies of national importance.

If, as the medical journals frequently argued, the medical profession aided the housing-reform movement, participation in that movement by the medical officers greatly enhanced the reputation of the medical profession. Certainly, as the *Medical Times* suggested, the association of doctors with local government gave the medical profession a 'national character which has been hitherto wanting.'[93] The office of medical officer of health, like that of the Poor Law medical officer, intertwined the doctor so closely in local and national government, and in legislative responsibilities, that it made state-directed medicine, in this case preventive medicine, a reality, and helped to create the atmosphere in which state curative medicine for the needy, and ultimately fully nationalized medicine, could be accepted. The role of the medical officers of health must, therefore, be seen as of the greatest political as well as the greatest social significance.

Despite the constraints upon them, the medical officers with their ever-increasing duties and powers may be taken as a barometer of the growing complexity of town life. Their rise to national importance was prompted by the process of urbanization. For the specialist skills which they injected into urban administration, and their dynamic belief in the preventive approach to urban ills were an integral part both of the late Victorian response to the urban challenge and the widespread desire to improve the quality of urban life. Their significance must, therefore, not only be measured by, but must also be seen as symbolic of, urban development in Victorian England.

Notes

1   The abbreviation M.O.H. is used throughout these notes, for both the singular and plural.

2   John Simon, *English Sanitary Institutions* (1890); Henry Jephson, *Sanitary Evolution of London* (1907); S. E. Finer, *The Life and Times of Sir Edwin Chadwick* (1952); R. A. Lewis, *Edwin Chadwick and the Public Health Movement, 1832–1854* (1952); and especially the brilliant biography by Royston Lambert, *Sir John Simon, 1816–1904, and English Social Administration* (1963).

3   *Report of the Speeches of E. Chadwick, Esq., Dr. Southwood Smith . . . and others at a Meeting held on the 17th August, 1847 . . .* (1847).

4   For the influence of the Health Section of the National Association for the Promotion of Social Science, and the remarkable role of doctors Rumsey and Stewart, see the introduction to Alexander P. Stewart and Edward Jenkins, *Medical and Legal Aspects of Sanitary Reform*, ed. M. W. Flinn (Leicester, 1969).

5   Quoted in E. A. Underwood, 'The Field Workers in the English Public Health Movement, 1847–1875,' *Bulletin of the Society of Medical History of Chicago*, vi (October 1948). The M.O.H. have not been completely ignored. See *British Medical Journal*, 11 January 1947, 58–9; W. S. Walton, 'The History of the Society of Medical Officers of Health, 1856–1956,' *Public Health*, lxix (May 1956), 160–226; C. F. Brockington, *Medical Officers of Health, 1848 to 1855, An essay in local history* (1957); Jubilee Number of *Public Health* (1906); and 'Our Medical Officers of Health, 1855–1860' [by students of the History Seminar of the London School of Hygiene and Tropical Medicine], *Public Health*, lxiii (June 1950), 175–9; Jeanne Brand, *Doctors and the State. The British medical profession and government action in public health, 1870–1912* (Baltimore, 1965) has some interesting material.

6   *Lancet*, 23 September 1843, 1902.

7   The Metropolis Local Management Act, 18 & 19 Vict., ch. 120, clause 132. For Simon's influence, and the inspiration of his example see Lambert, op. cit., pp. 204, 217, 230.

8   Simon, who was pathologist at St Thomas's, played an important part in the creation of the post. See C. F. Brockington, *Public Health in the Nineteenth Century* (Edinburgh, 1965), pp. 197, 199; H. C. Thomson, *The Story of the Middlesex Hospital Medical School* (1935).

9   The First Chair in Public Health was established at Edinburgh University in 1898 and in 1902 the John Usher Institute of Public Health was opened there.

10   *The Times*, 24 December 1855. The instructional minute was the work of Simon (Lambert, op. cit., pp. 244 ff).

11   Metropolitan Association of Medical Officers of Health, *Papers*, Session 1878–9, p. 9. See also Sir G. Newman, *The Health of the State* (1907), p. 21.

12   Mansion House Council on the Dwellings of the Poor, *Report for the Year Ending 1889*, p. 11. One M.O.H. described the typical inspector as 'an unskilled workman . . . an official recruited . . . from the ranks of ex-sailors, ex-policemen or army pensioners.' Quoted in Sir G. Gibbon and R. Bell, *History of the London County Council, 1889–1939* (1939), p. 59. In the view of one vestry clerk 'no special training is required [for an inspector]. If a man was endowed with common sense I think that

would be about as good a training as he could have.' *Parliamentary Papers (P.P.)*, 1884–5, XXX, Royal Commission (R.C.) on the Housing of the Working Classes: Minutes of Evidence (C. 4402), p. 663.

13 For the scope of their work, and their expected qualifications see: E. Smith, *Handbook for Inspectors of Nuisances* (1873), pp. iii–iv.

14 By contrast, St Giles's appointed two inspectors for its 54,000 people. See Vera Zoond, 'Housing Legislation in England, 1851–1867, with Special Reference to London' (unpublished M.A. thesis, University of London, 1932), pp. 129–30.

15 Gibbon and Bell, op. cit., p. 59; London County Council, *Annual Report M.O.H.*, 1894, Appendix 10, 1, 2; Ibid., 1898, p. 9; Duncan's staff in Liverpool in 1861 consisted of one Chief Inspector and four sanitary inspectors. See W. H. Frazer, *Duncan of Liverpool* (1947), p. 127.

16 Mansion House Council on the Dwellings of the Poor, *Report for the Year Ending 1892*, 5.

17 *Pall Mall Gazette*, 11 February 1884. The *Pall Mall Gazette* considered vestry inactivity to be the result more of ignorance than apathy or self-interest. But to one of the commissioners on the Royal Commission on the Housing of the Working Classes, to permit the vestries to appoint medical officers was akin to allowing the wolves to appoint shepherds. See R.C. on the Housing of the Working Classes, 1884–5, QQ. 507–12.

18 Quoted in Zoond, op. cit., p. 57. The officials in Bethnal Green were alleged to have wanted to 'shut out' from the post of medical officer 'all those doctors whose reports are troublesome and who are running about "stink-hunting" in the parish' (p. 133).

19 J. Liddle, 'What ought to be the Functions and Authority of Medical Officers of Health,' *Public Health*, ii (January 1869), 1–2.

20 Dr Edwin Lankester, 'Address on Health,' *Transactions of the National Association for the Promotion of Social Science (T.N.A.P.S.S.)* (1865), 74. See also Dr Littlejohn, *T.N.A.P.S.S.* (1880), 517.

21 E. Hart, *Local Government as it is and as it ought to be* (1885), p. 45; W. Farr, quoted by Jephson, op. cit., p. 189.

22 *Lancet*, 22 February 1868, 265.

23 *British Medical Journal*, 8 December 1888, 1315: Public Records Office (P.R.O.), Ministry of Health, 25, 50 (8708/81).

24 Quoted in Jephson, op. cit., p. 189. Rendle's resignation was supported by the other local medical officers and by Simon, and Rendle continued to be a member of the Society of Medical Officers of Health. See Jubilee Number of *Public Health* (1906), 30. Rendle attacked vestry apathy in his provocative *London Vestries and their Sanitary Work* (1865). On the other hand, one medical officer (Dr Goderich of Kensington) was asked by his vestry to resign because he was not doing enough! See Patricia E. Malcolmson, 'The Potteries of Kensington: a study of slum development in Victorian London' (unpublished M.Phil. thesis, University of Leicester, 1970), p. 129.

25 *Public Health*, lxiii (June 1950), 178. Of the five men, one had died, one had resigned, and another had emigrated, so that only two were not reappointed by their vestries. The high turnover of 'evidently capable men' in Wandsworth between 1872 and

1883 might indicate differences of opinion between medical officers and local authority. See Janet Roebuck, 'Local Government and Some Aspects of Social Change in the Parishes of Lambeth, Battersea, and Wandsworth, 1838–1888' (unpublished Ph.D. thesis, University of London, 1968), p. 170.

26 *Lancet*, 29 December 1855, 632–3, and 12 January 1856, 47.

27 *The Times*, 7 December 1855.

28 Ibid.

29 In 1900, of the fifty-two medical officers in London, thirty were associated with the Royal College of Surgeons and thirty with the Royal College of Physicians, twenty-seven were M.D.s, twenty-five had obtained the prestigious D.P.H. or Doctorate of Science in Public Health, twenty-four were prolific authors and a further eight had published. Among the more celebrated specialists were Ballard (Islington), Burdon-Sanderson (Paddington), Pavy (St Luke), Bristowe (Camberwell), Odling (Lambeth), Hillier (St Pancras), Liddle (Whitechapel), Buchanan (St Giles's). See Jubilee Number, *Public Health*, xviii (1906), 237; lxiii (June 1950), 176–7.

30 Wandsworth's instructions are most interesting: they stressed the value of the medical officer having a knowledge of vital statistics, otherwise, he may 'lead the board into absurd, possibly disastrous mistakes.' Also, 'the most important duty of the medical officer will be to prepare such reports as will convince the Public that what the Board propose to do ought to be done, and that the expenses they propose to incur will be more than counterbalanced by the benefit to be anticipated' (Roebuck, op. cit., p. 144).

31 I am indebted for the information on Littlejohn and the Edinburgh Town Council to Mr Hector Macdonald, whose doctoral dissertation on Dr Littlejohn (Edinburgh University) is in preparation.

32 J. F. B. Firth, *Municipal London* (1876), pp. 307, 408; *Lancet*, 22 March 1856, 322.

33 The M.O.H. for Oldbury was ousted by the efforts of the local Ratepayers' Protection Society, *T.N.A.P.S.S.* (1868), 474.

34 For a complete listing of the wages of medical officers at the end of the century, see London County Council, *Annual Report M.O.H.*, 1898, 10.

35 *Public Health* ii (January 1869), 1.

36 Frazer, op. cit., pp. 45, 47.

37 For an exception, see A. E. Harris, M.O.H. for Islington, *Annual Report M.O.H.*, 1898, 18, 19. Harris wanted to protect Islington from 'being invaded by swarms of people from other parts of London' and to 'keep Islington for the Islingtonians.'

38 The organization changed its title several times: Metropolitan Association of Medical Officers of Health (1866), Association of Medical Officers of Health (1869), Society of Medical Officers of Health (1873), and Incorporated Society of Medical Officers of Health (1891).

39 One member of the Society expressed the fear that the choice of meeting place would be frowned upon 'by some vestries who had a great dislike for centralization.' See *Public Health*, lxiii (June 1950), 178.

40 Simon's introduction to *P.P.*, 1857–8, XXIII, 'Papers Relating to the Sanitary State . . .' (2415) p.v. See also Gavin, *Unhealthiness of London . . .*, p. 34.

41 18 & 19 Vict., ch. 121, and 31 & 32 Vict., ch. 115. The official title of the Torrens Act was the 'Artisans' and Labourers' Dwellings Act.'

42 Quoted in Frazer, op. cit., p. 74.

43 The M.O.H. for Islington (1893), quoted in Jephson, op. cit., p. 379.

44 The Society of Medical Officers of Health was very much in favor of the extensive use of the 1866 Act (section 35), and hoped for a uniform system of registration and by-laws throughout London. See St Mary Abbots, Kensington, *Annual Report on the Health of St. Mary Abbots, Kensington*, 1884, 176. Under Fulham's by-laws all houses let above 3s. 6d. per week (unfurnished) and 5s. p.w. (furnished) were exempt from the by-laws governing houses let in lodgings. In Poplar the by-laws affected only those houses (and there must have been extremely few) let at under 3s. p.w. (unfurnished) and 4s. p.w. (furnished). These levels were ridiculously low. The City of Westminster, on the other hand, set its by-laws to govern all houses let at under 15s. p.w. (unfurnished) and 18s. p.w. (furnished). See: Vestry of the Parish of Fulham, *Annual Reports M.O.H.*, 1893, 38; Parishes of All Saints, Poplar, and Bromley St Leonard, *Annual Report M.O.H.*, 1898, 41; and City of Westminster, *Annual Reports*, 1903, 51.

45 Jephson, op. cit., p. 377.

46 London County Council, *Report of the M.O.H.*, 1896, Appendix IV, 1–2. For the development of public interest in housing reform in the 1880s see A. S. Wohl, 'The Bitter Cry of Outcast London,' *International Review of Social History*, xiii (1968), Part 2.

47 Jephson, op. cit., 375. For Dudfield's persistence in getting the Kensington vestry to put houses on the register, see Malcolmson, op. cit., p. 111.

48 London County Council, *Annual Report M.O.H.*, 1908, 68–9. Tottenham, *Report of the Health of Tottenham for the Year 1903*, 93; Willesden Local Board, *Sanitary Report for the Year 1913*.

49 Hammersmith Borough Council carried out well over 3,000 house inspections a year —about an average number at the end of the century. Hammersmith Borough Council, *Annual Reports*, i (1901), 277.

50 See Wohl, 'The Housing of the Working Classes in London, 1815–1914', in S. D. Chapman, ed., *The History of Working-Class Housing* (Newton Abbot, 1971).

51 *Second Annual Report M.O.H. to the Strand* (1858), 80, 72–4.

52 Metropolitan Borough of Stepney, *Annual Report on the Sanitary Condition of the Whitechapel District (of Stepney) for the Year 1900*, 4. The M.O.H. was Joseph Loane.

53 Simon, *Reports Relating to the Sanitary Condition of the City of London* (1854), pp. 44–5.

54 See for example, The Parish of St Pancras, *Second Annual Report of the Medical Officer of St. Pancras on the Sanitary Condition of the Parish during the Year, 1857*, 11. Liddle, *On the Moral and Physical Evils Resulting from the Neglect of Sanitary Measures* (1847), p. 6, and Strand District, *Second Annual Report . . .*, 73–4.

55 I am grateful to Dr George Rosen of the Yale University School of Medicine for helping to clarify this point.

56 Newman, *Some Notes on the Housing Question in Finsbury . . .* (1901), p. 8.

57 Quoted in Jephson, op. cit., p. 119.

58 *T.N.A.P.S.S.* (1864), 588.

59 London County Council, *Annual Report of the M.O.H.*, 1908, 47. Murphy drew up the following table:

Proportion of total population living more than 2 to a room (*in tenements of less than 5 rooms*)		Death-rate from all causes, 1855-92, per thousand
Districts with under 15		17·51
,, ,,	15 to 20	19·51
,, ,,	20 to 25	20·27
,, ,,	25 to 30	21·76
,, ,,	30 to 35	23·92
,, ,,	over 35	25·07

(London County Council, *Annual Report M.O.H.*, 1892, 10). Murphy always used his statistics cautiously, and emphasized that overcrowding was associated with 'other adverse social conditions,' such as poverty, bad working conditions, etc., which could affect the death-rate.

60   *Second Annual Report . . . Strand*, 71–2.

61   *Public Health*, vii (May 1895), 323.

62   Simon, *Public Health Reports* (1887), II, 207.

63   For the evidence concerning incest, most of which was, understandably, hearsay, see R.C. on the Housing of the Working Classes, 1884–5, QQ. 1525, 1954, 2163–5, 2228, 3355, 3690, 4989, 5872–5.

64   The Metropolitan Board of Works sold the land it cleared under the Cross Acts to model-dwelling companies—usually to the Peabody Trust—but the model dwellings erected were let at rents the laboring class could not afford.

65   D. M. Connan, *A History of the Public Health Department in Bermondsey* (1935), p. 134.

66   *Public Health*, vii (June 1895), 323; St James and St John, Clerkenwell, *Annual Report of the M.O.H., 1862*, 15.

67   *Public Health*, xxiv (September 1911), 459. No wonder one medical officer called regulations against overcrowding a 'royal game of "hunt the slipper"'—a living slipper, very dirty, of flesh and blood.' *Transactions of the Society of Medical Officers of Health* (1882–3), 83.

68   *Charity Organisation Reporter*, 18 March 1874.

69   Gibbon and Bell, op. cit., p. 38.

70   A. Wynter Blyth, 'An Account of the Work done in the Parish of St Marylebone under the Artizans and Labourers Dwellings Acts,' *Transactions of the Society of Medical Officers of Health* (1883–4), 36–7.

71   *Lancet*, 7 February 1874, 209.

72   *Copy of a Memorial on the Improvement of the Dwellings of the Poor in London to the Secretary of State for the Home Department . . .* (1874).

73   Quoted in *Public Health*, vii (June 1895), 324. For a criticism of laissez faire in housing see also *Medical Times*, 16 March 1850, 200; 22 October 1870, 477.

74   *Public Health*, xii (February 1900), 323; J. Sykes, *Public Health and Housing* (1901), pp. 188–9. Shaftesbury's Act of 1851 permitted local authorities to erect dwelling houses but was ambiguously phrased and, as Shaftesbury himself admitted, a total failure.

75   For the influence of the medical officers see City of Westminster, *Minutes of Proceedings*, 20 December 1900, p. 35; Chelsea Borough Council, *Minutes*, 1900,

p. 187 (the medical officer for Chelsea, Louis Parkes, was particularly influential); Kensington Borough Council, *Minutes*, 1900–1, p. 460; and Metropolitan Borough of Finsbury, *Annual Reports*, 1901–2, 105.

76 For a typical attitude towards the rates see Dr Parkes, the M.O.H. for Chelsea, *Public Health*, xxvi (June 1913), 271.

77 Bethnal Green, *Chief Inspector's Annual Report on the Work of the Sanitary Department, for the Year Ending 1905*, 7. For the relation between wages and rents see my articles, previously cited. For much of the nineteenth century, as one M.O.H. pointed out, external sanitary factors and not 'internal conditions arising from poverty' were assumed to be the sole cause of high death-rates in poor areas. See Newman, *Health of the State*, p. 184. But see also Dr Alison, 'On the Effects of Poverty and Privation on the Public Health,' *T.N.A.P.S.S.* (1857), 442, and the special section on poverty in E. Smith, *Manual for Medical Officers of Health* (1873).

78 *Public Health*, ii (January 1890), 277.

79 Ibid., xvii (February 1905), 287.

80 *Trans. Soc. M.O.H.* (1883–4), 39. For the 'no rent' movement of the East End see *Pall Mall Gazette*, 12 October 1883, 1 November 1883. Rent tribunals were established following the control of rents in 1915.

81 I am indebted to Mr Hector Macdonald for this statement about Littlejohn. See note 31 above.

82 Society of the Medical Officers of Health, *Reports*, Session 1868–9, 6.

83 The Select Committee on Artisans' and Labourers' Dwellings Improvement devoted much time to questioning the medical officers on the day-to-day working of the Torrens and Cross Acts.

84 Quoted in Jephson, op. cit., p. 218.

85 Metropolitan Association of Medical Officers of Health, *Papers*, Session 1878–9, 16.

86 The Local Government Board, under Simon and then Buchanan, was headed by medical officers of health. Buchanan did initiate enquiries into back-to-back housing.

87 For this team at the Privy Council see Lambert, op. cit., pp. 315 ff. and Brockington, *Public Health in the Nineteenth Century*, pp. 210 ff.

88 Newman, *The Building of a Nation's Health*, p. 18. It was Duncan's use of the Registrar-General's statistics that first brought him into prominence in Liverpool as a possible future M.O.H. See Frazer, op. cit., p. 28.

89 See, for example, H. Letheby, *On the Estimation of the Sanitary Condition of Communities and the Comparative Salubrity of Towns* (1874), 3, and *Public Health*, vii (May 1895), 321.

90 Lambert, op. cit., p. 264.

91 O. R. McGregor, 'Social Research and Social Policy in the Nineteenth Century,' *British Journal of Sociology*, viii (June 1957), 149.

92 The medical officers did not feature in many working-class novels. There is one notable exception, *Dives and Lazarus*, written by W. S. Gilbert's father, a man who took a great interest in both housing problems and medical matters. See also M. Brightfield, 'The Medical Profession in Early Victorian England, as Depicted in the Novels of the Period, 1840–1870,' *Bulletin of the History of Medicine*, xxv (May–June 1961), 238.

93 *Medical Times*, 13 December 1851, 616.

27　Disease, Debility, and Death

George Rosen

For the Victorians it was the age of great cities, their growth due largely to the immigration of millions who came for the most part from rural England and Wales, from the Scottish Highlands, and from Ireland. The raw industrial cities and towns into which these people poured were as unprepared to receive them as they were unprepared to live in an urban environment. By the 1840s it was evident that the consequences of this migration were nothing short of catastrophic. Lack of proper housing, overcrowding, inadequate environmental sanitation, polluted water supplies, and malnutrition combined to make the life of the city-dweller, particularly if new, and that of his family, hard, desperate, and hazardous to health and life. The situation was in large measure a consequence of the precarious economic situation of the workers. Not only the hard core of paupers, but very many more were subject to the shadow of economic distress and destitution.

To many observers of the Victorian city, the consequences of economic want, poor housing, defective sanitation, deficient nutrition were clear; they led to a waste of human life through disease, debility, and death. Dickens's account of the revenge taken by Tom-all-Alone's, a pestilential slum in the shadow of Southwark Cathedral, makes the point directly and explicitly:[1]

> He has his revenge. . . There is not a drop of Tom's corrupted blood but propagates infection and contagion somewhere. It shall pollute, this very night, the choice stream (in which a chemist on analysis would find the genuine nobility) of a Norman house, and his Grace shall not be able to say Nay to the infamous alliance. There is not an atom of Tom's slime, not a

cubic inch of any pestilential gas in which he lives, not one obscenity or degradation about him, not an ignorance, not a wickedness, not a brutality of his committing, but shall work its retribution . . .

A similar account was given more prosaically and precisely but quite as forcefully in official and unofficial reports. Cowan noted in 1840[2] that

> The rapid increase in the amount of the labouring population, without any corresponding amount of accommodation being provided for them; the density and still increasing density of that population; the state of the districts which it inhabits; the fluctuations of trade and of the prices of provisions, and the lamentable 'strikes' in consequence of combination among the workmen, by which the means of subsistence have been suddenly withdrawn from large masses; the recklessness and addiction to the use of ardent spirits, at once the cause and the effect of destitution; the prevalence of epidemic disease both among the adult and infantile portion of the community, have been the chief causes of the great mortality in the city of Glasgow.

The close connection between ill-health, death, and the evil brood engendered by poverty was noted as well by other observers and investigators, many of them physicians. Well acquainted with conditions in the Manchester slums, Richard Howard, surgeon to the Royal Infirmary and the Workhouse at Manchester, observed in 1838 that 'Although death directly produced by hunger may be rare, there can be no doubt that a very large proportion of the mortality amongst the labouring classes is attributable to deficiency of food as a main cause, aided by too long continued toil and exertion without adequate repose, insufficient clothing, exposure to cold and other privations to which the poor are subjected.' Furthermore, he asserted that the 'destitute are [fever's] most frequent victims' since 'in persons labouring under an impaired state of health from deficiency of food there is a remarkable susceptibility to the effects of contagion.'[3]

The points made by Cowan, Howard, and others were repeated many times in the course of the century. Indeed, the pioneer dietary surveys conducted by Edward Smith in the 1860s pointed to a clear association between ill-health and poor nutrition. The fact is, however, that little or no attention was given to these matters and it was not until seventy-five years later that effective action was taken.

Nevertheless, an increasing awareness was developing during the same period that the health of large sections of the population was worse than it had been at the beginning of the nineteenth century. The crude death-rate for the country as a whole had been declining from about 1780 to approximately 1810. Thereafter it began to rise again and continued to do so until the 1840s. Informed contemporaries noted this shift. The Census Commissioners called attention in 1831 to the rising mortality.[4] In 1849, the very knowledgeable William Farr, Compiler of Abstracts to the Registrar-General, wrote that 'Since 1816 the [statistical] returns indicate a retrograde movement. The mortality has apparently increased.' But Farr added that 'The health of all parts of the kingdom is not equally bad.' Variations in mortality were evident and he related them to a variety of factors. 'Upon looking generally at the health of the population,' he continued, 'it will be found that people suffer most in the great town districts . . . the returns . . . conspire in proving the prevalence of general causes of insalubrity operating with different degrees of intensity, but with much greater force than in other parts of the country.'[5]

In short, as increasing numbers of people were subjected to an unfavorable, and for some, lethal environment in the urban center, mortality rose. Moreover, there was a clear awareness that for every death there were many more cases of sickness. In 1836, T. R. Edmonds calculated a relationship between mortality and sickness at various ages, chiefly between fifteen and sixty. He concluded that for every annual death, two persons were suffering from illness severe enough to prevent them from working. He wrote: 'If, as is commonly the fact, the annual deaths between these ages amount to $1\frac{1}{2}$ per cent, there will be *constantly sick* 3 per cent of this part of the population. . . If the mean duration of an attack of sickness be assumed to be $36\frac{1}{2}$ days, the tenth part of a year, then 30 per cent of this population are yearly attacked by sickness.'[6] A decade later, William Farr, using sickness-rates obtained by F. G. P. Neison from reports of Friendly Societies, calculated that 'the numbers constantly sick in London were 122,000 and the annual attacks of sickness more than 1,220,000 during the seven years 1838–44.'[7] Despite their interest, however, these figures are of limited value. As Neison himself was aware, members of the Friendly Societies were not representative of all the workers or of the poor. Members either had more stable employment or were more provident.[8] Moreover, in view of the difficulty of establishing valid morbidity-rates even today, one can hardly expect more than rather crude results at a time when few data were available and analytic tools were less sophisticated. None the less, to many observers it was clear that the recorded mortality was only the tip of a vast iceberg of ill-health. Most evident were the acute communicable diseases and their consequences. Thus, in 1856, the medical officer of health of Clerkenwell commented that 'Those attacked do not simply recover or die. I shall not be exaggerating when I say that all recovering from these complaints [i.e. infectious diseases] are permanently injured.'[9]

Despite inadequacies of data and method, relations between social circumstances and differential morbidity and mortality in cities and towns continued to be studied throughout the Victorian period. The methods available for the study of health problems were critical observation, the survey, and, from the late 1820s onward, statistical analysis. The survey as a tool for medical and social investigation was well known and had been employed during the eighteenth and early nineteenth centuries, particularly in the form of the regional health survey or medical topography. Statistical methods were also eagerly accepted and applied with considerable vigor, so that increasing numbers of studies of health problems based on numerical data began to appear. Examples are the *Report on the Sanitary Condition of the Labouring Population* by Edwin Chadwick; the studies carried out at John Simon's instigation by the physicians associated with him during the 1860s at the Privy Council; contributions to the *Journal of the Statistical Society*; and the investigation of workhouses and provision for sick paupers by a commission appointed by the *Lancet* in 1866.[10]

These studies showed that differences in mortality-rates were directly related to socio-economic conditions; they pointed out those groups such as infants and children who were highly vulnerable; delineated the diseases or groups of diseases causing excessive mortality; investigated the possible causes of epidemics; and examined social problems such as prostitution, and the effects of industry on health. Based on a study of mortality in Glasgow for the period 1821–35, Edmonds reported that the marked increase in mortality was due chiefly to deaths among men in the age groups from thirty to sixty, commenting that this situation was 'just what might be expected to occur, on the supposition of the rising adult population possessing a lower degree of vitality than their immediate predecessors.'[11] Several years later, in 1842, Chadwick compared mortality-rates for different social and occupational groups in Manchester with their counterparts of Rutland, showing quite clearly that the former was a most unhealthy city for its inhabitants. This was confirmed by William Farr, who, discussing the period 1838–44, noted[12] that even though

> The population of Surrey exceeded that of Manchester, yet in 7 years 16,000 persons died in Manchester over and above the deaths in Surrey, the mortality in which from the poverty of the labourer, and slighter degrees of the influences so fatal in Manchester, is higher than it should be. There were 23,523 children under 5 years of age in Surrey, and the deaths of children of that age were 7,364; the children in Manchester were 21,152, the deaths 20,726. In the 7 years, 13,362 children in Manchester alone fell a sacrifice to known causes, which it is believed may be removed to a great extent and the victims in Liverpool were not less numerous. Other parts, and particularly the *towns* of England are similarly afflicted.

In short, as Farr put it, 'different classes of the population experience very different rates of mortality, and suffer different kinds of diseases. The principal causes of these differences, besides the sex, age, and hereditary organization, must be sought in three sources—exercise in the ordinary occupations of life—the adequate or inadequate supply of warmth and of food—and the differential degrees of exposure to poisonous effluvia and to destructive agents.'[13]

The point made by Farr was underscored throughout most of the nineteenth century by outbreaks of infectious disease, for this was a period of frightening epidemics. On four occasions during the century, Europe was scourged by severe invasions of Asiatic cholera. Other communicable diseases were continually present in the urban communities of the Victorian period, the most important of which were typhus and typhoid fevers, dysentery, tuberculosis, diphtheria, scarlet fever, smallpox and other diseases of infancy and childhood, and venereal diseases. Although communicable diseases remained in the forefront of attention throughout most of the period, the diseases of various groups of workers were increasingly investigated to provide an additional basis for public-health action.

The occurrence of disease in a given population at a specified time exhibits a characteristic pattern defined by causation, morbidity, and mortality as related to age, sex, social class, occupation, mode of life, and, more generally, to the culture and psychology of a society. The pattern of disease which characterizes any group of people is not a matter of chance. It is an expression of their interaction with their environment in its various facets, and from this viewpoint certain diseases or groups of diseases may be considered as most characteristic or indicative.[14] The action of George Eliot's *Middlemarch* is set around 1830, and in presenting Lydgate, the physician, she alludes to his interest in 'special questions of disease, such as the nature of fever or fevers.' This comment is not just a coincidental dab of local color, but rather a precise brush-stroke which defines Lydgate and his place within the medical profession. 'Fever,' the portmanteau term that included typhoid, typhus, and relapsing fevers, was a problem of major concern among physicians during the earlier nineteenth century. Indeed, from a public-health and medical viewpoint, the history of the Victorian city is to a considerable degree a history of 'fever,' the consequence of inadequate or absent community and personal hygiene.

The diseases in this as yet undifferentiated group had apparently subsided toward the end of the eighteenth century, though they remained endemic, but during the early decades of the nineteenth century there were severe outbreaks of 'fever' first in Ireland, then in Scotland and England. Physicians were aware of variations in symptoms exhibited by 'fever' patients, and that the clinical course of the illness was not the same in all those affected. The implications had been raised by John Huxham in 1739. 'I cannot conclude this Essay on Fevers,' he wrote, 'without taking notice of the very great difference there is between the *putrid malignant* and the *slow nervous Fever* . . . they resemble one another in some Respects, tho' very essentially different in others . . . Could we suppose both the one and the other to arise from contagion, (which is commonly the Case in pestilential and petechial Fevers).'[15]

During the first thirty years of the nineteenth century a group of French clinician-pathologists, chief among them Louis, Bretonneau, and Chomel, differentiated typhoid fever as a specific disease. However, acceptance of the distinction between typhoid and typhus fevers spread slowly in Britain, chiefly because of lack of agreement on etiology, symptomatology, and prognosis.[16] It was not until 1869 that typhoid and typhus were separated from the general category of 'fever' deaths for the purpose of death-registration. Thereafter, they were tabulated separately, but in referring to them before 1870 they must be considered collectively. However, there are indications in hospital records between 1849 and 1869 which make possible some judgment on the relative prevalence and significance of these conditions during these two decades.

The city of Glasgow is frequently mentioned in the early medical reports dealing with the 'continued fevers,' and with good reason. Typhus and typhoid fevers were endemic, and from time to time the former diseases erupted in serious epidemics. Indeed, 'fever' was so prevalent and appeared to have such a distinctive character that foreigners came to Glasgow to study it.[17] Although the number of hospital admissions cannot be used as direct evidence of the actual number of cases of the disease, nevertheless they appear to reflect its prevalence and over a period of time to indicate trends in its occurrence. The situation in Glasgow is revealed by the number of hospitalized cases of 'fever' from the turn of the century to 1839. As a proportion of all patients admitted to the Glasgow Royal Infirmary between 1795 and 1839, the number of 'fever' cases increased enormously: 1795–1809, 10·9 percent; 1810–24, 23·3 percent; 1825–39, 50·0 percent.[18] This trend may be seen as well in terms of absolute numbers. Until 1815, the number of 'fever' cases hospitalized annually from 1796 on ranged from a low of 16 to a high of 128, with an average for the period of 68. Thereafter the number of annual admissions increased sharply. There were 230 cases admitted in 1815 and the number rose to 1,371 by 1818, declining again to 229 in 1822. Thereafter the number of admissions increased steadily to reach 2,734 in 1832, fluctuated in the ensuing years but rarely dropped below 1,300, and reached the highest point in 1837 with 5,387 admissions. Hospitalization of 'fever' patients continued on a high level through the forties, as indicated by the following figures: 1846, 1,270; 1847, 4,732; 1848, 1,493; 1849, 510.[19] Admissions remained relatively high until the end of the sixties.

The rise and fall in the number of hospitalized 'fever' cases in Glasgow reflects the frequent epidemics of typhus fever. During the middle of the nineteenth century, Glasgow was probably the dirtiest and unhealthiest of all the British cities, and its wretched proletariat provided the human material which physicians investigated to untangle the mystery of the 'continued fevers.' According to the Scottish physician Neil Arnott in 1840, 'the great mass of the fever cases occurred in the low wynds and dirty narrow streets and courts, in which because lodging was there cheapest, the poorest and most destitute naturally had their abodes. From one such locality, between Argyll-street and the river, 754 of about 5,000 cases of fever which occurred in the previous year were carried to the hospitals.'[20] The reason for the difficulties in achieving precise definitions of the diseases subsumed under 'fever' are not far to seek. Typhus is basically a disease of the small blood vessels which are seriously damaged when invaded by micro-organisms called *Rickettsia*. Vessels of the brain and the skin are particularly liable to attack, thus producing the delirium and stupor so prominent in the course of the disease, and the characteristic spotted rash appearing on or about the fifth febrile day. Except for the rash, typhus has no characteristic symptoms or signs. The skin eruption appears to have been overlooked or was not mentioned by physicians, and it is indeed striking to note how late references to this phenomenon appear. According to Stewart, prior to 'a visit which Dr Peebles made to the Glasgow Fever Hospital in the spring of 1835, the exanthema of typhus, then found to be of general occurrence, had neither been looked for nor registered in that institution, and was received as a new discovery.'[21] A probable reason for this situation may be related to the transmission of the disease to man by the body louse. Generally, man is infected when rickettsia-laden louse feces are rubbed into the broken skin. Scratching the bites of lice or fleas facilitates the process. The bites of lice and fleas must have been quite common among 'fever' patients and it is possible that the typhus petechiae were overlooked among them.[22]

Evidence for the widespread prevalence of the louse in the population from which the fever patients came is provided by Stewart. 'It is well known,' he wrote,[23]

> that, for many years past, every resident clerk in the Glasgow Infirmary, with very rare exceptions, many students who frequented fever wards, several of the acting physicians, and almost all the nurses, have, at one time or other, been attacked with typhus, and that not a few have fallen victims; and Dr. Cowan in his pamphlet, entitled Statistics of Fever and Smallpox in Glasgow says, (p. 10), of the district surgeons, 'Few of those gentlemen escape an attack of fever.'

Louse infestation (*pediculosis*) occurs most often among poor people where a lack of facilities reduces the frequency of bathing, and of changing and washing clothing. Scratching and restlessness on the part of heavily infested persons cause lice to wander and to reach the outer garments whence they may be readily transferred to others. This is particularly the case when people are crowded together in dwellings under insanitary conditions, when louse infestation may increase to the point where endemic typhus becomes epidemic. Furthermore, lice are sensitive to temperature and leave a person with a high fever, or a cold cadaver, to settle in bedding or on other individuals. Thus, those who care for the sick and the dead are particularly likely to encounter infected lice and to become victims of typhus.

The role of the louse in the transmission of typhus, the nature of the causative organism, and the character of the essential lesion of the disease were all largely unknown during the Victorian period, and were not fully established until the twentieth century. The process by which these facts were discovered, and typhus and typhoid fevers were distinguished, was a gradual one to which French, American, and British physicians contributed. Among the last several Scots endeavored to explain why continued fever exhibited such varied clinical phenomena, and in the process developed the idea that there were actually two diseases. The first definite statement of this concept was made in 1835 by Robert Perry, physician to the Glasgow Royal Infirmary, and published the following year.[24] His conclusions were based on the observation of four thousand patients and three hundred autopsies. Perry stated that typhus was a specific disease caused by contagion which introduced an aminal poison into the body. It differed from typhoid which exhibited a definite pathology of the small intestine, as well as a different rash. A similar position was taken by another physician, H. C. Barlow, in a paper presented in 1840 before the Paris Medical Society.[25] After stressing the differences in symptomatology, he emphasized the presence of a particular anatomical lesion of the bowel in typhoid and the absence of any obvious gross anatomical lesion in typhus, concluding with the comment,

'Surely two diseases which differ in all these particulars cannot be identical.' Several months later Stewart discussed the symptoms and the skin eruptions, and emphasized the presence of the intestinal lesion in typhoid and its absence in typhus. Despite the clarity and logic of these papers, however, the concept which they advocated was not immediately accepted. Thus the author of an article in the *British and Foreign Medical Review* for 1844 discussing epidemic fevers in Glasgow, Edinburgh, Aberdeen, and other Scottish municipalities, concludes that 'the continued fevers . . . were the *same species* of disease, although *different varieties* of that species.'[26] However, the writer admits that the fever which occurred in Edinburgh in 1842–3 exhibited features distinct in certain respects from those of typhus, particularly relapses and jaundice.

These comments point to another factor that complicated the problem of 'fever,' namely the occurrence of relapsing or recurrent fever. The cause of relapsing fever is a spirochete which is conveyed from man to man by the body louse. Since typhus and relapsing fever are both dependent on the same vector, they may coexist in the same population though in differing proportions. The onset of the disease is sudden, and frequently accompanied by nausea and severe vomiting, a symptom which gave rise to the name 'gastric fever'; the fever continues for three to five days, and ends in a sharp crisis marked by copious sweating and exhaustion. After about a week the fever recurs, and there may be four, five, or even more relapses, whence the name of the disease. Some manifestations of relapsing fever are not unlike typhus. At the height of the fever, there may be dizziness, mental cloudiness, or delirium. A transitory erythematous rash also occurs and in severe cases there may be petechiae. Unlike typhus, however, in which jaundice does not occur, this manifestation develops in relapsing fever, and appears to have been very common in some nineteenth-century epidemics. At a time when the cause of the disease was still unknown and laboratory methods for making a specific diagnosis were not yet available, the confusion of physicians dealing only with clinical and post mortem findings is understandable. It was not until 1868 that Otto Obermeier showed that a spiral organism was consistently present in cases of relapsing fever, and that the disease was transmissible; these findings were not published until 1873.

By the middle of the century, however, medical opinion began to shift decidedly to an acceptance of the concept of distinct disease entities, rather than maintaining a single category of 'continued fever.' This shift was hastened by the support given to the former position by William Jenner (1815–98), professor of pathological anatomy at the University College, and later physician to Queen Victoria. Between 1849 and 1851, he published a series of twenty papers[27] in which he examined a series of sixty-six fatal cases, and on the basis of a rigid clinical and pathological examination separated typhus from typhoid fever. Moreover, he demonstrated the distinct nature of these diseases in his own person as he noted when he republished his lectures and essays in 1893: 'it was said at the time,"Before typhus and typhoid fevers can be said to be absolutely different diseases, someone must be found who has suffered from both," and I was the first, so far as I know, who at that time could be proved to have suffered from both.'[28]

About this time typhus fever began to be recorded separately from relapsing fever and enteric fever (typhoid) in hospital statistics, thus making it possible to study the prevalence of these conditions somewhat more accurately. The epidemic prevalence of the disease in London in 1848 is shown by the fact that 786 cases were treated at the London Fever Hospital that year. Cases declined in succeeding years but in 1856 at the end of the Crimean War admissions rose precipitously to 1,062. From 1861 there was another epidemic in England and Scotland, associated largely with the hardships arising from the Cotton Famine in Lancashire. The London Fever Hospital had 1,827 cases in 1862, 2,493 in 1864, and the number did not drop below 1,000 until 1870, when 631 cases were reported. There were similar increases in Glasgow, Liverpool, and other towns.[29]

After 1869, when typhus fever began to be tabulated separately in the Registrar-General's reports, it ceased to be epidemic, and thereafter the number of fatal attacks declined almost continuously. In 1869, there were 4,281 typhus deaths in England; by 1885 the number had dropped to 318. The corresponding rates per thousand living were 0·19 and 0·01. Individual cities reflected the general trend. London, for example, had 716 typhus deaths in 1869 and only 28 in 1885; during this period the death-rate per thousand living for typhus declined from 0·23 to 0·01. By 1906, three years before Charles Nicolle's discovery that the body louse transmitted typhus, the annual report of the London County Council stated that there were no more deaths from the disease that year.

How had this change come about, even though the cause of typhus remained unknown? These trends undoubtedly reflect in large measure the impact of the sanitary reform movement in the earlier part of the period. 'The discovery of the laws of public health,' the Registrar-General noted in 1871, 'the determination of the conditions of cleanliness, manners, water supply, food, exercise, isolation, medicine most favourable to life in one city, in one country, is a boon to every city, to every country, for all can profit by the experience.'[30] The leaders of sanitary reform believed they had discovered the laws of public health. Acting on the premise that a clean city is a healthy city, they undertook to clean up the physical environment, to provide pure water in adequate supply, to improve housing, and to provide unadulterated food on a regular basis—in short, to provide decent living conditions. It had long been noted that the occurrence and prevalence of typhus were closely related to the socio-economic circumstances of its victims. Typhus was found to be closely associated with poverty, destitution, poor housing, overcrowding, and poor personal hygiene, and was not inaccurately called the poor man's disease. It was not a characteristic health problem of the middle and upper classes of Victorian Britain, except for those, such as the clergy, physicians, nurses, and others, whose occupations brought them into contact with the sick, the dead, or their environs. Most municipalities throughout the Victorian period never even came within sight of overtaking problems of community hygiene and health. Nevertheless, enough positive change did take place to yield ascertainable benefits. Slum clearance, regulation of lodging houses, provision of public baths and wash-houses, increased use of cotton clothing, particularly underwear, and consequent improvement in personal cleanliness played their part in reducing the prevalence of typhus fever. Slum clearance tended to disperse workers to newer districts where they could live without crowding because new means of transportation also became available. In addition, as Creighton observed in 1894, 'food has been for a long time cheap and wages good . . . So long as our cheap supplies of food, fuel and clothing are uninterrupted, there is small chance of typhus or relapsing fever.'[31]

Seen in retrospect, such historical trends as the decline of typhus seem clear and straight, but the process from which they are abstracted was not so smooth. What looks like a steady, even advance over several decades is seen under closer scrutiny to consist of hesitant piecemeal changes, *ad hoc* expedients, and compromises resulting from bitterly waged campaigns against specific evils. Actions were taken by urban communities, or were forced upon them, to remedy specific and glaring sanitary deficiencies, without considering how far these were related to other problems. Nevertheless, the thread of continuity is not an illusion, an artifact of the historian. It is a reality derived from the circumstances that throughout most of the nineteenth century health-workers confronted substantially the same problems. The same undesirable characteristics and conditions that had been uncovered in urban communities by the classic investigations of the 1830s and 1840s were still being exposed thirty years later. What was different was that the sheer magnitude of the problems was no longer so overwhelming. Factual knowledge of such conditions and the conscience and drive to do something about them, combined with more knowledge as to causation, led officials and concerned citizens to redress such shortcomings. This pattern is illustrated by the history not only of typhus but also of typhoid, diarrhoeal diseases, and other preventable conditions. Indeed, John Simon classified the chief preventable diseases into four groups: the fevers, diarrhoeal diseases, pulmonary affections, and infantile disorders.

With the separation of typhus and typhoid after the middle of the century and their establishment as distinctive diseases, it becomes possible to study the prevalence of typhoid, how it arose and spread, and consequently how it might be prevented. After 1850, the medical literature is concerned less with symptoms and pathology and more with epidemic outbreaks and their causes. Moreover, typhoid fever was not a disease largely of the poor and the destitute, but attacked all social classes, reaching even into the Royal Family. Albert, the Prince Consort, died of typhoid in 1861 at the age of forty-two, and in 1871, when he was thirty, the Prince of Wales suffered a severe attack.

Typhoid fever did not become a reportable disease until 1889. Consequently, the incidence and prevalence of the disease cannot be known exactly for most of the Victorian period. However, it is possible to estimate the prevalence of the disease from the number of deaths. In 1869 the deaths from 'enteric and simple continued fevers,' which included typhoid and paratyphoid, numbered 13,969, and in the immediately ensuing years there was little decrease in the total. There were probably about six cases for every death, in all not quite 84,000 cases in 1869. During the five years 1871–5 the average annual number of deaths fell very slightly to 12,026; in the following five-year period (1876–80) the average dropped more significantly to 8,657; and in the period 1881–5 it fell to 6,671, despite a steady increase in population. During the subsequent five years (1886–90) the annual average deaths continued to drop but somewhat more slowly, numbering 5,681. This decline is paralleled by the decline in the number of deaths for London for the same period. Mortality-rates from typhoid fever for England and Wales during the last quarter of the nineteenth century highlight the decline more sharply. By decades the average annual death-rate per million persons was as follows: 1871–80, 332; 1881–90, 198; 1891–1900, 174. In short, over three decades the death-rate fell by slightly over 50 percent.[32] This decline, though marked, was not so dramatic as the drastic decline of typhus.[33] For social and biological reasons typhoid remained endemic and medically significant well into the twentieth century. This situation is reflected in the sixth edition of William Osler's *Principles and Practice of Medicine*, a leading text among British students, which appeared in 1905. In a volume of 1,100 pages, about fifty pages were devoted to typhoid fever and only four to typhus.

At the time when typhus and typhoid were being differentiated clinically and pathologically, evidence began to accumulate that there were important differences in the circumstances under which the two diseases occurred. The problem was enmeshed in the larger controversy over the origin and spread of infectious diseases. Basically there were two types of explanation: contagionist and non-contagionist, whose history throughout the centuries had been a series of ups and downs. In the course of time the two viewpoints merged in some degree to produce an intermediate position. Thus, for most of the nineteenth century three theoretical positions may be distinguished. First, there was the miasmatic theory that epidemic outbreaks of infectious disease were caused by the state of the atmosphere, corrupted by terrestrial exhalations or vapors. During the nineteenth century, this was generally held in the version that poor sanitary conditions leading to organic putrefaction produced a local atmospheric state that caused such diseases. Many of the sanitary reformers, among them Edwin Chadwick, Southwood-Smith, and Florence Nightingale, held this view. Then there was the view that specific contagia, probably animate, were the sole causes of infectious and epidemic diseases. This was the strict contagionist position taken by John Snow and William Budd, of whom more below, and the one best known today because of the great impact of the bacteriological discoveries at the end of the century. The third position, adopted by those who endeavored to conciliate or to compromise the miasmatic and contagionist theories, may be called limited or contingent contagionism. While admitting that infectious diseases were due to contagia, either animate or chemical, the proponents of this view held that the latter could not act except in conjunction with other elements, such as the state of the atmosphere, condition of the soil, or social factors. This was the most widely held theoretical position, and one of its prominent advocates was John Simon. Its popularity was due in large measure to its portmanteau character. Able to accommodate a variety of elements, some of them mutually inconsistent, this view persisted into the last decades of the century. Practically, limited contagionists tended to concentrate on cleaning up the environment and providing proper drainage, rather than on isolation or quarantine procedures. In comparing the experience of the City of London during the cholera epidemic of 1853–4 with that of 1849, John Simon expressed this view succinctly and pragmatically. He pointed out that there was 'less suffering in the City of 1854 than in the City of 1849, less in the City clean than in the City dirty, less in the City cared for than in the Metropolis neglected.'[34]

Around the middle of the century, however, evidence began to accumulate that contamination of drinking water by human fecal discharges in sewage caused typhoid and cholera, and that some agency resembling a living organism was the immediate cause in each disease. This view emerged from empirical studies by John Snow and William Budd in connection with epidemics of cholera and typhoid fever.

Cholera first appeared in England in 1831–2. The second invasion occurred in 1848–9, appearing first in September 1848, reaching its height between June and the middle of September 1849, and finally disappearing in December. Most deaths from cholera occurred during 1849, reaching a total of 53,293. In addition, there were 18,887 deaths from diarrhoea, not labelled cholera. The disease reappeared in London in August 1853, and by September it was prevalent in Newcastle, Gateshead, and other towns in Britain. Then it seemed that cholera would disappear—as it had previously. However, the disease hung on in London, and in the following year there was a recrudescence, leading by the end of 1854 to a total of 20,097 deaths for England and Wales. The fourth cholera epidemic from which Britain suffered in the nineteenth century first made its appearance in Southampton in July 1865. Cases occurred later that year in Southampton, Weymouth, Portland, Dorchester, and in other communities. The following year saw a full-blown epidemic with 14,378 deaths in England as a whole, 5,548 of them in London.[35]

The first important contribution to the etiology of cholera was made by John Snow (1813–58), a medical practitioner in London, who in his own day was better known as an anesthetist than as an epidemiologist. Indeed, his reputation was such that in 1853 and again in 1857 he administered chloroform to Queen Victoria when she was delivered. Snow had seen cases of cholera at Newcastle upon Tyne during the epidemic of 1831–2; when the disease recurred in 1848 he began actively to study it. He was then in London, and his first communication appeared there in 1849 as a pamphlet entitled *On the Mode of Communication of Cholera*. During the epidemic of 1854, Snow carried out a more systematic investigation, which involved also an outbreak among the consumers of water from a pump in Broad Street. In the course of his study, he examined the distribution of deaths from cholera in the southern sections of London, where drinking water was supplied by several private water companies. Snow showed that the number of deaths in each area corresponded to the degree of pollution of the part of the river Thames from which each company obtained its water. In 1855, Snow published a second, enlarged edition of his 1849 pamphlet, in which he set forth his definitive views on the etiology and spread of cholera.[36] The clinical features of the disease led him to infer that the poison of cholera enters the alimentary canal directly by mouth, and that this poison is probably a specific living being derived from the excreta of a cholera patient. Furthermore, he showed that cholera can be transmitted from person to person through soiling of the hands or through contaminated food and water. Finally, Snow pointed out that defective sewerage made it possible for the dangerous wastes from cholera patients to permeate the ground and to pollute wells or other supplies of water used by the community. Snow showed conclusively that the agent of cholera infection could be carried in water, but he did not identify it. Not until 1883 when Robert Koch isolated and cultivated *Vibrio cholerae* was the essential correctness of Snow's teaching established.

Simultaneous discovery is by no means uncommon in science; it is not surprising therefore to find that the views formulated by Snow had been developed independently by his countryman and contemporary, William Budd (1811–80), also a medical practitioner. In 1849, the year in which Snow's first communication appeared, Budd too published a pamphlet on *Malignant Cholera: Its Mode of Propagation and its Prevention* in which he advanced similar conclusions. In his view cholera was caused by a specific living organism, breeding in the human intestinal tract and disseminated by contaminated drinking water. Budd recognized that this view also applied to typhoid fever, which he studied for more than thirty years. Budd was interested in the problem of 'fever' and particularly in typhoid, of which he had had a very severe attack. Although a connection between the occurrence of typhoid and poor sanitation was generally accepted, there was a widespread belief in its spontaneous generation from dirt and filth. This was the doctrine supported by Charles Murchison (1830–79), physician to the London Fever Hospital (1856–70) and St Thomas's Hospital and author of the classic book on the *Continued Fevers of Great Britain* (1862). He believed that typhoid could arise spontaneously from filth, and therefore called it 'pythogenic' fever, meaning generated in rottenness. Budd emphatically rejected this idea and attacked it with slashing logic, using the 'Great Stink' during the hot months of 1858–9 as part of his argument.

That summer 'the sewage of nearly three millions of people had been brought to seethe and ferment under a burning sun, in one vast open *cloaca* lying in their midst,' and the stench from the Thames assumed the dimensions of a national catastrophe. In the public buildings along the river, rooms were rendered only barely tolerable by hanging blinds soaked with chloride of lime before every window and by the lavish use of disinfectants. Moreover, in the light of the generally accepted opinion on the relation between epidemic disease and vapors and gases derived from putrefaction, there were extremely gloomy predictions of pestilence on a vast scale. Meanwhile, Budd says, 'the hot weather passed away; the returns of sickness and mortality were made up, and, strange to relate, the result showed, not only a death-rate below the average, but, *as the leading peculiarity of the season*, a remarkable diminution in the prevalence of fever, diarrhoea, and the other forms of disease commonly ascribed to putrid emanations.'[37] Based on this episode and a great deal of other evidence, Budd concluded that the idea that a poison capable of producing typhoid fever is 'bred in every cesspool or ditch in which there may chance to be a heap of seething rottenness . . . will take its place in that limbo of discarded fallacies to which . . . other superstitions have long since been consigned.'[38] Budd was in no doubt as to the nature of the disease and the means of its spread. In the rules for preventing the disease which he drew up, Budd noted that 'the poison by which this fever spreads is almost entirely contained in the discharges from the bowels. These discharges infect—1. The air of the sick room. 2. The bed and body linen of the patient. 3. The privy and the cesspool or the drains proceeding from them. From the privy or drain the poison often soaks into the well, and infects the drinking water . . . In these various ways the infection proceeding from the bowel discharges often spreads the fever far and wide.' Or as he commented in the *Lancet* (15 November 1856) on a typhoid outbreak in the Clergy Orphan School in London, 'The sewer may be looked upon, in fact, as a *direct continuation of the diseased* intestine.'[39] As a result, Budd advised that the excreta of typhoid patients be disinfected so as to reduce the incidence of the disease.

However self-evident Budd's concepts of the nature and transmission of typhoid may appear now, they were not so regarded by his contemporaries, who accepted them only with reservations or refused even to consider them. Viewed objectively the contagionist and miasmatic theories were too evenly balanced for any clear-cut decision in favor of one or the other to be made on the basis of the existing evidence. Neither side had any knowledge of certain important links in the chain of infection, such as human or insect carriers, and both sides endeavored to deal with gaps in knowledge or inadequate evidence by analogical reasoning. Furthermore, there was still an inadequate appreciation and application of experimental methods, as well as the use of uncontrolled observations and unreliable information. In this situation, the standpoint adopted was not infrequently either a suspension of judgment or was determined by non-scientific, i.e., political, economic, or social factors.[40]

Whatever the precise means of spreading these diseases might be, the available evidence appeared to point to the need for proper sewerage and unpolluted water. John Simon, reporting to the Privy Council in 1858, emphasized that 'if only a few simple sanitary faults were corrected throughout the country,' the average annual mortality might be reduced by at least 100,000 lives.[41] The factual underpinning for this recommendation was provided by Edward H. Greenhow (1814–88), an outstanding member of a group of medical investigators, who under Simon's direction between 1858 and 1871 carried out epidemiological researches of lasting importance.[42] This was a major survey of the prevalence of diarrhoeal diseases ('alvine flux') in England and Wales, with specific attention to ten cities and towns with the highest mortality from this cause: Coventry, Birmingham, Wolverhampton, Dudley, Merthyr Tydfil, Nottingham, Leeds, Manchester, Chorlton, and Salford. Greenhow's lengthy survey, almost a hundred pages, was published in 1859 in Simon's Second

Report to the Privy Council. The detailed findings for each community were based on a personal field-investigation by Greenhow, in which he collected samples of the local water supply for analysis, examined the vital statistics, and visited the streets and districts with the highest mortality from diarrhoeal disease. He noted the tendency for excessive mortality from diarrhoea

> to prevail in places where human excrement is allowed to accumulate in cesspools, and privies. The facts of the case are so striking . . . that it is impossible not to admit the relationship as one of cause and effect. But the cause is not an exclusive one . . . The presence of faecal impurity infecting the atmosphere must, therefore, be classed only as a principal cause of diarrhoea, and the existence of other causes must be conceded.
>
> Instances were adduced in which the use of well water, contaminated by the percolation from sewers or cesspools, had caused diarrhoea and, in some cases, fatal diarrhoea.

The conclusions which Greenhow drew from his findings were that the excessive mortality was a consequence of two basic factors: '*a*, The tainting of the atmosphere with the products of organic decomposition, especially of human excrement: *b*, The habitual drinking of impure water.'[43] Moreover, he called attention to the appalling mortality from diarrhoea of infants and children under five, and linked this problem to the employment of mothers in factories, an evil which Simon was soon to investigate.

Emphasis on the need for correction of sanitary inadequacies did not remain without results. By 1866, Simon was already able to show statistically, from a study by George Buchanan (1831–95), another of his epidemiologic researchers, that installation of proper sewerage and water supply systems was reducing deaths from typhoid fever and diarrhoea, probably dysentery. Consequently, his prescription for continued improvement of urban health was more of the same. Simon urged 'that, by appropriate structural works all the excremental produce of the population shall be so promptly and so thoroughly removed, that the inhabited place, in its air and soil, shall be absolutely without faecal impurities; and that the water-supply of the population shall be derived from such sources and conveyed in such channels, that its contamination by excrement is impossible . . .'[44]

Nevertheless, though improvement was steady and cumulative during the later nineteenth century, outbreaks of typhoid fever continued to occur, even after the introduction of new sewerage and water-supply systems, a phenomenon which happened not infrequently in the new residential districts of growing urban centers and which thus affected members of the middle and upper classes. It should be made clear that working-class areas were also affected by town growth. At the end of the century, Creighton pointed out that since 1869, typhoid fever 'has been much more common per head of the population, in the quick-growing manufacturing and mining towns than in any other parts of England and Wales, the districts with the highest enteric death rates being the mining region of the East Coast from the mouth of the Tees to somewhat north of the Tyne, the mining region of Glamorgan, certain manufacturing towns of Lancashire and the West Riding of Yorkshire, and some districts in the valley of the Trent in Staffordshire and Nottinghamshire.' In part this was due to poorly situated sources of water liable to contamination, in part to shoddy workmanship in the installation of waterworks and sewerage pipes, and more generally to an incomplete understanding of the etiology, epidemiology, and pathogenesis of typhoid, dysentery, and other gastro-intestinal infections.[45]

The typhoid outbreak at Croydon is illustrative. The epidemic was probably due to a carrier who introduced the disease, which then spread along the lines of a new sewerage system, filtering through defective pipes to contaminate the water supply of the community. (The role of the carrier was unknown and was not established for typhoid fever until the first decade of the twentieth century.) The impact of such events on public opinion is reflected in popular novels such as those of Charlotte Yonge. In *The Three Brides* (1876) an outbreak of typhoid occurs after a property owner rebuilds his tenements with proper drainage, but the well that supplied the buildings becomes contaminated and is the focus from which the disease stemmed.[46]

> The focus of the disease was in Pettitt's well. The water, though cold, clear, and sparkling, was affected by noxious gases from the drains, and had become little better than poison; the air was not much better, and as several neighbouring houses, some swarming with lodgers, used this water, the evil was accounted for . . . Odours there had been in plenty from the untouched drainage of the other houses, and these no doubt, enhanced the evil; but everyone agreed that the bad management of the drains on Mr. Pettitt's property had been the main agency in the present outbreak.

The typhoid problem, however, was more complex than was first realized. Even in places where good sewerage systems and waterworks were installed, outbreaks still occurred. It was not until the last three decades of the nineteenth century that epidemiologic studies established the more obscure channels by which infection was conveyed to its victims; and such knowledge was made even more precise with the discovery of the typhoid bacillus by Carl J. Eberth in 1880, and the development of the diagnostic agglutination test for the disease by Gruber, Widal, and Grünbaum in 1896. Michael William Taylor, of Penrith, first incriminated milk as a transmitter of typhoid in 1858.[47] Not surprisingly, in the light of current opinion, little attention was given to the paper he published on the subject. In 1870, E. Ballard, medical officer of health for Islington, traced a typhoid outbreak to a specific milk service, where water used in the dairy had been taken from a tank in direct communication with old drains. Three years later (1873) Netten Radcliffe and W. H. Power traced a widespread epidemic of typhoid in West London to the use of milk from a large London dairy.[48]

The discovery was also made that human beings in apparent good health could themselves serve as carriers of pathogenic organisms. As early as 1855, Pettenkofer had suggested that healthy human carriers could transmit cholera, but this hypothesis was not substantiated until the end of the century. Indeed, the importance of the

406 *above* 'A Court for King Cholera,' from *Punch*, xxiii (1852), 139. At the left is a refuse heap; in the center forefront children are playing with a dead rat; and just behind them is a man with a flat-topped conical hat and a pipe representing an Irishman.

407 *below* From *Punch*, xxxv (1858), 5. This was the period of the 'Great Stink' when gloomy predictions of epidemics to come were prevalent, and the smell from the river so bad that the House of Commons had to have a special recess.

DIPHTHERIA,   SCROFULA,   CHOLERA

FATHER THAMES INTRODUCING HIS OFFSPRING TO THE FAIR CITY OF LONDON
(A Design for a Fresco in the New Houses of Parliament.)

THE GREAT LOZENGE-MAKER.

A Hint to Paterfamilias.

408 From *Punch*, xxxv (1858), 207. This was a reaction to the investigations which revealed how widely foods and drugs were adulterated, often with dangerous chemicals such as arsenic.

carrier in the spread of typhoid was not demonstrated until the first decade of the present century. Yet as knowledge accumulated and was applied, as cities and towns were cleaned up with greater or lesser rapidity, the incidence and prevalence, the morbidity and mortality from typhoid fever diminished. At any given time during the later nineteenth century, the typhoid situation was variable and spotty, but the long-term trend was downward, as revealed by the average annual death-rate per million persons in England and Wales: 1871–80, 332; 1881–90, 198; 1891–1900, 174.

John Bunyan had already characterized consumption as 'the captain of all these men of death', and it was an equally—if not more—lethal disease in the nineteenth century. Not so swift and dramatic in its attack as cholera, nor so clearly linked to poverty as typhus, nor to environmental filth as the enteric fevers, yet in its insidious way tuberculosis was without question a more effective killer of large numbers of people. Nevertheless, any attempt to specify precisely the incidence and prevalence of tuberculosis in the Victorian city confronts serious problems.

The first is that of diagnosis. Throughout most of the nineteenth century there was little diagnostic precision in dealing with tuberculosis, since there was no unified concept of tuberculosis as a disease resulting from infection with the tubercle bacillus. On the one hand, many wasting diseases of the pulmonary organs, e.g., abscesses, cancer, pneumoconiosis, were confused with tuberculosis. On the other hand, physicians were inclined to consider non-pulmonary forms of tuberculosis and their diverse pathological manifestations, such as the swollen lymph nodes of the neck in scrofula, as so many separate diseases. Robert Koch discovered the tubercle bacillus in 1882, but as late as 1908 Arthur Newsholme noted that belief in the separate origin of scrofula had only recently disappeared. This situation found its reflection in the wide variety of names used to designate the disease and its varied forms— phthisis, consumption, hectic fever, gastric fever, tabes, and scrofula. Not infrequently the victims were described with a genteel euphemism as 'going into a decline.'

The second problem is that trustworthy records of the numbers suffering from tuberculosis were not available until the twentieth century. Tuberculosis did not become officially reportable until 1908, and then only the cases under the care of Poor Law medical officers were reported. Only in 1912 did all cases become reportable. Consequently, any estimate of the dimensions of the problem of tuberculosis must depend on the numbers of fatal cases and death-rates. Reliable death-rates for tuberculosis are available in the Registrar-General's reports after 1850. In addition, it is possible to glean some data from hospital and dispensary records, from surveys such as those made under John Simon's direction in the sixties, as well as from non-medical, particularly literary sources. Furthermore, the characteristic clinical and pathological features of advanced 'consumption' or scrofula are easily recognizable. From the combination of such data it is possible to establish general trends of morbidity and mortality, and to identify other aspects of the tuberculosis problem.

Assessment of the incidence of tuberculosis must begin with the fact that up to the middle of the nineteenth century only figures for pulmonary tuberculosis are available from such sources as the London Bills of Mortality, and from studies by individual physicians such as Robert Willan (1801) and William Woolcombe (1808).[49] Since there are no accurate population figures until 1801, only the ratio of deaths from pulmonary tuberculosis (phthisis, consumption) to total deaths can be computed. On this basis Brownlee conjectured in 1918 that 'from the beginning of the 18th century to the beginning of the 19th century consumption increased in amount, and from the latter point steadily diminished' and that 'the probabilities that there was a large amount of phthisis in London are very great. In the first period for which accurate statistics exist, namely that between 1840 and 1850, the amount of phthisis was about half of that I estimate for the earlier epoch, and from this point the decline is sufficiently well proven.'[50] However, the Registrar-General's data after 1837 show that tuberculosis mortality continued on a high level into the forties, and a more recent study by McKeown and Record advances the view that the deaths did not begin to diminish appreciably until after 1847.[51]

From 1850 onward more or less accurate data are available on tuberculosis deaths (pulmonary and non-pulmonary). The downward trend is evident from the crude death-rates. Not only did the disease diminish but the rate of fall was higher during the third quarter of the century than during the last quarter. This decline in mortality occurred in both sexes and at all ages, though not at the same rate. From 1851 to 1863 deaths from pulmonary tuberculosis were highest among females, but after 1868 female mortality declined more rapidly than among males.[52]

To understand the significance of these trends they must be seen in a broader context. Before the twentieth century, tuberculosis, like so many other diseases, is believed to have exhibited a spontaneous ebb and flow in its prevalence and severity, to have gone through a series of epidemic waves or cycles. From this viewpoint the British experience in the Victorian period represents part of a long epidemic wave that rose in the eighteenth century, reached its peak sometime in the 1830s and 1840s, and then slowly subsided. This experience was not exclusively British, since records from western and central Europe and the eastern United States reveal a similar pattern during the nineteenth century.

The conception of tuberculosis as an infectious disease with a natural history must also take into account the social factors involved in its causation. Tuberculosis is an endemic disease, protean in its manifestations, slow and insidious in its progress, selecting its victims from among those whose resistance is diminished, and thriving in deprived bodies. In this connection, it must be emphasized that living conditions are of paramount importance in determining the tuberculosis experience of a population. Throughout most of the nineteenth century the disease almost exclusively affected urban communities, and certain conditions were regarded as favoring its occurrence and propagation. An urban community is a complicated structure within which no single factor operates alone to cause tuberculosis. As a result it is difficult to separate out the interlocking, interdependent, causative factors. One of the best studies of this problem was made by Bradbury who, in 1930–1, investigated the high incidence of

642

tuberculosis on Tyneside, specifically in the towns of Jarrow and Blaydon.[53] Bradbury concluded that the most important social factors were poverty, undernourishment, and overcrowding in dwellings. Poverty compels people to skimp on food and to live in small, overcrowded rooms. However, it must be emphasized that while poverty and tuberculosis are closely linked in an ugly alliance, poor people need not become tubercular. Poverty, poor housing, overcrowding, and malnutrition are significant but secondary. The important primary factor is the presence in close proximity to people who may be susceptible of an individual who expectorates tubercle bacilli, particularly a person with an open case of the disease. In a community where tubercle bacilli are widely disseminated, most people from time to time come in contact with individuals who spread the germ of the disease. On the whole, occasional fortuitous contacts are quite unimportant. Much more significant are close and regular contact for weeks or months, such as that between husband and wife, parent and child, or other persons living in the household such as lodgers or servants. Such contact may also occur in schools, places of employment, or in institutions such as hospitals. Lack of previous exposure to tuberculosis is a significant predisposing factor.

All these factors were present to an important degree in the Victorian cities and towns throughout most of the period, and made tuberculosis the important cause of illness and death that it was. Large-scale migration from rural to urban areas during the earlier nineteenth century brought millions of individuals into contact with city-dwellers among whom tuberculosis had long been prevalent under conditions favorable to the spread of the disease. Although not identical, the experience of the newcomers to the early Victorian city was not unlike that of non-white peoples, e.g. Africans, Amerindians, and Maoris, who encountered the tubercle bacillus for the first time, or whose contact with it has been relatively short as compared with that of Europeans.[54] For an optimistic observer the growth and development of early Victorian cities clearly indicated progress and the promise of increased well-being. From a less sanguine, more immediate viewpoint, they were disaster areas in which a vastly increased population of suffering humanity lived and worked under appalling conditions. Under the circumstances, environmental factors in the causation of pulmonary tuberculosis could hardly be overlooked, particularly since the atmosphere was considered an important factor in the etiology of disease. William A. Guy (1810–85), Professor of Forensic Medicine at King's College (1838–69), and one of Simon's investigators in the sixties, noted in 1844 that 'the chief cause of the great mortality is the defective ventilation of houses, shops, and places of work. Next to this in point of importance is the inhalation of dust, metallic particles, and irritating fumes.'[55] More specifically, Chadwick noted in 1842 that tailors frequently worked in 'large shops, where the men are crowded together in close rooms,' with the result that 'great numbers of them die of consumption.'[56] Similarly, consumption, asthma, and chronic hoarseness among women who worked in textile mills were attributed by other observers to breathing air choked with dust and fluff. Even worse-off during this period were needlewomen (dressmakers, seamstresses, and milliners) among whom consumption and poor eyes were common ailments.[57]

By the middle of the nineteenth century, a relationship between occupation and the occurrence of pulmonary disease was no new discovery. But there was no detailed investigation of specific occupations and of the health experience of workers engaged in them. This was provided by Greenhow in his studies of lung diseases in 1860 and 1861. Several years earlier, in 1856–7, he had made a comparative study of deaths in different parts of England, in which he analysed mortality statistics from pulmonary disease by occupation. Using the statistical analysis of mortality as a framework, Greenhow visited various towns and developed a picture of living and working conditions in different trades. The first report covered pottery workers (Stoke-on-Trent, Woolstanton); nailmakers, needle and fish-hook makers (Redditch, Alcester, Sheffield); tin and copper mining (Penzance, Redruth); lead mining (Reeth, Middleton, Pateley Bridge); weaving silk and wool (Pateley Bridge, Macclesfield, Leek, Leeds, Bradford, Stroud, Melksham); hosiers (Leicester, Hinckley); spinners of cotton and lace (Preston, Towcester, Newport Pagnell); straw plaiting (Berkhamsted); glovers (Yeovil); and agricultural workers (Saffron Walden). The second report dealt with cotton manufacture (Blackburn); lace making and hosiery (Nottingham, Radford, Basford); silk manufacture and watch making (Coventry); metal work and button making (Birmingham, Aston); metalwork, coal and iron-stone mining (Wolverhampton, Merthyr Tydfil, Abergavenny). The results supported the comments made by Simon in his Third Report to the Privy Council (1860)[58] to the effect that '*in proportion as the male and female populations are severally attracted to indoor branches of industry, in such proportions, other things being equal, their respective death-rates by lung-disease increased.*' Simon cited the result 'developed 17 years ago by the late Dr. Baly, in his admirable essay on the *Diseases of Prisons.*'[59] He found that pulmonary phthisis and scrofula,

> tubercular disease in all its forms, resulted from the long-continued influence of imprisonment on the bodily health. This influence appears to be partly physical and partly moral: among its component parts (with cold and poorness of diet) Dr. Baly enumerates *deficient ventilation, sedentary occupations, and want of active bodily exercise, and listless or dejected state of mind.* Of the points thus enumerated, there are some in which the life of textile factory-populations, and of certain other in-door work-people, is comparable to the life of prisoners. Taking, for instance, the case of girls and women who from childhood onwards sit ten hours a day or more, often in constrained postures, weaving or knitting at looms and stocking-frames, or plaiting straw, or stitching gloves, or lace-making:—this life, at its best, has to a great extent the evils of monotony, of deficient bodily exercise, of physical seclusion from sun and air, and of mental privation from what is beautiful and animating in external nature. And thus probably, even at its best, it tends to produce somewhat of vital depression, somewhat of mental and bodily etiolation, during which, especially with persons otherwise predisposed to scrofula, there is a heightened liability to tubercular disease . . .

From these considerations, it would of course not necessarily follow that an excess of phthisis, prevailing in our great centres of manufacture, is, in any practical sense preventable . . . But should it . . . appear that the production of disease in each phthisis-breeding employment depends in part on sanitary faults which might be eliminated from the employment (on defective ventilation, for instance, and other like influences), then at once the way would be opened to an improved economy of life in many branches of popular industry.

Greenhow's studies were soon followed by other investigations of occupational ill-health. The Sixth Report (1863) contained a large section on 'Hurtful or hurtfully conducted occupations,' dealing with metallic poisons (lead and mercury) and indoor industries (printers, tailors and dressmakers, including milliners). Edward Smith (1818–74), the physician whose pioneer dietary surveys have been mentioned, investigated the working conditions and health of tailors and printers in London, finding the former hideous, and a disproportionate amount of sickness and death in the health-states of these workers. Smith found that among tailors 'consumption and other forms of chest-disease constitute two-thirds of all the causes of death.' Phthisis was also widely prevalent among printers; in fact Smith believed that it was twice as prevalent there as in the general male population. The needlewomen were studied by William Miller Ord (1834–1902) who worked with John Simon for four years (1859–63), and later became a leading practitioner and consultant. Although Ord was unable to obtain precise statistical data, the health of these women was found to be quite poor. The illnesses which appeared to be most frequent among them were phthisis, chlorosis (anemia), hysteria, dyspepsia, headache, dizziness, and affections of vision.[60]

Tailors and dressmakers worked in a 'sweated' trade, and their plight had already attracted public notice in the middle of the century. Following the appearance of a series of revealing articles in the London *Morning Chronicle*, Charles Kingsley in 1850 published his pamphlet *Cheap Clothes and Nasty* in which he exposed the evils of the 'sweating system.'[61] Nothing much happened following those exposures. From time to time public concern about the problem revived, but the 'sweating system' was not brought under effective regulatory control until the twentieth century. Nevertheless, the dreadful disclosures of Simon's investigators in a variety of industries influenced the government and led to a number of important legislative enactments. Simon emphasized the imperative need for legislative intervention and in 1864, commenting on Smith's survey of printers and tailors, demanded action. 'Doubtless,' he said,[62]

> there may be some small technical difficulty in defining the exact line at which employers shall become subject to regulation. But I would submit that, in principle, the sanitary claim is universal. And in the interest of myriads of labouring men and women whose lives are now needlessly afflicted and shortened by the infinite physical suffering which their mere

employment engenders, I would venture to express my hope, that universally the sanitary circumstances of labour may, at least so far, be brought within appropriate provisions of law, that the effective ventilation of all in-door workplaces may be ensured, and that in every naturally insalubrious occupation the specific health-endangering influence may as far as practicable be reduced.

The reports of Simon's investigators reinforced the findings of Lord Shaftesbury's Children's Employment Commission (1861) which led to the Factory Act of 1864. All the labor laws enacted in Britain up to the early 1860s had been passed to protect workers in textile plants, and to a lesser degree those in mines. Beginning with the Act of 1864, however, industries other than textiles were included. Among these were the manufacture of matches, earthenware, percussion caps, and cartridges. This trend was carried further by the Factory Act of 1867 and the Workshop Act of the same year, which brought under control a large number of hitherto unregulated industries. Further Acts dealing with the prevention of lead poisoning (1883); ventilation, sanitation, and safety in factories; workmen's compensation (1897), as well as other matters, were enacted during the last three decades of the nineteenth century. By the end of the century there had been created a code of law intended to provide for the health and safety of industrial workers. Admittedly, certain groups, as, for instance, those in home industries, were inadequately protected, but a solid basis for further action was present. An important consolidatory Factory and Workshop Act was passed in 1901, bringing together all previous factory legislation and simplifying the procedure for establishing regulations in dangerous industries.

Although these measures cannot be accorded a primary role in the reduction of tuberculosis, the improvement of industrial conditions during the later nineteenth century is undoubtedly reflected in the declining tuberculosis mortality. Moreover, the discovery of the tubercle bacillus and the establishment of the communicable nature of the disease provided a surer basis for measures designed to prevent its dissemination to others. From this point of view the segregation of patients in hospitals and sanatoria was an important preventive measure which contributed to the decline of tuberculosis. Indeed, as we shall see shortly, it was the recognition of the specific nature of tuberculosis which helped to reduce its incidence among the more favored social classes of the Victorian community.

Tuberculosis did not respect social position, and in its ubiquity attacked ladies of fashion as well as prostitutes, gentlemen as well as unskilled laborers. Countless unavoidable contacts spread the disease throughout society, especially since the process of infection was not understood or only dimly comprehended. Tuberculosis was most frequently diagnosed in its later or terminal phases, a circumstance that contributed greatly to its spread, since close contact with persons in advanced stages of tuberculosis was accepted.[63] Such individuals lived as normal a life as they could almost to the end, thus spreading the tubercle bacillus to all round them. For years the children of the Brontë family were exposed to the 'chronic bronchitis' of their father, Patrick Brontë, from whom they acquired the fatal infection. Poor sanitary practices, such as drinking from common cups, promiscuous expectoration, nursing the sick and dying in unventilated rooms and without taking any measures to prevent infection, undoubtedly contributed to the ubiquity and intensity of contagion.

The inadequate treatment of tuberculous individuals was recognized at the end of the Victorian period to be a danger to others. Treatment in institutions was a means of preventing the dissemination of the disease. More affluent members of society could be treated at home, but this was hardly possible for the workers and the poor. Efforts to provide for such patients began in the eighteenth century but were only actively developed in the nineteenth century. Tuberculous patients were seen in general dispensaries and in the out-patient departments of general hospitals. Thus, among the medical cases treated at the Liverpool Northern Hospital during 1846 and 1847, diseases of the respiratory organs were most numerous and also most fatal, 'chiefly in consequence of the number of cases of pulmonary consumption admitted.'[64] For 1847 the Glasgow Infirmary reported seventy-nine patients suffering from phthisis, as well as twenty-two with pleurisy and a hundred and one with bronchitis, some of whom may have been tubercular.[65] During the three years 1839–41, 370 patients were treated for phthisis at the St Marylebone Infirmary in London, many of them paupers who received outdoor medical relief. One hundred of these patients died of consumption.[66] Nonetheless, existing facilities were inadequate to care for the large number of patients, and many institutions were reluctant and even refused to admit consumptives because of the chronicity and high mortality of the disease and because of some feeling that phthisis might be contagious.

This led to specialized institutions. By the 1840s there was a West London Dispensary for diseases of the chest, established 'to afford relief to the poor when labouring under the most prevalent of human afflictions, *the Diseases of the Chest*; and to preserve life, as far as it can be done by medical skill and care, from these, the most mortal of human maladies, viz. pulmonary consumption, diseases of the wind-pipe and air passages, and morbid affections of the heart.'[67] This institution was amalgamated in the spring of 1841 with the newly conceived Hospital for Consumption and Diseases of the Chest, later known as the Brompton Hospital, opened on 13 September 1842. After 1850, a large number of special hospitals for tuberculosis patients, all voluntary institutions, were founded.[68] The consumptive poor were treated in workhouse infirmaries if they were inmates, and those on outdoor relief were admitted. The increasing role of workhouse infirmaries in the care of the tuberculous poor may be seen from the following figures. In 1863–5, almost 20 percent of the deaths in the Clerkenwell, St Luke's, St Marylebone, Kensington, St Giles, and St George's Bloomsbury, Infirmaries was due to phthisis.[69] During the last third of the century this proportion rose in London and other cities. In 1889, of the total deaths from phthisis in London institutions, 31·4 percent occurred in workhouses, workhouse infirmaries, and sick asylums; in 1904 the proportion was 33·5 percent. In Sheffield this proportion was 6·3 percent in 1876–80 and 26·1 percent in 1901–5; in Salford 14·4 percent in 1884–90 and 27·6 percent in 1901–4, and in

Brighton 9·6 percent in 1866–70 and 20·2 percent in 1901–4. As Newsholme summed up the situation in 1908, after 1860 'a vast increase in the extent of segregation of tuberculous patients in workhouses and infirmaries took place,' which no doubt contributed to the increasing control of tuberculosis.[70] This separation of persons suffering from the disease removed numerous foci of infection and probably reinforced its downward trend. Recognition in Great Britain of the implications for community action of Koch's discovery of the tubercle bacillus acted in the same direction. Robert W. Philip (1857–1939), an Edinburgh physician at the Royal Victoria Hospital for Consumption, saw that 'If the community as such was to benefit practically by the discovery, there appeared to be need of centralized effort in order to ascertain the extent of tuberculosis in a district, and to devise means for its limitation and prevention.' Philip believed that the focal point of anti-tuberculosis work should be a dispensary under the direction of a medical officer of health. In addition there should be a sanatorium for selected patients to arrest early cases; a hospital for patients in advanced stages to limit infection; and an occupational colony for after-care and rehabilitation. The consequence was the opening in 1887 of the Royal Victoria Dispensary for Consumption, the first modern anti-tuberculosis clinic. This pioneer endeavor was followed in 1898 by the organization of the 'National Association for the Prevention of Consumption and other Forms of Tuberculosis' for the purpose of preventing the ravages of the disease in Great Britain. Its objectives were to educate the public concerning the propagation and prevention of tuberculosis, to influence Parliament and other public bodies in matters concerning prevention, and to stimulate action on a local level.[71]

One aspect of the tuberculosis problem which was not understood until the twentieth century was the relation of bovine tuberculosis to the disease in man. Cases of tubercular glands (scrofula) and joints, which were common in the Victorian period, were most often due to milk contaminated with the bovine strain of the tubercle bacillus. Whether tuberculosis in man could be contracted from infected cows was hotly disputed up to the end of the century. Various public-health officers drew attention to the danger of milk from tuberculous cows, and the report of the Departmental Committee on Tuberculosis recognized that a tuberculous cow in a dairy was a danger to consumers. But it was not until after the turn of the century, after a vast amount of evidence had been accumulated, that this view was finally accepted and appropriate action taken.[72]

Tuberculosis morbidity and mortality provide a rather sensitive index of living conditions in a community. The decline of the disease during the latter half of the century, despite inadequate understanding of its etiology and transmission, indicates that improving social conditions interacting with biological factors were bettering the health of the people in this respect. Moreover, by the end of the Victorian period, Britain had the basic elements of an antituberculosis program, which made it possible in the twentieth century to bring the disease under control and to counteract the effects of worsening conditions in time of war and economic depression.

Although the health of the population improved, this favorable trend did not develop uniformly at all ages. An aspect which remained unfavorable throughout most of the nineteenth century was infant mortality. At the beginning of the century the death-rate among children, especially in towns, was appallingly high. Throughout the century the infant mortality-rate for England and Wales remained at about the same level, fluctuating around 150 per 1,000 births. During the quinquennium 1841–5 the rate was 148 per 1,000 births; during the quinquennium 1851–5 it rose to 156. Not until 1901–5 did it drop to 138. Indeed, the infant mortality-rate seemed to rise during the later nineteenth century. According to William Farr, 'the death-rate of infants in England and Wales, in 1875 was 158 per 1,000, or 4 per 1,000 above the average rate in the 10 years 1861–70.' These average rates covered wide differences in the figures for various towns. Examining eighteen large towns, Farr found that the highest rates in 1875 varied from Leicester with 245 per 1,000 to Portsmouth with 133 per 1,000.[73] The situation was similar in Scotland, with infant mortality reaching a maximum of 138 per 1,000 live births in 1897 and, as in England, declining after 1900. It was higher in towns than in rural areas, ranging in 1863 from a low of 117 in Perth to 163 in Glasgow and 193 in Greenock. This general gradient continued to the end of the century. Infant mortality-rates were higher in large towns than in smaller towns, and in some, such as Aberdeen, the problem of infant deaths continued to present difficulties.[74]

Infant deaths occurred in all social classes, but the greatest number occurred among workers and the poor. Moreover, poverty and its attendant evils were compounded by scientific and medical ignorance of the physiology and pathology of infancy. In the course of the century various investigators deduced what they believed to be the causes of this enormous waste of life. John Bunnell Davis (1780–1824), an English physician who established a Universal Dispensary for Children in London, noted certain causes which were not alleviated until the end of the century. Writing in 1817, he attributed the high mortality among the infants and children who had attended the Dispensary over a period of fifteen years to improper feeding after weaning. He also pointed out that there was practically no medical care for infants and young children. In fact, some hospitals would not admit children under two. Recognizing the need for instruction of mothers, he distributed pamphlets to them and organized a group of domiciliary visitors.[75]

In 1844, the Rev. J. Clay, reporting on health conditions in Preston, noted that 'the mortality of the town chiefly predominates among the children of the working classes, the mortality among them increasing as the social condition of the parent sinks . . . additional causes are connected with the ignorance, indifference, neglect, or selfishness of the parents. Their ignorance leads them to give to their offspring the most improper food even when they are able to procure for them wholesome sustenance; and too often the child is destroyed by the gin poured into it with the intention to "nourish" it.' Clay refers to the widespread practice among the poor of giving beer, spirits, and various nostrums containing opiates to infants in order to keep them quiet. On the basis of an enquiry among the chemists and druggists of Preston, Clay reported that more than 1,600 families used Godfrey's Cordial, a popular compound containing opium, and that on an average each family consumed about half an ounce per week. Furthermore, it was known 'that druggists are often resorted to for medicine and advice by the poor, and probably in some or many cases assistance from such quarters may have been obtained for sick children; but after making all allowances, it is to be feared that, among certain classes of the poor, a great amount of infant death takes place without anything worthy the name of medical assistance having been obtained or even sought.' Thus, 'while 44·4 per cent of infantile death took place in the "worst streets," only 8·5 per cent died under the cognizance of the medical officers of the dispensary' despite the fact that medical care was free. To a very considerable degree these conditions stemmed from the employment of mothers. While working in the factory, the mother 'intrusts her infant to an old woman or young girl, who may also have the charge of other infants; and this general nurse, in order to fulfill her task with as much ease to herself as possible, drugs the unfortunate babes with "Quietness".'[76]

This aspect of the problem of excessive infant mortality, and its relation to the employment of mothers in factories was investigated by several of John Simon's collaborators. In the 1859 report to the Privy Council, Simon called attention to the extensive employment of women in factories as a root cause of infant mortality, and in 1861 Greenhow investigated this circumstance. He was asked to study the 'conditions of dwelling, nourishment, and tendance; and the influence exerted upon infantile mortality by the poverty of parents, illegitimacy of birth, and by the industrial occupation of mothers.' For the study he chose the factory towns of Coventry, Nottingham, Blackburn, Wolverhampton, Merthyr Tydfil, and Abergavenny, where the infant mortality-rates ranged between 180 and 220 per 1,000 live births. Greenhow's findings corroborated Clay's earlier testimony and provided more detailed evidence in support of the conclusion that 'infants are subject to some other causes of ill-health and mortality besides those to which the general population are exposed.' These causes arose from the employment of mothers, the improper feeding of infants, and the pernicious practice of pacifying infants by dosing them with opium mixtures.[77] The ubiquity of the practice and the fact that even physicians did not necessarily take it too seriously are reflected in Charlotte Yonge's *The Three Brides*. When Lady Charnock's baby is taken by the nursemaid to a public-house in the absence of the parents and is given a pacifying cordial, the mother, after retrieving her infant, rushes the child to a physician. The latter on hearing the story comments dryly: 'Well, then, it only remains to be proved whether an aristocratic baby can bear popular treatment. I dare say some hundred unlucky infants have been lugged out to the race-course today, and come back squalling their hearts out with fatigue and hunger, and I'll be bound that nine-tenths are lulled with this very sedative, and will be none the worse.'[78]

Infant mortality is a sensitive indicator of community health because it reflects the influences exerted by a number of social factors. It is particularly sensitive to environmental conditions, such as housing, sanitation, and pure food and water.

Housing is important because overcrowding favors the spread of respiratory infections and other conditions communicated by air-borne droplets, while lack of adequate washing facilities increases gastro-intestinal infection. The level of infant mortality is affected as well by a proper knowledge of infant nutrition and the availability of medical care. Most of these factors were unfavorable during the Victorian period, but were most adverse for the infants of poor women who worked. It is worth noting that when women were unemployed during the Lancashire cotton famine of 1861–4, infant mortality-rates declined because mothers were at home to take care of their children.

To deal with the problem of infant mortality, Simon proposed the establishment of nurseries in factories, and control of the sale of drugs. He was well aware, however, that these remedies were only ameliorative and did not strike at the heart of the problem. 'The root of the evil,' he wrote, 'is an influence with which English law has never professed to deal. Money is on one side; penury on the other. Domestic obligation is outbidden in the labour-market; and the poor factory woman, who meant only to sell that honest industry of hers, gradually finds that she has sold almost everything which other women understand as happiness. But the root of this evil is perhaps out of reach of law—certainly out of reach of remedies which I am competent to advise.'[79] Although Simon hesitated to draw the obvious conclusion, his associate Edward Smith did not evade the issue. In his survey of diets of the poorer working class, Smith commented on the employment of women in agriculture, but the point was equally applicable to women in cities who worked in factories. 'When the income attainable by the husband is sufficient to maintain his family in health and respectability, no doubt the out-of-door occupation of the wife and young children should cease . . . but the first question at present is, the obtainment by any means of sufficient money to maintain her family.'[80] To be sure, some mothers and 'nurses' were heartless, neglected the children, fed them improperly, and drugged them with opium, but these were consequences of the basic problem, poverty. As soon as the mother was able to rise after her confinement she had to go to work again, leaving her child to be cared for by anyone willing to accept it. Survival was the primary need. As Smith made abundantly clear, what was the matter with the poor was their poverty, a discovery which has recently been rediscovered. What was needed was an adequate family income; a higher standard of living including proper housing; a better diet including pure milk; knowledge of child care; and facilities to aid working mothers. None of these was present in the Victorian city as far as the workers and the poor were concerned, and it was not until the present century that real improvement occurred in the health of infants. Those who survived infancy were subject to the perils of various acute communicable diseases, chiefly scarlet fever (streptococcal disease), diphtheria, and smallpox.

Throughout their history, scarlet fever and diphtheria have been diseases of infancy and childhood—the period during which immunity to the toxins produced by the respective causative organisms is developed. During earlier periods there was some confusion between the two diseases, but by the end of the eighteenth century a clinical concept of scarlet fever had been rather generally recognized by physicians. Clinicians were clear about *Scarlatina simplex*, that is, mild scarlet fever without complications. Shortly after the turn of the century scarlet fever declined in virulence, and for about the first quarter of the nineteenth century there was small interest in a more precise understanding of the disease. In the thirties, however, there was a change for the worse. Scarlet fever began to increase in virulence, culminating in a period of some forty years (1840–80), during which there were frequent and severe epidemics in Europe and America.

In 1831 an outbreak of a very malignant type occurred in Dublin, and in 1834 Ireland was ravaged by the disease, which caused as many deaths as cholera had done in 1832.[81] The first great epidemic covering all of England occurred in 1840, a second came in 1844, and a third in 1848. The worst epidemics in England occurred during the period 1850–90. In England and Wales the annual average death-rates per million population were as follows during these forty years: 1851–60, 832; 1861–70, 972; 1871–80, 716; 1881–90, 338.[82] With respect to age incidence, almost two-thirds of deaths from scarlet fever were among those under five years of age.[83]

There is no question that a change occurred after 1830, and the disease became, as Charles Creighton noted, 'the leading cause of death among the infectious diseases of childhood,' and remained so until the last decades of the nineteenth century. After 1880 the severity of scarlet fever diminished. These trends may be interpreted in terms of our understanding of bacterial virulence, as well as of economic and social developments. One and possibly two generations of city-dwellers had acquired immunity to relatively avirulent streptococci in the early nineteenth century. Such immunity as had been developed to more virulent types during the later eighteenth century disappeared. As the population grew through internal increase as well as by recruitment from rural areas, the number of people susceptible to virulent organisms increased. Crowded together in the filthy, insanitary environment of the early-Victorian city, these people were inevitably exposed to infections. It was probably at some such point around 1830 that a more virulent type of streptococcus was introduced.

The transmissible nature of scarlet fever was in large measure accepted during the nineteenth century. Isolation and disinfection were the means employed to counteract the possibility of spread. It was believed that treatment at home of children affected by the disease led to a lower mortality than among those treated in hospitals, an observation no doubt due to the lack of cross-infections at home. Then it was observed that scarlet-fever epidemics could be produced among people supplied with milk from a common source. A physician, Michael W. Taylor, of Penrith, had described the first outbreak of this type in 1870. Gradually similar occurrences were reported by other observers, and at the International Medical Congress at London in 1881 sixteen cases were presented. The epidemic of milk-borne scarlet fever at Hendon in 1885 illuminated the problem by showing that infected milk produced the disease, and that the infective organisms could be introduced from sick cows or by the hands of milkers. Over fifty years of research, however, were required before the true nature of the mechanism by which the disease is produced became apparent. Streptococci were implicated in the causation of scarlet fever in the late nineteenth century but the biological activity which enables these organisms to cause disease was not yet understood.[84]

Diphtheria was undoubtedly present in Great Britain before the nineteenth century but it was confused with scarlet fever. Indeed, before 1860 the Registrar-General's returns list the two diseases together. However, it was not until the summer of 1855 that diphtheria began to receive serious attention as a separate condition. This was due to the pandemic of diphtheria which broke out at various points in Europe and North America about this time and soon spread to almost every part of the globe. During the earlier part of the nineteenth century France, Norway, and Denmark had been the only countries affected by epidemics of diphtheria, but after the fifth decade of the century the disease was to be found in all civilized communities of the temperate zone. Although the incidence and severity of diphtheria varied widely during this period, it was overwhelmingly a disease of childhood, not of adult life. A second epidemic wave appeared in Europe around 1890, which then declined steadily over the next thirty years.[85]

These trends can be seen in the death-rates from diphtheria (and croup)[86] from 1858 to 1894.[87] The statistics for the period 1886–94 seem to reflect the greater diagnostic precision which became possible after 1883, when Edwin Klebs announced that diphtheria was caused by rod-shaped bacteria, some exhibiting a clubbed form. Further findings by Friedrich Loeffler in 1884, and by Roux and Yersin between 1888 and 1890 led to efforts to create an artificial immunity to diphtheria, and from 1894 on diphtheria antitoxin came into general use. The decline in the croup death-rate appears to reflect greater diagnostic accuracy. Also following the introduction of antitoxin there was an increasing reduction in the case-mortality from diphtheria, especially if it was administered early.[88]

An additional factor which contributed to the handling of diphtheria was the creation of special hospitals for children. The first of these, the London Hospital for Sick Children in Great Ormond Street, was established through the joint efforts of two doctors, Charles West and Henry Bence Jones, and opened its doors to patients on 14 February 1852. Only ten beds were available at first and a larger number of children were treated as out-patients, but as time went on the hospital expanded to become a major teaching and research center.[89] Similar action was taken elsewhere. Children's hospitals were established in Liverpool, Norwich, Edinburgh, Glasgow, Manchester, Birmingham, Gloucester, Nottingham, and Brighton. More significant in terms of numbers of children involved were workhouse infirmaries and schools for pauper children. During the Victorian period, especially after 1850, they received increasing attention because conditions in them were generally atrocious. To a certain extent, the situation of the children may have been improved by removing them from the infirmary wards where they mingled with adult patients and sending them to the Poor Law schools. But as Hodgkinson observes, many schools soon became hospitals rather than educational establishments, in which ophthalmic infections, ringworm, and skin affections were highly prevalent. Moreover, without means of isolation the children easily acquired communicable diseases spread mainly by droplet infection, such as diphtheria, scarlet fever, measles, chicken pox, whooping cough, and smallpox. Except for smallpox, there was at this time no means available for the production of active immunity against these diseases. However, the very concentration of these children meant that they could not be neglected, but it was not until the end of the century that much was changed.[90]

Although it is not possible to consider them in detail, several other diseases and causes of ill-health should be noticed. One is smallpox, which was a continuing threat to the public health throughout the eighteenth and nineteenth centuries.[91] It smoldered endemically in city and town, flaring up recurrently into epidemic outbreaks. Jenner's discovery of vaccination in 1798 made prophylaxis and virtual eradication of the disease theoretically possible, but it was not until 1840 that the first Vaccination Act was enacted, providing for a system under which any person might be vaccinated at public expense. The local Boards of Guardians, the Poor Law authorities, were made responsible for its execution, since it was intended to protect the mass of the people. Members of the middle and upper classes were vaccinated by their private physicians, who performed about one-third of the annual vaccinations. The Act of 1840 was a consequence of the situation at the beginning of the Victorian period. According to the First Report of the Registrar-General, smallpox was then the fifth most fatal disease in Britain. Moreover, in view of the fact that an average of 12,000 people died annually during the epidemic of 1837–40, action to deal with preventable mortality was clearly necessary. This permissive legislation achieved some success, reducing the smallpox deaths to about 5,000 per year. Nevertheless, the situation was still quite unsatisfactory, and in 1853, after a study by the Epidemiological Society of London, a Vaccination Extension Act was passed which made it obligatory for parents and guardians to have infants vaccinated within four months of birth. In practice, despite a large increase in the number of infant vaccinations, the compulsory provision was not enforced. Nevertheless, the number of vaccinations remained high and the incidence of smallpox declined. Between 1841 and 1853 the average annual death-rate from smallpox per million people was 304; in 1855 after the Act became operative, the rate dropped to 132. Public-health reformers continued to work for further improvement of legislation to prevent smallpox, leading to the Vaccination Act of 1867 which introduced penalties for non-compliance, thereby arousing vociferous and fanatical opposition. Despite such attacks, however, vaccination stayed at high levels. In 1873, for example, 85 percent of the births were vaccinated, owing perhaps to the severe epidemic which struck England from the end of 1870 to the middle of 1873. The epidemic first appeared in London and Liverpool, and by the middle of 1871 had spread to the entire country. By the end of the epidemic in 1873, 44,079 people had died of smallpox in England, of whom 10,287 were from London. By comparison, the average annual number of deaths from smallpox in England during the period 1854–70 inclusive was 3,493.

During the last quarter of the nineteenth century, the effectiveness of the vaccination program declined. In 1897, of 823,506 surviving births, only 70·3 percent were vaccinated. This decline, which continued into the present century, was the result of several interacting factors. One was that immunity to smallpox was not fully understood. At the time of the 1870–3 epidemic, it was noted that a large proportion of the deaths occurred among persons over the age of fifteen who had been vaccinated. This finding was attributed to imperfect and inadequate vaccination, but it was not recognized that the immunity produced by vaccination was limited and did not confer life-long protection against smallpox. Furthermore, after 1873 smallpox declined in significance, and as the danger from the disease became more remote parents were less inclined to have their children vaccinated, or simply neglected to do so. As 'Lord' George Sanger observed early in this century, 'People in these days cannot imagine what the scourge was like, what a thrill of fear and horror it produced . . . In some places, notably in seaport towns, the slums of London, and other large cities, it lurked regularly, and people were, in a sense, accustomed to its presence. But now and again . . . it burst forth into a tremendous pestilence that stalked the length and breadth of the land.'[92] Behavior of this kind is not unknown at present and has been observed in connection with immunization against poliomyelitis, diphtheria, and other diseases. Among some persons this tendency was reinforced by active anti-vaccination agitation which became widespread during the late nineteenth century. These factors were even able to counteract the impact of large outbreaks of smallpox in London in 1901 and Liverpool in 1901–3. As a result, the Acts of 1898 and 1907 successively eroded the compulsory system which was finally abolished in 1948.

Rickets was another disease which affected large numbers of children, rich and poor, but unlike smallpox it did not occur in epidemics and attracted relatively little attention. As a result it is impossible to give any precise information concerning its incidence and prevalence. Samuel Gee, a leading clinician of the later nineteenth century and a member of the medical staff at the Great Ormond Street Hospital, wrote in 1867 that '30·3 percent of sick children under two years of age are rickety.' He also noted that while severer forms might occur largely among the poor, 'slight or even considerable rickets is really common in the children of the comparatively rich.'[93] These statements by Gee probably grossly underestimate the prevalence of rickets in the Victorian city. In part this was due to the confusion of infant scurvy and rickets. W. B. Cheadle drew attention to infant scurvy in 1878, and it was not until 1883 that Thomas Barlow published his classic paper clinically separating rickets from scurvy.[94] Nevertheless, the essential nature of rickets as a vitamin-deficiency disease produced by a combination of dietary and environmental conditions was not understood, but the first steps toward its elucidation were taken at this time.

Though not limited to the poor, rickets in Victorian Britain can be described as a disease of city slums, of ignorance, poor hygiene, and a paucity of sunlight. A study of the distribution of rickets in Great Britain, prompted by the Medical Congress of 1884, found that it coincided with the distribution of the industrial population. In the Clydeside, for instance, every child examined was found to be rachitic. Then, in

1889 William Huntly, a medical missionary, reported the absence of rickets among the masses in India, even though their diet was poor in animal fat, a deficiency which had been suggested by W. B. Cheadle as the major cause of the disease. Comparing climatic conditions in India and Glasgow, Huntly concluded that though diet might be involved causally in rickets, 'the absence of open-air exercise and sunlight appear as the main factors in accentuating the tendency to its production.'[95] Following up these observations, T. A. Palm studied the geographic distribution of rickets and found it most prevalent where sunlight was scarce.[96] Earlier in the century, John Hughes Bennett of Edinburgh published a book on cod-liver oil, *Treatise on the oleum fecoris aselli* (1841), in which he recommended the oil for the treatment of rickets. For a time, its therapeutic use became popular so that Gee wrote in 1868: 'In cod liver oil we possess a pharmaceutical agent worthy of a place beside iron, Peruvian bark and mercury.'[97] Thus, by the end of the century various studies and observations had shown that rickets tended to be most prevalent in technologically developed countries such as Great Britain, particularly in cities and towns, and that dietary elements were somehow involved in the pathogenesis of the disease. To reconcile the role of environmental factors such as sunshine with that of diet in the production of rickets was not possible at the close of the Victorian period. Indeed, it was not until the second and third decades of the twentieth century that this question was answered.

The problem of rickets also touches on one of the dangers to women of child-bearing age. Stunting of growth and deformation of the skeleton are consequences of rickets. Narrowing of the pelvis due to rickets in early life thus represented a hazard in pregnancy, and was one cause of maternal mortality. Another and more important cause throughout the period was puerperal sepsis. Infection during childbirth was a common hazard for women in the nineteenth century. In the forties and fifties the workhouse infirmaries had a high puerperal fever rate, but after the middle of the century, as they were cleaned up, there was a considerable improvement. Indeed, conditions were probably much worse in other hospitals, as revealed by the survey conducted for John Simon by Bristowe and Holmes in 1863.[98] The bacteriological discoveries toward the end of the century, after the work of Semmelweis and Lister, provided a basis for reducing puerperal infections, but much more was needed before the risks of childbirth could be eliminated or reduced to a minimum. Increased medical knowledge and changes in social life were necessary if women were to receive the best kind of care during pregnancy, parturition, and the postnatal period. This was still in the future and would come with a change in the social position of women.

Commenting on the survey by Henry Julian Hunter of infant mortality in five rural areas of eastern England, John Simon referred to the 'vast quantity of reckless fornication' among the migratory female workers. Simon might just as appropriately have used this phrase to describe another aspect of Victorian life—its illicit sexual behavior manifested particularly in prostitution. Whether prostitution was more widespread in mid-Victorian Britain than at any other time in the history of the kingdom may be debated, but there is no doubt that public opinion was greatly concerned about the problem. Prostitution is essentially an urban phenomenon, and its prevalence was closely related to the enormous urban growth of the nineteenth century and the social problems to which it gave rise. An unusually high proportion of prostitutes were initially domestic servants.[99] Of the 11,000 prostitutes who were inmates of the prison on Millbank during the eighties, at least 50 percent were estimated to have come from this source. The situation was clearly depicted by William Acton (1813–75), a physician who in 1857 gave the first candid, rational, and humane account of prostitution in England. In 1859, urging that 'fallen women' be rehabilitated through employment as wet-nurses, he wrote:[100]

> Remember, it is not street-walkers nor professional prostitutes we are speaking of. We are speaking of the young house-maid or pretty parlour-maid in the same street in which the sickly lady has given birth to a sickly child, to whom healthy milk is life, and anything else death. With shame and horror the girl bears a child to the butler, or the policeman, or her master's son. Of course she is discharged; of course her seducer is some-where else; of course, when her savings are spent, she will have to take, with shame and loathing, to a life of prostitution. Now, she is healthy and strong, and there is a little life six doors off, crying out for what she can give, and wasting away for the want of it, and in the nursing of that baby is a chance, humanly speaking, of her salvation from the pit of harlotry.

In his book on prostitution, Acton linked the situation of such women to their occupations and the low level of wages in certain trades. After they have been seduced, he said, 'Domestic servants, and girls of decent family, are generally driven head-long to the streets for support of themselves and their babies; needle-women of some classes by the incompatibility of infant nursing with the discipline of the work-shop.'[101]

The precarious economic situation of women workers, based on low wages, was depressed even further in some trades by seasonal unemployment, particularly in those connected with fashion and dress. Barmaids provided another large contingent of prostitutes, while still others were recruited from among seamstresses, laundresses, charwomen, and factory workers. At the very lowest level were the streetwomen of whom Taine wrote: 'This is not debauchery which flaunts itself, but destitution—and such destitution.'[102]

Overcrowded dwellings and common lodging houses certainly contributed to promiscuity. Regarding the latter Mayhew wrote, 'The indiscriminate admixture of the sexes among adults, in many of these places, is another evil. Even in some houses considered of the better sort, men and women, husbands and wives, old and young, strangers and acquaintances, sleep in the same apartment, and if they choose, in the same bed. Any remonstrance at some act of gross depravity or impropriety on the part of a woman not so utterly hardened as the others, is met with abuse and derision.' Conditions involving juveniles were if anything even worse. 'Three, four, five, six and even more boys and girls have been packed head and feet, into one small bed; some of them perhaps never met before. On such occasions any clothing seems often enough to be regarded merely an incumbrance. Sometimes there are loud quarrels and revilings from the jealousy of boys and girls, and more especially of girls whose 'chaps' have deserted or been inveigled from them. At others there is an amicable interchange of partners, and next day a resumption of their former companionship.' Among the statements which Mayhew took from various poor people is a moving account from a girl of sixteen, who was barely twelve when she became a street-walker, and which substantiates the preceding description. In her story are combined a lack of parental control due to the death of both parents; poor conditions of domestic service; the bad environment of the lodging house with its encouragement of loose living; as well as the prevalent connection with crime and drunkenness.[103]

A plentiful supply of such purchasable women and girls was thus available to satisfy the sexual needs of a large group of men in Victorian cities and towns. Small wonder that public opinion in the mid-nineteenth century became concerned with the state of affairs revealed by Acton, Mayhew, and others—by the extent of prostitution and its consequences, particularly venereal disease.

From the point of view of health, it was the diseases caused by prostitution, particularly as they affected members of the armed forces, which aroused the greatest concern. Beginning in 1864, three Contagious Diseases Acts were passed to deal with this problem. Most important was that of 1866, empowering military and naval authorities in a number of garrison towns to secure compulsory medical inspection of prostitutes, who if found to be infected with a venereal disease were to be detained in a hospital. About this time, a powerful association including many physicians and sanitary-reformers mounted a campaign to extend the compulsory provisions of the Contagious Diseases Act of 1866 to the civilian population. In support of the need for such action, it was claimed that one-fifth to one-third of the sick poor suffered from 'a contagious disease of the gravest character, which is constantly transmitted to offspring.' To deal with these claims and with the entire question, John Simon requested William W. Wagstaffe, a young surgeon at St Thomas's Hospital, to find out if venereal diseases were as prevalent as claimed by the advocates of compulsory inspection. In 1868, Wagstaffe examined attendance by age and sex at the out-patient clinics of the London hospitals for periods ranging from two or three days to one week, as well as the number of inpatients treated on a single day in some seven hospitals, including two workhouse infirmaries. A separate study to determine the prevalence of congenital syphilis was made at the Great Ormond Street Hospital. Finally, Wagstaffe estimated the amount of venereal disease among the sick poor receiving domiciliary care based on returns from medical officers of the large Lambeth Poor Law Union. His study revealed that the numerical 'evidence' advanced by the association was highly inflated. Among the adult sick poor 6·9 percent suffered from some kind of venereal disease, while information from the children's hospital for a ten-year period showed that only 1·5 percent had congenital syphilis.[104] Using these findings, Simon concluded that he could not recommend the extension of the Act of

1866 to civilians. He considered it neither practical nor desirable to institute government control of prostitution. The legislation was never extended, and increasing opposition to the compulsory examination of women eventually led to the repeal of the entire system in 1886. Thereafter, little or no action was taken by government to prevent or cure venereal diseases. Nevertheless, the medical and social problems remained. But it was not until the second decade of the twentieth century that effective knowledge and means were available to reduce the occurrence of syphilis and its later consequences.

The health situation in the Victorian city was a consequence of its evolution. The rapid aggregation of people in limited spaces was bound to produce stresses and strains and to create problems. The health of a population depends on many factors, among which a high place must be given to the standard of living, including as it does nutrition, housing, clothing, and medical care. What happened in the Victorian city in the thirties and forties was that the pressures of industrialization and of economic individualism, particularly when applied to people who were just becoming urbanized, created a state of cultural shock and depressed their living standards to such a degree as to create feelings of 'anxiety and apprehension amounting almost to dismay' in those about them.

The fear and dismay aroused by these developments had two aspects. One was a reaction to the different way of life of the workers and the poor, a sense that there was something unknown, mysterious, and dangerous about the lower orders of society, that the alleys and rookeries in which they lived were 'rife with all kinds of enormity.' These attitudes were not restricted to the British; they were shared with the French, the Americans, and the Germans. After all it was Eugène Sue who wrote *Les Mystères de Paris* in 1843, and Charles Loring Brace who produced *The Dangerous Classes of New York* in 1877. The culture of poverty, to use a current phrase, in its values, experience, and life style denied all that the middle class officially espoused and held dear.

Related to this psychological confrontation was the concern aroused by specific urban problems such as overcrowding, crime, destitution, alcoholism, prostitution, illegitimacy, and disease which seemed to be inextricably intertwined. Death and disease seemed to lurk in the houses and haunts of the poor, ready to emerge as epidemics to threaten the health and life of their betters. Thus, exploration of the dark alleys of poverty in the Victorian city went hand in hand with horrified and fascinated investigation of disease, particularly of those aspects which aroused public opinion through fear or because they seemed to lead to evil consequences of such magnitude that they could not be sustained. Various legislative enactments concerned with the public health were the result of reactions to revealed abuses and threats. Thus, the cholera epidemic of 1853 led to the Act of 1855, which consolidated and amended the Nuisances Removal and Disease Prevention Acts, and obliged local authorities to token action on sanitary matters. This was true as well of the Arsenic

Act of 1851 and the 1860 Act for preventing the Adulteration of Articles of Food and Drink.[105]

Whatever the motivation, action to deal with health problems had to be taken in terms of available knowledge, and it was precisely on this point that medical science was defective. Nevertheless, vaccination reduced the incidence of smallpox and the ravages of enteric infections were diminished by the drive for sanitation of the environment through the removal of filth and the provision of clean water. For the most part, however, improvement in the health status of the urban population, e.g., in regard to typhus fever and tuberculosis, was achieved essentially by improvement in the standard of living of the poorer and most numerous classes of the community. Real wages generally rose during the second half of the nineteenth century, largely as a result of cheap imported foodstuffs becoming available. Indeed, after 1870 the eating habits of British city-dwellers began to be transformed, and however uneven the improvement may have been, the trend towards better health was clearly established.

Notes

1   Charles Dickens, *Bleak House*, ch. 46.
2   Robert Cowan, 'Vital Statistics of Glasgow . . . ,' *Journal of the Statistical Society of London (J.S.S.),* iii (1840), 269.
3   Richard B. Howard, *An Inquiry into the Morbid Effects of Deficiency of Food* (1838), p. 38; Charles Creighton, *A History of Epidemics in Britain* (1894), II, pp. 167–74, 181–3, 191, 203–5. The benefits to health from proper nutrition were strikingly demonstrated in Britain during the Second World War. The policy of making diets on a health standard available to all the people without regard to ability to pay not only maintained public health but in many respects improved it. On this see: Ministry of Food, *How Britain Was Fed in War Time. Food Control 1939–1945* (1946), pp. 46–9; H. E. Mazee, 'Application of Nutrition to Public Health—Some Lessons of the War,' *British Medical Journal (B.M.J.),* 30 March 1946, 475.
4   T. H. Marshall, 'The Population Problem during the Industrial Revolution,' *Economic History,* i (1929), 453–4; *Parliamentary Papers (P.P.),* 1831, XVIII, Comparative Account of the Population of Britain, 1831, p. 15, cited by M. W. Flinn, ed., *Report on the Sanitary Condition of the Labouring Population of Great Britain, 1842* (Edinburgh, 1965), p. 14.
5   William Farr, *Vital Statistics,* ed. Noel A. Humphreys (1885), p. 150.
6   T. R. Edmonds, 'Statistics of the London Hospital, with Remarks on the Law of Sickness,' *Lancet,* ii (1835–6), 778.
7   Farr, op. cit., p. 153; F. G. P. Neison, 'Contributions to Vital Statistics . . . ,' *J.S.S.,* viii (1845), 290–343; ix (1846), 50–75.
8   Neison, op. cit., p. 303.
9   Henry Jephson, *The Sanitary Evolution of London* (1907), p. 118.

10 George Rosen, 'L. L. Finke on the Different Kinds of Geographies, but Chiefly on Medical Topographies and how to compose them,' *Bulletin of the History of Medicine (B.H.M.)*, xx (1946), 527–38; 'Problems in the Application of Statistical Analysis to Questions of Health: 1700–1800,' *B.H.M.*, xxix (1955), 27–45; *A History of Public Health* (New York, 1958), pp. 208–33.

11 T. R. Edmonds, 'On the Mortality at Glasgow and on the increasing Mortality in England,' *Lancet*, ii (1835–6), 353–9; 'On the Law of Mortality in each County of England,' ibid., i (1835–6), 364–71, 416.

12 Farr, op. cit., p. 159.

13 Ibid., p. 166.

14 For a discussion of this approach see George Rosen, 'People, Disease and Emotion: Some Newer Problems for Research in Medical History,' *B.H.M.*, xli (1967), 5–23.

15 John Huxham, *Essay on Fevers* (2nd edn, 1750), pp. 72–3.

16 See, for example, the discussion of fever in Robert James Graves, *A System of Clinical Medicine* (Dublin, 1843), pp. 41–64.

17 Alexander P. Stewart, 'Some considerations on the nature and Pathology of Typhus and Typhoid Fever . . . ,' *Edinburgh Medical and Surgical Journal (Edin. M.S.J.)*, liv (1840), 290; H. C. Lombard, 'Observations suggested by a comparison of the post-mortem appearances produced by typhous fever in Dublin, Paris and Geneva,' *Dublin Journal of Medical Science*, x (1836), 17, 101.

18 Cowan, op. cit., p. 271.

19 Ibid., Creighton, op. cit., p. 208.

20 Flinn, op. cit., p. 97. Neil Arnott (1788–1874) was one of three physicians employed by the Poor Law Commission to look into the prevalence and causation of preventable disease ('fever') in London, and whose study led to Chadwick's *Report* of 1842.

21 Stewart, op. cit., p. 316; John H. Peebles, M.D., was a Fellow of the Royal Colleges of Physicians of Edinburgh and Florence. See his 'Observations on Petechial Fevers and Petechial Eruptions,' *Edin. M.S.J.*, xliv (1835), 356, where he describes typhus fever as 'petechial contagious fever.'

22 H. E. Sigerist, *Civilization and Disease* (Ithaca, 1943), p. 119. See Charles Murchison, *A Treatise on the Continued Fevers of Great Britain* (1862), p. 131.

23 Stewart, op. cit., pp. 296–7.

24 Robert Perry, 'Observations on Continued Fever, as it occurs in the City of Glasgow Hospitals,' *Edin. M.S.J.*, xlv (1836), 64; see also A. L. Goodall, 'Glasgow's Place in the Distinction Between Typhoid and Typhus Fevers,' *B.H.M.*, xxviii (1954), 140–53. In Philadelphia, the American physician W. W. Gerhard concluded independently that typhus and typhoid were distinct diseases, and also published his results in 1836.

25 H. C. Barlow, 'On the Distinction between Typhus Fever and Dothienenterie,' *Lancet*, i (1839–40), 838–41.

26 Cormack, etc. on the 'Endemic Fever of Scotland,' *British and Foreign Medical Review*, xviii (1844), 179–97. For Stewart see note 79; also Goodall, op. cit., pp. 149–50. Alexander P. Stewart (1813–83), studied at Glasgow, Paris, and Berlin and received his degree of M.D. in 1838. He practised in London and was active in sanitary reform there; see Alexander P. Stewart and Edward Jenkins, *The Medical*

and *Legal Aspects of Sanitary Reform* (1867, reprinted Leicester University Press, 1969).

27 *Medical Times*, xx–xxiii (1849–51).

28 William Jenner, *Lectures and Essays on Fevers and Diphtheria* (1893).

29 Creighton, op. cit., pp. 209–11; R. Thorne Thorne, *The Progress of Preventive Medicine during the Victorian Era, 1837–87* (1888), p. 14.

30 Jephson, op. cit., p. 118.

31 Creighton, op. cit., p. 215; Thorne, op. cit., pp. 17–22.

32 Thorne, op. cit., p. 24; Creighton, op. cit., pp. 212–13, 216, 218–19.

33 Typhus fever did not totally disappear in Britain during the nineteenth century, but it no longer had any serious epidemiologic importance after 1900.

34 Royston Lambert, *Sir John Simon, 1816–1904, and English Social Administration* (1963), p. 204.

35 Thorne, op. cit., pp. 53–8.

36 *Snow on Cholera, being a Reprint of Two Papers by John Snow, M.D. together with a biographical memoir by B. W. Richardson, M.D.* (New York, 1936).

37 William Budd, *Typhoid Fever, Its Nature, Mode of Spreading, and Prevention* (1874, reprinted New York, 1931), pp. 141–3.

38 Ibid., p. 153.

39 Ibid., pp. 176, 181.

40 Stewart, op. cit., pp. 10, 14.

41 *Report of the Medical Officer of the Privy Council, 1858* (1859), p. 27.

42 C. Fraser Brockington, *Public Health in the Nineteenth Century* (1965), pp. 192–278.

43 *Second Report of the Medical Officer of the Privy Council, 1859* (1860), pp. 89–90, 160.

44 Ibid., p. 34.

45 T. Sheriff, 'Account of a Remarkable Outbreak of Enteric Fever,' *Edinburgh Medical Journal (Edin. M.J.)*, xi (1865), 525–30; Article 'Hygiene,' *Chambers' Encyclopedia* (1906), VI, p. 42.

46 Charlotte M. Yonge, *The Three Brides* (New York, 1876), p. 391. In this passage there seems to be an echo of Greenhow's description of the water from the public pump in Well Street, Coventry, which was 'palatable, cool and refreshing in hot weather,' but which on analysis was found to be polluted. These themes occur in other novels by Miss Yonge, e.g., *The Young Stepmother, or a Chronicle of Mistakes* (1861) and *The Trial: More Links of the Daisy Chain* (1864). See G. Battiscombe and M. Laski, eds, *A Chaplet for Charlotte Yonge*, (n.d.); Alethea Hayter, 'The Sanitary Idea and a Victorian Novelist,' *History Today*, xix (1969), 840–7.

47 'The Infection of Fever by Ingesta,' *Edin. M.J.*, May 1858.

48 Thorne, op. cit., pp. 26–7; E. Ballard, *Medical Times and Gazette*, ii (1870), 611; *Reports of the Medical Officer to the Local Government Board*, ii (1873), 193.

49 Robert Willan, 'Report of Diseases in London,' in *Miscellaneous Works* (1821); W. Woolcombe, *Remarks on the Frequency and Fatality of Different Diseases . . .* (1808).

50 John Brownlee, *An Investigation into the Epidemiology of Phthisis in Great Britain and Ireland*, Parts I and II, National Health Insurance, Medical Research Committee, Special Reports, Nos 18, 46 (1918–20).

51 T. McKeown and R. G. Record, 'Reasons for the Decline of Mortality in England and Wales during the Nineteenth Century,' *Population Studies*, xvi (1963), 113.

52 See H. T. Bulstrode, *On Sanatoria for Consumption and Certain other Aspects of the Tuberculosis Question*, Supp. Rep. Med. Off. L. G. B., 1905–6 (1908), cited by Gregory Kayne, *The Control of Tuberculosis in England Past and Present* (1937), pp. 9–10.

Table 27.1   *Crude death-rates per million living*

	1858–60	1901–5
Phthisis	2,565	1,215
Other tubercular and scrofulous diseases (excluding Lupus)	739	523
Diseases of the respiratory system	3,265	2,476*

*Excluding Croup

Table 27.2   *Quinquennial death-rates per 10,000 living*

Year	Total deaths	Average annual death-rate per 10,000 living for each quinquennial period
1840	59,923	38·8 (1838–42)
1853	54,918	28·0 (1851–5)
1858	50,442	26·0
1863	51,072	25·2
1868	51,423	24·4
1873	51,355	22·1
1878	52,856	20·4
1883	50,053	18·3
1888	44,248	16·3
1893	43,632	14·5
1898	41,335	13·2
1903	40,132	12·1 (1901–5)

Table 27.3   *Mortality from phthisis per 10,000 living at each age*

	10–15	15–20	20–25	25–35	35–45	45–55	55–65	65–75	75 and over
Males									
Decennium 1851–60	76	240	405	403	402	384	335	239	93
Year 1901	19	80	167	215	289	313	252	159	60
Decline (percent)	75	67	59	47	28	19	25	33	35
Females									
Decennium 1851–60	129	352	430	458	419	313	239	164	72
Year 1901	40	100	129	164	186	149	112	83	31
Decline (percent)	69	72	70	64	56	52	53	50	57

53 F. C. S. Bradbury, *Causal Factors in Tuberculosis* (1933); see also P. D'Arcy Hart and G. Payling Wright, *Tuberculosis and Social Conditions in England* (1939).

54 S. Lyle Cummins, *Primitive Tuberculosis* (1939); J. B. McDougall, *Tuberculosis: A global study in social pathology* (Edinburgh, 1950).

55 Kayne, op. cit., p. 60.

56 *Rep. San. Cond.*, 1842, pp. 168–9.

57 Wanda F. Neff, *Victorian Working Women* (New York, 1929), pp. 39, 122–4.

58 Dr Greenhow's Report on Districts with Excessive Mortality from Lung-Diseases, *3rd Rep. M.O. Privy Council, 1860*, pp. 102–94; continued *4th Rep. . . . 1861*; for Greenhow's studies on miners' diseases see George Rosen, *The History of Miners' Diseases. A medical and social interpretation* (New York, 1943), pp. 365–76.

59 *3rd Rep. M.O. Privy Council, 1860*, pp. 30–3.

60 Report by Dr William Ord on the sanitary circumstances of dressmakers and other needlewomen in London, *6th Rep. M.O. Privy Council, 1863*, pp. 362–82; Report by Dr Edward Smith, F.R.S., on the sanitary circumstances of printers in London, ibid., pp. 383–415; Report of Dr Edward Smith, F.R.S., on the sanitary circumstances of tailors in London, ibid., pp. 416–30.

61 Charles Kingsley, *Cheap Clothes and Nasty* (1850); Kingsley also dealt with this topic in *Alton Locke*.

62 *5th Rep. M.O. Privy Council, 1862*, p. 10; *6th Rep. M.O. Privy Council, 1863*, p. 31.

63 The intimate relationship between Bertrand Russell's mother and his brother's tutor, who had advanced pulmonary tuberculosis, is a case in point. See *The Autobiography of Bertrand Russell 1872–1914* (1967), p. 17.

64 James Turnbull, 'Report of the Medical Cases treated in the Liverpool Northern Hospital during 1846 and 1847,' *Edin. M.S.J.*, lxx (1848), 40–101.

65 John Charles Steele, 'View of the Sickness and Mortality in the Royal Infirmary of Glasgow during the Year 1847,' *Edin. M.S.J.*, lxx (1848), 145–69.

66 R. Boyd, 'Pathological Contributions and Vital Statistics,' *Edin. M.S.J.*, lviii (1842), 72–112; lx (1843), 110–64.

67 Maurice Davidson and F. G. Rouvray, *The Brompton Hospital. The story of a great adventure* (1954), p. 9.

68 Western Hospital for Incipient Consumption, Torquay (1850); City of London Hospital for Diseases of the Chest, Victoria Park (1851); National Hospital, Bournemouth (1855); Mount Vernon Hospital for Consumption (1860); Home for Consumptive Females, Portman Square, London (1863); Liverpool Hospital for Consumption (1864); Royal National Hospital, Ventnor (1867); Manchester Hospital for Consumption (1875); St Joseph's Hospital, Chiswick (1875); St Michael's Home, Axbridge (1878); St Catherine's Home, Ventnor (1879); Hahnemann Home, Bournemouth (1879); Eversfield Hospital (1884); Manchester Sanatorium, Bowden (1885); Mildway Convalescent Home, Torquay (1886). See H. T. Bulstrode, *On Sanatoria for Consumption and Certain other Aspects of the Tuberculosis Question*, Supp., Rep. M.O., L.G.B., 1905–6 (1908).

69 *Lancet*, ii (1865), 14.

70 Kayne, op. cit., p. 43; A. Newsholme, *The Prevention of Tuberculosis* (1908).

71 Thomas Ferguson, *Scottish Social Welfare 1864–1914* (1958), pp. 429–30; Rosen, *History of Public Health*, pp. 385–6.

72 Ferguson, op. cit., pp. 421–3; W. M. Frazer, *A History of English Public Health, 1834–1939* (1950), pp. 260–2.

73 Farr, op. cit., pp. 190–1; Frazer, op. cit., pp. 78, 244.

74 Thomas Ferguson, *The Dawn of Scottish Social Welfare. A survey from medieval times to 1863* (1948), pp. 301–2; *Scottish Social Welfare 1864–1914*, pp. 535–6.

75 J. B. Davis, *A Cursory Inquiry into some of the Principal Causes of Mortality among Children, with a View to Assist in Ameliorating the State of the Rising Generation in Health, Morals and Happiness* (1817).

76 *First Report of the Commissioners for Inquiring into the State of Large Towns and Populous Districts* (1844), I, pp. 182–4.

77 *4th Rep. M.O. Privy Council, 1862*, pp. 496–8, 651–9. See also M. Hewitt, *Wives and Mothers in Victorian Industry* (1958), particularly chs 7, 9–10.

78 Yonge, *Three Brides*, p. 357. See also 'The Public Hygiene of Great Britain,' *British and Foreign Medical Review*, xviii (1844), 504; Dr Christison on Poisons, ibid., xx (1845), 332.

79 *4th Rep. M.O. Privy Council*, p. 499.

80 *6th Rep. M.O. Privy Council*, p. 262.

81 H. H. Scott, *Some Notable Epidemics* (1934), p. 166.

82 Creighton, op. cit., pp. 726–7.

83 Ibid., p. 729.

Table 27.4 *Mean annual mortality from scarlet fever per million living at successive age-periods 1859–85, in England and Wales*

Age	Males	Females
0–1	1,664	1,384
1–2	4,170	3,874
2–3	4,676	4,491
3–4	4,484	4,332
4–5	3,642	3,556
0–5	3,681	3,482
5–10	1,667	1,613
10–15	346	381
15–20	111	113
20–25	59	77
25–35	36	58
35 and upwards	13	15
All ages	778	717

84 Thorne, op. cit., pp. 30–7; Frazer, op. cit., pp. 178–80; George Rosen, 'Acute Communicable Diseases,' in W. R. Bett, ed., *The History and Conquest of Common Diseases* (Norman, Oklahoma, 1954), pp. 26–38.

85 H. Haeser, *Geschichte der epidemischen Krankheiten* (Jena, 1865), pp. 660–4; A. Hirsch, *Handbook of Geographical and Historical Pathology*, 3 vols (1886), III, pp. 81–100; Creighton, op. cit., pp. 734–44; A. Newsholme, *Epidemic Diphtheria* (1898), pp. 117–20, 121–2; Rosen, 'Acute Communicable Diseases,' pp. 6–26.

86 Croup is a popular term used for respiratory tract infections in young children characterized by stridulous breathing, and was often applied to cases of diphtheria. The term is vague in its meaning, but most probably refers to diphtheria in earlier literature.

87 Newsholme, op. cit., p. 31.

Table 27.5 *Annual death-rate from diphtheria and croup per million persons living, 1858–94, in England and Wales*

Period		Diphtheria	Croup	Diphtheria plus croup
Three years	1858–60	372·3	274·7	647·0
Five years	1861–65	247·6	287·6	535·2
	1866–70	126·8	208·0	334·8
	1871–75	120·8	184·2	305·0
	1876–80	121·8	154·2	276·0
	1881–85	156·2	163·4	319·6
	1886–90	169·6	125·8	295·4
Four years	1891–94	251·2	74·0	325·2

88 Simon had drawn up a schedule in 1858 for an epidemiologic study of diphtheria which Greenhow carried out in 1859. The results appeared in the *Report* to the Privy Council for 1859, and E. H. Greenhow, *On Diphtheria* (1860). However, this investigation did little to elucidate the problem of diphtheria.

89 Thomas T. Higgins, *Great Ormond Street, 1852–1952* (1952); *An Appeal to the Public on behalf of Sick Children* (1850), reviewed in *Edin. M.S.J.*, lxxiii (1850), 481–3.

90 Ruth G. Hodgkinson, *The Origins of the National Health Service. The medical services of the New Poor Law, 1834–1871* (Berkeley and Los Angeles, 1967), pp. 550–6.

91 For the following discussion of smallpox see Thorne, op. cit., pp. 5–14; Frazer, op. cit., pp. 71–2, 169–72; Lambert, op. cit., pp. 250–7, 587–8.

92 'Lord' George Sanger, *Seventy Years a Showman* (1926), p. 62. Sanger is discussing an epidemic of smallpox in 1833 in which his sister was attacked. To protect the other children in the family, Sanger's father inoculated them with matter taken from the pustules of the sick child. This method of prophylaxis, called variolation, was introduced into England in the eighteenth century, though it had long been used in various forms in different parts of the world, especially in the East.

93 S. Gee, *St. Bart's Hosp. Rep.*, iv (1868), 69–80.

94 T. Barlow, *Medico-chirurgical Transactions*, lxvi (1883), 159–220.

95 W. Huntly, *Investigation into the Habits and Diet of the Natives of Rajputana with reference to the Etiological Treatment of Rickets* (Ajmere, 1889), p. 23, cited by A. White Franklin, 'Rickets,' in Bett, op. cit., p. 195.

96 T. A. Palm, *Practitioner*, xlv (1890), 270, 321.

97 Iron was used in the treatment of anemia, Peruvian bark (cinchona) for malaria, and mercury for syphilis.

 98 Hodgkinson, op. cit., pp. 549–50; *6th Rep. . . . to the Privy Council, 1863*, pp. 467–753.

 99 Steven Marcus, *The Other Victorians. A study of sexuality and pornography in mid-nineteenth-century England* (New York, 1966), pp. 128–30.

100 W. Acton, 'Unmarried Wet-Nurses,' *Lancet*, i (1859), 175–6; James Laver, *The Age of Optimism: Manners and morals, 1848–1914* (1966), p. 92.

101 William Acton, *Prostitution, Considered in its Moral, Social and Sanitary Aspects . . .* (2nd edn, 1870), p. 29.

102 *Taine's Notes on England*, pp. 96, 34, 36.

103 Henry Mayhew, *London Labour and the London Poor* (1861), I, pp. 412–14.

104 Report by Mr William W. Wagstaffe on the Quantity and Kinds of Venereal Disease under Treatment at certain Charitable Institutions in London, *11th Rep. M.O. Privy Council, 1868*, pp. 78–91; Frazer, op. cit., pp. 200–4.

105 A. H. Hassall, *Food and its Adulteration* (1855); E. G. Clayton, *Arthur Hill Hassall, Physician and Sanitary Reformer* (1908); John Burnett, *Plenty and Want. A social history of diet in England from 1815 to the present day* (1966), pp. 77–90.

28 Training Urban Man

A hypothesis about the sanitary movement

Richard L. Schoenwald

It is customary to treat the great sanitary reformers as men who investigated and began to solve problems which mainly belonged to engineering or to politics. The cities were full of stinks; horse droppings accumulated in the streets; human feces lay heaped in slum courts or moldered sickeningly beneath middle-class and aristocratic —even royal—dwellings.[1] Then Edwin Chadwick and his snooping cohorts appeared. Unlike most of their contemporaries, they found dirt horrifying, and they vigorously promoted technological, legislative, and administrative devices intended to reduce some of the filth generated in growing cities.

This picture is far too simple: it has no psychological dimension. The reformers were presuming to deal with aspects of human behavior which modern men feel to be very intimate, very personal, very much their own. The history of the sanitary movement has been written so far without any consideration of the attitudes and feelings of the ambitiously controlling reformers, or of the population which had to be induced to alter its behavior and accept external control.[2] In a campaign which dragged on into the twentieth century the great vision of the reformers did triumph. Today the man who asserts most imperiously that his home is his castle can only do so by forgetting that his throne is plugged into a network of municipally maintained means for removing, forever, products of his own royal self.

The task of the nineteenth century was to teach men that they must change fundamentally, and to show them that they could.[3] The sanitary demands increasingly made on dwellers in Victorian cities helped them to become conscious of having a self which needed and repaid watching and regulating. As they grasped this new truth, fitfully and resistingly to be sure, they proceeded with making these selves more productive and more disciplined than the insides of any creature ever known to history.

The first section of this paper uses material from several fields to analyse how sanitary discipline readies people for altered conduct. The second part discusses the origin and establishing of sanitary reform as measures intended, both consciously and unconsciously, to make men learn to act differently from their sad predecessors mired in ages past.[4]

At the end of the nineteenth century Sigmund Freud constructed a psychology which sought to explain how human beings could become so miserable, so deprived, so much in want of satisfaction.[5] Once upon a time the infant had managed to gain intense pleasure from the retaining and then the expelling of feces. The build-up and the reduction of tension as feces accumulated and were then discharged followed a rising and falling curve which Freud considered identical with the pattern evident in sexual satisfaction. Too soon civilization closed in on the child, and towering authorities dictated that he must abandon the joy which he had found in storing feces and then parting from them as he, and only he, pleased.

Freud sometimes spoke as if he considered excretory processes and products to be equally important, and sometimes as if he gave highest significance to the process or to the products alone.[6] Leading commentators on Freud's work have underscored his concern both with process and product.[7] The present paper deals primarily with process, with actions and attitudes which involve a product. Decades ago, when Freud was restoring respectability to excretion after the moralizing ravages of the late-eighteenth and nineteenth centuries, he had to speak rather favorably, and even fondly, of wastes as a product. Now it is much clearer that excretion represents a process in which attitudes and emotions develop that are transferable to other behavioral processes whose products resemble excrement only in sharing the label 'products.'[8]

A pleasurable way of acting can never be wholly abandoned, Freud maintained; it can only be pushed aside, temporarily held down, publicly forbidden. Civilization decreed that a good and civilized nineteenth-century child must conceal his pleasurable gain in the process of excretion, and disavow his fondness for the product which made the process possible. Yearning for the good old days and their freedom, the child could gain disguised satisfactions through character traits established during the battle to 'get him trained.' He might become willful ('I won't give out'), orderly ('You told me to be clean, and I'll be very clean, but only on the outside'), or parsimonious ('You told me to give it up, but I'll find a way to keep this precious stuff all, all, all for myself.')[9]

Freud's account of lost pleasures combines unmistakable regret with recognition that civilization must exact such a price. For Freud there is no doubt that civilization is certainly worth controls on random defecating and indiscriminate orgiasticizing. Man's energy is limited, as Freud knew, because he was thoroughly steeped in nineteenth-century thermodynamics. If man—the run-of-the-lot worker, the herd-creature—only plays, he will not toil, and in his sporting he will wreck utterly the culture painfully created by the few already initiated into the wisdom of renunciation.[10] In the 1890s Freud had rediscovered and made conscious the message of order, pacification, and routinization brought by the sanitary movement half a century earlier.

Freud's preoccupation with modern life as a series of deprivations, clamp-downs, and shuntings into substitutes kept him from being very concerned with how men did learn to carry on what they called civilization. Since the time of his greatest discoveries, psychology has given much more attention to the capacities for learning which make men distinctively human. Freud's dramatic scenario becomes much more plausible when taken as a program for learning.

Every society inducts its young into membership by making them learn its ways. Every known human society makes its young learn some regulations for the controlling of wastes.[11] In the process of socializing the child—of making him a social and sociable animal—learning to curb and regulate the excretory functioning of his body constitutes his earliest extensive set of responses to purely external demands.[12] Voluntary control of excretion depends upon learning to interpret both internal and external signals: how pressing the need, how suitable the time and place. Depending on the climate and the level of cultural development, the child must master as well procedures for unfastening and fastening clothes, and for using various technological devices.

The demanding, complex, and lengthy learning necessary for self-regulation frequently begins before the child can exercise real command over language.[13] The child who lacks ready use of language grants to such learning a largely unconscious grip over himself. In his pre-verbal innocence he acquiesces in the establishment of habits which he may never be able to criticize, or even force into his awareness as behavior that is not eternal. The devoted pressure of a mother who values neatness, punctuality, precision, and discipline can go far to ensure the child's learning to be like such a parent.[14]

The young child takes in as much as he can of what his parents say, preach, and prescribe. He gains also from perceiving what they do, and trying to model himself on what he thinks must be good ways of acting: how hard *they* press, how anxiously concerned *they* become, how eager *they* are to get things over and done with, how satisfied *they* are willing to feel. Through the parents as reflectors, the child catches the culture's conception of how to make, to do, to achieve. In his first efforts toward learning to control his body's output the child is gaining basic conceptions of how to work.[15]

Ways of acting learned early acquire a supportive moral coloration. On the basis of the prescribed regulation of bodily processes the child learns to label actions as good, evil, or indifferent: being clean and predictable ('regular') means being good, being messy means partaking of evil.[16] The child learns to turn up his nose at objects, people, or ideas which do not smell right. As he learns to turn away and avoid contact and contamination, he is learning how to repress. He is learning to push away the enticing prospect of behavior into which he would have let himself go had not the society around him wanted him to bar such conduct.[17]

Learning that some smells are good, and that others are bad, re-enacts the great scene in man's developmental history when he began to walk erect. He could not maintain erect posture and still yield to the array of tempting aromas at ground level which drew his less highly developed animal forebears. In this crisis men came to renounce such attractions by learning to turn away: repression of old desires constituted a large part of what being man-like meant, initially.[18]

With the coming of urban life, both in its first appearance in the ancient world and its flourishing in the modern, this crisis must have been played through again. The second time, however, would prove less disruptive than the first, for the anatomical evolution which sealed man as human had destroyed, long before, most of his smelling sensorium.[19] Smell for town dwellers would constitute a sense activatable by strong stimuli, a part of themselves useful in underscoring a point being driven home to, and being driven into, a child: when you smell that strong smell of which you are so proud, which comes from the mess of which you are so proud, you are nothing but an animal! Stand up straight and act like a human being! You have to live with other people, with lots of them in big cities, and you have to learn that they can't find your smells as beguiling as you do, or everyone will be down on all fours, and riot and rampage will run in the streets! Turn your nose away from the smell of lower parts, turn your eyes and your mind to higher things!

The child must learn that what is inside him becomes bad when he lets it out, and he can only redeem its resultant badness by learning to dam and damn its seductiveness, and by letting his precious substance out in a ceremoniously sanctified manner. If a child can manage enough control to find the odors of others disgusting, and even his own odors at times less than intoxicating, he should be learning to leave the other atoms in his social universe pretty much alone.[20] If a child can manage enough control to situate his inner products only in certain specified external locales, he should be on his way to learning something about the nature of the station in life to which he has been called: inner stability portends outer steadfastness.

The learned voluntary regulation of excretory behavior customarily leads, then, to effects on adult activity. Psychoanalysis has used the rubric of 'anality' to designate feelings and meanings related to the production of wastes which persist in every adult's life. These feelings and meanings may be transformed into attitudes toward work, into the harshness with which an individual watches himself, into the rage or apathy which comes to be characteristic of an individual living within a network of demands and prohibitions. Successful parents induct children into a ritual which persists without their presence, the excretory receptable or the outside world's job sufficing to trigger responses lovingly implanted. A ritual has been created in which the feeling of doing the job as the parental gods commanded tempers the inextinguishable fury of balked, restrained, citified man.[21]

CHRISTMAS DAY'S BIRTH-DAY.

THE 25th of December you will hold in especial honour. As early as 4 a. m. I—CHRISTMAS—shall expect to be greeted by the "wobbling" of the pudding in the boiler, whilst all sorts of delicious odours will steal even through the key-holes, making sweet the out-door air. At early light, the Robin Redbreast—the unpaid Christmas minstrel—shall whistle you a blithe and jolly song! Your house will, I know, be green as a bower with holly. Holly that typifies green spirits and red hearts. You will make the poor's-box at church rattle rejoicingly; you will call up smiles and thanks from astonished crossing-sweepers. You will carve your turkey with a fearless hand, for you have subscribed a goose—a piece of beef or so—to the table of your poorer neighbours. You will help yourself twice to pudding, for have you not made at least one *pudding* smoke elsewhere? You will let your eye rejoice in the beeswing of "*that* particular port," for you have warmed the toes and noses of at least a few old folk, with some humming ale. And in this way you will double every enjoyment of the Birth-day of CHRISTMAS, by enjoying the enjoyments you have bestowed upon others. At this season let not the high forget the low. Let the Head of Gold bear in special memory the Feet of Clay.

HINTS ABOUT FIRE.

In case of fire, whatever may be the heat of the moment, keep cool; let nothing put you out, but find something to put out the fire; keep yourself collected, and then collect your family. After putting on your shoes and stockings, call out for pumps and hose to the firemen. Don't think about saving your watch and rings, for while you stand wringing your hands, you may be neglecting the turncock, who is a jewel of the first water at such a moment. Bid him with all your might turn on the main.

WISE SAWS BY AN OLD FILE.

Coal is the real philosopher's stone. It is the ballast of the good ship *Britannia*, which would be assuredly scuttled without it.

The true glory of England consists in her coal, and alas! how much of it, like other kinds of glory, is destined to end in smoke.

RAG FAIR.

It is a puzzle to know why the Lord Mayor's Procession is still continued every month of November, for its excessively seedy state quite rips up the old excuse that it is done merely "for the *show* of the thing."

How to Procure Golden Dreams at Will.—Take a rock in a Californian "cradle."

CALUMNIATED CREATURES.

The pig is generally accounted the emblem of all that is dirty; yet it is a severe hardship to this interesting animal to be deprived of his wash; and the same thing, *mutatis mutandis,* may be said of the London Alderman.

TAVERN WINE MEASURE.

2 Sips	make	1 Glass.
2 Glasses	. . .	1 Pint.
1 Pint	makes	1 Quart Bottle
1 Bottle		One Ill.

Good Wishes for Christmas.—May the overnight face over the punch-bowl bear the morning's reflection in the looking-glass.

The Least Objectionable Soup for Cannibals.—A Broth of a Boy.

What nation was most prominent in the Continental troubles? Hallucination.

To make Tea go further than usual.—When you put the water to your tea, add a spoonful of the best Gunpowder into the pot, and having set a light to it, you will find your tea go a great deal further than you expected.

Habit of the Ground Beetle.—To creep into the coffee-mill.

A new Reading of an old Request to John O'Connell.—"Shut up your (agi) tator trap."

409 'Sanitary and Insanitary Matters,' from *Punch*, xviii (1850), Almanack. '. . . At this season let not the high forget the low. Let the Head of Gold bear in special memory the Feet of Clay.'

THE WATER THAT JOHN DRINKS.

This is the water that JOHN drinks.

This is the Thames with its cento of stink,
That supplies the water that JOHN drinks.

These are the fish that float in the ink-
-y stream of the Thames with its cento of stink,
That supplies the water that JOHN drinks.

These are vested int'rests, that fill to the brink,
The network of sewers from cesspool and sink,
That feed the fish that float in the ink-
-y stream of the Thames, with its cento of stink,
That supplies the water that JOHN drinks.

This is the sewer, from cesspool and sink,
That feeds the fish that float in the ink-
-y stream of the Thames with its cento of stink,
That supplies the water that JOHN drinks.

This is the price that we pay to wink
At the vested int'rests that fill to the brink,
The network of sewers from cesspool and sink,
That feed the fish that float in the ink-
-y stream of the Thames with its cento of stink,
That supplies the water that JOHN drinks.

410 *left* 'The Water that John Drinks,' from
Punch, xvii (1849), 144–5.

411 *above* 'Edwin Chadwick Esq., one of the
Metropolitan Sanatory [sic] Commissioners,' from
Illustrated London News, xii (1848), 39. The date
is 22 January.

THE ALDERMAN AND THE APOTHECARY.

Ald. I do remember an Apothecary,

*   *   *   *   *   *

And if we need an Officer of Health
To toil upon the lowest salary,
This object is the very man for us.

*   *   *   *   *   *

Come hither, Sir; I see you are hard up:
Hold.   There are fifty and a hundred pounds
Per annum, for your wages.   Let us have
Your service to explore the sinks and sewers
Of our foul city and its liberties

Apoth. The pay is very small   and the employ

Is death to many a man that works at it.

*   *   *   *   *   *

My poverty, and not my skill, consents.
    Ald. We pay thy poverty and not thy skill

Shakspeare (a little altered.)

412 *left*   From *Punch*, xv (1848), 173. The stage directions for this melodrama on the incompetence of politically-chosen officers of health, given on another page, read simply 'SCENE—*The City of London. A Street in the Slums.*'

413 *above*   'Intramural interment—a scene in the Strand,' from *Illustrated London News*, xv (1849), 161. Burial of the dead inside the walls of churches and churchyards, already jammed with the remains of earlier generations, kept London constantly supplied with fresh infection, according to many reformers and observers.

of space after the mode used
by Mr. Sopwith, the engineer.
Each square of the subjoined
plate represents an acre. The
extent of squares coloured
shows the extent of ground
occupied by each religious denomination. The blank spaces
show the extent of deficiency
of public ground for the burial
of the population in single
graves.

CHURCH OF ENGLAND
PAROCHIAL
BURIAL GROUNDS.
Burials 191 per acre.

PROTESTANT DISSENTERS'
BURIAL GROUNDS.
Burials 246 per acre.

PRIVATE OR TRADING
BURIAL GROUNDS.
Burials 405 per acre.

JEWS' BURIAL GROUNDS.
Burials 33 per acre.

ROMAN CATHOLICS'
BURIAL GROUNDS.
Burials 1043 per acre.

414 *above* 'View of the extent of intra-mural
burial ground provided, as compared with the
quantity required for the metropolis, at the
standard of 110 per acre.' From *Parliamentary
Papers*, 1843, XII, Report from the Poor Law
Commissioners on the Sanitary Condition of the
Labouring Population of Great Britain: Supplementary Report on . . . Interment in Towns by
Edwin Chadwick [509], p. 272.

415 *right* 'Bethnal Green Parish . . . Mortality
from four classes of Disease . . . during the year
ended 31st December 1838,' portion of a map
from Report on Interment in Towns, 1843,
between pp. 160–1. Houses heavily hatched were
occupied by tradesmen and shopkeepers; those
more lightly shaded were occupied by weavers
and laborers. Crosses mark the streets in which
five or more deaths occurred from contagious
and epidemic diseases, diseases of the brain and
nerves, diseases of the lungs, and diseases of
the digestive organs.

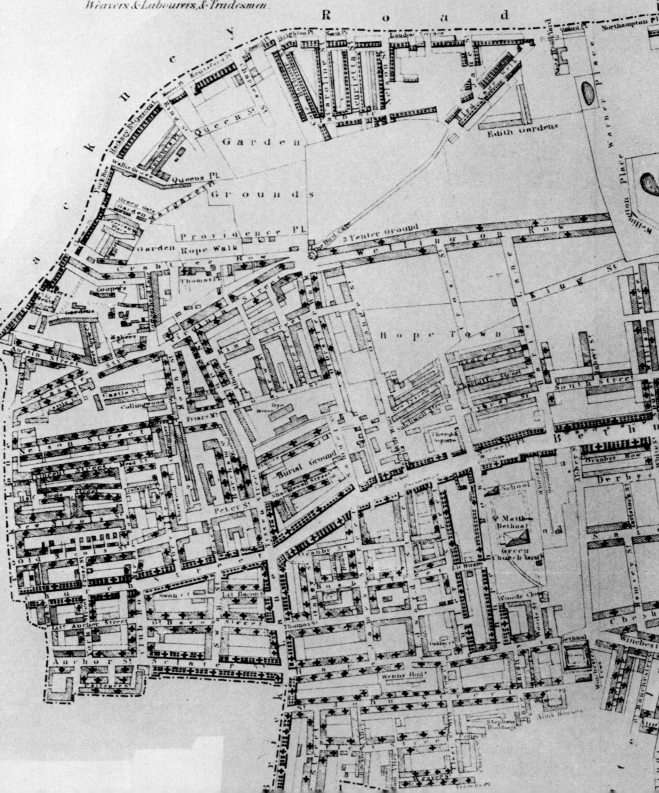

Map of
BETHNAL GREEN PARISH,

Shewing the Mortality from four classes of Disease in certain localities during the year, ended 31st Dec. 1838, distinguishing the Houses occupied by Weavers & Labourers, & Tradesmen.

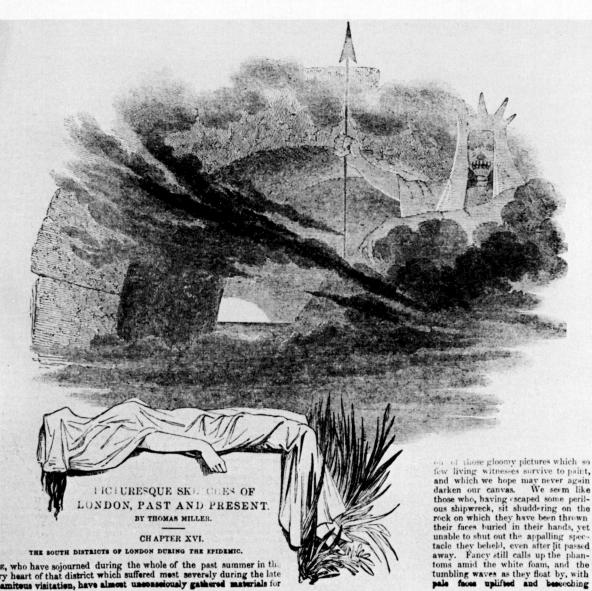

416 *above* 'Picturesque Sketches of London,' from *Illustrated London News*, xv (1849), 285. The article, written during the cholera epidemic, was published on 27 October. Its content is as harrowing as the illustration suggests. The artist is not known but Thomas Miller (1808–74) was a prolific and popular writer, chiefly on account of his books about the countryside. The series of articles from which this illustration comes dealt, except for this one, with antiquarian and romantic aspects of London.

417 *left* 'London with a Clean Front On,' from *Punch*, xx (1851), 83. This illuminated initial leads on: 'Our good city of London is determined to deck itself out for the forthcoming Exhibition in its very best.' The invocation to the government to do as well as private individuals in preparing for the event listed such projects as the completion of the Marble Arch or throwing St Paul's open to foreigners without charging them for entrance. With savage irony the specter of the drains was totally ignored.

CHOLERA PREVENTED.—ASIATIC CHOLERA TINCTURE, in conformity with the Instructions issued by the Government Board of Health.

The ASIATIC CHOLERA TINCTURE is infallible as a remedy for the Cholera (whether Asiatic or English) when taken according to the directions of Dr Jacques Lenae, with attention to the Government General Instructions, a copy of which is furnished with each bottle.

No person should be without this invaluable Medicine, which affords immediate relief in Diarrhœa, Flatulency, Cholic, and Bowel Complaints. In bottles, at 2s 9d, 4s 6d 11s, and 21s, duty included.

Also, ANTI-CHOLERA FUMIGATORS, for purifying the air of apartments and sick chambers, and destroying the Malaria of this fearful disease. Boxes at 6d, 1s, and 2s 6d ; or carriage free at 1s, 1s 6d, and 3s.

GRATIS.—The Government Instructions may be had on application. If sent to the Country an envelope, with a stamp affixed, must be forwarded.

Money orders to be made payable to Dr JACQUES LENAE, Asiatic Cholera Tincture Depot, 44 Coleman-street, City.

418 *left* From an advertisement page of the *Economist*, vi (1848), 1436.

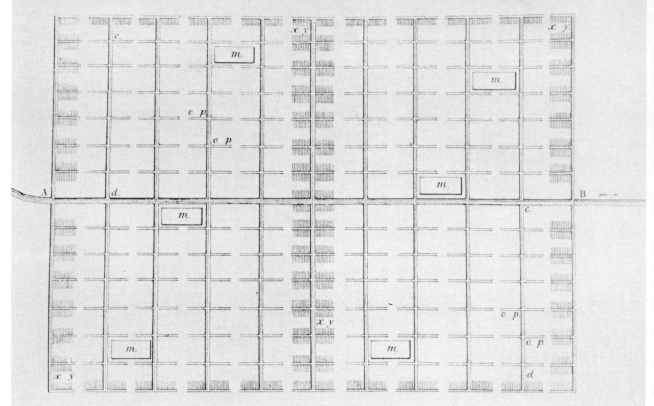

PLAN OF SEWERAGE.

A B. *First Class Sewer, or Main Drain.*   o p. *Third Class Sewer, or Street Drain.*

c d. *Second Class Sewer, or District Drain.*   x y *Fourth Class Sewer, or House Drain.*

m m. *Blocks of Houses.*

419 *above* 'Plan of Sewerage,' from a Communication from Captain Vetch, R.E., included
in the Appendix to Chadwick's Report of 1842,
pp. 388–9. The plan was conceived as a form of
military strategy. 'The sewers of a city or town,'
its author explained, 'may be conveniently
divided into four classes: First, the main drain or
sewer, and this, whether natural or artificial,
being fixed, becomes the basis of the system, and
upon it the second drains or district class will be
directed: these again will receive the third class
or street drains; and lastly, the house or fourth
class drains, will be discharged into the street
drains. In small towns, only the third and fourth
class drains will be required; in large towns,
three classes of drains may be necessary; and in
great cities, all the four classes will be required.'

420 *right* 'Subway for sewage, gas, and water
supply,' from *Illustrated London News*, xxiii
(1853), 367. A scheme, approved by the
Metropolitan and City Sewers Commissioners, for
dealing with major and minor sewers but still
dependent on manual labor for handling the
sewage and extracting commercial value from it.
It also aimed at saving much of the loss of gas—
said to amount to as much as one-third of that
manufactured—due to badly jointed underground pipes.

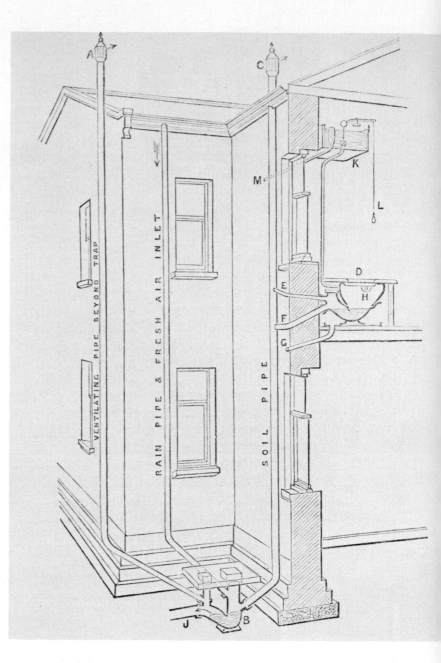

421–2 The guidance given to speculative builders in the most celebrated series of manuals printed in the Victorian period, *Weale's Rudimentary Series*, was comprehensive and completely lacking in mystery. 'The closet "H" here shown [right] has no working parts about it to get out of order, while *the water in the trap* is above the floor and *in sight*. So there are no out-of-view dirt-collecting corners about it to stink. . . I may here again condemn the dangerous unhygienic pseudo-water-saving policy of restricting the water-flush of a closet to only two gallons. Four gallons a flush would be more sensible.' That controversy is being conducted still. These illustrations come from the volume entitled *Plumbing* (4th edn, 1883), by William Paton Buchan, first published as a series of articles for 'the young apprentice-plumber' in the *Building News* for 1872 and as a book in 1876.

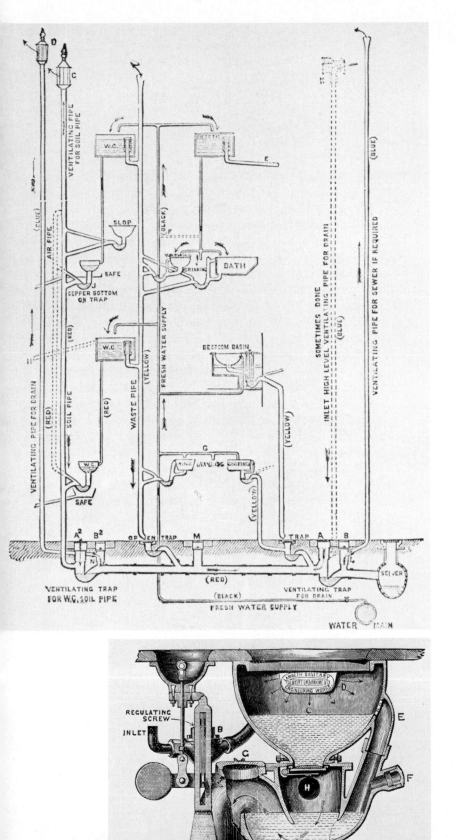

423 *left* Doulton's best valve closet, having the advantage of ventilation and a means of unblocking obstructions. Sanitary engineering became increasingly complex as it struggled to serve the needs of more and more people. From Eardley F. Bailey-Denton, *A Hand Book of House Sanitation* (1882), p. 61.

424 'The Prince of Wales starting up the main-drainage works at Crossness,' from *Illustrated Times*, new series, vi (1865), 225. A moment to celebrate as 'the first pumpful of sewage was lifted into the reservoir, there to lie until the turn of the tide, when it would be discharged into the Thames to be carried down in the vast volume of the river, to which, many as are the gallons of the sewage, it is little more than a drop in the bucket.' This was the culmination of plans to dispose of all London's wastes beyond its own reach. The pumping station was richly ornamented and the whole architectural effect declared to be 'extremely good' (p. 226).

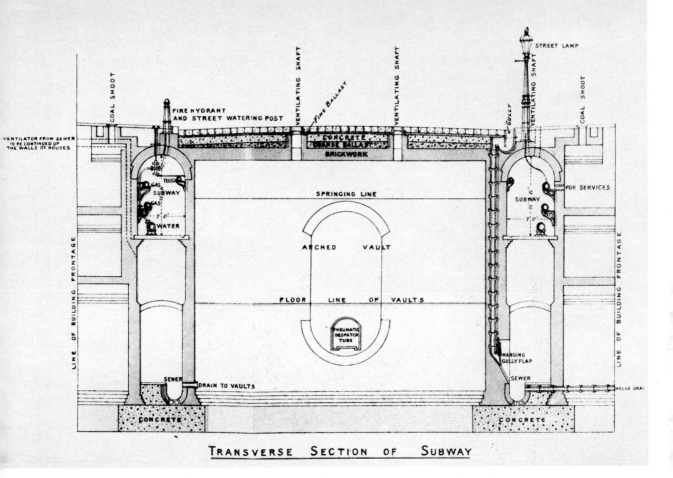

COAL SHOOT

VENTILATOR FROM SEWER
TO BE CONTINUED UP
THE WALLS OF HOUSES

LINE OF BUILDING FRONTAGE

FIRE HYDRANT
AND STREET WATERING POST

VENTILATING SHAFT

Fine Ballast

VENTILATING SHAFT

GULLY

VENTILATING SHAFT

STREET LAMP

COAL SHOOT

LINE OF BUILDING FRONTAGE

CONCRETE
COARSE BALLAST
BRICKWORK

GAS
TELEG.
SUBWAY
GAS
WATER
7'.0"

SPRINGING LINE

ARCHED   VAULT

FLOOR   LINE   OF   VAULTS

PNEUMATIC
DESPATCH
TUBE

SUBWAY
7'.0"

FOR SERVICES

HANGING
GULLY FLAP

SEWER   DRAIN TO VAULTS

SEWER

HOUSE DRAIN

CONCRETE

CONCRETE

TRANSVERSE   SECTION   OF   SUBWAY

425   Holborn Viaduct subway. An early
example of a completely unified system of
underground services requiring the minimum
human attention, opened in 1869. From
Parliamentary Papers, 1906, XLIII, Royal Commission on London Traffic: Maps and Diagrams
[Cd. 2799], plate xcv.

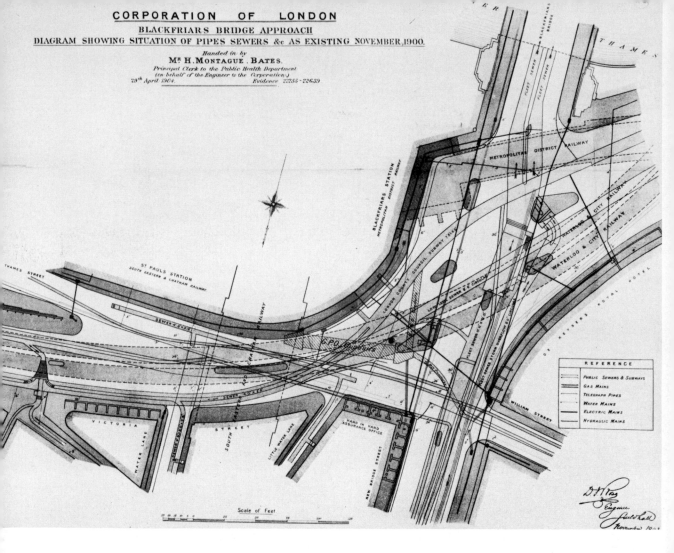

426 Blackfriars Bridge Approach, 1900. One access point to the commercial capital of the world seen from below street level. The City of London itself had had a dwindling night-time population for nearly half a century. Its essential functions were being systematically controlled and directed with increasing authority. From R.C. on London Traffic, plate xcii. See also no. 242.

No investigator has yet shown a tight linkage between specific modes of excretory training and specific modes of behavior in later life. Existing studies make dubious the possibility that such a tidy connection can ever be effected.[22] There is, however, no real need to know precisely how George Washington or Josiah Wedgwood or Henry Ford was sat upon the potty. The absence of such intimate detail about a few particular figures cannot invalidate the likelihood that a culture or a social group presses a multitude of parents to teach children to be disciplined and rule-observing through learning to be self-cleaning. Excretory regulation constitutes an essential segment of the drill needed to fashion a 'trained' person, an individual increasingly sought and likely to be found in an English city from the 1830s onward.[23]

The sanitary reformers understood the problem of dealing with urban masses during advancing industrialization to be the question of the imposition of order on a large scale. Somehow they came to realize that self-control for waste disposal would provide a foundation for other controled behavior. Industrialization in Britain beyond the initial stages required the presence of large numbers of people in cities, and also required the establishment and maintenance of order so that both production and consumption could go forward.

The condition to bring about is order. 'If we picture a number of things that can be distributed in a variety of ways within a given space, we may say that the fewer places these things can occupy the more orderly the system; the more places the things can occupy the more disorder. "A place for everything and everything in its place," should express the quintessence of orderliness . . .'[24] Orderliness means that men have learned some relatively effective ways of binding energy; they counter the universe's general and natural tendency to disorder. They oppose letting time, money —and wastes—ooze away indifferently.

Human beings have always fought entropy, attempting to enlarge the store of energy available for useful purposes.[25] After the late-eighteenth century men became increasingly more successful in this struggle. They discovered that they could channel amounts of energy staggeringly greater than those commanded by any of their ancestors. They found themselves confronted by the need to learn to be more orderly so that they could produce and consume economic goods more efficiently.

'Dirt is matter in the wrong place,' Freud quoted parenthetically in discussing anality.[26] The anthropologist Mary Douglas has explained more fully how dirt gets to be dirty. By crossing boundaries which should not be crossed, dirt has violated the prescriptions of the surrounding culture. Men are always trying to organize each other, by setting bounds, and by treating trespasses on these bounds as pollutions. To maintain itself a society must proclaim that things have their right places, whether within the biological organism or the social. Disorder means a weakening of strength at margins; excessive helter-skelteredness can lead to dissolution. The control of disorder means the labeling of intrusive and displaced matter as dirt. Such matter then becomes taboo, and recognizable only with much discomfort, as in the revulsion which accompanies hunting for a lost object in trash already consigned to the pale of non-existence. Bodily products such as tears, saliva, and breast milk can trigger a reaction like the aftermath of an unbeliever's crossing a temple gate, because the body is like society: the bounds of each can be overstepped only at the risk of incurring social sanctions against the violation of order.[27]

Then conduct learned in terms of the individual body can also function as behavior learned with regard to the body politic. The orderly body in the orderly society: thus should run the fundamental, unconscious presupposition of an industrialized world. As the body is, within, so will the state be, without.[28] In one kind of unconscious fantasy things which are evil are derived from products which presumed to cross bodily apertures: anything which could desert the wonderful and infatuating body must become bad.[29]

A deep and bitter conflict is taking place. The putting out of energy necessary in learning to gauge and behave within boundaries set by others runs counter to a tendency which would retain all energy within the bounds of the self. This tendency Freud called 'narcissism'; he meant a basic desire of the individual to keep his priceless energy invested in his own exalted being. This desire could be called self-love, and in its purest form would permit no energy to be allocated for activities related to anything outside the self. If energy simply stuck to the walls of organismic containers, life would become impossible. Freud believed that most energy remained narcissistic, or directed within the self, but that throughout life some of it was loaned to external figures and activities.[30]

The sanitary reformers had to reckon with vast human self-intoxication. Yet the nineteenth century demanded both the curtailing of unboundedness and widespread acknowledgment of the futility of being self-contained. Men must learn the role of factory-hand or foreman, not lapsing lazily into that of the navel-contemplator who punches no time-clock and earns no piece-rates. Society must arrange both for disciplined retention and scheduled letting go, by ordaining the orderliness which stores materials for the factory and then sends them through. In some cases of flight from society in mental illness, excretory functioning undergoes severe impairment; most people learn to conquer their fear of surrendering parts of their infatuating selves to be taken away forever, because they have learned to feel enough assurance that other parts will remain. Being social means sharing other people's notions of what can be clung to, and what must be sacrificed.[31]

The death of agrarian and handicraft existence, and the slow creation of the world of ever-rising productivity, show the gradual learning of new boundaries. Cultures too lovingly attached to the human body could not mobilize themselves psychically to create machines operating effectively 'out there.' Antiquity's machines were modelled too closely on human functioning because men could not curb their narcissism.[32]

Industrialized society rests on order;

order means everything in its place;

dirt is whatever is not where it should be;

the meanings of dirt held most deeply because learned earliest relate to bodily operations;

then a society bent on order should put the body into order by putting order
   into the body;
society gains order by 'training.'[33]

The control of excretory behavior furnished the most accessible approach on a mass basis to inculcating habits of orderliness. The sanitary reformers wanted to break man's self-indulgent unboundedness by making him learn certain ways of behaving which he would repeat every day of his existence. They determined to remove with impersonal finality the products of his body. If man could be forced to yield to interference in such a sensitive domain, he could be made to acquiesce in any kind of control: he could be made to learn many ways of binding his energy, he could be pressed into modernity. The many decades of struggle required to establish sanitary reform, and the ferocious determination of an Edwin Chadwick needed to get it going, show the immense weight of the old psychic ways.

Edwin Chadwick's mother died when he was a child. In his desolation, amid a family without close emotional ties, Chadwick salvaged an image of his mother which enabled him to become an active and significant adult.[34] A close associate wrote: 'he remembers that she was, by nature, a sanitarian *pur et simple*. Morning and evening ablution of unquestionable quality was the rule with her for her children, and in all domestic affairs she played the housewife's part with thrift and gentleness.'[35] Chadwick's destiny remained unclear for a time. He went through lengthy training to become an attorney, and later decided that he preferred being a barrister. A friend who was an actuary asked him to consider an official statement that although the social condition of the middle classes had improved, their life expectancy had not. At first Chadwick found himself fascinated by the mathematical aspects of the problem, but as he worked along, 'a new train of reasoning came into his mind, which, in the end, developed into what he called the "sanitary idea," that is to say, the idea that man could, by getting at first principles, and by arriving at causes which affect health, mould life altogether into its natural cast, and beat what had hitherto been accepted as fate, by getting behind fate itself and suppressing the forces which led up to it at their prime source.'[36]

'The sanitary idea' gripped Chadwick completely because it enabled him to undo his mother's death by affirming that what she had lived for still lived—in him: 'For some reason, which he has often told the writer of this memoir he never understood, the sanitary idea became dominant in his mind, and he became impressed with the conviction that if sanitation were carried out in its completeness, disease, which was the cause of all death before the appointed time, would itself die.'[37] Thus the sanitary movement, to the vital extent to which it was identical with Chadwick, cannot be seen merely as a set of technical rules. The movement embodied a faith in the reordering of life so powerful that new ways of living would give man sway over death itself. No mother would be cut down untimely; death, rendered stingless, would be compelled to acknowledge a devoted son's victory.[38]

From the early 1820s Chadwick had been a member of Benthamite circles; between 1830 and Bentham's death in 1832, he worked closely with the patriarch of reasoned order himself. Then he began his years of concern with Poor Law reform and administration. In the decade after 1828 'the sanitary idea' became deeply fixed within Chadwick, a process which paralleled his growing knowledge of the waste and suffering wrought by disorder throughout England.[39]

The first generation of great industrial enterprisers began a battle about 1750 which lasted for two centuries, struggling titanically to counter disorganization, insouciance, and sprawl, by locating things and men in proper, neat places and roles. Men like Josiah Wedgwood succeeded in curbing their feelings and fantasies sufficiently to mobilize their intelligence so that they could create machinery, and the means for the further creation of machinery, without crippling fears that they were destroying the value of their own bodies. They had to perform a similar function for their workmen, instilling habits which would change easily sated and generally unconcerned slovens into operators gearing the rhythms of their bodies to the pulsing of machines. Wedgwood wanted to 'make such *machines* of the *Men* as cannot err.'[40]

The first and second generation of trainers managed to succeed with relatively small numbers of workers, but numbers large enough to begin a recognizable industrializing process. As the process accelerated, 'mechanization takes command,' in Siegfried Giedion's memorable phrase. The burgeoning demand for goods, and the locational freedom afforded by sources of power movable at man's will, led increasingly to the abandonment of the countryside. In the towns the old problem remained: countryfolk still had to be changed into workers concerned about coming to work on time, concerned about arriving sober and reasonably fit, concerned about caring for their tools and the quantity of their output, concerned about looking forward to tomorrow and next month and next year. Now a further problem developed, because these workers had to learn how to live amid the cities whose attractions they increasingly sought.[41] Din and hurly-burly, and the pressing upon them of many other bodies, replaced the relative quiet and the small cast of characters of settled rural life. No city's population, clearly, could consist of recently arrived bumpkins alone; as already settled townsmen moved to a new district, they must have experienced some difficulty and uncertainty in getting the hang of new ways.[42] Much had to be learned by many, and it remained unclear whether they would master what they needed to make their own.

Children working alongside their parents underwent the factory master's training just as their elders did. The factory was their home, the place where they learned to act, more or less, like socialized creatures. Neil Smelser has shown that the introduction into the cotton industry in the 1820s and 1830s of more complex machinery which had to be manned by men served to drive women and children out of the factories. The modern working-class family was coming to be defined as a unit in which the father went to work, and the mother and children found themselves cooped up in a 'home.' There the children had to learn somehow some ways for getting along in an urban setting often quite foreign to the mother's understanding.[43]

In 1833 Chadwick served as a Royal Commissioner appointed to investigate the condition of children in factories. He saw clearly that limiting their hours, or excluding them altogether, would accomplish little if it simply meant 'intrusion of them into the streets in a state of idleness and demoralization.'[44] A decade later he wrote that 'Instead of giving the reduced hours of labour to efficient schools, the reduction has in fact turned the children in many places out into the streets and swollen the ranks of juvenile delinquents.'[45]

As Smelser has argued, the installation of expensive, complicated machinery which had to be operated by adults, and the need of men to assert and protect their independence as the indispensable wage-earners in a family, made the departure of children from the factories inevitable.[46] Yet just as clearly, no network of schools or other agencies existed for bending and tempering hordes of children. Not only was it certain that they would spend their childhood on the streets, breeding filth and crime and disorder, but also it was fully as uncertain how the ever-larger work force of practical, tidy, calculating adults would be recruited.

Chadwick beheld England jeopardized, yet not beyond rescue through heroic action. '"He looked",' B. W. Richardson recalled being told, '"for every opportunity that should give an historical future to a peculiar and sensitive posture".'[47] His constant referring to bad habits, or poorly anchored good habits, shows his awareness that Englishmen had to be remolded at very deep levels.[48] Resources for education were scanty. 'For some reason, which he has often told the writer of this memoir he never understood, the sanitary idea became dominant in his mind . . .' Chadwick's mother spoke to him again and again a message of exhortation to cleanliness. The maintaining of outward cleanliness would remake the inner man into an ambitious, disciplined Briton—just like Edwin Chadwick. If sanitary reform could induce men to abandon anarchy in an area of their lives prized most highly as theirs to rule as they alone willed, they could then be led to learn many other orderly ways of behaving. Chadwick and his fellow sanitary reformers would turn out to be parents to a nation's parents, instilling patterns of action that would be transmitted from generation to generation.[49]

'If sanitation were' to be 'carried out in its completeness,' some human and mechanical elements were indispensable. Chadwick fanatically mistrusted the presence of the necessary degree of fanaticism for change in anyone but himself. Most politicians and physicians lacked the honesty, the devotion, and the knowledge to carry out the tasks which he saw pressing to be completed. To combat their slothfulness and their lack of useful training, Chadwick proposed to create a new figure, the medical officer of health. He would be armed with legal power sufficient to clean up a district and keep it clean, enabled to do so by a fusion of medical, engineering, and administrative skills.[50]

Reasonable and admirable as the existence of such officials might be, English society and its educational institutions in the first half of the nineteenth century produced too few. Until that society made its schools graduate far more sanitarians, an effective and reliable non-human solution would have to be found. Beneath every city Chadwick foresaw a network of pipes so fully branched that no man could declare himself free of its tentacles. Sewers below, and the water closet above: no exemption for rank, sex, age, all conforming and all performing with discipline, not once a year or once a month, but several times each day.[51]

Advocates of order as it became tangible in larger numbers of factories faced a critical problem: now that men had begun to realize that capacities for production and accumulation could far surpass the capabilities of mere human bodies, they had to be prevented from relapsing into their earlier slothful pleasure with themselves. The age needed mechanisms appropriate to a second stage of industrialization; it needed means for interference with more and more of anyone's life. At the same time, the real nature of this interference would have to be concealed, or men whose narcissism had been too painfully curbed might revolt. Then it would seem wise to promote and cultivate a fantasy in which each man inhabited a universe in which he could make as much as he wanted. The crescendoing chanting of laissez faire, 'Let me make without stint,' deadened the noise of social engineers like Chadwick, intent on hammering together new restraints, but concerned also lest total achievement ever slip.

The concept of 'making more' demands a curb on narcissistic satisfaction with what is already possessed. The old world in which custom dictated wages, the world in which what a man makes stays with him, as in the privy, must yield to the world of enterprise, in which men learn not to cling to what they have made. They must come to terms with the reality of sewers. If wastes cannot be accumulated as a challenge to the eternal transitoriness of existence, perhaps money can be piled up. Men will strive mightily to make their bruised narcissism persist in a monument of some kind. The secret of the Industrial Revolution consists in altering the design of the monuments.[52]

Lacking the personnel to create new urban men, Chadwick determined to make urban man over impersonally. His schemes were bound to provoke opposition fully equal to their grandiosity, but with unconscious wisdom Chadwick divined the basic nature of the opposition. A population forced to desert forever some of its most valued productions would howl in protest, or laugh, or simply resolve to vote for inaction as the only suitable rejoinder to such an outrageous scheme. Chadwick understood unconsciously that he was attacking men's narcissism with painfully wounding results, and he proposed to redeem thwarted self-love, thus short-circuiting his opposition.

Chadwick caught a vision of what lurked beneath an adult's acceptance of the need to part from indisputable proofs of his productive powers. Chadwick sensed still living on in the adult a deeply fixed image of himself as a creature who produced infinitely, but never lost what he produced because he had no boundaries to be violated. He was like a magically self-closing hoopsnake, rolling along with his tail happily clamped in his mouth. That mythical being serves to depict metaphorically an existence which does not acknowledge mouth or anus as distinct and unfortunately limited anatomical features. At this primitive level the psyche knew no difference between food and wastes; nothing was ever wasted, nothing perished because the loss of something dearly valued, in a separation later called either death or the carrying on of civilized life, could not be pictured. There was no death of self or of loved things outside the self—like mothers—because 'outside the self' had no meaning. Secure in absolute control, the psyche knew only eternal bliss.[53]

Later, reality would make its inroads. Men would replace loving absorption in excrement with disgust. Yet the flushers of sewers interviewed by Henry Mayhew testified to the continued existence of the hoopsnake. They countered the old yearning to assert unendedness through ingesting excrement by taking a drop of rum and a bite to eat before they began their work.[54]

Chadwick understood that the hoopsnake demanded its due. A child praised for dutiful performance in a water closet must then experience bafflement, and even rage, as testimonies of his goodness whirl downward to extinction.[55] If human wastes never vanished utterly, but instead remained as good and important objects, the narcissism of men who unknowingly valued excrement would suffer less scarring. Chadwick in fact proposed to systematize and universalize an existing practice, the use of sewage as agricultural fertilizer. The idea was not new at all, but the zeal with which Chadwick propagated it had no precedent. He turned all of his ingenuity to dealing with the countless technical problems created. At one time he planned and tested a barge as a means of spraying suitably aged and deodorized sewage on crops growing along the banks of a waterway.[56]

Chadwick saw that men could never be made wholly new, though urbanization called for such a metamorphosis. Yet they could be redeemed in large part from the undisciplined ways, the confusion of inner and outer, the suffusion of their universe by filth: 'What avails it to send a Missionary to me, a miserable man or woman living in a fœtid Court, where every sense bestowed upon me for my delight becomes a torment, and every minute of my life is new mire added to the heap under which I lie degraded?'[57] An astute combination of unrelenting external pressure, and sops tossed to the old narcissistic demons growling within, could drive men to behave in some ways quite different from those to which they had been accustomed. Triumph lay near:[58]

> The Engineering means for the supply of Water have been developed . . .
> The establishment of the economy and the efficiency of the constant supply
> will when fully considered be found to be a great work. The completion of
> what I venture to call the venous and arterial system of Towns; the
> carrying water into every house, the removal of all excreta in suspension in
> water by means of the soil pan etc., the proof that the water closet may be
> made mechanically cheaper than the cesspool . . . the evidence as to the
> application of liquid manures . . . are also subsequent advances. With this
> we complete the circle and realize the Egyptian type of eternity by
> bringing as it were the serpent's tail into the serpent's mouth.

Chadwick's career showed him not only trying to gain the ends for which his mother had lived, but also using extraordinary energy and resourcefulness in a series of important posts to which he was called. Other sanitary reformers lacked his driving intensity, or allowed themselves to be scattered in a variety of reforming endeavors, or missed the opportunities for legislative impact and administrative power which were Chadwick's.[59]

Assuredly the reformers took whatever help they could find, and they did not battle unaided.[60] A very evident feature of anality is a product with unmistakable properties of bulk and odor. Given the establishment of efficient ways to deal with anality's embodiment, a growing city would become more livable, both at the level of sheer survival and in terms of any pleasure beyond mere existence. The rise in the numbers and skill of the medical profession, despite Chadwick's reservations about their hideboundedness, helped further action directed toward the investigation and control of dirt. Increasing sophistication in statistical procedures cut the likelihood that mortality figures could be shrouded over in decorous silence. The solution of some crucial technological problems, such as the production of non-porous pipe for the efficient transport of wastes, coincided with the height of Chadwick's reforming activity.[61]

The reformers gained more directly from the first modern cholera epidemics, which struck the West in 1831–2 and 1848–9. These holocausts brought terror in the localities which they hit, and then some determination to enquire and search for understanding, and even mastery.[62] Theories of causation differed widely, but many views attributed disease to the prevalence of dirt. The real intellectual difficulties involved in deciding among competing theories increased greatly because of unacknowledged contributions by the hoopsnake. That deep and ancient set of feelings kept men from admitting the likelihood of taking in bad products from outside, such as water tainted by sewage, without simultaneously affirming the probability that bad stuff would be transformed, once it got inside. Frederick Accum, who led the attack on the adulteration of food, could not bring himself to believe that filth in the Thames meant that its water should not be drunk: the massiveness of the Thames, and the constant motion provided by the Thames, afforded surety enough. Men had not yet been won over sufficiently to guidance by outer reality so that they could overpower the hoopsnake in important parts of a lifetime; they had not yet been trained to curb the effectiveness of denial as a mechanism for defense against that reality. Perceptions and valuations of the citizenry which endured the 'Great Stink' of 1858 resembled somewhat, in their narcissistic coating of invulnerability, the reactions of many cigarette smokers a century later as they read statistics about lung cancer.[63]

Chadwick grasped the impossibility of confronting England with tortuous choices among explanations of disease, and he saw, too, the limits beyond which more reports of overflowing privies would prove redundant, or boring. He recognized that men had arrived, for the most part, at an unsensing accommodation with stenches. His mission then became to enforce a very conscious recognition that bad odors belong to anality, to being undisciplined and untrained. He devised a simple doctrine:

'all smell is, if it be intense, immediate acute disease, and eventually we may say that, by depressing the system and making it susceptible to the action of other causes, all smell is disease.' The first great anal crisis of humanity ended with an incomplete resolution. Men stood erect, renounced sniffing like a dog, and then fell back onto a dungheap. Now Chadwick determined to interfere in men's lives and to end that crisis finally. Men would be forced to gain a new control by gearing their bodies into the venous-arterial network. They would be compelled also to acknowledge their lapses and inefficiencies whenever a tell-tale cue appeared: smell.[64] That signal would announce invariably and unmistakably an individual's failure in socially desirable self-regulation.

As the nineteenth century advanced, men would agree to being left alone less and less.[65] Chadwick recognized the crucial factor: interference and regulation do not simply run in one direction, from officialdom outward. Men accept thorough-going control only when they have learned, deep down, to live with it as part of their universe. Now began a profound reversal of history: men would consent to disciplining their own feelings of grandiose self-sufficiency; they accepted the demise of close rural dependence on their fellows, and its replacement by urban separateness, lessened somewhat by crowding; they prepared to practice self-control in the service of orderliness; they gave in and signified their readiness to give out energy in the cause of production for a distributing system which they could not see—like a sewer system.

Never before the urbanizing decades of British history in the nineteenth century had a systematic attempt been made to interfere with an intimate human function. In no society before the nineteenth century were the dwellings of many inhabitants of all social classes equipped with privies or water closets. Chadwick proposed to abolish a part of life hitherto accepted as everlasting: open sewers, bad drains, ladies and gentlemen relieving themselves in the bushes in Hampton Court Park.[66]

To take Exeter as an example: its townspeople in the twelfth century used 'a stream, recorded unequivocally as the Shitbrook . . . as a receptacle for the human refuse of the city.' Later, before 1467, common latrines called '"the Pixey or Fairy House"' were built. The well-to-do who dwelt in castles or in houses with stone walls could command the convenience of garderobes which emptied through channels built into the thick walls. When smaller dwellings built of wood became dominant, the garderobe declined. More public latrines were built, but most Exeterians 'had to fend for themselves, in their own back gardens or in the nearest open spaces.' The manufacturing and trading classes used a chamber pot or a close stool, a variant of the pot. [67]

An alternative to traditional means for dealing with wastes appears once before the end of the eighteenth century. In 1596 Sir John Harington published a design for a water closet which could be installed at a cost of thirty shillings. The closet led to a cesspool, so that emptying and transport would be required, but otherwise the advantages in cleanliness and in the reduction of odors were undeniable. Sir John included his plan in a piece of bravura writing intended narcissistically to show off his talents as a Renaissance man. He wanted to parade his ability to apply elaborate stylistic treatment to any topic, including the description of a quite practical invention. Sir John could control and channel his narcissistic feelings sufficiently so that he could imagine a new way for dealing with wastes, if he got the credit. His posterity lacked such flexibility. In the two centuries which followed, few copies of Sir John's model seem to have been built. Men were not ready to accept the limitation of narcissism inherent in conceiving impersonal sanitary devices, and then turning them into reality. Men were not willing yet to part with the notion of themselves as inevitably dung-laden, and hence dung-surrounded, creatures. Only after 1775 did the issuing of patents for improvements to the water closet begin.[68]

In Chadwick's time the onrush of industrialization and the rampages of cholera led to a clear statement of alternatives: in the modern world, interference or death. By the end of the nineteenth century most men were agreeing to be told what to do in order to remain alive. The violent opposition which Chadwick faced is well typified in the reaction of Herbert Spencer, who reworded the statement of alternatives and cried out that interference meant death. The inviolability of human faculties, of a man's means of making and doing for himself, stands at the core of *Social Statics*, Spencer's first book. He was working on this book during the great cholera epidemic of 1848–9, amid a stricken nation put in charge of the General Board of Health.

The vicissitudes of his own development had made Spencer excruciatingly sensitive to the threat of interference. Let adults be interfered with, he came to believe, and they would be reduced to childish incompetence. Interference could acknowledge no bounds; therefore let it not exist at all. An instance such as the operation of Chadwick's Board of Health during the cholera epidemic showed the criminal futility of direction from outside. The Board should have suppressed intramural interments, for which it thought it had power enough, but instead 'it occupied itself in considering future modes of water supply and devising systems of sewage.' Its 'sanitary guardianship did no good, but it may be, even harm,' because a society could only command a limited amount of energy: then force drained off to serve the ends of interference necessarily reduced the amount available elsewhere.[69]

Spencer was arguing here for unlimited human endeavor, which included untrammeled narcissism. To the end of his life he maintained that sanitary problems would be solved quickly and neatly if men of intelligence attacked them. Spencer even tried his hand at 'A Solution of the Water Question' which included adopting Chadwick's proposal to use sewage as manure.[70] For his audience he provided a service like that afforded by many other opponents of sanitary reform, by elaborating an ideology which protested the unnaturalness of interference with men's bodies, and hence with men's lives generally.[71] Spencer had sensed that the issue in sanitary reform was not the disposal of wastes. Fundamentally the issue was the desire of someone—the government, or that fanatic Chadwick—to force him to perform in a manner officially prescribed, and not freely chosen. Spencer actively countered the devious schemes of devilish administrators by asserting the ineradicable rightness of the small, untrained child's freedom to make what he pleased, when, as, and if he pleased. His rhetorical exertions eventually brought an enthused following, only worn away at last when demands for discipline proved more essential to a bustling society than calls for the maintenance of imperiously unpredictable willfulness.

A more passive kind of opposition to the sanitarians is evident in the different rates of growth in sanitary facilities for various cities. Some writers have described a 'pervasive apathy' about sanitary improvement, and they have gone on to discount the movement as a major factor in reshaping life in British cities.[72] It is true that in 1911 Manchester had water closets in less than half its houses, mostly in the newer and better-class areas; other dwellings were graced by pail closets, ash-boxes, ash-bins, midden privies, wet middens, and dry middens. In Crewe, a planned town, water closets were still unusual in 1875. Yet more populous places had been sewered by the end of the eighties.[73] Two great problems remained, one at each end of the sewer line, and both foreseen by Chadwick: the continuing need for compulsion to make builders and owners install water closets, and the lack of satisfactory techniques for sewage treatment. By 1951 the median percentage of households with water closets for the 157 largest towns of England and Wales was 97.[74]

If sanitation could yield such grand results in terms of productivity and stabilization, why was no campaign mounted for 'One man—one w.c.'? Though Chadwick and his contemporaries and successors discerned much, they could not see the full range of possibilities for behavioral alteration now so clear after a century of work in psychology, sociology, and related fields. They could urge and hector, but they could not pinpoint the precise behavioral gains which they sensed to be attainable.[75]

Given all of the difficulties amid which they struggled, including shortages of money and personnel and technology and good temper, they did succeed in carrying their message rather far.[76] They faced, after all, a population addicted to denial, fond of fatality in its view of the world, and always ready to debate whether the bogey of centralization would consume them tomorrow or next week. Sanitary facilities increased and improved steadily as time went on, into the twentieth century. It may be that what the Age of Chadwick and the Age of Simon wrought was sufficient for the needs of the work force and urban British society of those decades. As demand increased for better control of one's character, in the service of rising on the ladder, sanitation increasingly became part of the package used to attain such an inner state. The formal benefits of sanitary discipline were called for, in the sense of a supply of adults inwardly ready to perform a series of more and more taxing parts.

The water-closet and the sewer as bringers of order do not ensure the disappearance of crime, or laziness, or untidiness. They underscore and reinforce the restraints and controls necessary to keep an industrialized society producing and consuming. They have a cosmic impact because they remake part of the daily universe for urban men. Chadwick understood that he had a great task, a task not finished in his time: to make men learn to love as parts of themselves a thousand limits within which they must learn to live.

Notes

1   F. M. Jones, 'The Aesthetic of the Nineteenth-Century Industrial Town,' in H. J. Dyos, ed., *The Study of Urban History* (1968), p. 183; Arthur Redford, *The History of Local Government in Manchester* (1939–40), II, pp. 130–70, an excellent account of the prevalence of wastes; Henry Mayhew, *London Labour and the London Poor* (1861), II, p. 402.

2   The historical, psychoanalytic, and social science literature all lack any treatment of the deeper psychology of the sanitary movement. A. A. Brill, a psychoanalyst, does refer to 'the beginning of sanitation' as a cause for 'the repression of pleasure in smell'—'The Sense of Smell in the Neuroses and Psychoses,' *Psychoanalytic Quarterly* (*P.Q.*), i (1932), 38. It is surprising to find so little on the psychology of sanitation in the growing literature about modernization. See Margaret Mead, ed., *Cultural Patterns and Technical Change* (Paris, 1953), pp. 239–43, and M. B. Clinard, *Slums and Community Development* (New York, 1966), pp. 78–81, 210–13, 215, 254–6.

3   G. M. Young, *Victorian England* (2nd edn, 1953), p. 186; G. Kitson Clark, *The Making of Victorian England* (1962), pp. 63–4; R. L. Schoenwald, ed., *Nineteenth-Century Thought: The discovery of change* (Englewood Cliffs, 1965).

4   I offer the interpretation of the sanitary movement in Britain at which I have now arrived. Some points, such as the psychology of centralization, will receive further consideration in a biography of Herbert Spencer on which I am working.

5   E. Fromm, *Escape From Freedom* (New York, Toronto, 1941), p. 295; D. Riesman, *Individualism Reconsidered* (Chicago, 1954), pp. 359–62; D. Bakan, *Sigmund Freud and the Jewish Mystical Tradition* (Princeton, 1958); J. H. van den Berg, *The Changing Nature of Man*, trans. H. F. Croes (New York, 1961).

6   *The Standard Edition of the Complete Psychological Works of Sigmund Freud* (Freud), (1953 onward), VII, p. 186; IX, pp. 169–75; XII, pp. 335–7; XXI, pp. 99–100, n. 1.

7   E. Jones, *Papers on Psycho-Analysis* (5th edn, 1948), pp. 413–37; W. C. Menninger, 'Characterologic and Symptomatic Expressions Related to the Anal Phase of Development,' *P.Q.*, xii (1943), 161–93.

8   This view follows P. Heimann, 'Notes on the Anal Stage,' *International Journal of Psycho-Analysis*, xliii (1962), 406–14.

9   Freud, X, p. 248; XVII, p. 129, 133; XXI, p. 96.

10 On the restricting of gratification as a socially useful incitement, see P. E. Slater, *The Glory of Hera* (Boston, 1968), pp. 457–9; on the breakdown of some controls related to excretion, in a time of acute social disintegration, see the reports of the use of feces and urine as weapons during the convention of the Democratic Party in Chicago, 1968: [D. Walker], *Rights in Conflict* (Report to the National Commission on the Causes and Prevention of Violence, reproduced, Philadelphia [1968], pp. 135–6, 147, 153, 156, 173, 184).

11 R. R. Sears, and others, eds, *Patterns of Child Rearing* (Evanston, Ill., White Plains N.Y., 1957), pp. 104–5; J. W. M. Whiting and I. L. Child, *Child Training and Personality* (1953), p. 62.

12 L. Andreas-Salomé, '"Anal" und "Sexual",' *Imago*, iv (1916), 250; Freud, VII, p. 187, n. 1. It has been argued that the untrained infant enjoys genital stimulation as he is being changed and is learning that he can gain a reward for parting with his

bodily products: L. S. Kubie, 'The Fantasy of Dirt,' *P.Q.*, vi (1937), 412–13; B. Bettelheim, *The Empty Fortress* (1967), pp. 262–3.

13 J. Dollard and N. E. Miller, *Personality and Psychotherapy* (1950), p. 137.

14 H. Beloff, 'The Structure and Origin of the Anal Character,' *Genetic Psychology Monographs*, lv (1957), 141–72.

15 I. Hendrick, 'Work and the Pleasure Principle,' *P.Q.*, xii (1943), 322–3; E. H. Erikson, *Identity and the Life Cycle* (New York, 1959), pp. 66–70.

16 S. Ferenczi, 'Psycho-Analysis of Sexual Habits,' trans. E. Glover, *Further Contributions to the Theory and Technique of Psycho-Analysis* (1950), pp. 265, 267; Dollard and Miller, op. cit., pp. 140–1; G. R. Taylor, *The Angel-Makers: A study in the psychological origins of historical change, 1750–1850* (1958), pp. 164–5.

17 S. Freud to W. Fliess, 14 November 1897, in Freud, *The Origins of Psychoanalysis* (*Origins*), trans. E. Mosbacher and J. Strachey (New York, 1954), pp. 231–2; Heimann, *Int. J. Psycho-Anal.*, xliii, 413; 'Maxwell Gitelson: Analytic Aphorisms,' *P.Q.*, xxxvi (1967), 262.

18 Freud to Fliess, 11 January 1897, *Origins*, pp. 186–7, and also pp. 231–4; Freud, X, p. 248, XI, p. 189, XXI, pp. 99–100, n. 1, 105–7, n. 3; A. Ehrenzweig, *The Psycho-Analysis of Artistic Vision and Hearing* (New York, 2nd edn, 1965), pp. 64–70, 80–1, 220–1, 260–1, 268; Ehrenzweig, *The Hidden Order of Art* (Berkeley, 1967), pp. 184–5, 217–18.

19 W. La Barre, *The Human Animal* (Chicago, 1954), pp. 33, 35–6.

20 The study of man's ability to maintain varying distances from his fellows in cities has scarcely begun: R. Frankenberg, *Communities in Britain* (Garden City, N.Y., 1966), pp. 286–92; E. T. Hall, *The Hidden Dimension* (Baltimore, 1966), pp. 29, 36–7; Lt M. J. Horowitz, USNR, and others, 'Body-Buffer Zone: Exploration of Personal Space,' *Archives of General Psychiatry*, xi (1964), 651–6; M. J. Horowitz, 'Spatial Behavior and Psycho-pathology,' *Journal of Nervous and Mental Disease*, cxlvi (1968), 24–35; R. Sommer, *Personal Space: The behavioral basis of design* (Englewood Cliffs, N.J., 1969); J. A. Banks, 'Population Change and the Victorian City,' *Victorian Studies* (*V.S.*), xi (1968), 281–2, 289.

21 An adaptation of the views of E. H. Erikson, 'The Development of Ritualization,' *Philosophical Transactions of the Royal Society of London*, Series B, No. 772, ccli (29 December 1966), 337–8, 342–3.

22 Whiting and Child, op. cit., pp. 117, 311–13; J. M. W. Whiting, 'Socialization Process and Personality,' in F. L. K. Hsu, ed., *Psychological Anthropology* (Homewood, Ill., 1961), pp. 366–8; R. W. White, *Lives in Progress* (2nd edn, New York, 1966), p. 333.

23 One investigator reports that until the middle of the eighteenth century, doctors rarely specified an age for the start of 'toilet training'; until then, she suspects, it began at about one year, and during the nineteenth century the age descended steadily to six months or less. Unfortunately, sources printed in England are used only for 1550–1800, and thereafter American publications supply the data: A. Ryerson, 'Medical Advice on Child Rearing 1550–1900' (unpublished Ed.D. thesis Harvard University, 1960), pp. 10–11, 97, 99–100. It seems likely that the English middle class similarly lowered the age for the onset of excretory regulation. J. C. Loudon, *An Encyclopedia of Cottage, Farm, and Villa Architecture and Furniture* . . .

(1839), p. 1087: 'Infants of ordinary health and strength' would be placed on a chair equipped with a matted seat and a night pan when between three and four months old.

24   H. F. Blum, *Time's Arrow and Evolution* (3rd edn, Princeton, 1968), p. 201.

25   Dr Stanley Rudin of the University of Cincinnati suggested considering the problem of wastes in terms of entropy. On entropy see S. W. Angrist and L. G. Hepler, *Order and Chaos* (New York, 1967), pp. 146–7, 160. On the condition of energy and the fate of man, see L. A. White, *The Science of Culture* (New York, 1949), pp. 363–93.

26   Freud, IX, pp. 172–3, 173, n. 1; the quotation is in English in the original, and no source is given.

27   Mary Douglas, *Purity and Danger* (1966), pp. 2–5, 40, 113, 115, 121, 160.

28   Ibid., p. 115; H. F. Searles, *The Nonhuman Environment in Normal Development and in Schizophrenia* (New York, 1960), p. 395.

29   Kubie, *P.Q.*, vi, 388–96, 416–18; Kubie, 'Body Symbolization and the Development of Language,' *P.Q.*, iii (1934), 443–4.

30   Freud, XIV, pp. 73–102; C. Brenner, *An Elementary Textbook of Psychoanalysis* (New York, 1955), pp. 112–13; Grace Stuart, *Narcissus* (1956).

31   Bettelheim, op. cit., pp. 35, 111–13, 262; Marion Milner, *On Not Being Able to Paint* (New York, 1957), p. 150.

32   Ferenczi, 'Concerning the Psychogenesis of Mechanism,' trans. J. Suttie, *Further Contributions*, p. 390; V. Tausk, 'On the Origin of the "Influencing Machine" in Schizophrenia,' trans. D. Feigenbaum, *P.Q.*, ii (1933), 556, n. 1; H. Sachs, 'The Delay of the Machine Age,' trans. M. J. Powers, *P.Q.*, ii (1933), 404–24.

33   See also W. A. Davis and R. J. Havighurst, *Father of the Man* (Boston, 1947), p. 171; D. R. Miller, G. E. Swanson, and others, *Inner Conflict and Defense* (New York, 1960), pp. 394–5; D. Bakan, *The Duality of Human Existence* (Chicago, 1966), pp. 85–7; J. H. van den Berg, *The Psychology of the Sickbed* (Pittsburgh, Louvain, 1966), p. 49.

34   R. A. Lewis, *Edwin Chadwick and the Public Health Movement 1832–1854* (1952), p. 5, n. 1; 'Death of Sir E. Chadwick,' *The Times*, 7 July 1890. See also R. W. White, *Ego and Reality in Psychoanalytic Theory* (New York, 1963), pp. 141–50.

35   [Sir] B. W. Richardson, *The Health of Nations* (1887), I, p. xxiv. *The Times*, 1 August 1854, in its leader on Chadwick's fall from power, caught him as an overwhelmingly mothering figure: 'It was a perpetual Saturday night, and Master John Bull was scrubbed, and rubbed, and small-tooth-combed, till the tears came into his eyes, and his teeth chattered, and his fists clenched themselves with worry and pain. Certainly cleanliness is a beautiful thing, but then mortals must be won to the ways of cleanliness. History tells us, indeed, of whole tribes being conquered and baptized in a day. England, however, had not been conquered by Mr. CHADWICK; and when he sent his priests to take us by force we resented his compulsory ablutions.'

36   Richardson, op. cit., I, p. xxvii, for the quotation; [E. Chadwick], 'Life Assurances—Diminution of Sickness and Mortality,' *Westminster Review*, ix (1828), 384–421; S. E. Finer, *The Life and Times of Sir Edwin Chadwick* (1952), p. 29, n. 2; A. Briggs, 'The Welfare State in Historical Perspective,' *Archives européennes de sociologie*, ii (1961), 230–1.

37   'Obituary. Sir Edwin Chadwick, K.C.B.,' *Lancet*, 12 July 1890, p. 99.

38 When men really put into practice their knowledge of how to prevent disease, 'we may hope then to see the approach of those times when, after a life spent almost without sickness, we shall close the term of an unharassed existence by a peaceful euthanasia' [E. Chadwick], *Report . . . on an Inquiry into the Sanitary Condition of the Labouring Population of Great Britain . . . (Report . . . San. Cond.)* (1842), p. 356; here, at the end of a section on the need for a responsible, independent Medical Officer, Chadwick is quoting a report by a Dr Wilson. Chadwick wished to keep his mother alive until he, rather than fate, decreed that she might leave this world. To the extent that he was powerless to dictate the circumstances of her being placed in the grave, he was driven to assert a kind of control by attacking the scandalous ways in which other corpses were deposited: see Lewis, op. cit., p. 68, on Chadwick's report of 1843 on interment in towns. Later Chadwick claimed that an improved mode of burial which he advocated would exercise a beneficient moral influence on the living: *Parliamentary Papers (P.P.)*, 1850, XXI, Report on a General Scheme for Extramural Sepulture (1158), p. 122.

39 Lewis, op. cit., chs 1, 2; Finer, op. cit., pp. 16, 34, 154–7, 161.

40 N. McKendrick, 'Josiah Wedgwood and Factory Discipline,' *Historical Journal*, iv (1961), 34; [Sir] E. Roll, *An Early Experiment in Industrial Organization* (1930); P. Shashko, 'Nikolai Alexandrovich Mel'gunov on the Reformation and the Work Ethic,' *Comparative Studies in Society and History*, ix (1966–7), 263, n. 2; E. P. Thompson, *The Making of the English Working Class* (1964), pp. 359ff., 365, 409–10; E. P. Thompson, 'Time, Work-Discipline, and Industrial Capitalism,' *Past and Present*, No. 38 (1967), 69, 73, 90; S. Pollard, *The Genesis of Modern Management* (1965), pp. 173–4, 181–5, 195–6, 207–8; Phyllis Deane, *The First Industrial Revolution* (1965), pp. 150, 268; A. Briggs, *The Age of Improvement* (1959), p. 61.

41 Banks, *V.S.*, xi, 280, 284.

42 H. J. Dyos, 'The Slums of Victorian London,' *V.S.*, xi (1968), 28–30.

43 N. J. Smelser, *Social Change in the Industrial Revolution* (1959), pp. 268–9, 190–1, 193–4, 199. For a summary of the argument in this book, see Smelser, *Essays in Sociological Explanation* (Englewood Cliffs, 1968), pp. 82–8.

44 Finer, op. cit., p. 68.

45 Finer, ibid., p. 65. An unpublished manuscript by Chadwick, 'A Short Sketch of E. C.'s Career' (Chadwick Papers, University College, London; dated by Finer, p. 10, n. 3, about 1860), shows clearly (p. 3) the association in Chadwick's mind, as he recalled the enquiry into the factories in 1833, of changes in the structure of the labor force, the need to educate the manufacturing population, the necessity for interference by the state to gain this end, and the likelihood of mob violence unless education provided restraint. On his awareness of a factory as a socializing influence, and his recognition of the dangers inherent in the closeness of uneducated families to each other, see *Report . . . San. Cond.*, pp. 243, 274. The inspectors proposed by Chadwick to see that the Factory Act was carried out (Finer, p. 58) reproduce in part his mother's concerned watchfulness. On the usefulness of being watched, see *Report . . . San. Cond.*, p. 234.

46 Smelser, *Social Change*, pp. 210, 212, 223–4, 238, 297–8.

47 Richardson, op. cit., I, p. xiii.

48 *Report . . . San. Cond.*, pp. 4, 203, 232, 370–2; *P.P.*, 1845, XVIII, Royal Commission

on the State of Large Towns and Populous Districts: Second Report (602), pp. 61, 76; *P.P.*, 1850, XXI, Report of the General Board of Health on the Epidemic Cholera of 1848 & 1849 (1273), p. 148; *P.P.*, 1852, XIX, General Board of Health: Minutes of Information Collected with Reference to Works for the Removal of Soil Water . . . (1535), pp. 8–9; *P.P.*, 1854, XXXV, Report of the General Board of Health on Administration of the Public Health Act . . . from 1848 to 1854 (1768), p. 33. The long section on 'Domestic mismanagement, a predisposing cause of disease,' in Chadwick's famous 1842 sanitary report (pp. 137–53) suggests that he was contrasting his mother's very evident ability to implant orderly habits with the incapacity of many working-class wives: see Frances Collier, *The Family Economy of the Working Classes in the Cotton Industry, 1784–1833* (1965), p. 53; J. P. Kay, *The Moral and Physical Condition of the Working Classes Employed in the Cotton Manufacture in Manchester* (2nd edn, 1832), pp. 6, 25, 69.

49   The sanitarians did not doubt that their doctrines of cleanliness could and should affect an entire population: see *P.P.*, 1837–8, XXVIII, Appendix (A.), Fourth Annual Report of the Poor Law Commissioners, Supplement No. 1: N. Arnot [sic], and J. P. Kay, 'Report on the Prevalence of certain Physical Causes of Fever in the Metropolis . . . (147),' pp. 68, 83; *P.P.*, 1847–8, XXXII, First Report of Commissioners Appointed to Inquire Whether and what Special Means may be Requisite for the Improvement of the Health of the Metropolis (888), pp. 10, 21.

50   Lewis, op. cit., pp. 58, 75, 77–81; C. F. Brockington, *Public Health in the Nineteenth Century* (1965), p. 136.

51   On economic costs, administrative feasibility, and the prospective gain in reformed habits, see *P.P.*, 1844, XVII, First Report . . . the State of Large Towns and Populous Districts (572), pp. 22–3; *P.P.*, 1845, XVIII, Second Report . . . Large Towns . . . (602), pp. 61–2; R. A. Church, *Economic and Social Change in a Midland Town* (1966), pp. 185, 187.

52   E. J. Hobsbawm, *Labouring Men* (1964), pp. 347, 349; Freud, IX, p. 175; XVII, pp. 127–33; E. R. Kittrell, '"Laissez Faire" in English Classical Economics,' *Journal of the History of Ideas*, xxvii (1966), 616, 618.

53   R. L. Schoenwald, 'Town Guano and "Social Statics",' *V.S.*, xi, Supplement (1968), 699; E. Neumann, *The Origins and History of Consciousness*, trans. R. F. C. Hull (New York, 1954), pp. 5ff.; W. La Barre, *They Shall Take Up Serpents* (Minneapolis, 1962), p. 105; Marion Milner, *The Hands of the Living God* (1969), pp. 156–7.

54   Mayhew, op. cit., II, p. 430; O. Fenichel, *The Psychoanalytic Theory of Neurosis* (New York, 1945), p. 139; Freud, XI, p. 189; N. O. Brown, *Life Against Death* (Middletown, Conn., 1959), pp. 293, 299–301.

55   Bettelheim, op. cit., p. 112.

56   Chadwick, *Report . . . San. Cond.*, pp. 51–2; *P.P.*, 1846, X, Select Committee on Metropolitan Sewage Manure (474), pp. 110–11, 117; Lewis, op. cit., pp. 54, 122–3. Prince Albert was one of many who worked on the problem of utilizing sewage as fertilizer: *P.P.*, 1852, XIX, Minutes of Information Collected by the Board of Health on the Practical Application of Sewer Water and Town Manures to Agricultural Production (1472), pp. 63–4.

57   *The Speeches of Charles Dickens*, ed. K. J. Fielding (1960), p. 129.

58   Chadwick to Lord Francis Egerton, 1 October 1845, Chadwick Papers, University

College, London; see also Finer, op. cit., pp. 222–3, 234. Kubie, *P.Q.*, vi, 420: Egyptian mummies were bent so that the head and a food container were near the excretory organs, 'as though self-perpetuation in immortality was to be achieved by reingesting one's own excrement.'

59 G. F. A. Best, *Shaftesbury* (1964); Mrs C. L. Lewes, *Dr. Southwood Smith* (1898); F. Smith, *The Life and Work of Sir James Kay-Shuttleworth* (1923); [A. Briggs], 'A Health Centenary,' *The Times*, 29, 30 April 1948.

60 B. Keith-Lucas, 'Some Influences Affecting the Development of Sanitary Legislation in England,' *Economic History Review*, second series, vi (1954), 290–6; E. P. Hennock, 'Urban Sanitary Reform A Generation Before Chadwick?' *Economic History Review*, x (1957), 113–19; Briggs, *Age of Improvement*, pp. 33–4, 46–7; Kitson Clark, op. cit., pp. 98–9, 102. Chadwick's predecessors could not be successful because they were so concerned with the products of excretion, rather than with excretion as a process freighted with heavy emotional investment.

61 E. Chadwick, *Report on the Sanitary Condition of the Labouring Population of Gt.* [sic] *Britain*, ed. M. W. Flinn (Edinburgh, 1965), pp. 18–19, 21, 26; D. M. Vaughan, 'Justice to the Past in the Teaching of Social History,' *History*, new series, xxxii (1947), 51–6; Kitson Clark, op. cit., pp. 80–1; T. C. Barker and J. R. Harris, *A Merseyside Town in the Industrial Revolution* (1959), pp. 318–19; Finer, op. cit., pp. 298–9. A. Kira, *The Bathroom* (Ithaca, 1966), p. 4: '. . . technology is to a large degree a variable which can be speeded up or slowed down according to the social and cultural demands of an era.'

62 N. Longmate, *King Cholera* (1966); R. H. Mottram, 'Town Life,' G. M. Young, ed., *Early Victorian England* (1934), I, pp. 155–66; A. Briggs, 'Cholera and Society in the Nineteenth Century,' *Past and Present*, no. 19 (1961), 74–96; R. E. McGrew, 'The First Cholera Epidemic and Social History,' *Bulletin of the History of Medicine* (*B.H.M.*), xxxiv (1960), 61–73; C. E. Rosenberg, 'Cholera in Nineteenth-Century Europe: A Tool for Social and Economic Analysis,' *Comparative Studies in Society and History*, viii (1966), 452–463.

63 E. H. Ackerknecht, 'Anticontagionism between 1821 and 1867,' *B.H.M.*, xxii (1948), 588–9; W. L. Burn, *The Age of Equipoise* (1964), p. 203; O. Temkin, 'An Historical Analysis of the Concept of Infection,' [History of Ideas Club, Johns Hopkins University], *Studies in Intellectual History* (Baltimore, 1953), pp. 145, 147; Lewis, op. cit., pp. 42, 51, 163–4, 191, 193; C. Macnamara, *A History of Asiatic Cholera* (1876), pp. 178–82; G. Godwin, *London Shadows* (1854), p. 66; H. W. Dickinson, *Water Supply of Greater London* (1954), pp. 107–8, 122; R. Lambert, *Sir John Simon* (1963), pp. 50–1; P. E. Brown, 'John Snow—The Autumn Loiterer,' *B.H.M.*, xxxv (1961), 526–8; Anna Freud, *The Ego and the Mechanisms of Defence*, tr. C. Baines (1946), pp. 89ff.; B. D. Lewin, *The Psychoanalysis of Elation* (1950), pp. 52–4; S. J. Sperling, 'On Denial and the Essential Nature of Defence,' *Int. J. Psycho-Anal.*, xxxix (1958), 33, 36; F. Accum, *A Treatise on Adulterations of Food . . .* (2nd edn, 1820), pp. 62–5; A. H. Hassall, *Adulterations Detected* (1857), does not mention the problem of water, but his *Food: Its adulterations, and the methods for their detection* (1876), includes a long section on water, pp. 15–91, condemning the use of water polluted by sewage although it had been filtered by the usual methods of the water companies: p. 32; E. W. Stieb, with G. Sonnedecker, *Drug Adulteration*,

Detection and Control in Nineteenth-Century Britain (1966), p. 184. Resistance to vaccination in the later nineteenth century involved emotional confusion over the effectiveness of a bad outer stuff provoking a good inner result: R. M. MacLeod, II, 'In the Interests of Health: State Medicine, Social Policy and the Power of Public Opinion in the Late-Victorian Vaccination Services' (unpublished B.A. Honors thesis, Harvard University, 1963), pp. 3, 70, 175–6; Burn, op. cit., pp. 157–8; C. Braithwaite, 'Conscience in Conflict with the Law,' *Durham University Journal*, new series, xviii, no. 2 (1957), 66; L. G. Stevenson, 'Science Down the Drain,' *B.H.M.*, xxix (1955), 19.

64 *P.P.*, 1846, X, Select Committee on Metropolitan Sewage Manure: Minutes of Evidence (474), p. 109, for the quotation; Finer, op. cit., pp. 298, 300; H. Gavin, *Sanitary Ramblings* (1848), p. 79; 'England's Drear and Dirty Land,' *The Times Literary Supplement*, 6 January 1966, 12: Chadwick never accepted the germ theory, and was still advocating the effectiveness of soap and water against epidemics a few months before his death in 1890 (another unconscious tribute to his mother's impact); Temkin, op. cit., pp. 131–2. For other examples of making people aware of the badness of excretory odors which they had previously accepted, see R. R. Beardsley and others, *Village Japan* (Chicago, 1959), p. 88, and J. H. Cassedy, 'The Flamboyant Colonel Waring,' *B.H.M.*, xxxvi (1962), 165–6. Professor L. Jarrard, a physiological psychologist at Washington and Lee University, has pointed out in conversation the ability of people to adapt very quickly to horrendous smells, and soon fail to notice them, as in the American Civil War and in Korean prison camps.

65 Chadwick-Flinn, *Report . . . San. Cond.*, p. 42; W. A. Guy, *Unhealthiness of Towns. Its Causes and Remedies* (1845), pp. 25–6; Briggs, op. cit., p. 335. On house-to-house visitation by inspecting personnel in times of crisis, a technique vigorously advocated by Chadwick, see *P.P.*, 1849, XXIV, Report of the General Board of Health on . . . . the Execution of the Nuisances Removal and Diseases Prevention Act, and the Public Health Act . . . (1115), p. 17; *P.P.*, 1854, XXXV, Report . . . on the Administration of the Public Health Act . . . , p. 10.

66 L. Mumford, *The City in History* (1961); L. Wright, *Clean and Decent* (1957); G. Sjoberg, *The Preindustrial City* (1960); S. Marcus, *The Other Victorians* (1966), p. 98. J. Pudney, *The Smallest Room* (1954), and R. Reynolds, *Cleanliness and Godliness* (1943) are of little value in this context. M. W. Barley, *The House and Home* (1963) is carefully written and very well illustrated.

67 D. Portman, *Exeter Houses 1400–1700* (1966), pp. 15–16, 50–1.

68 Sir J. Harington, *A New Discourse of a Stale Subject, Called the Metamorphosis of Ajax*, ed. E. S. Donno (1962), pp. 18–19, 22, 161, 172, 175, 183, 192–6, 211; Lynn Thorndike, 'Sanitation, Baths, and Street-Cleaning in the Middle Ages and Renaissance,' *Speculum*, iii (1928), 201–2; E. L. Sabine, 'Latrines and Cesspools of Medieval London,' *Speculum*, ix (1934), 303–6, 313, 321; Wright, op. cit., pp. 71–5, 106; H. A. J. Lamb, 'Sanitation. A Historical Survey,' *Architects' Journal*, lxxxv (1937), 385–403; R. M. Frye, 'Swift's Yahoo and the Christian Symbols for Sin,' *Journal of the History of Ideas*, xv (1954), 201–17; Mrs C. S. Peel, 'Homes and Habits,' *Early Victorian England*, I, pp. 85–8.

69 The quotations are from ch. 28, section 6, of *Social Statics*. For the argument in the preceding two paragraphs, see Schoenwald, *V.S.*, xi, 691 ff.

70 'A Solution of the [London] Water Question,' letter signed H. S., *The Economist*, 3 January 1852, 10–11 (reprinted in *Various Fragments* [1910], pp. 253–8), *The Economist*, 24 March 1849, p. 328, for a report probably by Spencer on the Metropolitan Sewage Manure Company; *Essays* (1901), III, pp. 231, 238, 247; *The Study of Sociology* (1910), p. 3 and n. 1; *Social Statics, Abridged and Revised; together with The Man versus the State* (New York, 1896), pp. 323, 343–7, 350–1, 356–7 (references are from *The Man . . .*); *Facts and Comments* (1910), pp. 218–24.

71 For studies of the opposition to fluoridating water as a threat to control over the individual's innermost being, see W. A. Gamson, *Feelings of Helplessness and the Anti-Fluoridation Attitude* (mimeograph, Harvard University School of Public Health, 1960); A. L. Green, *The Ideology of Fluoridation Partisans* (mimeo., Harvard Sch. P. H., 1958); B. D. Paul, *Fluoridation of Community Water Supplies* (mimeo., Harvard Sch. P. H., 1958); J. Marmor, and others, 'Psychodynamics of Group Opposition to Health Programs,' *American Journal of Orthopsychiatry*, xxx (1960), 340.

72 W. Ashworth, *The Genesis of Modern British Town Planning* (1954), p. 65 for the quotation, also pp. 62, 75–6, 82; S. Pollard, *A History of Labour in Sheffield* (1959), pp. 8, 93.

73 Redford, op. cit., III, p. 128; II, pp. 143–4, 147, 156–60, 379, 401; W. H. Chaloner, *The Social and Economic Development of Crewe 1780–1923* (Manchester, 1950), pp. 126, 49, 55, 57, 121, 123, 125–9, 182–4, 186, 285; W. M. Frazer, *A History of English Public Health 1834–1939* (1950), p. 131. For additional data on the continuing increase in sanitary facilities, see R. Newton, *Victorian Exeter* (Leicester, 1968), pp. 136, 169, 243–4, 253, 259–61, 308; Pollard, op. cit., pp. 95–6, 190–1, 256; A. T. Patterson, *Radical Leicester* (Leicester, 1954), pp. 142, 169, 188–9, 336–42, 370, 379; R. Turnor, *The Smaller English House 1500–1939* (1952), p. 172; J. Prest, *The Industrial Revolution in Coventry* (1960), pp. 38, 41–2; Gwen Hart, *A History of Cheltenham* (Leicester, 1965), pp. 304, 339–43; W. Lillie, *The History of Middlesbrough* (1968), pp. 405, 407; Lambert, op. cit., pp. 58, 454–60, 605–6; H. J. Dyos, *Victorian Suburb* (Leicester, 1961), pp. 145–6, 148; Barker and Harris, op. cit., pp. 171, 299–304, 398–400, 416, 466; B. S. Rowntree, *Poverty* (2nd edn, 1902), pp. 184–5, 199–204; Church, op. cit., pp. 10, 345; E. C. Midwinter, *Social Administration in Lancashire, 1830–60* (1969), pp. 63–120; H. Cantril, ed., *Public Opinion 1935–1946* (1951), p. 580.

74 A. P. Stewart and E. Jenkins, *The Medical and Legal Aspects of Sanitary Reform* (1867, repr. 1969), pp. 8, 31, 45, 76, 81–2; J. Rawlinson, 'Sanitary Engineering: Sanitation,' in C. Singer and others, eds., *A History of Technology* (Oxford, 1958), IV, pp. 512–19; as an example of the difficulties involved in sewage treatment, see C. Gill and A. Briggs, *History of Birmingham* (1952), I, p. 427; C. A. Moser and W. Scott, *British Towns* (1961), p. 10.

75 The sanitarians would subscribe to Samuel Smiles's aim, 'to show his audience that "their happiness and well-being as individuals in after-life must necessarily depend upon themselves—upon their own diligent self-culture, self-discipline and self-control—and, above all, in that honest and upright performance of individual duty which is the glory of character".' Quoted, K. Fielden, 'Samuel Smiles and Self-Help,' *V.S.*, xii (1968), 165. Men in the nineteenth century, however, could not find out very easily or very reliably the extent to which one method might succeed more

rapidly or more lastingly than another, how increased and unsupervised privacy for bodily functions, for example, might heighten independence in other aspects of behavior: see M. Langford, *Personal Hygiene Attitudes and Practices in 1000 Middle-Class Households* (Ithaca, 1965), p. 17; Kira, op. cit., p. 56; Burn, op. cit., pp. 268–9. Social engineers in the twentieth century increasingly can choose whether to utilize or ignore childhood training: Ryerson, op. cit., pp. 160–1; D. C. McClelland, *The Achieving Society* (Princeton, 1961); McClelland, D. G. Winter, and others, *Motivating Economic Achievement* (1969).

76 Burn, op. cit., p. 288; *P.P.*, 1854, XXXV, Administration of the Public Health Act, pp. 13–14; D. Roberts, *Victorian Origins of the British Welfare State* (1960), p. 288.

29   Prostitution and Paterfamilias

Eric Trudgill

Observers of the extent of prostitution in nineteenth-century London were distinguished more by their number than their numeracy. The lowest tallies were those of the Metropolitan Police, which never went above 10,000, but which, as the police were quick to emphasize, excluded many clandestine and part-time prostitutes. The highest were those of the fourth estate, which occasionally reached 120,000, and owed more perhaps to intuition than arithmetic. Almost every round number between these poles received its advocates at some time or another, and some enjoyed a longevity that showed a notable disregard for such variables as a change in population or society's sexual habits. 50,000 was a regular favourite: Johann von Archenholz heard it in the 1780s, Frederick von Raumer in the 1830s, Hippolyte Taine in the 1860s,[1] and it was still going strong in the latter years of the century. But the most popular guess of all was 80,000. This was firmly entrenched by 1830, and despite frequent sniping from sceptics for nearly seventy years, it was still sufficiently common in 1907 for a rescue worker to think it worth demolishing.[2]

Amidst all this statistical confusion one fact is very clear: that prostitution in London, whatever its exact dimensions may have been, was very extensive, so extensive as to cause contemporary observers great anxiety and distress. In May 1859 the *Edinburgh Medical Journal* (xlvii, 1,008) pointed out the difficulty of achieving any degree of statistical precision, but went on:

> Let any one walk certain streets of London, Glasgow, or Edinburgh, of a
> night, and, without troubling his head with statistics, his eyes and ears

> will tell him at once what a multitudinous amazonian army the devil keeps in constant field service, for advancing his own ends. The stones seem alive with lust, and the very atmosphere is tainted.

Statistics were doubtful, but not the evidence of eyes and ears. To anyone who wished to look, *The Times* had remarked the previous year, it was plain that 'in no capital city of Europe' was there 'daily and nightly such a shameless display of Prostitution as in London':[3] an unpalatable fact for a nation that liked to think it led the world in morals as in affluence, but a fact that had been obvious for several decades. In December 1815, not so very long after the celebrations for Britain's victory over the French, a victory that was often ascribed to her superior morality, the *Anti-Jacobin Review* (xlix, 628) complained stiffly that

> notwithstanding our lofty pretensions to the character of a religious and moral people, there is no capital in Europe where prostitution is suffered to display itself in so shameless a manner as in London: Paris, though a sink of profligacy, is infinitely more decent in the above respect. There too the theatres are free from those disgraceful scenes which render those of London unfit to be entered by a modest woman.

Foreign visitors, one can appreciate, found the situation somewhat bewildering: they were astonished that a country so strait-laced in other respects should be so permissive in this. The German Pückler-Muskau, though certainly not a prude, was genuinely shocked by what he saw in the 1820s:[4]

> It is most strange that in no country on earth is this afflicting and humiliating spectacle so openly exhibited as in the religious and decorous England. The evil goes to such an extent, that in the theatres it is often difficult to keep off these repulsive beings, especially when they are drunk, which is not seldom the case.

How was it, wondered foreigners, that the British paterfamilias with his cult of domesticity, with his determination to avoid anything in public discourse that might bring a blush to the cheek of modesty, could yet allow the streets and places of public amusement in his capital to be infested with open harlotry? Local observers, too, often found the situation rather puzzling. A writer in the *Lancet* (7 November 1857) remarked

> The typical Pater-familias, living in a grand house near the park, sees his sons allured into debauchery, dares not walk with his daughters through the streets after nightfall, and is disturbed from his night-slumbers by the drunken screams and foul oaths of prostitutes reeling home with daylight. If he look from his window, he sees the pavement—his pavement—occupied by the flaunting daughters of sin, whose loud, ribald talk forces him to keep his casement closed . . . Yet he refuses to sanction any practical means for remedying the evil, or to lend his aid to its reform.

Generalizations such as this need to be taken with some caution: the typical paterfamilias hardly lived 'in a grand house near the park'; and if he found his pavement full of prostitutes, usually in fact he would be in the van of any movement to displace them—in the interest of property values as well as morals. But whilst recognizing the enormous variety of middle-class attitudes and behaviour towards the prostitute, and the shifting pattern of these variations in the course of an entire century, we may still profitably discuss, I think, a generalized paterfamilias and his remarkable indulgence to the harlot. Through all the diversities and changes in nineteenth-century sexual attitudes there runs the constant paradox that baffled foreign visitors: that the respectable British father, whilst believing that his country enjoyed better morals and more freedom than anywhere else in the world, could yet allow his freedom and that of his family to be severely restricted by the operations of common prostitutes.[5]

In the first half of the century, for example, many respectable fathers were obliged to deny themselves and their family the pleasures of the theatre. The saloons of theatres at this time were full of prostitutes openly plying their trade, frequently with the collusion of the managements, who far from discouraging them were often alleged to sell them cut-price season-tickets. Macready, it is true, the famous actor-manager, succeeded in purifying both Covent Garden and Drury Lane, but the *Theatrical Journal* in congratulating him (27 July 1844) still felt forced to describe the other theatres as 'great public brothels . . . the very hot-beds of vice . . . houses of illfame on a *large scale*. For an innocent girl to enter the saloons was of course quite out of the question: apart from other considerations she might be mistaken for a prostitute herself by some undiscerning gallant. But nowhere in the theatres was she safe from the sight of vice: even in the auditorium she would be unlikely to miss the boisterous activity of harlots in the second tier of boxes. An American visitor of the thirties commented sardonically:[6]

> How edifying to the young boarding-school misses who might be present.
> It was not necessary that they should go into the saloon, or look in as they
> passed, or observe what was going forward in the stairway and surrounding
> galleries; everything was visible, and necessarily visible too, from their
> seats.

After 1850 the prostitute took her trade to the casinos, night-houses, and pleasure-gardens that were coming into vogue, like the Argyll Rooms, Kate Hamilton's, and Cremorne, and left the more prosaic theatre to be enjoyed by paterfamilias and his family. But when these resorts began to enter an eclipse around 1870, she moved to the promenades of music-halls, like the Alhambra and later the Empire. Here again paterfamilias and his ladies suffered a restriction of their pleasures: even the Empire, which had the most decorous promenade of any music-hall, was not a respectable place for most fathers to take a wife or daughter.

The legitimate West-End theatres by this time had been purified within, but many of the streets outside them, especially after the performance, were still thick with clamorous prostitutes. For by far the greater part of the century the route from

St Paul's Churchyard to Regent's Park through Fleet Street, the Strand, the Haymarket, Regent Street, and Portland Place—was a thoroughfare for harlots that imposed strict restraints upon all respectable heads of families. To conduct a wife or daughter through these streets at night was to encounter dozens of unmistakable prostitutes accosting almost every man who passed and possibly jostling and insulting any lady. There were some areas, indeed, that paterfamilias would skirt even when by himself: in the Haymarket, for example, at mid-century he would be lucky to escape physical molestation without abandoning the pavement for the middle of the street.[7] Even daylight presented certain difficulties: a gentleman might well think twice before treating ladies to a stroll through the red-light district around Portland Place or, later in the century, the area around Charing Cross station. Fashionable shopping centres like the Strand or Regent Street furnished the biggest problems of all: to allow ladies to wander through them unattended, window-gazing at their leisure, was to risk their being not only scandalized by streetwalkers, but, what was worse, accosted as such themselves. As late as the 1890s, when the streets in general were more decorous, it was inadvisable for a respectable woman to walk alone in Piccadilly, Regent Street, the Strand, or Leicester Square. 'Although I was quietly dressed,' wrote Mrs Peel, a Fleet Street journalist at that time, 'and I hope looked what I was, a respectable young woman, there was scarcely a day when I, while waiting for an omnibus, was not accosted.'[8] A correspondence in *The Times* in January 1862 puts the picture nicely in perspective. A 'Paterfamilias from the Provinces' had been outraged to find that two ladies of his family had been followed and accosted in Oxford Street, owing perhaps to their inadvertent intrusion upon the wrong side of Regent Street, the pavement that the prostitutes had seized as their own exclusive property. The *Saturday Review*, in hazarding this explanation (1 February), showed no surprise at the ladies' difficulty and very little sympathy: the best solution it could offer was for them to dress thoroughly unbecomingly, to procure poke bonnets, to stint their skirts to a moderate circumference, and to cultivate sad-coloured under-clothing—the best solution, that is, until the nation solved the problem through the statute book.

Twenty years earlier, in fact, an attempt had been made towards this end. In 1842 the Committee of the London Society for the Protection of Young Females produced a Bill which, though it would not directly restrict the amount of street prostitution, would help to control the situation generally by giving the police more power over brothels. But the Government refused to introduce it in the Commons. After the Society had carefully reframed the Bill under the guidance of specialists in penitentiary work, the Bishop of Exeter introduced it in the Lords in 1844. It passed its first two readings without difficulty, but on its third, after a proposal that the question be deferred for more considered judgment and a hint from the Duke of Wellington that the Government might at some time take up the matter, the Bishop withdrew the Bill altogether. A few militants kept up the pressure for a year or so, but without much success; the issue was effectively dead. Forty years later the process was repeated. Between 1882 and 1885 the Criminal Law Amendment Bill, a roughly similar measure, was passed three times in the Lords only to hang fire in the Commons; and in May 1885, when it was talked out one night in the Commons, it appeared to have gone the way of its predecessor.

Parliament's inertia in this matter was often subjected to bitter criticism. Some critics accused politicians of a cowardly, wilful blindness, of acting as though no such thing as prostitution existed; an accusation that does not seem very consistent with the alacrity with which the Contagious Diseases Acts were passed in the 1860s, to control venereal disease in the prostitute population. Others were still more scathing in their charges:[9]

> How can *they* be expected to legislate freely on the subject,—how can they fail to be shy of restrictive and punitive measures,—who are conscious, possibly, that any law, approaching in its principle and in its execution, to impartiality, must first affect themselves?

These words were written by a clergyman of the forties. But the accusation he makes was even more common in the eighties, and not without cause—only weeks before the Criminal Law Amendment Bill was talked out in the Commons the Home Office appears to have been complicit in the extraordinary lenience shown to Mrs Jeffries, a high-class bawd with many aristocratic clients.[10] But cynical self-interest as an explanation of Parliament's inaction seems hardly adequate. With both Bills it was not the allegedly libertine Lords but the Commons of the respectable Peel and Gladstone that was obstructive. Public opinion, not the machinations of evil men, was the real key to the problem. The Government, once W. T. Stead had roused the people in July 1885 with his 'Maiden Tribute' articles in the *Pall Mall Gazette*, took up the Bill with almost unseemly haste. But why did paterfamilias require Stead's sensational promptings to make him call for legislative action? The problem of prostitution had needed tackling throughout the century.

To an extent here, in the case of paterfamilias rather than his statesmen, the charge of wilful blindness was well-founded. Many Victorians had a talent for not seeing the unpleasant obvious. In some cases paterfamilias might be moved by a feeling of shame: the *Standard* (5 March 1858) explained society's toleration of prostitution as being largely due to

> a very respectable, moral, and middle-aged race. They may, it is true, have been guilty of certain short-comings in their youth, but they have now left all that sort of thing, and find it convenient to forget the existence, if they could, of those poor creatures with whom they have sinned; and never on any occasion to allude to, much less would they think of legislating upon, a subject so indelicate in its nature, and so fraught with disagreeable reminiscences . . .

In other cases he might be moved, especially with materfamilias jogging his elbow, by an exaggerated deference to feminine modesty. In May 1855 Mrs Oliphant expressed a fairly widespread view about prostitutes and purity: 'every pure feminine mind, we suppose, holds the faith of Desdemona—"I do not believe there is any such woman".'[11] But Nelsonian blindness of this order can never have been particularly easy to achieve, and by the mid-fifties was virtually impossible. Even if paterfamilias and his ladies kept aloof from the indecent parts of London, they would still find it hard to evade the whore in literature and in the papers. The fictional prostitute had come a long way from the reticent ambiguities of the thirties, from Dickens's girl in 'The Pawnbroker's Shop' in *Sketches by Boz* or Nancy in *Oliver Twist*. By June 1859, indeed, she had become so vividly familiar that *Tait's Edinburgh Magazine* protested that 'the subject of the "Social Evil" has been overdone'. In these years too the occasional press complaints of earlier years about the state of the streets and theatres had given way to such an absorption in the problem of prostitution that the *Saturday Review* was led to complain that 'the Social Evil question has become a very popular one—too popular by half'.[12] In the face of such exposure, evasion, for whatever motive, was not a very practical proposition. 'Prostitution', wrote Miss Mulock in 1858, 'in country cottages as in city streets, in books, newspapers, and daily talk, meets us so continually that no young girl can long be kept ignorant of it.'[13] Why then did paterfamilias not take action to cleanse society of this evil? The prostitute in his streets was a constant stain on his country's honour, a constant source of temptation to his son, distress to his daughters, and inconvenience and embarrassment to himself; so why did he not support the efforts of moral vigilantes to drive her off the streets? To this, paterfamilias might reply, he did support them—twice. On two major occasions public opinion was mobilized in an attempt to solve the problem.

The first instance began in 1812. In that year the Guardian Society formed a Committee to discover the best means of both driving prostitutes from the streets and supplying a refuge for those who wished to reform—a two-fold programme that was copied shortly by the Philanthropic Society's Fund of Mercy. By December 1813 a group of citizens had been stimulated by this activity to present a petition to the Lord Mayor and the Court of Common Council, signed by more than 2,000 householders calling for energetic civic intervention. In October 1814 the Mayor, encouraged by the report of a special committee he had appointed, had a proclamation published in the press and put up in every watch-house expressing his determination to apply to prostitution the utmost rigour of the law. By the end of 1815 a new and very active Mayor was busily prosecuting brothels and committing streetwalkers to Bridewell in droves, and the press was full of enthusiastic letters and articles upon the subject. On 11 February 1816 the *Sunday Monitor*, which had been running a series of lengthy progress reports, rejoiced that 'the nuisance of the prostituted streets is nearly removed'. A critic of the Guardian Society commented cynically the following year:[14]

> a stranger, coming at that period to town, would have concluded that in a short time, London would be the purest city in the universe. What was the result of all this, however! Why, that, in a short time, within a little

month, the papers dropped the subject, and the business was forgotten; nay, in spite of the continued exertions of the Lord Mayor, the streets soon became as much infested as before.

The stone of Sisyphus was back where it had started; and there it remained for another forty years, until the vestry of St James's began to move it.

In the summer of 1856 a deputation went to the Home Office from St James's, Westminster, to plead for greater police control of prostitution; and the Home Secretary promised to investigate the matter. But two weeks later he simply reported that he was satisfied with the present arrangements. In the summer of 1857, however, the vestry and its colleagues in St Marylebone began to make some headway by engaging public interest in their efforts, thereby putting extra pressure on the authorities. By the end of October the *Lancet* was claiming that there was scarcely a journal of repute which had not begun to advocate the need for some practical reforms; and although this was a sizeable exaggeration at that moment, by January 1858 it had become much more like a fact. A series of meetings under the auspices of the Society for the Suppression of Vice and then a convention organized by St James's for the leaders of other metropolitan parishes to co-ordinate their programmes, were enough to produce a minor flood of letters, articles and editorials in the press. With public opinion seemingly behind them, the vestrymen looked to be making genuine progress. But soon the movement had lost the impetus it had gained. In March 1858 a deputation went to the Home Office to plead for stricter law enforcement; and the new Home Secretary, like his predecessor, promised to investigate the matter. But, as before, nothing materialized. Public interest fizzled out. And, once more, the vigilantes were back almost exactly where they had started. In October 1857 the St James's vestry had succeeded in closing the Argyll Rooms, a favourite resort of London's harlots and their clients; in October 1858 the Argyll was re-opened, and became as notorious as ever. The *Saturday Review* on 12 September 1863 gave the scene an ironic backward glance:

> Five years ago, there was a great ripping-up of the skirts of society . . .
> The 'Social Evil' was elaborately investigated from the sentimental, the
> classical, the philanthropic, the medical, the religious, and the statistical
> points of view; and sometimes the writer so warmed with his subject that
> the glowing descriptions which were intended to point a moral had them-
> selves a mischievous pruriency . . . And then, amid much excited writing
> and highly-coloured purposeless description, all practical results were
> gradually lost sight of, until at length the subject, worn threadbare,
> gradually dropped out of notice.

It would be wrong to underestimate the truth of this observation. In 1857–8, as in 1815–16, the press interest in prostitution reform was doubtless partly spurious: some papers clearly took up the issue less from moral zeal than from an enthusiasm for a topic that was both novel and mildly prurient, or from a desire not to get out of step with their competitors. At the same time it would be wrong to underestimate the integrity of both press and paterfamilias. Some of the papers, through silence or explicit statement, had shown a coolness about the reformers from the beginning, and the dwindling of public interest in the movement seems to have been less the result of boredom than a growing recognition that these sceptics were being proved right, that mere law enforcement was not an effective solution: the whores chased out of the City in 1816 simply settled in the suburbs until the wave of repression ended; 'what is cut down in one parish', noted the *Saturday Review* (16 October 1858), 'grows up in the next—the weeds are only transported from Norton-street to Brompton.' Paterfamilias, if not sceptical about the reformers' strategy from the beginning, soon learned to become so. In 1857 Dr Acton, a leading authority on prostitution, chided him for denouncing the casinos and night-houses for which the prostitute had abandoned the theatre: 'He rails and preaches against vice when he ought, as I view it, to thank her for doing what he could obtain of her neither by persuasion nor by force, I mean putting herself in a corner.'[15] The closing of the Argyll Rooms by the vestry had taken place a few weeks before. When they re-opened a year later local people were unanimous in saying the locality had grown worse. 'Last year, in a transport of moral and popular indignation, we closed the Argyll Rooms because they were the focus of all metropolitan vice. This year we open them, because, on the whole, it is better that the vicious population should be brought together than that it should be let loose on society.'[16] Many erstwhile enthusiasts for reform had made the chastening discovery that the problem was much bigger and more complex than they had thought, that legal sanctions could only work if society underwent profound economic and social changes, and that intervention for the moment might do more harm than good.

If paterfamilias felt that the Social Evil was temporarily incurable, he had ample grounds for his belief. To begin with, a revolution was required in the condition of the poor. Large numbers of women were forced on to the streets by poverty —by atrociously low wages, by unemployment, or by improvidence. In the hopeless squalor at the base of the social pyramid, prostitution was an accepted occupation that rarely attached any shame to its practitioners. For, as the *Leader* instructed its middle-class readers (28 April 1860), morality meant very little to women in these conditions:

> Neglect, starvation, ignorance, vice, filth, and disease have surrounded them from infancy. They have been brought up with scarcely an idea of modesty or personal reserve; and the language to which they have habitually listened has been of the foulest and most blasphemous description. Intoxicating drink has formed the only, or almost the only pleasure of the class to which they belonged.

A perhaps more important factor than squalor and destitution was the drabness of existence for many respectable working women: for domestic servants and factory girls, for instance, working very long, hard hours for little pay and little recreation. In the provinces especially, with their comparative austerity, life was often, as the

Saturday Review put it, 'one dreary routine of work, work, stitch, stitch, church-and-chapel-going',[17] a tedium that prostitution offered to replace with fancy clothes, gay living, and financial independence.

Prostitution in London was particularly attractive, for besides the appeal of its amusements there was the comfort of its size, giving fallen women of this type a greater safety from disturbance by police or reproachful past acquaintances. London, too, encouraged an exceptional demand for prostitution. As the centre of the country's railway system, as the biggest commercial sea-port in the world, it had inevitably a large shifting population of likely customers: of immigrants from Ireland and the Continent; of soldiers and sailors; and of middle-class tourists and business travellers looking for amusement and with few respectable friends in town, perhaps, to prevent them finding it on the streets. London, moreover, through its size offered its own respectable citizens a comforting anonymity for their misconduct. And it was this middle-class involvement in prostitution, as much as working-class conditions, that made paterfamilias suspect the efficacy of using only the law to repress the harlot. Not only the economic and social conditions of the workers, but the sexual attitudes of much of the bourgeoisie would have to change before legal sanctions could be successful.

This latter transformation seemed as unlikely as the former, for the standards of masculine morality to which the Victorians officially subscribed were perhaps more difficult to observe then than at any other time in history. Late marriage, for example, was extremely common among the middle classes, from choice or from necessity; and for these men prolonged chastity involved not only the psychological pressures on male virginity and the denial of pleasure that obtain in any period, but in the light of much current medical opinion a serious danger to their health. Masturbation, doctors warned, would lead to untold horrors, from dyspepsia to insanity and death. But perfect continence too was a hazardous undertaking: even conservative medical opinion was sometimes forced to admit that it led to impotence, and some doctors claimed it led to spermatorrhoea, a dread disease invented by the Victorians as one of the symptoms of self-abuse. Dr George Drysdale in his *Elements of Social Science* (1854), which went through thirty-five editions in fifty years, paints a nightmare picture of the results of both celibacy and masturbation, and prescribes free love as the perfect panacea. Orthodox practitioners doubtless shuddered at this suggestion; but some of them in the privacy of the consulting-room unquestionably recommended prostitution to certain patients, and other celibate sufferers, one imagines, made out their own prescription.

The married man too, paterfamilias himself, was subjected to special pressures that made him aware of the utility of the prostitute. For one thing there was his wife's frequent conjugal incapacitation in an age when (up to the eighties at least) contraception was little used. For another there was the near-impossibility of divorce at a time when marriage, especially for women, was often a loveless arrangement of convenience—of securing wealth and status or avoiding the stigma of spinsterhood. But perhaps more important, there were the marital problems peculiar to the

Victorians. Disillusionment with marriage is common to any period, but it was all the more likely in an age when affianced couples might often have exceptionally idealistic expectations, and yet, through the restrictions of social conventions, know little of each other's innermost personality. Wives, moreover, were expected to be angels, but their training from childhood too often gave them an intellectual, emotional, and physical insipidity that could only bore or irritate their disappointed husbands. Even successful marriages could put the husband's fidelity under strain: for so ingrained was the middle-class belief in a pure woman's asexuality that few married couples, it seems, could give themselves really freely to sexual pleasure. Freud put this particular husband's dilemma very succinctly:[18]

> Full sexual satisfaction only comes when he can give himself up wholeheartedly to enjoyment, which with his well-brought-up wife, for instance, he does not venture to do. Hence comes his need for a less exalted sexual object, a woman ethically inferior, to whom he need ascribe no aesthetic misgivings, and who does not know the rest of his life and cannot criticize him.

The prostitute, in short, was a natural corollary of the Victorians' idealistic view of feminine purity.

Many Victorians, without Freud's perception, were shrewd enough to see this connection clearly. Some even argued that prostitution was not only inevitable because of society's economic structure, it was also in fact desirable because of society's marriage system: without this channel for middle-class men's illicit sexual indulgence the purity of the home, the peace and chastity of British maids and matrons would be undoubtedly less secure. The typical paterfamilias would probably not go this far. But, if he rejected the desirability of prostitution whilst ruefully accepting its temporary inevitability, he would often at least concede that it was socially very useful. And this awareness made him unenthusiastic as well as sceptical about the use of the law to repress it. His toleration of the prostitution in his streets stemmed less, I suspect, from the cowardly evasion of an unpleasant topic than from a painfully honest confrontation—the wilful blindness, especially on the question of legislative reform, being often a cover for his awareness of society's need and guilt. Until society transformed the situation of the poor and the working conditions of female labour, until society's marriage system—which was itself in some measure little more than legalized prostitution—was freed from its dependence on the harlot, it was ethically very dubious to harass and victimize her. Indeed, paterfamilias could be forgiven for letting compassion in some cases run to sentimentality, for seeing her as a martyr: in Lecky's famous words, as 'the eternal priestess of humanity, blasted for the sins of the people'.[19]

Sometimes, in fact, this conscience and compassion made for outright opposition to the moral reformers, perfectly respectable citizens being led to champion the prostitute's right to be seen in public places, to protect her from the operation of the law. 'Many a gentleman of character', it was remarked in 1858, 'had passed a night in a police cell for interference in the defence of prostitutes against the police'[20]—a spirit of gallantry that was still in evidence in 1895, when an Oxford scientist, Professor Lankester, and a distinguished actor-manager, George Alexander, were prosecuted in successive months for protecting harlots from harassment by the law.[21] The police understandably were often slow to risk the odium that arresting prostitutes might bring them, especially when they might not always be supported by the courts. *The Times* (21 February 1844), reported that a London alderman named Farebrother had rejected a petition from some citizens who had been disturbed by the activity of prostitutes at night: 'These poor creatures must be somewhere ... and why, if acts of disorder were not proved against them, should they be punished with imprisonment, or with the bad treatment which they often suffered without being brought before magistrates at all ? He for one would not imprison a wretched woman merely because she was brought before him by a policeman.' On some occasions the policeman, and more especially his instigators, the moral reformers, received much worse than mere obstruction in their efforts: they could be subjected to the most bitter vilification, particularly from those who so accepted the necessity of prostitutes as hardly to suffer any inconvenience from encountering them. In 1848, for example, the tradesmen of Regent Street, who had fought a long, costly, and unavailing battle against the prostitutes in their midst, took the drastic course of having John Nash's beautiful Quadrant demolished by Act of Parliament. In the controversy that followed, a writer to *The Times* (2 December 1848) exploded:

> It is the curse, Sir, of this nation to be beset with a myriad of canting hypocrites with great pretensions to religion and morality, but totally devoid of godliness and charity. That the condemned Quadrant afforded a temporary shelter from the pitiless storm to the houseless wanderer was sin enough in the eyes of these shopkeeping Philistines ... but, Sir, I appeal to you, I appeal to every London pedestrian, whether they ever suffered any annoyance, in any way, from the helpless creatures here attacked ? ... No. But this afforded your would-be saint an occasion to exercise his persecuting spirit too favourable to be lost.

The same accusations of hypocritical cant, of houseless wanderers being cast to the mercies of pitiless storms, the same protestations that self-righteous prudery was grossly exaggerating a trivial inconvenience, were heard forty-six years later, when in 1894 some moral vigilantes, led by Mrs Ormiston Chant, sought to drive prostitutes from the Empire Theatre by abolishing its promenade. The newspapers were full of such letters as this, angrily attacking busy-body 'Prudes on the Prowl':[22]

> How long is this great London of ours, so proud and yet so patient, to wait for that strong and irresistible voice of public disapprobation, that mighty roar of disgust, which is heard today in private in every assemblage of commonsense men and women, protesting against and execrating the tyranny of the self-satisfied minority ? How long are we

patiently to endure the shrill shriek of the emancipated female, to say nothing of the prurient grass widow? How much longer must we listen to the impudent piety of these provincial pedlars in social purity, who come red-hot from their Chicago platforms and tinpot tabernacles to tell this London of ours how she is to amuse herself and how she is to dispose of and harass and drive from pillar to post those unfortunate outcasts, whom we always have had, and always shall have, amongst us?

The 'self-satisfied minority' was not in fact particularly self-satisfied. Mrs Chant, far from being a fanatical persecutor of defenceless outcasts, had been deeply involved for many years in welfare work to rescue fallen women—like most of the vigilant pressure groups before her, from the Guardian Society to the Salvation Army. Nor in fact was her movement a minority: for despite the opposition it encountered it was quickly endorsed by the general public in the L.C.C. elections. History was on the vigilantes' side, and as England passed into the twentieth century, prostitution became progressively more discreet, less public, in its conduct. Its decline, however, in both extent and flagrancy, was less the result of any social purity crusade than a general change in social conditions. As the masses' living and working conditions improved, as they adopted new standards of moral respectability, the supply of prostitutes was inevitably reduced. And as middle-class thought gradually became more liberal on such subjects as contraception, marriage, and divorce, and especially the social role and sexual nature of women, the demand for prostitutes fell off proportionately. The social factors that had stopped paterfamilias from putting a curb on public prostitution were now a thing of the past. So indeed was he. And his death, the dissolution of Victorian idealism about the family and the home, the end of the cult of fervent domesticity, was itself one of the main causes of the decline of prostitution. Ironically, as the nation became less preoccupied with the purity of the home, the purity of the streets became at last a practical proposition.[23]

Notes

1 See von Archenholz, *A Picture of England* (1789), II, p. 75; von Raumer, *England in 1835* (1836), II, p. 24; H. Taine, *Notes on England*, trans. Edward Hyams (1957), p. 37. The police estimates are given and usefully discussed in William Acton, *Prostitution Considered in its Moral, Social, and Sanitary Aspects . . .* (1857), pp. 15–19, and 2nd edn (1870), pp. 3–7.

2 See William J. Taylor, *The Story of the Homes* (1907), p. 23.

3 8 January 1858, p. 6.

4 *A Regency Visitor: The English tour of Prince Pückler-Muskau*, ed. E. M. Butler (1957), p. 84.

5 In a short essay such as this a great deal must perforce be omitted from discussion: I can do little more than glance, for example, at such huge topics as Victorian sexual behaviour, the 'double standard', the Contagious Diseases agitation, the

reclamation movement, and the prostitute in fact and fiction, all of which would in some measure qualify, without substantially altering, the picture I am presenting of prostitution and paterfamilias.

6   [Alexander Slidell], *The American in England* (1835), II, pp. 211–12.

7   For a graphic description of the Haymarket in the sixties see the *Saturday Review*, xiii (June 1862), 644.

8   Mrs C. S. Peel, *Life's Enchanted Cup* (1933), pp. 105–6.

9   Ralph Wardlaw, *Lectures on Female Prostitution* (1842), pp. 93–4.

10 There is a useful account of this affair in Giles Playfair, *Six Studies in Hypocrisy* (1969), pp. 98–100.

11 *Blackwood's Magazine*, lxxvii (1855), 560.

12 6 October 1860.

13 Dinah Mulock, *A Woman's Thoughts about Women* (1858), p. 285.

14 S. T., *An Address to the Guardian Society*, reprinted in the *Pamphleteer*, xi (1818), 227–8.

15 Acton (1857 edn), p. 101.

16 *Saturday Review*, 16 October 1858.

17 Ibid., 20 October 1866.

18 Sigmund Freud, 'Contributions to the Psychology of Love', *Collected Papers* (1924–50), IV, p. 210.

19 W. E. H. Lecky, *The History of European Morals* (1869), II, p. 283.

20 *Globe*, 15 January 1858.

21 Cyril Pearl, *The Girl with the Swansdown Seat* (1955), discusses these cases, pp. 210–11. Pearl's book in fact, with all its inaccuracies of substance and facetiousness of tone, is the most helpful of modern discussions of Victorian prostitution; and I am greatly in its debt. The reader may also find useful material in Peter T. Cominos, 'Late-Victorian Sexual Respectability and the Social System', *International Review of Social History*, viii (1963), 18–48, 216–50; Fernando Henriques, *Modern Sexuality* (1968); Ronald Pearsall, *The Worm in the Bud* (1969); Keith Thomas, 'The Double Standard', *Journal of the History of Ideas*, xx (1959), 195–216; and Patricia Thomson *The Victorian Heroine* (1956). Maurice J. Quinlan, *Victorian Prelude* (New York, 1941) and the chapter on 'Love' in Walter E. Houghton's *The Victorian Frame of Mind* (New Haven, 1957) are the best general treatments of Victorian sexual attitudes. O. R. McGregor, 'The Social Position of Women in England, 1850–1914; A Bibliography', *British Journal of Sociology*, vi (1955), 55–6, surveys some of the primary material on Victorian prostitution.

22 *Daily Telegraph*, 13 October 1894. The writer ironically was Clement Scott, who three years earlier had distinguished himself by leading, in the *Telegraph*, the hysterically prudish attack on Ibsen's *Ghosts*.

23 For amplification of these generalizations see my study, 'Madonnas and Magdalens: The origins and development of Victorian sexual attitudes in literature and society' (unpublished Ph.D. thesis, University of Leicester, 1972).

30   The Culture of Poverty

Gertrude Himmelfarb

The 'Condition of the People' was as much a set topic for Victorians as it has since become for historians. It was the subject of Royal Commission reports and parliamentary debates, statistical analyses and sensationalist exposés, sermons, articles, novels, even poems. The historian would seem to be well served by this abundance of material. Yet he would be wise to approach it warily. And not only for the usual reasons—doubts about its accuracy, consistency, and bias—but also because it is not always clear what all of this evidence is about, what subject it is that is being elucidated.

The variety of titles under which the subject was discussed is itself suspect; in place of 'the People' one may read 'the Labouring Population,' or 'the Labouring Poor,' or 'the Poorer Classes,' or 'the Working Classes,' or, more grandly, 'England.'[1] Contemplating these alternatives, the historian may find himself attending less to the question of the Condition of the People than to the question of the identity of the People who were so variously and, as it appeared, synonymously described. And the question of identity, in turn, raises that of image. Was there a common image that would account for the assumption of a common identity? The questions are of some importance, not only in defining and clarifying the subject of the Condition of the People—what condition and which people—but also in understanding what was or was not being done about that Condition and those People. For there is no doubt that the way the People were perceived played a large part in the way they were treated, in the kinds of legislation, the modes of administration, the types of philanthropy, the forms of public policy and private behavior which so materially affected their Condition.

Questions of identity and image persist even when the subject appears to be more carefully delineated, more precisely located in time, place, and rank. Henry Mayhew's *London Labour and the London Poor*, published in the middle of the century, would seem to be sufficiently well-defined. Referring explicitly and exclusively to the metropolis, it has only a partial relevance to the larger body of urban labor and poor, and no necessary relevance to the much more considerable body of rural labor and poor. And certainly in comparison with studies purporting to deal with 'the People' or 'England,' it suggests a commendable clarity and specificity. It also has the virtue of being eminently readable, indeed one of the most fascinating social documents of the century. Mayhew's work, therefore, may well serve as a case study of the ambiguities both of the historical situation and of the historical enterprise.

The most obvious ambiguity lies in the title itself. Were the two categories, 'Labour' and the 'Poor,' meant to be conjunctive or disjunctive? And how do the subtitles of the several volumes relate to the overall title? The first three volumes were subtitled: 'The London Street Folk; comprising Street Sellers, Street Buyers, Street Finders, Street Performers, Street Artisans, Street Labourers'; and the fourth, 'Those That Will Not Work, comprising Prostitutes, Thieves, Swindlers, Beggars.' [2] These subtitles obviously do not add up to the title either in its conjunctive or disjunctive sense. And it is the subtitles rather than the title which accurately describe the plan of the work and the bulk of its contents.

Unfortunately this difficulty cannot be resolved, as one might think it could be, by simply ignoring the title and concentrating on the substance of the work. For in fact the ambiguity is of the substance of the work. It is not just a question of setting the record straight, of putting aright those contemporaries and historians who used the work as a source of information about London Labour and the London Poor, even Labour and The Poor, instead of about the London Street Folk. One would also have to put Mayhew aright; for he too seems on occasion to have been a victim of the same confusion. What is important is not so much the confusion itself as its significance, the reasons why so many people found it possible to identify the Street Folk with the Labouring Poor, why even those who were aware of the distinction tended to ignore it at crucial moments.

The anomaly of the title may in part (but only in part) be accounted for by the peculiar publication history of the work. In September 1849, in the midst of one of the worst cholera epidemics of the century, Mayhew published an article in the *Morning Chronicle* describing the most severely ravaged area of London. 'Jacob's Island' had long been infamous as one of the vilest slums of London; it was there that the cholera epidemic of 1832 had broken out, and, more memorably, that Dickens had located the grisly scene of Bill Sikes's death in *Oliver Twist*. One wonders whether Dickens had been inspired by earlier newspaper accounts of the epidemic, or whether Mayhew, in writing his account, was inspired by Dickens. In any event, Mayhew's article apparently suggested either to him or to the publishers of the *Chronicle* the idea of a series on the condition of the poor.

Half a dozen years earlier, Mayhew, then on the staff of *Punch*, had witnessed the enormous success of Thomas Hood's 'Song of the Shirt,' and the success of *Punch* itself largely as a result of having printed it; the fact that the poem had been published over the objections of most of the staff, including Mayhew himself, may have impressed him all the more with the public appeal of the Condition-of-England question. The *Chronicle*, for its part, had long been distinguished by its concern for social reform. It was, therefore, entirely in keeping with the paper's character, as well as Mayhew's, to undertake a series on 'Labour and the Poor.' The series, the announcement read, would provide 'a full and detailed description of the moral, intellectual, material, and physical condition of the industrial poor throughout England,' and would 'equal, perhaps surpass, official or Parliamentary reports in impartiality, authenticity, and comprehensiveness.'[3]

For about a year, at first twice weekly and then once a week, Mayhew's three to four thousand word articles appeared under the by-line of the 'Metropolitan Commissioner.'[4] (On alternate days, under the same general heading of 'Labour and the Poor,' two other correspondents reported on the industrial areas outside of London and on the rural districts; still other series appeared on conditions abroad, particularly in France and Belgium.) In his first article, Mayhew explained his intention of enquiring into the 'condition of the poor of London': 'Under the term poor I shall include all those persons whose incomings are insufficient for the satisfaction of their wants—a want being, according to my idea, contradistinguished from a mere desire by a positive physical pain, instead of a mental uneasiness, accompanying it.' He categorized the poor as the 'honest' (subdivided into the 'striving' and the 'disabled') and the 'dishonest'; or alternatively as those 'who *will* work' (including the 'poorly paid' and the 'improvident'), those 'who *can't* work,' and those 'who *won't* work.'[5]

It was apparently Mayhew's original intention to deal with all these groups and in approximately that order. Had he done so, he might have fulfilled at least part of the promise of his title; we might then have had a conspectus of the Poor as a whole and of that part of Labour that was poor. To a certain extent, his *Chronicle* articles do provide some of the raw materials for such a conspectus. But even here the emphasis was on the poorest of the poor and on the 'slopworkers' among the laborers (those working in the cheapest branches of each trade). Thus the subject of his first article was the Spitalfield weavers, who had the double advantage for his purpose, he explained, of being confined to a single area and therefore easily visited, and of being 'notorious for their privations.'[6] Similarly, a later article on the needlewomen excluded the milliners and dressmakers, on the ground that they were 'somewhat better paid than the generality of other needlewomen.'[7]

The *Chronicle* articles, however weighted, were nevertheless on the general and recognizable subject of Labour and the Poor. The next stage of the publication history of this work saw a further departure from the sense of the title. Having resigned from the *Chronicle* in October 1850, Mayhew undertook to publish the series privately in the form of weekly twopenny pamphlets. The first of these appeared in December 1850, the last in March 1852. These pamphlets were bound together in two volumes in 1851 and 1852. In 1861–2 a four-volume edition was published (and reprinted in 1864) consisting of the two original volumes of 1851–2, a third more rambling and disorganized, and a fourth which was largely the work of collaborators and was exclusively on the subject of beggars, prostitutes, and thieves.[8] Thus Mayhew's work as we now know it, as almost all historians and commentators have known it, and as most contemporaries knew it (except for those who happen to have read the *Chronicle* in 1849–50), corresponds to the later pamphlets and volumes rather than to the original newspaper articles.

To be sure, the pamphlets and volumes did draw upon some of the *Chronicle* articles. But only upon some of them. From the beginning of the pamphlet series, Mayhew took as his explicit theme the street-folk, reprinting or adapting from the *Chronicle* the articles on the street-hawkers and hucksters, dock-laborers and flower-girls, and omitting (except for passing references) those on the Spitalfield weavers, the needlewomen and tailors, boot-makers and carpenters.[9] With the addition, in the later volumes, of more extensive material on street-traders and street-criminals, the work became even further removed from the 'industrial poor' that the *Chronicle* had spoken of, or from the *London Labour and the London Poor* of the title.

About the same time that Mayhew's first volume was being published, there also appeared, as it happened, the results of the census of 1851. This census is of particular importance in English social history, since it was the first to treat in some detail such subjects as religious affiliations and practices, the first to single London out for separate consideration, and because it was altogether more satisfactory than any previous one. It is also instructive as a contrast or corrective to Mayhew's work. For it gave as the largest occupational groups in the metropolis: domestic workers (200,000, or one-tenth of the total population of London), building workers (60,000), tailors, dressmakers, and milliners (60,000), shoemakers (40,000), etc.—none of whom figured in Mayhew's work. Included in the census figures were the self-employed and better-paid artisans; but these—the 'labour aristocracy,' as recent historians have designated them—constituted no more, according to Mayhew himself, than one-tenth of the laboring population.[10] The rest, and surely the vast bulk of domestic workers, indubitably belonged to Labour and the Poor, however that category may be understood.

But it did not take the census to reveal just how limited was the population with which Mayhew dealt. Mayhew himself was explicit enough—and not only in subtitles and chapter titles but in numbers and ratios. Repeatedly in the first two volumes he gave the total of street-folk as approximately 50,000, this figure including men, women, and children. And, lest there be any doubt about their relative numbers, he specified, in the opening pages of Volume I and again of Volume II, that these 50,000 represented 'a fortieth part' of the population of the metropolis.[11] Volumes III and IV added other groups of street-laborers (dockworkers, transport workers, etc.) and non-laboring street-folk (prostitutes, beggars, criminals, paupers). But even assuming that the addition of these groups doubled the original number, Mayhew's population still constituted only about one-twentieth of the population—which is far short of anything that could reasonably come under the category of Labour and the Poor. Mayhew protested, and quite rightly, that most of his street-folk were missing from the census.[12] But if the census had its non-persons, Mayhew as assuredly had his—and in even larger numbers.

More important, however, than the question of numbers is that of characterization. For Mayhew's street-folk were not only quantitatively distinct from the population of laboring poor; they were qualitatively distinctive, indeed a race apart. And here too Mayhew could not have been more explicit. The very first pamphlet, which was also the opening chapter of the first volume, was entitled, 'Of Wandering Tribes in General.'[13] And the opening sentences set the theme: Mankind had always consisted of 'two distinct and broadly marked races, viz., the wanderers and the settlers—the vagabond and the citizen—the nomadic and the civilized tribes.' Each of these tribes, or races, had its 'peculiar and distinctive physical as well as moral characteristics.' Physically the nomadic race was distinguished by 'a greater relative development of the jaws and cheek bones.'[14] Morally the differences were no less conspicuous:[15]

> The nomad then is distinguished from the civilized man by his repugnance to regular and continuous labour—by his want of providence in laying up a store for the future—by his inability to perceive consequences ever so slightly removed from immediate apprehension—by his passion for stupefying herbs and roots, and, when possible, for intoxicating fermented liquors—by his extraordinary powers of enduring privation—by his comparative insensibility to pain—by an immoderate love of gaming, frequently risking his own personal liberty upon a single cast—by his love of libidinous dances—by the pleasure he experiences in witnessing the suffering of sentient creatures—by his delight in warfare and all perilous sports—by his desire for vengeance—by the looseness of his notion as to property—by the absence of chastity among his women, and his disregard of female honour—and lastly, by his vague sense of religion—his rude idea of a Creator, and utter absence of all appreciation of the mercy of the Divine Spirit.

It was curious, Mayhew remarked, that no one had thought to use this universal distinction to explain 'certain anomalies in the present state of society among ourselves.' Yet the distinction, he insisted, did apply as much to the English metropolis as to the interior of Africa or Arabia. Like the Bushmen and Bedouins, the London street-folk were noted for the 'greater development of the animal than of the intellectual or moral nature of man ... for their high cheek-bones and protruding jaws—for their use of a slang language—for their lax ideas of property—for their general improvidence—their repugnance to continuous labour—their disregard of female honour—their love of cruelty—their pugnacity—and their utter want of religion.' And lest there be any doubt of which Londoners he was talking about, he specified that they included pickpockets, beggars, prostitutes, street-sellers, street-performers, cabmen, coachmen, watermen, sailors, 'and suchlike.'[16]

If Mayhew found it curious that no one before him had thought to study the London street-folk from this point of view, we may find it still more curious that Mayhew himself has been studied to so little effect. For in spite of subtitles and chapter titles, of figures on the number of street-folk and graphic descriptions of their nature, Mayhew's work continues to be interpreted as an enquiry on the subject of London Labour and the London Poor. E. P. Thompson has described Mayhew's book as 'the fullest and most vivid documentation of the economic and social problems, the customs, habits, grievances, and individual life experiences of the labouring people of the world's greatest city of the nineteenth century.'[17] And the introduction to an American reprint of the work praises him for having 'uncovered and codified data on the modern proletariat that whole municipal and federal agencies are only now beginning to assemble.'[18]

In view of Mayhew's own description of the street-folk, it is surely bizarre to identify them with 'the modern proletariat'; Marx himself would have been more likely to characterize them, with all the contempt reserved for that term, as 'lumpen-proletariat.' (In fact, as Mayhew presented them, they seem to have been less a class in the Marxist sense than a species in the Darwinian sense.) And it is only a little less bizarre to find one-fortieth (or even one-twentieth) of London's population equated with the 'labouring people of the world's greatest city,' and to find the problems, customs, life-experiences, etc. of Mayhew's 'nomadic race' equated with the problems, customs, life-experiences, etc. of the 'labouring people.' Yet such statements, from reputable and ordinarily authoritative sources, cannot easily be dismissed—not only because they are apt to influence future commentators and historians, nor because they are typical of the judgments of lesser commentators and historians, but also because they reflect something in the work itself which is conducive to this kind of interpretation; and, more important, because the work itself reflects something in the times, something in the subject, which permits the confusion of street-folk with the laboring poor. For even more curious and significant than this confusion on the part of historians is a similar not uncommon confusion on the part of contemporaries.[19]

On the simplest level, part of the confusion, as has been suggested, can be explained in terms of the peculiar publication history of the work. Those contemporaries who had read or heard of the *Morning Chronicle* articles may have carried over into their reading (or non-reading, as was often the case) of the later pamphlets and volumes the impressions and expectations derived from those early articles. Much the same process of assimilation may have occurred in the case of those few historians familiar with the early articles.[20] Mayhew himself encouraged this confusion by opening his first volume with the announcement that the completed work would constitute 'a cyclopaedia of the industry, the want, and the vice of the great Metropolis.'[21] It was all too easy for the reader to take the promise for the fact. (One reviewer was so dazzled by the idea of a 'cyclopaedia' that he assumed it would be 'alphabetically arranged,' as if this would be an added warrant of its comprehensiveness and definitiveness.[22])

Another source of confusion—more excusable on the part of the contemporary reader than of the professional historian—is the massiveness of the book, with its profusion of facts, figures, tables, charts, life-histories, interviews, and the like, all of which seem to add up to something like the promise of the title and preface. The ordinary reader, assaulted by so many numbers and impressive charts, was apt to overlook the occasional reference to 'one-fortieth' buried in the text (which lacked even the visual distinctiveness of arabic numerals). Nor was he likely to perform the arithmetical calculations which would put those figures in proper proportion to the whole. Moreover, the very profusion of statistics had the illusory effect of suggesting a profusion of people. Somehow the number of tons of shipping handled annually in the London docks, the pounds of refuse collected annually from the London streets, the miles of streets yielding that refuse, were insensibly fused with the numbers of people engaged in loading those ships, collecting that refuse, cleaning those streets. Mayhew was, as his editor justly remarked, 'obsessed with statistics'—although those statistics were not always such as to give his work the 'coherence and authority' claimed for it.[23] What the statistics did do, however, was to give his subject a weightiness it might not otherwise have had, to create an impression of magnitude which facilitated the identification of the street-folk with the laboring people as a whole.

This inflation of subject was compounded by faulty statistics and faulty logical deductions from the statistics. The first volume, of 1851, contained two pages of errata with about eighty items. Both the mistakes in the text and the appended errata (to say nothing of a host of unacknowledged mistakes) were reproduced in every subsequent edition, including the most recent. The other volumes contained no such lists of errata but quite as many mistakes. Typical was one table enumerating the hackney-drivers, stage-drivers, etc., licensed in each year from 1843 to 1850, including a column designated 'total,' in which the figures for all the years were added together to produce a grand total that was most impressive but completely meaningless.[24] (It is as if one were to add together the census figures for each of eight years to arrive at the total population.) Similarly, tables on poor relief and the incidence of crime were presented as evidence of the pauper or criminal population, without any indication of the amount of recidivism—the same person receiving relief or committing crimes more than once during a given period. One of Mayhew's most dramatic figures—that 14 percent of the population of England 'continue their existence either by pauperism, mendicancy, or crime'[25]—contains half a dozen fallacies, starting with a simple arithmetic miscalculation, and including the use of questionable sources, the collation of data pertaining to different periods and otherwise not comparable, and the adding together of several categories to produce the 14 percent as if

713

each were distinct and mutually exclusive—as if paupers did not also, on occasion, figure among the crime statistics, or beggars on the pauper rolls.

When the reader was not being overwhelmed by statistics of this sort, he was being overwhelmed by images, descriptions, case studies, and life histories. The last were presented either in the neutral tones of a commentator or in the dialect—the 'unvarnished' language, as Mayhew put it—of the subject;[26] in either case the emotional impact was all the greater for the apparent objectivity of the narration. One need not suppose that this was the result of any conscious strategy on Mayhew's part—although one of his friends, describing Mayhew's procedure, said that the 'picturesque specimens' brought to the *Morning Chronicle* office told their stories not to the stenographer who was present, but to Mayhew, who then redictated them to the stenographer, 'with an added colour of his own.'[27] But, consciously or not, he could hardly have helped adding such color. He was, after all, a skilful, professional writer trying to reach the largest popular audience. Each article or pamphlet had to make its point and create its effect quickly and dramatically. However scrupulous he may have been in handling his material, however much he may have resisted making a good story better, he could not have helped but make the most of his material, choosing true stories that made good reading rather than true ones that were dull, interspersing dramatic episodes with pedestrian ones so as to give authenticity to the one and drama to the other. Even if every detail had been true (and from the nature of the sources and of the medium this is unlikely), the whole would have added up to something more than the truth—as Mayhew's street-folk seemed to add up to rather more than one-fortieth of the population.

Paradoxically, the very boldness of color, and the extravagance and exoticism of the details, lent verisimilitude to the work. If it resembled fiction, this could only be because, as the cliché had it, truth was stranger than fiction. Contemporary reviewers often compared it with fiction or romance, and almost invariably in the most favorable sense. The *Morning Chronicle* was proud to quote the comment of its rival, the *Sun*: 'At this auspicious moment the *Morning Chronicle* has published a series of revelations of London life—revelations so marvellous, so horrible, and so heart-rending, that few histories can equal, and no fiction surpass them.'[28] And one of Mayhew's colleagues on the *Chronicle*, the novelist Thackeray, wrote a similar tribute in *Punch*:[29]

> What a confession it is that we have almost all of us been obliged to make! A clever and earnest-minded writer gets a commission from the *Morning Chronicle* newspaper, and reports upon the state of our poor in London; he goes amongst labouring people and poor of all kinds—and brings back what? A picture of human life so wonderful, so awful, so piteous and pathetic, so exciting and terrible, that readers of romances own they never read anything like to it; and that the griefs, struggles, strange adventures

here depicted exceed anything that any of us could imagine. Yes; and these wonders and terrors have been lying by your door and mine ever since we had a door of our own. We had but to go a hundred yards off and see for ourselves, but we never did . . . We are of the upper classes; we have had hitherto no community with the poor. We never speak a word to the servant who waits on us for twenty years. . . Some clear-sighted, energetic man like the writer of the *Chronicle* travels into the poor man's country for us, and comes back with his tale of terror and wonder.

It would be interesting to know whether Mayhew was inspired by Thackeray's comment to write the kind of preface he did to the first volume of *London Labour*. For there is a clear echo of Thackeray in Mayhew's image of himself as a 'traveller in the undiscovered country of the poor,' bringing back information about people of whom as little was known as of 'the most distant tribes of the earth,' and presenting facts 'so extraordinary' that they might well be suspected of being the kind of tales that travelers were wont to tell.[30] Whatever Mayhew's intentions, the effect of this image was surely to disarm suspicion. If it was a distant and hitherto undiscovered country that Mayhew was reporting from—and the description of the street-folk as species more akin to the Bushman and Bedouin than to the civilized Englishman reenforced this image—anything was possible; indeed the most extraordinary things were most credible, testifying as they did to the uniqueness of the species, the remoteness of the country. It was in this spirit that one reviewer greeted the work, paraphrasing Mayhew's prefatory remarks as if they were self-evidently true:[31]

He has travelled through the unknown regions of our metropolis, and returned with full reports concerning the strange tribes of men which he may be said to have discovered. For, until his researches had taken place, who knew of the nomad races which daily carries on its predatory operations in our streets, and nightly disappears in quarters wholly unvisited by the portly citizens of the East as by perfumed whiskerandoes of the West End? An important and valuable addition has thus been made to our knowledge. In a volume replete with curious facts, authenticated by absolute proof, as well as by the high character of the author, we have a description of a class of the population perfectly marvellous to contemplate.

The suspension of disbelief induced by the metaphor of the unknown country meant not only that the most dramatic and exotic facts could be taken as true, but also that those dramatic and exotic facts could be assumed to be true of a large class of people. If the street-folk could have remained unknown for so long, why not the 'poor' as well? How was one to know that the characteristics of the former were not those of the latter? Thackeray, horrified to learn of the 'wonders and terrors' lurking, unknown to him, not a hundred yards from his door, was prepared to believe that the 'upper classes' had never had any community with 'the poor,' had never spoken a word to their servants, knew nothing of their tradesmen or workmen—and that, therefore, Mayhew had indeed reported accurately upon 'the state of our poor in London.' He was so appalled by his own evident ignorance that it did not occur to him that if he had never spoken to his servants, neither, apparently, had Mayhew.

There is, however, some excuse for Thackeray, his comments having been evoked by the *Morning Chronicle* articles, which did cover a wider range of Labour and the Poor than the later pamphlets or volumes. What is interesting is that both the pamphlets and the volumes, in spite of their specific and dramatic focus on the street-folk, should have elicited much the same reactions as had the articles. A reviewer of the first volume, having paraphrased Mayhew's most extreme judgments of the street-folk ('more degraded than the savages of New Zealand, than the blacks of the Great Karroo, or the insular communities of the Pacific . . .'), having remarked upon their peculiar racial attributes ('greater development of the animal than of the intellectual or moral nature . . . high cheek bones and protruding jaws . . .'), and having even specified their numbers ('upwards of fifty thousand individuals, or about a fortieth of the inhabitants of London'), concluded by recommending Mayhew's 'noble work' as 'a history of the poor in the nineteenth century.'[32] Another reviewer reversed the order, opening with a statement that seemed to suggest a work of the largest scope— 'an inquiry into the actual condition of the London poor' (in the second sentence this became 'the million poor of London')—and ending up with the casual remark that so far (the first volume and about half of the second) the work was still entirely devoted to the street-folk.[33]

Still another reviewer made a point of the fact that the work dealt with those who 'derive their living from the streets,' 'a class decidedly lower in the social scale than the labourer.' But his brief comments on Mayhew came in the course of an article on 'The Charities and the Poor of London,' which repeatedly referred to 'the metropolitan poor' and 'the London poor.'[34] Moreover, one of the main themes of this article was the intimate relationship between poverty on the one hand and crime and a generally uncivilized condition on the other, so that the force of the earlier class distinction was dissipated:[35]

> Guilt and poverty are closely connected. Misconduct leads to poverty,
> poverty tempts to crime. To discriminate between them would be as hard
> a task as that imposed by the Lord Mayor on the mutinous scavengers
> when they remonstrated that they were hired to remove the dirt, but not
> the snow . . . It matters not with what views the philanthropist begins
> his task. The humane are anxious to supply the physical wants of the poor,
> the statesman tries to raise their social condition, the missionary sighs to
> enlighten their spiritual darkness. The means which all must employ are
> the same. If they would christianize, they must civilize. If they would feed,
> they must reform. In short, charity must embrace every effort which
> benevolence can devise to rouse the slothful, tame the brutal, instruct the
> ignorant, and preach the Gospel to the native heathen.

The paradox of Mayhew's work—that the image derived from a relatively small, highly distinctive group of moral and social 'aliens' should get superimposed on the entire class of London Labour and the Poor—has so far been accounted for in terms of the work itself: the history of its publication, the expectations aroused by its title, the encyclopedic-like massiveness of the work, the inflationary effect of its statistics and style, and the blank check of credibility normally extended to the traveler in unknown lands. But the paradox is so great that it could hardly have been generated, still less sustained, by this work alone. And indeed, the work, whether in the earlier series or in the complete edition, was not nearly so often referred to as might be thought. There is, for example, no mention of Mayhew in the letters, memoirs, or biographies of many of his contemporaries who might be expected to have spoken of him: Dickens, George Eliot, Mrs Gaskell, Disraeli, Gladstone, Bright, Mill, Marx, Engels.[36] And there were prominent journals and newspapers that never reviewed or even alluded to his work. To be sure, books do not have to be read or reviewed to be influential. But the paucity of references and reviews does suggest a more limited influence than might be supposed.

Mayhew was, in fact, less influential than symptomatic. If he did not create a novel image of the poor, he did reflect, disseminate, and perpetuate a not uncommon image. The impressionable reader may have been taken in by Mayhew's claim to originality, but one reason why he was taken in was precisely because Mayhew was not all that original, because enough of his 'unknown' world was familiar from other sources to make it credible.

One might plausibly suppose that a major source of this image was the actual condition of the poor at the time, the extreme impoverishment and debasement of the 'Hungry Forties.' Yet it is now generally accepted that the forties were not nearly so hungry as they were once made out to be, and that the late forties were less hungry still. But if the time was not one of acute hunger, it was one of anxiety and crisis: the Irish famine, the financial crisis, revolutions on the Continent and the fear of revolution at home, and, climactically and most disastrously (for London slum-dwellers at any rate), the cholera epidemic.

This atmosphere of anxiety and crisis, a sense of psychic and social dislocation, pervades all of Mayhew's work. The 'miasma' of noxious vapors which contemporaries held responsible for the epidemic seems to have infected the very pages of his book. Although his article on Jacob's Island was not reprinted in the pamphlet series or in the later volumes, the memory and impressions of that visit to the most wretched of all slums at the worst of all times may well have affected his vision of the slum-world in general—and not only his vision but also his expectation, so that he later looked for similar cases of desperation and degradation. Or perhaps he simply felt impelled to sustain the dramatic pace of that initial article. For whatever reason, the life of the street-folk, as Mayhew described it, had all the symptoms of an epidemic situation—feverish, frenetic, anxiety-ridden, demoralized, and dehumanized. The society he depicted was in a visible state of dissolution, the people in a morbid, pathological condition, a condition that was permanently critical, imminently fatal.

But the forties were not only a decade of crisis. They were also a decade of reform—actual reforms, proposals for reform, and most important in this connection, revelations of the need for reform. Paradoxically, this movement for reform intensified the sense of crisis and reenforced the most extreme image of pathological poverty. The famous Blue Books—Royal Commission and Select Committee reports on sanitation, housing, health, interment, and the like—presented the Condition of the People in terms not very different from Mayhew's; indeed Mayhew himself drew upon the Blue Books for his own work. The reports were ostensibly intended to elicit the condition of the laboring classes as a whole. But inevitably the tendency was to emphasize the worst conditions of the lowliest poor. In part this was the result of an obvious strategy—to attract attention and promote the desired reforms; in part the result of an entirely natural and unconscious disposition towards the dramatic. Even the actual reforms provoked by the reports, reforms intended to ameliorate the worst of those conditions and to some degree at least having that effect, had also the unwitting side-effect of focusing attention on those conditions, thus perpetuating the image of unredeemed and unredeemable poverty.

The most influential of these reports was *The Sanitary Condition of the Labouring Population of Great Britain*, published in 1842 and extensively discussed in parliament, the press, and the journals. In view of the astonishment later expressed by Thackeray and other readers of Mayhew's work over the existence of an unknown world in their very backyards, it is interesting to find the report, a decade earlier, making the same claim to the discovery of the same unknown world:[37]

> The statements of the condition of considerable proportions of the
> labouring population of the towns into which the present inquiries have
> been carried have been received with surprise by persons of the wealthier
> classes living in the immediate vicinity, to whom the facts were as strange
> as if they related to foreigners or the natives of an unknown country . . .
> The inhabitants of the front houses . . . have never entered the adjoining
> courts, or seen the interior of any of the tenements, situated [sic] at the
> backs of their own houses, in which their own workpeople or dependents
> reside.

Edwin Chadwick, author of the Sanitary Report, invoked the metaphor of the unknown country for much the same reason as Mayhew later did: to account for the public's ignorance of the shocking conditions described in that report—the foul odors of open cesspools; the garbage, excrement, and dead rats rotting in the streets; the filth and scum floating in the river; the sewage that passed as drinking water. If it was not an entirely successful metaphor (surely the smells at least must have reached the front houses and given the rich a whiff of the world behind them), it did serve to distract attention from the question of the actual extent and pervasiveness of those conditions. How considerable, in fact, were the 'considerable proportions of the labouring population' who were subjected to these noisome conditions? The report did not say. But it did have the effect of irrevocably associating the 'labouring population' of the title with the most vivid, the most dramatic, and the most disagreeable scenes depicted there. And because those scenes were so much worse than anything the reader could be presumed to have witnessed—hence the metaphor of the unknown country—the report also had the effect of making 'foreigners,' aliens, out of the 'labouring population' who lived in such unnatural and repulsive circumstances.

Mayhew's work was, in a sense, a dramatic rendition of the Sanitary Report. Where the report merely had the laboring classes living in the midst of rubbish, filth, offal, and excrement, Mayhew's street-folk, or at least the more memorable of them, lived *off*, actually made their livelihood out of that rubbish and filth.[38] In grisly and fascinating detail, Mayhew described the several varieties of 'street-finders': bone-grubbers, rag-gatherers, rat-catchers, sweeps, scavengers, dredgermen, and, most unforgettably, the 'pure-finders' ('pure' being the euphemism for dog's dung, which was used in the tanning of leather).

There is a curious and disturbing correspondence between the 'sanitary condition' described by Chadwick and the human condition described by Mayhew. And there is the equally disturbing habit of contemporaries of using the same word to describe both: 'residuum' referred to the offal, excrement, and other waste that constituted the sanitary problem, and was also the name applied to the lowest layer of society that constituted the social and political problem. In Mayhew's work, the two usages of the word dramatically, tragically merge.

The Sanitary Report was, in effect, a sequel to the Poor Law Report—and not only because Chadwick happened to be the author of both, but because his experience with the administration of the New Poor Law had made him acutely aware of the relationship between debility and pauperdom. And as the Poor Law Report inspired the Sanitary Report, so it also inspired, although more subtly and obliquely, Mayhew's work.

One of the main purposes of the Poor Law Report was the elimination of what it called the 'mischievous ambiguity of the word poor'—the popular tendency to confound the 'poor man' with the 'pauper,' the former earning his subsistence by his own labor, the latter being sustained by private or public charity.[39] Of the common varieties of pauper—the aged, the infirm, abandoned children, and the 'able-bodied'—the report was particularly concerned with the last, its primary purpose being to distinguish the 'able-bodied pauper' from the 'independent labourer.'

In insisting upon that distinction, the report was seeking to discredit and abolish the Speenhamland policy: the giving of allowances, or 'aids-in-wages,' to laborers whose earnings fell below a given standard. The implication of Speenhamland was that laborers and paupers were, in principle at least, undifferentiated, both being potentially or actually dependent upon relief, and both being presumed to have the same minimum standard of subsistence. Whether Speenhamland had the actual effect, as the report claimed and as historians long assumed, of 'pauperizing the poor'—making more laborers dependent upon relief than would otherwise have been the case—has recently been disputed.[40] But it did have the effect of obfuscating a distinction that had never been very clear, of making pauperdom as normal, almost as respectable, as poverty, and of assimilating pauper and poor within a single class.

The Poor Law of 1834, which incorporated all the recommendations of the report, was (like Speenhamland) far less effective in practice than its supporters claimed at the time or than historians once believed. But it did succeed in dramatizing and popularizing an image of pauperdom that became as much a part of the social reality as the law itself. The report had distinguished between 'the two classes' of independent laborers and able-bodied paupers.[41] And the law had tried to give substance to that distinction by strictly limiting relief to paupers and by giving it to them in such a way as to create an unmistakeable gulf between them and the independent laborers. Thus the famous principle of 'eligibility': that the condition of the pauper receiving relief be less 'eligible' (i.e. desirable) than that of the independent laborer. And thus the workhouse principle: that relief be given the able-bodied only within the confines of the workhouse, which would have had the literal, physical effect of segregating him from the independent poor. And thus, too, the 'workhouse test,' the ultimate deterrent to discourage the poor from crossing over into the world of the pauper.

In accentuating the differences between the two classes, the report also accentuated the image of pauperdom. The pauper was regarded as not simply poorer than the poor; he was presumed to be qualitatively different. Indeed, even if the pauper were richer than the independent laborer (as he might be, the report claimed, under the old Poor Law), his condition was nevertheless worse: 'In every district, the condition of the independent labourer [was] strikingly distinguishable from that of the pauper, and superior to it, though the independent labourers were commonly maintained upon less money.'[42] Not only the pauper's condition but also his character and manner of life were distinctively worse than the independent laborer's—and for no other reason than that of dependence. The laborer turned pauper lost his previous 'air of content and cheerfulness'; he became 'dirty, ill fed, discontented, careless and vicious,' his wife 'dirty, and nasty, and indolent,' his children 'neglected, and dirty, and vagrants, and immoral.' Paupers were typically 'callous of their own degradation,' given to 'indolence, improvidence, or vice.'[43]

The Poor Law was concerned with paupers, and agricultural paupers for the most part; Mayhew with the street-folk of London. Every commentator on Mayhew has remarked upon the compassion he evidently felt for his subjects; few commentators on the Poor Law would think to credit it with that particular trait. In principle and in detail, Mayhew was opposed to much, if not all, of the New Poor Law. Yet Mayhew's work is extraordinarily reminiscent of that law. Both display what might be called the paradoxical effect of differentiation: the sharper the differentiation between the subgroup and the larger group, the more dramatic the image of the former in contrast to the latter, the more inevitable it was that that dramatic image should be transposed to the larger group. Thus the poor became saddled with the supposedly worst attributes of the pauper.

Indeed Mayhew's street-folk were even more sharply differentiated from the laboring poor than were the paupers. The new law made of the paupers a class apart;

Mayhew made of his subjects a race apart. The harshest Poor Law Guardian would not have ascribed to his charges (at least not publicly) the distinctive racial and physical features with which Mayhew endowed his. And in moral and social qualities, his street-folk were more than a match for the paupers. The costermongers, the largest group among them, were 'a foul disgrace . . . utterly creedless, mindless, and principleless . . . [a] vast dungheap of ignorance and vice . . . a social pestilence in the very heart of the land . . . dangerous classes . . . one and all ready, upon the least disturbance, to seize and disable their policeman.'[44] The street-children were remarkable for their 'extraordinary licentiousness'; 'nothing can well exceed the extreme animal fondness for the opposite sex which prevails among them'; their 'unnatural precocity,' Mayhew suggested, should cause us to revise our notions of the age of puberty.[45] The dockers were animal, mechanical, natural, barely human: 'a human steam-engine . . . a striking instance of mere brute force with brute appetites . . . as unskilled as the power of a hurricane.'[46] And the vagabonds, wandering through the country were 'a stream of vice and disease—a tide of iniquity and fever.'[47]

Yet it cannot be emphasized enough that such comments, however numerous and abrasive, were significantly different in tone and intention from similar comments voiced by Chadwick or Senior. If Mayhew sometimes ascribed the unsavory qualities of his street-folk to innate racial or moral dispositions, he as often ascribed them to the unfortunate circumstances of environment. On one page the typical dock-laborer was said to have been 'shut out from the usual means of life by the want of character';[48] while several pages later his miseries were attributed not to 'any particular malformation of his moral constitution' but to the 'precarious character of his calling':[49]

> His vices are the vices of ordinary human nature. Ninety-nine in every hundred commit similar enormities. If the very winds could whistle away the food and firing of wife and children, I doubt much whether, after a week's or a month's privation, we should many of us be able to prevent ourselves from falling into the very same excesses.
>
> It is consoling to moralise in our easy chairs, after a good dinner, and to assure ourselves that we should do differently. Self-denial is not very difficult when our stomachs are full and our backs are warm, but let us live a month of hunger and cold, and assuredly we should be as self-indulgent as they.

Similarly the description of the costermongers as 'a foul disgrace . . . a vast dungheap . . .' was followed by a paragraph of explanation that was nothing less than extenuation: 'It would be a marvel indeed if it were otherwise . . .That they are ignorant and vicious as they are, surely is not their fault . . . We should have been as they are, had not some one done for us what we refuse to do for them. . .'[50]

Sometimes the fact of race or innate character was presented as its own excuse: how can men who 'are as much creatures of the present as the beasts of the field' be expected to be provident? But again, in the very next sentence, it was the hazards of weather and occupation that made them improvident.[51] Even the subject of race took on a different aspect towards the end of the first volume, when he distinguished among those '*bred* to the streets,' those who '*take* to the streets,' and those '*driven* to the streets.' Of these, only the second were responsible for their condition, since only they were 'wanderers by choice, rather than wanderers by necessity.' And although he was candid enough about the vices of this group—they were predatory, dishonest, immoral, with 'the instincts of the brute or the artifice of the demon'—he was at pains to point out that they were the least numerous of the three groups, that they were no more predatory or dishonest than 'a large portion of even our wealthy tradesmen,' and that they were in any case 'worthy of our pity.'[52]

One sometimes has the impression that Mayhew was deliberately bringing out the worst in his street-folk in order to claim for them the same compassion and concern that most reformers reserved only for the 'deserving poor.' In another work he explained why the 'undeserving poor' had a greater claim to sympathy than the 'deserving':[53]

> Are we all so immaculate that we have no sympathy but for the *deserving* poor. Is our pity limited merely to those only who suffer the least, because they suffer with an unaccusing conscience; and must we *entirely* shut out from our commiseration the wretch who is tormented not only with hunger, but with the self-reproaches of his own bosom.

And not only sympathy but also assistance ought to be given in such a way as to respect the nature of those in need of it. 'If anything effectual is to be done in the way of reforming you,' he told an audience of parolees, 'Society must work in consonance and not in antagonism with your nature.' And having defined that nature as the 'love of a roving life,' he then proposed his own scheme of reform: the establishment of 'poor men's markets' where 'you are allowed to roam at will unchafed by restraints not congenial to your habits and feelings.'[54]

For the common variety of reformer, who sought to re-form the undeserving in the image of the deserving, Mayhew had no more respect than the reformer himself had for the objects of his benevolence:[55]

> Philanthropists always seek to do too much, and in this is to be found the main cause of their repeated failures. The poor are expected to become angels in an instant, and the consequence is, they are merely made *hypocrites*. Moreover, no men of any independence of character will submit to be washed, and dressed, and fed like schoolboys; hence none but the worst classes come to be experimented upon. It would seem, too, that this overweening disposition to play the part of *ped-agogues* (I use the word in its literal sense) to the poor, proceeds rather from a love of power than from a sincere regard for the people. Let the rich become the advisers and assistants of the poor, giving them the benefit of their superior education and means—but *leaving the people to act for themselves*—and they will do a

great good, developing in them a higher standard of comfort and moral excellence, and so, by improving their tastes, inducing a necessary change in their habits. But such as seek merely to *lord it* over those whom distress has placed in their power, and strive to bring about the *villeinage* of benevolence, making the people the philanthropic instead of the feudal, serfs of our nobles, should be denounced as the arch-enemies of the country. Such persons may mean well, but assuredly they achieve the worst towards the poor. The curfew-bell, whether instituted by benevolence or tyranny, has the same degrading effect on the people—destroying their principle of self-action, without which we are all but as the beasts of the field.

On specific policies of reform Mayhew was similarly at odds with most reformers. He condemned the New Poor Law for its workhouse principle, which served only to make labor repulsive and degrading. He condemned the principle of eligibility, which sought to make the condition of the pauper less eligible instead of making the condition of the laborer more eligible. He opposed the attempts to encourage emigration, arguing that what was needed was not fewer workers but higher wages. He criticized Shaftesbury's Ragged Schools for being ineffective and even counter-productive, for serving as schools of crime instead of reformation.

Yet in spite of all these differences of attitude, intention, and policy, Mayhew shared with the conventional reformers—indeed he carried further than they did—the one idea that may have been more decisive than all their differences. This was the idea of a 'class' of paupers, a 'race' of street-folk, uncivilized and unsocialized. And precisely because Mayhew's work was written under such different impulses and intentions, its effect in reenforcing the prevailing image of that class may have been all the greater—still more, because it came at a time when the Poor Law itself was being increasingly evaded and discredited. By the late forties, it had become abundantly clear that paupers and poor could not be so tidily divided and segregated as either the report or the law had envisaged. Relief was being given to the able-bodied outside the workhouses; it was being given on a much larger scale than had been anticipated; and there was more popular and even parliamentary sentiment against the law than at any time since its passage.

Precisely at that time Mayhew came along and, with the most laudable intentions and in the most generous spirit, portrayed a class with all the stigmata of the pauper class. And because his was an ambiguous class, neither pauper nor the conventional 'deserving' poor, and because he claimed for it all the compassion generally accorded to the deserving poor (and for all the other reasons already discussed that made for a confusion of categories), those stigmata were insensibly transferred to the whole class of the poor.

As the Sanitary Report was a sequel to the Poor Law, so the Poor Law was, in a sense, a sequel to Malthus's *Essay on Population*. And Mayhew's work displays the same paradoxical affinity to Malthus's as it does to the Poor Law. In intention and policy Mayhew was utterly opposed to Malthusianism (or what was taken as such). The cause of low wages, he insisted, was not the over-supply of labor but the under-consumption of the produce of labor, and the remedy for the lower classes consisted neither in curbing nor transporting population but rather in the payment of higher wages.[56]

Mayhew rarely referred to Malthus by name, although he did often refer to and quote from Adam Smith, John Stuart Mill, J.-B. Say, and other political economists. Yet his work had far more in common with Malthus than he may have liked to think. Indeed, it is as if he had set out to write the book that Malthus had said was wanting. In his *Essay*, Malthus had observed that the 'laws' of population had previously gone unrecognized because the histories of mankind were almost always the 'histories only of the higher classes,' so that there were few reliable accounts of 'the manners and customs of that part of mankind' where the pressures of population upon food were most keenly felt—the 'lower classes of society.'[57] It remained for Mayhew to write that account.

The effect of Mayhew's work was unwittingly to confirm in fact what he disputed in theory and policy. The world he described was quintessentially Malthusian. His street-folk occupied that marginal area of society where population pressed hardest against the means of subsistence, producing all the misery and vice that Malthus had ascribed to that situation. Indeed the refrain, 'misery and vice,' appears as often in Mayhew as in Malthus. If Mayhew was able to inject into his account moments of gayety and high spirits, if his street-folk sometimes seemed to revel in their misery and vice, this only testified to the extent to which they were abandoned in vice—or so the Malthusian (and often Mayhew himself) saw it. And although Mayhew denied the causal connection between overpopulation and low wages, he dramatically attested to the facts of overpopulation and misery in his memorable description of the dockyards:[58]

> In the scenes I had lately witnessed the want has been positively tragic, and the struggle for life partaking of the sublime... It is a sight to sadden the most callous, to see thousands of men struggling for only one day's hire; the scuffle being made the fiercer by the knowledge that hundreds out of the number there assembled must be left to idle the day out in want. To look in the faces of that hungry crowd is to see a sight that must be ever remembered ...
>
> The scenes witnessed at the London Dock were of so painful a description, the struggle for one day's work—the scramble for twenty-four hours' extra-subsistence and extra-life were of so tragic a character, that I was anxious to ascertain if possible the exact number of individuals in and around the metropolis who live by dock labour ... At one of the docks alone I found that 1823 stomachs would be deprived of food by the mere chopping of the breeze ... That the sustenance of thousands of families should be as fickle as the very breeze itself; that the weathercock should

be the index of daily want or daily ease to such a vast number of men,
women, and children, was a climax of misery and wretchedness that I
could not have imagined to exist; and since that I have witnessed such
scenes of squalor, and crime, and suffering, as oppress the mind even to
a feeling of awe.

Darwin himself could not have portrayed better the struggle for existence; indeed had
Darwin not found inspiration for his theory in Malthus, he could well have done so in
Mayhew.[59]

If the struggle for existence was waged on the dockyards, the common lodging-
houses where many of the dockers lived exemplified those 'checks to population'
which Malthus had made so much of and which were the basis of Darwin's theory of
natural selection. Mayhew described the crowded rooms emitting 'so rank and foul a
stench' that he was sickened by 'a moment's inhalation of the fetid atmosphere,'[60]
with the occupants exhibiting every variety of wretchedness and degradation—
drunkenness, brutality, violence, criminality, apathy, and despair—the whole range
of misery and vice which constituted Malthus's 'positive' checks to population.
The common lodging-houses were the extreme case of such checks, as the dockers
represented the extreme case of misery and vice. But to one degree or another, all of
Mayhew's street-folk may be taken as an object lesson in Malthusianism: the misery
and vice that shortened, prevented, and degraded life among the lower classes.

In Mayhew's world, as in Malthus's, the extremes of poverty coexisted with the
extremes of wealth. Malthus had made a great point of this in his quarrel with Adam
Smith. Against Smith's proposition that the increased wealth of the nation necessarily
benefited all classes alike, Malthus argued that an increase of wealth in the form of
manufactured goods rather than food (as was likely in Britain) could only have an
adverse effect on the poor, since it would result in an increase in population without a
corresponding increase in the means of subsistence. Thus the rich would get richer
while the poor got poorer. This was exactly the situation which Mayhew found in the
docks of London:[61]

> The docks of London are to a superficial observer the very focus of
> metropolitan wealth. The cranes creak with the mass of riches. In the
> warehouses are stored goods that are as it were ingots of untold gold . . .
> There are acres upon acres of treasure, more than enough, one would
> fancy, to stay the cravings of the whole world, and yet you have but to
> visit the hovels grouped round about all this amazing excess of riches to
> witness the same amazing excess of poverty. If the incomprehensibility of
> the wealth rises to sublimity, assuredly the want that co-exists with it is
> equally incomprehensible and equally sublime.

There is another less obvious but ultimately more important affinity between
Malthus and Mayhew. Malthus had opposed the New Poor Law for the reason that he
opposed any Poor Law: because however 'less eligible' the condition of the pauper
might be, however much he might be segregated from the independent laborer, any

money or food given to the pauper left so much less for the laborer. Moreover, since such a policy would lead to an increase of population without any increase of subsistence, the whole body of the poor would bear that additional burden. In effect, Malthus was saying that there were not 'two classes' but only one, and that the whole of the poor would be pauperized by the operation of a Poor Law.

The New Poor Law was passed in contravention of Malthus and in the conviction that the two classes could be kept separate, that relief could be given on such terms as to prevent the pauper from impinging on the condition of the poor. In a sense Mayhew's work seemed to bear out Malthus's fears. For just as the New Poor Law failed in practice to maintain the distinction between its two classes, so Mayhew, having first distinguished so sharply between the street-folk and the rest of the poor, then blurred that distinction. This is not to say that Malthus was confirmed in actuality, that the poor were actually pauperized as a result of the New Poor Law, still less as a result of Mayhew's work. But it does suggest that the distinction itself—whether Mayhew's or the Poor Law's—had the *conceptual* effect of pauperizing the poor by first creating the most distinctive, most dramatic image of the lowest class, and then imposing that image upon the lower classes as a whole.

A similar effect can also be seen in the work of other of Mayhew's contemporaries, who, for all their differences, shared essentially the same conception of poverty, the same image of the poor. One can see this, for example, in Shaftesbury's speeches on the 'Dwelling Places of the Working Classes.' The speeches, under this or similar titles, were pleas for the regulation and inspection of the common lodging-houses, which were inhabited by transients, casual laborers, and those reduced to the lowest level of existence, and which so often degenerated into the dens of iniquity depicted by Mayhew. But these common lodging-houses were hardly the typical 'dwelling places of the working classes.' Shaftesbury was as well aware of this as anyone. He opened one speech by distinguishing between the 'stationary' and 'migratory' elements in the cities, the former occupying ordinary lodging-houses (one or two rooms per family) and the latter the common lodging-houses (some containing fifty to one hundred men in a room). But in the course of the opening paragraph, he moved rapidly from the former to the latter, with the rest of the speech devoted to descriptions of the worst kinds of common lodging-houses and recommendations for their control.[62] Thus the agitation for the reform of these wretched conditions had the paradoxical result of reenforcing the image of an utterly degraded and alien class—particularly since the middle-class audience to which it was directed, knowing (or convinced that it knew) nothing about the dwelling-places of the working classes, was prepared to believe the worst.

Shaftesbury himself is an excellent example of the reformer whose conscious purpose may well have been at odds with his unintended effect. His intent was reformist, meliorative, and preeminently humane. But what inspired his reformism and humanitarianism—and what distinguished him so markedly from either Chadwick or Mayhew—was his Evangelicalism. And that Evangelicalism, which made him so zealous a reformer, also colored his image of those in need of reform. To the reform-minded Evangelical, original sin was not only the primal, metaphysical condition of man; it was also the actual, existential condition of a social class. As Gladstone sought out fallen women and tried to convince them of their evil ways, so Shaftesbury sought to redeem the class of fallen men. In good Calvinist fashion, he attributed the 'deep moral and physical degradation' of the lowest class to their state of 'practical heathenism,' 'a heathenism as complete as if they were found in California or Timbuctoo.'[63] And in good Victorian fashion, he found it easy to make the transition from the part to the whole—from the 'thousands' of heathen-vagabonds 'in our highways and hedges, in our streets and alleys, in our courts and lanes,' to the 'large mass of the people of these realms' whose spiritual and intellectual condition was so debased, and finally to the 'labouring classes' whose 'social condition' he was ostensibly describing.[64]

In 1853 *The Times* paid tribute to Shaftesbury:[65]

> To purify the inferno that reeks about us in this Metropolis, to recover its inmates, and to drive the incorrigible nucleus into more entire insulation, is one of the labours to which Lord Shaftesbury has devoted his life; and we can never be sufficiently obliged to him for undertaking a task which, besides its immediate disagreeableness, associates his name with so much that is shocking and repulsive.

Like the Poor Law reformers, Shaftesbury may have sought to 'drive the incorrigible nucleus into more entire insulation.' But his effect may have been quite the opposite: to associate all the poor, as he was himself associated, with 'so much that is shocking and repulsive.'

One could cite other evidence to the same effect: Carlyle, for example, who had the most rigorous and puritanical idea of the virtue of work and who therefore might have been expected to distinguish most sharply between the working class and what we would now call a 'lumpen' class; but who was also so obsessed with what he took to be the Condition of the People that he was convinced that the working class was becoming morally pauperized.[66] Or Dickens, whose most memorable characters and scenes were Mayhewian (or perhaps Mayhew's were Dickensian), so that it is these that give his work its distinctive quality; yet who made an obvious effort to de-Mayhewianize them in the end, to redeem his heroes by having them give up their exotic ways—in effect, to take them off the street and make of them respectable indoor folk.[67] Or all those books whose titles were more memorable than their contents and conjured up the most lurid vision of the metropolis: *The Rookeries of London, The Sorrows of the Streets, Ragged London, Sanitary Ramblings, Night Side of London, London's Shadows, Sinks of London Laid Open.*[68]

One could also cite rarer instances of the opposite tendency, attempts to resist the melodramatic, to keep in mind the distinctions and relative numbers of Mayhewian poor and laboring poor. There were those who charged Mayhew with exaggeration and misrepresentation. It is interesting that most of these criticisms were directed against the *Morning Chronicle* articles, particularly the accounts of the needlewomen and tailors. *The Economist* objected that Mayhew had grossly underestimated the workers' earnings by relying entirely on their own statements without checking the employers' records.[69] The *Athenaeum* suspected that the articles had been written 'for the mere sake of effect,' but found the published volume more subdued in tone and the information 'more copious and precise.'[70] The *Edinburgh Review* first criticized Charles Kingsley for accepting at face value the *Chronicle* articles;[71] and then, in a review of still another book, questioned not the literal validity but rather the significance of Mayhew's portraits of the 'class of beings *below* the working classes, permanently and almost hopelessly degraded.'[72] 'They are true as scenes,' it objected. 'Are they true as general delineations? Are they *specimens*, or *exceptions*? How deep do these miseries go? Are they characteristic of a class, or only of individuals of that class?'[73]

The questions, of course were rhetorical, the reviewer having little doubt that Mayhew's scenes were not typical, that the misery was neither so deep nor so widespread as might be thought. But why, he went on, were such scenes so commonly misrepresented? Why was the condition of England so often made out to be much worse than it was, worse, indeed, than it had been in the past? Perhaps, he suggested, it was precisely because the condition of England had so considerably improved, both materially and morally, that contemporaries were dissatisfied with those lesser evils that remained. People acquired a heightened sensitivity to suffering. Conditions once accepted as normal were now found to be intolerable. Miseries once hidden from view were exposed in the very process of remedying them. The very facts of progress were introduced as evidence of regression.

Another and diametrically opposed view of the social reality was put forward by the Christian Socialist J. M. Ludlow in *Fraser's Magazine*. After citing the *Morning Chronicle* articles as evidence of the deplorable condition of 'Labour and the Poor' (the title of his article), Ludlow faced the obvious objection: 'Still, it may be said, Your accounts apply only to the emphatically underpaid and suffering classes. Starvation wages and unwholesome diet are not the characteristics of the bulk of London workmen.' This objection he promptly disposed of:[74]

> But what if they be the characteristics of a daily-increasing class?—if the fallen condition of the Spitalfields weaver be only the full-developed type of what is everywhere taking place? . . . So that, whilst the poor are getting poorer, the comparatively well-off are either sinking into poverty or becoming the mere parasites of labour, swelling the helplessness or sharpening the tyranny.

This mode of reasoning is obvious and familiar. The idea of 'immiseration,' as it is now called, has as ancient and respectable a lineage as the idea of progress. But in this context and at this time, we are inevitably reminded of Marx. There is no evidence that Ludlow had yet read the *Communist Manifesto*, and of course, his own brand of socialism was decidedly un-Marxist. Yet the echoes of the *Manifesto* are uncanny, not only in the ideas of the pauperization of the proletariat and the proletarianization of the 'comparatively well-off,' but also of the 'tyranny' accompanying this process. In this scheme of things, Mayhew's poor represent the proletariat *in extremis*, in the final stages of a degenerate and decadent capitalism.

Few contemporaries were as pessimistic about the future as Ludlow. Much more common was the sense of a precarious present. In the future, most people thought, the condition of the poor would probably get better, but in the here and now there was the persistent threat that it might get worse. The poor were seen as living on the edge of a precipice from which at any moment they might topple off into the abyss below. Even if relatively few actually toppled off, the fact that anyone might do so was an integral part of their social condition if only because it was a vital part of their consciousness—and not only of their consciousness but also of the consciousness of the upper classes. As the poor lived out their lives in the knowledge and fear of the abyss, so the rich lived in the knowledge and fear of that other 'nation' which had so tenuous a hold on respectable society. And their fear was not only for those who might actually lose their hold, but also for the avalanche that they might precipitate, an avalanche that might bury under it all of society.

The English, it has been noted *ad tedium*, never went through the experience of a French Revolution. But they did experience the fear of revolution. And those who did not themselves experience this fear often utilized and played upon it for reasons of their own. Charles Kingsley, in the pamphlet about which the *Edinburgh Review* had complained, described the conditions of the 'sweated' tailors in tones much more extravagant than the articles by Mayhew upon which the pamphlet was ostensibly based:[75] 'What is flogging, or hanging, King Ryence's paletot or the tanneres of Meudon, to the slavery, starvation, waste of life, year-long imprisonment in the dungeons narrower and fouler than those of the Inquisition, which goes on among thousands of free English clothes-makers at this day?' From this intolerable condition, combined with the greater education of workers, he predicted the direst consequences: 'The boiler will be strained to bursting pitch, till some jar, some slight crisis, suddenly directs the imprisoned forces to one point, and then—what then? Look at France, and see.'[76]

Mayhew spoke of the 'dangerous classes'—the costermongers in particular, who were, upon the slightest pretext, prepared 'to seize and disable their policeman.'[77] But not even the costermongers, still less the poor in general, were anything like the '*classes laborieuses et classes dangereuses*' that the Parisian poor were reputed to be.[78] Nor were they nearly so violent as they had been a century earlier. It may be that the improvement in public order and morality on the part of all classes, which began to be visible about the middle of the nineteenth century, made the crime and prostitution in the urban slums all the more conspicuous.[79] Similarly it might be said that precisely because the opportunities for civilization and socialization seemed so much greater, so much more available, the lapses from civilized, socialized behavior were all the more inexplicable and terrifying.

In 1833 de Tocqueville visited England. Two years later he wrote a 'Memoir on Pauperism' which opened with a curious and typically Tocquevillian observation. Why was it, he asked, that the most impoverished countries of Europe had the fewest paupers, while England, which was the most opulent country, had the most paupers? His answer, in effect, was that it was opulence that created pauperdom: those who by other standards would have been considered opulent, by the standards of opulence were considered so intolerably poor as to require relief.[80]

In current sociological parlance, this is now known as the 'theory of relative deprivation,' a corollary of which goes under the name of 'the revolution of rising expectations.' There is no doubt that Victorian England was peculiarly and critically affected by the phenomena of relative deprivation and rising expectations. And it was the rich as much as the poor who were affected by them—the 'rich' in this context being those who wrote about the poor: the authors of books and articles, the compilers of reports and members of commissions, the public speakers, organizers of charities, and Members of Parliament who were so largely preoccupied with the Condition-of-England question. It was their sense of the deprivation suffered by the poor, their expectations of how the poor should be living and behaving, which helped to shape their conception of poverty and their image of the poor.[81]

What has here been discussed, then, is a kind of identity crisis, a crisis afflicting not only those whose identity was at stake, but also those who were trying to define that identity and define themselves in relation to it. One is reminded of the master-slave relationship described by Hegel, in which each partner can find self-consciousness only through the consciousness, the recognition, of the other, and where the failure of that mutual recognition dooms the master as much as the slave to a state of bondage and of self-alienation.

Thus it was that the Victorian poor were, in a sense, the victims of the exacerbated sensibilities of the rich. The 'revelations,' as they were invariably called, of a Mayhew or Malthus, of a Sanitary or Poor Law Report, each came as a shock, as if such revelations had never been revealed before, as if the 'unknown country' had never been traversed before. And each shock, because it was not really a shock, further exacerbated the sensibilities, deepened the sense of guilt. Perhaps to atone for that guilt, as in an orgy of self-flagellation, perhaps to displace that guilt upon those seemingly responsible for it, the rich were prepared to believe the worst of themselves for having tolerated such conditions, and the worst of the poor whom they presumed to be living under those conditions.

One can speculate about other circumstances, other symbolic acts of displacement: the sexual impulse, for example, that caused the rich to create a class of 'other Victorians' who seemed to be liberated from the constraints of civilization, a civilization far more constraining than it had previously been.[82] The street-folk, as Mayhew described them, enjoyed a sexual freedom and license that might well have been the envy of those who could only indulge their 'secret lives' indoors, indeed behind locked doors, and for whom the streets, the open and public display of vice, must have been the one unattainable, unsatisfiable desire. If I have not here made more of the connection between the 'social problem' of poverty and the 'social evil,' as it was commonly called, of prostitution (or for that matter, of criminality in general), it is because I have not wanted to distract attention from poverty as such, or to make the image of poverty even more dramatic then it was. But certainly the connection was there, in Mayhew's work and elsewhere, and certainly the image of uninhibited sexuality was part of the contemporary image of poverty.

If this discussion of Mayhew seems in some respects to deflate his work, to make it appear less original in conception, less consistent and systematic in development, less comprehensive in scope, by the same token it may acquire greater importance as a representative and most revealing expression of the temper of the time. Diminished in numbers, the Mayhewian poor may find themselves enhanced in significance. In cold, hard actuality, they were nowhere near the 'London Labour and the London Poor' of the title, nothing like the 'labouring people of the world's greatest city of the nineteenth century,' still less the 'modern proletariat.' Then, as now, what passed as 'the culture of poverty' was the culture of a small subgroup of the poor. Yet that culture, or more precisely the image of that culture, was of momentous consequence in shaping the lives not only of the poor but of society as a whole.

Notes

(Some of these notes have been abridged for reasons of space. They will appear in more extensive form in a forthcoming work by the author, of which this chapter is part.)

1 See, for example, the titles of articles in the first few volumes of the *Journal of the Statistical Society of London*, from 1838. The singular form, 'working class,' never appears there and rarely elsewhere, although it does, of course, in Engels's work.

2 These are actually sub-subtitles, the complete title reading: 'London Labour and the London Poor; Cyclopaedia of the Condition and Earnings of Those That *Will* Work, Those That *Cannot* Work, and Those That *Will Not* Work.' After this there followed, in bold capitals, 'The London Street Folk,' with the remainder of the subtitle, 'comprising . . .' in smaller type. These were the titles of the 1851–2 edition as well as that of 1861–2 and 1864. The pagination in this essay follows the Dover edition reprint (New York, 1968) of the 1861–2 edition.

3 *Morning Chronicle (M.C.)*, 18 October 1849, 4. The Jacob's Island article had appeared on 24 September.

4 There seems, however, to have been no secret about Mayhew's identity. References to the articles in other journals frequently mentioned his name.

5 *M.C.*, 19 October 1849, 5.

6 Ibid., 23 October 1849, 5.

7 Ibid., 23 November 1849, 5. His figures here are revealing, for of the total number of needlewomen—33,500—20,800 were the excluded milliners and dressmakers, which left 13,900 in the slop-trade; and of the latter 11,400 were below the age of twenty, leaving (although Mayhew did not make explicit this final calculation) 2,500 adult women in the group he was describing.

8 Volume III includes some material dating from 1856 when Mayhew resumed publication of these pamphlets.

9 The more conventional trades make brief appearances in the second volume, in illustration of the problems of casual and surplus labor (pp. 297–322), and in the third volume in a chapter on the 'Garret-Masters,' the makers of cheap furniture (pp. 221–31).

10 Mayhew himself sometimes included 'artisans' among the poor and sometimes also the 10 percent of the artisans whom he described as the 'society men' of their trades (III, p. 221).

11 *London Labour*, I, p. 6; II, p. 3.

12 Ibid., II, p. 1.

13 The phrase 'wandering tribes' was often used at this time to describe the vagrants. But Mayhew used it generically, so to speak, to characterize the street-folk as a whole.

14 *London Labour*, I, p. 1.

15 Ibid., p. 2.

16 Ibid., pp. 2–3.

17 E. P. Thompson, 'The Political Education of Henry Mayhew,' *Victorian Studies*, xi (1967), 42. This article is an abridged version of one of the introductions to a selection of Mayhew's *Morning Chronicle* articles on the trades of London, which are being reprinted now for the first time, under the title *The Unknown Mayhew* (1971), ed. E. P. Thompson and Eileen Yeo. Unfortunately, this volume appeared too late for consideration here.

18 John D. Rosenberg, introduction to the Dover edn, I, p. vi.

19 This is not to say that all commentators and historians have been guilty of this confusion. The *Edinburgh Review* at the time was not (see notes 71–3). And among recent historians, H. J. Dyos has been sensitive to the actual subject matter of the work ('The Slums of Victorian London,' *Victorian Studies*, xi (1967), 12–13). For the most part, however, non-historians have proved to be more alert to the distinction between the Mayhewian poor and the conventional laboring poor. (E.g., the poet W. H. Auden reviewing the recent reprint of Mayhew, in *New Yorker*, 24 February 1968; the sociologist Ruth Glass, 'Urban Sociology in Great Britain,' *Current Sociology*, iv (1955), 43; A. F. Wells, *The Local Social Survey in Great Britain* (1935), pp. 21–22. Robert Mackenzie and Allan Silver, *Angels in Marble: Working class conservatives in urban England* (Chicago, 1968), p. 75). Curiously, it has been Mayhew's editors who have most often perpetuated the confusion (note 18 above): Peter Quennell, ed., *Mayhew's London* (1951), p. 18; John Bradley, ed. *Henry Mayhew's London* (Oxford, 1965), pp. viii–ix.

A curious misreading of Mayhew appears in a recent essay on 'Irish Slum Communities in Nineteenth-Century London,' by Lynn H. Lees. The author quotes Mayhew repeatedly to illustrate the prevailing English image of the London Irish as a degraded and savage race. She complains that such an image 'would have enraged observers if applied to the English working class,' and that these English observers deliberately ignored the fact 'that large numbers of English laborers lived in exactly the same way as many of the Irish did.' (*Nineteenth-Century Cities: Essays in the new urban history*, ed. S. Thernstrom and R. Sennett (New

Haven, 1969), pp. 359, 361.) Yet Mayhew himself amply demonstrates that the English had precisely the same image of their own lower classes.

20 This would seem to apply especially to Thompson. More than most historians, Thompson is well aware of the differences between the *Morning Chronicle* articles and *London Labour*. Had he chosen to describe the *Chronicle* articles as 'the fullest and most vivid documentation . . . of the labouring people,' the judgment would have been perhaps excessive but not altogether inappropriate. But it was *London Labour* that he described in those terms. Perhaps this came about because he wanted to include in his analysis not only the *Chronicle* articles, but also the endpapers of the pamphlets, where Mayhew replied to correspondents and expressed himself on such subjects as the causes of low wages. But to include the endpapers meant to include the pamphlets and hence the volumes of *London Labour* which were a reproduction of the pamphlets—a reproduction, however, that omitted both the endpapers and the articles on the more conventional types of 'labouring people.' Towards the end of his essay, Thompson gives some intimation of this difficulty:

> Somewhere in the late 1850's he seems to have given up the effort to comprehend or to offer remedies. The published volumes in the early 1860's held onto his old positions but showed little advance on the material already gathered by 1851. The working trades were in many cases dropped from the book to make room for the more colourful (and perhaps saleable) traders.
>
> (pp. 81–2)

But the 'working trades' were dropped, not in the 'late 1850's,' but at least as early as December 1850, when Mayhew explicitly chose as his subject the street-folk. They were dropped from the very pamphlets whose endpapers Thompson finds most rewarding.

There is another difficulty in Thompson's analysis. Even if he were to distinguish more carefully between the early articles and later volumes, the fact remains that the 'historic' Mayhew—the Mayhew that most contemporaries and almost all historians have known—is the Mayhew of *London Labour*. (The endpapers in particular were most ephemeral and least known.) Thompson may succeed in constructing for us another and perhaps more worthy Mayhew. But the new Mayhew is necessarily of less interest to the social historian.

More questionable still is Thompson's assertion that Charles Booth, in the late 1880s, 'rediscovered' the poverty (or the 'consciousness of poverty'—it is not clear which Thompson intends) that Mayhew had earlier discovered (p. 62). Surely this is to miss the essential difference between Mayhew and Booth—and, indeed, between mid-century and late-century society. Booth's was no 'rediscovery' of Mayhew's but rather the discovery, or uncovering, of a quite different species and consciousness of poverty.

21 *London Labour*, I, p. xv.

22 'Recent Aspects of Socialism,' *British Quarterly Review*, xi (1850), 419.

23 *London Labour*, I, p. viii.

24 Ibid., III, p. 347.

25 Ibid., p. 429.

26 Ibid., I, p. xv.

27 H. Sutherland Edwards, *Personal Recollections* (1900), p. 60.

28 *M.C.*, 18 December 1849, 6. The *Eclectic Review* recommended it as 'more entertaining than any fiction' ('Mayhew's Revelations of London,' xciv (1851), 436).

29 *Punch*, xviii (1850), 93.

30 *London Labour*, I, p. xv.

31 *Eclectic Review*, xciv (1851), 424–5.

32 Ibid., 424–5, 436.

33 *Athenaeum*, xxiv (1851), 1199–1201.

34 *Quarterly Review*, xcvii (1855), 411, 409.

35 Ibid., 414.

36 This is not to say that these contemporaries did not know of Mayhew or had not read him. For example, his name appears in none of the standard works by or about Shaftesbury. Yet we know from other sources that the two engaged in open and public controversy with each other.

37 *Report on the Sanitary Condition of the Labouring Population of Great Britain*, ed. M. W. Flinn (Edinburgh, 1965), p. 397.

38 The Sanitary Report was, of course, aware of the occupations of the bone-grubbers and pure-finders. At one point it even raised the question of their loss of employment if better modes of street-cleaning were adopted (pp. 164–5). But for the most part the Report was concerned with conditions, Mayhew with occupations.

39 *Report from His Majesty's Commissioners for Inquiring into the Administration and Practical Operation of the Poor Laws* (1834), p. 278.

40 Mark Blaug, 'The Myth of the Old Poor Law and the Making of the New,' *Journal of Economic History*, xxiii (1963); 'The Poor Law Report Re-examined,' ibid., xxiv (1964).

41 *Poor Law Report*, p. 89.

42 Ibid., p. 88.

43 Ibid., pp. 87, 93, 264.

44 *London Labour*, I, p. 101.

45 Ibid., p. 477.

46 Ibid., III, p. 301.

47 Ibid., p. 397. Note the epidemic metaphor here and in the reference to 'social pestilence' quoted above.

48 Ibid., p. 303

49 Ibid., p. 310.

50 Ibid., I, p. 101.

51 Ibid., I, p. 101.

52 Ibid., pp. 320–2.

53 Henry Mayhew and John Binny, *The Criminal Prisons of London and Scenes of Prison Life* (1968; reprint of 1st edn of 1862), p. 52.

54 *London Labour*, III, p. 432.

55 Ibid., II, p. 264.

56 These views are expressed only in passing in *London Labour* (e.g., II, p. 268), but are the main themes of his letters to correspondents on the endpapers of the pamphlet series.

57 T. R. Malthus, *On Population* (New York, 1960, reprint of 1st edn of 1798), pp. 15–16.

58 *London Labour*, III, pp. 303–4, 307–8.

59 There are even echoes of Mayhew's prose in Darwin. The 'feeling of awe' described here by Mayhew when he witnessed the 'sublime' struggle for life recalls the last paragraph of the *Origin of Species*, with its testimonial to the 'exalted object' served by the war of nature, the 'grandeur in this view of life.'

60 *London Labour*, III, p. 305.

61 Ibid., p. 308.

62 *Speeches of the Earl of Shaftesbury upon Subjects having relation chiefly to the Claims and Interests of the Labouring Class* (1868), pp. 269–80 (8 April 1851).

63 Ibid., p. 191 (25 May 1845). See also p. 226 (8 May 1848).

64 Ibid., p. 191 (25 May 1845).

65 J. Wesley Bready, *Lord Shaftesbury and Social and Industrial Progress* (1926), p. 104.

66 E.g., *Latter-Day Pamphlets* (New York, 1897), p. 286.

67 The case of Dickens is most interesting but too complicated to go into here. A recent article, trying to establish Dickens's indebtedness to Mayhew for some of the characters in *Our Mutual Friend*, is more revealing in showing how Dickens transformed those characters, if indeed he borrowed them in the first place. (See Harland S. Nelson, 'Dickens's *Our Mutual Friend* and Henry Mayhew's *London Labour and the London Poor*,' *Nineteenth Century Fiction*, xx (1965), 207–22.)

68 Thomas Beames, *The Rookeries of London* (1850); M. and S. Barber, *The Sorrows of the Streets* (1855); John Hollingshead, *Ragged London* (1861); H. Gavin, *Sanitary Ramblings* (1848); J. E. Ritchie, *Night Side of London* (1857); George Godwin, *London's Shadows* (1854); *Sinks of London Laid Open . . . with Flash Dictionary* (1848).

69 *The Economist*, viii (1850), 1265.

70 *Athenaeum*, xxiv (1851), 1199.

71 *Edinburgh Review*, xciii (1851), 8.

72 Ibid., 322. (Both reviews were by W. R. Greg.)

73 Ibid., 324.

74 *Fraser's Magazine*, xli (1850), 8.

75 Charles Kingsley, *Cheap Clothes and Nasty* (1850), p. 3.

76 Ibid., p. 31.

77 *London Labour*, I, p. 101.

78 Louis Chevalier, *Classes laborieuses et classes dangereuses à Paris pendant la première moitié du xixe siècle* (Paris, 1958). The contemporary use of the phrase, 'dangerous classes' was common (e.g. Mary Carpenter, *Reformatory Schools for the Children of the Perishing and Dangerous Classes . . .* (1851)). But even in England it was more often used of the French than of the English lower classes. In the *Sanitary Report*, Chadwick had a long discussion of the Paris water-carriers, scavengers, etc., whom he took to be much more 'dangerous' than their London equivalents. (*Report*, pp. 161ff.)

79 J. J. Tobias, *Crime and Industrial Society in the Nineteenth Century* (1969), pp. 122ff.; Harold Perkin, *The Origins of Modern English Society 1780–1880* (1969), p. 169.

80 *Tocqueville and Beaumont on Social Reform*, ed. Seymour Drescher (New York, 1968), pp. 1–27.

81 The question of how the poor regarded their own condition is quite different and,

fortunately for purposes of this study, less urgent. Less urgent, because this paper has been concerned with the image of the poor which was largely the creation and concern of the non-poor; and 'fortunately' less urgent, because information about how the poor regarded themselves is vastly more difficult to come by. The opinions of the poor would have to be filtered either through the minds of the 'rich,' in the above sense, or of the supposed 'spokesmen' of the poor, who, by virtue of being spokesmen, may be presumed to have ideological, social, or personal characteristics significantly different from those of the large body of poor.

82 I am here using the term, 'other Victorians,' in a different sense from that of Steven Marcus in the book of that name (New York, 1966). His 'other Victorians' represented primarily the underworld of the upper classes, mine the underworld of the lower classes.

VII   A New Earth

31 Literary Voices of an Industrial Town
Manchester, 1810-70

Martha Vicinus

Nineteenth-century Manchester was very vocal about the facts of change. From the early writers on factory conditions and from the laissez faire economists and social and political commentators we can piece together a fairly complete picture of the facts of a city in shock.[1] But, somewhere in the middle ground of our picture, there is the forgotten man of letters—an articulate figure who can tell us much about the Victorian city. How did he feel about the shocking changes in his physical and mental world? By looking at a part of Manchester's nineteenth-century literary output we can learn something of how individuals and classes faced or denied the facts of an industrializing city. Not many people nowadays, if asked to list native writers, could do much better than mention Mrs Gaskell or George Gissing (who fled Manchester in 1876 after being expelled from Owens College). A few might remember Harrison Ainsworth, but he spent his whole literary life in London. Many would argue that the only really important literary contributions to the Manchester picture are the early studies of manufacturing, such as Samuel Bamford's autobiography, describing the last days of handloom weaving, or the first efforts of the Manchester Statistical Society.[2]

Manchester, however, had other literary voices. These voices were directed as much against the nature of factory work as against the city itself, and, from our point of view, writers often seemed to react against the effects rather than the causes of industrialization and urbanization. In the first half of the century Manchester's writers sought refuge in an idealized past or a world of the literary imagination, but in time they found both the language and the subject-matter to explain, define, and even celebrate the advantages of Manchester and its people. The responses of those who aspired toward a creative interpretation of their condition, and who sought to improve it through literature, tell us in part how *change*, the defining quality of Manchester, came to be accepted, and the old rural culture altered to suit the new conditions.

Manchester's writers never lacked at least a coterie of loyal readers, but it was an easy matter to lament 'the want of taste for literature in Manchester,' as one bookseller, J. S. Gregson, described the situation in 1825:[3]

> The all-absorbing feeling of the bulk of the inhabitants, is a desire to acquire wealth; and everything is deemed worthless in their estimation, that has not the accomplishment of this object for its end. Now, this insatiable passion for gain cannot co-exist with a love of literature or the fine arts; it must either preclude a taste for the refined pleasures of the mind,—or a taste for the latter will destroy, or at least greatly impair, the more grovelling and sordid propensities of our nature... A thorough Manchester man sees more beauty in rows of red brick than he would in groves and 'alleys green'; he hears more music in the everlasting motion of the loom than he would in the songs of the lark or the nightingale.

That wealth was pursued regardless of personal cost was a repeated complaint among those early commentators, who viewed Manchester with a mixture of dismay and admiration.[4] While men might look with awe on economic and social changes and even conclude that they were for the best, artistic values remained essentially a reaction to these changes. Gregson's typical call for literature set in Nature rather than in the city reveals both an inability to see beauty in new places and a desire for a traditional literature that would evoke set responses in the reader. Rather than give red brick and looms literary stature, Gregson prefers to return to those subjects already conducive to 'a taste for the refined pleasures of the mind.' This narrow definition of literature persisted throughout the century, in spite of the existence of weaving- and factory-verse which had absorbed the new images of the power-loom, albeit not of the city, and was widely read by the working class of Manchester.

Gregson and his contemporaries did not consider weaving-songs and dialect poems literature. For the working class these songs and poems served as valuable links between the traditional handloom-weaving culture of Lancashire and the new industrial culture of the cities and towns. Despite severe economic and social dis-location during the early part of the century, the traditional Lancashire culture proved flexible enough to absorb and reflect many of these changes and their impact upon the working class. During these years large numbers of broadsides accurately describing and analyzing the changes which working men and women were forced to undergo in their work appeared on the streets of Manchester, Salford, Oldham, Bolton, and other industrial towns. Moreover, the handloom weaver remained throughout the century a symbol of a happier age which had been destroyed by the factory system; Lancashire workers in hard times repeatedly compared their situation with that of their weaver forefathers, seeing in the death of handloom weaving a precursor to their own struggles.[5]

Although Samuel Bamford and many other handloom weavers looked back on the years 1790–1810 as the 'golden age' when the weaver had been free from the petty tyrannies of the factory overseer,[6] the reality was one of increasing control over the weavers by the 'putter-out,' a middleman who set the prices and fines for piece work. When handloom weaving came to compete with factory work the putters-out became more ruthless in their exploitation by cutting rates and raising fines.[7] At first the machinery was not capable of weaving finer goods, and so weavers changed over to the luxury market, and wove complicated patterned cloth. Since the looms needed for such work were expensive and delicate, in Manchester and other cities by the 1820s weavers worked together under one master in a kind of primitive factory of eight or ten looms. Ironically, in fighting the factory system, they tied themselves to a form of it.[8] As one popular broadside described the situation:[9]

> Come all you cotton-weavers, your looms you may pull down;
> You must get employ'd in factories, in country or in town,
> For our cotton-masters have found out a wonderful new scheme,
> These calico goods now wove by hand they're going to weave by steam.
>
> In comes the gruff o'erlooker,* or the master will attend;
> It's 'You must find another shop, or quickly you must mend;
> For such work as this will never do; so now I'll tell you plain,
> We must have good pincop-spinning,† or we ne'er can weave by steam.'
>
> .   .   .   .
>
> The weavers' turn will next come in, for they must not escape,
> To enlarge the master's fortunes they are fined in every shape.
> For thin places, or bad edges, a go,‡ or else a float,§
> They'll daub you down, and you must pay threepence or else a groat.
>
> If you go into a loom-shop, where there's three or four pairs of looms,
> They are all standing empty, incumbrances of the rooms;
> And if you ask the reason why, the old mother will tell you plain,
> My daughters have forsaken them, and gone to weave by steam.
>
> So, come all you cotton-weavers, you must rise up very soon,
> For you must work in factories from morning until noon;
> You mustn't walk in your gardens for two or three hours a-day,
> For you must stand at their command, and keep your shuttles in play.

* o'erlooker: overseer, the poet is describing conditions in the spinning section of the mill.
† pincop-spinning: a 'pincop' is a pearshaped cop, or roll, of yarn used for the weft in a power loom.
‡ go: break or tear.
§ float: the passing of weft threads over a portion of the warp without being interwoven with it.

Poetry of this type, although written by one person, is not individualized, but is the response of a member of a particular group; its chief function is to describe accurately a well-known situation for that group. The emotional emphasis of this poem, as with all consolatory verse of the period is on the loss felt by the weavers rather than the new conditions themselves. The old freedoms of combining weaving and gardening, or walking about, or working late at one's own pace were severe losses for persons who did not customarily divide their work and leisure into the precise components demanded by the factory system. No effort is made to dramatize the conflict between the old handloom-weaving days and the new, nor to suggest further action; indeed no wider economic or social context is presented. The handloom weaver is caught between the loss of freedom through entry into the factory and the indignities suffered at the hands of the putter-out. There is no solution to his dilemma; the inescapable answer is 'you must work in factories from morning until night.'

The loss felt by the handloom weavers had little to do with the city itself and the changes in living habits it entailed. The emphasis in this poem and other traditional broadside verse was on work and courting rather than day-to-day problems of living, home life, or the general environment. The limitation of this song, and others like it, rests in the failure to describe individual responses to living conditions that had changed as radically as working conditions. Local weaving-songs continued to sell in the form of penny broadsides throughout the century in Manchester (but in time the impersonal factory verse and courting lament were replaced by the highly personal yet stereotyped songs of the music-hall and dialect works by such men as Edwin Waugh and Ben Brierley).[10]

Manchester's 'literary' writers, on the other hand, were on the side of Gregson. Although there were relatively few of them at the beginning of the century, some fifty-odd published volumes of poetry during the period 1821–41.[11] These authors found Lancashire ballads and prose too limited in scope and character to express their personal desires and aspirations, and so turned to imitating major English writers of the past, especially Shakespeare, Milton, and Thomson. While a few wrote an occasional poem in dialect,[12] they made no effort to enrich or alter the comic and satiric attitude which characterized most local dialect works. Most of these writers wrote familiar essays, fictionalized sketches, and romantic tales, but they all preferred lyrical poetry to other genres as being more elevated and truer to their personal sensibilities. For some twenty years the dominant literature of Manchester dealt with 'alleys green,' and left untouched both the existing weaving-culture and everyday events in the city and factory.

All these writers came from the middle and working classes; few had any advantages as to education or literary culture, but they were impelled by a love of reading and a desire to express themselves in poetic form. As John Evans proudly declared in his descriptive survey of Manchester writers, 'Our Lancashire authors are essentially men of self-education and self-advancement,' and their productions are 'the emanations of studious pastimes.'[13]

While proud of their elevated use of leisure time, many writers would have leapt happily into full-time writing, and several attempted to do so. Indeed, those who took writing most seriously changed jobs frequently, either from temperamental difficulties or because they lacked the skills necessary to continue long in any position.[14] For example, John Bolton Rogerson (1809–59), originally articled to a solicitor, wrote for and edited a series of short-lived journals, published numerous volumes of poetry, essays, and tales, and worked off and on as a book-seller.[15] When he died of rheumatism only a collection taken among his literary friends prevented his family from entering the workhouse.[16] Charles Swain (1803–74), apprenticed in his uncle's dyeworks, managed to escape after ten years to the more congenial and healthy labor of a lithographer. He achieved enough fame locally as 'Manchester's Tennyson' to be called upon regularly as a speaker,[17] but his conservative political views made him unpopular with some literary men.[18] Richard Wright Procter (1816–81), who used the pen-name 'Sylvan,' seems to have balanced his work and 'studious pastimes' more happily than most. He supplemented his income as a barber by running a small lending library, initially made up of his own personal collection. He was soon known as a book lover, and his place became a favorite with those who enjoyed his assistance and interest. Living longer than most of his contemporaries, he published an anthology of their poems (1855) and, in the 1860s and 1870s, a series of reminiscences about old Manchester streets and characters.[19]

The Manchester poet who attracted the most attention during the late 1830s and early 1840s was John Critchley Prince (1808–66). Prince was truly a product of the new industrial city—or perhaps its victim. His alcoholic father beat him whenever he found him reading, because he thought books were dangerous and unnecessary for a working man. Apprenticed to his father's dying trade of reed-making, Prince never learned another skill, and so was unemployed or underemployed most of his life. At eighteen he married, and soon had three children. In 1830, desperate for work, he walked and begged his way to Mulhausen where he had heard conditions were better. He was unsuccessful there, and finally made his way back to Lancashire many months later only to find his family in the poorhouse and his only son dying of malnutrition.[20] Nevertheless, throughout his life Prince wrote very little about his personal sufferings and his problems in adapting to industrialization, but celebrated instead in poem after poem the moral joys of literature, and its power to keep men from evil. As he described his own situation in an essay on 'poesy,'[21]

> I cannot easily express how much I have been indebted to it, as a source of pure intellectual enjoyment, for years of many sorrows, many baffled hopes, and many vain endeavours to rise above the evils of my station in society. Poesy has been the star of my adoration, affording me a serene and steady light through the darkest portion of my existence; a flower of exquisite beauty and perfume, smiling amid a wilderness of weeds; a fountain of never-failing freshness gushing forth in an arid desert; a strain of witching and every-varying melody, which so softens my heart with sympathy, so strengthens my mind with fortitude, that I bless God for

743

having made me susceptible of feelings so elevating, so humanizing, so
divine!

In 1841 friends made it possible for him to publish his poems, under the title *Hours
with the Muses*. The book was hailed as the work of a totally self-educated man, and,
as such, a mark of both intellectual progress and success for the working class. While
the *Westminster Review* dourly warned Prince to keep a steady job,[22] the uniform
praise and excellent sales encouraged him to hope for a more congenial job than
reed-making. When nothing better than fifteen shillings per week as a postman
was forthcoming, Prince retreated angry and disappointed. The last twenty years of
his life were spent cadging drinks from the sympathetic in return for a few lines of
verse.[23]

The poets of those years saw the imagination as the only effective escape from the
city. They rarely described the city or industrialization except in terms of their own
horrified rejection of its more savage aspects, such as prostitution and drunkenness.
There could be no compromising between the purity of the literary imagination they
created and the sordid reality of their urban environment.

The abstract world of the imagination was linked with and defined by means of
descriptions of natural scenery. The countryside was rarely an identifiable place, but
rather was symbolic of the natural order and harmony lost in the city; the seasonal
changes, the round of farming chores, and the church calendar all became representative of a past—or an imagined—world of meaningful order and obedience. As
Prince described this world:

> Once more the ponderous engines are at rest,
> Where Manufacture's mighty structures rise:
> Once more the babe is pillowed at the breast,
> Watch'd by a weary mother's yearning eyes;
> Once more to purer air the artist flies,
> Loosed from a weekly prison's stern control,
> Perchance to look abroad on fields and skies,
> Nursing the germs of freedom in his soul,—
> Happy if he escape the thraldom of the bowl.
>
> .   .   .   .
>
> God of the boundless universe! I come
> To hold communion with myself and Thee!
> And though excess of beauty makes me dumb,
> My thoughts are eloquent with all I see!
> My foot is on the mountains,—I am free,
> And buoyant as the winds that round me blow!
> My dreams are sunny as yon pleasant lea,
> And tranquil as the pool that sleeps below;
> While, circling round my heart, a poet's raptures glow.
>
> .   .   .   .

> Behold the lordly mansion's splendid pride,
> The peasant's cottage with its zone of flowers,—
> The shepherd's hut upon the mountain's side,
> Keeping lone watch through calm and stormy hours,—
> The clustered hamlet, with its quiet bowers,—
> The pastor's snug abode, and gothic fane,—
> The crowded city, with its thousand towers,—
> The silvery-sheeted lake, the opening plain,
> And, mixed with farthest sky, the blue and boundless main.[24]

So run three of the fifty-six stanzas in Spenserian rhyme that make up 'The Poet's Sabbath.' The most striking characteristic of this poem is the amount of periphrasis and personification. Prince cannot say 'factories,' but must say 'Manufacture's mighty structures,' not a 'church,' but a 'gothic fane.' This avoidance of the word itself to describe an object is partially an effort to show the poet's imaginative powers, but it also serves to keep a distance between the poet-observer and the thing observed. The cumulative effect is one of reified human emotions; emotions have been identified with objects external to the poet, and are a part of an imaginative world that bears little relation to any real world.

Prince's view of society was traditional; he accepted its order as God-ordained. The classes of society, for example, named in the third stanza by means of their dwellings, are seen not as products of man's labor, but as part of Nature; although these social divisions are the result of human attitudes and actions, they are described as outside of human control. Yet the poet himself has created this reified world, and sees himself as a participant in it. The crucial point is that the poet can control the world of his imagination, but the price he must pay is to turn his emotions into describable objects. The result is a perfectly self-contained poetic world perfectly separate from the city—or the country—and its realities.

The other possible escape for a writer of this period was through companionship with like-minded persons. For several years writers in Manchester met in pubs, stationery shops, and homes to discuss the latest works from London and their favorite authors, and to compare their own works. The most famous was a group which met at the 'Poet's Corner,' the Sun Inn, Long Millgate. Some forty to fifty people attended from time to time, under the aegis of Prince and Rogerson, during the years 1840–3. In 1841 the more regular 'members' declared themselves the Lancashire Authors Association, formed for 'the protection and encouragement of British authors,' and for 'the meeting of men of congenial ideas and sentiments.'[25] They elected officers and discussed the founding of a suitable journal and the means by which they could make Lancashire writers better known beyond the confines of the county.

A special soirée was held 24 March 1842. Over a dozen persons wrote poems for the occasion, songs were sung and messages read from well-wishers, including Isabella Varley (afterwards the authoress Mrs Linnaeus Banks), who hid behind a velvet curtain to listen to the evening's entertainment.[26] A particularly warm toast was made to George Falkner, then editor and publisher of *Bradshaw's Journal* (1839–43), the only weekly catering to local literary interests that willingly published the writings of the Sun Inn group.[27] The evening was fully reported in the *Manchester Guardian* (30 March 1842), and later *The Festive Wreath* (1842), edited by Rogerson, was published containing all the verses written for the occasion. The Association, however, never went beyond its original prospectus, nor was a journal started; enthusiasm could go far, but the Manchester of the 1840s did not have the readership to support either literary men or a literary journal of their type.

While the Sun Inn writers rarely published their own works as penny broadsides, and refused to take seriously contemporary Lancashire dialect writers, they counted among their number Alexander Wilson, who wrote and sang dialect songs in Manchester pubs. His favorite topics were the local sights and current events, such as the opening of the Liverpool & Manchester Railway, the Kersal Moor Races, and the early balloon ascents.[28] His song for the March evening was called 'The Poet's Corner,' and describes each person present and the general atmosphere of the evening ('A PRINCE of *more worth* than the prince lately born/ We've a beautiful SWAIN as e're traversed the plain,' etc.).[29] As a comic entertainer Wilson was a link between the old-fashioned broadside-sellers who hawked their wares on street corners and the music-hall artistes who sang popular songs and had a comic routine. He offered light relief in an otherwise solemn evening, but he also reinforced the attitudes of those present that the local and popular could never be true art. His function as a comic character of good heart was as narrowly defined as the verse he wrote and sold.[30]

While Wilson wrote solely about local events, other Sun Inn poets were edging toward a poetry that included commentary on the city. John Bolton Rogerson published in 1842 a long poem entitled 'A Voice from the Town' in which he describes the virtues and vices of town living. The only virtues he finds are his friends' companionship and his humble home. The main emphasis of the poem is on the evils of the gin-palace and the prison van. His diction and language are often artificial and falsely poetic, but the final effect is quite powerful, in a manner reminiscent of Milton's Hell. The city in one section is seen as an extension of a nightmare where the reality of a drunken brawl blends with his dream of climbing cliffs and crossing deserts:[31]

> Now whilst my mind is scarcely dispossess'd
> Of the wild phantoms of my dreadful dream,
> Again I hear a loud and piercing shriek,
> And bitter curses borne upon the wind;
> Words hiss upon mine ear, whose very sound
> Strikes on the mind like to a poison'd shaft,
> Wounding and shattering pure and virtuous thoughts.
> The words are breath'd by lips which God design'd

Should utter only syllables to bless,
And soothe man's heart, as oil the billowy sea;
'Tis woman's voice that mingles with the blast—
Fierce imprecations from a female tongue,
And passionate bursts of scorn and reckless rage,
And impure thoughts in horrid language drest,
Like pestilential taint, pollute the night,
Blent with some drunken ruffian's hoarse deep oath,
Perchance the prelude to a fearful blow . . .
                —I court again repose:
Than such reality more welcome sleep,
Throng'd though it be with angry, vision'd fiends.

We have moved away in this poem from Prince's reified world to one where human beings are both responsible for their actions and unable to control them; the streets of the city are as disordered and uncontrollable as a nightmare, yet the people in this vision are seen to be the cause of their own downfall. A complete reading of 'A Voice from the Town' brings only one solution for the sober and, in this case, the sensitive poet: to retreat to the refuge of dreams or, alternatively, to the family and friends. Already we can see the separation of the respectable from the savage both physically and metaphorically. Rogerson's selective vision and rejection of the city, with his equally selective acceptance, was consonant with a larger movement to escape the impact of industrialization and urbanization through moral righteousness, family love, and personal education.

A contemporary critic praised Rogerson for his honest treatment of drink and imprisonment as poetry conducive to social improvement, but added that the subject was 'certainly an uncouth and unpoetic theme.' Attitudes, however, were changing. This same critic went on to concede that 'the humblest son of toil, who resides in the lowest cellar or loftiest garret of a populous town, has his own little world of affections, cares, projects, successes and disappointments,' which are 'as worthy of the historian's or poet's pen' as larger events.[32] This concession is a step toward recognizing the value of a literature about the common people of a 'populous town,' though hedged by strictures concerning the proper style and language. To take the most dramatic sights of a large industrial town—its drunken men and women and those being driven to prison—was but a short step toward finding drama in less obviously emotional events and sights. The change was made easier by the placement of the family and the home as moral centers worthy of the most serious artistic considerations, though these subjects in turn became a means to avoid writing about the city itself. While high art was still controlled by those who wrote about Nature, Rogerson and others, perhaps simply from more varied interests or imagination, were beginning to write about the city and to find their work acceptable among readers and critics.

When the bookseller Gregson had called for a greater appreciation of literature in Manchester he was looking more to a potential readership than at the problems an author might face in living and writing in the city. Gregson seems to have believed that if Mancunians could only be made to appreciate Nature in art more and money less, all would be well for the refinement of the city. The situation was more complicated, however, for those who had either to find poetry in red bricks or retreat imaginatively to alleys green. Both the anonymous author of 'Hand-Loom vs. Power-Loom' and the poets of Prince's circle some twenty and thirty years later felt deeply alienated from their work and their environment. The acceptance and resignation of the earlier poem, however, were replaced with rejection and escapism. The Manchester poet of the 1830s and 1840s saw himself as a product of the city, not as a producer of or participator in its work; he longed to escape from a life over which he had no control. Even those who wrote about the drunken throng created a physical escape for themselves through the home, friends, or even emigration to the New World.

Those themes first explored by Rogerson in his poetry were carried further by prose writers in the 1840s. The world of the everyday Manchester resident became the province of fiction writers. As Mrs Gaskell (1810–64) said, 'I bethought me how deep might be the romance in the lives of some of those who elbowed me daily in the busy streets of the town in which I resided.'[33] *Mary Barton*, published in 1848, was the first full-length novel written by a Manchester resident to deal with the city's working class and its problems. Although Mrs Gaskell was not from Manchester, nor did she have any contact with the city's literary men,[34] she was an acute and sympathetic outsider. Her ministrations to the poor, part of her duties as a Unitarian minister's wife, gave her a far closer knowledge of the urban poor than other nationally known novelists; nevertheless, she was writing primarily as a middle-class outsider for a middle-class audience. Many of her descriptive passages are more than a trifle self-conscious in their itemization of prices, rents, clothing, and other material objects. She was equally given to reminding her educated readers of the necessity for human sympathy and the reasons for the bitterness of so many working men.

Mrs Gaskell's limitations as a novelist can be set aside in comparison with her achievement in *Mary Barton*. She took Manchester and its local culture seriously, and her influence on other Manchester writers, though largely indirect, was enormous. She frequently quoted Lancashire weaving- and factory-songs and made special efforts to reproduce Lancashire dialect accurately (with the assistance of her husband, she glossed the more alien words for her national audience). At a time when southerners looked upon industrial workers as little better than heathens, and Manchester's own writers scarcely looked beyond the scenes of drunken brawling, Mrs Gaskell's serious treatment of working-class individuals stands out above her obvious faults. In a characteristic passage, Mrs Gaskell presents the reader with Margaret's fine rendering of an old weaving song:[35]

> Margaret, with fixed eye, and earnest, dreamy look, seemed to become
> more and more absorbed in realising to herself the woe she had been
> describing, and which she felt might at that very moment be suffering, and
> hopeless within a short distance of their comparative suffering.

Suddenly she burst forth with all the power of her magnificent voice, as if a prayer from her very heart for all who were in distress, in the grand supplication, 'Lord, remember David'. Mary held her breath, unwilling to lose a note, it was so clear, so perfect, so imploring. A far more correct musician than Mary might have paused with equal admiration of the really scientific knowledge with which the poor depressed-looking young needle-woman used her superb and flexible voice. Deborah Travis herself (once an Oldham factory girl, and afterwards the darling of fashionable crowds as Mrs Knyvett) might have owned a sister in her art.

In scenes such as this Mrs Gaskell brought the reader closer to the potentialities and limitations of industrial urban life than any previous Mancunian writer had done. Moreover, she combined characterization of an individual with that of a culture; Margaret's singing is unique, as we see from Mary's admiration and the author's comments, and yet her songs are sung by all the members of her class and are part of the living traditions of Manchester. The plea for understanding is made indirectly through the presentation of great talent in the midst of poverty, and through the comments in parentheses that one Lancashire girl actually achieved worldly success because of her exceptional musical talents. Margaret is linked both with her local culture, represented in the songs she sings, and with the wider world, represented by her talent and connection with Deborah Travis.

Mary Barton opens with a walk through Greenheys Field, 'but half an hour' from the center of Manchester. The countryside was still readily accessible, but it was no longer a part of daily life. Many characters came from the hills and moors surrounding Manchester, and their talk was of a happier bygone time. This sense of a better, more regulated past was a recurrent theme in all Manchester literature. Paradoxically, as city life became more acceptable as subject-matter, nostalgia for the rural past became more marked.

While the working class kept alive its rural heritage through the continuation of customs, superstitions, and songs, many members of the middle class found their entry into the past through antiquarianism. As early as 1829 John Roby (1793–1850), probably under the influence of Sir Walter Scott, collected tales about the knights, fairies, and 'boggarts' (goblins) of Lancashire, publishing in all four volumes, costing two guineas each.[36] One essayist described his work as a 'fair, sound, and honest record of facts, mingled with pleasing touches of fancy, and spirited dashes of imagination.'[37] The amount of fancy and imagination was criticized by later collectors of tales, but Roby retained his popularity; in later years his volumes were reprinted in cheap editions for the working class.[38] Roby seems to have set the tone, if not the standard, for subsequent collectors. His emphasis was on past traditions and lore, as if Lancashire customs were all in the past and not in the process of change and replenishment within the cities.

The most famous collectors of the late nineteenth century were John Harland (1806–68), a *Manchester Guardian* reporter who had consistently supported Manchester letters since he had first begun working on the paper,[39] and his assistant T. T. Wilkinson. Harland and John Crossley, a solicitor and essayist, started the Chetham Society in 1844 (prospectus, 1842) to publish manuscripts and incunabula related to Lancashire. Wilkinson and Harland collected Lancashire lore, legends, and songs, publishing each in a separate volume.[40] Their attitude toward the material they found was divided. They delighted in its richness and the number of parallels between Lancashire's legends and classical myths, but they also proudly announced in one preface that thanks to education Lancastrians had 'divested themselves of many of the grosser superstitions which formed a portion of the popular faith of their immediate precedessors.'[41] While distressed that folklore was dying out even in the remoter villages, they were pleased to find education replacing the very superstitions they were seeking.

An interest in Lancashire lore led naturally to an interest in the county's dialect. The rise of philology as a serious study encouraged local men of learning to examine the speech of those about them more carefully. The initial enthusiasm of the English Dialect Society, founded in Cambridge in 1873, was carried on in Manchester, where the Society moved in 1876. For sixteen years J. H. Nodal, editor of the *Manchester City News*, a weekly specializing in Manchester and Lancashire doings of the past and present, supervised the publication of dialect glossaries, which led to the publication of the *English Dialect Dictionary* in 1896.[42] Although there was a nominal recognition of the difference between an urban Lancashire dialect, filled with words referring to various parts of factory machinery, city customs, and so-called impurities of accent, the main emphasis of the dialecticians, as of the antiquarians, was on capturing the rural dialect before it died.

One of the results of this attitude was a seeking out of working-class writers who had retained those characteristics most prized by the dialect scholars. Those who remembered and wrote about the rural past were imitated by the educated—a reversal in roles from the earlier part of the century. How strongly this affected the kind of literature written during the period 1850–80 is difficult to gauge. Although scholars were in some position to commission work,[43] the major audience for dialect literature remained the general public, and in particular the better-off factory worker. Nevertheless, without the encouragement of the antiquarians, folklorists, and philologists, Lancashire dialect literature would not have become so well known and respected.

We find, for example, such men as Edwin Waugh (1819–90) achieving considerable fame and attention as an authentic moorland poet from both those who attended his popular readings and the dialecticians. Although he spent most of his adult life in Manchester, all of his poems deal with Rochdale and the surrounding countryside where he was born and reared. Waugh wrote dialect verse and stories through the 1850s, achieving fame and a moderate fortune with the publication of the temperance poem 'Come Whoam to thi Childer an' Me' in 1856.[44] For the next twenty years he pursued a career as a journalist and speaker, earning £2 and £3 for an evening's entertainment.[45] He was elected to the board of the English Dialect Society and was frequently consulted in preparing the glossary of Lancashire words. When his health began to fail in 1876 a committee took over the copyrights of his books and gave him a guaranteed income. Then in 1886 influential friends were able to place him on the Civil List to receive a pension of £90 a year. He died honored by his county and his country. In the *Saturday Review*'s obituary, he was praised because[46]

> His ditties have sweetened the bitter lot of some; have given pleasure to many; have provoked wholesome laughter and honest tears; and have strengthened the love of home and its homely virtues among the Lancashire folk. What more shall we ask of a poet or of a people? And what higher praise can we give him?

Waugh did not seek to write authentic reproductions of earlier dialect poetry. Rather, he skilfully combined old customs, and rural settings with the new attitudes of his age.[47] In his courting poem 'Th' Sweetheart Gate,' for example, he describes the courtship of a working man in a small town, but the attitudes of the narrator are thoroughly Victorian:[48]

> There's mony a gate* eawt of eawr teawn-end,—
>   But nobbut one† for me;
> It winds by a rindlin' wayter side,‡
>   An' o'er a posied lea;
> It wanders into a shady dell;
>   An' when I've done for th' day,
> I never can sattle this heart o' mine,
>   Beawt§ walkin' deawn that way.
>
> .   .   .   .
>
> When th' layrock's finished his wark aboon,¶
>   An' laid his music by,
> He flutters deawn to his mate, an' stops
>   Till dayleet stirs i'th sky.
> Though Matty sends me away at dark,
>   I know that hoo's reet‖ full well;
> An' it's how I love a true-hearted lass,
>   No mortal tung** can tell.

* gate: road, way
† nobbut one: nought but one
‡ rindlin' wayter side: musically wandering water side
§ Beawt: without
¶ th' layrock's finished his wark aboon: when the lark has finished his work above
‖ hoo's reet: she's right
** mortal tung: mortal tongue.

> I wish that Michaelmas Day were past,
> > When wakin' time* comes on;
> An' I wish that Candlemas Day were here,
> > An' Matty an' me were one;
> I wish this wanderin' wark were o'er,—
> > This maunderin' to an' fro;†
> That I could go whoam‡ to my own true love,
> > An' stop at neet an' o'.§

Waugh, like the earlier Manchester poets, Prince and the anonymous author of 'Hand-loom vs. Power-loom,' relied upon familiar references to evoke emotional responses from his readers. He reminds his predominantly city audience of a happier past when they might have courted by a sweetheart gate, or perhaps of a day spent happily in the country (until the very end of the century, the country was within a half hour's walk for most factory workers, even in the heart of Manchester). Those familiar escapes from the city—the countryside and marital bliss—have been grafted onto a more realistic presentation of persons and places. The familiar and the homely have replaced 'the refined pleasures of the mind,' but the city is still successfully evaded as a place with which the poet and his readers must come to terms.

Waugh's poetry is a comfortable expression of the idealized real—it is a reflection of the happier parts of his readers' lives, mingled with cheerful optimism and homely advice for the unhappy times. The special vocation of the poet, in the mind of writers like Prince, has been replaced by the role of a person who gives folks 'a lift on the way,' as Waugh describes himself in one poem. Dialect meant a limiting of one's audience to those who saw themselves as members of a special group, and who looked for a literature written specifically about and for them. The primary function of literature had come to be an accurate re-creation of an alternative world, be it the home, country courting, or a walk on the moors.[49]

The interest in Lancashire's dialect literature and past customs naturally enough revived interest in the formation of an association of local writers. Waugh and some other writers had been meeting for a time at the Clarence Hotel, when with several businessmen in 1861 they changed their informal gathering to the Manchester Literary Club. For a number of years it remained chiefly a group of men who met weekly to dine and talk about literature, but eventually the leadership passed from the hands of those primarily interested in creative writing to those concerned with literature as an avocation and study. A long-time member described the Club as 'Business men with an interest in literature in the midst of a great commercial city, whose ideal was to do what it can to keep the mind of the city true to the higher and more unselfish forms of mental activity, to see that the "humanities" hold their

* wakin' time: the time when workmen begin working by candlelight
† maunderin' to an' fro: wandering aimlessly
‡ go whoam: go home
§ at neet an' o': at night and all.

ground along with science and material considerations.'[50] Membership varied from fifty to eighty for the better part of the century; finances were strong enough to publish the transactions of the Club from 1873–4 in the form of the Manchester Literary Club *Quarterly*. The majority of the essays published were concerned with such problems as 'Who will posterity remember, George Eliot or Thomas Carlyle?' but there was a plentiful number of essays on Lancashire literature, and, toward the end of the century, frequent reminiscences of earlier members, such as Waugh and Brierley.[51] J. H. Nodal, in addition to his duties for the Dialect Society, was also Secretary of the Club; his influence was such that much of the Club's time and efforts went toward compiling a bibliography of all local literature, a glossary of Lancashire words, and a bibliography of members' works.[52] If the Club never became the Lancashire Literary Association dreamed about in 1842, it still served, and serves, a valuable function in providing a place for businessmen to meet authors and to discuss literature.

In the early days of the Club, writers such as Edwin Waugh and his friend Ben Brierley (1825–96), the other major dialect writer of the time, felt quite at home and frequently wrote satiric verse about one another as well as other Club members.[53] Brierley, primarily a prose writer, began life as a bobbin winder for his handloom weaving family in the same village as Elijah Ridings; in his autobiography he speaks of how the knowledge of Ridings' publications spurred him and his friends to try their hand at writing.[54] When still under twenty-one he worked as a warehouseman for a silk-weaving firm in Manchester, walking the four-and-a-half miles there and back daily. His early interest in literature found an outlet in publishing verse in the poetry column of local papers and writing sketches for his friends to dramatize. In 1855 he published a short sketch about a working man's day in the country, 'A Day Out, or a Summer Ramble to Daisy Nook,' and its immediate popularity launched him into a career of journalism, fiction writing, and public reading. For sixteen years he published and wrote a dialect weekly, *Ben Brierley's Journal* (1869–85), which sold for threepence. He rose to be a town councillor for a working-class ward in the city of Manchester (1875–81) and throughout his life was a respected and widely admired member of the working class.[55] In 1885 when the savings bank that he had invested in failed, a special testimonial dinner was given, with an honorarium of £650. He was eulogized by those present for having helped 'to crystallize and preserve the speech of their fathers and of their own childhood,' once again emphasizing the connection between the rural past and Lancashire literature of his own time. Lest the moral of his writings and life be forgotten, the same speaker added, 'The poor for whom he has written and striven have received from his life and writings many a lesson of honesty and frugality and unaffected simplicity which only come with force from Mr. Brierley and such as he.'[56]

Brierley, by no means the skilled author that Mrs Gaskell was, remains important because he was a spokesman from and for the working class. Although as eager as she to draw lessons from his stories and to explain his characters to his readers, he speaks as only an insider can. Like Edwin Waugh's, most of Brierley's works were set in the past, or in a vague mixture of the past and present; nevertheless, his attitude about the past was ambiguous. As someone who could remember many a hungry, cold winter, and who had never received any formal education beyond a dame's school, he could speak acidly of such times as 'when we had to stare through a haupenny candle fro' neet to mornin', singin' "Britons never shall be slaves", an' leatherin'* away at one's loom as if we'rn feightin'† a battle—an o for t'just get a mess o' thick porritch o' th' week day, an' a quartern o' bacon,‡ cut up int' dominoes, ov a Sunday.'[57] But, in another, more nostalgic story, describing the weaving village of 'Treadlepin Fold,'§ Brierley praises the folk of the old days:[58]

> They were content, poor fellows, to toil day and night at the loom, sing 'Britons never shall be slaves', and pocket indifferent legislation, with now and then a stout gamble, and, for the rest, let the world take any course it might. So long as they could by honest means obtain the wherewithal to keep body and soul together their loyalty was unbounded.

It would be an easy matter to claim that Brierley told the 'truth' when he used dialect, and what the well-educated wanted to hear when he wrote Standard English. Both stories, however, were meant for the same audience, those established factory workers to whom Waugh addressed himself, as well as those particularly interested in local culture and the Lancashire dialect. Probably Brierley and his readers believed in both pictures: fiction has always permitted the mixing of past and present.

While accepting the benefits of education and greater opportunity, the Manchester readers of the 1860s and 1870s still longed for a simpler, more secure past. The ideal was surely Brierley's favorite character, Ab-o'-th'-Yate, a handloom weaver from 'Walmsley Fowt [Fold]' who lived close enough to Manchester to participate in many of its events, such as the opening of the Town Hall in 1877, and who still had all the advantages of the old village life. Constantly involved in minor scrapes and adventures, Ab is a comic figure of great shrewdness and sympathy—indeed, like Waugh's creations, someone a Lancashire reader could identify with and admire, yet he could not possibly have existed at the time Brierley was writing.

Brierley's most significant accomplishment was to portray the factory worker in transition, though relatively few of his stories are concerned with urban problems. He was much happier drawing portraits of rural weaving-folk, happy Sundays in the country, or hard-won contentment by the family hearth. In his story 'Out of Work,' however, he writes about the unemployed with sympathy and understanding. A country lass is saved from a fearful life by an out-of-work laborer and is conveyed to the country squire who has long loved her from a distance. To add to the romantic complications, in case the hero is too mundane, he had come from the same village as Jenny and had loved her once himself, but he had not spoken for fear of offending her.

* leatherin': working as fast as possible so as to raise a sweat
† feightin': fighting
‡ quartern of bacon: a quarter pound of bacon
§ Treadlepin Fold: A treadlepin holds the treadle (a lever worked by foot to reproduce a rotary motion) to the loom. A fold is an area, turning, or corner, usually referring to a village.

Stiffy, the laborer-hero, is forced to live in a place Brierley called 'Bedlam,' scathingly described as *home*:[59]

> From the circumstance that there once existed in this locality a mountain of refuse dug out of a contiguous coalpit, the atmosphere about it seems to think it has a right to be offensively grimy even at this day, and to extend its influence to the habits of some of the more favoured denizens. The sanitary reformer would be mobbed if he was seen to poke his sleek and healthy face in this region of privileged squalor. . . It has been said that at one time children born in this place came into the world web-footed, like ducks, that they might 'baddle' in the pools and muddy kennels which, at that period, abounded in Plattington. Be it true or otherwise, there is one thing to be said in partial extenuation. Poverty and dirt were always allied. Grind a man down, and self-neglect, and a corresponding degree of dislike to wholesome appearances is sure to follow.

The fever that sweeps Bedlam, and the consequent aid given to the poor by the poor is reminiscent of Mrs Gaskell, but the difference lies in Brierley's ironic treatment of the condition of the inhabitants, such as the 'web-footed' children, and of the supposed solution, the sanitary reformer. Irony of this sort comes from someone who has participated in 'privileged squalor.' Unlike much of the poetry written about the city, he has avoided the obvious evils of drink, and has emphasized the difficulties of an average good-hearted worker who cannot find decent housing with his limited income.

While Brierley had come from the working class, he was also an example of self-help and success. His solution for the ills of Bedlam is the same as Mrs Gaskell's: not economic or political reform, but love. She had urged greater love between all classes and all individuals; he subscribes to the Victorian ethic of the loving family as a protective barrier against the horrors of Bedlam-city:[60]

> Bedlam, however, was not a social desert without its oasis. Stiffy's home glimmered out in the cloudy void like a green spot upon which a streak of refreshing sunlight had settled. It was a home that you would think ought to have had more genial companionship that could be found among squalid dens, where vice and unkindly feelings gendered and grew in festering loathsomeness. It was a home that ought to have had such associations as green meadows, blossoming hedgerows, gardens, the song of the wild bird, and the breadth of the sweet moorland breeze. But had it been placed among the wigwams of some savage tribe it would have been just the same, for *woman* had made it what it was; and she has the power to make such a place a Paradise or Pandemonium, whichever she wills.

The ills of Bedlam cannot be changed by economic theories, or even improved housing; it lies within the individual will of each working-class wife to make a small garden of her home. The impact of the city slum can be absorbed by viewing it as an aberration to be ignored from within the safety of Stiffy's home. It is only from this refuge that Brierley and his readers are more able psychologically to accept the seemingly unchangeable Bedlam. There has been a crucial change in the thirty years since Rogerson and Prince wrote and lived in Manchester. In the life they described, worldly success came only by possessing innate goodness and protecting it through a total avoidance of the evils of the city. Stiffy, on the other hand, succeeds through living in the midst of evil and constantly testing his hard-won decency and goodness. He actively participates in the life of the city while resisting its temptations, and therefore feels more ready to accept its constrictions and to work within them. The growing acceptance of the city is clearly, if obliquely, reflected in this story.

The metaphor of the garden used to describe Stiffy's home was a recurrent image throughout the latter half of the century. Gregson's call for a literature based on 'alleys green' has in part been answered by taking nature into the home, behind the red bricks, so that a metaphoric refuge has been created. By the 1870s, Manchester's literature did not so much make possible 'the refined pleasures of the mind,' as insure a carefully guarded respectability and self-pride that prevents the 'grovelling propensities of our nature' from entering the family. Local writing from this time simply follows the lead of Mrs Gaskell, Waugh, and Brierley. Mrs Linnaeus Banks's *The Manchester Man* (1876) is set in the days before and after Peterloo; it is a labored historical reconstruction, centering on the successful rise of an orphan apprentice. The city is mentioned only in terms of historical places and events but never as a growing, developing place in which persons must work and live. If anything, dialect literature grew progressively less concerned with the everyday lives of Manchester working people and more with the rural past—as the country grew more remote from the city, so too did the stories.[61]

The writers of Manchester had before them an entirely new area of human experience to describe and analyze. That they largely failed to do so is in part an indication of their own limitations as creative writers and thinkers, but even more it reveals how difficult it was for sensitive and articulate individuals to come to terms with the urban experience, and how difficult it was, and still remains, to describe the city and its impact upon people. The measure of their success should rather be that they could rediscover the old dialect literature of the past, and alter it so as to fit the new needs of a society seeking not realistic descriptions of poor housing and crowded streets, but an idealized mirror of their happier moments.

Notes

1   Asa Briggs calls Manchester 'the shock city' of the early nineteenth century. See *Victorian Cities* (1965), p. 51.
2   See Samuel Bamford, *Autobiography*, 2 vols (Middletown, 1838–41, 1848–9).
3   'On the Want of Taste for Literature in Manchester,' *Gimcrackiana* (Manchester, 1833), pp. 157, 159.

4   Travelers' comments on Manchester abound. The most famous are A. de Tocqueville, *Journeys to England and Ireland* (ed. J. P. Mayer, 1958); L. Faucher, *Études sur l'Angleterre*, 2 vols (Paris, 1845); and W. Cooke Taylor, *Notes of a Tour in the Manufacturing Districts of Lancashire* (1842).

5   See such poems and songs as Samuel Bamford's 'My Wynder' (1843), Ben Brierley's 'The Weaver of Wellbrook' (*c*. 1875), R. R. Bealey's 'My *Piece* is o bu' Woven Eawt' (after 1865), all in John Harland and T. T. Wilkinson, eds, *Ballads and Songs of Lancashire, Ancient and Modern*, 3rd edn (1882).

6   Samuel Bamford, *Early Days*, ed. W. H. Chaloner (1967), pp. 96–115.

7   Sim Schofield, *Short Stories about Failsworth Folk* (Blackpool, 1905), p. 17, tells a traditional story of these days, when a weaver was fined sixpence apiece for two small holes. The weaver asked if the fine was the same no matter what the size of the holes; when the answer was yes, he proceeded to tear the holes together, and thereby saved himself sixpence.

8   Duncan Bythell, *The Handloom Weavers* (Cambridge, 1969), pp. 83–5.

9   Harland and Wilkinson, op. cit., pp. 188–9. The editors date this song from 'a transitional era in weaving.' Bythell argues that the handloom weavers were not seriously affected by the power-loom until the 1820s; while this may be true economically, the large number of songs about the power-loom replacing the handloom written before 1820 indicate that psychologically the factory system made an early and lasting impact on handloom weavers.

10   'Jone o' Grinfilt, Jr.' (also known as 'The Owdem Weaver') was still being sold in the streets of Manchester in the 1860s; it dates from around 1815. For a discussion of broadside literature in Lancashire, see Martha Vicinus, 'A Study of Nineteenth Century Working Class Poetry,' *An Anti-Text in Literature*, ed. Paul Lauter and Louis Kampf (New York, 1972). Fred Leary, in an unpublished scrap-book entitled 'Manchester Ballads,' Manchester Central Reference Library, has transcribed a number of the more interesting broadsides he found still being sold in the 1880s and 1890s. The last hawker in Manchester, whom he had not seen 'in some years' in 1893, was to be found on Shudehill or in Ancoats Lane with a long sheet of calico on which he had fastened his broadsides. He then carried obscene cards and engravings in his pockets from which he made his primary profit. It was unclear to Leary whether he died or was arrested for trafficking in obscene goods.

11   The most famous of these were Samuel Bamford, *Hours in the Bowers* (1835), Rev. William Gaskell, *Temperance Rhymes* (1839), Maria Jane Jewsbury, *Phantasmagoria, or Sketches of Life and Literature* (1825) and *Lays of Leisure Hours* (1829), John Jones, *The Cotton Mill* (1821), Rev. Richard Parkinson, *Poems, Sacred and Miscellaneous* (1832), John Critchley Prince, *Hours with the Muses* (1841), Elijah Ridings, *The Village Muse* (1831), John Bolton Rogerson, *Rhymes Romance and Revery* (1840), Charles Swain, *The Mind and Other Poems* (1831, rev. edn, 1842), and an early anthology of Manchester poets, James Wheeler, ed., *Manchester Poetry* (1838). All these books were published in Manchester.

12   See Elijah Ridings, ed., *The Lancashire Muse: Containing humorous specimens of the Lancashire dialect* (Manchester [1853]) which contains poems by Tim Bobbin, Bamford, Ridings, and Alexander Wilson as well as several anonymous works.

13   *Lancashire Authors and Orators* (1850), p. 260.

14 The fullest discussion of Manchester writers of this time is to be found in John Evans, op. cit., and Richard Wright Procter, *Literary Reminiscences and Gleanings* (Manchester, 1860) and *Memorials of Bygone Manchester* (Manchester, 1880). Also see Henry Fishwick, *The Lancashire Library* (1875) and John R. Swann, *Lancashire Authors* (Manchester, 1924).

15 Evans, op. cit., pp. 240–6 and Procter, *Memorials*, pp. 157–71.

16 See Samuel Bamford, unpub. Diary, 28 February 1858 to 26 December 1861, Manchester Central Reference Library. An undated comment in March or April 1859 remarks that Rogerson's furniture had been seized for debts and that his son was dying of consumption, so Bamford suggested to Ben Brierley that they raise money by means of a public reading.

17 He was the only local poet present, for example, at the Athenaeum soirée of 23 October 1845. See *Report of the Proceedings connected with the Grand Soirée of the Manchester Athenaeum, held on Thursday, October 23, 1845* (Manchester, 1845), pp. 7, 9, for a list of dignitaries present. Swain lectured on literature at the Royal Institution and the Manchester Athenaeum in the late 1840s (see Evans, op. cit., p. 262).

18 See Bamford, Diary, 11 October 1858. An honorary dinner for Bamford was proposed on his return from London after an absence of seven years. All his old literary friends were to come, including Swain, until Bamford indicated that he 'did not suppose Swain would accord with the political feelings which would be expressed.' Swain did not attend, to Bamford's relief. On the other hand, in Edwin Waugh's personal papers, Manchester Central Reference Library, there is an undated letter from Swain suggesting that he, Brierley, Chattwood, and Bealey join him for a day in the near future. All these persons were early and active members of the Manchester Literary Club (see pp. 752–3 above).

19 His works include some autobiographical comment. See also W. E. A. Axon, 'Introduction, In Memoriam—R. W. P.,' *The Barber's Shop*, rev. edn (Manchester, 1883). For Procter's own publications, see *Manchester in Holiday Dress* (1866), *Memorials of Manchester Streets* (Manchester, 1874), and *Our Turf, Our Stage and Our Ring* (Manchester, 1862).

20 R. A. Douglas Lithgow, *The Life of J. C. Prince* (Manchester, 1880), pp. 7–9, 20–30, and [George F. Mandley], 'A Sketch of the Author's Life,' *Hours with the Muses* (Manchester, 1841). The Manchester Central Reference Library has an extensive collection of Prince's letters, scrapbooks, and personal papers, all of which give an invaluable picture of his difficulties.

21 'Random Thoughts on Poetry,' *Hours with the Muses*, 6th edn (1857), pp. xxii–xxiii (originally published in 1841).

22 The critic commented, 'Had such a volume of poetry as the one before been produced twenty years ago by a poor cotton weaver, its author would have been accounted a prodigy. As it is, he must be content to take his stand amongst the numerous *Dii minores* who overflow the realms of print: to him, poetry must be its "own exceeding great reward",' *Westminster Review*, xxxv (1842), from a cutting in Prince's commonplace book, 'The Olio,' Manchester Central Reference Library. *Hours with the Muses* went through three editions of 750 copies each within eighteen months.

23 Lithgow, op. cit., pp. 174–218, and Procter, *Reminiscences*, pp. 185–9.

24 *Hours with the Muses*, pp. 26–7.

25 Lithgow, op. cit., pp. 128–32, Procter, op. cit., pp. 179–80.

26 See Procter, op. cit., pp. 124 ff., and 'Poetic Festival,' *Manchester Guardian*, 30 March 1842.

27 In 1842 when Prince was offered a government position in Southampton, Falkner offered to help him pay his way by writing a series of letters, 'Rambles of a Rhymester.' After Prince turned down the postmanship Falkner continued to assist him in a number of ways, even though other men of influence had deserted him. See Lithgow, op. cit., pp. 140–58.

28 See John Harland, ed., *The Songs of the Wilsons, with a Memoir of the Family* (Manchester [1842]).

29 In addition to being published in *The Songs of the Wilsons* and *The Festive Wreath*, the poem came out as a penny broadside. Mrs Linnaeus Banks's personal copy with a biographical comment about William Earnshaw, the landlord of the Sun Inn, is in the Manchester Central Reference Library.

30 In Rogerson's *A Voice from the Town and Other Poems* (London, 1842), p. 26, he described Wilson as 'That strange, eccentric wight . . . one whose humorous strains are often heard—/ Relish'd most when chanted by himself.'

31 *A Voice from the Town and Other Poems*, p. 36.

32 'New Books,' *Bradshaw's Journal*, iii (1842), 222.

33 'Preface,' *Mary Barton* (1906 edn), p. lxxiii.

34 For her Manchester circle, see Esther Alice Chadwick, *Mrs. Gaskell, Haunts, Homes, and Stories* (1913), pp. 130–88, Elizabeth Haldane, *Mrs. Gaskell and her Friends* (1930), pp. 30–56, and A. B. Hopkins, *Elizabeth Gaskell: Her life and work* (1952), pp. 297–321. The only extant letter from a working man which Mrs Gaskell received praising her for the fidelity with which she drew working men is Samuel Bamford's, written 9 March 1849, in the collection of her letters, John Rylands Library, Manchester. In his old age Bamford was very testy about a supposed slight on her part. See his Diary, 16 March 1859.

35 *Mary Barton* (1906 edn), p. 39.

36 'The Publishers' Preface to the Fourth Edition,' *Traditions of Lancashire*, 5th edn (1872), pp. x–xi.

37 Evans, op. cit., p. 237.

38 The 4th (1866) and 5th (1872) editions sold for 10s. 6d. for two volumes, containing all of Roby's work. See 'Publishers' Preface,' *Traditions*, pp. ix–x.

39 See T. T. Wilkinson, 'Memoir of John Harland,' *Lancashire Legends* (1882), pp. xv–xxxv, and Donald Read, 'John Harland: "The Father of Provincial Reporting",' *Manchester Review*, viii (1958), 205–212.

40 *Ballads and Songs of Lancashire, Ancient and Modern*, rev. edn (1882); *Lancashire Folk-Lore, Illustrative of the Superstitious Beliefs and Practices, Local Customs and Usages of the People of the County Palatine* (1867); and *Lancashire Legends, Traditions, Pageants, Sports &c. with an Appendix containing a Rare Tract on the Lancashire Witches* (1873). See also W. E. A. Axon, *The Folk Song and Folk Speech of Lancashire* (Manchester, 1871). Folk customs and lore were also closely linked with rural rambling. A number of books on botany and Lancashire wildlife were

published during these years. See, for example, Leo H. Grindon, *Manchester Walks and Wild Flowers* (1858), later expanded and published as *Country Rambles, Manchester Walks and Wild Flowers* (1882). More recently published is Sylvia L. Corbridge, *It's An Old Lancashire Custom* (1952), *A Lancashire Miscellany*, ed. James Bennett (Oldham, 1960), and the works of Ammon Wrigley for which see n. 61.

41   *Lancashire Folk-Lore*, p. 11.

42   See the preface to the *English Dialect Dictionary* (Oxford, 1896), p. vii.

43   Prince Louis Buonaparte seems to have gone throughout northern England commissioning dialect versions of 'The Song of Songs.' No systematic study of his results has been made, and I have not been able to find out how much he paid his writers, or how *authentic* the results were, since several persons were asked to write versions in different dialects.

44   For a short biographical sketch of Edwin Waugh, see George Milner, 'Introduction,' *Collected Edition* (Manchester [1892], in *Lancashire Sketches*, First Series). Reminiscences of Waugh abound in the pages of the *Manchester Quarterly*. The most informative are James T. Foard, 'Edwin Waugh,' *Manchester Quarterly*, xvii (1890), 197–204, and Abraham Stansfield, 'Recollections of Edwin Waugh,' *Manchester Quarterly*, xxxvii (1911), 434–6. See also Ben Brierley, *Personal Recollections of Edwin Waugh* (Manchester [1890]); a long obituary in the *Manchester City News*, 3 May 1890; and a perceptive early review of his first volume of poetry, *Lancashire Songs*, in the *Manchester Examiner*, 5 February 1859. Waugh's personal papers, commonplace book, and diary (21 July 1847–10 February 1851) are in the Manchester Central Reference Library. There are also three letters in the Chetham Library, Manchester.

45   According to Ben Brierley, *Personal Recollections* (p. 8), he and Waugh were each paid 31s. 6d. plus their fare for an evening's reading in Stockport, but with their overnight expenses and meals 'when we got back [to Manchester] we hadn't even the price of a cab.' For a similar discussion of the problems of giving readings, see Bamford, Diary, passim. He and Brierley gave a reading together 30 January 1861, grossed £1.0s.2d., with expenses of 12s., but on 23 July 1859 he comments 'Gave three readings at Oldham. Gross £16.18.2, Net £14.8.9.' Bamford, a friend of Brierley's, also indicates a good deal of ill-feeling and distrust between Waugh and Brierley, who outwardly found it to their advantage to appear as close friends. Bamford, however, is not to be trusted completely. He heartily despised Waugh and never lost an opportunity to score against him. For comments, see 19 September 1858, 20 October 1858, 2 December 1858. Bamford particularly hated the fact that at the time Waugh was being lauded for his picture of family happiness in 'Come Whoam to thi Childer an' Me' he was living with another woman and had left his wife and children in the Marland Workhouse. See 19 September 1858. For Waugh's version of why he left his drunken wife, see his Diary, passim.

46   10 May 1890, pp. 572–3.

47   Milner, op. cit., pp. xxxii–xxxiii.

48   *Poems and Songs* (Manchester [1892]), pp. 36–8. Originally published 1859.

49   Waugh does treat factory life and poverty in a few of his poems, though he leaves the nature of the work and place quite vague, except in 'The Little Doffer,' set in

an early mill before the Child Labour Acts. See 'God Bless These Poor Folk,' 'Hard Weather, Winter 1878–79,' and 'The Factory Bell.'

50 John Swann, *Manchester Literary Club: Some notes on its history, 1862–1908* (Manchester, 1908), p. 7. For a statement of purpose, see *Proceedings of the Manchester Literary Club 1873–74* (Manchester [1875]), p. xii; the same issue contains a complete membership list, rules, and reports of the previous year's sessions.

51 For reminiscences, see the references to Waugh, above, and Joseph Weir Hunter, 'The Clubs of Old Manchester,' *Manchester Quarterly*, iii (1875–6), 7–32.

52 For the publications of members, see *Manchester Quarterly*, ii (1874–5), iii–xi, and regularly thereafter. Also see W. E. A. Axon, *The Literature of the Lancashire Dialect: A bibliographical essay* (1870).

53 See R. R. Bealey's 'Our Folk' (Manchester [1869–73?]) and Ben Brierley's 'What ails thee, Ned?' untitled poem, in *Personal Recollections*.

54 Ridings (1802–72), a silk handloom weaver and a Peterloo veteran, drifted from job to job in Manchester, never settling down or succeeding in a new trade. He published verse prolifically and finally ended life selling his volumes and a few second-hand books at a stall. Failsworth, the home of Ridings and Brierley, was a small silk-weaving village with a considerable history of Radical politics and poetry. Sim Schofield, *Failsworth Folk* (p. 32), mentions six poets, plus 'a number of very minor ones.' In 1884 eleven 'Peterloo veterans' from the village posed for their picture at a reform demonstration for extending the franchise (see Schofield, p. 64). For details about Brierley's early life, see 'Failsworth, My Native Village,' *Ab-o'-th'-Yate Sketches and other Short Stories*, ed. James Dronsfield (Oldham, 1896), III, pp. 253–61, and *Home Memories and Recollections of a Life* (Manchester, 1886), pp. 2–53.

55 *Home Memories*, pp. 72–99; Brierley, *Some Phases of Municipal Life* (Manchester, 1879); Edward Mercer, 'Brierley as a Writer of Fiction,' *Manchester Quarterly*, xxvi (1900), 454–6; Thomas Newbigging, 'A Reminiscence of Ben Brierley,' *Manchester Quarterly*, xxviii (1902), 447–51; James Dronsfield, 'Preface,' *Ab-o'-th'-Yate Sketches*, I, pp. v–xxv. The total lack of comment about Brierley's political career leads one to conclude that he left no mark on the town council.

56 Ben Brierley Testimonial Fund, Newspaper cuttings, n.d., n.p., Manchester Central Reference Library.

57 'Owd Times an' New,' *Ab-o'-th'-Yate Sketches*, II, p. 132.

58 'Treadlepin Fold,' *Ben Brierley's Lancashire Stories* (Manchester, 1884), III, p. 6.

59 'Out of Work,' *Lancashire Stories*, VI, pp. 76–7.

60 Ibid., pp. 77–8.

61 See May Yates, ed., *A Lancashire Anthology* (Liverpool, 1923) for the later developments. Ammon Wrigley (1862–1946) of Saddleworth, was a poet of the moors and an antiquarian, living far from the city but much admired by Manchester writers as one of the last authentic voices of Lancashire dialect. See his *Songs of the Saddleworth Dales* (1903), *Saddleworth Superstitions and Folk Customs* (Oldham, 1908), *Lancashire Idylls* (1942), and his autobiography, *Rakings Up* (1945).

32 Areas of Urban Politics
Leeds, 1830-80

Derek Fraser

Political party feeling prevails to a mischievous extent at Leeds—the parties
are nearly balanced and it is scarcely possible to take any step in Leeds Township
without exciting strong party feeling.[1]

There is much more to urban politics than supplementary evidence about national
politics. Politics is about the pursuit and exercise of power: it is also about conflict
and debate over policy. A proper study of urban politics will seek to explain how
urban society organized its power structure and to show how this is related to wider
views about national and local policy. We know far too little about the political
structure of specific localities both rural and urban, because so much local history has
been written to illustrate or confirm national developments.[2] To what extent the
same analytical tools are required to study urban and county politics remains an
open question. There are certain themes common to both but it does appear that the
county political system was inherently less diffuse, its institutional structure less
complex than that prevailing in Victorian cities. Basically, we need a model of
urban politics.

In this chapter such a model will be suggested to explain the institutional
structure of politics in Victorian Leeds and it will be based on an attempt to chart *all*
the avenues through which politics ran. It is contended here that a fourfold model
be used and that political activity be examined in four related, though distinct fields:
(a) township and parochial administration, (b) municipal government, (c) parliamentary elections, and (d) political agitation. We thus trace the ripples in the political
pool from the minor offices of street-sweeping, through the seat of local power in the
town council, out to the nations' legislature, and beyond to the sort of programme
that people believed ought to be implemented in the national interest.

Leeds was in 1831 a bustling town of some 123,000 people whose population had grown no less than 47 percent in the previous decade and whose traditional power structure was now threatened by underlying economic changes. Still unrepresented in parliament and governed by a self-elected Corporation, Leeds had grown as a commercial rather than a manufacturing centre and its woollen merchants had by the eighteenth century gained a dominant position in the West Riding wool trade. It specialized in the finishing trades of woollen-cloth production and in the marketing of finished cloth. Three-quarters of all cloth passing through Leeds was exported, and good communications, especially via waterways, enhanced its geographical location between contrasting regions: 'with a vast manufacturing district on one side and a rich agricultural district on the other Leeds is calculated to form the most advantageous depot for the commodities which they respectively produce.'[3] In the eighteenth century the élitist social and economic structure of the town, based on the dominance of woollen merchants, was faithfully mirrored in the oligarchy of the Leeds Corporation, which had originally been created to maintain exclusive control over the local trade.[4]

In the half-century from the end of the American war Leeds woollen merchants found themselves challenged by new entrants to the trade who showed less of the traditional caution in grasping for the fruits of the expanding American market. At the same time technological changes in wool production were undermining the dominance of the merchants and a few, like the famous Benjamin Gott, went into the manufacture of woollen cloth themselves. The whole Leeds economy was diversifying as flax-spinning, engineering, coal-mining, and tanning developed along with a host of consequent tertiary industries.[5]

None of these newer occupations was exclusively filled by men hostile to the Corporation. Indeed, Gott was a Tory Anglican and the co-options of the last years of the old Corporation indicate a widening occupational spread. Yet large numbers both of the newer merchants (who were taking the places of those traditionalists whose sons were entering the gentry and the professions) and of the manufacturers in the newer trades, were Whig or Radical in politics and Dissenters in religion. In wealth they could rival or even surpass the traditional oligarchy, yet socially and politically they were still outsiders. There were no avenues for social and political advancement within a closed corporation, and no seats in parliament. Hence successful businessmen aspiring for local positions of influence and dignity invaded the only area of political control open to them, the institutions of parochial administration. The battle against the Tory oligarchy would begin here and in this disequilibrium between the economic and political structure the political system of Victorian Leeds was born.

It has normally been argued that the politicizing of the minor local offices was a development of the later 1870s and a result of widespread imitation of the Birmingham caucus as a mode of organizing local politics. Indeed, the activities of the Leeds Liberal Association have been quoted as evidence of this tendency.[6] Yet in fact the immersion of the minor parochial offices in the Leeds political cauldron had occurred half a century earlier. This had been noticed by the Municipal Corporations Commissioners:[7]

> The ill effects of the present exclusive system are rendered strikingly apparent from one circumstance in this borough. In cases where the election is popular as in the choice of the Commissioners under the local acts the persons selected are all of one political party professing the opposite opinions to those entertained by the majority of the corporation: which is accounted for by the necessity of balancing the influence of the corporation at the same time it is said to show the inclination of the majority of the town. This choice of Commissioners exclusively from one party is admitted to be undesirable but is justified as being resorted to in self defence.

In Newcastle a complicated method of election enabled some degree of popular control to seep into an unreformed corporation. In Nottingham proscribed Tories who faced a Whig corporation gained entry to the junior council, even though real power remained with the aldermen and senior councillors of the 'clothing'.[8] In these two places some participation *within* the existing municipal system was possible: in Leeds it was not. Hence a Liberal vestry emerged as a counterweight to a Tory corporation and the scramble for the spoils of *all* local offices became a feature of the political system of Victorian Leeds.

The parish of Leeds, which was coextensive with the nineteenth-century borough, had traditionally been divided into Leeds township and the ten out-townships of Chapel Allerton, Potter Newton, Holbeck, Hunslet, Beeston, Wortley, Armley, Farnley, Bramley, and Headingley-cum-Burley (see Maps XIV–XV). Many of the local offices such as those of highway surveyor and Poor Law overseers were fragmented and their jurisdiction applied only to their local township. For the office of churchwarden, the first local office to be politically contested, each out-township nominated a warden whose name would be confirmed, along with those of the eight wardens for Leeds township, by the ratepayers in the vestry of the parish church. The office of churchwarden had the three characteristics which made it an administrative post worthy of political combat. Its intrinsic status was high while other superior offices were out of reach. It carried with it considerable power (not only over church affairs, in this instance, but also over the Poor Law). Finally, it enabled men to implement policies for which they were already campaigning by way of political agitation, in this case the abolition of church rates.

From 1819 Edward Baines, a Liberal Independent and editor of the *Leeds Mercury*, began a campaign to open up parochial administration to public view. Votes of money were withheld by the vestry until accounts were published, in an attempt to highlight extravagance, and Liberal Anglican churchwardens began to be elected in order to encourage economy. When John Armitage Buttrey became senior churchwarden in 1828 a reign of economy began and expenditure was reduced by up to two-thirds within five years.[9] Tory Anglicans, like Henry Hall, a wealthy wool merchant, and Robert Perring, editor of the *Leeds Intelligencer*, led a spirited counter-attack in the mid-1830s. They contested the election of 1833, went to the Court of King's Bench over their inability to get a poll in 1834, and finally successfully demanded a poll in 1835. While Anglicans saw this dispute as an attack by Dissenters upon the Church, Liberals emphasized the question of economy in church rates. The building of three new parliamentary churches in the 1820s had placed added burdens on the rates and Baines was confident about an appeal to the pockets of the voters:[10]

> The Tories have often talked of turning out Mr Buttrey but they
> have never yet succeeded indeed the parishioners unless they prefer
> extravagance to economy will never allow it. Nor would a poll by plurality
> of votes save them for the Tories around them would rather pay 300£
> a year than 1500£ and many would vote for Mr B. on that ground.

This proved to be a judicious prophecy and the Tories were defeated in the poll by three to one.[11] The contest, which had all the paraphernalia of a Parliamentary election—coloured handbills and bunting, canvassers and placards—indicated that very real power and very real issues were involved at this level of Leeds politics. In Manchester the churchwardens later became a Conservative stronghold in opposition to a new Liberal corporation: in Leeds the roles had been reversed.

The office of churchwarden was a great breeding-ground for future Liberal politicians in Leeds and no less than five of those elected in 1835, including Buttrey, entered the council when the corporation was reformed. Two of them had particularly distinguished municipal careers. Joseph Bateson, a wool merchant, was alderman from 1838 to 1862 and while mayor in 1850 gave the most splendid ball in living memory. Peter Fairbairn, a self-made Scot who founded the great engineering empire which later became Fairbairn Lawson, matched his soaring business career with progress upward in local politics, first as churchwarden, then councillor, later alderman and mayor—a career finally sealed by a knighthood for entertaining the Queen on her visit to open the Town Hall.

These men were Liberal Anglicans, while the majority of their political colleagues were Dissenters, whose main aim in capturing the churchwardens had been to abolish church rates. This did not immediately follow the Liberal accession, since many believed that the churchwardens could not fairly be expected to bear the financial burdens themselves, and the last church rate was accordingly levied in December 1835, demanded by Liberal churchwardens and granted by a Liberal vestry.[12] The vestry was not so pliant two years later when the new right-wing vicar of Leeds, Walter Farquhar Hook, tried to bully ratepayers into the grant of another rate.[13] From 1836 Dissenters were elected churchwardens, indemnified by their friends for the necessary expenses of running the Church, and even Hook had to accept enforced voluntaryism to the extent that the parish church was rebuilt in 1840 by private subscription rather than church rates. Even the pressing need for new burial-grounds could not induce the ratepayers to grant another rate.

Though Hook had acknowledged the demise of church rates he continued to identify himself with the Tory Party by such acts as his flamboyant return from a

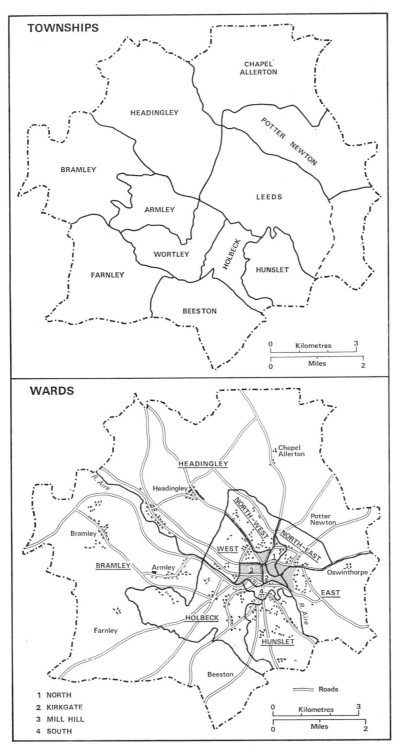

XIV and **XV** The townships and wards of Leeds

Continental holiday to vote in the 1841 election. Liberals therefore felt that they must 'in pure and necessary self defence elect Dissenters to be Churchwardens'.[14] A majority of Chartists were elected as churchwardens in 1842 and while the Liberals did make a token challenge in the following year they were quite happy, so long as there were no church rates, to leave what were in reality tedious and humdrum duties to these humble men. When the Tories regained control after twenty years in 1847 it produced no reaction from the Liberal side, who declined to aid the Chartists in an attempted poll. This contrasts sharply with the later action over the office of highway surveyor which, because of the highway rate, remained of some importance. By about 1850 the three characteristics mentioned earlier no longer applied to the office of churchwarden. Its status was debased; its power had been reduced to laundering surplices and sweeping the church; and church rates had been abolished in Leeds. The office could safely be left in the hands of communicants, and the annual election of churchwardens ceased to have any more general significance than the appointment of trustees in Mill Hill Unitarian Chapel. The office of churchwarden had been removed from the political scene.

One of the attractions of that office in 1830 had been that it held the balance of power in the so-called workhouse board which administered the Poor Law in Leeds township. The workhouse board comprised thirteen overseers *appointed* by the magistrates, twelve trustees of the workhouse elected by the vestry, and the eight township churchwardens. This system, which had evolved in the early eighteenth century, 'contained the Intelligence and philanthropy of men of all parties in the service of the town and has given the Ratepayers a wholesome influence over the expenditure of their money'.[15] The overseers were always predominantly Tory, the trustees Liberal, so that the churchwardens, Tory up to 1827 but Liberal after that, tipped the scales of power.

The accession of the Liberal 'economists' under Buttrey thus removed the Poor Law as well as parochial administration from Tory control—and of course far more money was spent in poor relief than in maintaining the church. This led to violent arguments on the board and Robert Baker reported,[16]

> The Boardroom has long been a sort of arena for party politics on a small scale; . . . of late politics have run high with us, the Trustees and Churchwardens chosen by the people in Vestry have been a little opposed to the overseers chosen by the magistrates and to such a pitch has this feeling been carried that public poor law business has been very much neglected and very bad feeling has existed.

The Tory attempt to win back the churchwardens in the years 1833–5 was as much as anything a means of resolving the deadlock on the workhouse board. When this failed the Tories resorted to law and found that in fact the overseers were the only legal instrument of Poor Law administration and that 'Trustees sat on the Workhouse Board by courtesy; the Churchwardens by *usurpation*'.[17]

The Tory victory in confirming the overseers in sole control was a pyrrhic one, because the new Liberal magistrates of 1836, the much criticized 'Russell justices', replaced Tory overseers by Liberal ones, the immediate consequence of which was the notorious 'Heaps job'. George Evers, the inefficient Tory treasurer of the workhouse board, was replaced at double his salary by Christopher Heaps, himself one of the Liberal overseers.[18] While the spoils of power were so obviously being allocated on party lines, political pressures could not be removed, but a *via media* was found when the Peel Government appointed nine Tory magistrates in 1842 and the practice began of nominating an equal number of overseers from each party. This balance was carefully maintained, especially after 1867 when the overseers, by then merely poor-rate collectors, had the burden of drawing up even bigger voting lists. This helped to insulate the overseers from the party politics of the town and they reported to their superiors that 'to preserve unity of feeling and to avoid any political bias the magistrates have elected an equal number of persons professing opposite political sentiments, and the harmony which has existed amongst the overseers has never been interrupted'.[19]

The sole rule of the overseers came to an end in December 1844 when the new Poor Law was introduced into Leeds. This had first been tried in 1837 with an attempted election which had ended in fiasco. Both in 1837 and in 1844 the guardians' elections were fought on party lines, justified as ever by the needs of self-defence. In 1837 Perring had written, 'it is at all times desirable that party politics should be excluded from matters connected with parochial affairs but the grasping spirit of our political opponents turned the election of every petty parish officer into a question of party.'[20] By 1844 all local power was in the hands of the Liberals and the Poor Law election followed close on the heels of a refusal by the Liberal majority on the council to share the aldermanic honours between the parties. Tories, like the Liberals twenty years earlier, thus pursued political power through the Poor Law as a compensation for their disappointments in the town council.

They were certainly well rewarded, for until 1876, when the better organized caucus approach produced dividends for the Liberals, there were only three occasions (1853, 1854, and 1859) when the board of guardians had a Liberal majority. The spoils could thus be distributed under Tory patronage and the notorious Heaps and four of his underlings were dismissed and replaced by Conservatives. In particular the important office of clerk to the guardians went in 1844 to John Beckwith, reporter for the *Leeds Intelligencer* and leader of the Tories at many vestry meetings. When he died in 1856 he was succeeded by Henry Lampen, secretary of the Leeds Conservative Association. Only with the appointment of Lampen's successor in 1878—John King, formerly a superintendent of out-relief at Liverpool—was this key post allocated without reference to politics.

Lampen, though a political appointee, proved to be most impartial in his administration, unlike Beckwith who was severely censured by the Poor Law Board for the way in which he handled the complicated guardians' elections. A big Poor Law enquiry in 1852 revealed that voting-papers had been tampered with in order to maintain a Tory majority and Liberals were shocked at the gross corruption revealed.[21] Yet their motives in attacking Beckwith were not entirely disinterested, for the Poor Law was a Tory island in a Liberal lake or, as it was aptly put, 'they do not like the Clerk. Of course they don't, I believe his is almost the only Tory appointment in the borough'.[22]

The enquiry of 1852 produced a rare flash of enthusiasm by Liberals for the responsibility of Poor Law administration and in 1853 they won all eighteen seats on the board of guardians. In general, however, Liberals were prepared to allow the Tories to dominate the board and after their two years in control they contested only half of the seats in 1855. The mid-Victorian years saw an overwhelming Liberal majority within the town council, and the decline in contested guardians' elections (only one in 1863) was a sign of declining Liberal concern with the Poor Law.

For a time, party labels ceased to be used in rendering the election results, yet in Leeds there was no getting away from politics and—as the *Mercury* explained on the occasion of a nine-nine election result[23]—

> The Board has been made political and the gentlemen who have now
> obtained seats there have done so as the representatives of their respective
> parties . . . It is not a question of politics or of no politics but simply whether
> the Conservatives or the Liberals are to have the power of giving the
> casting vote on all questions of public policy.

Poor Law policy then, if not Poor Law administration, was to be determined by political attitudes and each year the official party agents, Elihu Finnie for the Liberals and J. Brook for the Conservatives, were in attendance when the voting-papers were cast up. Though politics were studiously avoided within the board, the external popular view of the guardians was inherently political and, as one guardian explained, having been censured for introducing a political matter, 'politics were mentioned outside in reference to the Board though he agreed very improperly'.[24]

The return to a more overt political battle occurred in the 1870s by which time the board had even more power to exercise. In 1869 the Leeds Union had been enlarged to include the out-townships of Potter Newton, Chapel Allerton, and Headingley and the neighbouring districts of Roundhay and Seacroft, which produced a board of thirty-one guardians. In 1874 the work of the Liberal caucus produced a prestigious conquest. William Middleton, formerly a pawnbroker, who, apart from a year's absence in 1859, had been the guardian for North East ward since 1855 and who had been chairman of the board for fifteen years, was defeated and his defeat signalled a more aggressive approach by the Liberals. When the ensuing battle raged over Middleton's vacant chair, James Craven defended the participation of the Liberal Association: 'they did meet and would continue to meet and they would continue to be a power at the board. They meant to be represented there not in a political sense but they wanted the best men in the right places.'[25] Middleton managed to return for a further three-year spell 'via the back door' with a safe seat at Roundhay, but the Liberal advance could not be averted and in 1876 the Liberals regained control of the board. By that time it was clear that

770

elsewhere as well as in Leeds the boards of guardians were part of the political battle. Recent surveys of the Poor Law in the West Riding, Lancashire, and the North East have not been much concerned with politics, concentrating mainly on social administration.[26] There were certainly political contests in Nottingham in 1846 and Beverley in 1869, and Poor Law affairs dominated Gateshead politics in the years 1849 to 1852.[27] It is not yet clear whether Leeds was distinctive in politicizing the Poor Law throughout the half-century under review.

The enlarged powers of the guardians contrasted with the fate of two other township institutions whose powers were amalgamated into the Corporation. These were the improvement commissioners and the highway surveyors, whose offices were abolished in 1842 and 1866, respectively. It was through the Improvement Act of 1824, which led to the demolition of the Moot Hall in Briggate, that Liberal Dissenters had first gained some share in local government. Since magistrates sat *ex officio* as commissioners it was necessary for Liberals to monopolize the elected posts. Without ever becoming a matter of contested elections the improvement commissioners became a Liberal stronghold, so that, for instance, all but three of the nineteen commissioners elected in 1833 can be positively identified as Liberals.

Political controversy entered the arena in the mid-1830s with the abortive attempt by the commissioners to provide Leeds with a much-needed water supply. Internal dissension, mainly over technical matters, forced the abandonment of the scheme and called into question the whole principle of public control for social utilities: 'It is time to give over this wretched farce. Let the Commissioners stick to their sweepings and their drains and leave *pure* water alone, because this is a soilable article. In a word Leeds can only be properly supplied by a Joint Stock Company.'[28] Opinion in Leeds polarized along political lines, most Tories favouring a joint stock company, most Liberals a publicly controlled scheme financed out of a contingent rate on real property. The debate raised important ideological issues and a Radical editor wrote: 'The Joint Stock Company is just a scheme for throwing the town of Leeds bound hand and foot into the power of these men to do as to them seemeth good. The public have over them no control and their scheme is just a monopoly of one of the necessaries of life.'[29] On one side were George Goodman, Baptist woolstapler, four times mayor and later M.P. for Leeds, and Baines junior, who led what might be termed embryonic collectivists who wished to organize a public utility by public control and the redistribution of wealth through taxation. On the other side were Tory wool-men like Richard Bramley and Henry Hall, together with Tory doctors like Adam Hunter and William Hey, who led what might be called the individualists—mostly capitalists who saw the profit motive as the main guarantee of efficiency.[30]

In the end a compromise was found, but not before the improvement commission election of 1837 had been fought on the water question, giving the Tories their first majority. A four-year period of office was made possible by packing the vestry with a bizarre alliance of Operative Conservatives and hackney-carriage proprietors, and by a legal decision annulling a Liberal victory in 1840. The 1839 commissioners remained in office for two years, clinging to power like leeches and diminishing in numbers because of the vestry's refusal to appoint replacements until all of the 'usurping commissioners' resigned.[31]

The Liberal commissioners of 1841 were succeeded by a Chartist body which fought valiantly to retain the powers of improvement commissioners within the vestry. The anticipated Improvement Act, which was the belated fruit of Robert Baker's statistical enquiry of 1839, raised the whole question of where the powers should reside. The Chartist commissioners, led by Joshua Hobson, sought to retain democratic control by the massed ratepayers in popular assembly in the vestry. The Leeds Improvement Act of 1842, however, vested all powers in the town council and so the commissioners disappeared.[32]

It was no coincidence that this Act, which removed an important area of local administration from Chartist control, should be followed immediately by a successful Chartist challenge for the board of surveyors of highways. The highway surveyors had always been lowest on the list of priorities for those who had political aspirations and until the Chartist move in the 1840s the office has not been politically contested. The board's duties were the humble ones of highway maintenance, but its powers did include the right to levy a highway rate. Once more the political system of Leeds produced a situation where men, denied access to superior offices by their social and political status, made a political battleground wherever they could pitch their tents. With the improvement commission gone and the council susceptible to only marginal Chartist influence, the Chartist rank and file turned to those offices still accessible, the churchwardens and the highway surveyors. In Oldham and Merthyr Tydfil the social structure produced a high political system dominated by proletarian control: in Leeds it produced the politicizing of the township institutions.[33]

William Brook and his fellow Chartist surveyors received no serious challenge to their power between 1843 and 1852 and illustrated by their efficient administration that humble men could manage local affairs. A trip to London by the surveyors on 'a bootless errand unless it was to see the Great Exhibition without making much demands on their own pockets' aroused controversy and produced a spirited Tory attack in 1852.[34] The Liberals, who had been prepared to allow the return of Tory churchwardens, were not so complacent about the highway surveyors and they supported the Chartists in what was seen as a straight Liberal-Tory struggle. Three years later another row, this time over the canvassing activities of a man employed on the stone-heap, led to a similar alliance against a Tory attack.

The victories by poll in 1852 and 1855 confirmed control in the hands of Chartists and Radicals and when the euphemistic terms 'old' and 'new' commissioners were used in other political contests (as in 1854, 1860, 1861) it was invariably an attempt to graft a more respectable membership on to the board. According to Robert Meek Carter, a prominent mid-Victorian Radical, this was inappropriate since 'the gentleman part of such bodies did not do the work and would not do the work. No the work must be done by plain practical hardworking men like himself . . . the barristers the lawyers and the physicians were the worst attenders on any committee.'[35] The last contested election occurred in 1861 when a Liberal councillor John Wales Smith unsuccessfully proposed a completely new board. During the last five years of its existence the board comprised a coalition of mostly lower-class Liberals and Radicals who worked harmoniously together. Carter's hopes about its social composition were fulfilled and the last board of 1866, for instance, contained nine tradesmen/craftsmen, eight retailers, and only two professional men. To the last the board of surveyors of highways remained the political resort of the humble.

Three years after the council levied its first highway rate following the amalgamation of powers, a new area of extra-municipal administration was opened up. The election of the first Leeds school board under the 1870 Education Act put to the test (as had the first Poor Law election in 1844) all those pious statements about removing politics from local government. In October 1870 a compromise was agreed upon by all interested parties, which would have avoided a contest. Within a fortnight John Barran, wealthy clothier, twice mayor and Liberal M.P. for Leeds from 1876 to 1885, announced on behalf of the Leeds Reform League that the compromise would have to be repudiated.[36] Finnie, the Liberal agent, and Frederick Spark, proprietor of the *Leeds Express*, became the organizer for the Liberal party's official list and thereafter school board elections in Leeds were fought on grounds partly political and partly religious.

The school board was a prime example of the politicizing of an institution primarily because of *policy*. It was not, as with the other institutions, that unfulfilled social and political aspirations had to be satisfied, but that the contesting parties disagreed fundamentally over the educational and particularly the religious policy which the Leeds school board ought to pursue. Indeed, the political composition of the board is best understood in terms of religious policy rather than in terms of the normal party labels which never quite fitted the realities of its power structure.

Table 32.1 *Composition of the Leeds school board, 1870–85*

Year	Church	Liberal/Unsectarian	Denominational	Independent
1870	7	6	2	—
1873	5	8	2	—
1876	5	8	2	—
1879	5	3	4	3
1882	5	8	2	—

Table 32.1 analyses the composition of the board after each triennial election, using the categories which make most sense. The Church party was predominantly Conservative yet their leader and first chairman of the board, Sir Andrew Fairbairn, inheritor of the great engineering empire, was a Liberal. The Dissenters and official Liberal candidates tended to coalesce in support of a policy of unsectarian religious education, while those designated Denominational were openly supporters of their

own schools (two Roman Catholics in each election joined by two Wesleyans in 1879). The Independents were a real entity only in the very bitter election of 1879 when there was considerable fragmentation of political opinion.[37]

School board elections posed some severe organizational problems, particularly on the Liberal side. In 1870 the official Liberal list stood independently of the Denominational candidates, even though there was agreement over policy. From 1873, however, Liberals and unsectarian Dissenters worked in harmony and nominated by prior agreement a combined list. It was the refusal of the Wesleyans to work within this scheme that led to the disunity of 1879. The Church party for its part had occasional problems. Fairbairn was an official Church candidate in 1873 but was omitted from the Conservative list and in 1876 an extreme right-wing Church candidate, William Jowitt, forced an election in contravention of an agreement between the parties for the unopposed return of the old board.

More important than the need to regulate nominations was the need to organize the allocation of votes. With each ratepayer having fifteen votes to cast, votes could be wasted in excessively large majorities. The question was whether the Liberal party in Leeds was 'as capable of organizing its forces as is the Liberal party in Birmingham'.[38] Initially Dissenters were advised to cast all their votes for their own denomination's candidate. This did not prove successful and it was not until 1882 that Liberals began to use the principle of ward adoption, which produced spectacular results. In 1882 Liberal voters were advised to plump for one adopted candidate by casting all of their fifteen votes for him and this produced majorities of between 8,000 and 17,000 on these plumpers alone.[39]

Almost inevitably the opening up of a new area of local expenditure produced accusations of extravagance. The board was accused by the Leeds Ratepayers Protection Society of purchasing costly sites and building magnificent schools. As ever, these 'economists' were led by Archie Scarr, a wealthy, rough and ready fruit merchant from Kirkgate market, who also attacked the board inside the council chamber in 1878. The board elected in 1879 was perhaps inhibited by this campaign, tending in any case to starve the non-sectarian board schools, and the economy drive produced one spectacular martyr when Fairbairn resigned in April 1878 over an increase in salary for the board's secretary.[40] In general, however, educational progress was made in Leeds by the school board:[41]

> It has not treated the children of the working classes as paupers and
> criminals for whom the barest and most tasteless sustenance would suffice.
> On the contrary it has sought to equip them fully for the battle of life so that
> even the poorest and humblest among them might have a fair start in the
> race of existence.

Thus an institution of parochial and township administration could affect the lives of Leeds citizens in very basic ways; hence the importance of this area of Leeds political activity.

Feeling also ran high in the town council which was, from the time of municipal reform, a battleground in the political war between the parties. There were many who were prepared to argue that politics should not enter into local government, that the good of the local community should be the sole concern. In the divisive political atmosphere of Leeds this was impossible, and in any case many believed politics to be an intrinsic part of municipal government. George Goodman believed that politics brought 'a spirit of competition, vigilance and . . . energy into the service of the public', while thirty years later John Darnton Luccock, the longest-serving member of the council, confirmed 'this was a political body . . . the Councillors were elected because they had certain political opinions . . . To suppose that gentlemen were sent there merely to make sewers, to light lamps and to cleanse the town was to take a very poor view of the duties devolving upon the Council.'[42] Party political conflict made sense within the political structure of Leeds and if men were not to be chosen on political grounds, then fluctuating municipal issues might produce strange electoral war cries. When the biggest issue of local concern was whether Boar Lane should be rebuilt straight or crooked, an anonymous writer highlighted the incongruity of the slogan 'Rush to the polls and vote for the straight street and down with all dog legs'.[43]

The Leeds town council thus became the Leeds House of Commons and a mere pontoon for shifting the loose baggage from side to side of the political stream. Liberals and Radicals, denied participation prior to 1835, wished it to be so in order to make their newly-won power manifest. There was no better way of reminding their displaced rivals that 'we're the masters now' than by a political distribution of the spoils of power, which in turn further exacerbated political relationships. A critic complained that the new Liberal majority had 'been so immediately governed in all its acts and appointments of paid and honorary public servants by party distinctions and political predilections that any attempt on our part to discard politics when treating of Municipal affairs would be utterly futile.'[44]

It was generally realized by both supporters and opponents of municipal reform that a wider disbursement of municipal honours was expected as the first fruits of the new system, and Joseph Parkes had freely acknowledged, 'Liberals are naturally looking to the Municipal patronage—county attorneys to Town Clerkships—Liberal bankers to Treasurerships etc. etc . . . it is human nature.'[45] In Birmingham an opponent of incorporation detected the main motivation of its supporters in a search for 'power and influence and some share of the loaves and fishes of official rank', while a Leicester doggerelmonger put the same point in verse

> Indeed the Rads are working hard
> Each in his own vocation
> To get a finger in the pie
> Of a *party* Corporation.[46]

Men whose economic status had encouraged frustrated social and political ambitions revelled in the exercise of power once their political influence could truly mirror their wealth.

In Leeds the political distribution of spoils was openly acknowledged. The old town clerk was induced by a paltry salary to resign in 1836 and his post went, subsequently with an inflated salary, to Edward Eddison, a Liberal solicitor who had acted with James Richardson in the revision court. Richardson was appointed clerk of the peace, succeeded on his death in 1861 by his son Hamilton Richardson, also an active Liberal partisan. When Eddison resigned in 1843 because of ill-health he was replaced by John Arthur Ikin, first secretary of the West Riding Reform Registration Association. Baines initially got the Corporation printing-contract and the council wished to appoint as recorder his son Matthew Talbot Baines, who in the event took a similar post at Hull as his father's position as M.P. debarred him from Leeds.[47]

Seats on the bench were generally regarded in mid-Victorian England as legitimate rewards for party loyalty and they have been aptly termed 'the spoils of the game'.[48] Table 32.2 illustrates the system at work and particularly highlights the grossly partisan character of the first two commissions which reflect the political complexion of the government of the day. The creation of the 'Russell justices' in 1836 did more than anything else to rub salt in the wounds of the displaced Tories of the old corporation, who sent a deputation to London to protest about their exclusion.

Table 32.2 *The political composition of the Leeds bench*

	Liberal	Conservative
Magistrates appointed 1836	19	3
1842	0	8
1848	7	4
1855	8	6

Baines provided Russell with the names of a couple of moderate Conservatives to add to the list but also reminded him where his true loyalties lay by successfully urging the inclusion of Darnton Lupton, although he was only thirty, whose 'services to the Liberal party in Leeds have been valuable'.[49] Baines had no difficulty in justifying the appointments of 1836—previous proscription required massive counteraction:[50]

> Almost everywhere the Lord Lieutenants, the County Magistrates, the Clergy, the Police, the functionaries of our Law Courts from the Judges on the Bench to the humblest officer and all the endless train of dependants on each, including the publicans, the *employés* of the Corporations etc., have within living memory been of the Tory party.

The mayoral chain and the aldermanic robe had also been denied to prominent Liberals and Dissenters in Leeds and this too had to be rectified. In Gateshead a Liberal/Radical majority appointed one Tory mayor in the first twenty-two years, but even this small concession was refused in Leeds and there was no Conservative mayor in the sixty years from 1835. The first few mayors of the reformed corporation illustrate the opening of the honorific gates to proscribed Dissenters. George Goodman, a Baptist, was followed by Dr James Williamson, an Independent, Thomas Tottie, a Unitarian, and James Holdforth, a Roman Catholic. Thereafter there were three years of Wesleyan rule and, during one period of five years in the 1840s, four Unitarians came from Mill Hill Chapel, earning for that place of worship the title 'the Mayor's nest'. Liberal Anglicans such as H. C. Marshall, Joseph Bateson, John Hope Shaw, and Peter and Andrew Fairbairn eventually had their turn.[51] By the 1870s the civic chair was being allocated by rotation on the basis of seniority so that in 1878 the main recommendation for the moderate Liberal Addyman was that 'he was not the senior Alderman but he was the senior Alderman of those who had not filled the Mayor's chair'.[52]

As the mayor was almost always appointed from among the aldermen, Conservatives had little chance of progress since they were generally excluded from that honour as well. The initial gesture of appointing four Tory aldermen in 1836 was intensely unpopular among Liberal and Radical voters and, in a council atmosphere poisoned in the later 1830s by the alienation of the borough fund by the old corporation, this generosity was not repeated. Two Liberal solicitors, Tottie and Shaw, frequently pleaded the case for a division of the Corporation honours, but all they could show for their efforts was one Tory alderman in the 1840s—and even he was only elected in mid-term as a replacement for a deceased Liberal. Thus, from the later 1830s to the mid 1890s, there was only this one Conservative alderman.

The caucus organizing municipal affairs was by no means a creation of the late-Victorian period, for it was a feature of Leeds municipal politics from 1835, necessitated by the need for prior organization of the spoils. In order to channel honours in the appropriate direction business had to be arranged beforehand. At one of the earliest meetings of the new council a Tory complained, 'if gentlemen were to come there with measures cut and dried it was all a farce coming there to discuss them' and one anonymous partisan claimed that the council was managed 'in the laboratory behind the curtain'.[53] In the later 1830s Perring continually attacked 'the *Caucus* which meets at the "Reform Registration Rooms" in the Commercial Buildings to dictate the measures of the Whig majority', while in the mid-1860s Henry Price, an aggressive Tory doctor who was councillor for Mill Hill from 1861 to 1870, was a persistent critic of the prior organization of council affairs, 'the business having been done in the back room in Bond Street out of which many things emanated which had better not see the light'.[54]

Men enter politics to *do* something as well as to *be* someone and if the opening up of municipal government had meant in Leeds merely an alternative distribution of honours, then it would have been valid to ask 'what boots it to the people whether a fool wear a blue cap or a yellow one'. One voter had commented 'I care nowt about what colour they wear; it's not blue nor yellow 'at makes 'em better or warse'.[55] From the outset Liberals acknowledged that the aim of a reformed corporation was, in the words of Goodman, to 'effect a material improvement in the condition of the burgesses . . . and promote those objects which would tend to their happiness and prosperity'.[56] How much had been achieved by 1880?

If Leeds had not completely conquered its public health problem by 1880 it had certainly gone a long way towards it, the immensity of the task being the main stumbling block.[57] Otherwise Leeds could compare favourably with other large cities such as Liverpool, Sheffield, Manchester, Newcastle, and even Birmingham. There had been the building of Armley Gaol, the Town Hall, and a new Leeds Bridge; major improvements in Boar Lane, Albion Street, and Briggate; the extension of the public highways and the purchase of Roundhay Park. Important Improvement Acts had been passed in 1842, 1848, 1866, 1870, and 1877, and the council had provided a sewerage scheme, water-supply, and gas. In 1870 the council's powers and activities were described thus: 'It controls the highways throughout the borough, supplies water and gas, directs street sweeping, deals with slaughter houses and lodging houses, regulates smoke consumption, controls the markets, provides recreation grounds and now has added public libraries.'[58] The civic gospel may have emanated from Birmingham but Leeds was a leading disciple of it in the North.

The most obvious result of all this activity was an enlarged borough debt and increased rates. In 1842 the debt was £15,700 and the total borough rates 2s. 4¼d.; by 1867 the debt was £801,150 and the rates 3s. 4½d. Further increases stemmed from the purchase of the gas-works in 1870 and Roundhay Park in 1871. Such increased costs produced periodic cries for economy and retrenchment in the 'spending propensities' of the corporation, although this never became the divisive and dominant issue that it did at Leicester.[59]

These were nervous public reactions to sudden increases in powers and expenditure, and invariably followed some great scheme of improvement. Thus the 1843 and 1849 examples of 'economist' activity were the result of the Improvement Acts of the previous year, and in the early 1850s the Town Hall became the test case for people who were worried about the total borough debt. Fears were mixed with grudging admiration for a council which could in one day vote to spend £400,000.[60] The decade prior to the Privy Council inspection of 1865 was free from cries for economy, but these revived strongly in 1868 as a consequence of the 1866 Improvement Act and the great Washburn scheme for water supply which alone cost over £300,000. G. A. Linsley, a pawnbroker and Liberal councillor for West ward from 1862 to 1868, together with Archie Scarr, the fruit merchant, led the economist campaign of the later 1860s. Though a lot of noise was made and an economist was returned for both Hunslet and Holbeck in 1870, Scarr's main campaign in West ward from 1869 to 1871 failed and he eventually entered the council in 1872 for North East, by which time the fears of extravagance had subsided once more.[61]

Popular pressure for economy was the price which had to be paid for the introduction of the representative principle into local government. The main case for municipal reform in Leeds had lain in the self-elective, oligarchic nature of the corporation, and frequently recurring fears of centralization were based on a desire to preserve democratic local self-government. The general will had to prevail and good sense conquer short-sighted economy, which was usually what happened. The elective principle enabled a new area of political combat to be opened up and this can be measured in terms of political parties.

The bald fact of Liberal control from 1835 to 1895 hides two great upsurges of Conservative strength which nearly brought victory. The initial election of December 1835, in which the Liberals won forty-two of the forty-eight seats, seemed to ensure long-term control, yet by 1841 the council was delicately balanced thirty-two to thirty-two, despite the Liberal monopoly of all sixteen aldermanic seats. In 1841 in Leeds and in 1844 in Nottingham the expected Tory victory did not materialize and these two boroughs did not follow Liverpool and Exeter into the Tory camp.[62] Thereafter there was no real Conservative challenge for thirty years, with the number of Conservative seats fluctuating between eight and sixteen. In the early 1870s, partly as a result of political activity by the licensed victuallers, there was a Conservative revival, and by 1874, again a year of aldermanic elections, the end of the Liberal regime was possible. In fact the Liberals won eleven to five in 1874: had the result been reversed Conservative aldermen would have been elected and Conservative control established.[63] Instead the Tory challenge withered away and by 1880 Liberals dominated the council by fifty-three to eleven.

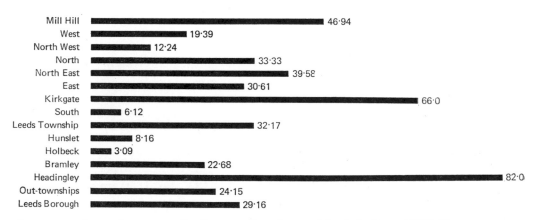

Percentage share of seats won by Conservatives in municipal elections, 1835–80

Moving from chronology to geography we can see from the diagram the overall result of all elections between 1835 and 1880, based as it is on the wards introduced in 1835 and replaced in 1881 (see Map XV). The pattern of voting may be compared with Table 32.3 which attempts some relative assessment of the wealth of each ward. It will be seen that the three wealthiest wards (Mill Hill, Kirkgate, and Headingley) were the three most successful wards for the Conservatives, while two of the safest Liberal wards (Hunslet and Holbeck) were near the bottom of the social ladder. However, before we advance over-simplified relationships between social class and municipal voting we should recall that Conservative strength in Mill Hill (in any case less than 50 percent) was not substantially greater than that in North East, the

779

poorest ward in the town. When the richest and poorest wards of Leeds could return roughly similar numbers of Conservative councillors over about half a century, one should beware of forging iron links between wealth and voting.

Table 32.3   *Economic status of Leeds wards (average per capita rateable value in £)*

		1841	1871
1	Mill Hill	11·94	23·69
2	Kirkgate	7·52	11·21
3	Headingley	6·27	4·39
4	South	3·82	3·94
5	West	3·67	3·33
6	Bramley	2·82	2·78
7	North West	2·78	2·37
8	North	2·24	2·16
9	Hunslet	2·23	1·92
10	Holbeck	2·11	2·20
11	East	1·83	1·67
12	North East	1·49	1·38

Municipal voting gives an added dimension to the political analysis of parliamentary election results; this is the third and most familiar area of political activity surveyed here. A comparison of ward voting-patterns shows a close correlation at the extremes between municipal and parliamentary results, Liberals doing well in South, Hunslet, and Holbeck wards, Conservatives in Headlingley and Mill Hill. However, other wards displayed considerable discrepancies between the two types of contest. Superficially, the *overall* results seem roughly similar since the 29·16 percent of council seats won by Conservatives in the borough between 1835 and 1880 are echoed by the fact that, between the first parliamentary election in 1832 and the redistribution of seats in 1885, Conservatives won eleven out of thirty parliamentary seats contested. Yet *a priori* one would not expect the fragmented ward elections for councillors, which allowed the distribution of political strength to be reflected in the results, to have produced similar results in parliamentary elections, where all voting had to be centred on one contest. When it is recalled that the vital Liberal municipal victories of 1841 and 1874 occurred in years of Conservative success at parliamentary elections then it becomes clear that Conservative municipal weakness masked parliamentary strength.

While nearby Radical boroughs like Bradford were living proof of the almost unbreakable link between the great cities and Liberalism, Leeds distinguished itself by its large and persistent Conservative minority.[64] Liberals, of course, won most of the seats (about two-thirds) and no election in Leeds between 1832 and 1885 failed

to return at least one Liberal M.P. Yet at the same time only five contests failed to
return at least one Conservative and there was a long list of defeated Liberal visitors
to Leeds: Lord Brougham's brother William in 1835, the Radical Josephs, Hume in
1841 and Sturge in 1847, the great Gladstonian Liberal W. E. Forster in 1859, and
Lord John Russell's eldest son Viscount Amberley in 1865. Indeed, Leeds was the
first of the newly enfranchised industrial boroughs to return a Conservative when
Sir John Beckett, of the famous Leeds banking family, was returned in 1835, following a spectacular success in objecting to Liberal compounded ratepayers at the
previous revision.[65]

In order to judge the relative strength of the parties in the period as a whole, a
particular statistical mode of rendering the results has been utilized in Table 32.4.
The problem is that between 1832 and 1867 Leeds was a dual-member borough and
that the contending parties did not always put up the same number of candidates.
Hence to compute the share of poll on the basis of the total votes cast (our contemporary method) would distort the picture, since some voters plumped for one candidate while others split their votes between two. The problem is even more acute
between 1867 and 1885 when the so-called minority clause of the second Reform Act
gave Leeds a third seat but restricted voters to no more than two votes each. The
result at Leeds was to ensure that neither party was completely defeated or completely victorious.

Table 32.4 shows share of poll, assuming a contest between leading Liberal and
leading Conservative, which gives a picture of the optimum voting strength achieved
by the parties at each election except 1847, when there was a 51 percent cross-party
vote. This statistical method is not biased by the unequal number of candidates nor
by the minority clause, and enables a comparative survey to be made, using the
same scale throughout the period. The figures for 1834, 1857 (ii), and 1876 are actual
results for by-elections where only one seat was being contested. Only in 1852, 1868,
and 1880 did the Liberals achieve a share of over 60 percent, and in the latter two
dates the minority clause presented the Conservatives with one seat.

Table 32.4   *Conservative share of poll at Leeds elections, 1832–80 (assuming
leading Liberal against leading Conservative)*

(percent)

1832	44·11	1852	32·57	1868	37·19
1834	49·56	1857 (i)	48·99	1874	49·13
1835	51·84	1857 (ii)	50·07	1876	45·24
1837	46·45	1859	49·56	1880	35·09
1841	50·39	1865	51·42		

The situation of balance, slightly tilting towards the Liberals, is echoed in the
voting patterns derived from poll books.[66] Conservative strength of the order of

two to one was evident in the law and medical professions, while Liberal strength at the ratio of three to one was revealed in the three key Leeds industries of wool, engineering, and flax. In general, Conservatives were able to beat the Liberals three to two in the craft/trade/retail groups such as hatters and curriers. This general pattern may be compared with a very significant analysis of council membership. In 1841 when the council was evenly divided the proportion of each party falling in each occupational group was as follows:

Table 32.5 *Distribution of council membership by occupational group, Leeds, 1841*

		Liberal	Conservative
		(per cent)	
I	Gentry and Professional	34·3	34·3
II	Merchants and Manufacturers	56·3	40·7
III	Craft/Retail	3·1	18·7
IV	Drink/Corn interest	6·3	6·3

Broadly speaking the parties were similarly composed, with a greater inclination to the Liberals in group II and to the Conservatives in group III.[67]

This picture is reinforced by an examination of the individuals who were prominent in Leeds politics. Every occupational group was represented in each party. Tory doctors like the Heys, Adam Hunter, and Henry Price faced Liberal colleagues James Williamson, Robert Baker, and Samuel Smiles. Liberal solicitors such as T. W. Tottie, James Richardson, and John Hope Shaw confronted Tories such as Edward Bond, John Atkinson, and Benjamin Cariss. Many of the new engineers were Liberals, such as the Fairbairns, the Kitsons, Taylor Wordsworth, and Maclea and March, but Conservatives had supporters in this growing trade in Samuel Lawson, the Cawoods, and the Beecrofts and Butlers of Kirkstall Forge. The traditional wool oligarchy of Leeds had been Tory, but Liberals such as the Luptons, the Stansfelds, George Goodman, and Henry Dixon created woollen empires in the nineteenth century. If the most famous flax-spinning family were the Marshalls, they were opposed politically by J. R. Atkinson and W. B. Holdsworth. The list could go on and on: there was even a Tory equivalent of the notorious Archie Scarr, William Wray, also a fruit merchant who was uncouth but wealthy and who faced continual jibes from more respectable folk. It was certainly the impression of contemporaries that parties did not represent different social and economic interests and James Garth Marshall, M.P. for Leeds from 1847 to 1852, wrote,[68]

> I should be sorry to see the Whigs entirely merged in the Conservatives.
> I do not like party divisions to run by classes and not by principles:
> all the aristocracy and landed gentry on one side, the democracy and town
> people on the other: or all church against all dissent. Our old party
> organisation was far better.

The key phrase is the last: politics in Leeds as Marshall knew them were not 'run by classes'.

What mattered in Leeds politics was opinion and belief. Men differed politically not because of social class or connection or interest group but because of issues of conscience, policy, and ideology. Nurtured by a sophisticated and influential press, Leeds thus became an active centre for the fourth area of urban politics, political agitation. An enormous variety of movements found support in Leeds from the years of Catholic emancipation in the 1820s through to the 'Bulgarian bosh', as one opponent called it, of the later 1870s. Thomas Plint, a leading Anti-Corn Law man, was right when he said in a self-congratulatory manner, 'Leeds had always been the leading town in these great movements and what great movement was there that had not had its strongest support in Leeds? It had been foremost for 90 years in all works of charity, enlightenment and right legislation'.[69] Out of the cauldron of political agitation which included such diverse questions as factory reform, co-operation, Poor Law, Corn Law repeal, operative Conservatism, pacifism, and temperance it would be fair to highlight two dominant issues which captured Leeds opinion in the half-century under review: these were the suffrage and religion.

The period opened with the struggle for the Reform Bill, followed during the 1830s by a series of abortive Radical movements. Leeds provided its own hybrid attempt at class co-operation in the age of the Chartists with the 'new move' of 1840 led by Hamer Stansfeld, J. G. Marshall, and Samuel Smiles. At that time Baines junior was opposed to further reform and was a stern critic of Stansfeld and his friends, but after the Chartist period Baines was one of the national leaders of the combined middle- and working-class Radical assault on the suffrage in the 1850s and 1860s. Two discoveries by middle-class Radicals underlay the new alliance. The first was a realization that an extended suffrage would not necessarily swamp an urban constituency with working-class voters. The second was a growing awareness of the non-revolutionary character of the British working class, many of whom were, in the words of Baines, 'readers, thinkers, members of Mechanics Institutions, teachers in Sunday Schools and enrolled in clubs of mutual assurance or as depositors in Savings Banks'.[70] The propertied middle classes had no need to fear for, as a Leeds councillor explained, 'the men who formed their cooperative societies and mechanics institutions, the 250 or 300 thousand men who were training youths in the Sunday schools . . . he did not think that these men could be considered dangerous'.[71]

Leeds was thus in the van of the movement to extend the suffrage and its other great concern on both sides of the political fence was religion. 'Church in danger' was a powerful rallying cry for Conservatives especially during the 1830s, and the Dissenting attack upon church rates and then upon the established church itself produced an inevitable Conservative reaction. From the later 1840s the whole debate on religion centred on the question of education. If currency was the great

'Brummagem' question and free trade essentially the product of the Manchester School, then the distinctive badge of Leeds was Voluntaryism. Even the great Voluntaryist Edward Miall acknowledged the pre-eminence of Baines on this issue as the 'fire from Leeds' spread throughout the country in 1847.[72] Baines and the Voluntary party in Leeds took up a fixed stance against state education and presented the Conservatives with a seat in Leeds in 1847 and the West Riding in 1848 by splitting the Liberal party on the education question. The Dissenters eventually accepted the 1870 Education Act but, as we have seen earlier, they continued the battle for unsectarian education into the 1870s.

This battle was finally fought out in the school board and thus we have come full circle back to the petty offices of Leeds politics. The fourfold model of urban politics, namely (a) township and parochial administration, (b) municipal government, (c) parliamentary elections, and (d) political agitation, has been illustrated by the workings of the political system of Leeds over half a century. The comment quoted at the head of this chapter, indicating that political partisanship was an important variable in producing the vitality of the system, should not deter researchers from applying the model to other Victorian cities. We know far too little about other places to be sure how typical Leeds was, but if this pattern were repeated elsewhere it would lead to the conclusion that the politicizing of the minor institutions was not the product of the 1870s but of the power structure half a century earlier. Men created the boundaries of political activity according to the prevailing institutional structure, and thus in Birmingham street commissioners, in Manchester police commissioners, became the vehicle for oligarchy in the absence of a corporation. Urban politics ought to be studied in this wider fourfold context because activities in these related areas were all part of the same process. The local ward activity had its place in the wider world, and as one Leeds partisan put it, 'The Whigs of North West ward were part and parcel of a mighty power which was at work in the British Dominions that was attempting the separation of Church and State and the ultimate destruction of the Protestant Religion.'[73] The microcosm mirrored the macrocosm as the renewed national alliance of middle- and working-class Radicals for further reform was illustrated in Leeds by Liberal support for Chartist highway surveyors in a township poll of 1852. Municipal and Parliamentary contests were fought on the same lines since, as the *Mercury* put it, 'the names of Liberal and Conservative are accepted by both sides as embodying a distinct policy in Municipal as in Parliamentary Government'.[74] All these elements combined into one political current which depended for its strength and character on *all* of them. Herein lies the essence of urban politics in Victorian England.

Notes

1   Public Record Office (P.R.O.), Poor Law Correspondence, M.H. 12/15225, Report of Inspector, 24 August 1841.

2　For a somewhat rare attempt to examine local politics exhaustively (which was criticized because it looked at local history through national eyes) see A. T. Patterson, *Radical Leicester* (Leicester, 1954). Most studies of local politics do not have Patterson's range and treat only part of the political structure. See, by way of example, B. D. White, *A History of the Corporation of Liverpool* (Liverpool, 1951); R. Newton, *Victorian Exeter* (Leicester, 1968); G. W. Jones, *Borough Politics: A study of the Wolverhampton town council 1888–1964* (1969); J. M. Lee, *Social Leaders and Public Persons: A study of county government in Cheshire since 1888* (1963); A. H. Birch, *Small Town Politics* (1959); M. I. Thomis, *Politics and Society in Nottingham 1785–1835* (Oxford, 1969); C. Gill and A. Briggs, *A History of Birmingham* (Oxford, 1952); G. Williams, ed., *Merthyr Politics: The making of a working class tradition* (Cardiff, 1966); J. R. Vincent, *Poll Books* (Cambridge, 1967); H. Pelling, *The Social Geography of British Elections* (1967); T. J. Nossiter, 'Elections and Political Behaviour in County Durham and Newcastle 1832–1874' (unpublished D.Phil. thesis, University of Oxford, 1968); V. I. Tunsiri, 'The Party Politics of the Black Country' (unpublished M.A. thesis, University of Birmingham, 1964).

3　*Leeds Mercury*, 29 December 1849. For a general survey on the history of Leeds see M. W. Beresford and G. R. J. Jones, eds, *Leeds and its Region* (Leeds, 1967).

4　See J. Wardell, *Municipal History of the Borough of Leeds* (Leeds, 1846), pp. xxxi–xliii, lxii–lxxxii for the original charters of incorporation.

5　R. G. Wilson, *Gentleman Merchants: The merchant community in Leeds, 1700–1830* (Manchester, 1971); W. G. Rimmer, 'The Industrial Profile of Leeds 1740–1840', *Publications of the Thoresby Society*, l (1967), 130–57.

6　H. J. Hanham, *Elections and Party Management* (1959), p. 391.

7　*Parliamentary Papers* (*P.P.*), 1835, XXIII, Royal Commission on Municipal Corporations in England and Wales, First Report (116): Leeds Report, p. 6.

8　M. Cook, 'The Last Days of the Unreformed Corporation of Newcastle Upon Tyne', *Archaeologia Aeliana*, xxxix (1961), 207–28; M. I. Thomis, *Politics and Society in Nottingham 1785–1835* (Oxford, 1969), pp. 114–42.

9　*Leeds Mercury*, 12 February 1839, gave the figures for the annual Church rates as: 1828: £1642; 1833: £974; but according to C. M. Elliott, 'The Economic and Social History of the Principal Protestant Denominations in Leeds 1760–1844' (unpublished D.Phil. thesis, University of Oxford, 1962), p. 180, these figures do not take account of amounts carried forward. Elliott's figures are 1827: £1526; 1833: £614.

10　Leeds Archives Dept, Baines MSS., Edward Baines to Edward Baines junior, 15 March 1834. Fuller details of these disputes are given in my article 'The Leeds Churchwardens 1828–1850', *Publications of the Thoresby Society*, liii (1970), 1–22.

11　Leeds Parish Church, Vestry Minute Book 1828–1844, p. 111.

12　*Leeds Mercury*, 5 December 1835; Vestry Minute Book 1828–1844, p. 123.

13　W. R. W. Stephens, *Life and Letters of W. F. Hook* (1878), p. 377, claims, 'The day was gained. The rate was passed.' It was in fact refused: see Vestry Minute Book 1828–1844, pp. 166–7; *Leeds Mercury*, 12, 19 August 1837.

14　Ibid., 26 March 1842.

15　Vestry Minute Book 1828–1844, p. 125.

16　P.R.O., M.H. 12/15224, R. Baker to Poor Law Commission, 18 March 1836.

17   *Leeds Intelligencer*, 26 December 1835.

18   *Leeds Mercury*, 28 October, 4 November 1837. For a fuller discussion of the administration of the Poor Law in Leeds see my article 'Poor Law Politics in Leeds 1833–1855', *Publications of the Thoresby Society*, liii (1970), 23–49.

19   Leeds Archives Dept, Ramsden Papers, L.C.A. Box 47 B.2, Memo to Poor Law Board from Leeds Overseers, 15 August 1859. (Professor M. W. Beresford kindly supplied this reference.) See *Leeds Mercury*, 8 April 1868, for remarks of the Chairman of the Magistrates on this matter.

20   *Leeds Intelligencer*, 7 January 1837.

21   P.R.O., M.H. 12/15230, Report of H. B. Farnall, July-September 1852.

22   Anonymous letter to *Leeds Intelligencer*, 24 July 1852.

23   *Leeds Mercury*, 21 April 1860.

24   Ibid., 18 April 1872.

25   Ibid., 23 April 1874.

26   M. E. Rose, 'The Administration of the Poor Law in the West Riding of Yorkshire' (unpublished D.Phil. thesis, University of Oxford, 1966); E. C. Midwinter, *Social Administration in Lancashire 1830–1860* (Manchester, 1969); N. McCord, 'The Implementation of the 1834 Poor Law Amendment Act on Tyneside', *International Review of Social History*, xiv (1969), 90–108.

27   *Nottingham Review*, 17 April 1846; *Leeds Mercury*, 17 April 1869; F. W. Rogers, 'Mayoral Elections and the Status of the Mayoralty in Early Victorian Gateshead [1835–1856]', *Gateshead and District Local History Society Bulletin*, No. 2 (1968), 31.

28   *Leeds Intelligencer*, 26 September 1835.

29   *Leeds Times*, 10 December 1836.

30   For a fuller review of the issues raised by the water question see my article 'The Politics of Leeds Water', *Publications of the Thoresby Society*, liii (1970), 50–70.

31   Leeds Civic Hall, Proceedings of the Commissioners, 2, 29 January, 26 March, 13 April 1840; Vestry Minute Book 1828–1844, pp. 203–4, 210–11, 213–15.

32   The Improvement question is fully discussed in my article 'Improvement in Early Victorian Leeds', *Publications of the Thoresby Society*, liii (1970), 71–81.

33   J. Foster, 'Nineteenth Century Towns—A Class Dimension' in H. J. Dyos, ed., *The Study of Urban History* (1966), pp. 281–99; G. Williams, ed., *Merthyr Politics: The making of a working class tradition* (Cardiff, 1966).

34   *Leeds Intelligencer*, 3 April 1852.

35   *Leeds Mercury*, 1 April 1854.

36   Ibid., 7 November 1870.

37   Ibid., 17–25 November 1879.

38   Ibid., 22 November 1873.

39   Ibid., 21 November 1881.

40   See the exchange of letters between Fairbairn and Jowitt in *Leeds Mercury*, 4, 14 April 1878.

41   *Leeds Mercury*, 17 November 1879.

42   Ibid., 15 October 1836, 30 March 1866.

43   Letter from 'A Ten Pounder' in *Leeds Mercury*, 10 November 1866.

44   *Leeds Intelligencer*, 2 March 1838.

45 Joseph Parkes to Lord Brougham, 18 August 1835, quoted by G. B. A. M. Finlayson, 'The Municipal Corporations Commission and Report 1833–1835', *Bulletin of the Institute of Historical Research*, xxvi (1963), 51.

46 *Birmingham Advertiser*, 2 November 1837; *Leicester Herald*, 19 December 1835.

47 For biographical details of the legal men mentioned here (and of many others mentioned in this chapter) see R. V. Taylor, *Biographia Leodiensis* (1865), *Supplement* (1867).

48 J. R. Vincent, *The Formation of the Liberal Party* (1966), p. 126.

49 P.R.O., Home Office Papers, H.O. 52/31, R. Hall and A. Titley to Lord John Russell, 29, 31 January 1836.

50 *Leeds Mercury*, 16 January 1836.

51 Leeds Civic Hall, Council Minutes, Vols 4–9.

52 *Leeds Mercury*, 11 November 1878.

53 Ibid., 16 January 1836; 'Thoughts on the Town Council', No. 7 in *Leeds Intelligencer*, 17 September 1836.

54 *Leeds Intelligencer*, 17 November 1838; *Leeds Mercury*, 11 November 1862.

55 *Northern Star*, 7 November 1840; University of London Goldsmiths Library, Oastler White Slavery Collection, *The Factory System* (1831), p. 12.

56 *Leeds Mercury*, 27 January 1838.

57 For a review of activity here see J. Toft, 'Public Health in Leeds in the Nineteenth Century' (unpublished M.A. thesis, University of Manchester, 1966).

58 *Leeds Mercury*, 29 October 1870.

59 Patterson, op. cit., pp. 332–52.

60 *Leeds Times*, 6 September 1851.

61 For Scarr see H. Yorke, *A Mayor of the Masses* (Leeds, 1904).

62 For the general background to these cities see R. A. Church, *Economic and Social Change in a Midland Town* (1967); R. Newton, *Victorian Exeter* (Leicester, 1968); B. D. White, *A History of the Corporation of Liverpool* (Liverpool, 1951).

63 For a survey of the crucial 1873 to 1875 period see J. S. Curtis, *The Story of the Marsden Mayoralty* (Leeds, 1875).

64 For Bradford see D. G. Wright, 'Elections and Public Opinion in Bradford 1832–1880' (unpublished Ph.D. thesis, University of Leeds, 1966).

65 For the results at Leeds see W. W. Bean, *The Parliamentary Representation of the Six Northern Counties of England* (Hull, 1890), pp. 911–29; J. Mayhall, *Annals of Yorkshire* (Leeds, 1875). For details of the revision see Thoresby Society, Reports in the Revision Court (with MS. note by Edward Bond).

66 A full set of Leeds poll books exists for the period 1832–68 but only that for 1834 gives occupations. For the rest directories have been used.

67 For a fuller discussion of these and other issues see D. Fraser, 'Politics in Leeds 1830–1852' (unpublished Ph.D. thesis, University of Leeds, 1969).

68 Sheffield Public Library, Wentworth Woodhouse MSS.G7(d)—by kind permission of Earl Fitzwilliam and the Trustees of the Fitzwilliam Settled Estates—J. G. Marshall to Earl Fitzwilliam, 29 November 1848.

69 *Leeds Mercury*, 3 August 1850.

70   Baines MSS., bundle 26, printed letters of Edward Baines to the Leeds Working Men's Parliamentary Reform Association, 1 January 1864.

71   *Leeds Mercury*, 30 March 1866.

72   See ibid., 30 October 1847, for remark of Miall on the pre-eminence of Leeds on the education question.

73   *Leeds Intelligencer*, 1 December 1838.

74   *Leeds Mercury*, 1 November 1877.

33 Orange and Green
Belfast, 1832-1912

Sybil E. Baker

1832 was the cholera summer in Belfast. Of the 60,000 inhabitants almost 3,000 had been stricken.[1] It was, nevertheless, better to risk fever in the town than hunger in the Irish countryside of the 1830s, where the soaring population had brought 'the pressure and danger of want' without the alleviation of any Poor Law.[2] Along the roads of Ulster were passing 'great numbers . . . like the swarming of a hive' to Belfast.[3] Those with capital or ambition—more generally the Nonconformists—embarked for Canada; or remained to seek their fortune in the town's expanding commerce, or to gain entry to the relatively small group of skilled crafts which served the foundries, building trade, and wooden-shipyards.[4] With them, however, came the lowest ranks of Ulster's rural society, the Episcopalian and Catholic labourers or weavers—lured either by the prospect of employment in the thriving port and in the industrial construction which accompanied the transfer from cotton to linen spinning, or by the hope of setting up their looms again closer to the output of the mills. Failures already in the battle to secure a living from Ulster's land, they carried the ethnic violence of her land-wars, the sectarian passion of the 1790s, and the economic bitterness of the dispossessed into their new urban environment. For all these people there were only two shades in the spectrum of Ulster's society and politics—Orange and Green.

The Orange Order, founded in the sectarian-economic competition of County Armagh in 1795, had been given the approval of the gentry as a defence against the '98 Rebellion. Drawn increasingly, however, from the poorest social order—'small weavers, living on low wages, or servants of husbandry . . . few of the Orange farmers owned three acres apiece . . .', it was now regarded by the Presbyterian farmers and the urban middle classes with contempt.[5] Nevertheless the Orange yeomen and militia, followed by the weavers, had carried the Society into the old Liberal strongholds of the United Irishmen—down the Lagan Valley, around and into Belfast.[6] By the 1830s more than half the lodges in Ireland were in this north-east region, and the Order's greatest urban strength lay in the thirty-two lodges of Belfast.[7] Their Catholic counterpart, the Defenders or Ribbonmen, had spread wherever the Orange organization threatened or where the Catholic navvy travelled. Since it was secret and oathbound, without the publicity or restraints of the Orange Order's open constitution and aristocratic Grand Lodge, the Government had greater difficulty in assessing its strength.[8] But as early as 1825 it had sufficient numbers in Belfast to threaten to mount a rival procession to the Orangemen's parade on the Twelfth of July.[9]

Despised by the respectable Protestants, banned by the Catholic clergy, the Societies persisted, for they reflected at its most violent and pugnacious level the ethnic rivalry of Ulster. Even the Party Processions Act of 1832 failed to suppress their parades. Orangemen continued throughout the 1830s to demonstrate their strength on the Twelfth: Ribbonmen marched to St Patrick's Day fairs; and both factions used funerals, elections, and religious processions as legitimate evasions of the ban on parades.[10] For parades were at the very centre of the territorial, and with it the political and economic, struggle. 'Where you could "walk" you were dominant, and the other things followed.'[11]

The election of December 1832 decided that in Victorian Belfast that dominance would be Orange. The Reform Party, the descendants of that Dissenting liberalism which had marked the eighteenth-century Presbyterian town, failed to reverse the monopoly of the Tories, whose downfall they had long awaited. Belfast Conservatism, born of the sectarian excesses of the '98 Rebellion, nourished by the fears of Catholic Emancipation, and wedded to the prosperity of the Union with Britain, won over in the election a significant section of the enfranchised middle classes—the bourgeois Methodists and the evangelical wing of the Presbyterians. For them Reform represented no longer the defeat of the Episcopalian Ascendancy, but '. . . the Repeal of the Act of Union—the dissolution of the connexion betwixt England and Ireland, and the establishment of the Italian Church . . .'[12] In the next thirty years the eloquence of their Conservative Presbyterian spokesman, the Rev. Dr Cooke, made the defence of Protestantism, and not the fraternity of Wolfe Tone, the political shibboleth of Belfast's Nonconformity.

Nonconformity, however, was not yet prepared to assume in 1832 that political Protestantism implied the acceptance of Orangeism. The respectable Conservative and Reform voters deplored the Orange and Green mobs which had paraded the town since nomination day and intimidated the hustings. The new Member, Emerson Tennent, a last-minute convert to Conservatism from Reform, retained enough of

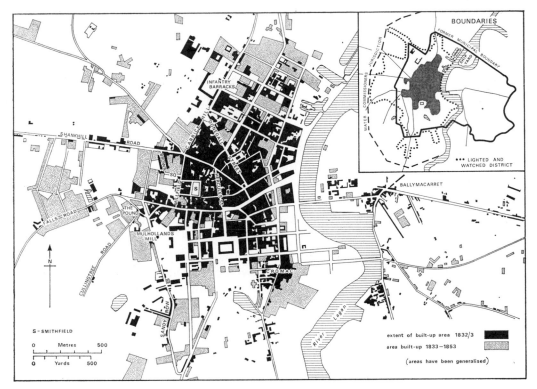

XVI and **XVII** The growth of the built-up area of Belfast between 1832 and the extension of the municipal boundary in 1853
Source: *Parliamentary Papers*, 1859, X, Royal Commission on Municipal Affairs of the Borough of Belfast: Minutes of Evidence (2526, Sess. I)

his earlier Liberal principles to reject at first the proposal of the Orange weavers of Sandy Row that they should celebrate the victory with a chairing.[13] But drink had been flowing freely in Sandy Row, and a second, more insistent deputation made him yield—with one stipulation: that there should be no party tunes or emblems.

His aristocratic fellow Member, Lord Arthur Chichester, son of the local magnate, the Marquis of Donegall, did not share Tennent's bourgeois distaste. Before his committee rooms the parade assembled on Saturday to hear District-Master Boyce address them from Lord Arthur's window. As the mob waved their Orange kerchiefs and the bands played 'The Protestant Boys' and 'The Boyne Water', he 'flourished his stick exultingly, and told them that the Protestants had gained this victory, and that they would continue to maintain their ascendancy; they had trodden down their enemies, and they would keep them down.'[14] At three o'clock, and in this spirit, the processionists moved off, dragging at their head in the carts with their elaborately decorated chairs their noble representative and the apprehensive Tennent. Along the triumphal route through the centre of town the windows of the middle-class houses were crowded with cheering ladies and gentlemen, waving handkerchiefs and hats to the bowing Members.[15]

There were signs, none the less, that trouble was expected. Shopkeepers had shuttered their premises, and the route had been carefully planned to avoid Hercules Street, where the butchers' shops marked the fringe of the Catholic quarter.[16] (See Map XVIII.) One skirmish had taken place in the street already that day, when an Orange mob armed with bludgeons had attempted to traverse it. Now Colonel Coulson with an escort of Constabulary rode at the head of the procession, determined to see that the safe and less provocative route was maintained.

As he reached the further end of Donegall Street, where the parade was to turn back, away from the enticements of the Catholic district, towards the centre of town, Coulson could see at the entrance to Hercules Street a hostile waiting crowd. Behind the jeering butchers' boys pressed the Catholic residents of the narrow streets and rookeries of Carrick Hill—women carrying stones in their aprons, men armed with sticks, crutches, and iron spikes. Coulson wheeled towards them to form a barrier with his men.

The processionists may have believed, as they later asserted, that Coulson was leading them into the street; or they may have been spoiling for another fight. As a shower of stones flew over the heads of the Constabulary, the men dragging Lord Arthur's carriage pulled it resolutely towards the Hercules passage, and the Catholics rushed forward. Ripping the chair from its cart, the butchers with hatchets, knives, and axes began to smash the timber, while Lord Arthur was pulled backwards to safety. Tennent in the second chair was less fortunate, being carried forward into the street in the rush, and making his escape through the open door of the Post Office into a back alley and timber-yard.[17]

Behind him all was confusion. The stewards who had escorted the parade had dropped their white wands and were hurling back the Catholic missiles. One processionist had stepped into a house in Donegall Street and, emerging with a gun, began to fire. Oblivious of the paving stones soaring over him, a man, stripped to the waist, continued to saw busily at the spokes of Lord Arthur's cart. Coulson's description of the Hercules mob as 'murderous' is credible. One Protestant related in evidence later how, having been felled by a butcher with a cleaver, he was surrounded by a crowd crying, 'Kill him! Finish him!', and another leapt upon his throat; but the sound of gunshots distracted his assailants and, with one last blow from a woman with a butcher's skewer, he was able to crawl away.[18]

The Constabulary now were in complete disorder—one horse on the ground, and the Chief Constable defending himself from an adversary who wielded a piece of spiked railing painted green. They could hear answering shots beginning on the Hercules Street side. In spite of this no one had read the Riot Act, for though the Sovereign, the town's Chief Magistrate, had struggled into the mêlée, he had been confronted by a man with a hatchet leading a group shouting 'Kill him!' and had beaten a hasty retreat.[19]

One constable, however, had broken away—racing towards the barracks with the news that 'they were all a'killing at the head of Hercules Street'.[20] From the other end of the street police reinforcements at last advanced. Half-way down, ignorant of the lack of warning, they opened fire. Twenty shots were sufficient to send the mobs scurrying for shelter, but two young boys and two old men had been fatally wounded—their deaths, the subsequent inquest found, 'inflicted by certain policemen at present unknown'.[21]

Tennent in his victory speech had urged that the town's first election should end the era of party rivalry in Belfast, so that its citizens might be 'forgetful of all our late dissensions, and again united in one common cause, the promotion of peace, the concord and prosperity of our native town'.[22] The ferocity displayed by the factions; the inability of the political leaders to restrain their followers; and the inadequacy and loss of control of the police boded ill for his pious hope of concord.

His second wish for prosperity was fulfilled amply in Victorian Belfast. Conveniently sited to channel the increasing Irish Sea traffic between agricultural Ireland and industrial Britain, and to share in the textile-engineering-shipbuilding economy of Northern Britain, Belfast had become by the end of the century both the major port and the industrial capital of Ireland. By 1901, with a population of 350,000, it was the eighth city of the United Kingdom. Its growth-rate—multiplying by five in the Victorian era—was remarkable in Britain, but phenomenal in the declining population and industrial stagnation of Ireland. Dublin, isolated from the traffic of Liverpool and Glasgow and with few manufactures, had multiplied by a mere 1·7. Only by counting its outlying suburbs could it claim at the end of the century a slight numerical advantage over the rival mushroom city of the North.[23]

The contrast in economic growth between the national and regional capitals was paralleled by their ethnic composition. In the first half of the nineteenth century Dublin had become predominantly Catholic. Only 30 percent of its citizens were Protestant in 1841 when it elected the Nationalist leader, Daniel O'Connell, as its first Catholic Lord Mayor.[24] But Belfast was a northern rather than an Irish city. Its industrial expansion was fed by a small but significant flow of British entrepreneurs and skilled labour, and, above all, by the migrating population of Ulster. Only 3 percent came from the other Irish provinces; 7 percent were British-born; 90 percent of its people were of Ulster stock.[25] Drawn from the cleft society of the Ulster Plantation, the urban migration of the descendants of British Protestant settler and Irish Catholic native made it unlikely that Belfast would follow the religious transformation of Dublin, or achieve so painlessly a new ethnic balance.

By the end of the 1830s the enmity between the Orange and Green factions had reached a new peak of rural disorder . . . 'both parties are most anxious to annihilate each other if they possibly could . . . when their blood is up . . . and they have weapons in their hands.'[26] In their new industrial environment the atavistic struggle for socio-economic and political dominance was heightened by the race for the numerical control of the town. Catholics had been 6·5 percent of its population in the middle of the eighteenth century; in 1834 they were 31 percent: by 1848 some 43 percent.[27] The hopes or fears of a Catholic engulfment permeated mid-century Belfast, and help to explain the violence with which each group sought to establish its territorial dominance.

Distinctive occupations formed the basis of Belfast's ethnic neighbourhoods (see Map XVIII). North of the band of Catholic labourers, which stretched from the infantry barracks to the docks, was the new and more prosperous territory of the Orange ships' carpenters. The Orange weavers of Ballymacarett were separated by

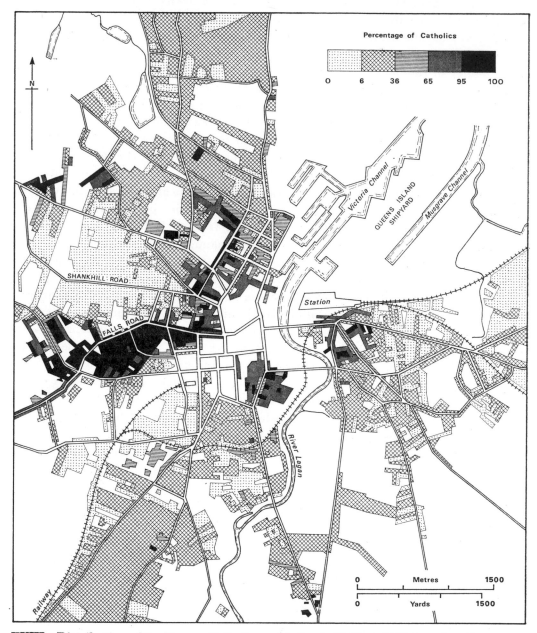

XVIII Distribution of the Roman Catholic population in Belfast, 1911, based on the religious proportions of each street. Source: Census Returns, 1911

the river from the Catholic market-men and navvies of Cromac. To the west, between the Orange weaving-districts of Brown Square and Sandy Row, lay the original Catholic quarter around the markets of Smithfield and the weavers of Millfield. It was here in the western suburbs, where the small streets were springing up to serve the linen mills and foundries of the Antrim streams, that competition for employment was most direct and territorial rivalry most intense. In the thirties and forties, as the expanding Catholic population pushed south-west across the Pound, the Protestant districts on its borders were clearly failing to hold their own in the race for dominance in the key industrial area.

When Sandy Row raised its Orange arch for the Twelfth in 1835, a Green arch fluttered derisively from the Pound, forcing the magistrates to demolish both. With an exultant Pound pressing behind the soldiers, it required three cavalry charges and an infantry volley to bring down the Orange garland. While Sandy Row counted its dead and wounded, the Millfield Boys bearing green branches had slipped quietly northwards from the soldiers to terrorize and loot Brown Square.[28]

Orange fears were not allayed by the withdrawal of their aristocratic leadership.[29] When the Grand Lodge placated the Government by dissolving itself in 1836 the Belfast lodges continued to meet secretly, displaying their flags and emblems in the backrooms of public-houses, and watching uneasily the signs of growing Ribbonism in the town.[30] By 1839 the Ribbon headquarters was thought to be in Belfast, for the harbour and railway construction had brought an influx of Catholic navvies—a close-knit and pugnacious labour force, which used Ribbonism as a closed shop to exclude the Protestant labourer.[31] Not until 1843 did the Orange lodges find a means to regroup openly under the guise of the Belfast Protestant Operatives Society. At its soirées, surrounded by Orange flags and portraits, they drank toasts to 'The Protestant Ascendancy' and 'William's Pious Memory' and vowed 'to put things right at the next elections'.[32] Belfast's Catholic workers, confident of their increasing numbers and buoyed up by the enthusiasm for O'Connell's Repeal of the Union which was sweeping the South in the summer of 1843, were more than ready to take up the challenge of the Operatives. The Twelfth of 1843 would decide whether Orangeism or Repeal would dominate in West Belfast.

As the Twelfth week-end approached and the skirmishings of the boys culminated in the burning of the effigies of William and O'Connell, it was difficult for the authorities to determine which faction was the aggressor. When house-wrecking began on Friday evening on the fringes of Sandy Row and the Pound, each district claimed to be terrified of the other. But it seemed to a Constabulary officer that it was the Catholic party which was 'making the loud cry and giving the big nip'.[33] On Saturday night when a crowd of 600 met to do battle with sticks and stones on the field where Mulholland's Mill divided their territory, Sandy Row found itself outnumbered two to one. 'The number of the Repeal Party continued to increase vastly, and it became necessary for the Protestants to join with the Police, in order to protect the neighbourhood and the Police themselves.'[34] A week later the Pound pressed home its victory by transforming a funeral to the Catholic graveyard of Friar's Bush into a grand

Repeal demonstration of 5,000–6,000 along the very borders of its rival. Marching 'under captains of twenties, captains of fifties, and captains of hundreds', it was the most impressive and ominous organized display of Catholic force which Belfast had witnessed, and in the fighting which accompanied its return the offensive and the advantage lay clearly with the Repealers.[35]

Belfast Catholicism was in the ascendant. Protestant children were attacked on their way to school that August, and a grand Orange anti-Repeal meeting planned for September was abandoned because of fears of disorder.[36] When the lapsing of the Party Processions Act in 1845 allowed the Orange lodges to resume their Twelfth parades, they travelled discreetly out of town.[37] But even this did not satisfy the militant Ribbonmen, of whom there were estimated to be 1,000 in Belfast in 1845.[38] When the 1,500 Orangemen returned from Lisburn on the Twelfth of 1846 they found the Repealers waiting with green boughs and drums, and order was not restored until dark.[39] In the 1847 election the navvies took the day off from cutting the new Lagan channel to riot in the Court House, and they formed the few armed clubs which prepared in Belfast for the '48 Rebellion.[40]

But there was little thought of fighting among the Famine migrants who crowded through Belfast in the next few years. Hunger had broken finally the attachment of the Irish Catholic for his native soil. The United States and not the hostile northern city was his lode-star in the next half-century. In the 1850s the ethnic tide was turning in Belfast—a process accelerated by the opening of the town's first iron-shipyard in 1853.[41] The expansion of shipbuilding and engineering in the next fifty years provided the skilled crafts, and with them the Trade Union organization against the threat of cheap Catholic labour, which continued to draw the Ulster Protestant to the city. Frustrated by the lack of opportunity, the more ambitious urban Catholics joined the stream of rural emigration. By 1900 Belfast's Catholic proportion had dropped to one quarter.[42]

1852 marks the return to confident aggression by the Protestant mob. The Twelfth of that year coincided with polling in the parliamentary election, where a crushing defeat for the Liberal candidates sealed the dissolution of the uneasy alliance of Presbyterian entrepreneurs and Catholic workers.[43] Parades had been banned once more by a new Party Processions Act of 1850, but Sandy Row had other plans to celebrate its victory. On the night of the Twelfth, the first shots were heard in the small streets of Cullingtree Road which led into the Catholic quarter. Warned by these, the Pound was ready by dawn to meet the attackers with stones and firearms.[44]

> One man made himself very conspicuous by the almost unremitting fusilade he kept up from the windows of his house . . . the horrors of the scene almost transcend description. At the moment of the savage conflict the peals of thunder which had been heard at intervals during the day increased in loudness, the lightning flashed vividly and in quick succession, while the screams of women, and the savage shouts of the insane wretches engaged in deadly contest, completed a scene which few who beheld can ever cease to remember.

The arrival of the police and military put the parties to flight, but one man had been killed, and no one could assess how many were injured, for the wounded were carried away to be treated privately.

It had been no more than a night's battle, but it set a more violent and mischievous form upon the hostility of West Belfast. The resort to guns had introduced a dangerous rural weapon into the narrow streets. In the succeeding riots the relationship between the two communities would be further embittered by the memories of their dead. The success of the night's intimidation, moreover, in enforcing large-scale evacuation of families from the mixed territories between the districts was even more tragic, for it involved the innocent and law-abiding and penalized those who practised toleration, or sought integration outside their own community. 'Large numbers of persons, the majority Catholics, have fled their houses in the greatest consternation—carrying all their moveables with them. Some streets are depopulated of the greater part of their inhabitants.'[45] The old rural evil of house-wrecking had been little more than a minor element in the early urban riots. From 1852 it was to prove a persistent and successful factor in enforcing the physical and social segregation of Belfast's religions.

The decennial riots which accompanied Belfast's expansion and prosperity varied only in duration or intensity from the pattern of sectarian hostility, political tension, and ethnic intimidation set in mid-century. For the Belfast worker they became as much a part of his urban environment as its industrial success.

> Belfast's a famous northern town,
> Ships and linen its occupation;
> And the workers have a riot on
> The slightest provocation.[46]

That provocation was persistently the challenge of the right to 'walk'.

In 1864 the Repeal procession in Dublin to lay the foundation of O'Connell's statue incensed the Belfast Orangeman, denied the right to parade his own streets.[47] For five days following the return of the Repealers from Dublin on 9 August, Sandy Row and the Pound were in riot. Mill girls beat each other; running gun-battles disrupted the streets; houses, churches, and chapels were wrecked.

The Catholics, however, had their militant defenders in the Irish navvies of Cromac, 400 of whom had arrived recently to work on a new graving dock and bridge, and among whom militant Fenianism was strong.[48] On Lady Day, 15 August, to celebrate their holiday and avenge the burning of a penitentiary, they marched across town to attack the day-school in Brown Square. Summoned by the screams of the children, the workers from a nearby foundry drove off the attack; but the march of the navvies had drawn into the conflict the skilled workmen, already hostile to the navvy labour threat. Next day the ships' carpenters dropped tools to make their own march to Brown Square, and on their return through town made good their promise of protection by breaking into the gunsmiths' and hardware shops for weapons. On the 17th, while the Constabulary were concentrating on an arms search, 500 of the shipyardmen, armed with guns and adzes,[49] descended upon the unsuspecting navvies on the slobland and drove several hundreds into the mud and rising tide[50] (see Plates 428–9).

> The navvies fought like bull-dogs, but we swore to put them down—
> The assassins of the children—the despoilers of the town!
> Some struggle in the deadly gripe, some load away and fire,
> Ho! Ho! the Navvies show their backs and down the bank retire;
> Some leap into the river, some are scrambling through the mud,
> And our noble fellows follow to the margin of the flood!

The following day the right to walk through the town was asserted more triumphantly, when 5,000–6,000 men, many openly armed, followed the funeral of John M'Connell, a riot victim from Sandy Row, and, defying the route of the magistrates and the escort of cavalry, forced the hearse up to the entrance of Hercules Street before proceeding more decorously upon their way (see Plate 430). Sandy Row had avenged at last the Pound funeral of 1843. By the end of the week the Protestant hysteria had been sated, and a subdued town was left to count the cost of the fortnight's rioting—316 injured, 98 with gunshot wounds, and 11 dead.[51]

The extent of the savagery brought one positive measure from the Irish Executive. In 1865 a quota of the Irish Constabulary replaced the Belfast local police. The permanent presence of a body of the national gendarmerie, armed and trained to quell the Irish land troubles, might instil respect in the turbulent spirits of this urban industrial population. The new police might chasten, but they could not cure the enmity of Belfast's factions. The Commissioners who examined the '64 Riots had concluded with the pessimistic warning that '. . . the increase of physical force on the side of Roman Catholics . . . will tend to provoke trials of strength and . . . make collisions more fierce and bloody than heretofore'.[52]

Their fears proved sound. In 1872 the Orange Order had won at last the repeal of the Party Processions Act. That summer the Lambeg drums beat outside the Chapel of the Holy Cross and Orangemen wearing their regalia made their first open Twelfth parade through Belfast for twenty years. But the legacy of Fenianism had made the diminishing Catholic community defiant, and they were not disposed to permit 'a mob of fanatics to taunt us': '. . . the Catholics of this great town will not allow themselves to be trampled on . . . we must claim equality and assert our right to it, as we are the great majority of the population of this country.' When the speakers at a rally on 23 July called for a parliament at College Green, 10,000 answered with the cry 'Home Rule'. To counter the Twelfth they planned a Fenian Amnesty march for Lady Day, the anniversary of the navvies' march of 1864.[53]

This 'March to Hannahstown' of 1872 erupted into the worst violence the town had yet seen. For nearly a fortnight, flying mobs wrecked houses and battled with each other and the police. It required 2,000 extra police and military, the Inspector General, four Government Magistrates, the closure of the public-houses, the banning of the sale of firearms, and finally the exhaustion of the rioters to restore calm.

837 families had been evicted; 1 constable had been killed and 73 seriously wounded; no one was sure how many civilians were injured or dead.[54]

If the first rumblings of Home Rule had exposed the weakness of the Castle's new measures to maintain order, the next two decades, in which Home Rule became an imminent possibility, proved that the Royal Irish Constabulary alone could not contain the Orange and Green tension. In 1886 that tension had reached a new height and had infected the middle classes, who saw in the Home Rule Bill before Parliament not only a political, but also a social and economic reversal in Belfast. Protestants feared they might be called upon to defend their 'altars and firesides'.[55] Catholic labourers that spring were rumoured to be holding raffles for the future ownership of the factories. In June the city was awake at dawn to hear the result of the Third Reading of the Bill, and the shipyardmen cheered on their way to work. Relief and frustration exploded in three months of rioting until 'the rain took the heart out of the fighting' between the 'Islandmen' of the shipyards and the navvies; between the new Orange and Green districts of the Shankill and the Falls; most of all between the Protestants and the Police[56] (see Plates 431–3).

Chief Secretary Morley's public promise that he would tame Belfast Unionism with the Constabulary had rebounded.[57] When the country reinforcements, ignorant of the topography and uncertain of the temper of the crowds, had panicked and fired recklessly and indiscriminately, the Protestant animosity had been diverted to the 'Tipperary Buckshots' and 'Morley's Murderers'.[58] Of the 2,000 policemen in Belfast that summer 371 had been injured and two killed. But the civilian casualties were much greater and not easily forgiven. There had been 30 public inquests and 'many other lives were lost, the bodies being secretly buried by their friends'.[59] The 1886 shootings sealed the antipathy of the Belfast Protestant to the R.I.C. Never again did the Castle dare to flood Belfast with country police. In 1893 for the Second Home Rule Bill it was the military who cordoned the shipyards and kept the Falls and Shankill apart.[60]

The defeat of the Second Bill forced Belfast's Catholics to look once more to their own exertions to secure equality within the city. Led by their Bishop, the Most Rev. Dr Henry, they formed the Catholic Association in 1896 to win through the influence of the Irish Party at Westminster two Catholic wards in the extension of the municipal boundary of that year, and to continue with a campaign against discrimination in public employment.[61] The combination of religion and politics debased the Green cause as it had the Orange.[62] From the sectarian propaganda of the Catholic Association sprang the rival Belfast Protestant Association with its virulent preacher, Arthur Trew.[63] The defence of religion inflamed the political and ethnic conflict of the processions at the end of the century.[64]

Marches to Hannahstown by the Ancient Order of Hibernians; torchlight processions by the '98 Centenary Clubs; Trew's anti-ritualist demonstrations; Twelfth parades; Lady Day excursions; embarkation marches; Ladysmith, Mafeking, and Pretoria; bands with their followers playing nightly through the town—Belfast's mobs had never exerted with such tireless vigour their right to parade the streets.[65]

The Vicar of Belfast wrote despairingly to the Chief Secretary, 'The leaders of the mob now openly boast that they and not the police are masters of the city, and it seems to many that their words are not without foundation.'[66] Every outburst increased the confidence with which the rioters defied authority. 'I don't know', the Attorney General told the Commons, 'the precise number of police who could effectively restrain a Belfast mob; I wish I did.'[67]

It was not the best climate in which to introduce Belfast's first Catholic religious procession for fifty years: but Bishop Henry, too, had been infected by the passion to 'walk'. On 9 June 1901 15,000 Catholics marched to a Corpus Christi service—silently, without bands, and with furled banners.[68] Trew was not among those who threw stones or beat the marchers with umbrellas and sticks, but his influence in inciting the attack was undisputed. 'The Pope's Brigade', ran his B.P.A. posters, 'is preparing for an illegal procession through the streets of this Protestant city . . .'[69] By 14 June the Catholics had been driven from the shipyards, and the Castle had determined that Trew must be prosecuted.[70] Trew's venom had persuaded the riotous Protestant that the Catholic priest had taken over his streets: his prosecution convinced the respectable Protestant that the Catholic politician had taken over the Castle. The Orange clerics wove the religious and political fear into their Twelfth sermons. 'They lived in a land where the majority belonged to what they considered an alien religion. The Roman Catholics were never satisfied until they got the power into their own hands.'[71] Bonfires on the Falls celebrated Trew's imprisonment at the end of July, but on the Island 'Trew for ever' was chalked upon the walls, and cordons of military with fixed bayonets guarded the Catholic workers.[72]

The Victorian era closed in Belfast upon two communities intransigent in their politics; intolerant in their religion; inured to the violent ethic; trusting neither the English parliament to promote their interests, nor the Irish Executive to protect their safety. The Orange and Green causes had been born in violence. Dominance and not integration was their goal: force and not persuasion their ultimate weapon. In 1914 as they waited for the passing of the Third Home Rule Bill Belfast's communities prepared for civil war.

'Home Rule is coming' defiantly adorned the gables of the Pound, but its inhabitants had evacuated their children and had measured anxiously the range of a rifle shot from its borders.[73] 3,500 Irish Volunteers with 250 rifles were a poor defence against Belfast's 24,000 Ulster Volunteers—fully armed and prepared to use those arms to assert their right to self-determination.[74] On the night of the Bill's last passage through the Commons bonfires burned in the heart of the Pound, but its approaches were guarded by the priests with their street committees. Every policeman in the city manned the line between the Shankill and the Falls; but there was not a soldier in Belfast, and the Castle hoped desperately that it would not have to call for the regiments waiting with their special trains at Holywood, Carrickfergus, and Dundalk.[75] Only the British army could impose a Dublin Catholic parliament upon the northern city, and in that battle Belfast's isolated Catholics would be the first victims.[76] For the Victorian years had made Belfast not only the economic capital of

427 *above* The Belfast riots, 1864: fight in front of St Malachy's Chapel, being attacked by Protestants in retaliation for damage done by Catholics on their own edifices. From *Illustrated Times*, new series, iv (1864), 165.

428 *below* The riot at Thomson's Bank, 1864. Shipyard carpenters drive navvies into the mud. From a watercolour. A drawing of this scene was reproduced in *Illustrated Times*, new series, v (1864), 152.
Ulster Museum

429 *above* Riot at Sandy Row, 16 August 1864. In driving a Sandy Row mob back from the Pound, a line of Royal Irish Constabulary open fire from the Boyne Bridge and kill John M'Connell, one of their leaders. From a watercolour. This, too, was reproduced in *Illustrated Times*, new series, v (1864), 152.
Ulster Museum

430 *below* Funeral of M'Connell. Shots are being exchanged between the funeral party and the Hercules Street mob. From *Illustrated Times*, new series, v (1864), 145.

431 *above* Mob wrecking the tramway depot at Milltown, 1886. From *Illustrated London News*, lxxxix (1886), 196.

432 *right* The islandmen threatening the police on their way home from the shipyards, going up North Street, 1886. From *Illustrated London News*, lxxxix (1886), 193.

433 *above* Bower's Hill Barracks, Shankhill Road, on the morning after the besieged Royal Irish Constabulary had shot dead seven Protestants, 9 June 1886.
Photo: R. J. Welch
Ulster Museum

434 *below* The people of Nelson Street beneath their Orange Arch, *c*.1900.
Photo: R. J. Welch
Ulster Museum

Ulster's regionalism, but also a Protestant citadel where Unionism would be violently upheld. One quarter of the population of Ireland was Protestant: a little more than half of Ulster; three quarters of Belfast. Hardened and embittered by a century of urban conflict, Belfast Protestantism would accept no longer a Government which did not reflect its interests. In 1920 it secured those interests when Belfast became the capital of the Northern Ireland Orange city-state.

Violence was a characteristic of the early frontier of urbanization. Other British cities suffered the brutalizing effects of industrialization and the political tension of the unenfranchised. Belfast was not the only town to have its Reform election riot. In Sheffield five people were shot dead. But in Britain political and economic conflict in the new urban society were fused in the Victorian class struggle with its safety valves of social mobility and industrial negotiation. The political arena of the urban workers moved from the streets to parliament with the Second Reform Act. Finally, local unarmed police won a grudging respect for the relative impartiality and efficacy of the rule of law, and Chief Constables depended increasingly upon the co-operation of neighbouring forces rather than the military to curb incipient disorder. Only once in the last thirty years of Victoria was the army obliged to open fire upon a British mob.[77] It is Belfast's failure to establish such a variable conflict basis, to accept democratic rather than violent means of decision, and to be persuaded of the capacity and compass of the representatives of the law, which makes it a peculiar, and therefore a significant Victorian city.

There was neither mobility nor negotiation to blur the edges of Belfast's conflict grouping, for the barrier of the Reformation was as effective as colour in preserving the ethnic distinction of Irish and British, and on their attitude to the Union there was no room for compromise. Distance and time allowed British cities to absorb the ethnic and political tensions of the Irish immigration into the national framework. Only in Ireland could the Union continue of overriding political importance, and only in Ulster was there an ethnic population-balance to maintain so large and dissident a minority in its growing linen-towns. Ethnicity remained in Belfast the paramount classification and determined the economic and political struggle. There were no bread riots, no Chartists, no threat to the middle classes like Hyde Park or Trafalgar Square. Only once in the Victorian era did class alignment threaten to break temporarily the rigidity of sectarian embattlement, when, in 1841, the starving Ballymacarett weavers were accused of wishing 'to sell the Orange cause for a big loaf'.[78] The Belfast riots are distinguished in that they were waged consistently between two ethnic groups of workers, and in that they were prolonged and intensified into the twentieth century.

Their persistence and their escalation, however, were fed by the fears, grievances, and frustrations of much wider sections of the community. The Catholic middle class shared the resentment against political and economic discrimination which deprived them, as a body, of municipal and parliamentary representation and closed the paths to advancement in the town's commerce, technology, and professions. Their declining numbers and their estrangement from the Liberal Party gave them no hope of securing either of Belfast's parliamentary seats until the four divisions of the 1885 Redistribution Act created the delicately-balanced constituency of West Belfast. Their municipal ostracism lasted longer. Only three Catholics sat on the Town Council before 1897.[79] Towards their opponents' supporters the Tory rate collectors displayed a remarkable leniency in pressing for payment before the electoral lists were drawn.[80] Moreover, the £10 Irish municipal franchise was weighted against the Catholics who were disproportionately the poorer citizens.[81] When they obtained the special extension to Belfast of the British municipal household franchise in 1887, they had still to combat the ward alignment by which the Corporation in 1837 and 1853 had dispersed the Catholic and Liberal vote.[82] In 1896 this grievance was met at last when Westminster forced the Council to accept the predominantly Catholic areas of Falls and Smithfield as two of its fifteen wards in its Boundary Extension Bill.

They had less hope of combating occupational discrimination through parliament. Poverty clung to Belfast's Catholic migrants. In 1853 they were 48 percent of the workhouse inmates: fifty years later they were still 46 percent—although their proportion in the town had declined to 24 percent.[83] At the end of the century they remained more heavily weighted in the unskilled than the skilled trades, more likely to be manual than white-collar workers. They were, for example, 47 percent of the barefoot women spinners, but 29 percent of the 'superior' women weavers; 41 percent of the dockers, but 7 percent of the shipwrights; 32 percent of the general labourers, but 13 percent of the commercial clerks. Where Orange political influence was strongest—in employment distributed by the local public boards—their disadvantage was clearest. They were, for example, only 15 percent of the tramway workers and 8 percent of the municipal clerks and officials.[84]

The Protestant middle class, on the other hand, had fear as well as grievance to sharpen their animosity. The fear of a Catholic engulfment in mid-century had bred their policy of political and socio-economic containment. Time and the population of Ireland were not on their side. 'Did you ever hear', queried one of the Select Committee in 1834, 'a desire expressed on the part of Roman Catholics that the ascendancy of numbers should prevail over the ascendancy of property?'[85] Belfast's prosperity was based upon the Union with Great Britain. It was Home Rule, not Catholicism, argued the Belfast Unionist, that he strove to hold at bay.[86] If his methods were scarcely democratic, neither were those of his opponents. Belfast Catholics sought majority rule in Ireland but opposed it in Belfast. In the Castle and, from 1885, in the Irish Party at Westminster, Belfast's minority had allies to impose terms. They had blocked, for example, two essential Improvement Bills—main drainage in 1886 and the boundary extension in 1896—to win Catholic political representation.[87] After the Local Government (Ireland) Act of 1898 gave the Catholics control of the Corporations and County Councils outside the North, they used the threat of reprisals against Belfast's Protestant discrimination. When the Catholic nomination for High Sheriff had been outvoted in the Council in 1903, a Nationalist Councillor 'could assure the Protestants that their friends in other parts of Ireland would suffer for their action there that day'.[88] The campaign for a Catholic quota of public employment increased the Protestant suspicion that ethnicity and not ability would determine the social stratification of Home Rule.[89]

There was, moreover, some justification for the Protestant belief that anti-Catholic discrimination was not the main determinant of their existing stratification. Protestant dominance in the town's business and skilled trades was strengthened undoubtedly by the employers' hostility to Home Rule employees, and by the Trade Unionists' barriers against Catholic labour. But it was a Nonconformist dominance—based on the eighteenth-century capital and initiative of the Presbyterian entrepreneurs, and supported by the puritan ethos of education, apprenticeship, and self-help of the nineteenth-century nonconformist migrant. In 1861 the illiteracy rate for Belfast Catholics was 30·2 percent; for Episcopalians 14·9 percent; Presbyterians 8·2 percent; Methodists 6·5 percent. Although the Catholic and Episcopalian rates had been reduced to 12·2 percent and 8·4 percent by 1901, the capital and drive of the Dissenting social *mores* was still evident. There were only 5 percent more Presbyterians than Episcopalians by 1901, but they had three times as many doctors and grocers and twice as many carpenters.[90]

Religious hostility might not account for economic disparity, but it was the force which deepened the intransigence of the political creeds. For the nineteenth-century Catholic, 'Faith and Fatherland' were entwined. The moral righteousness of the oppressed strengthened Catholic ethnicity. 'On our side is Virtue and Erin: on theirs is the Saxon and Guilt.'[91] The Famine fear of 'Souper' proselytism increased the Church's opposition to educational integration.[92] The Belfast Hierarchy lent its support to the widening of the cultural gulf in the Gaelic Revival.[93] Belfast priests checked off their congregations at the polling booths.[94] They had cherished the sorrows and fears of their people too long to see those of the Protestants.

Protestant intolerance drew upon the arrogance of the Established Church and the fundamentalism of Ulster's Nonconformity. Calvinism had left its legacy in these northern Ironsides, who would have approved Senator Goldwater's dictum that, 'Extremism in the defence of liberty is no crime.'[95] A line of Orange demagogic politician-preachers ensured that the defence of Protestant liberty would be a clarion call in nineteenth-century Belfast. The grandiloquent oratory of the Rev. Dr Cooke nursed the infant Conservative Party and defied O'Connell.[96] The energy and sectarian intolerance of the Rev. Dr Drew sustained mid-century Orangeism.[97] The Rev. Hugh Hanna carried the pulpit battle into the streets.[98] The Rev. Dr Kane welded the Orange Order into the constituency machinery of the Unionist Party.[99] They preached violence and deplored its outcome. 'They could lead a mob', it was said of Kane and Hanna in 1886, 'but not control one.'[100]

Political resentment and religious suspicion widened the social, if not the physical segregation of middle-class Catholic and Protestant. Educated in their own schools, teacher-training, or university colleges; patronizing their own shops and employing their own professions; playing separate games, reading different newspapers; much of their social and cultural activity linked to their churches; a great part of Belfast's white-collar workers and middle class, and most of their wives and children, knew 'the other sort' only as stereotypes—alien, if not suspect. Louis MacNeice wrote of his Edwardian rectory childhood that 'The cook Annie, who was a buxom girl from County Tyrone, was the only Catholic I knew, and therefore the only proof that Catholics were human.'[101] Isolated, moreover, in their middle-class suburbs from the riots and evictions of West Belfast, few had ever seen a stone thrown. Violence is acceptable when it is remote and directed against a fleshless enemy.

The result was to create not merely a middle-class toleration for the violence of the rioters, but a political and religious chauvinism which did little to ameliorate the social conditions in which rioting was bred. Few British cities carried into the twentieth century so obdurate a policy of municipal *laissez-faire* in social welfare. In 1848 Belfast's fever incidence over the past thirty years had been second only to Dublin in the United Kingdom.[102] Fifty years later it had the highest typhoid death-rate of eighty-two of Europe's largest towns; and the *Lancet* blamed its sanitary officials who were 'not always selected for their technical competence, but rather because they held a prominent position in church or chapel and had been able to render eminent service at election times'.[103] Private housing was plentiful, at least for those who could afford it, but it was the political balance which determined to whom it should be let and which slums should be razed in West Belfast.[104] Estate agents asked prospective tenants for a line from their clergymen.[105] The Corporation decided to demolish the Catholic rookeries of Carrick Hill after a Nationalist was returned for the division of 1886.[106] In that western maze of workers' streets and factories the children had one park—an acre given by a private benefactor.[107] Between the Public Baths Act of 1847 and the belated adoption of the Free Libraries (Ireland) Act of 1855 in 1882, neither the Belfast worker's health nor his recreation had laid a heavy burden on the rates. £200 spent on pictures completed the Victorian municipality's provision for his culture.[108]

Not all the blame can be laid upon the local authorities. It would have required determined pressure from central government to break the vicious circle, in which ethnocentrism dulled Belfast's public conscience, and meagre physical and cultural welfare contributed to frustration, boredom, and rioting and again renewed ethnic antagonism. Such central initiative was at best spasmodic. More often the Irish Executive, geared to a declining, impoverished rural population, failed to treat separately the peculiar needs of rapid urban growth, or to insist upon reforms which the town's prosperity might have afforded. Fear, for example, of subsidizing a nation of pauper farmers made the Irish Poor Law Board oppose out-relief in general—even for the short-time and temporary depressions of the linen-city.[109] Belfast's out-relief, 7 per 1,000 against Glasgow's 80, was the lowest rate in the United Kingdom in 1901.[110] It is probable, therefore, although comparisons are difficult, that the distress in the poverty level which remained outside the workhouse was more acute in Belfast than generally in British cities.

It was at this level also that national provision for education was most wanting.

Although state support for primary education came early in Ireland in 1831, the Churches or private individuals had first to build the schools. Where Belfast's growth had outstripped the provision of the Churches or the resources of the poorer congregations the schools could not be built or enlarged. The inadequacy was greatest among the poorer (and often only nominal) Episcopalians, for the Established Church, like the political Establishment, was slow to adapt its administration to urban growth. Catholics and Nonconformists, therefore, saw no need to make good the deficiencies of the wealthier church by supporting a demand for municipal schools upon the rates.[111] In 1899 72 of Belfast's 191 schools were admitted to be grossly overcrowded.[112] By 1913, when Birrell declared that 'no city in the Empire was worse supplied with schools or more in need of education . . .', Belfast could provide places for no more than 69 percent of its primary schoolchildren.[113] The National Commissioners had envisaged the schoolhouse as in part an instrument to discipline Ireland's rural insubordination. A significant section of the industrial capital's most unruly children had a scanty acquaintance with that regular discipline.

Nowhere was the Irish national framework less appropriate for Belfast's industrial growth and ethnic rivalry than in the provision of its police. By the end of the nineteenth century it was the only major city in the United Kingdom which did not maintain its own urban force. Even Dublin had its Metropolitan Police. The Royal Irish Constabulary adapted slowly to the duties of a city role. Its rule of transfer on promotion gave Belfast too few senior men with local knowledge.[114] Its need to enforce general order in Ireland prevented its Belfast quota keeping pace with the town's expansion.[115] Belfast, save at times of tension, was consistently underpoliced.[116] In addition, docks, barracks, prison, and the availability of temporary employment ensured that there were more habitual criminal and political suspects under police surveillance in the city than in the rest of Ireland; and during riots this criminal element seems to have exacerbated violence.[117]

A more important contribution of the police to Belfast's climate of disorder lay in their failure to win the co-operation and respect of both communities. The Ulster County Constabulary of the 1830s was in great part Orange.[118] 'Here is the Protestant Police', the mob had cried in Hercules Street.[119] The Belfast local force, established in 1845 and appointed by the Council, continued to be suspect to the Catholics. In 1857 its Superintendent was the Master of an Orange lodge: and in 1865 155 of its 160 members were Protestant, 'of which a great many of them are or have been Orangemen'.[120] In the 1864 riots it was the Protestant desperadoes who answered the call for Special Constables—an experiment so disastrous that local magistrates would not risk repeating it for fifty years.[121] When Catholic complaints against the town force led to its disbandment in 1865, the national Constabulary which replaced it was equally repugnant to the Belfast Protestant. The Royal Irish Constabulary, recruited from a predominantly Catholic Ireland, transferred frequently to prevent local attachments, proclaiming its basic military purpose in its weapons, drill, and defensive barracks, remained an alien and unwelcome garrison—a sign of the town's subjection to Dublin Castle. After the 1886 riots the Protestant hostility to the Peelers or Buckshots could erupt at any provocation. At those times only the soldiers, who were regarded as fellow British Protestants, could enter the shipyards or the Shankill.[122] Equally disastrous was the hostility of the local magistrates, whose pleas for their own, or a more urban force, or even an enlarged quota, met stubborn resistance in Dublin.[123] By 1900 the police issue had strained to breaking point relations with the Castle. Mayor and magistrates refused advice from the police and took a perverse delight in demonstrating that only they and the military could control the town.[124] When extra drafts from the Castle failed to curb the Home Rule pogroms of 1912 it was on the police issue that the Unionist Corporation made its final break with the Executive by refusing to pay any longer for reinforcements of a force it disowned.[125]

Even a universally respected police force would have had difficulty quelling Belfast's natural exuberance. 'The Belfast worker, of whatever politics, took a dose of R.I.C. about the Twelfth of July just as he would take a course of sulphur and treacle in the Spring.'[126] For the Irish traditionally liked a good fight. A Presbyterian Doctor of Divinity, much revered in 1910, had been observed as a young man in 1864 sprinting up Donegall Place pursued by the military.[127] In 1886 a clergyman reported that his Shankill congregation were 'particularly anxious for the enjoyment of stone-throwing'.[128]

Riots and revivals were the emotional release in an impoverished working-class culture where politics and religion were the only respectable activities. Nowhere was the bleakness of Belfast's industrial life more evident than in the linen industry's dependence upon cheap child and female labour.[129] Nearly 30 percent of Belfast's women linen workers in 1907 were married or widowed.[130] Tied to mill or factory from childhood to old age, the West Belfast women waged the same socio-economic battle and erupted in the same sporadic savagery as their men. When they did not throw stones they gathered them, and they attacked each other in the mills.[131]

Working mothers and the precocious independence of half-timers were one factor in Belfast's juvenile delinquency problem. 60 percent of the employees in Mulholland's Mill in 1836 were children. There were still 3,000 half-timers in the mills in 1901.[132] Another factor was the seven-year apprenticeships which survived in engineering and shipbuilding into the twentieth century, and which, as in Glasgow, prolonged the dependence of the 'corner boys' and 'clans', whose penury and boredom engaged the police in constant skirmishes.[133] Every riot found the 'urchins of ten to twelve years', the 'boys and girls', or the 'juvenile hooligans' to the fore.[134] If the city did not provide recreations, a Reformer cautioned, those who could not pay for their own amusement would create it on the street.[135] Sectarian anti-socialism and puritanism neglected the warning. Dance-halls were frowned upon. 'Plays inflame the passions, excite the imagination and depict vice.'[136] The Council rejected the intent of a charitable bequest to provide Sunday music for the workers in the parks.[137] The Belfast juvenile continued to dance behind the Orange and Green bands in the streets.[138]

The Belfast adult worker had another recreation. 'It may be said that the popular amusements are public houses and churches. When Belfast is not getting converted she is getting drunk.'[139] The Belfast migrant brought with him a liking for hard liquor which industrial conditions did not assuage. 'In the morning it is a general practice for mechanics to take a glass of whiskey before they go to work.'[140] In the provision yards the employers encouraged their workers through the busy season with two-and-a-half glasses of whiskey per day.[141] Smuggling in the early century; illicit stills in the 1830s; the distilleries' 'gallon for the King and another for the Queen'; and the low Irish spirit-duty ensured a cheap supply.[142] When the tax was made uniform throughout the United Kingdom in 1859, Belfast's predilection was well established. In 1836 there had been one pub for every 100 persons; by the twentieth century temperance campaigns had reduced this to one for every 328.[143] The other three notoriously heavy-drinking cities, Dublin, Liverpool, and Glasgow, had respectively one in 250, 300, and 600.[144] But the type of drinking and not the number of licensed premises was the real determinant. Only Glasgow shared Belfast's high whiskey-drinking reputation.[145] Like Glasgow, too, puritanism had made perpendicular drinking and not conviviality, the feature of the Belfast pub.[146] Drunkenness remained a persistent Belfast problem and an important element in rioting, which reached its crescendo after the Saturday pay. Public-houses were the first buildings to be looted. In 1872 rioting decelerated once the Mayor had closed the pubs.

If spirit-drinking made Belfast riots more violent, firearms made them more deadly. The Ulster settler, like the American, preserved his belief in the right and the need to bear arms. In the rural disorders of the 1830s the Belfast gunsmiths were sending over by the cartload Ulster muskets 'equal to any firelocks I ever saw come out of the Tower', for even the poor could pay for them by instalments through the Orange and Ribbon gun-clubs.[147] The rural migrants of the forties carried many of those muskets back into Belfast. In 1857 gunmen lined the ditches between Sandy Row and the Pound for a two-hour battle; and the Catholics set up a gun-club to prepare for the 1858 Twelfth.[148] Proclamations and arms searches had little effect. Guns were merely hidden to be brought out when needed, like that of Mrs Mullins of the Pound in 1864. 'Her husband had taught her to use a gun when he first brought her to Belfast. So, when she heard that the shipwrights were coming, she put her three children in the piggery at the back of the house, loaded her gun and went off to defend the church.'[149] Rifle clubs maintained the skill.[150] The Home Rule crises renewed the purchase of party and private arms. In 1913 the police reported that there were 10,000 rifles hidden in the city and both sides were equipping themselves privately with revolvers.[151] The Lord Mayor told the Commons that 'on a contingency there would be 30,000 revolvers on the streets of Belfast', but many seemed to be there already.[152] Football mobs fired into the air at half-time, and 'life was more exciting than it is in Cinema films of the wild and woolly West'.[153]

In this climate of political intransigence, economic competition, religious intolerance, social impoverishment, and atavistic violence, the Orange and Green societies were the motive force. As Belfast adjusted to the Home Rule conflict, their numbers and political influence increased. The new Unionist Party turned to the Orange lodges to supply the constituency machinery for the extended franchise of 1884. In return the Belfast Grand Lodge nominated two of the four Conservative candidates of 1885.[154] Political expediency had restored Orange middle-class leadership; the Home Rule Bills swelled the ranks. The town which had referred to its Orange lodges in 1825 as 'surviving dreggs' was proud in 1884 to be called 'the citadel of Orangeism' and in 1913 contained 18,800 in the Order.[155] The various shades of Green into which Ribbonism had divided took longer to coalesce and become generally acceptable. In 1896 the seven Belfast lodges of the Ancient Order of Hibernians were 'of a very low class and no respectable Nationalist appears to sympathise with the movement'.[156] By 1906, however, the A.O.H. had proved its electoral value to the Nationalists by winning the West Belfast seat for its new President, Joseph Devlin, and the Hibernians as a party machine grew rapidly in the next few years.[157] As religiously exclusive and discriminatory as the Orange Order, they 'made it difficult or uncomfortable for Catholics of the working or professional classes to prosper outside their ranks', and they countered the Orange influence in Belfast's public appointments by Devlin's 'almost complete ascendancy over the Irish Government during the Liberal administration in patronage and other matters'.[158]

Their effect was to fasten upon Belfast's politics not only a more rigid sectarianism, but also their apolitical doctrine of ultimate physical force. As early as 1883 some Orangemen were advocating a call to arms.[159] The Orange Manifesto of 1910 warned that should they fail to carry the British election they must prepare for a martial struggle in Ireland.[160] The Green societies were infused more covertly with the tenet of rebellion. In 1864 the Belfast Fenians counted upon securing the armoury of the Antrim Rifles for the prospective rising.[161] Their dedication to insurrection continued in the secret Irish Republican Brotherhood, whose leader in Belfast at the end of the century was also the Vice-President of the A.O.H.[162] In 1906 he advised the northern Brethren to join the Hibernians 'as it was very useful for revolutionary purposes'.[163] Upon his I.R.B. successor, rather than upon Belfast's Nationalist M.P., Joseph Devlin, devolved the responsibility for organizing the defence of the city's Catholics in 1914.[164] Unionist and Nationalist had harnessed violence to their politics. In 1914 the city's political future had moved from Westminster to the streets of West Belfast.

There a century of Orange and Green rivalry had conditioned its communities to violent confrontation. The influence of the lodges upon Belfast's working classes had always exceeded their numerical strength, for they reflected much wider circles of family, neighbourhood, and trade, and crystallized sectarian competition and ethnic enmity. Their indoctrination fed prejudice. Their disciplinary codes enforced chauvinistic intolerance. Their celebrations taunted the opposition to retaliation. Their ballads perpetuated an impassioned urban folklore where victories on seventeenth-century battlegrounds and nineteenth-century brickfields were entwined. Separate education began the ethnic isolation: the culture of the lodges turned it into ethnic alienation (Plate 434).

Above all they imposed their concept of territoriality upon the city. Their parades constantly tested the area of that territorial domination, with its implicit economic and political advantage. To trail one's coat is an Irish humour. Every riot followed an infringement or extension of the right to walk. With every riot voluntary evacuation or intimidation redrew the territorial borders and reinforced neighbourhood identity. Churches, schools, employment, and a natural preference to live amongst one's own kind contributed to the physical segregation of Belfast's communities, but it was the Victorian riots which drove so clear a line of demarcation between the Orange and Green territories of West Belfast. It was the Orange and Green electoral lists which forced two such hostile peoples to live so close together and so evenly matched. For a century their belligerents had forayed and retreated, perfecting an urban guerilla warfare which grew more dangerous and less controllable as their territory and their numbers increased. Across the border of the Ulster capital the shock troops of the Falls and Shankill were to continue to wage their battles for the dominance of Ulster into our own day.

Notes

1 *Guardian and Constitutional Advocate*, 11 December 1832.
2 *Parliamentary Papers*, (*P.P.*) 1835, XXX, Royal Commission (R.C.) on the Condition of the Poorer Classes in Ireland: Third Report, Part I, Appendix (C)(35), p. 38; *P.P.*, 1835, XVI, Select Committee (S.C.) on the Nature, Character and Tendency of Orange Lodges, Associations or Societies in Ireland (476), p. 47.
3 Ibid., p. 247.
4 Ibid., pp. 246–7.
5 *P.P.*, 1835, XV, S.C. on Orange Lodges (377), p. 129; M. W. Dewar, J. Brown, S. E. Long, *Orangeism: A new historical appreciation* (Belfast, 1967), p. 139.
6 Ibid., p. 107.
7 S.C. on Orange Lodges (377), p. 38.
8 Ibid., pp. 153, 296, 352, 382; *P.P.*, 1835, XVI, S.C. on Orange Lodges (476), p. 228.
9 *Irishman*, 15 July 1825.
10 S.C. on Orange Lodges (377), pp. 317–18, 357, 373–4, 384–5, 406–8; ibid. (476), pp. 134, 136, 167, 296, 397–406, 414–15.
11 Dewar, Brown, Long, op. cit., p. 118.
12 *Guardian and Constitutional Advocate*, 21 December 1832.
13 Public Record Office (P.R.O.), Northern Ireland, Jonathan Cordukes' Papers, D.861/2.
14 *Northern Whig*, 24 December 1832.
15 *Guardian and Constitutional Advocate*, 24 December 1832.
16 *Belfast Commercial Chronicle*, 24 December 1832.
17 *Belfast News Letter*, 25 December 1832.
18 *Guardian and Constitutional Advocate*, 28 December 1832.
19 *Belfast News Letter*, 28 December 1832.
20 Ibid.

21 *Northern Whig*, 24, 27 December 1832.

22 *Belfast News Letter*, 25 December 1832.

23 Sir C. A. Cameron, *Report upon the State of Public Health and the Sanitary Work etc. performed in Dublin during the year 1914* (Dublin, 1915), pp. 12–13.

24 R. B. McDowell, *Social life in Ireland 1800–1845* (Dublin, 1951), p. 18.

25 *P.P.*, 1912–13, CXVI, Census Returns for Ireland, 1911: Province of Ulster, City of Belfast (Cd. 6051–I), p. 31.

26 *P.P.*, 1839, XI, S.C. (H. of L.) on the State of Ireland since 1835 in respect of Crime and Outrage (486–II), p. 704.

27 H. A. Cronne *et al.*, eds, *Essays in British and Irish History in Honour of James Eadie Todd* (1949), p. 220; *Henderson's Belfast Street Directory 1850* (Belfast, 1850), p. 13; *Northern Whig*, 17 April 1852.

28 *Belfast News Letter*, 14, 17 July 1835.

29 Private Collection of A. M'Clelland, Belfast, Minutes of Grand Lodge of Ireland 1835–1921 (1838), p. 2.

30 *Northern Whig*, 27 August 1840; *Belfast News Letter*, 29 September 1843.

31 S.C. on Crime and Outrage (486–I), p. 73; *P.P.*, 1852, XIV, S.C. on Outrages (Ireland) (438), pp. 87–8, 145, 150, 168, 340.

32 *Belfast News Letter*, 4 March, 10 November, 20 December 1843.

33 *Northern Whig*, 29 July 1843.

34 Ibid.

35 *Northern Whig*, 14 September 1843; *Belfast News Letter*, 15 September 1843.

36 *Belfast News Letter*, 15 August 1843; *Vindicator*, 22 July 1843; *Northern Whig*, 22 August 1843.

37 *Belfast News Letter*, 1, 8, 15 July 1845.

38 Ibid., 19 September 1845.

39 Ibid., 14 July 1846.

40 Ibid., 6 August 1847; D. Gwynn, *Young Ireland and 1848* (Cork, 1949), pp. 140–1; D. J. Owen, *History of Belfast* (Belfast, 1921), p. 276.

41 W. E. Coe, *The Engineering Industry of the North of Ireland* (Newton Abbot, 1969), p. 79.

42 *P.P.*, 1902, CXXVI, Census Returns of Ireland for 1901: Province of Ulster, City of Belfast (Cd. 1123(a)), p. vii.

43 *A Brief Historical Sketch of Parliamentary Elections in Belfast from the First General Election under the Reform Act till 1865* (Belfast, n.d.), p. 39.

44 *Northern Whig*, 15 July 1852.

45 Ibid.

46 I skipped to this verse myself in the school playground in the 1930s and think it probably began as a street ballad.

47 T. Henry, *History of the Belfast Riots* (1864), p. 11.

48 I. B. Cross, ed., *Frank Roney, Irish Rebel and Californian Labour Leader: An autobiography* (Berkeley, 1931), pp. 56–9. T. Henry, op. cit., pp. 7, 16.

49 *P.P.*, 1865, XXVIII, R.C. respecting the Magisterial and Police Jurisdiction, Arrangements and Establishment in the Borough of Belfast (3466), pp. 1–13.

50 A. M'Clelland Collection, Orange ballad, 'The Battle of the Navvies', by One of the Carpenters.

51 R.C. on Magisterial and Police Jurisdiction (3466), pp. 13–15, 382.

52 Ibid., p. 17.

53 *Belfast Morning News*, 3–24 July, 9, 13 August 1872.

54 City Hall Belfast, Town Clerk's Letter Book 1857–80, Castle to Mayor on causes and course of 1872 riots and conduct of Magistracy, fol. 110.

55 *Belfast News Letter*, 5 January 1886.

56 F. F. Moore, *The Truth about Ulster* (1914), pp. 56–8, 61; State Paper Office (SPO) Ireland, Chief Secretary's Office Registered Papers (CSORP), 15601/1912.

57 *P.P.*, 1887, XVIII, R.C. on Belfast Riots: Minutes of Evidence (C.4925–I), pp. 373, 403.

58 R. J. Adgey, *The Arming of the Ulster Volunteers* (Belfast, n.d.), pp. 4–5.

59 SPO Ireland, CSORP 15601/1912.

60 Ibid.

61 F. J. Whitford, 'Joseph Devlin, Ulsterman and Irishman' (unpublished M.A. thesis, University of London, 1959), pp. 26–8; *P.P.*, 1892, XI, S.C. on Belfast Corporation (Lunatic Asylums etc.) Bill (228–Sess. 1), pp. 331–6, 374.

62 *A Statement of the Municipal Grievances of the Roman Catholic Ratepayers and Inhabitants of Belfast* (Belfast, 1896), passim. For a refutation of some of its statistics see Alderman Haslett's evidence before the 1896 Hybrid Committee, *Belfast News Letter*, 19 May 1896.

63 A brief account of the B.P.A.'s working-class origin and objects is given in *Belfast Protestant Record*, iv (June 1901).

64 SPO Ireland, Miscellaneous Notes B Series, No. XV, July–August 1896, p. 56.

65 The mounting files in the Chief Secretary's Office between 1897 and 1901 reveal the Castle's anxiety about containing rioting and unease about Trew. SPO Ireland, CSORP 11665, 11740, 15358, 15483/1900, 12018/1901, 11935/1912. P.R.O., Intelligence Notes B Series 1897–1900, C.O. 903/6; P.R.O., Inspector General's and County Inspectors' Reports, C.O. 904/68 and 70.

66 SPO Ireland, Miscellaneous Notes B Series, No. XXXVIII, March–June 1899, p. 11 in CSORP 13517/1901.

67 Hansard, 4th series, LXXX, 9 March 1900, 491.

68 *Daily Mail*, 13 June 1901; SPO Ireland, CSORP 11764/1901.

69 *Belfast News Letter*, 22 June 1901.

70 Hansard, 4th series, XCV, 14 June 1901, 430–61; SPO Ireland, CSORP 12018, 12385, 13517, 13881, 20512/1901.

71 *Belfast News Letter*, 8 July 1901.

72 SPO Ireland, CSORP 11935/1912; *Irish News*, 31 July 1901; *Belfast News Letter*, 1 August 1901.

73 National Library of Ireland, George Berkeley Papers, MS. 10,923, ch. 8.

74 Ibid., ch. 5, pp. 5–6.

75 SPO Ireland, CSORP 8550/1914.

76 SPO Ireland, CSORP 8733/1914; P.R.O., Crime Special Branch, 14 July 1913, C.O. 904/90; A. T. Q. Stewart, *The Ulster Crisis* (1967), pp. 124–5, 144–6, 150–60, 218.

77 *P.P.*, 1908, VII, S.C. on Employment of Military in cases of Disturbances (236), p. 369.

78 *Northern Whig*, 10 June 1841.

79 *Belfast News Letter*, 6 May 1896.

80 *A Brief Historical Sketch of Parliamentary Elections in Belfast*, pp. 98, 103; *Northern Whig*, 3 August 1847; *P.P.*, 1864, VI, S.C. on Belfast Improvement Bill (348), pp. 89–92.

81 R.C. on Magisterial and Police Jurisdiction: Minutes of Evidence (3466–I), pp. 363–4.

82 *A Brief Historical Sketch of Parliamentary Elections in Belfast*, p. 97; S.C. on Belfast Corporation Bill, pp. 276, 331, 349, 374; *Belfast News Letter*, 7 May 1896.

83 J. S. Reid, *History of the Presbyterian Church in Ireland*, ed. W. D. Killen (Belfast, 1867), p. 515; P.R.O. Northern Ireland, Minutes of the Belfast Board of Guardians, 9 December 1903, BG. VII/A/73.

84 Census of Ireland, 1901, Belfast, passim.

85 S.C. on Orange Lodges (476), p. 231.

86 S.C. on Belfast Corporation Bill, p. 300; *Northern Whig*, 14 January 1896.

87 *Northern Whig*, 22 June 1886; *Irish News*, 2 January, 16 March, 3 June 1896; F. J. Whitford, op. cit., p. 39; T. J. Campbell, *Fifty Years of Ulster 1890–1941* (Belfast, 1941), p. 46.

88 *Belfast News Letter*, 24 January 1903.

89 *Northern Whig*, 30 November 1911; *Belfast News Letter*, 14 February 1912.

90 Census of Ireland 1901, Belfast pp. 47, vii, 16–21.

91 T. Moore, 'The Song of O'Rouarke', *Irish Melodies and Songs* (1887), p. 130.

92 *P.P.*, 1856, LIII, Correspondence between the Commissioners of National Education in Ireland and the Committee of the Lancasterian Industrial National School, Belfast, relative to the charges made by the Rev. Dr Denvir against the system of management of that school (88), pp. 449–54; T. J. Campbell, *Fifty Years of Ulster*, pp. 186–8; *Irish News*, 20 May 1902, 5, 14, 16 October 1903.

93 *Irish News*, 16 December 1904.

94 *Belfast News Letter*, 27 November 1885.

95 Quoted in H. G. Nicholas, *Violence in American Society* (1969), p. 8.

96 J. Porter, *The Life and Times of Dr. Cooke* (Belfast, 1875), passim; *The Repealer Repulsed: The repeal invasion of Ulster* (Belfast, 1841), passim.

97 P.R.O. Northern Ireland, The Annals of Christ Church from its Foundation in 1831, Abraham Dawson MS, T.1075/11/150.237, pp. 159–163.

98 *P.P.*, 1857–58, XXVI, R.C. on the Origin and Character of the Riots in Belfast in July and September 1857 (2309), pp. 13–15.

99 *Belfast News Letter*, 13 April 1885.

100 *P.P.*, 1887, XVIII, R.C. on Belfast Riots: Minutes of Evidence (C. 4925–I), p. 324.

101 F. L. MacNeice, *The Strings are False: An unfinished autobiography*, E. R. Dodds, ed. (1965), p. 41.

102 A. J. Malcolm, *Report on the Sanitary State of Belfast* (Belfast, 1848), p. 3.

103 *Lancet*, 25 December 1897.

104 City Hall Belfast, Local Government Board Inquiries on the 1911 Housing of the Working Classes Improvement Scheme, Nos 32, 39, 46, 49.

105 City Hall Belfast, Local Government Board Inquiry 10–13 March 1914, p. 287.

106 *Belfast News Letter*, 7, 15 May 1896.

107 *P.P.*, 1902, XLIX, Inter-Departmental Committee on the Employment of Children during School Age, especially in Street Trading in the large Centres of Population in Ireland (Cd. 1144), p. 336.

108 *Nomad's Weekly*, 24 March 1906.

109 P.R.O. Northern Ireland, Minutes of Belfast Board of Guardians 1908, Principle to be followed on Workhouse Test, BG. VII/A/81, fol. 576.

110 *Labour Gazette*, December 1901, 386.

111 *Northern Whig*, 13, 14, 23 October 1899; *Belfast News Letter*, 10 November 1902.

112 City Hall Belfast, Special Reports, 19 October 1899.

113 Hansard, 5th series, LV, 8 July 1913, 229–30.

114 SPO Ireland, Police Inquiry 1906, pp. 59, 116.

115 SPO Ireland, CSORP 19676/1901.

116 *Belfast News Letter*, 7 July 1835; *Northern Whig*, 29 July 1843; *Irish News*, 3 December 1912.

117 SPO Ireland, CSORP 6781/1904; R.C. on Magisterial and Police Jurisdiction: Minutes of Evidence (3466–I), pp. 301–2; *Belfast News Letter*, 12 June 1901; *Northern Whig*, 13 June 1901.

118 S.C. on Orange Lodges (476), pp. 145–6.

119 *Northern Whig*, 24 December 1832.

120 R.C. on Magisterial and Police Jurisdiction (3466), pp. 5–6.

121 A. M'Clelland Collection, Orange Ballad, 'The Belfast Special Boys and King Mob'; P.R.O. 'Notes on Police', 'B' Specials 1922, C.O. 906/27; R. J. Adgey, op. cit. p. 10.

122 SPO Ireland, CSORP 15358/1900, 15601/1912.

123 City Hall Belfast, Town Clerk's Special Letter Books, 1857–80, fol. 113; 1880–7, ff. 190–1, 231, 248.

124 SPO Ireland, CSORP 13517/1901 and 11935/1912.

125 *Irish News*, 3 December 1912; *The Belfast Book; Local government in the City and County Borough of Belfast* (Belfast, 1929), pp. 156–8.

126 L. Doyle, *The Spirit of Ireland* (1935), p. 7.

127 *Northern Whig*, 11 November 1910.

128 R.C. on Belfast Riots: Minutes of Evidence (C. 4925–I), p. 242.

129 D. L. Armstrong, 'Social and Economic Conditions in the Belfast Linen Industry, 1850–1900', *Irish Historical Studies*, vii (1951), 260–1; *P.P.*, 1914, XXXVI, Departmental Committee on Humidity and Ventilation in Flax Mills and Linen Factories (mainly in Ireland): Minutes of Evidence (Cd. 7446), pp. 153, 184.

130 *P.P.*, 1909, LXXIX, Summary of Returns of Persons employed in 1907 in Textile Factories (Cd. 4692), p. 858.

131 Green Ballad, 'The Heroes of Hardinge Street', in G. D. Zimmerman, *Irish Political Street Ballads and Rebel Songs* (Geneva, 1966), p. 108; *Belfast News Letter*, 14 July 1835; *Irish News*, 27 April 1893; SPO Ireland, CSORP 11935/1912, 19 August 1896; R.C. on Magisterial and Police Jurisdiction: Minutes of Evidence (3466–I), p. 283.

132 *P.P.*, 1836, XXX, R.C. on Poorer Classes in Ireland: Third Report, Part I, Appendix (c) (35), p. 41; Inter-Departmental Committee on Street Trading (Cd. 1144), p. 284.

133 SPO Ireland, CSORP 29776/1902; P.R.O. Inspectors' Reports, April 1902, C.O. 904/75; SPO Ireland, Police Inquiry 1906, p. 138.

134 *Belfast News Letter*, 17 July 1835; R.C. on Magisterial and Police Jurisdiction: Minutes of Evidence (3466–I), pp. 283, 349; R.C. on Belfast Riots: Minutes of Evidence (C. 4925–I), p. 382; *Northern Whig*, 1, 4 November 1901.

135 *Belfast News Letter*, 18, 24, 26 June 1901.

136 Ibid., 16 September 1901.

137 Ibid., 2 August 1901.

138 SPO Ireland, Police Inquiry 1906, pp. 15, 55.

139 *Nomad's Weekly*, 17 August 1907.

140 R.C. on Poorer Classes in Ireland: Part I, Appendix (c) (35), p. 57.

141 *P.P.*, 1834, VIII, S.C. into Extent, Causes and Consequences of the Prevailing Vice of Intoxication among the Labouring Classes of the United Kingdom (559), p. 396.

142 T. M'Tear, 'Personal Recollections of the Beginning of the Century', *Ulster Journal of Archaeology*, 2nd series, v (1899), 212–13; S.C. into Intoxication (559), p. 393.

143 R.C. on Poorer Classes in Ireland: Part I, Appendix (c) (35), p. 57; D. Kennedy, 'The Catholic Church', in T. W. Moody and J. C. Beckett, eds, *Ulster since 1800*, 2nd series (1957), p. 177; Hansard, 5th series, LIV, 30 June 1913, 1499.

144 L. Paul-Dubois, *Contemporary Ireland* (Dublin, 1908), p. 363; E. C. Midwinter, *Victorian Social Reform* (1968), p. 102; *Nomad's Weekly*, 12 April 1908.

145 F. F. Moore, *The Truth about Ulster*, p. 121.

146 J. Cunnison and J. B. S. Gillfillan, eds, *The Third Statistical Account of Scotland, Glasgow*, p. 622.

147 S.C. on Orange Lodges (377), pp. 225, 266, 311, 321, 362.

148 A. Boyd, *Holy War in Belfast* (Tralee, 1969), pp. 29, 33, 35, 43.

149 Ibid., pp. 70–1.

150 R.C. on Belfast Riots: Minutes of Evidence (C. 4925–I), p. 60; R. J. Adgey, op. cit., p. 6.

151 P.R.O., Inspectors' Reports, C.O. 904/91; ibid., Crime Branch Special, C.O. 904/120.

152 Hansard, 5th series, XXXVIII, 7 May 1912, 289; P.R.O., Intelligence Notes 1913, C.O. 903/17.

153 J. W. Good, *Ulster and Ireland* (Dublin, 1919), p. 268.

154 *Belfast News Letter*, 13 April 1885.

155 *Northern Whig*, 7 July 1825; A. M'Clelland Collection, *The Ulster Counter-Demonstration by a Leinster Loyalist* [pamphlet] (Dublin, 1884), p. 14; P.R.O., Inspectors' Reports, Crime Branch Special, C.O. 904/90.

156 SPO Ireland, CSORP 1935/1912.

157 SPO Ireland, Crime Branch Special, 308/s, 1452/s, 1996/s, 2079/s, 247/s.

158 H. A. Robinson, *Memories Wise and Otherwise* (1923), p. 146.

159 A. M'Clelland Collection, *The Orange Secret* [pamphlet] (Belfast, 1883).

160 B. MacGiolla Choilla, ed., *Chief Secretary's Office Dublin Castle Intelligence Notes 1913–1916, Preserved in the State Paper Office* (Dublin, 1966), p. 16.

161 I. B. Cross, op. cit., pp. 86–9.

162 P.R.O., Intelligence Notes, Miscellaneous Notes B Series, C.O. 903/6, No. XXIV and No. XXVIII.

163 Ibid., Crime Branch Special, C.O. 904/117.

164 Ibid., C.O. 904/118, 119, 120; National Library of Ireland, George Berkeley Papers, MS. 10,923, ch. 5, pp. 4–6, 37–8; MS. 7888, pp. 37–8, 47, 50.

34 Challenge to the Church
Birmingham, 1815-65

David E. H. Mole

The Victorian city was as much an enigma for the churches as it was in other respects. Its growth and the new sort of life which it brought took men by surprise. The only precedent was London, which had always been regarded as an exception; apart from that, a city meant somewhere like Norwich or Exeter, crowded with churches and chapels. Nevertheless the churches behaved as though the new cities differed from the old only in the matter of size. Nonconformity long imagined that the gathered church, traditionally independent, was equal to the challenge; Methodism never succeeded in making the leap from the industrial village to the new city; the Roman Catholic authorities found themselves overwhelmed by the influx of Irish immigrants and the hostility of the English natives; and the Church of England tried to cope in the traditional way by dividing the cities into sub-districts, each of which could reproduce the ideal society of the rural parish.

Dissenters were perhaps more at home in the towns than Churchmen. For them city air was free air, and although they might be excluded from some areas of urban society they found there power and influence and some freedom from the unwelcome interference of the clergyman of the Established Church. It was therefore natural that they should see in the development of urban England a movement which would be essentially beneficial to them. They took for granted the basic Christian character of the nation, and they tended to define themselves in relation to the Established Church. What they looked for was freedom—freedom to establish themselves as true churches of God, ordering themselves according to his will apart from the interference of magistrate and squire; freedom to preach the Gospel and to establish new congregations, and freedom to enjoy the full benefits of citizenship regardless of creed. In the new towns it seemed as though they would be able to pursue their aims with more success than in the rural areas. In view of this it is not surprising that they tended to think of the towns as their areas of strength. When they talked of church extension they were usually thinking of the establishment of churches in the country-side, where the Anglican squire and parson seemed to be in control, rather than in the towns. That is not to say that any simple division could be made, with the Church strong in the countryside and Dissent strong in the towns: that is one of the myths that current research has exploded. There were towns strong in Churchman-ship and rural areas where Nonconformity was in the ascendant. But the idea must have come from somewhere, and its origin surely lies in the fact that in the towns Churchmen were often on the defensive and Dissenters on the attack.

Early in the nineteenth century the demands of the new towns were beginning to be heard in church circles, and the progress of the Evangelical revival brought fresh resources to meet them. The freer organization of the Dissenters gave them something of an advantage over the Church of England. They were not encumbered with the legal rigidity of the Establishment, and they could establish churches with-out concerning themselves with parish boundaries, consecrated buildings, or the rights of incumbents and patrons. They also lacked the psychological encumbrances which bound Churchmen: fear of novelty, fear of losing respectability, and suspicion of lay leadership. On the other hand, they generally lacked organization, except for the connexional Methodists. Each congregation was expected more or less to stand on its own feet, and Churchmen were quick to point out that this meant that Dissenters were poorly equipped to deal with church provision in the areas of urban poverty. The usual Nonconformist answer was the founding of societies: the founding of town missions and church-building societies was the application of traditional methods to the challenge of the towns. There is also some evidence that the growth of denominational structure was occasioned by the needs of church extension, but here it was the rural rather than the urban areas which were in the minds of Dissenters.[1]

The Church of England was affected by two developments in the nineteenth century. One was a movement away from it, a growth of religious indifference, growth in the power of Dissent, decline in the Church's political and social influence. The other was a revival within its life, arising partly from the pressure of outside criticism, partly from a movement of renewal dating from the eighteenth century. The Industrial Revolution, and the new urban areas which it created, reinforced these developments even if they did not cause them. They challenged the Church's understanding of itself, as well as its traditional place in English social and political life, for the Established Church could not claim to be the national church if it was incapable of serving the new England. The towns also demanded a change in the Church's traditional institutions and organization, for they put great strain upon them. Such things as the parish, the parson's freehold and private patronage, the diocese and clerical training had to be adapted to deal with new conditions. And, most difficult of all, there had to be a change of attitude on the part of those who had a stake in the ecclesiastical situation.

By the 1860s it was a commonplace among Churchmen that the previous half-century had seen 'a blessed change' in the condition of the Church of England. According to the accepted story, a church which had slumbered in worldliness and idleness had been awakened by the attacks of its enemies and the earnestness of its friends into setting its house in order. In place of deserts of churchless suburbs there had arisen a multitude of Gothic towers and spires; in place of absentee incumbents there were industrious and conscientious pastors; in place of a desultory performance of legal obligations there were numerous schemes for improving the religious and moral life of the people. The picture is an exaggerated one, of course. In the earlier period there had been very many who had taken their Christianity seriously, and, although the reforms of the nineteenth century may have saved the Church from formal disestablishment, they did not halt the growing separation between the church and the nation. Nevertheless, the achievement of that half-century was a significant one. It can be seen in programmes of church extension, in higher standards of pastoral ministry, and in the development of a new pattern of parochial life which persisted into the middle of the twentieth century.

The revival of parish life and schemes for parochial betterment had their origins back in the eighteenth century.[2] In the nineteenth century the movement gathered momentum, though it had to wait for the passing of a generation or more before it could be regarded as dominant. The parochial vision was essentially rural in origin and conception, and it retained its rural preconceptions even when it was transferred to the different conditions of the cities. The overwhelming preponderance of rural parishes gave to the Church of England a rural bias, even when the population was becoming rapidly urbanized. The ideal clergyman had his roots in the country parson of George Herbert and the reformed pastor of Richard Baxter, and parochial reform meant the provision of spiritual oversight by an incumbent known personally to his parishioners, with whom he was in close contact. Even a successful city parson like W. F. Hook believed that the best training for a young clergyman was in a rural parish, for it was there that the essential character of the Church's work was to be most purely experienced. Obviously it was impossible for the city clergyman to behave as though he was a rural one, but he tried hard. He was the hub of the parish, the chairman of all the parochial organizations. The assistance of lay members of his church was conceived as giving him extra eyes and ears (and mouths, too, it was hoped) rather than as any apostolate of the laity. In the same way social criticism, when it went against the fashionable social attitudes of the day, took the form of Tory Radicalism, which was essentially a countryman's dislike of urban conditions and of city customs.

All the same, the city could not be treated in the old way. It was as true for the churches as for everything else that differences in size made a difference in quality, and the story of the first half of the nineteenth century was the gradual realization of the fact by churchmen. New conditions meant new methods, better organization, a new mentality. They meant that church life, evangelism, church extension, social action, must all be different from their counterparts in rural England.

It is extremely difficult to generalize about the cities, and earlier judgments are having to be revised in the light of the great variety which further research is disclosing. Not until all sorts of questions have been asked of a great many different areas and societies will generalization become possible again. What follows is only a rough attempt to describe one city in the light of some of the evidence, and no general conclusions about the Victorian city should be drawn from it.[3]

In Victorian Birmingham the churches found themselves existing within a prosperous and expanding commercial and industrial community.[4] Steady growth in the eighteenth century had made the town the fourth largest in the kingdom, and with the end of the Napoleonic wars the rate of expansion increased. The 1820s brought a boom in building, both in the centre and on the outskirts. Georgian Birmingham still retained some aspects of a country town, with large gardens even in the centre and a comfortable professional quarter in the High Town round St Philip's Church, but as the Victorian age drew near factories and warehouses arose in the gardens behind the houses, and the wealthier families moved to new houses nearer the green fields. The countryside itself was receding fast. In 1815 it came to within half a mile of the Bull Ring on the south, and the built-up area of the town was only two miles across at its greatest extent. The activities of the builders soon altered that. In spite of occasional periods of slackness in trade, there was a general and sustained rise in prosperity. More and more immigrants arrived in Birmingham, and by 1870 there was a solid area of bricks and mortar for five or six miles across the town, with tentacles spreading out across the countryside towards the neighbouring villages. A single decade could produce whole suburbs where before there had been only green fields. The rate of development astonished contemporaries and confronted them with physical and social problems which baffled them.

The growth of the town and its surroundings rendered obsolete the traditional pattern of local secular and ecclesiastical government. At the time when country and diocesan boundaries had been formed, the Birmingham area had been relatively unimportant, and the centres of government were some miles away, at Worcester, Warwick, Stafford, and Lichfield. As a result, boundaries zig-zagged across an area which had become economically united. The town was situated on the very edge of the diocese of Lichfield and Coventry, in a pocket of Warwickshire almost surrounded by similar pockets of Worcestershire and Staffordshire. In 1830 it was still governed more or less as an ordinary rural parish (except for its Streets Commissioners), with no corporation of its own and only a handful of local magistrates. Ecclesiastically it was part of a largely rural diocese stretching from the edge of North Wales to the Northamptonshire border south-east of Rugby. When in 1837 it was transferred to the Worcester diocese, it still did not really belong: it was on the edge of the diocese and it was different from the rest. Not until 1905 did it receive its own bishop.

The town's prosperity was based very largely upon a wide variety of light metal industries in which the typical unit was the small workshop, owned by the master-workman and attached to the family home. It was maintained that this produced a close personal relationship and community of interest between master and men, and that it was responsible for a remarkable degree of co-operation between the middle and lower classes, forming the basis for a popular Liberalism which determined the politics of the town.[5] Above and alongside the small manufacturers were the merchants and capitalists who made the town the 'Midland Metropolis' and who provided its political leadership, men like the bankers Attwood and Spooner and the merchants Scholefield and Sturge. The society which these men created was a prosperous and self-confident one, energetic and proud of its achievements. Within the town there was a strong element of Radicalism, impatient of tradition and of the traditional leaders of society, sceptical of religious dogmas and suspicious of organized religion, particularly of the Established Church. Within Dissent, even where religious principles were firmly held, there was a strong attachment to religious equality, and the town prided itself on its tolerance and variety of denominations. 'In this town', declared Charles Pye in his *Description of Modern Birmingham* in 1819, 'every individual worships his maker in whatever way his inclination leads him without the least notice being taken or remarks made; if a person's conduct is exemplary, or if he does not give way to any vicious propensities, no one will interrupt or interfere with him.'

Within this urban society there were two 'establishments' living in uneasy co-existence. They are easier to describe in general terms than to define rigidly in categories, for objections can be made to any definition. On the one hand there were the leading Churchmen, who included prominent professional men—lawyers, doctors, bankers, schoolmasters, and (naturally) parsons—as well as many manufacturers. Prominent in parish vestries and as governors of King Edward's School, they may be assumed to have had a certain social standing because of their association with elements dominant in contemporary English society. On the other hand there were prominent Dissenters whose wealth and influence placed them in a local position which was on the whole more significant than that of the Churchmen. Since the beginning of the eighteenth century they had controlled parish government: the High Bailiff was always a Churchman, but the Low Bailiff was always a Dissenter, and it was the Low Bailiff who had the greater power. This unwritten tradition is a testimony, both to the tension which existed between Church and Dissent and to the *modus vivendi* which regulated it in pre-Reform Birmingham, except for a brief period around the time of the 'Church and King' riots of 1791. It is significant that the Street Commissioners included both Churchmen and Dissenters, and that their last chairman was a Quaker.

This strength of Nonconformity depended upon two things—the social weight of its leading members, and the radical atmosphere of the town which tended to swing public opinion behind the advocates of Dissent. The population as a whole was not particularly Nonconformist compared with that of other large towns. In the census of 1851 almost half the churchgoers were Anglican, a higher proportion than in other towns of comparable size, and considerably higher than in Leeds or Manchester. But when it came to a showdown between Church and Dissent, Dissent was likely to win. Not until the closing years of the century, after the break-up of the Liberal Party, did the Churchmen come back into their own, and by then it was a very different world.

In the ranks of Dissenters there was a wide variety of forms, from the traditional bodies of Roman Catholics and Protestant Dissent, through the many types of Methodism, to the small modern sects of Swedenborgians, Mormons, and Brethren.[6] Most ancient, and highest in the social scale, were the Unitarians and Quakers. The Old and New Meetings had been founded as Presbyterian churches in the later seventeenth century, but later, like so many others of their kind, had adopted first Arianism and then Unitarianism in the middle of the eighteenth century. Of almost equal antiquity was the local meeting of the Society of Friends, whose place of worship in Bull Street dated from 1703, and burial ground in Monmouth Street from even earlier. These two denominations included among their adherents families of great wealth and importance in the town: among the Unitarians the inter-related families of Kenrick, Beale, Ryland, Phipson, Smith, and Hutton, and among Quakers Cadbury, Barrow, Lloyd, and Sturge. Although jealous and suspicious of the Established Church, the Unitarians and Quakers were an accepted part of the social establishment. As men of influence—traders, bankers, capitalists, factory owners, and landowners—they took part in the government of the parish and acted as Street Commissioners. Their politics in this period tended to be moderate, Whig rather than Radical, and the Quakers were still uneasy as to whether or not political agitation was permissible. The Radical activism of the Sturge brothers brought them rebukes from their fellow-Quakers. The leading Unitarians were at first suspicious of the Birmingham Political Union (which was led by an Anglican Tory-Radical) and they joined it only when it was already popular. Hugh Hutton, minister of the Old Meeting from 1822 to 1851, played a small part in the Reform agitation when he acted as chaplain to the Birmingham Political Union and wrote its hymn, but after 1832 he withdrew from active politics and devoted his energies to his duties as pastor and scholar. At the New Meeting the ministers Samuel Bache and the elderly John Kentish belonged as much to the eighteenth century as to the nineteenth.[7]

Generally lower in the social scale than the Unitarians and Quakers were the Evangelical Dissenters. The oldest congregation among them was the Cannon Street church of Particular Baptists, formed in 1737.[8] The Independent Church in Carrs Lane owed its formation to a secession of the orthodox members of the Old Meeting in 1747 in protest against the minister's Arianism. Both Baptists and Independents were profoundly influenced by the Evangelical Revival, which brought them new life, more members, and more chapels. Carrs Lane church under John Angell James and R. W. Dale became nationally famous far beyond the bounds of Congregationalism.[9] Methodism also was established in the town, though it seems never to have supplied quite the same strength of political leadership as the other major denominations.

820

Among Methodists the Wesleyans were strongest: for much of the period they remained sympathetic towards the Church of England, and as late as the 1830s Churchmen scarcely considered them as Nonconformists. On public occasions they were ready to co-operate with Churchmen, and it was a Wesleyan mayor, Sir John Ratcliff, who in the 1850s defied the anti-clerical tradition of the borough by appointing as his chaplain the Vicar of Edgbaston, Isaac Spooner.[10] Primitive Methodism was less important: indeed, the local historian of the movement declared in 1882 that 'Birmingham, for Primitive Methodism, has been like the seed sown on hard and rocky places'.[11] A Primitive Methodist preacher visited the town in 1824, and in 1828 there was one circuit with a travelling preacher and less than two hundred members, but this connexion, which claimed to be 'the working-man's church', had only three places of worship at the time of the 1851 census, with 656 sittings and a total attendance of 1,053, though this was before the opening of its principal chapel on Gooch Street in 1852. There were other Methodist connexions represented in the town, but none of them of any importance.[12]

The Roman Catholics built an unobtrusive chapel (St Peter's) near Broad Street in 1786, and followed this in 1809 with another (St Chad's) in Shadwell Street. The priest of St Peter's was less self-effacing than his chapel: T. M. M'Donnell was an Irishman of eloquence and great energy, both in the superintendence of his own flock and in political and religious controversy. He was a friend and supporter of Daniel O'Connell, and a member of the governing council of the Birmingham Political Union, and he secured for his denomination a voice in public life. His life of unceasing controversy earned him the hatred of many Anglican Churchmen, and in the end his own superiors moved him to a quiet life in Torquay. Birmingham was an important centre for the Roman Catholics, with St Chad's Cathedral (consecrated 1841) in the town, and Oscott College in the near neighbourhood, but the number of Roman Catholics actually resident in Birmingham remained relatively small for many years. In the 1851 census their proportion to the whole population was far smaller than in Manchester or Liverpool, smaller even than in Bristol or Wolverhampton. Nevertheless their numbers did increase steadily, as also did the provision of churches for them. They were significant enough in the town for there to be a No-Popery riot in 1867, when they besieged the Protestant lecturer Murphy, and were in turn attacked by a Protestant mob, which sacked the Irish quarter. And they had in Edgbaston the distinguished figure of John Henry Newman, though his presence was generally discreet and not particularly influential.

It was natural that an expanding town, receiving immigrants from all over the British Isles, should display such a wide variety of denominations. The religious life of the town was marked by all the vigour which one would expect in a thriving society of such diversity. But the majority of the working classes, though avowing membership of some religious body, were by accident or design lost to organized religion, and were scarcely or never seen in the churches or chapels, for whom they formed a vast and increasing mission field. If religion was strong, so also was religious indifference, and there was a multitude of people for whom there was no place in church, and no parson to visit them, while they for their part apparently entertained little desire to bridge the gap which separated them from the churches.

The Church of England was poorly equipped to deal with the challenge of the large and expanding Birmingham of the nineteenth century. Its organization was outdated. Not only did the diocesan system ignore the city's new importance: the local parish system also was based on a society that had long passed away. The old parish of Birmingham covered the centre of the town on the left bank of the river Rea and also a large area to the north-west, the wide expanse of the newly enclosed Birmingham Heath. The population was large, but there were only two parish churches, St Martin's and St Philip's, and the various chapels which had been built had perpetual curates but no cure of souls. As the town spread northwards and eastwards, an increasing number of people belonged to the parish of Aston. This was a vast parish whose area was still largely rural, extending eastwards for some miles through several small hamlets and villages, but its south-western boundary ran very near to the centre of the city and included part of the old manor of Birmingham. Even in the Middle Ages the position had been regarded as anomalous, and the hamlet of Deritend had built its own chapel. To the south-west lay the parish of Edgbaston, in 1815 still entirely rural, but about to be developed as a high-class residential district.

These three parishes all contained ancient parish churches, adapted and modernized in the eighteenth century, but quite unable to contain more than a tiny proportion of the population. Their accommodation was supplemented by chapels of ease, for which there was an increasing demand, but even these were insufficient for the growing town. If the Church of England were to remain the church of the people, it needed to make adequate provision for their accommodation in church, and in an expanding town this meant a sustained programme of church building. Unfortunately the situation had already got out of hand by 1800. To provide an effective pastoral and parochial ministry for everyone it would be necessary not merely to keep pace with the amazing growth of population in the nineteenth century but also to make up the deficiency of the previous century.

The shortage of accommodation was made worse for the poor by the high proportion of seats, in both Anglican and Dissenting churches, which were reserved in return for pew-rents. In St Martin's there was even a tradition of privately owned pews. Nor were the standards of pastoral ministry high. The rectors of the two important churches were absentees. The rector of St Philip's divided his time between lectureships in London and livings in the country, and he made only occasional visits to Birmingham: this state of affairs lasted until his death in 1844. The rector of St Martin's, Charles Curtis, resided until his death in 1829 at his other rectory at Solihull: he was not popular in Birmingham, and had caused much ill-will by enforcing the payment of Easter dues from recalcitrant parishioners. Both these rectories were well endowed, and St Martin's was getting richer as a result of the rising value of land in Birmingham.

The response of the Church of England to the challenge of the new towns lay in the development of the urban parish. The parochial system, properly reformed and extended, was seen by many Churchmen as a source of new life and as a means of supplying the needs of urban society. They said that if only there were more churches and clergymen there would be less need for prisons and workhouses. The correctly functioning parish, with its pastors and district visitors, its benevolent societies and its schools, and all its other agencies for doing good, would relieve, guide, and elevate the population of its surrounding district, thereby restoring a diseased society to health.

One basic need was the provision of new churches. At the beginning of the century Christ Church was built in a crowded part of Birmingham, specifically for 'the Artificers and Handicraftsmen' of the district. It was declared a 'free church' in which private pews would be confined to the galleries, and no charges were to be made for seats or benches in the main body of the church. Although a special Act of Parliament was required, it was essentially a private piece of church extension, in keeping with eighteenth-century practice, and it suffered from the drawbacks of that system. It took from 1805 to 1813 to progress from laying the foundation stone to the consecration of the church, and the spire and portico were not complete until 1815. It was comparatively expensive (£26,000) and it was built in difficult times, but, even allowing for that, the support from local subscribers must be considered poor, and the church was burdened with debt. An attempt in 1817 to pay off the debt and to purchase a parsonage house by means of a parish rate encountered violent opposition and was withdrawn. Christ Church was a sign that a new approach was needed in the matter of church extension.[13]

The story of church building in Birmingham between 1815 and 1865 divides into four parts. The first period was dominated by the Parliamentary Church Building Commissioners, who were a godsend for Birmingham. In the 1820s they built four large churches—one in the centre of the town and three on the outskirts—and for the first time for a century it seemed that the provision of churches might meet the increase of population. A large proportion of the seats was free—nearly half in one church, and in the other three more than two-thirds. The rapidity with which they were built contrasted with the painfully slow completion of Christ Church. But state aid was not to continue in such fashion. The parliamentary grants would not last at such a rate, and in the changed political circumstances after 1830 further grants were extremely unlikely. It became necessary to build more cheaply: there is a remarkable difference between the cost of St Thomas's, 1826–9 (£14,263) and that of the next Birmingham church, All Saints', consecrated 1833 (£3,820). From this time onwards the Commissioners were unwilling to undertake the responsibility for building, preferring instead to give grants towards churches built on local initiative with largely local money.[14]

The second period, covering most of the 1830s, was a transition period, marked by the foundation of diocesan building societies. The Lichfield diocesan society was formed at a meeting in Birmingham in 1835, and it contributed towards six new or

1815

ASTON

HOCKLEY

ASHTED

DERITEND

EDGBASTON

	Built-up area

●	Baptist	▲	Methodist
✛	Catholic Apostolic	⌐	Presbyterian
+	Church of England	◆	Roman Catholic
◨	Congregationalist/Independent	▮	Society of Friends (Quakers)
☆	Jewish	✪	Swedenborgian
◣	Latter Day Saints (Mormons)	U	Unitarian et sim

| 0 | Metres | 2000 |
| 0 | Yards | 2000 |

XIX Religious denominations in Birmingham, 1815

extended churches in the Birmingham area, despite the fact that the town was transferred to the Worcester diocese following Bishop Ryder's death in 1836.[15]

The third period was that of the Ten Churches Scheme, inaugurated by the rural dean of Birmingham in 1838. He said that while the population of the town had quadrupled since 1780, the number of churches had little more than doubled, so that

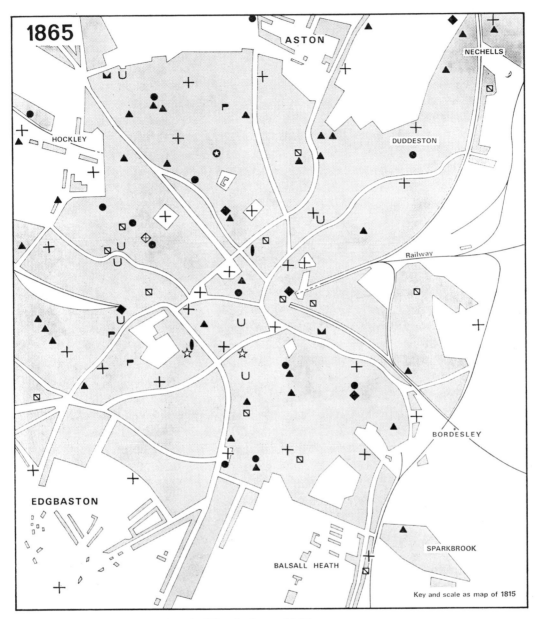

XX Religious denominations in Birmingham, 1865

there was accommodation for less than one-seventh of the inhabitants. One-third of this accommodation, and four-fifths of the provision for the poor, had been provided by parliamentary grants, while Bishop Ryder's Church (1838) had been built mainly from sources outside the town. It was therefore time for the town to help itself. He proposed the erection of ten new churches in the next five years, to

825

supply the poorer parts of the borough with churches each costing about £3,000 and holding a thousand worshippers. Each new church would receive an endowment of £1,000 and would be assigned a pastoral district.[16]

The appeal met with an immediate response. Within a month £8,000 had been subscribed. The first church was begun in October 1839 and was consecrated a year later, and the second church followed soon after. Then came delay over a suitable site for the third church, and over a year passed before its consecration. The gap before the consecration of the fourth church was longer (one and three-quarter years), and the gap before the fifth even longer still (two and a quarter years). Church building then ceased for a time. Instead of ten churches built in five years there had been only five churches built in ten years. Building costs had kept fairly close to the estimates, but the early enthusiasm had waned, and in the absence of any tradition of sustained giving the subscriptions had fallen off considerably. Meanwhile the town had grown so fast that in 1847 the local Church of England Lay Association recorded 'the painful conclusion that, even since the establishment of the Birmingham Church Building Society, we have not kept pace, year by year, with the increasing population, much less have we done anything to retrieve former neglect'.[17]

The fourth period was that of a new Church Building Society which was founded in 1851. It was less centrally directed than its predecessor and more dependent upon the exertions of individual parishes, but its fortunes were much the same. Despite a wide range of initial support, the new society was weak from its early days. It was never given full support by the laity; its meetings and work were spoilt by disagreements among the clergy; and according to the minute-book the committee met irregularly with poor attendance. In view of all the dissensions and discouragements it is surprising that any churches were built at all, but a new church was consecrated about every two years. Nevertheless, the Church was still losing ground. A local critic pointed out that in 1851 there had been accommodation for 13·3 percent of the town's population, but in 1864 for only 12·16 percent—for 36,073 out of 296,606. The clergy made yet another fresh start. In 1865 the Birmingham Church Extension Society took over the work of the old Society in the hope of doing better, yet it had to announce with regret a year later that its appeal for support had 'failed to secure anything like the measure of success which has crowned similar efforts in other large towns', and with the population increasing by 8,600 each year the prospect was poor.[18]

The pattern of church provision since 1815 had been fairly consistent. On the one hand, the number of churches within the town and Edgbaston had increased from nine to more than three times that number—no mean achievement. On the other hand, the population which the churches were meant to serve had increased still faster, so that the overall result suggested failure rather than success. Despite its great wealth, Birmingham had not given very much towards the building of churches, or towards the staffing of them. It was dependent upon grants from outside the town, and a good deal of the money given locally came from a small group of wealthy and generous individuals. Gradually over the years churchmen came to expect less from their efforts; churches were smaller, and extension was viewed not as the creation of new congregations but as the provision of a building and a district for a congregation that already existed. The initiative for building a new church had to come from the locality itself, and a regular congregation was required to provide the pew rents which made up a good proportion of the incumbent's stipend. It was likely that first there would be services in rooms licensed for public worship; then a mission room or hall would be built; a congregation would be established under an assistant curate; and finally a permanent church would be consecrated and would be given a legal district, often with the curate as the first incumbent.[19]

Ideally a new church meant a new parish, staffed by resident clergy, and perhaps also by paid lay agents, with a wide variety of parochial activities. Unfortunately new churches were not all immediately given pastoral districts, for there were great difficulties in the way of creating new parishes. In this matter the Establishment weighed very heavily upon the Church, for throughout the eighteenth century special Acts of Parliament were necessary, and parliament was scrupulously jealous for the rights of incumbents and patrons. Only one new parish was formed in that century—St Philip's, under an Act of 1709 (7 Anne, ch. 13)—and even then it remained part of St Martin's parish for rates, including church rates, and the rector of the new parish was bound by a clause in the Act to pay £15 yearly to the rector of St Martin's in compensation for the latter's loss of income. The Church Building and New Parishes Acts of the nineteenth century provided machinery for the creation of pastoral districts and new parishes, but the law was very complicated and obscure. It was necessary for Thomas Moseley to resign and be re-appointed to the rectory of St Martin's in order that three new churches might become separate rectories in the early 1830s. There were many other churches in the town, some of them older than these three, which were still without parishes. For the sake of greater efficiency and pastoral convenience, the clergy of Birmingham parish met together towards the end of 1829 and agreed to divide the greater part of the parish into small districts, each incumbent becoming responsible for the area around his own church or chapel, but this arrangement did not alter the hard legal facts, and it was many years before some of the areas became official ecclesiastical districts.[20] And each new parish required a suitable endowment, which was an added burden on to the cost of building. Rectors of St Martin's helped in some cases by giving part of their own endowments. For Aston parish an Act of Parliament in 1832 (2 Will. IV, ch. 2) gave the patron the right to assign part of the tithes and vicarial dues towards the endowment of churches in the outlying townships of the parish, naming among others the chapels of Ashted, Bordesley, and Deritend, but the difficulties were such that little advantage seems to have been taken of the Act. In 1837 the vicar of Aston wrote to the trustees of the estates belonging to St John's chapel, Deritend, suggesting that the living of Deritend be made into a vicarage under the new Act, but the trustees replied that they had no money available for the purpose.[21] By the 1840s it became usual for a district to be assigned shortly after the consecration of a church, with a small endowment provided by the local Church Building Society or the Ecclesiastical Commissioners.

These institutional changes would have been worthless without a higher standard of pastoral ministry. Over the years there was a noticeable change in what was expected of a clergyman. This change was not the monopoly of any one ecclesiastical party, but in Birmingham it coincided with the ascendancy of the Evangelicals. In the 1820s the patronage of St Martin's and three daughter churches came into the hands of Evangelicals, who in 1837 set up a trust to secure 'a succession in perpetuity of holy and devoted Ministers'. They said that they had 'resisted repeated opportunities of disposing of these Livings to great pecuniary advantage' and that they regarded the patronage as a stewardship from God, to be exercised to his glory and for the spiritual welfare of the inhabitants. In appointing to a benefice, the trustees were enjoined to lay aside all personal considerations, to elect 'a man of God in deed and truth', and to be guided only by his qualifications for the parish to which the appointment was to be made.[22]

The Evangelicals had a high seriousness about their ministry. The arrival of Thomas Moseley as rector of St Martin's in 1829 had an immediate effect upon the parish. There were more services, a greater emphasis on preaching, a rector permanently resident in the town, a conscientious discharge of official duties, and the encouragement of religious societies. It was under his guidance that the clergy of the town met together and divided the old parish between them unofficially, and when the three new rectories were formed he endowed them with portions of his own glebe-land and of the rectorial tithes.[23] Unfortunately his ministry was marred by political warfare (he was pelted in the streets for refusing to let the Birmingham Political Union ring the church bells for partisan purposes) and by the long and bitter controversy over church rates, which so dispirited him that he withdrew from active life, and in 1846 he resigned because of illness.[24]

The Evangelicals were also responsible for the introduction of visiting schemes on a wide scale. *Aris's Birmingham Gazette* of 4 January 1830 carried a statement informing the public of a system arranged 'on a plan adopted in some other parts of the kingdom', to provide incumbents with the assistance of visiting societies from their own congregations. 'A regular and systematic plan of pastoral superintendence' followed the lines of Thomas Chalmers's organization in Glasgow, combining the investigation of physical needs and the distribution of charity with moral exhortation, tract distribution, and evangelism.[25] Similar schemes, with the use of paid agents, were used by both Churchmen and Dissenters in the Town Mission, founded in 1838, and in connection with individual churches.

Between the 1830s and the 1860s a standard parochial pattern was established in the majority of urban parishes. There was a resident incumbent with one or more curates, and in Evangelical parishes a scripture-reader or two. Parochial life centred on the parish church and the church school, with mission rooms or halls spread about the parish, some of them forming growing points for new parishes, others acting simply as meeting places for parochial organizations or as 'halfway houses' for people who could not yet be induced to attend services at the parish church. The parochial organizations were many and various. Some were social agencies, providing savings clubs and sickness benefits. Others were a means of fellowship for church members, to teach them the faith, to bring together those of the same age or of similar interests, and to attract the outsider. Some were local auxiliaries of home and foreign missionary societies. Some were visiting societies. All these activities, together with Sunday schools, gave ample scope for lay participation in the Church's work, and some of them provided opportunities for lay leadership. A similar pattern was to be found in connection with churches of most denominations. The Unitarians gave more attention to adult education and 'useful knowledge'; churches of a more Evangelical character paid greater attention to evangelism: variations naturally occurred from church to church, but the general pattern was so widely accepted that one finds it reflected even in non-religious bodies.[26]

Outside the church organizations lay the vast masses who rarely went to church. By the middle of the century the churches were all debating the missionary situation which lay at their doors, and in 1861 *The Mission and Extension of the Church at Home* was the subject for the Bampton Lectures by the Archdeacon of Coventry, John Sandford. The 1851 census of attendance at religious worship was both a consequence of, and an added stimulus to, this general discussion. The census figures have to be handled with care, but they do provide a general picture of church attendance and denominational allegiance.[27] In Birmingham they seemed to indicate that probably three-quarters of the citizens regularly abstained from public worship. Churchmen were soon pointing the moral: John Cale Miller, rector of St Martin's from 1846 to 1866, told the Church Pastoral-Aid Society in 1855 that 'the Church . . . has now to gird herself to a work among her HOME HEATHEN as truly Missionary as is work in her outposts in the Punjaub or amid the Dyaks of Borneo . . . A vast work has she yet to do ere she stands forth in our midst in truth, as in name, the Church of ENGLAND, the Church of the people, the Church of the poor.'[28]

The situation led to much heart-searching among Churchmen. Miller welcomed the signs of awakening in the churches—cottage and schoolroom lectures, open-air preaching, town missions, scripture-readers, tracts, and the many schemes and societies. But he was aware of the great gap between the Church and the ordinary people.[29]

> The very fact that we have been a Church established by law, and, to a great extent, the Church of the aristocracy and higher classes, while it has given us, in some respects, a great vantage ground, has, in others, been a snare . . . We have stood upon our dignity. We have a morbid horror of being *vulgar*. Our ministers have not been trained for a work among 'the common people'; and 'the common people' have soon discerned their want of adaptation to their wants and tastes.

Within the churches the pew system had been a fruitful source of class consciousness. The old system of the private ownership of pews was disappearing fast by the middle of the century: the ecclesiastical authorities disliked it, and the law was found to be a useful ally in extinguishing it. But the renting of pews remained prominent in both Church and Dissent. Nonconformists recommended pew rents to Churchmen as a more satisfactory source of income than church rates. There was a general feeling that the churches belonged to the pew-holders, the upper and middle classes, and that the working classes were present as guests, welcome or unwelcome. When Thomas Nunns left St Bartholomew's in 1843 to go to Leeds, the address which accompanied his church's parting gift made the distinction between the 'we' of the church and 'the humbler members of your congregation'. It spoke of the regular and large attendance of the poor, but these poor were clearly regarded as attenders rather than as an integral part of the church.[30] Dr T. R. Tholfsen cites a similar case from Dissent: Timothy East of Ebenezer Chapel, 'in order to preach to "the mechanics", used to pitch a tent in various parts of the town, in addition to Tuesday evening sermons for them in the chapel. That is, the working men remained in a separate category.'[31] It is of course debatable which came first, the distinctive treatment of the working classes or their withdrawal from ordinary services, but either way the distinction existed. Too much distinction was considered wrong: Birmingham clergy always rejected the idea of 'ragged churches' (an echo of 'ragged schools'), which would have segregated the poor completely by inviting them to worship in separate, and shoddier, buildings. Mission services and working-class missionaries were an attempt to attract them without setting them in an inferior order. The upper and middle classes were not entirely insensitive to the feelings of the working classes. That is why it was the *best* seats in Christ Church which were free, and why many advocated providing pews at rents sufficiently modest for working men to afford them and thus to have a sense of belonging to the church, though in this case they evidently had in mind a different type of person from 'the poor' for whom the ragged church might cater. There were also free seats for them. In the 1851 census nearly half of the accommodation was considered to be free, for not only were the new buildings supplied with a good proportion but the older churches were adapted to provide more.[32]

Some clergymen had success among the working classes. Where working men met with sympathy and understanding they were often prepared to attend church. Thomas Nunns at St Bartholomew's (1834–43) sympathized with working-class sufferings and had a large and regular attendance of poorer parishioners.[33] The Tory-Radical G. S. Bull managed to fill St Thomas's Church, and it was said that he had a genial humour 'which endeared him to the working classes, in whom he always took an especial interest'.[34] Above all, John Cale Miller of St Martin's was said to have obtained the sympathy of the working classes to a considerable extent.

Miller was the outstanding Anglican clergyman in Birmingham in the middle of the century. His preaching attracted large congregations to St Martin's, which became in fact as well as in name the most important parish church in the town. He had an eye for current events and a flair for organization which enabled him to take note of other men's ideas and to use them to such good effect that they often became associated with his name. He was one of the first to substitute shorter and more specialized services for the old pattern of mattins, litany, and ante-communion, and to introduce evening communion in 1852. He became such an enthusiastic supporter of open-air preaching that he became credited with its revival in Anglican circles, though it is clear from his own words that other Birmingham clergymen had preceded him. He found it exhausting work, but 'the working classes and the poor assemble in decorous, grateful, attentive auditories', and he claimed that as a result outsiders, including working men, were brought into the Church. He realized that the Church could not hope to speak to working men before it had their confidence. In the past it had failed to sympathize with them: they needed more than an occasional visit which was 'too often insulting in its very patronage and condescension'. It was not enough to be condescending and to practise charity. 'We must go among them; we must improve their dwellings; we must provide them the means not only of mental self-improvement, but of physical recreation.' In 1854 he established at St Martin's a working-men's association on a wider basis than was usual for such institutions, with educational lectures, classes and discussions, newspapers and books, quarterly tea- and music-parties, and savings clubs. He believed its value to lie, not so much in what was provided, as in 'the cultivation and exercise of sympathy with the Working Classes'. He was also aware that in evangelism the working people were best approached by members of their own class, and to that end he organized a band of working men as missionaries among their neighbours.[35]

Too often in the past the working classes had found sympathy lacking among church leaders. Clergymen and ministers repeated what the political economists told them, that poverty was a permanent and unavoidable feature of human existence, and they found suitable Biblical texts to support the statement.[36] The unfortunate impression which this created was likely to be encouraged by attempts to commend Christianity on the grounds of moral influence and social utility, as a means of keeping the poor contented and meek. The Churchmen seemed primarily interested in order, the Nonconformists in liberty: what the working classes looked for was a mitigation of their poverty.

Within the framework of the old conception of social order Churchmen sought to practise Christian principles. Charity and the relief of suffering were in the forefront of their work, not only when there was great distress but also at all times. They supported local charitable institutions with their time and their money; they provided food and clothing for the deserving poor; they honoured employers like William Chance and R. W. Winfield who provided schools for their factory children; they collected money in church for good causes. When in the middle of the century it became fashionable to collect information about the conditions of the urban poor, the clergy from their intimate knowledge played a prominent part equalled only by the doctors. Local clergymen were among those who read papers at the first meeting of the National Association for the Promotion of Social Science which took place in Birmingham in 1857.[37]

Together with charity went the message of self-improvement. The churches

831

were leading advocates of savings clubs, and it was said that there were more wealthy sick-clubs connected with religious bodies in Birmingham than in most towns.[38] The supporters of one Provident Association declared that 'if similar institutions were established in the several parishes in the kingdom, it would do more to improve the moral and social welfare of the working classes, and to diminish pauperism, than any legal enactments that could be passed'.[39] The rector of St Philip's, G. M. Yorke, took a special interest in the work of ragged schools, reformatories, and the education of the very poor. Churchmen were among the supporters of the municipal provision of public parks, baths, and libraries. Above all, the work of education absorbed the time, attention, and energies of the churches. By 1850 almost every parish had its Sunday and day schools, for which the incumbent usually made himself responsible, and they were considered an almost indispensable part of the parish. In some of the poorer areas they must have been a heavy drain on the clergyman's energy.

One great drawback of the parochial system, as it was practised in the nineteenth century, was the strain which it imposed upon the incumbent. The increasing duties and the high conscientiousness of Victorian clergymen made enormous demands upon their time and energies. Everything in parochial life centred on them—the management of church schools, the chairmanship of parochial organizations, the direction of district visiting, and the conduct of services—while the parish's ever-increasing need of money made them feel that begging was the chief element in their duties. It was too much for an incumbent to fulfil the old idea of pastoral oversight, for however hard he worked there were still important things left undone. 'A clergyman attends upon the sick and dying,' said Thomas Nunns, 'visits, in his ministerial capacity, the members of his congregation; superintends his schools. This is all he does, and (with little exceptions not worth noticing) this is all he can do.'[40] All this left the clergyman with little or no time for study or for the ordinary life of society, and too often he lacked an intelligent understanding of the contemporary scene. Evangelical clergymen in particular now paid the price for their earlier condemnation of worldly society and secular study. Competent and positive preaching existed, but it lacked the attractiveness and modernity which congregations desired. It tended to degenerate into the 'common-places' and the 'time-honoured conventionalities' of which a local reporter complained around 1870. The popularity of the unorthodox preacher George Dawson arose partly from his sympathy with the age and his ability to give it the sort of addresses which it liked. Too many clergymen resorted to denunciation. 'We were treated once more to a denunciation of "modern scepticism" which, to judge from the frequency with which it is alluded to, seems to be a peculiar terror to Birmingham clergy', said the writer of *Pulpit Photographs*. 'If, instead of continually scolding the sceptics, the clergy would meet them on disputed points and beat them by fair argument . . . we should all be somewhat wiser, and, probably, a good deal better . . . If the Church wants to battle successfully with her intellectual foes she must put up intellectual men to do the work.'[41]

By 1865 the main outlines of institutional change within the churches were complete. Within Nonconformity the modern denominational structure had come into existence. Within the Church of England the urban parish had appeared. There were new churches, new parishes, and new church schools. Change was now easier, services were different, and the movement had begun to bring some form of synodical government into the Church. For the rest of the century the churches turned their attention more positively towards the society in which they were placed. Already by the 1850s a new spirit is discernible among churchmen of all denominations, drawing them towards three areas of concern. Miller was reported as having said in 1853, at a meeting in support of the Saturday half-holiday, that: 'it was a happy thing that the religious part of the community were now aware that they have been too neglectful of questions of this nature, which had no small influence on the moral and spiritual interests of the masses. Where there were filthy lodging-houses, necessitating indecency and dirt, there the Minister, the Scripture-Reader, or the Missionary, might labour in vain.'[42] During the same decade it was borne in upon them that the position of the churches in the nation demanded the evangelization of the masses.[43] And about the same time George Dawson was drawing their attention to 'The Demands of the Age' upon the Church,[44] demands which were becoming increasingly loud and which called for a new type of urban clergyman, professionally trained and socially relevant.[45] These were the outlines of the developments in late-Victorian Birmingham—social reform, evangelism, and adjustment to the new culture.[46]

Notes

1 Denominational histories by Nonconformists during the nineteenth century gave little attention to the problems of urban society, but concentrated more on theological, biographical, and political matters. During this century the development of denominational government has been described in Albert Peel, *These Hundred Years—the Congregational Union, 1831–1931* (1931), and E. A. Payne, *The Baptist Union: A short history* (1959). R. Tudur Jones, *Congregationalism in England, 1662–1962* (1962), is more general in scope.

2 For a description of this revival, see G. F. A. Best, *Temporal Pillars*, especially ch. 4 (Cambridge, 1964).

3 A general introduction to the subject is given in Standish Meacham, 'The Church in the Victorian City', *Victorian Studies*, xi (1968), 359–78. Studies of particular cities and areas include: E. R. Wickham, *Church and People in an Industrial City* (1957); E. T. Davies, *Religion in the Industrial Revolution in South Wales* (Cardiff, 1965); Stewart Mechie, *The Church and Scottish Social Development, 1780–1870* (1960); R. B. Walker, 'Religious Changes in Cheshire, 1750–1850', *Journal of Ecclesiastical History (J. Eccles. Hist.)*, xvii (1966), 77–94; R. B. Walker, 'Religious Changes in Liverpool in the Nineteenth Century', ibid., xix (1968), 195–211.

4 The standard history of Birmingham is Conrad Gill & Asa Briggs, *History of Birmingham* (1952). Valuable references to contemporary life can be found in J. A. Langford, *A Century of Birmingham Life, 1741–1841* (Birmingham, 1868), and *Modern Birmingham and its Institutions 1841–1871* (Birmingham, 1873, 1877). A good deal of information about the churches can be found in the Victoria County History volume on the city of Birmingham (*V.C.H. Warwickshire*, VII). A vast amount of material is gathered together in the Birmingham Collection of the Central Reference Library in Birmingham: this contains minute-books, pamphlets, programmes, maps, parish magazines, newspapers, and books. The library is also the home of the Birmingham Diocesan Record Office.

5 Asa Briggs, 'Thomas Attwood and the Economic Background of the Birmingham Political Union', *Cambridge Historical Journal*, ix (1948), 190–216. For an earlier contrast of Birmingham and Manchester, see A. W. W. Dale, *Life of R. W. Dale of Birmingham* (2nd edn, 1899), pp. 136–7.

6 For a contemporary portrait of Nonconformity, see John Angell James, *Protestant Nonconformity: A sketch of its general history* (1849).

7 Catherine Hutton Beale, *Memorials of the Old Meeting House and Burial Ground, Birmingham* (Birmingham, 1882); Herbert New, *The New Meeting and the Church of the Messiah, Birmingham* (Birmingham, 1912).

8 A. S. Langley, *Birmingham Baptists Past and Present* (1939).

9 A. H. Driver, *Carrs Lane 1748–1948* (Birmingham, 1948).

10 Langford, *Modern Birmingham*, I, p. 452.

11 George Davies, *A Sketch of the Rise and Progress of Primitive Methodism in and around Birmingham* (Birmingham, 1882), p. 18.

12 Ibid., pp. 16–23; *Parliamentary Papers* (*P.P.*), 1852–3, LXXXIX, Report on the Census of Religious Worship, p. ccliii.

13 43 Geo. III, ch. 117 and 50 Geo. III, ch. 130; R. K. Dent, *The Making of Birmingham* (Birmingham, 1894), pp. 278–9; Birmingham Central Reference Library, Birmingham Collection 660234, Christ Church Minute Book 1803–1858, pp. 227–44.

14 M. H. Port, *Six Hundred New Churches* (1961), p. 113.

15 *Aris's Birmingham Gazette*, 2 February 1835, 2 January 1837, 30 January 1837; *Birmingham Journal*, 28 January 1837, 4 February 1837; William Beresford, *Lichfield* (n.d.), pp. 279–80.

16 *Aris's Birmingham Gazette*, 8, 15, 22 October, 5 November 1838; John Garbett, *An Appeal for the Erection of New Churches in Birmingham* (Birmingham, 1838).

17 Church of England Lay Association for Birmingham and its Vicinity, *8th Report* (Birmingham, 1847), 15. Compare *Birmingham in Miniature* (Birmingham, 1851), p. 38.

18 Birmingham Collection 234450, Birmingham Society for the Building and Endowing of Churches within the Borough, Minute Book 1851–62; Nash Stephenson, *Church Accommodation in the Rural Deanery of Birmingham* (Birmingham, 1864); J. C. Miller, *The Church of England in Birmingham* (Birmingham, 1864); Birmingham Church Extension Society, *Appeal by the Committee . . . in Behalf of a new Plan of Operation* (Birmingham, 1866).

19 Compare church extension in London: P. J. Welch, 'Bishop Blomfield and Church Extension in London', *J. Eccles. Hist.*, iv (1953), 203–15 and 'The Difficulties of

Church Extension in Victorian London', *Church Quarterly Review*, clxvi (1965), 302–15. For Scotland, see J. H. S. Burleigh, *A Church History of Scotland* (1960), pp. 319–28.

20 *Aris's Birmingham Gazette*, 23 November 1829; R. K. Dent, *The Making of Birmingham* (Birmingham, 1894), p. 405.

21 Birmingham Collection 443354, Minute Book of the Trustees of the Estates belonging to St John's Chapel, Deritend, 1822–41, p. 105.

22 Birmingham Collection 359505, *A Brief Historical Sketch of St Martin's Birmingham* (Birmingham, 1852), p. 7.

23 *Aris's Birmingham Gazette*, 23 November 1829; Dent, op. cit., p. 405; C. M. Marsh, *The Life of the Rev. William Marsh, D.D.* (1867), p. 143.

24 C. M. Wakefield, *Life of Thomas Attwood* (1885), p. 159.

25 For the system as operated by Chalmers, see William Hanna, *Memoirs of the Life and Writings of Thomas Chalmers* (Edinburgh, 1850), II, passim.

26 Despite Canon Charles Smyth's remark ('The Evangelical Movement in Perspective', *Cambridge Historical Journal*, vii (1943), 161) that 'The creation and working of the urban parish constituted one of the most important achievements of the Church of England in the nineteenth century', the urban parish still awaits its historian. Information can be gleaned from the biographies of urban clergymen like Chalmers, Hook, and Bickersteth. For an idealized picture of a Birmingham Evangelical clergyman of the 1830s, see *Memoir and Correspondence of the Rev. John George Bray* (1841), and *The Faithful Pastor Delineated: Five sermons preached at Christ Church, Birmingham, on the occasion of the death of the Rev. John George Bray* (n.d.).

27 Census of Religious Worship; K. S. Inglis, 'Patterns of Religious Worship in 1851', *J. Eccles. Hist.*, xi (1960), 74–86; W. S. F. Pickering, 'The Religious Census of 1851 —a Useless Experiment?', *British Journal of Sociology*, xviii (1967), 382–407; D. M. Thompson, 'The 1851 Religious Census: Problems and Possibilities', *Victorian Studies*, xi (1967), 87–97. The Congregationalists had already begun debating their lack of success among working men—see the *Congregational Year Book* for 1848, and Edward Miall, *The British Churches in Relation to the British People* (1849).

28 J. C. Miller, *The Church of the People* (1855), p. 11.

29 Ibid., pp. 11–14.

30 *Aris's Birmingham Gazette*, 21 August 1843.

31 T. R. Tholfsen, 'The Artisan and the Culture of Early Victorian Birmingham', *University of Birmingham Historical Journal*, iv (1954), 162. For a Scottish example of the middle-class captivity of the churches, see A. Allen McLaren, 'Presbyterianism and the Working Class in a Mid-Nineteenth Century City' (Aberdeen), *Scottish Historical Review*, xlvi (1967), 115–39.

32 But some were probably returned as free when they happened merely to be unlet.

33 *Aris's Birmingham Gazette*, 21 August 1843.

34 J. M. Brindley, *Church Work in Birmingham* (Birmingham, 1880), p. 38; *P.P.*, 1859 (session 2), V, Select Committee on Church Rates: Report, p. 134. See also J. C. Gill, *The Ten Hours Parson*, (1959) and *Parson Bull of Byerley* (1963).

35 *Dictionary of National Biography* (1909), XIII, p. 414; J. C. Miller, *The Dying Judge's Charge* (1854) and *Home-Heathen* (1854); D. E. H. Mole, 'John Cale Miller: A Victorian Rector of Birmingham', *J. Eccles. Hist.*, xvii (1966), 95–103.

36 As an illustration of this, see J. B. Sumner's views in R. S. Dell, 'Social and Economic Theories and Pastoral Concerns of a Victorian Archbishop', *J. Eccles. Hist.*, xvi (1965), 196–208.

37 Langford, op. cit., I, pp. 442–3. For examples of the principles and practice of charity, see the establishment of parochial visiting societies (*Aris's Birmingham Gazette*, 23 November 1829, 4 January 1830); the advertisement of the newly-formed local Society for the Suppression of Mendicity (*Aris's Birmingham Gazette*, 11 January 1830); and the report of the St Peter's District Visiting Society for 1844 (Birmingham, 1845). Outside Birmingham, see Kathleen Heasman, *Evangelicals in Action* (1962); K. C. Pringle, *Social Work of the London Churches* (Oxford, 1937); Margaret B. Simey, *Charitable Effort in Liverpool in the Nineteenth Century* (Liverpool, 1951).

38 Tholfsen, op. cit., pp. 157–8.

39 *Aris's Birmingham Gazette*, 8 July 1844.

40 Thomas Nunns, *A Letter to the Right Hon. Lord Ashley* (Birmingham, 1842), p. 52.

41 *Pulpit Photographs*, 2nd series (Birmingham, 1872), ch. 10.

42 *Aris's Birmingham Gazette*, 13 June 1853. It was symptomatic of the change that was coming over the churches that John Sandford's Visitation Charge as Archdeacon of Coventry in 1867 was entitled *Social Reforms, or, the Habits, Dwellings, and Education of our People*.

43 On the national level, this concern led to the Report of the Select Committee of the House of Lords on Divine Worship in Populous Districts (*P.P.*, 1857–8, IX).

44 George Dawson, *Sermons on Disputed Points and Special Occasions* (1878).

45 J. C. Miller, *The Defective Ministerial Training of Our Universities* (1857).

46 For national studies on the churches in the later Victorian cities, see Owen Chadwick, *The Victorian Church* (1970), II, esp. chs 5, 7; K. S. Inglis, *Churches and the Working Classes in Victorian England* (1963); and for contemporary accounts of the Church of England the various Church Congress reports.

35 Catholic Faith of the Irish Slums
London, 1840-70

Sheridan Gilley

> But - but - but! There are the Irish courts — there are the famishing souls —
> there are your little ragged thousands! Everything in England is crying out,
> Blood! Blood! Blood! The precious Blood! . . .
> (Father Frederick Faber to Lady Georgiana Fullerton, 12 March 1852.)

The drift of Irish paupers into the slums of Victorian cities gave the Roman
Church in England an entirely new task: the care and cure of hundreds of thousands
of souls where there had been only tens before, and the consequent need for a popular
urban ministry hitherto unknown within the rural and aristocratic world of genteel
English Catholicism. As religious endeavour of this popular sort must have its place
in an urban history which would embrace the response of all kinds and conditions of
men to the new urban life, so there is good reason for the appearance in a collection
of urban essays of a study of one such religious response: the method evolved by the
Church of Rome for the salvation of the souls of its Irish poor in the slums of Victorian
London. The social historian of religious movements among the Victorian proletariat
has a vast field to cover, and among a wide range of possible topics, a number of
scholars have recently made a beginning by describing the nineteenth-century
Churches' response to the half-heathen multitudes of the Victorian urban poor.
'Poor' is of course the least precise of social terms, encompassing a great range of
occupations and degrees of affluence and insecurity. But as the Churches conceived
the notion of a 'mission to the poor', so the word may stand for the purpose of a
sketch of the Roman Church's mode of restoring its Catholic faith to the nominally
Catholic Irish poor.

For its missionary activity the Roman Church found models to follow in the
modern forms of non-Catholic association: self-help and friendly societies, public-
house clubs, and, paradoxically, temperance organizations. There were other influences acting upon it in the Romantic feudal dream of restoring an imaginary

medieval class union of rich and poor, and in the popular French and Italian forms of religious devotion so beloved by the new Ultramontanes who avowed a fiercely emotive loyalty to the Papacy, and above all, to the private person of His Holiness. The example of the Continental Catholic mission was especially potent, for it implied a higher standard of sacerdotal ministry and pastoral care for the underprivileged, a consciousness of a specifically urban ministry unknown to English Catholics hitherto, and the repudiation of the emotional dryness and class-consciousness of English Catholicism, especially as it was reflected in class segregation in the seating arrangements in the London Catholic chapels. This sense of need for new methods for the mission to the Irish was especially the achievement of Nicholas Wiseman, who in 1847 became Vicar Apostolic of the London District, and, in 1850, Cardinal Primate of a restored Catholic hierarchy, as Archbishop of Westminster. At a lower level, the movement ran an uneven course from one London church to another, but its tendency is clear: towards the limitation of class distinctions in seating in order to attract the Irish, and the introduction of Ultramontane devotions in revival services in order to reclaim them.

Though its origins are obscure, the first such experiment in mass conversion was undertaken during the first year of Wiseman's episcopate in London by Joseph Hodgson, a young English secular, who during March and April 1848 evangelized the colony of dock-labourers, 'pedlars and hucksters', and worse, of Tooley Street, Southwark, near the London Bridge railway station. Hodgson said daily Mass and preached in the evening in a room which had once been an anatomy school, and was still occasionally used for tanning. He attracted congregations of five hundred every weekday, while on Sundays, wrote an observer, 'the room is crowded to suffocation. There are not a dozen seats . . . but the poor people stand in rows packed together . . . It is literally the preaching of the gospel to the poor, almost for the first time'—in a London Catholic chapel. This was a pardonable exaggeration, proclaiming the dawn of a new era of missionary zeal, 'for it is not too much to say that few of all these crowds visit church or chapel from one year to another'.[1]

'We understand', the *Rambler* continued, 'that it is Dr. Wiseman's wish to establish many such missions, one after another, in the most destitute parts of London', adding that Wiseman himself had twice been to Tooley Street to preach, 'to the extreme joy of the listening poor'.[2] The work was obviously too great for one man unaided, and Hodgson was soon joined by an English convert, the Honourable George Spencer, who was the son, brother, and uncle of successive Earls Spencer, and who, after some years as a secular priest, had become a Passionist. Spencer and a brother Passionist—one Father Gaudentius, an Italian—employed the device of *svegliarini*—emotional preaching in the streets, Italian-style—to great effect, and gave later revivals a model to follow.[3]

There were many such in the following decade, perhaps the largest of them conducted by the priests of the Redemptorist order in the East End: grandiose affairs which began with the confirmation of five hundred children, and counted as many as ten thousand communions. One such mission to the men of dockland concluded in a chapel crowded to suffocation with a wild masculine outpouring of emotion as all 'burst forth into one long continued wail and lament' for their sins during the closing sermon.[4] In the same vein were the terrifying hell-and-horror sermons preached by the redoubtable Redemptorist Father John Furniss to Soho children.[5]

Even the Jesuits staged similar spectaculars, and Bishop Thomas Grant of Southwark paid them fulsome tribute in 1859, after a mission to the slums round his cathedral.[6] The formerly Anglican Hathaway and Christie led the cathedral clergy in *svegliarini* in English and Irish, instructed adults and children for confirmation, solemnized common-law marriages, dispensed two thousand communions, and crammed a congregation of four thousand into St George's to renew their baptismal vows with lighted candles in their hands. This was a service they performed again, in the East End in 1860, with a gathering of comparable size.[7] More dramatic still was the Passionist mission to the Surrey dockland of Rotherhithe in 1861. The overflowing crowd on the final night was harangued by Grant outside the church, where the impact of the events of the mission—Solemn Benediction and Papal Blessing and the confirmation of a hundred and sixty adults and children—was reinforced by indulgences offered for kissing a ten-foot cross on a high brick platform, with the scourges hanging from the arms, the sacred monogram nailed above the red thorn crown, and the lance and sponge affixed to the pole.[8]

This kind of service bore many of the marks of Protestant revivalism, for Evangelicals and Ultramontanes touched at a number of points, in their call of the agonized conscience to repentance in the midst of scenes of mass fervour, cathartically relieved in the ecstasy of promised forgiveness through the all-atoning Blood of the Lamb. An uncertain tradition maintains that Wiseman himself recognized and approved this emphasis upon the Atonement among the Yorkshire Methodists, whom, it was said, he declared he loved for preaching from the pulpit the sacrifice which he offered at the altar.[9] These likenesses impressed many sometime Evangelicals, who had become High Churchmen in the 1830s, and were attracted to Rome in the 1840s partly by the emotive and enthusiastic strain in Ultramontane piety, and partly by its most un-Anglican want of *disciplina arcani*, a dignified restraint in devotion and theology. This was the pattern of conversion of the Redemptorist missioner Thomas Livius, of the vacillating Richard Waldo Sibthorp, and of Frederick William Faber of the London Oratory. In his eight large theological tomes, in his many hymns—and not least in his work among the poor—Faber displayed both an Evangelical fervour and an Ultramontanism which too often found expression in Mariolatry and gross superstition. But it has not hitherto been sufficiently understood that there is a key to his eccentricity in his conviction that all religious methods were right and good which won souls lost in the spiritual destitution of the great English cities. So he was glad to confess his debt to Nonconformity, explicitly preferring 'the pattern of the Wesleyans and Whitfieldians to the calm sobriety and subdued enthusiasm of the Protestant Establishment', and thought the English poor instinctively right for honouring 'the coarse tyranny' of an unprepossessing Methodism above 'the mild, considerate and good-natured rule of Anglicans', because the one knew, and the other abhorred, 'the catholic view of the use of excitement in things spiritual'. In similar vein, he considered that 'the solemn tones of the Divine Office, sung in choir' were of infinitely less value for reclaiming the illiterate than 'the vernacular hymn set to the tune of a drinking song, or a procession with an image in petticoats', and, as a Roman Catholic, he shuddered on taking a backward glance at the refined gentility of Anglo-Catholicism. 'Instead of tutoring the people in a right religious taste, and keeping alive a healthy and wholesome tone of ecclesiastical aesthetics among the lower orders,' he argued, it was rather the Catholic missionary's duty 'to get the masses to gather, to bring them within earshot of his vulgar sermons, to excite them to a feverish sorrow for sin by any spiritual claptrap he can hit upon . . .' Any Anglican, he continued, who had to serve in 'the confessional of any one of our huge towns for a week . . . would come out of the ordeal with more apostolic vulgarity than the worst of us.' The Established Church could not exploit popular piety because it could not share it: it

> would fair educate the masses, give a tone to society, moralize multitudes, or
> veil their immoralities. It is not with sin as sin, or with souls as souls,
> that it deals; whereas this is just the work of the [Roman] Church. Get a
> man out of his sins anyhow, whether it is by making him laugh, or by
> making him cry . . . Get him out of his sins, get him under the drip of the
> Precious Blood . . .[10]

In part because of this utter indifference to the outward forms of respectability, which was of a piece with his repudiation of Anglican reserve, Faber enjoyed considerable success with the poor. So he thawed one impassive slum congregation which had heard his impassioned preaching in stony silence, by throwing himself on his knees before them, crying, 'How can I touch your hearts? I have prayed to Jesus; I have prayed to Mary; whom shall I pray to next? I will pray to *you* my dear Irish children, to have mercy on your own souls.'[11] His enthusiastic temper and its meaning for the Ultramontane revival is well summed up in his letter to his penitent the Countess of Arundel and Surrey, on the Drury Lane retreat of 1852:[12]

> The mission has begun with immense consolations. Thanks to the Precious
> Blood, many most unhappy women . . . were on their knees before the
> crucifix, sobbing and beating their breasts. You know it [the mission]
> is in the very heart of London's worst dens of iniquity. We have got about
> a hundred and fifty masses promised, and several convents are praying.
> Mind and pray hard; tell our dear Lord He must give grace now, without
> measure, without measure, without measure! No common supply will do.
> Oh if you saw that mass of poor creatures, you would yearn for their souls.
> The heavens must positively rain Precious Blood . . .

This is, of course, part of the spirit of revival, to verge upon the blasphemy of forcing grace from the Deity; but Faber cared not, if sinners were thereby saved.

But to reclaim the Irish, the Church had also to transform its churches, which combined the class exclusiveness of an Anglican proprietary chapel with the devotional ethos of a Dissenting meeting-house. There were no statues; the first in London—of Our Lady—was set up in 1844 in St Mary's, Chelsea, to be a wonder and delight to the parish poor.[13] The churches were kept locked during the day; the Rosary and scapular were curiosities; weekday evening services were virtually unknown. Benediction was meagre and rare, it was recalled of St Patrick's, Soho: 'a few dismal candles cast a dim light over a scanty congregation, on a few days, and that only in Lent.'[14] Save at the four great feasts of the Church, there were few lay communicants. Even more inhibiting was the class segregation in seating arrangements decreed by Protestant example and by a noble musical tradition. The Bavarian Embassy chapel was better known as 'the shilling opera-house'; the talents of the organist Vincent Novello had won St James's, Spanish Place, a special eminence as a place of entertainment.[15] There were close connections between the Italian opera and the Sardinian Embassy chapel, where the clergy charged the enormous sum of ten shillings a seat for the Requiem staged for the soprano Grisi, when all the performers in her company sang. Even on less extraordinary occasions the chapels were normally divided into an 'enclosure' before the altar rails—or locked pews which were let out for sixpence or a shilling; a second enclosure behind it, for servants and tradesmen; and further from the altar still, and extending to the door, the 'body' of the church, usually without seats, standing-room for the poor, who might even there be charged an entrance fee of a penny. In St Patrick's, Soho, they took communion at a second altar rail, shut off from the enclosure by a glass screen.[16] This left the galleries furnished with hard, backless benches, which, when not reserved for children, were sold at each service at a lesser rate; and a Tribune in the chancel, which had thrones for the Ambassador and clergy in the Embassy chapels and for other notabilities elsewhere, and were often accessible by private doors.[17] These arrangements mirrored the separation of masters and servants in the manor chapels of the Catholic gentry, but the projection of the impersonal class-relationships of a great city into worship could only smack of callousness.

As new churches were opened in the 1840s, there were Catholics to demand that they should be free, and to declare with a wealth of illustration that pew rents were Protestant, and yet scandalized Protestants; that they were unknown on the Continent, and in England kept the Catholic and Anglican poor from both the Catholic chapel and Anglican church. An unsegregated church, it was claimed, could rely on Celtic coppers if it only chose; and if rich and poor mingled freely together, the poor would give in a golden rain of pence. For as the outcome of immigration from Ireland, a host of new shrines would rise in the slums under an impulse which was free and popular, and truly Catholic and Roman—and medieval, but modern as well thereby.[18]

So in the revivalist atmosphere of the early 1840s, it was a matter of frequent Catholic and Protestant comment that the Irish were usually too far from the altar and pulpit to hear or see service or sermon, and their solid and passive endurance of a ceremony at once invisible, inaudible, and incomprehensible was a source of wonder to some Tractarians.[19] The first effective effort to remedy this condition came in

1849. 'What does our divine Redeemer give as the great distinguishing mark of his mission . . . ?' asked the convert John Moore Capes in a campaign against pew rents in 1849; '*pauperes evangelizantur* . . . But look around upon the churches of this city . . . no part of St. George's is open without payment at High Masses or Vespers on Sundays, and . . . those who cannot pay sixpence or a shilling are never able to attend these services'. Worse, in the pro-cathedral, St Mary, Moorfields, 'in a small space under the organ gallery which will not contain a tithe of the thousands of poor belonging to the district, these children of the church, so dear to the heart of Jesus, are compelled to *stand*, while from a pulpit at the extreme end of the building a gospel is preached, which it must be physically impossible for them to hear . . .'[20]

> Any Irish bricklayer's labourer, who would contribute as much as one or two
> guineas a year in a church where there are no fixed payments at all
> is found . . . not to give a shilling where even the slightest distinction is set
> up between the children of wealth and the children of poverty. The surest
> way to keep the Irish poor in a state of personal uncleanliness, is to pew
> them up, all huddled together close to the doors and under the galleries
> of our crowded chapels . . . We have the utmost faith in the purity and
> genuine refinement of the poor . . . If the churches were only to respect their
> own good sense and good feeling, all would be well.[21]

This confidence was not always shared. The second national Synod of the new hierarchy in 1855 wished 'that many of these methods of maintaining the church were done away with, yet experience has taught that it is as yet impossible altogether to dispense with them', a sentiment embodied in decrees regulating door money, family pew rents, and seat fees, and requiring episcopal approval to increase or abolish them.[22] This uneasy compact with Mammon may have eased the conscience of clerics like Frederick Oakeley of Islington, who judged that 'nothing less than the virtue of Saints will enable a person of refined and sensitive feelings, not habituated, as priests are, to such trials, to endure the repugnance . . . created by the proximity of our squalid poor . . .'[23] He recommended instead a church divided into free and appropriated seating by the central aisle, so that the pauper half of the congregation might be as near the altar as their wealthy neighbours, without passing on their wandering fleas. As insects can jump the width of an aisle, this probably proved impractical, and at Islington, Oakeley found a neater solution in a special 'working-man's mass'.[24]

Thus if the open Continental churches always had champions, pew rents survived to give them offence.[25] Some chapels made a judicious compromise; they charged nothing at the early services, and received their big Irish influx at ten a.m., before the quality arrived for High Mass at eleven.[26] Even a congregation as impoverished as St Anne's, Spitalfields, continued to pay door money—and even required some rented seats—which brought in forty pounds a year,[27] while in the 1850s, at Wapping, where Father William Kelly preferred house collections to an entry fee, and was careful to tax no man beyond his power to pay, there was free standing room for

400 worshippers, but a penny was demanded for a seat at the Low Mass, and two-pence at the High.[28]

But some change for the good there was, in St Mary, Moorfields,[29] St Mary, Chelsea,[30] the Bavarian Embassy chapel,[31] and, most dramatically, in St Patrick's, Soho. 'It was in the year 1847, that the revival touched St. Patrick's,' wrote its historian. There was a new devotion to the Blessed Sacrament, while 'Communions on common Sundays became as numerous as . . . on Easter Day. But it was not until 1860 that the new spirit had free play'—when a new parish priest, Thomas Barge, greatly multiplied the number of Masses and 'short popular devotions' led by a surpliced choir. There was every effort to make them 'accessible to the people at large. Accordingly, as much as possible, the Church has been made free . . .' The body of the chapel was thrown open to all comers at every service, and, the Tribune excepted, all seating became gratis on weekdays. The old divisions—Enclosure, Galleries, and Tribune—remained, and were let for a penny, threepence, and sixpence at Low and High Masses on Sundays and St Patrick's Day; but the glass screen was removed, together with the second communion rail. The change effected a 'wonderful external development' of prayer to the Virgin, while along the aisles rose a city of side-altars and statues. In 1869, the Jesuits conducted a successful mission. 'Each court and alley—each house—almost each room was visited.' Great crowds over-flowed the chapel for three weeks, night after night; there were 2,500 communicants, and '700 out of the Church', it was reported, 'had made their peace with heaven.' Barge also abolished the monastic offices inappropriate to uneducated taste and 'suited more for the Cathedral than for a poor parish church; . . . the consequence has been, that in place of a few adorers, we have had multitudes': a model parish, and despite their fleas, a model congregation.[32]

It is also possible to chronicle in some detail this process of Ultramontane uplift in the subdivision of the parish of Lincoln's Inn Fields, in which Continental, English, and Irish influences all had their place. The renewal of the Catholic religious life of the area began in 1840 with a census, undertaken by two laymen, of the children in the district not receiving a Catholic education. They joined with an Irish chaplain at the Sardinian Embassy to rent a room which served as mass-house and poor-school; and in 1842, the mission was erected into a permanent parish served by two Spanish priests, first from a former workhouse, and, in 1847, from a converted dissenting chapel.[33] Their work was supplemented in 1849 by five more small temporary day schools established in the scattered Irish courts by John Kyne, another ecclesiastic attached to the Sardinian chapel, to give an elementary religious and secular educa-tion to three hundred Irish adults and children.[34] Kyne enrolled fifty intelligent Irish artisans as his teachers, and combined this modest experiment with the idea of the court mission, which mingled preaching with simple devotions in the open air. The first such revival, pioneered by Kyne's friend Hodgson in 1848, culminated in 1849 in a series of retreats to the poor of Charles Street, Drury Lane. Many of Hodgson's hearers were new arrivals from Ireland, for whom the district provided temporary accommodation before their migration east or south; others were prostitutes, a number of whom were reclaimed and given refuge at the Hammersmith House of the Good Shepherd.[35] Services were held in a large and rickety room which collapsed under the weight of its enormous congregation; more injuries resulted from the stampede occasioned by a malicious cockney who shouted 'Fire'; Hodgson was himself near mental breakdown, though assisted by Kyne and two fellow priests from the Sardinian Chapel, both Italians, Faa di Bruno, a secular, and Dr Melia, a Pallotine. But they were all opposed by their Rector, William O'Connor, who, though Irish-born, shared the older clergy's hostility to innovation, and now fought his subordinates' attempts to make the chapel, above all else, a church for the poor.

O'Connor's character summed up the conflict between old traditions and new needs with peculiar clarity. The adventurous activities of Hodgson and Kyne smacked to him of ecclesiastical anarchy. 'I esteem missions', he told Wiseman, 'because I believe this to be the means of bringing back the poor . . . but . . . they must be conducted with utility—with propriety & *order* & it is a matter of notoriety that in this mission these three requisites are eminently wanting. My principle is obedience . . . we want *cool* & *sound* heads . . . otherwise your Lordship's whole district will be in confusion and your chapels deserted by the stranger, by the *sober* & *calm*.'[36] And, he might have added, by the wealthy; for, special musical services for non-parishioners aside, parochial pew rents alone brought in a hundred pounds a year. The chapel had two-and-a-half thousand seats, five hundred of them free: only two and a half thousand of the poor could attend the five Sunday morning Masses, while the enclosure and galleries for which fees were charged at sixpence and threepence a head were often almost empty.

Hodgson's missions so increased Mass attendance as to make these class distinctions intolerable. On 'Sunday evening last the chapel was so crammed that it was impossible to get a single person more into any part of it,' he told Wiseman. 'Hundreds listened outside & hundreds were obliged to go away . . .' At the morning service, 'Father Kyne was doomed to see the crowds of poor packed into the only space allotted to them—compelled to *fight* their way . . . to the Holy Communion.'[37] How, he asked, was he to demand money from a congregation which included so many unemployed?

Wiseman's sympathies in the controversy were all on the side of the radicals, against O'Connor. He advised the Rector:[38]

> Reserve what is simply sufficient for the better classes that come to the Chapel and throw the rest open to the poor, at the lowest rate possible: make it the Chapel of the poor. Then set to work to make the poor come and fill it, go among them, give them abundant opportunities of instruction, plenty of time for confession, early masses (especially on holidays) for communion, multiply devotions, as the Via Crucis, confraternities etc., make the Chapel a home to them . . .

This was advice which the Rector was apparently forced to follow; at the very least, he installed a goodly number of new free benches, and could claim that most were 'unappropriated' on Census Sunday.[39]

Wiseman also urged him to 'rouse the lukewarm by retreats, & awaken sinners by strong and repeated warnings at their very doors',[40] an injunction which the Cardinal obeyed himself in at least one such mission, conducted by the Italian seculars of the Sardinian chapel to the Orchard Place rookery of Calmel Buildings near Portman Square, a community which, as a source of moral pestilence, may be traced back at least to the 1790s,[41] and which in the early 1840s was paid the compliment of a harrowing denunciation by Mathew.[42] Catholic activity in the district was partly in tribute to this notoriety, and partly a response to the local Protestant ragged school. Indeed the zealous Faa di Bruno provided *The Times*[43] and other anti-Catholic papers with excellent copy by entering *vi et armis* an Evangelical class to take down the names of its Irish pupils, a visit followed by the predictable assault of an Irish mob throwing mud and manure.[44] The climax to the mission was an evening service conducted from a platform in the centre of the court by Wiseman himself. 'Every window was filled with tiers of faces', he wrote to Monsignor Talbot. There were three thousand spectators; the rooftops and parapets were crowded with men and women holding candles; the windows and walls were lit with lamps in the Italian fashion—'it had the appearance of a street Madonna festival in Rome.'[45] Wiseman's train included children rescued from the Evangelicals, now singing hymns to the Virgin; and the Cardinal exacted from the excited crowd a promise to drink in moderation and to shun the Protestant schools. Well might he rejoice in so Latin an expression of popular faith: a Roman means to a Catholic end.

His triumphant mood was infectious. It inspired a scheme to tax Irishmen all over England to build a cathedral to St Patrick on Saffron Hill, dominating St Paul's,[46] and sustained the roving missionary priests. Kyne harangued the faithful from Hatton Garden to Great Wild Street, the notorious rookery north of Lincoln's Inn, while Joseph Hodgson ranged even further afield from Lincoln's Inn to Southwark[47] and Spitalfields, which he evangelized in January 1849 from a makeshift presbytery in a coal cellar.[48] In the July of the same year, in the Strand, his anarchistic indifference to the parochial rights of the local Oratorians stirred Faber to fury and provoked an anxious letter to Newman,[49] and in 1852, in the east-central rookery of Bunhill Row, he helped found the chapel of St Joseph's.[50] A like freedom from churchly restraint marked the mission preached in 1850 to the courts of Islington by Oakeley and two young Oxford convert friends who were shortly to enter the Society of Jesus. They gathered a congregation by ringing a cowbell in the High Street, where the unorthodox publicity of their proceedings caused questions to be asked in the House of Commons.[51] Another revival was preached in Islington two years later by the re-founder and 'Apostle' of the Roman Church in Cornwall, Father William Young, who had shared Hodgson's coal-cellar lodgings in Spitalfields,[52] and in Islington said Mass and heard confessions in the courts and tenements, concluding the mission in the church after Sunday vespers with a custom unknown to Old Catholicism, a distribution of thousands of scapulars of the Passion and Our Lady of

Carmel. Such was the pitch of Marian enthusiasm thereby aroused that a statue of the Virgin hitherto placed high in the church beyond the reach of vulgar piety was now 'vested in a handsome cope of blue and silver', and mounted on a low pedestal, so that the poor might 'delight in kneeling at the feet, which they often kiss with deep devotion'.[53]

These manifestations of proletarian taste transformed the outward aspect of the city missions with cheap and gaudy church furniture—'Stations of the Cross, groups of the Holy Family, statues of the Blessed Virgin and St. Joseph, and everything else that may be a source of devotion or enjoyment to the poor'. Slum priests believed that the Irish 'who see nothing in their miserable dwellings but wretchedness and desolation, feel the greatest delight . . . in . . . all those objects of devotion which gladden the eyes and the hearts of Catholics in foreign countries . . . they, and they alone, really enjoy them . . .'[54] Thus the change in ethos made the London chapels 'mass-houses for the masses' for the first time; from a tasteful Anglican point of view these were 'thoroughly vulgar': a visual impression reinforced by 'a faint odour of stale incense, probably mingled with gas; and . . . the not so agreeable after-smell of unwashed humanity.'[55]

From the early 1840s, this quest for the dramatic and colourful in the indulgenced devotions of the Counter Reformation also found expression for the first time in England in the formation of Confraternities, Sodalities, and Guilds. The first such lay brotherhood in London was the work of the assistant priest of the Virginia Street parish, Father John Moore, who in 1842 established an association combining pious innovation with social utility, a 'Guild of Our Lady and St Joseph', which for a shilling a month gave its members free medical attention and burial, and brought them together for special masses and non-liturgical prayer. This wholesome discipline assisted the coal-whipper dock-labourers of the East End to escape the bondage of their public-house employers, under an Act of Parliament passed in 1843 to give them a trade union organization and a special public employment office under government control. Moore's Guild also collected the pence of the five to six thousand Wapping Catholics for the chapel building fund, and paraded through dockland singing litanies, the women 'in green dresses, with sashes, and white leghorn bonnets; the males in green cloaks, trimmed with fur, white collars'—and mortar boards.[56] The Guild was established in other parishes, which found this pseudo-medievalism irresistible,[57] though elsewhere Continental institutes served as a model: in Poplar, the Arch Confraternity of the Immaculate Heart of Mary with a hundred members derived its forms in 1843 from the celebrated lay society in Paris,[58] and Deptford followed suit in 1846 with a Confraternity of the Scapular.[59] Though the Guilds were to fail as benefit societies, they survived through many reorganizations as devotional associations, and by 1860 their popularity had carried all before them as a sacerdotal means of reclaiming the poor.

Thus in the cathedral of St George's, Southwark, in the 1850s there were societies for devotion to the Blessed Sacrament, to the Sacred Heart of Jesus, the Passion of Our Lord, the Rosary, and the Immaculate Heart of Mary for the Conversion of

Sinners, while the Holy Guild of St George and the Blessed Virgin prayed for the dead. 'A great number of the poor Irish', it was noted, 'belong to these confraternities, which are found to be most effectual means of preserving their faith.'[60] In some parishes, the confraternities controlled every aspect of parochial life. They raised money for new churches, compiled the population censuses which helped the priesthood collect the pauper's pence,[61] taught in evening and Sunday schools, and reinforced in rather mechanical fashion the post-Tridentine Catholic obligation of weekly mass attendance and annual communion and confession. In the parish of St John's, Islington, where the really ragged poor were enrolled in guilds, the more respectable in confraternities, Oakeley reflected with satisfaction on the control which these associations gave him over 'forty boys and young men attached to the church . . . completely under our eye, and, as I may say, under our thumb.'[62] And so it was an axiom with the parish priest of St Patrick's, Soho, that 'The State of a Congregation may be Measured by the State of its Confraternities', and members were assured that the 'road to heaven will lie open before them. Let them live up to their rules, God will do the rest;' or, more positively still, that *an individual regular to the rules of a Confraternity can scarcely be lost.*'[63]

The confraternities had an equally significant social role, for ecclesiastics were suspicious of the Celtic gregariousness manifest in a wide range of Irish organizations *extra ecclesia*, and offering a purely secular salvation.[64] Such were the first Hibernian Societies, in the late 1830s;[65] the embryo waterside trade unions and Repeal movement of the early 1840s;[66] the Provident Societies of the 1850s;[67] and the Brotherhood of St Patrick, which was in ill-odour in the Church for its Fenian sympathies in the early 1860s.[68] Perhaps most important, because they served as the basis for other forms of association, were the Irish clubs which met in public-houses for mere conviviality, and which sometimes figure among the parochial penny-collecting agencies.[69] Indeed, clerics were well accustomed to taking collections in pubs,[70] and showed considerable imagination in putting secular associations to good religious use, and in diverting the violent vigour of Irish community life to orthodox ends. This skill was apparent in the Catholic Young Men's Societies of the early fifties,[71] and in certain crises in the Church at large, as in the slum branches of the Peter's Pence associations of 1860, which arose to pay for the Papal army assembled to defend the Temporal Power,[72] and less directly, in the band of Irish vigilantes 'ever ready for a fray, especially in so good a cause',[73] who guarded St George's, Southwark, during the Papal Aggression, and who, disciplined and drilled at a mere twelve hours' notice, marched forth, three hundred strong, from three East End parishes, in white sashes cut out from seventy yards of ribbon, to marshal the crowds around Wiseman's grave at Kensal Green.[74]

Confraternities were unstable institutions none the less, dissolving and then in a fresh burst of zeal, reforming in a new devotional mode under a new devotional name.[75] These vicissitudes of parochial organization are well illustrated by the chequered progress of the London Catholic Temperance Associations, which were sometimes coterminous with the confraternities,[76] and which appear in the late 1830s[77] under the impulse from Ireland of Father Theobald Mathew's first temperance campaigns. In January 1840, they united in a 'Metropolitan Roman Catholic Total Abstinence Society'[78] which could boast ten branches when it welcomed Mathew to London in 1843.[79] He gathered most of his sixty to seventy thousand pledges at open air meetings in slum areas: Hackney, the Barbican, Bermondsey, Deptford, and the Commercial Road,[80] where he was received by the coal-whippers' trade union, for at least three years the object of Catholic teetotal enterprise,[81] accompanied by Moore's Holy Guild in their eccentric uniform. It was 'the only religious meeting I ever saw in Cockneyland which had not plenty of scoffers hanging on its outskirts', wrote Mrs Jane Carlyle.[82] At similar gatherings elsewhere, Catholic aristocrats—the convert Marchioness of Wellesley, Mrs Edward Petre, Lady Bedingfeld, the Honourable Stafford Jerningham, and the Earl of Arundel and Surrey, took the pledge and received Mathew's medal in noble example to the Irish faithful, who were also edified by the conversion of one Jeremiah John Kelly, 'formerly a publican and coal-merchant in Shadwell', and among the coal-whippers 'a very unpopular character. . .'[83]

This fervour was not always lasting: many Irish labourers worked in trades controlled by publican-employers who forced them to drink or starve.[84] But though the London temperance associations perished with many other such voluntary organizations in the economic distress of the mid-1840s,[85] Mathew's campaign made a permanent impression upon some London parishes, leaving in its wake a large body of convinced teetotallers,[86] and becoming an accepted part of missionary activity, especially in the East End.[87] Thus some form of temperance pledge was administered to candidates for confirmation, to prospective members of devotional societies, even in the open-air revivals,[88] while clerical concern with popular insobriety on the greatest of Hibernian festivals gave rise to the Truce of God, a promise of total abstinence on St Patrick's Day, and during the two days following: a custom which was not, as has been claimed, established by Manning as Archbishop of Westminster,[89] but was in force as early as 1860.[90] Again in 1860, the Metropolitan Catholic Total Abstinence Society was refounded by the French Marists, who united five temperance fraternities, each with its own uniform, brass or drum and fife band:[91] a model which in the early sixties might be found in at least eleven parishes.[92] In some, sacramental theology and social utility reinforced each other, and in the pro-cathedral of St Mary, Moorfields, the annual renewal of a pledge of total abstinence for a year was reinforced by an oath to receive communion monthly, thereby bringing 'large numbers to their religious duties, who before seldom visited a church'.[93]

Such local fervour was sustained by Father Richard Richardson's 'Catholic Association for the Suppression of Drunkenness',[94] which had Manning's blessing for an advanced auxiliary programme of government-approved penny savings-banks and sick and burial clubs for Irishmen sufficiently sober and frugal to profit by them. Members had to renew an annual pledge of total or partial abstinence from drink before the priest-president of the local branch, and to receive communion on the feasts of the Assumption, Whitsun, the Immaculate Conception, and St Patrick's

Day. Each member had his place in an elaborate hierarchy of officers and stewards distinguished by cards and medals according to seniority of membership; could draw spiritual profit from a rich treasury of indulgences, also available to wealthy lay associates; and enjoyed the special protection of Mary Immaculate, who appeared on the medals, and was to be invoked in the hour of temptation. Richardson was fertile in schemes for Marian societies with a social end,[95] and in 1877 preached a 'Holy War against Drunkenness' all over London.[96] But in 1872 Manning had founded the League of the Cross, which he directed with a sureness of aim that earlier Catholic effort lacked, though it had created a tradition on which to build.[97]

The long-term effect of this religious adventuring is not to be weighed up here. It is now fashionable to decry the importance of missionary activity for maintaining religious practice, as if men were religious by social habit, regardless of the Church's anxiety to keep them. But it may still be asked how much the Roman Church in modern England owes to its Victorian pioneers. Nineteenth-century religious zeal does not guarantee twentieth-century religious prosperity: that notion is disproved by the decay of other denominations, once equally zealous. But if religious endeavour is not a sufficient condition for the survival of a religion, it may in testing circumstances be a necessary one. And as the Irish did not fall away from a Church which made no effort to reclaim them, so the labour of the priests of the Victorian slums perhaps explains something of the hold on the Anglo-Hibernian working class which the Church of Rome in England still retains.

Notes

Abbreviations

A.P.A.	Archivae Provinciae Angliae of the Society of Jesus, Farm Street, Mayfair
M.A.	Archives, St Mary, Moorfields
S.A.	Parish papers, Spitalfields
S.P.	St Patrick's, Soho
W.P., A.A.W.	Wiseman Papers, Archdiocesan Archives of Westminster

1 Cited H. J. Coleridge, S.J.: *Life of Lady Georgiana Fullerton* [from the French of Mrs Augustus Craven] (1888), p. 273.

2 *Rambler*, i (1848), 195–6.

3 On the early Passionist missions in London, see Conrad Charles, 'The Origins of the Parish Mission in England and the Early Passionist Apostolate', *Journal of Ecclesiastical History*, xv (1964), 72–4.

4 *Tablet*, 3 February 1855; 11 April 1857.

5 L. G. Vere, *Random Recollections of Old Soho* (1908), p. 94, S.P. Fr John Furniss, *The Sight of Hell*, Book X in *Books for Children* (Dublin, 1858); on his work elsewhere in England and in London, see Rev. Thomas Livius, C.S.S.R., *Father Furniss and his Work for Children* (1896), pp. 20, 42–5.

6 Grant to Cardinal Prefect (Barnabo) of Propaganda 5 April 1859; sent by the Cardinal to the Society: *College of St Ignatius* A.P.A.; cf. the Jesuit mission to Islington, *Tablet*, 11 March 1865.

7 *Tablet*, 30 June 1860.

8 *Universe*, 2 November 1861; on a similar Passionist mission to Baldwin's Gardens, *Universe*, 23 May 1863.

9 Cited, without reference, in J. K. Mozley, *Doctrine of the Atonement* (1915) p. 203.

10 *An Essay on Catholic Home Missions* (1855), pp. 7, 31, 64, 68–9, 41.

11 J. E. Bowden, *The Life and Letters of Frederick William Faber* (1869), p. 391.

12 Faber to Lady Arundel, 29 November 1852; ibid., pp. 392–3.

13 A. M. Clarke, *Life of the Hon. Mrs. Edward Petre* (1899), p. 101.

14 *Parish Report 1870*, p. 9. S.P.

15 B. Ward, *Catholic London a Century Ago* (1905), pp. 129–30.

16 Vere, op. cit., p. 83. S.P.

17 Ward, op. cit., pp. 45–6.

18 'John' in the *London and Dublin Orthodox Journal*, xi (28 November 1840), 344–7. See also 'Vesper', xi (19 December 1840), 391–3; 'Philalethes', xi (26 December 1840), 406–7; 'John', xii (12 January 1841), 5–8; 'Vesper', xii (9 January 1841) 25–7; 'John', xii (16 January 1841), 35–8.

19 See E. F. S. Harris, *From Oxford to Rome, and how it fared with some who lately made the Journey* (1847), p. 204. R. W. Vanderkiste, *Notes and Narratives: Six years' mission, principally among the slums of London* (1852), p. 112.

20 *Rambler*, iv (1849), 467–8.

21 Ibid., iv (1849), 84; 86–7.

22 Decree viii, *Second Synod of Westminster* (1855).

23 *Rambler*, iv (1849), 209.

24 *Tablet*, 18 May 1850.

25 B. Bogan, *The Great Link* (1948), pp. 292–4.

26 *Religious Census Returns*, H.O. 129, 4–6.

27 *Copie d'un Rapport addressé au R.P. Provincial sur la mission de St. Anne Londres août 1877*. S.A.

28 Kelly to Wiseman, 5 April 1856, A.A.W.

29 Rev. Canon W. Fleming, 'The History of St Mary Moorfields' [typescript], p. 48; cf. *Tablet*, 5 September 1857.

30 W. J. Anderson, *A History of the Catholic Parish of St Mary's Chelsea* (1938), pp. 61–2.

31 *Religious Census Returns*.

32 *Parish Report, 1870*, pp. 9–10; *1862*, p. 17; *1869*, pp. 4–5; *1870*, p. 5. S.P.

33 *Catholic Standard*, 23 March 1850.

34 *Tablet*, 5 June 1847.

35 *Rambler*, i (1848), 242–3, 268.

36 O'Connor to Wiseman, 4 September 1849, W.P., A.A.W.

37 Hodgson to Wiseman, September 1849, W.P., A.A.W.

38 Wiseman to O'Connor, 26 August 1849, W.P., A.A.W.

39 *Religious Census Returns*.

40 Wiseman to O'Connor.

41 M. Dorothy George, *London Life in the Eighteenth Century* (1966 edn), pp. 122–3; Bogan, op. cit., p. 54.

42 *Parliamentary Papers*, 1847, VI, Select Committee (House of Lords) on Colonization from Ireland: Report (737), p. 1.

43 *The Times*, 26 July 1851.

44 The Catholic version of the incident is in the *Tablet*, 2 August 1851; the Protestant in the *London City Mission Magazine*, xvi (1851), 252.

45 Wiseman to Talbot, 3 August 1851, *Dublin Review*, clxiv (1919), 23.

46 *Tablet*, 1 June 1850.

47 *Catholic Standard*, 26 January 1850.

48 Rev. W. Salmon, S.M., *A Short History of the Parish of St Anne's Spitalfields* (1950), p. 4.

49 B. Dalgairns to Newman, 9 July 1849, July–August Oratory Letters, Birmingham Oratory.

50 *Tablet*, 31 January 1852.

51 W. Ward, *The Life and Times of Cardinal Wiseman* (1913), II, p. 157.

52 Salmon, op. cit.

53 *Tablet*, 17 January 1852.

54 John Kyne, Appeal for the Saffron Hill Mission, *Tablet*, 10 June 1854.

55 Peter Anson, *Fashions in Church Furnishing 1840–1940* (1965), p. 195.

56 From a description of the ceremony in which O'Connell was invested as a member of the order. See *Tablet*, 23 March 1844.

57 On the Kensington and Richmond Holy Guilds, *Tablet*, 18 March 1843; Chelsea, *Tablet*, 23 March 1846; the Warwick Street Guild of the Holy Family, *Catholic Standard and Weekly Register*, 17 November 1849; Islington, *Tablet*, 1 June 1850; and on Somers Town, *Tablet*, 17 January 1852. *Third General Meeting of the Society of St Vincent de Paul 1846*, p. 14, Archives of the Society of St Vincent de Paul.

58 *Tablet*, 26 August 1843, 11 November 1843.

59 Ibid., 27 June 1846.

60 Ibid., 1 August 1857; cf. *Catholic Directory 1862*, pp. 158–9.

61 See account of Poplar census in *Tablet*, 4 October 1856.

62 *Tablet*, 16 December 1854.

63 *Parish Report, 1862* p. 4; *1864*, pp. 4–5; *1869*, p. 5. S.P.

64 Cf. Manning's letter to Fr Chaurain of Spitalfields, 11 January 1884, S.A. on a Hibernian Club which met in a tavern for social amusement.

65 See Lynn Lees, 'Social Change and Social Stability among the London Irish', (unpublished Ph.D. thesis, Harvard University, 1969), p. 328.

66 There were at least a dozen Repeal wards in Irish districts in London in 1843; cf. *Tablet*, 1 July 1843.

67 Cf. *Tablet*, 19 January 1856, on the Irish Provident Society of London, founded November 1854; also the society for South London, *Tablet*, 13 January 1855, and the parochial benefit society of Bunhill Row, *Tablet*, 15 May 1858.

68 At least fifteen metropolitan branches of the Brotherhood were enumerated in the *Irish Liberator*; 14 November–5 December 1863.

69 Cf. Fr W. Marshall on Deptford poor schools, *Tablet*, 4 March 1843. Also the *Minutes of Proceedings relating to certain repairs at the chapel of St Mary Moorfields October 1839–September 1840*, M.A.

70 Cf. Kelly in *Tablet*, 24 April 1858.

71 Founded with Wiseman's encouragement by Dr William O'Brien, of the Irish All Hallows Missionary College, in 1848; their growth was mainly in the North, but there was at least one branch in London, at Saffron Hill, under Kyne: *Tablet*, 5 April 1856. On the need for further such associations in London, see *Universe*, 6 April 1861.

72 *Tablet*, 9 June 1860; 25 August 1860; 15 September 1860.

73 E. S. Purcell, *Life of Cardinal Manning, Archbishop of Westminster* (1895), I, p. 671.

74 Kelly in *Tablet*, 11 March 1865.

75 So Moore refounded his Holy Guild in 1847 as the 'Society of the Divine Infant Saviour and his Virgin Mother', *Tablet*, 25 December 1847.

76 Cf. William Kelly's Temperance Society and Holy Guild in Hammersmith. *London and Dublin Orthodox Journal*, 4 February 1843, on the meeting of an East End Total Abstinence Association, which was apparently identical with the local 'Guild of St Joseph and Our Blessed Lady'.

77 The first reference to Catholic temperance activity encountered by Dr Brian Harrison of Corpus Christi College, Oxford (to whom I am grateful for this and other information), is to Fr Sisk of Chelsea, in the *New British and Foreign Temperance Intelligence*, 10 November 1839.

78 See *Tablet*, 12 August 1843, for the Society's history.

79 In the parishes of Moorfields; Southwark; Chelsea; Deptford; Lincoln's Inn; Somers Town; Vauxhall; Farringdon; Warwick Street; Virginia Street, and Saffron Hill: *Tablet*, 1 August 1840; 5 August 1843; 12 August 1843; 19 August 1843.

80 See Fr Augustine, O.F.M. Cap., *Footprints of Father Mathew* (Dublin, 1947), pp. 290–302.

81 See the work of Thomas Doyle and the Moorfields clergy, *Tablet*, 1 August 1840.

82 Cited Augustine, op. cit., p. 293.

83 *Tablet*, 5 August 1843.

84 Cf. Mayhew's account of the Irish dock-labouring ballast-men in *Life and Labour of the London Poor* (1861), III, pp. 278–81.

85 See the 'Catholic Teetotal Abstinence Association' meeting announced in *Tablet*, 17 July 1847, 'to revive the Temperance Societies, which have lately in a great measure fallen away . . .'

86 Mayhew, op. cit., I, p. 114. See also *Universe*, 16 February 1861.

87 See the German total abstainer, and Whitechapel priest, James Jauch, to Wiseman, 29 September 1847, W.P., A.A.W. So, too, the Marists began work in Spitalfields soon after their arrival in 1850. See also *Lamp*, 2 October 1852.

88 Cf. *Biography of Father Lockhart* (1893), pp. 78–9.

89 By V. A. McClelland, *Cardinal Manning, his Public Life and Influence 1865–92* (1962), p. 202.

90 *Tablet*, 10 March 1860.

91 See *Lamp*, 9 February, 6 April 1861.

92 Thus in the *Universe* there are references to temperance societies in the parishes of Spanish Place, 23 February 1861, 4 January 1862; Soho, 12 January 1861, 26 January 1861, 18 May 1861, 4 January 1862; Baldwin's Gardens, 2 March 1861, 4 January 1862, 21 February 1863; Islington, 23 February 1861; Hatton Garden, 1 August 1863; Bermondsey, 29 August 1863; Somers Town, 9 March 1861; Spitalfields,

23 February 1861; St George's, Southwark, 13 April 1861; Lincoln's Inn, 3 January 1863; and Bunhill Road, 4 January 1862.

93 *Tablet*, 30 January 1864.

94 Fr Richard Richardson, *Catholic Association for Suppression of Drunkenness, under the Protection of Our Lady of the Immaculate Conception* (1867), pp. 1, 32, 23–4, 13–16, 26.

95 Cf. his 'Guild of Our Lady, For Mutual Assistance in Time of Sickness, Old Age and Death', *The Rainy Day* (1868); and its expansion as the *Catholic Sick and Benefit Club: or, The Guild of Our Lady* (1875).

96 *Parish Report, 1877*, p. 7. S.P.

97 A tradition which Manning at least acknowledged of Spitalfields and St Peter's, Hatton Garden: see *The Temperance Speeches of Cardinal Manning* (1894), pp. 17–18, as cited Augustine, op. cit., pp. 301–2. In the tradition of the parish of Camberwell, founded by a French secular, Charles Burke, *History of the Camberwell Catholic Mission 1860–1910* (1910), pp. 25–6. For the development of Catholic temperance activity under Manning, see A. E. Dingle and B. H. Harrison, 'Cardinal Manning as Temperance Reformer', *Historical Journal*, xii (1969), 485–510.

36 Feelings and Festivals
An interpretation of some working-class religious attitudes

John Kent

Many Victorian observers agreed that the urban working class was indifferent to religious institutions and did not in general attend places of worship. Friedrich Engels, for example, said that working man 'does not understand religious questions, does not trouble himself about them ... All the writers of the bourgeoisie are unanimous on this point, that the workers are not religious, and do not attend church.'[1] It is interesting to note the similarity of expression between Engels who said (in 1845) that the typical worker 'lives for this world and strives to make himself at home in it',[2] and that of another well-informed observer, Horace Mann, who wrote (in 1853), in his study of the results of the Religious Census of 1851, that the workers 'are unconscious secularists—engrossed by the demands, the trials, or the pleasures of the passing hour'.[3] 'In cities and large towns', Mann said, 'it is observable how absolutely insignificant a portion of the congregation is composed of artisans.'[4] The census revealed a clear difference between the habits of town and country. Professor Inglis has estimated that if one adds all attendances on the chosen Sunday (30 March 1851) together and expresses them as a percentage index of the total population, just under 50 percent attended services in towns of more than 10,000 people, but that about 71 percent did so in the smaller towns and rural areas.[5] In the large manufacturing districts and in parts of London this figure dropped below 40 percent: examples are Sheffield 32 percent, Oldham 33 percent, Manchester 34 percent, Birmingham 36 percent, Bolton 36 percent, Newcastle 39 percent, Halifax 41 percent, Stockport 42 percent, Liverpool 45 percent, and Leeds 47 percent.

Finally, Charles Booth, the sociologist, describing London at the end of Queen

Victoria's reign, said that the religious institutions of the capital left the great mass of the working people untouched. He thought that ardent secularism might have declined among them since the 1880s, but that neither the classical orthodoxy of Protestantism nor revisionist attempts to make Christianity more acceptable to the lower classes had succeeded: the humanitarianism of the clergy was welcomed but their doctrinal teaching did not appeal any the more to the working class. Booth's evidence suggested to him one important change since the 1840s: that articulate urban workers had lost whatever confidence they had previously had in the churches as a means of social improvement; they were committed instead to trade unionism and political action.[6]

Not all modern historians would agree that nineteenth-century religion had so little effect. Mr E. P. Thompson, for example, ignores the opinions which Engels accepted and assumes that in the first half of the century, at any rate, the working class was sometimes deeply affected by religious forces hostile to social change. This was the allegedly counter-revolutionary role of the Methodist societies in the industrial areas, a role used by Mr Thompson to explain why no proletarian revolution took place in this period.[7] It is true, of course, that the early working class had to be disciplined before it would accept long hours of work under factory conditions with very brief weekend rests and little in the way of annual holiday; but one does not need to invoke Methodism to explain how this was done; Methodism played only a minor part in the process. The employers used beatings (especially of children in the textile mills), dismissal or threats of dismissal, blacklisting of awkward men in a whole area, heavy fines for absenteeism, the break-up of unions, and even the building of factory villages, as methods of negative discipline. Incentive payments were the chief positive approach; drinking and swearing were tackled through fines. These pressures affected the whole labour force; religion—Methodist or otherwise—only a minority.[8]

In this same period, between 1800 and 1850, the Church of England had made an immense effort to reform itself in the growing urban areas by the provision of more churches and schools: 2,029 new churches were built between 1831 and 1851, 849 of which were situated in Cheshire, Lancashire, Middlesex, Surrey, and the West Riding of Yorkshire, areas where the population was rapidly increasing.[9] In a recent study, however, Richard Soloway has concluded that this Anglican reform movement failed to bring the Church of England closer to the urban working-class population. He regards as the overall explanation the degree to which the clergy were unable to separate themselves from upper-class society whose attitudes and anxieties they closely mirrored. When the bishops, for example, analysed the religious situation 'they often drew critical and perceptive conclusions about the relationship of social and economic problems to the effectiveness of their Church. There they stopped, however, unwilling or unable to take the next logical step: the proposal of a solution or policy that might have made them appear genuinely interested in the total welfare of the labouring masses they endeavoured to reach.'[10] To provide more buildings, more priests, and more layworkers did not answer. Both Léon Faucher and his translator agreed about what happened in the largest towns of the industrial north on a Sunday:[11]

> Place yourself in Briggate, at Leeds; Mosley Street at Manchester; Lord Street or Dale Street at Liverpool; of what description are the families you see, walking along in silence, and with a reserved and formal attitude, towards the churches and chapels? You cannot be deceived, they belong almost exclusively to the middle class. The operatives loiter on the threshold of their cottages, or lounge in groups at the corners of streets until the hour of service is terminated, and the public houses are opened. Religion is presented to them in such a sombre and gloomy aspect; it succeeds so well in addressing neither the senses, the imagination nor the heart, that it remains the exclusive patrimony of the rich.

In the first half of the nineteenth century, then, it became possible that the transmission of church-going as the normal form of religious expression might break down altogether as far as the working class was concerned. The possibility was latent in the statements of observers like Engels, Faucher, and Mann; it was also clear in the fact that in a town like Sheffield, which had a population of 135,310 in 1851, the real number of men, women, and Sunday School scholars who went to church or chapel or meeting-room on Census Sunday was as low as 29,000, the vast majority of them not working-class. Contemporary explanations varied. Faucher thought Protestantism, with its emphasis on the Bible and its dearth of festivals, unsuited to the workers in general.[12] Engels thought that faulty education saved them from religious prepossessions.[13] Widest of the mark was C. J. Blomfield, who insisted, as Bishop of London from 1828 to 1856, that more buildings and more free sittings would solve the problem. At a more general level, Richard Soloway has recently suggested[14] that

> the laxity of 18th century parochial religion had permitted generations of English labourers to grow up with only the most superficial association with the national Church . . . When thousands upon thousands of labourers migrated to the growing manufacturing towns they easily shook off what remnants of the Anglican faith might still have remained . . . In many parts of industrial England, and in some rural areas as well, generations grew up in an environment virtually cut off from any meaningful association with a religious body . . . they grew to maturity in a non-church going culture.

Something more drastic than eighteenth-century parochial laxity was involved, as far as the bigger cities were concerned. Primitive Methodism, for example, which is usually accepted as a working-class religious movement, certainly began as a rural revolt against the inadequacies of the Anglican parish system in Devon and Cornwall, some parts of the Midlands, and Yorkshire. In the 1851 census the denomination returned a total attendance figure of 268,555, a figure which implies a community of about 180,000 people if one makes the one-third deduction suggested above. But if one then looks at the eight largest towns of the period, Birmingham, Bradford, Bristol, Leeds, Liverpool, Manchester, Sheffield, and Wolverhampton (all of which had more than 100,000 inhabitants and which together contained one and a half million people), one finds a total Primitive Methodist attendance of only 19,986 (the corrected figure would be a little over 13,000). This means that in 1851 only 7·4 percent of Primitive Methodist attendances were to be found in the major cities.[15] In other words, even where a non-Anglican form of religious activity had apparently overcome the consequences of the weaknesses of the eighteenth-century Establishment, it still proved difficult to transfer this solution to an urban situation. In his discussion of the census returns Horace Mann showed himself impressed by the progress of the Latter Day Saints (or Mormons) who reported 222 places of worship and about 35,626 total attendances.[16] For the moment the Mormons were a name to conjure with, and one finds Mayhew, for instance, saying that 'neither the Latter Day Saints, nor any similar sect, have made converts among the coster-mongers'.[17] Mann thought that exciting adventist preaching and a claim to infallibility had given the Mormons significant importance among the working classes: time did not confirm, however, that Mormonism had a special advantage in the towns.

There is some evidence, therefore, that in the first half of the nineteenth century the churches were failing to form the habit of church-attendance in the majority of the urban working class, and that new sects which grew out of the religious tradition, such as the Mormons and the Primitive Methodists, showed no unusual ability to cope. Indeed, the formation of religious sects can hardly be described as more than a peripheral answer to the religious problems of the nineteenth-century city. In some working-class autobiographies, like that of Joseph Gutteridge, one finds an interest in Spiritualism: this Coventry ribbon-weaver had been interested in the cult from 1851, but became more interested after his wife's death in 1855: he said that survival after death, which the churches had tried to prove from their so-called sacred writings, the Spiritualists had proved by scientific demonstration.[18] Here again the potential for growth was slight: when Mudie-Smith compiled his survey of the religious life of London in 1904 he listed only about twenty small Spiritualist churches in the whole capital, and some of these were certainly not working-class in their composition.[19]

At the same time it is important to recognize that in this treatment of the problem of Victorian popular religion we are, for the moment, accepting the common Victorian middle-class opinion that if the urban working class in general did not attend church services or belong to some Christian denomination then it was not 'religious'. Some Victorian writers took this non-religiousness for granted and offered explanations for it. In the *Diocesan Report on the Condition of the Bristol Poor* (1885), for example, it was stated that one reason why religious institutions had so little effect on the poor was the lack of privacy in which the poor lived: 'Individuals among them are rarely alone, except in the streets. Perhaps some religious influences may touch their hearts, but they are soon crowded out by the continual contact with others, by the ceaseless worry of their daily cares, by the dreary round of their daily struggles, under the stupefying strain of which their sense of their own personality, let alone the touch of religious influences, becomes obliterated . . . The indifference of the poor is not to religion only, but often to all except those interests that affect their daily life, its needs and toils.'[20] To be religious, in the sense that the writers of this not insensitive Report used the term, meant both denominational allegiance and church-attendance; they believed that the pressures of neighbourhood and economic anxiety stifled a working-class desire, however slightly felt, to belong to religious associations. The growth of cities had itself made the situation worse, ecclesiastical observers believed: thus W. D. Maclagan wrote, in 1870:[21]

> When times of commercial prosperity and the development of trade and of locomotion had drawn the people more and more to the great centres of commerce and manufacture, and the population gathering and increasing had far outgrown the provision of their spiritual need, it is easy to see how the artisan and the labourer fresh from the country village where at least they might find room and often sought it in the House of God, should gradually lose the habit of worship and devotion where there was neither place for them to worship nor pastor to lead them in the ways of God. It is in a great degree to this one cause that we owe the present habits of the poorer class in our large cities as regards the services of the Church. It has become the custom not only of the individual but of the class to which he belongs to neglect habitually the public worship of God.

The drift of these arguments seems convincing as long as one accepts their terms: in the first place, the exclusion of any political element, and then the assumption that religious behaviour inevitably entails denominational loyalty and church-attendance. (Maclagan was explicit about this, saying that 'whatever one may believe as to the existence here and there of men, or more rarely of women, who while they forsake the assembling of themselves together are yet diligent in private devotion and in the study of God's word, there is no one who seriously believes this to be the case with the mass of persons of whom we are now speaking'.[22]) One has also to remember, however, the significance of these arguments for those who employed them. If, as was constantly argued, working-class indifference to organized religion had largely been caused by the chaotic expansion of nineteenth-century cities and by the slowness with which the churches had adapted structurally to the changing situation, then it should not prove impossible to transform the position by making the churches more efficient. A modern church historian, Professor Owen Chadwick, is in line with this Victorian conclusion when he asserts that, although the attack of working-class progagandists upon Christianity was in a sense more powerful in 1890 than it had been in 1840—because it had better weapons and could reach every village in the country—yet the working man was not deeply moved by these activities: 'he was indifferent and not hostile'.[23] Analyses which emphasized the social causes of religious indifference had the advantage, from the clerical point of view, of suggesting that there was no 'religious crisis' as such among the poor.

Not all the evidence pointed to the same conclusion, however. Thomas Wright, for example, who published *Habits and Customs of the Working Classes* in 1867, *The Great Unwashed* in 1868, and *Our New Masters* in 1873, was not especially concerned with religion.[24] In *Our New Masters*, however, he deliberately replied to the ecclesiastical interpretation of working-class absence from public religious services. He quoted the Archbishop of York (the Evangelical William Thomson), who had told a meeting of the Scripture Readers' Union at York that in one district, out of two thousand families, 914, or nearly a half, had declared when questioned that they did not go to church at all. So that, York continued, 'One half of them had been accustomed to live, and had settled down to live, in a state which professed no hope hereafter, and confessed no God here.'[25] Wright commented that this attitude to church attendance was preached to the working classes by most Scripture Readers and did much to keep the poor out of the churches. 'Their common sense still tells them that to make church-going the be-all and end-all, as a test of religion, is to confound religion with one of its most mechanical sides.' They 'do not regard public worship as an essential of religion, but only as an optional accessory.'[26] Nor was this reaction to be summed up entirely in a dislike of the clergy, always the favourite targets of the anti-religious writers. The poor, Wright said, were willing enough[27]

> to believe in the good intentions of the individual parsons, scripture readers, district visitors, and self-commissioned amateurs of philanthropy who aim at the spiritual and moral elevation or regeneration of the masses, and so largely be-visit, be-lecture, be-tract, and be-question the members of the masses . . . What makes them cold or resentful to their reproaches is the belief that they never 'tackle' rich sinners . . . and take liberties with the poor man that they themselves would see as liberties, did they think of applying them to the rich.

Wright thought that this working-class sense of a divided society was fundamental to the religious, as to most other, issues. Towards the end of *Our New Masters* he gave another example of what he meant. At the time of the Prince of Wales's illness in 1871 the Archbishop of Canterbury caused prayers to be said for his recovery. The working class tended to judge such an official action in terms of what was likely to happen when there had been, for instance, a mining disaster.[28]

> The thing has been known throughout the land; and it has been known too that the exploring workmen would be engaged in their labours of mercy throughout the Sabbath; but the Primate who commanded the special prayers of the Church for the recovery of the Prince never called for public prayer that the entombed miners might be saved alive to their families. It may be that the Primate and the Church hold that the life of a prince is of more value, is more worthy to be prayed for, than the lives of any number of miners. So do not the working-classes, however. They mark things as these and inwardly digest them, and the result is that they are surprised that clergymen should be astonished that they do not attend

church; that they have but scant respect for any formalised religion—but scant belief in the professions of those practising, or even really believing, what they preach.

Here Wright was talking about a working-class feeling of social and political separateness which could amount to the hostility (in the case of religion) which Professor Chadwick is perhaps too quick to discount: the working man who, in Wright's phrase, thought of himself as 'the Ishmael of modern society',[29] was bound to see organized religion in such social and political terms.

In such a discussion, however, one is using church attendance and denominational affiliation as measure of Victorian religion; one is applying, that is, middle-class, clerical standards to working-class religious practice. In the towns, at any rate, in the first half of the century, when the pattern was set, the social unity which such an approach implies did not exist. In 1842, for example, Samuel Wilberforce, then the Archdeacon of Surrey, said that 'the tendency of all things round us is to break our people into separate and unsympathising classes, and thus to sow amongst us broadcast the deadly seeds of intestine discord. The unity of the Church's worship, in which rich and poor might mix together freely, would be a blessed safeguard from this danger.'[30] Writing a generation later Thomas Wright agreed that Christianity was desirable as a social cement, in order to soften the bitterness of the social struggle, but the gap between the two men and the two worlds which they represented was shown by Wright's definition of Christianity, which Wilberforce would never have accepted as adequate. Wright said that Christianity should not be thought of as a religion of 'mere creeds, rites and church-going',[31] but as the religion of Christ, the Christianity of the Sermon on the Mount, an exhortation concerned, as far as he understood it, with conduct, not dogma.

This anti-dogmatic emphasis was characteristic of working-class representatives later in the century. Thus Thomas Powell, the Bookbinders' representative before the Royal Commission on Elementary Education Acts in 1887, told Canon Gregory, an old-fashioned defender of Anglican claims to educate the poor, and a strong advocate of what amounted to compulsory Christianity for the working classes, that 'there are a great many things which are presumed to be belonging to religion which are altogether unnecessary to religion; there are a great many dogmas welded in'.[32] Powell wanted more Board Schools because their theoretically non-dogmatic religious teaching was preferable in his eyes to the teaching of Anglican doctrine. In this view he agreed with the other chief working-class representative called before the Commission, Thomas Smyth, a plasterer from Chelsea, who said that he also preferred the Board Schools to denominational schools because 'there is not any particular form of dogma taught'.[33] Smyth nevertheless thought that there were limits to the value of the Board Schools' religious teaching because 'it is liable to become the reflex of the teacher's own dogmatism, however guarded against'.[34] He said that the teachers should 'inculcate morality without the aid of religious teaching at all'.[35] The comment suggested the extent to which he identified the word 'religious' with 'denominational' and so with 'dogmatic'. He was quite specific in his criticism: 'There is a large army of professors of religion of various creeds, with very little to do in this country, or at least if they have much to do they neglect it ',[36] and they should try to convert people to their own way of thinking without benefit of the educational system.

Here there was certainly articulate dislike both of theological, as distinct from moral, instruction, and also of the organized churches. For this the education controversy was partly responsible: Thomas Wright had said in 1873 that this denominational squabble was doing religion no good in the eyes of the poorer classes—'it increases and embitters the feeling of contempt for creeds, already so largely existing in the minds of the working classes, and intensifies their dislike to and suspicion of "parsons".'[37] His statement was borne out by the evidence given to the Cross Commission in 1887.

There is some evidence, however, that the growth of factories and urban development in general was also partly responsible. The bringing together of large groups of working-class people in similar streets, factories, and workshops produced a psychological situation different from that of the equivalent agricultural labourers, always more thinly scattered on the ground, often living in scattered cottages, and isolated even from one another by many of the jobs they did. When Augustus Jessopp talked about the religious experiences of the Norfolk Primitive Methodist agricultural labourer in the last quarter of the nineteenth century he was usually reporting the imaginative adventurers of a man working by himself, hedging and ditching, for instance, or ploughing a field. This kind of rural society was not inimical, in the nineteenth century, to the formation of small, intense religious societies.[38] Urban workers associated much more closely: even unionism, which grew steadily in the Victorian industrial world, proved permanently difficult to establish in agriculture (and it is interesting that much of the impulse towards it came from men accustomed to the close, warm association of the chapel-society).[39] In the country, Primitive Methodism had started as a protest against the organized religious tradition: in the towns, in the denser fabric of industrial society, a similar antipathy towards organized religion was freer to show itself, externally as non-attendance at churches, internally as the distrust of extremes of articulate belief. The agricultural labourer who became a Primitive Methodist in the mid-nineteenth century was making a gesture against the way in which rural society was organized as a whole; he was not felt by his fellows to be repudiating his class. In the towns, however, the partial separation from working-class culture which followed from a man's joining one of the major religious denominations was a serious matter: Charles Booth wrote at the end of the century that in Woolwich 'the spirit of the Arsenal and of factory life in general is felt to be adverse to religion; units cannot be isolated from their surroundings; neighbours are also fellow workers. A man has to fight against his whole environment in attaching himself to a church.'[40]

It is significant, therefore, that when one turns for information to nineteenth-century working-class autobiographies and diaries one finds men like William Swan,

Joseph Gutteridge, and James Hopkinson,[41] all of them working men from towns and all of them interested in religion, though in rather different ways—Gutteridge, in particular, was a good example of the self-educated Victorian, unsettled religiously by eighteenth-century rationalism as well as by nineteenth-century science—were all of them lone wolves in their working lives as far as was possible for them. Swan (1813–80) was a London breadmaker; he supported himself and a family through great hardship and frequent unemployment. His diary gives the impression of a man who did not ever come to terms with his working-class surroundings, but sought in various Baptist chapels a more congenial society. Even this often became difficult. In 1843, for instance, he recorded that 'What with an increasing family, and uncertain work, and a hard man for my landlord so that I often had to pay rents whether I got my lodgers' money or not, I became scarcely able to keep a decent suit of clothes to go to chapel in.'[42] This was a genuine Victorian problem; Swan seems to have solved it temporarily by attending chapels where he was unknown. He certainly found the atmosphere of the bakery hostile: thus in 1864, and not for the first time, one finds him complaining that he had been stood off when the other men were kept on.[43]

This sense of living in an environment hostile to extremes of articulate belief was just as strong in the world of Joseph Gutteridge (1816–99) who, like Swan, knew poverty both in his youth and old age, and who felt himself to have been set apart from his fellows by virtue of his enquiring mind and heterodox religious opinions.[44] As a young man he was forced by adversity to work as a journeyman weaver in a Coventry ribbon factory; he did not want to do this because of 'a dislike for factory life on account of the low moral status of those employed there'.[45] He really wanted to work at home with a loom (and, one suspects, a mind) of his own. He soon lost the job when the firm went bankrupt, but said that 'the scenes witnessed at this factory were of so demoralising a character that nothing short of absolute want would have induced me to work in such a place again'.[46] One has no evidence in Gutteridge's autobiography for the existence of the factory as the centre of some kind of 'organic' working-class culture of which he wanted to be a part; at the same time, his moral strictures are interesting in as much he was not simply repeating nineteenth-century Evangelical attitudes.

Finally, there is James Hopkinson (1819–94). When he finished his apprenticeship as a cabinet-maker in Nottingham in 1840 his father paid for an 'outing' supper which cost between £6 and £7:

> at mid-day the men and boys came from all parts of the large workshops and drank my health, and then ranged themselves in a circle with me in the centre. Each man had in his hand a hold-fast . . . which sounds like a deep-toned bell when it is struck with a hammer. With these they rang me out of my time . . . After supper they all stood up with their glasses filled to the brim and sang 'Here is a health unto he who is now set free who was once an apprentice bound, T'is all for his sake that this holiday we make, so let his health go round.'

He and his father made short speeches in reply after which they crept away from 'the smoking and singing and disgusting and filthy conversations and jests usual on such occasions'.[47] This account was written down many years after the event—probably about 1880—and should therefore be treated with some caution, but Hopkinson's later development—he became a Baptist and a small shopowner—suggests the kind of gap which he at least believed must always have existed between him and the working class in which he grew up. And this again illustrates the general point that, whereas in the country a man might become a Primitive Methodist without entirely losing his working-class identity (at any rate down to about 1860), it was difficult, on the other hand, for a worker in the towns to become a member of one of the major religious groups without seeming to defy and even to dissociate himself from his working-class surroundings. The evidence suggests that in the first half of the nineteenth century, when Primitive Methodism first established itself in the countryside, the religious movement was riding on a wave of general social protest among the agricultural labourers, and that the comparative rural stagnancy of Primitive Methodism in the last quarter of the century resulted from the chapels losing contact with this demand for change: in the towns, on the other hand, the growing working-class political movement of the second half of the century did not seem to seek religious forms of expression and therefore did not reinforce either church or chapel. This is not to say that there were not those at the time who felt that some connection ought to exist, but the abject failure of the Labour Church Movement, started by John Trevor of Manchester in 1891, underlined the separation. The urban worker of the late-Victorian period had lost faith in religious institutions as sources of social change.[48]

There is another side, however, to the passage quoted above from Hopkinson. Even if, as has been suggested so far, the majority of urban workers came more and more to reject the middle-class idea of 'religion' (denominational allegiance and regular Sunday worship, together with financial support of a minister and buildings), they retained something of a traditional belief in the value of ritual, including religious ritual, for the celebration of special occasions, whether connected with work or with domestic life. Hopkinson's 'outing' supper was a secular example of this, but it is also clear that working-class parents, in the town as well as in the country, commonly had their children baptized. One should not press the significance of this conformity to convention too far: the performance of ritual, secular or sacred, does not require any profound belief in its doctrinal implications: the performance is more important than the meaning of the performance. Infant baptism, in any case, had gathered many superstitions about it, so that all kinds of anxiety might become attached to its omission.[49] Nevertheless, whatever the motives in individual cases, the association of birth, marriage, and death with ritual of a religious kind remained part of the nineteenth-century workers' mind. The kind of occasional use of religious ritual which this attitude involved annoyed the professional clergy, who were apt to deny it any 'religious' content; it seemed natural to the workers, however.

Nor were these the only religious forms with which working-class people in the towns celebrated special occasions. An attenuated form of the Harvest Festival enjoyed some popularity. Charles Booth, for example, recorded an Anglican vicar in outer North London who said that although in his parish not more than ten working men ever attended the Eucharist 'the Church is always crammed at Harvest Festivals': it is in line with what has just been said about the professional clergy that he commented that their presence was 'a relic of superstition'.[50] Nostalgia may have operated, certainly. Harvests had traditionally been occasions to be celebrated with dancing, drinking, and eating, at once a pagan and secular ritual. In the eighteenth century the clergy still tolerated this, even where their own farms were concerned. Thus William Cole wrote in 1766:'I got in all my Hay . . . They made a sort of Procession, with a Fiddle and a German Flute, Jem dressed out with Ribbands and Tom Hearne dancing before the last Cart, I giving a good supper to all my Hay makers and Helpers, being above 30 Persons in the Kitchin, who staid 'till one.'[51] By the 1840s, however, a more socially aggressive rural clergy wanted to curb the excesses of the countryside as they saw them: hence the Harvest Festival, of which several clergymen claimed to be the originator, including G. A. Denison, incumbent of East Brent in Somerset from 1845 to 1896, who by 1883 was organizing a two-day festival, complete with steam merry-go-round, football, vast evening dances in a marquee, and exclusively teetotal drinks.[52] More characteristic is Kilvert's account (Tuesday, 3 October 1871):[53]

> A note from Jane Dew of Whitney Rectory asking me to attend their Harvest Festival this afternoon. The service began at 2.15. After Church the whole parish, men, women and children, dined in the Rectory yard under a pent-house of beams and tarpaulin, near 200 people. After dinner all the men played or rather kicked football at each other and then till it grew dark, when the game ended in a royal scuffle and scrummage. Cold supper at 7.

Transposed to an urban setting the Festival became a Sunday preaching service in a church decorated with flowers, fruit, and vegetables: in *Orthodox London* (1875), Maurice Davies described such an event at St Paul's, Walworth, where the preacher honoured the occasion by pointing out that there could be no harvest of our souls without self-discipline, and everybody sang 'Raise the Song of Harvest Home', a hymn first published by Henry Alford in 1844.[54] Even in this emasculated form, however, the festival filled the Walworth church, as though the urban poor still relished a reminder of its recent past.

The other special occasion on which the poor still sometimes went to church was at the New Year. At Nine Elms, for example, in south-west London, Charles Booth found a Primitive Methodist minister who spoke of people crowding to a New Year's service, many of them drunk and very noisy, but still familiar with old hymns and quietening down once they were allowed to sing them; further north, in Haggeston and Hackney Wick, New Year's services proved just as attractive.[55] This was in the late 1890s, but a generation before, when St Alban's, Holborn, had just been built as an Anglo-Catholic offering to the London poor, A. H. Mackonochie and A. S. Stanton, the priests in charge, found a New Year's service forced upon them by their new parishioners. Stanton said:[56]

> Father Mackonochie had objected to the service as unliturgical. He said there was no Catholic precedent for it. So we had gone to bed; but the crowd in Brooke Street increased, and the bell of the Clergy House was perpetually rung and the demand shouted, 'Aint you going to have a service?' So having got the Vicar's leave I got up and opened the church and let the people in. They filled the church to the doors, and ever afterwards the service was continued, and without announcement or bell the church is always filled. What good is this service? Ah, what indeed? But the question goes further than 'this service'. The poorest come . . . in a way they come at no other time; God won't bless them in the year, they think, if they don't . . . Afterwards, when any help is wanted, the plea 'We were at your New Year's service' is often urged.

Stanton's comment hit off the combination of superstition, special celebration, and social insurance (before the coming of the Welfare State the very poor had good reason to maintain some contact with the Church as a potential source of charity) which seems to have been involved. He came closer to understanding this than did most of his clerical contemporaries, for most of whom the New Year's service was only tolerable as part of a pattern of regular church attendance. They were right in the sense that going to the New Year service might be 'religious' but was by no means necessarily 'Christian'. As Mackonochie said, the service was an innovation, usually referred back to eighteenth-century Wesleyan origins.[57]

In the late-nineteenth century, then, the question of the working-class attitude to institutionalized religion was ceasing to be of importance to the working class. Back in the years 1815–48, when the new cities were at their most chaotic, it had looked as though working-class Christianity would vanish, simply because the means were lacking to hand on even the rudiments of western religious culture from one generation to another. This was no longer the problem in the 1890s; the churches had improved their urban plant; the Board Schools had begun to supplement the denominational educational system. Charles Booth said of the Board Schools of East London that 'they were by no means without a religious tone, and their Bible teaching, though undogmatic, is very thorough'.[58] Contact with the tradition had been restored. What was vanishing now was any response other than that of indifference. The failure of the 'nondogmatic' Labour Church Movement has been noted. Ardent anti-religious propaganda was no more attractive. The Salvation Army's attempt to maintain at an urban working-class level the revivalistic tradition, to which the Americans Moody and Sankey had given a fresh lease of life among the chapel-going public in the 1870s, was not much more popular. As Percy Alden pointed out in the Mudie-Smith survey, the weakness of the Salvation Army in East London was extraordinary:[59]

The attendances in 1886 were 3,123; in 1903 they have doubled, it is true, and are now 6,376; but this is a wretchedly inadequate total for a population of nearly a million after all these years of unremitting work, and points to some serious weakness in Army methods. Even from the total we have given we fear we must deduct a considerable number of persons who attend the services held in shelters. While attendance may not be compulsory, it is more or less regarded as such by all those who use the shelters . . . When we remember that the Congress Hall in Linscott Road, Hackney, furnishes 2,549, and Mare Street, Hackney, 708, we can easily see how powerless the Salvation Army is in the remaining districts of the East End. But for their social work and the great hall at Clapton the Salvation Army would have been wiped out.

The Army's early expansion was not confirmed by lasting success in depth. The power of the idea of evangelical 'conversion' had waned throughout the century.

Even so one must be cautious before one identifies this indifference to religious institutions and middle-class definitions of properly Christian behaviour with an absence of religious feeling in a more general sense. Thomas Wright, for instance, insisted on the way in which the poor hung on to a belief in the underlying rationality and justice of the world order: 'Though there is much in their life that at times is almost enough to drive them to doubt the existence of a principle of eternal justice, they do firmly believe in it; believe that though it is often set aside here, it will be asserted hereafter. Such a belief is to them a hope.'[60] The existence of this attitude is part of what may be called the 'explanatory' function of religion. Joseph Gutteridge's passionate interest in both science and spiritualism was an articulate example of the same search for order and meaning. Even the journal of William Swan, a regular attender at chapels through most of his life, suggests that his primary impulse towards religious behaviour was a similar need for reassurance in the midst of a very wretched life. It is important to bear in mind that all these varieties of individual behaviour were possible.

Nevertheless, indifference prevailed. City and factory shaped a working-class culture unlike that of the village. The basis was a working-class housing area which had no real country equivalent. Factory and housing conditions made possible a new kind of proletarian solidarity about both work and leisure. People found themselves given the relative freedom of a money economy and so able to choose their own activities, especially at the week-end. They had to form their own social pattern: in the past they had not thought of the village church as a social centre for them, and once in the town they did not often choose the local church as a social focus. As one reads Charles Booth's study of the religious life of London at the end of the nineteenth century a clear picture of the resulting working-class Sunday emerges. Sunday was the day for relaxation, when the men stayed in bed in the morning or took the dog for a walk while the women prepared the one set dinner of the week; a slow recovery followed (the children were still sometimes packed off to Sunday School), and then came visiting, chiefly family visiting for the rest of the day. 'They thank Cobden and Bright and everybody but God for their prosperity,' lamented the Deptford vicar of St Luke's, 'those who can afford it buy a piano, and on Sunday evening you can hear them singing the latest music hall ditty.'[61]

From chaos to indifference: in the course of the nineteenth century the Protestant churches had almost lost any claim to express the religious aspirations of the working class. The Victorian period saw the drying-up of organized, institutionalized popular religion. The poor still made use of the existing churches to celebrate birth, marriage, and death, often mixing superstition with religious ritual. One may doubt how what we have called 'explanatory systems' of a religious type actually affected working-class behaviour; on the other hand, they were certainly there.

Notes

1 Friedrich Engels, *The Condition of the Working Class in England*, ed. E. J. Hobsbawm (1969), p. 155. It is with this widespread indifference that I am concerned, not with national groups like the Irish Catholics in England.
2 Ibid., p. 155.
3 Horace Mann, *Census of Great Britain, 1851, Religious Worship* (1853), p. 158.
4 Ibid., p. 158. For modern discussions of the census, see K. S. Inglis, 'Patterns of Religious Worship in 1851', *Journal of Ecclesiastical History*, xi (1960), 74–86; David M. Thompson, 'The 1851 Religious Census: Problems and Possibilities', *Victorian Studies*, xi (1967), 87–97; W. S. F. Pickering, 'The 1851 Religious Census —a useless experiment?', *British Journal of Sociology*, xviii (1967), 382–407.
5 Inglis, op. cit., p. 80. The census did not distinguish those who attended once from those who did so two or three times. Mann thought that a deduction of about one-third would give a fair approximation to the number of people actually involved. Such a correction would reduce Sheffield, for instance, from 32 percent attendance to about 21 percent. Not all towns were as low, for Bristol's percentage was 56, and that of Cambridge was 68. But the census does not suggest that concentration on London has made modern scholars exaggerate the religious indifference of the Victorian period.
6 Charles Booth, *Life and Labour of the People in London*: third series, *Religious Influences* (1902), VII, p. 422ff. Booth did not think that London workers were impressed by either Anglo-Catholic socialism, or by the Nonconformist 'social gospel', which traced the evils of man to drink, gambling, prostitution, a landed aristocracy, and the lack of an international court.
7 E. P. Thompson, *The Making of the English Working Class* (1968), especially pp. 385–440. In this impression he replied to criticisms made to the first impression of the book (1963) by R. Currie and R. M. Hartwell ('The Making of the English Working Class?' *Economic History Review*, 2nd ser., xviii (1965), 633–43). On the subject of Methodism he did not answer their objections convincingly.
8 Cf. Sidney Pollard, 'Factory Discipline in the Industrial Revolution', *Economic History Review*, 2nd ser., xvi (1963–4), 254–71.

9 Mann, op. cit., pp. xxxix–xli.

10 R. A. Soloway, *Prelates and People: Ecclesiastical social thought in England, 1783–1852* (1969), p. 429. Dissenting ministers did not easily identify with the urban working class either, though the social causes were not the same as in the Anglican case. The early nineteenth-century Primitive Methodist minister, for instance, had a rural background and did best in small towns and in the countryside. Between 1831 and 1851 the number of Anglican clergy rose from 10,718 to 17,621. For all that is said on religion in the cities here, see especially *Parliamentary Papers* (*P.P.*), 1857–8, IX, Report of Select Committee (S.C.) (H. of L.) on Deficiency of Means of Spiritual Instruction and Places of Divine Worship in Metropolis, etc. (387). This dealt not only with London, but also with Bradford, Leeds, Liverpool, Manchester, etc. The evidence makes quite clear how baffled the Anglican leaders were by the problems of expanding cities, and how the pew-rent system was still a major cause of half-empty churches in down-town areas in the mid-century. The sections on Liverpool and Manchester are especially revealing.

11 Léon Faucher, *Manchester in 1844*, translated by a member of the Manchester Athenaeum (1844), p. 54.

12 Ibid., p. 53.

13 Engels, op. cit., p. 155.

14 Soloway, op. cit., p. 445.

15 *Census*, 1851, *Religious Worship*, Summary Tables, Table F, pp. cclii–cclxxii.

16 Mann, op. cit., pp. cxi–cxii.

17 Henry Mayhew, *London Labour and the London Poor* (Dover edn, 1968), p. 22. Originally published in 1861, this section was probably written about ten years before.

18 Valerie Chancellor, ed., *Master and Artisan in Victorian England* (1969), p. 171, which contains the autobiography of Joseph Gutteridge, 1816–99 (first published in 1893).

19 R. Mudie-Smith, ed., *The Religious Life of London* (1904), pp. 503, 518. He instances the pattern of suburban Camberwell, where there was a New Jerusalem Church with 45 morning attenders, Christadelphians with 49, and two Spiritualist Churches with 13 and 39 (p. 206).

20 *Diocesan Report on the Condition of the Bristol Poor* (Bristol, 1885), p. 193.

21 A. Weir and W. D. Maclagan, eds, *The Church and the Age* (1870), p. 429. These were High Church essays; Maclagan, later a bishop, wanted to unite sacramentalism and revivalism as a solution to the problem.

22 Ibid., p. 426.

23 A. Symondson, ed., *The Victorian Crisis of Faith* (1970), p. 93.

24 Thomas Wright often wrote under the pseudonym, 'The Journeyman Engineer'. He also published novels, *The Bane of a Life* (1870) and *Grangers Thorn* (1872). He was clearly well-versed in working-class affairs.

25 Wright, op. cit., p. 87.

26 Ibid., p. 90.

27 Ibid., p. 157.

28 Ibid., p. 330.

29 Ibid., p. 17.

30 Samuel Wilberforce, *A Charge delivered at the Ordinary Visitation of the Archdeaconry of Surrey, November, 1842* (1842), p. 19.

31 Wright, op. cit., p. 104.

32 *P.P.*, 1887, XXX, Royal Commission (R.C.) on Elementary Education: Minutes of Evidence (C. 5158), Q. 52,905.

33 Ibid., Q. 52,252.

34 Ibid., Q. 52,299.

35 Ibid., Q. 52,308.

36 Ibid., Q. 52,334.

37 Wright, op. cit., p. 138.

38 Augustus Jessopp, *Arcady for Better or Worse* (1890), pp. 65–82, 'Arcady in some phases of her faith'. Jessopp was a Norfolk rector, local historian, and contributor to the *Nineteenth Century*, for which he often wrote about rural England; he was virtually the only nineteenth-century Anglican to make more than a passing reference to the Primitive Methodists.

39 See, for instance, the autobiography of George Edwards, *From Crow-Scaring to Westminster* (1922): Edwards, the principal founder of the Agricultural Workers' Union, was a Norfolk Primitive Methodist lay preacher.

40 The roots of the Woolwich situation were in the 1850s, when the Crimean War caused the rapid expansion of the area; the parish church was then one and a half miles from the mass of the people and would hold only 350. 'They come and labour like beasts of burden, and no man cares for their souls, and they die as beasts, not knowing where they go,' William Acworth, the Woolwich incumbent told the House of Lords Select Committee of 1858 (cf. note 10). He said that the men of the Arsenal did not go to church. The government had built a school for the boys, who worked from six in the morning to eight in the evening making cartridges, and Acworth used the building for Sunday services to which he drew women and children. During the war 'The men were employed by the temptation of double wages on Sunday.' In 1858 he was still trying to raise money for a new parish church which would have held 540 adults and 400 children (see S.C. on means of Divine Worship, QQ. 1,358–98). See also Booth, third series, V, p. 85.

41 Guida Swan, ed., *The Journals of Two Poor Dissenters, 1786–1880* (1970): William's was the second journal, the first being that of his father. See Chancellor, op. cit., for Joseph Gutteridge; and J. B. Goodman, ed., *Memoirs of a Victorian Cabinet Maker* (1968) for James Hopkinson.

42 Swan, op. cit., pp. 53–4.

43 Ibid., p. 71.

44 'Our little world was strictly orthodox', he wrote, 'and it required a large amount of moral courage to publicly acknowledge oneself to be out of agreement with accepted religious beliefs' (Chancellor, op. cit., p. 120).

45 Ibid., p. 122.

46 Ibid.

47 Goodman, op. cit., pp. 57–8.

48 For Trevor, see K. S. Inglis, *Churches and the Working Classes in Victorian England* (1963), pp. 215–49; also Trevor's book, *My Quest for God* (1897). There may have been more than 100 Labour Churches for a brief period, but only 20 to 30 lasted for

a significant length of time. Trevor's periodical, the *Labour Prophet*, sold 6,000 copies in 1894, but died out in 1898. The Movement had two points important from the viewpoint of this essay: there was to be no formal ministry, and no dogma apart from the broad claim that the aims of the Labour Movement were in line with the moral and economic laws of God; nor was there any ritual beyond the structure of the barest preaching service. But people who did not want institutionalized religion did not want an institutionalized form of that rejection.

49 In Lambeth, at the close of the nineteenth century, it could be stated that 'amongst the mass of the population the only religious observance at all common is churching' (Booth, op. cit., third series., IV, p. 41). Here also the ceremony—one of ritual purification—survived because of superstitions about the awful consequences of its omission.

50 Booth, op. cit., third series, I, p. 26.

51 F. G. Stokes, ed., *The Blecheley Diary of William Cole, 1765–7* (1931), p. 75.

52 L. E. Denison, ed., *Fifty Years at East Brent. The letters of George Anthony Denison* (1902), p. 278.

53 William Plomer, ed., *Kilvert's Diary, 1870–1879* (1967), p. 149.

54 C. M. Davies, *Orthodox London, Second Series* (1875), pp. 338–47. Davies was a religious journalist who specialized in describing the varieties of religion in the 1870s.

55 Booth, op. cit., third series, V, p. 26.

56 G. W. E. Russell, *Arthur Stanton* (1917), p. 72.

57 That is, to the Wesleyan 'Watchnight' service, a vigil originally held at any time; it became a New Year celebration, however. This suggests the survival of a primitive sense of the need to greet the new year with appropriate ritual, an ancient, pre-Christian idea. Cf. Mircea Eliade, *Cosmos and History* (1959).

58 Booth, op. cit., third series, I, p. 29.

59 Mudie-Smith, op. cit., pp. 25–6. Cf. Inglis, pp. 175–215.

60 Wright, op. cit., p. 88.

61 Booth, op. cit., third series, V, p. 23. As he said elsewhere, on the banks of the Lea on a fine Sunday morning 'man and pipe and dog form a purely working-class picture' (third series, I, p. 104). In *The Great Unwashed* (1868), Thomas Wright said that 'if a workingman does not attend a place of worship from an active feeling of religion, he need not do so from any reasons of caste. It is not essential to his maintenance of a character of respectability' (p. 92).

37   The Way Out

Stanley Pierson

'The great cities of the world,' John Ruskin wrote in 1879, 'have become loathesome centres of fornication and covetousness—the smoke of their sins going up into the heaven like the furnace of Sodom and the pollution of it rolling and raging through the bones and souls of the peasant people around them.'[1] The language and the imagery are peculiarly Ruskinian, and extreme; few Victorians were so one-sided. But the view of the city as a mainly evil growth was widespread in the period. Indeed, one of the striking features of the Victorians, engaged in developing the first predominantly urban society, was the reluctance of many of them to accept the outcome of their own energies.[2]

The strong nineteenth-century bias against urban life was probably in part due to the success of the landed aristocracy in accommodating itself to economic change and thereby maintaining much of its social and political pre-eminence. But Victorian hostility to the city arose more directly out of the shock administered to older social and cultural forms by the combined impact of economic and demographic change. As the most obvious manifestation of these changes, the large city became a central symbol for the Victorians, serving with the symbol of the machine to provide a focus for the feelings aroused by a transformation which though often exhilarating was also bewildering and frightening.[3] This symbolic city was not the complex growth of history or the outcome of distinct economic and social needs; it was a creature of the imagination. Various images were employed to describe it, usually fearful and hostile. To one observer, for instance, the cities were like 'giant octopuses . . . running out their suckers . . . into the surrounding country.' Another described the city as 'an elephantiasis sucking into its gorged system half the life and the blood and the bone of the rural districts.'[4]

This essay explores several patterns in the Victorian response to the city. First, it examines those forms of thought which envisaged and to some extent produced a radically de-urbanized existence. Secondly, it deals with a series of episodes in which manufacturers left industrial cities so as to continue their enterprises in more favorable economic and social circumstances, these efforts being conciliatory toward the urban process and the economic and social realities behind it. Finally the essay discusses the nature of the compromise which characterized the late-Victorian response.

These patterns of flight and reconciliation unfolded most clearly within the middle classes, or more accurately, within their more prosperous sections. The landed class lacked the incentives, the lower classes the resources, to share significantly in the process. Moreover, the Victorian city was largely the creation of the middle class; it mirrored their economic successes just as it reflected their apparent political and cultural failings. These changes were especially evident in cities most dominated by the production and distribution of goods, cities such as Manchester, Liverpool, Glasgow, Leeds, and Birmingham. They bore most clearly the marks of that process which Karl Polanyi in *The Great Transformation*, called 'disembedding' —the process through which economic activity freed itself from many of the traditional social controls and assumed a comparatively autonomous development. The outcome was a sense of the rapid deterioration of living conditions and the first and most substantial form of the flight—the retreat of the middle classes to the suburbs. The retreat to the suburbs has been treated elsewhere in these volumes, but one aspect of that retreat, the attempt to recover something of the older rural life, opens up a promising avenue for an explanation of the phenomenon of flight.

H. G. Wells argued shortly after the turn of the century that the yearning for the countryside was in fact the most powerful of the forces drawing men away from the cities. It was made up, he contended, of a passion for nature, the charm of cultivation and gardening, and the craving for 'a little private imperium such as a home or cottage on its own grounds affords.'[5] But some years earlier H. D. Traill had questioned the depth of this feeling. He acknowledged that it was 'the thing' for a man 'chained to his labouring oar in the great city' to profess an enthusiasm for the country.[6] He noted the 'multiplication of cottages, bungalows and villas standing in their own park-like grounds.' But, he argued, conversations with suburban house agents would demonstrate the transient and shallow character of the enthusiasm.

> . . . all over the rural environs of London, out to a radius of twenty miles or so, a perpetual process of disenchantment is going on in the minds of the emigrants from the metropolis; these districts are continually receiving the influx of a stream of restless towns-people who think that they long for a life of repose and quiet and who are continually sending back again an efflux of bored 'suburbans' who have found that all they really wanted was a 'little change.'

Traill concluded that the 'rush of townsmen into the country' was simply another sign of 'modern unrest' and the 'feverish search for excitement and novelty.' The suburban spirit was remote from the genuine 'rural spirit' for the latter was not, he argued, primarily an affair of transitory emotion, but of a 'permanent mental state' centering on the contemplative faculty.

Traill recognized that here, as in so much of the life of the period, the Victorians were given to sentimentalism, to emotions which were not firmly connected with internal convictions or outer circumstances. But, however one judges the force of this nostalgia for the countryside, it was a pervasive feature of Victorian thought and culture. And their modes of self-understanding, particularly as they relate to social change, reveal much about the inner refusal of so many Victorians to come to terms with urban realities.

The Victorian middle classes possessed two alternative ways of explaining and assessing the social transformation in which they were caught up. In Utilitarianism middle-class intellectuals were formulating a system of attitudes and values which affirmed many of the emerging characteristics of urban life. Romanticism, in contrast, registered the sense of menace which the city presented to older social values and customs. While Utilitarianism provided the outline of a philosophy for urban man, Romanticism furnished the elements of an ideology of flight. The difficulties of the former help to explain the gathering force of the latter in the late-Victorian years.

Bentham and his disciples provided a theoretical account and justification of a way of life in which economic transactions occupied the central place. Utilitarian morality was, in Halévy's terms, the economic psychology of the middle class 'put into the imperative.'[7] The Utilitarians also stressed the drive, closely associated with the new capitalists, to grasp the natural world, society, and even man's personality in quantitative and measurable terms. Nature so viewed was emptied of its former moral and religious significance and subordinated to man's practical needs; social relations were reduced to the impersonal and the repetitive; and the individual personality was encouraged to suppress the spontaneous and the emotional in favor of the logical. Utilitarian man was autonomous, basing his decisions not on the values and attitudes implanted by tradition and grasped intuitively, but rather on the anticipated consequences of his actions.

The Utilitarian stress on economic rationality, the impersonality of social relations, and individual autonomy, foreshadows the emphasis found in later attempts to epitomize the urban mentality. Georg Simmel, writing in 1905, described the man of the metropolis as dominated by the intellect, occupied mainly with abstract monetary relationships, and inclined to reduce all of reality to the objectively measurable. A generation later Louis Wirth sharpened Simmel's portrayal by indicating the ways in which city life promoted a greater social heterogeneity and a greater specialization of economic function.[8] It is true that Simmel's and Wirth's accounts go beyond the Utilitarian scheme. But they were both confirming at critical points the insights of middle-class intellectuals in the first half of the nineteenth century.

Yet the Utilitarian formulation was deductive and limited; it did not describe real individuals or the actual social process. For Mill, in a process of painful discovery, its rationalistic and analytical approach to man failed to account for basic values or to nurture the moral will and imagination necessary to sustain a reforming social mission. These apparent defects were as crucial to the Utilitarian approach to urban reform as they were in its individual psychology. For, unless the Utilitarian reformer smuggled in values or ideals from outside his system of thought, he was committed by it to the ends implicit in the existing urban process. While this commitment made possible a kind of improvement which was gradualist and pragmatic, it provided little comfort for those who recoiled from the deepening miseries and horrors in the large cities. Moreover, reformers of Utilitarian bent were themselves as often as not to follow the flight into Romantic patterns of thought.

The English Romantics, like their counterparts on the Continent, were struggling to repair the multiple ruptures—psychological, social, and cosmological—which were becoming so apparent in Europe at the close of the eighteenth century.[9] Initially their social and political outlook, inspired by the French Revolution, was hopeful, even millennial in nature. But this mood soon passed and the leading figures of the English movement, Wordsworth and Coleridge, sought to recover in the sphere of the imagination the unity and harmony which they thought history was denying them. The inner retreat of Wordsworth was especially significant and foreshadowed the withdrawal, at least in the imagination, of many members of the middle class in the face of the emerging urban world. More than any other figure Wordsworth supplied the vocabulary and spiritual model for an ideology of flight.

Wordsworth placed the good life firmly in the countryside where men could receive the moral and spiritual influences which Nature could bestow. Indeed, Nature assumed for the early Wordsworth the educative role hitherto assigned to the Church. It taught the virtues of the rural village community where social relations were personal and spontaneous, and life was regulated by the perennial cycle of the seasons. Wordsworth presented a sentimental and idealized view of a social order which was passing, and this view strongly condemned the 'dissolute city' where men like Michael's son Luke gave themselves 'to evil courses.'

The myth of rural goodness and urban evil pervaded poetry and much of fiction almost to the end of the century.[10] Victorian literature was, at least with respect to the city, a literature of evasion and regression. It failed to bring aesthetic perceptions to bear on the actualities of the city, when, by portraying the dilemmas of the people living there, it might have served to dispel something of the strangeness and menace of the urban world. But in its evasiveness and its regressiveness the literature of the Victorian middle class suggests the deeper reverberations of the shock of urbanization.

In a perceptive series of articles R. A. Forsyth has examined various ways in which the Victorian poets and writers struggled with the crisis of sensibility produced by the rise of the industrial city.[11] He has contrasted the retreat of William Barnes into the 'fastnesses of Edenlike Dorset' with the immersion of James Thomson in the despair of his dreadful city. Forsyth argues that the characteristic response of the Victorian writer was one of ambivalence—the coexistence within the individual of opposed traits, attitudes, and sentiments. And he concludes that ambivalence was not evasive but rather an 'adjustment device,' permitting 'some small area for psychic manoeuvre' for those who were struggling 'towards a new structure of feeling' based on an urban way of life.

Ambivalence is a useful concept in dealing with the Victorian responses to the city. It particularly suits the man of the suburbs. For in the 'area of psychological manoeuvre' provided by the suburb he could retain some of the securities felt in a rural environment without giving up his position in the urban business world. And yet, although ambivalence would play a role in a process of reconciliation, it was not necessarily a stage towards the acceptance of urban patterns of thought and behavior. It might mean the opposite—an intensification of the conflict between the new values and the old, and indeed, in itself a process of regression. It could mean a reversion not only to archaic social forms but also to those mythical or archetypal patterns of a harmony with Nature in which from time immemorial men have sought to escape from the pain of history. This 'mythological flight from the ravages of time,' which Walter Ong has seen as a characteristic movement for the traditional poet, was also the strategy of one current of British Romanticism.[12] The strategy produced, in fact, a counter-attack on urban industrial society, first through the fashioning of archaic myths and then through the development of a social program designed to free men completely from the curse of the great cities. Another result was a repudiation of those liberal political institutions which became in the course of the nineteenth century the chief means of adjusting national policy to the social realities of the cities.

The key figures in this development were Carlyle and Ruskin, for they transferred the Romantic ideology of flight onto the broader plane of historical interpretation and recast the symbols of the early Romantics into comprehensive social myths. These myths would gain in significance as the new patterns of urban life settled down ever more firmly around the Victorians. And in the closing decades of the century they would help to inspire a series of attempts to break away and develop new modes of human settlement outside the great cities.

Although Carlyle did not use the city as a distinctive category in his social criticism, his work is an intrinsic part of Victorian urban criticism. His response to the social changes of the thirties and the forties was initially ambivalent. His Calvinistic background made him particularly sympathetic to the ascetic, work-centered ethic of the new capitalists, while he retained from his Scottish boyhood a deep belief in the virtues of the rural community. Much of his early writing was directed toward the task of leavening capitalism with traditional forms of social responsibility. But that balance was not deeply felt and his early letters from London record his sense of shock, and yet awe, at the 'wild, wondrous chaotic den of discord . . . of men and animals and carriages and wagons, all rushing they know not whence.' Before long Carlyle was convinced that London-born men were 'narrow-built;

consistently perverted men, rather fractions of a man.'[13] And his fundamental antagonism to the ethos of the industrial or commercial city was increasingly pronounced. His attacks on Utilitarianism and what he called the mechanical spirit were aimed at precisely those forms of thought and behavior which the city encouraged. Carlyle praised the kind of society in which men shared common religious and moral values and were bound together by feelings of personal loyalty, a society exemplified most clearly in his portrayal of twelfth-century England in *Past and Present* (1843).

Carlyle's mythical reconstructions served him well in his indictment of the cruelties and inhumanities of the early-Victorian industrial city. He drew back, however, from any serious analysis of objective social and economic forces, relying instead on moralistic exhortation to remedy social evils. But when at mid-century he began to attack contemporary institutions more directly, the archaic and moralistic spell he had cast over the wealthy classes of London began to lose its power. In the years ahead he was more and more estranged from the main developments of British life. Having lost hope in the recovery of a spiritual solidarity, and unable to perceive what new forms of social integration might characterize an urban-based society, Carlyle began to look toward authoritarian means to counter the anarchy he saw inevitably approaching. He anticipated, in fact, those leaders in the twentieth century who would resort to totalitarian techniques in order to impose archaic fantasies on societies caught up in the almost unbearable social tensions of a comparable transition.

The hatred of the city, implicit in Carlyle's writings, became fully explicit in Ruskin. Here there was little sign of ambivalence toward social change. Moving from an essentially Wordsworthian or Romantic apotheosis of Nature, initially qualified by evangelical Christianity, Ruskin developed a social vision which stood in ever sharper opposition to the movement of British institutions. His studies of Venetian art and architecture had convinced him that the evils of Victorian society could be traced mainly to the machine and the attendant division of labor. And on the basis of this mythical simplification of the historical process he launched his critique of industrial society. The large industrial cities were simply the most glaring manifestation of Britain's degeneration. They were for Ruskin 'foul and vicious,' 'smoking masses of decay,' and 'spots of dreadful mildew, spreading by patches and blotches over the country they consume.'[14] He warned artists and architects to flee from them, for the hope that they could provide genuine conditions for art was mere 'vanity.'

Perhaps it was Ruskin's acute sensitivity which led him to such violent opposition to Victorian institutions. No one insisted so devastatingly on the inner vacuity of the middle-class pursuit of productivity. And in his recoil from the city he reverted not simply to preindustrial urban models but to some mythical ideal of pastoral harmony. For some Victorians such a myth could cushion the shock of fundamental social change; for Ruskin it meant an intensification of conflict and eventually a divorce from social and economic reality. The divorce found visible form during the seventies in his Guild of St George and the agricultural community it started near

878

Sheffield. The experiment quickly broke down, but it became, along with Ruskin's writings, an important source of inspiration to a number of late-Victorians who were in flight from urban and industrial society.[15]

By the 1880s few could deny the social impotence of the rural vision. Hence the effort of William Morris to rescue the ideal by attaching it to Marxism and the revolutionary energies which that creed promised. Ideological impulses within Marxism encouraged the project, but it was incompatible with the social and economic realism of that system of thought and it soon collapsed. In Morris's Socialism the Romantic regression ended virtually in anarchism and in an almost total repudiation of liberal political forms. Morris could envisage the day when the Houses of Parliament would be converted into a 'Dung-Market.' Yet despite the debacle of his Socialist work, the archaic and mythical vision of Morris survived to become one of the most vital impulses in the popular Socialist movement of the nineties. It was a central feature in what was by far the most successful piece of popular Socialist propaganda published in Britain—Robert Blatchford's *Merrie England* (1894).

Blatchford had come to Socialism out of the sense of shock and shame produced by a tour of the Manchester slums. Although his version was highly eclectic it drew its basic orientation, including a deep hostility towards politics, from Morris. Blatchford's vision was, as the title 'Merrie England' suggests, nostalgic. He looked forward to an England which was mainly agricultural, had abandoned the idea of serving as the workshop of the world, and was self-supporting. 'Merrie England' would be free from large-scale industry and great cities, and return to a decentralized order of more or less self-contained communities.

There were scattered efforts by Socialists in the nineties to implement the rustic vision. Indeed, it was in this context that the phenomenon of flight found its more extreme expression. Few working-class Socialists possessed the means that were usually required to launch community experiments, but there was the example of Edward Carpenter, the prominent Socialist writer and lecturer whose rural retreat at Millthorpe near Sheffield had become a place of pilgrimage and a source of inspiration for many Socialists and other reformers. Carpenter attempted to support himself and a companion by growing vegetables and making sandals. And he unfolded in his long poem, *Towards Democracy*, a vision of life which entailed not only a recovery of the old ties with the earth but the return to an almost primitive mode of existence.

Socialists participated in a variety of experiments designed to restore man to a harmony with Nature and his fellows. One member of the Bristol group pursued the dream all the way to the slopes of the Sierras in California. Others took part in the agricultural colony organized in the early nineties by H. V. Mills at Starnthwaite. There were also ties between the Socialists and the Cosme Colony, a settlement in Paraguay started by a group from Australia. 'Do we not know,' one of the members wrote back to the English sympathizers, 'that the modern city is unnatural, and that street and road and lane and alley have not been twisted further from their original significance than man has in them from his moral life.' The city, he declared, 'must go.'[16]

879

The most radical and self-conscious rejection of the ethos of city life was inspired by the spread of Tolstoy's ideas in the late nineties. Tolstoy's gospel, often echoing Ruskin's, condemned modern industry and technology, affirmed a life of close proximity to Nature, and assured men that the Sermon on the Mount provided a practical ethic. It appealed particularly to those Socialists who, in the aftermath of the election of 1895, were disenchanted with politics. At Purleigh in Essex, where the first of the Tolstoyan colonies was founded, the largest group comprised refugees from London's commercial life.[17] They attempted to build there a community animated by principles antithetical to those of the world of urban commerce. In contrast to the competitive, specialized, and impersonal routines of the city, the life they set out to live was cooperative, based on agriculture, and governed by primary affections. Indeed, the bolder spirits in the group were determined to view no one as a stranger and to admit all applicants into the community without considering their qualifications. Disagreements over this issue led to a schism and the formation of other groups. The most important of these was Whiteway, located in Gloucestershire, which, after a stormy beginning and some compromises with the prevailing mores of economic life, survived into the 1930s.[18]

Tolstoyan groups in the North of England carried their hostility to conventional commerce directly into its urban strongholds. A convert in Leeds, D. B. Foster, later a Lord Mayor of the city, joined a friend in an attempt to run a bicycle shop without recourse to regular hours or the normal work disciplines. In Blackburn the Tolstoyan proprietor of an electric shop set out to conduct his business in such a way as to avoid sullying his hands with money.[19]

Nearly all of these experiments had expired by the end of the century. But the romantic and archaic impulses out of which they arose continued to play a role in the Socialist movement, finding expression in its arts and crafts groups and exercising some influence on the Guild Socialists in the years just before World War I, and later still in the work of Middleton Murry. Outside the Socialist movement the quest can be followed in the life and work of D. H. Lawrence.[20]

The patterns of flight which have been examined—the move to the country, the retreat of the literary imagination, and the escape into archaic modes of social life—could be supplemented by studying the patterns of nineteenth-century emigration, and even more fruitfully by considering the various schemes for land reform in the Victorian period, particularly the early projects of the Chartist leaders; the plans to provide allotments for the poor; and the later movements for land nationalization.

The next section of this essay turns, however, to a development in which the industrial city was being rejected by the very men whose economic leadership had often been most responsible for its growth—the manufacturers. Their form of flight was prompted mainly by the failure of the city to provide the living and working conditions necessary for the expansion or proper continuance of their economic enterprises. They sought and to some extent found alternatives to the city. But mainly they were engaged in a work of reconciliation. Not only did they combine the economic benefits which proximity to a city gave them with the advantages of the open areas outside, they also sought a synthesis of old and new values. Indeed, the builders of the model factory communities present still another form of the Victorian ambivalence—the attempt to blend traditional moral and aesthetic values with those nurtured by an industrial and urban civilization.

The earliest forms of the factory village preceded the full onset of urbanization. They developed out of the efforts of manufacturers to combine technology, labor, and the other economic resources in the most efficient way. These villages mirrored even more clearly than the industrial cities the way in which economic considerations, or what Sidney Pollard has called 'managerial necessity,' could mold social life. The position of the factory, transport facilities, the housing arrangements for the workers, and provisions for basic services and governance were all closely geared to the goal of profit making. According to Pollard the framework of these early communities was made up mainly of compulsion and fear. The bitter pressures of competition together with the difficult adjustments entailed in the new work discipline left the manufacturers little scope 'for originating and putting into practice any coherent philosophy of their own.'[21]

Robert Owen was the obvious exception. His model factory community at New Lanark, while not economically successful in the long run, indicated that profit-making did not preclude a concern for the health, social welfare, and educational advancement of the workers. His combination of skilful industrial management and humanitarian feeling offered a creative approach to many of the emerging problems of an industrial and urban society. Yet Owen turned his back on the new social order. His later career as the leader of a millennial movement may be explained in terms of his own messianic bent, or in terms of the resistance which his reforming ideas encountered from the established order. But it also provides an example of the way in which a man whose philosophical outlook was essentially Utilitarian might succumb to romantic and nostalgic impulses. For Owen's communal experiments were cast in the archaic mold; the way of life to which he was drawn was primarily agricultural and, indeed, pastoral in aspiration.[22]

The split between the Romantic and the Utilitarian sides of Owen's thought widened in the work of his more prominent disciples. John Minter Morgan extended the Owenite reach after lost social forms with his scheme to create 'self-supporting village' communities. And he diluted the Utilitarian ideology of Owenism by restoring Christianity to its former place as the main source of morality and social discipline. Once more the spires of the Church of England would rise above the cottages clustered about.[23] James Silk Buckingham, in contrast, attempted to bring the Owenite creed back into a positive relationship to industrialization and urbanization. His conception of a model city—Victoria—owed much to Morgan's ideas and retained, in its plan for a central park and its surrounding green belt, rural elements. But its rigorous geometric form, its employment of iron and glass in construction, its acceptance of industry, and the functional relationships which dominated the plan, all pointed toward the future. Although Buckingham's model was never given practical expression, it influenced later attempts to view the city in terms of its more positive human and social possibilities.[24]

Meanwhile several early Victorian manufacturers in the North were exploring a middle ground between the complete dictation of profit making and the reversion to a non-industrial and non-urbanized existence. Walter Creese has described them as the 'Bradford-Halifax school of model village builders.'[25] Though it was not a school in any self-conscious or programmatic sense of the term, its three leaders, Titus Salt, Edward Akroyd, and Francis Crossley, all bore the stamp of a particular economic, geographical, and cultural region. They were wealthy woolen manufacturers who were deeply involved in the intense religious and political life of the West Riding of Yorkshire. They built their model villages in the years between 1850 and 1870 because they were dissatisfied with the living and working conditions of the main manufacturing centers, Bradford and Halifax.

The villages which resulted are interesting from several standpoints. They indicate how privately amassed capital could alter urban conditions in a way that was virtually impossible amid the conflicting economic interests, the institutional inertia, and the accumulating problems of the industrial centers. Such action was in part enlightened self-interest. But it also reflected strong moral and religious conviction and the desire to use profits to enhance the welfare of the workers. Most significant in terms of the themes of this essay was the manner in which a retreat from the city based mainly on economic or utilitarian considerations led to a conscious recovery of social and aesthetic values drawn from the past. Indeed, these manufacturers set out to reinstate a form of social responsibility derived from feudal traditions.[26] But they were also attempting to reconcile the social solidarity and paternalism of the past with the modern drive toward economic rationality and individualism. The most ambitious attempt to synthesize the two patterns was started by Salt in 1850.

Saltaire was located three miles outside of Bradford. It was the most geometric and functional of the West Riding communities and expressed Salt's own feeling for line and form. Economic considerations were primary in the development of Saltaire. First came the factory, located so that it would have easy access to both rail and water transport. Housing for the workers followed, constructed according to relatively high standards of health and comfort, and yet permitting a fairly high density of population. Salt also ensured a high level of services for his community; he set up a steam laundry, built schools and churches, and promoted cultural and recreational facilities.[27]

Behind its almost stark utilitarian posture, however, Saltaire incorporated much that was traditional. Indeed, its primary inspiration had come from the model factory community which Disraeli presented in *Sybil*. And there was something of 'noblesse oblige' in Salt's close supervision of his venture. He was not disposed, like some of the earlier community builders, to impose his religious views on the citizens of Saltaire, but his prohibition of public houses betrayed more than a hint of moral paternalism. 'Drink and lust,' he said, 'are at the bottom of it all.' The size of Saltaire, about forty-four hundred persons by 1880, no doubt restored some of the social restraints common to the tight rural community of the past and absent in the dense populations and the anonymity of the city. Salt exercised aesthetic controls, too; clutter and ungainly lines of washing were not allowed to interrupt the clean lines of street and building. But he did not, like other model community builders, introduce natural forms of beauty. Perhaps there was no need. Saltaire was situated alongside the river Aire, facing the rural scenery of the Yorkshire moors, with easy access to the wilds of Shipley Glen. During the late sixties, however, a fourteen-acre park was completed across the river from the town, with provision for various forms of recreation.

Akroydon, started in the early sixties, was located on a hillside near Halifax. In the matter of architecture Akroyd, with his archaic social vision, hoped to heal 'the breach in feeling between the ancient village and the new industrial age.' In contrast to the Neo-Renaissance architecture which suited Salt's more functional tastes, Akroyd employed a domestic Gothic style native to the area. 'Intuitively this taste of our forefathers,' he declared, 'pleases the fancy, strengthens house and home attachments, entwines the present with the memory of the past.'[28] The attachment of the worker to Akroydon was also strengthened by the privilege of home ownership, still rather rare among city workers, with Akroyd himself supplying the down payment if necessary. The houses were compactly arranged around a central park and a monument on which was inscribed a long quotation from Wordsworth's 'Excursion.' Outside the plan there were allotments for vegetables.

The Crossley West Hill Park Estate, begun two years after Akroydon, by attaching the gardens to the individual homes, carried further the desire to reconcile the life of the rural cottage and the industrial city.[29] The estate was, moreover, on the edge of Halifax, in an area which, along with the Crossley mills, possessed other evidences of the family's efforts to enhance the beauty of the neighborhood. The large 'People's Park' was the most conspicuous. It was, as Sir Francis expressed it, an attempt 'to arrange art and nature that they should be within the walk of every working man in Halifax; that he shall go and take his stroll there after he has done his hard day's toil, and be able to get home again without being tired.'[30] His Romantic faith in the restorative powers of Nature may have been excessive. But the remark expressed rather well the way in which the impulse to take flight into the countryside could also be redirected toward the task of interrupting the grim march of an economically impelled urban expansion.

In time that march would engulf all of these communities. Even Saltaire, the most distant of the villages, was gradually surrounded by the advancing suburbs of Bradford and Shipley. By then, however, the cohesion of purpose and design which had marked its birth had long since been lost. Indeed, that cohesion nowhere long survived the passing of the men from whose will and vision it derived. But the Bradford-Halifax villages exemplified well two important features of the mid-Victorian years—the emergence of a new social will in the industrial cities of the North and the strong tendency to seek in rural experiences and natural forms the means of urban regeneration.

These features were also prominent in the two major examples of the planned industrial community in the late-Victorian years—Bournville and Port Sunlight. Like their predecessors in the West Riding they originated in the dissatisfaction of manufacturers with living and working conditions in large cities.[31] In 1879 George Cadbury and his brother decided to take their chocolate works out of Birmingham into the country four miles away. A few years later W. H. Lever, a soap manufacturer in Liverpool, began to develop his plan for Port Sunlight on the marshy flats of the Mersey in Cheshire. Both men chose their sites with a careful eye for their economic utility, but they also took advantage of the aesthetic possibilities of the surrounding countryside. Bournville settled easily into the gentle contours of its landscape but the architects at Port Sunlight had a more difficult time, for their imposed forms did not harmonize readily with an area dominated by low tidal flats and ravines. The two villages presented, however, the distinct social and aesthetic outlooks of their founders.

Lever and Cadbury leaned in opposite directions in the continuing tension between the Utilitarian and the Romantic orientations toward the city. Lever had a more positive view toward urbanization. He believed that men preferred to live in cities or towns because they provided the greatest scope for personal development and social interests. At Port Sunlight he provided living conditions which were clean, healthy, and efficient, and instituted the social controls, absent in the large cities, necessary to maintain these conditions. He also made room in his conception for values which were rural and traditional. There were allotment gardens for those who wanted them, and he encouraged his builders to draw on the vernacular cottage architecture of Lancashire and Cheshire. Port Sunlight was still, moreover, a village; it was designed to recover something of the former intimacy of social intercourse and the closer bonds between employer and employee.

Cadbury's point of view, more nostalgic and sentimental, was expressed at Bournville in his preoccupation with the garden plot. Not only was there a garden adjacent to each house, it was also often planted before the tenant moved in. Cadbury advanced many arguments on behalf of the garden. He believed that work in the garden would counter the excessive specialization of factory labor. He was convinced that young and old alike would profit from contact with the soil, fresh air, and growing things. And there were also utilitarian, patriotic, and social arguments. Produce from the garden would add a significant increment to the householder's income; work in the garden would improve his capacity for military service; and the very presence of the garden would strengthen family life by keeping the husband away from the pub. Cadbury was too gentle and tolerant a man to impose his principles heavy-handedly, though in Bournville as in the other model industrial communities it was not difficult to find signs of moral paternalism. It would be inaccurate, however, to see Cadbury's paternalism as mainly archaic. Like Lever he had left the city in order to regain a control over the working and living environment, and the communal regulations instituted at Bournville and Port Sunlight represented significant moments in the growth of a British tradition of town planning.

The builders of the model communities were insisting on the value of the rural landscape and the village ideal even as they identified themselves with the advancing economic technology and organization which promoted the growth of cities. Their attempts to combine the realities of industrial and urban development with the advantages of the countryside represented, in fact, a characteristic Victorian response to the problem of the city. Indeed, some of the most prominent Victorians believed or at least hoped that this pattern would become the normal development of the great cities. 'Years of thought' had convinced Charles Kingsley that the only remedy for the 'worst evils of city life' was a 'complete interpenetration of city and country.' He foresaw the city going out into the country in the form of model lodging-houses—'huge blocks of buildings!' which would be situated in the hills or areas outside the present cities so as to benefit from the 'free and pure country air.'[32] Francis Newman, in contrast, urged a more radical interpenetration of city residences with rural spaces. 'It is not parks and gardens that we want in the middle of the town to serve merely as lungs,' he wrote in 1881, 'but rather rustic fields to be manured and cropped, at short intervals, under public and compulsory rules.'[33] Shortly after the turn of the century H. G. Wells predicted that the great population centers would disperse; the old terms 'town' and 'city' would become obsolete as people spread out more thinly into what he called 'urban regions.'[34]

> As one travels through the urban region, one will traverse open, breezy, 'horsy' suburbs, smart white gates and palings everywhere, good turf, a grandstand shining pleasantly; gardening districts all set with gables and roses; holly hedges, and emerald lawns; pleasant homes among heathery moorlands and golf links, and river districts with gayly painted boat-houses peeping from the osiers. Then presently a gathering of houses closer together, and a promenade and a whiff of band and dresses, and then, perhaps, a little island of agriculture, hops or strawberry gardens, fields of gray-plumed artichokes, white painted orchard, or brightly neat poultry farm . . . The same reasoning that leads to the expectation that the city will diffuse itself until it has taken up considerable areas and many of the characteristics, the greenness, the fresh air, of what is now the country leads us to suppose also that the country will take to itself many of the qualities of the city. The old antithesis will, indeed, cease, the boundary lines will altogether disappear; it will become merely a question of more or less populous.

A few years before Wells wrote his prospectus of urban development, Ebenezer Howard presented a version of 'interpenetration' which, through its impact on twentieth-century thinking about the city, demonstrated the enduring appeal of this late-Victorian conception. Howard's idea of the 'garden-city' represented in fact a climactic statement of the Victorian attempt to overcome the opposition between the city and rusticity. Howard's life and his social vision provide a recapitulation of a number of the patterns which have been surveyed in this essay.

Born in the lower-middle classes in London at mid-century, Howard entered the section of urban society which Kingsley saw as the city's most distinctive creation—the clerks. Before he was twenty, however, he took flight from London, emigrated to the American Midwest, and attempted a new life as a farmer. The venture failed and after a period in Chicago he returned to London and to his work as a clerk. During the eighties and nineties he exemplified a development in British life through which many energetic young men of the lower-middle classes in the cities were being drawn into a new social, political, and cultural awareness. Howard was influenced by the same writers and inspired by many of the same hopes as Shaw, MacDonald, Webb, Wells, Blatchford, and other figures who would play important roles in the making of the Socialist movement and the alteration of the Liberal party. Howard, like his more famous contemporaries, transformed the myriad ideas of this late-Victorian urban milieu into a distinctive vision. It first appeared in a small book, *Tomorrow*, published in 1898.[35]

Howard's vision of the future city was deeply Romantic. For the key to the urban problem was 'how to restore people to the land' and bring them once again into a redeeming contact with the countryside.[36]

> The country is the symbol of God's love and care for man. All that we are
> and all that we have comes from it. Our bodies are formed of it, and by it are
> we warmed and sheltered. On its bosom we rest. Its beauty is the inspiration
> of art, of music, of poetry. Its forces propel the wheels of industry.
> It is the source of all health, all wealth, all knowledge. But its fulness of
> joy and wisdom has not revealed itself to man. Nor can it ever, so long as
> this unholy, unnatural separation of society and nature endures.
> Town and country '*must be married*', and out of this joyous union will spring
> a new hope, a new life, a new civilization.

The vision owed much to Ruskin. At the head of the first chapter Howard placed a passage from *Sesame and Lilies*, in which Ruskin called for limited and compact towns 'kept in proportion to their streams and walled round' with a 'belt of beautiful garden and orchard round the walls, so that from any part of the city perfectly fresh air and grass and sight of far horizon might be reachable in a few minutes' walk.' This was the basic form of Howard's proposed garden-city. It would be carefully planned on a thousand-acre site within a six-thousand-acre area, restricted to a population of thirty thousand, and carefully balanced between agriculture and industry. The ownership and control of the entire urban district would be vested in the municipality itself, which would then lease out plots to private individuals; the unearned increments from the growth and prosperity of the town would return to the community. The archaic, almost medieval, cast of Howard's conception indicated his debt not only to Ruskin but also to Carlyle and especially Morris. Howard was not a Socialist in any strict meaning of the term. But like many of the romantic Socialists of the nineties he showed a cooperative and communitarian bent which rested on a Tolstoy-like faith, freed from older theological notions of sin and evil, in the power of man to break through into a full realization of the ethic of the Sermon on the Mount.[37]

Yet Howard's essentially Romantic outlook was qualified by a Utilitarian and practical strain. He drew on the emigration proposals of Gibbon Wakefield and the ideas of John Stuart Mill and Alfred Marshall—all working out of a Utilitarian tradition of social and economic thought—designed to relieve the congestion of the cities. And, while Howard's hatred of London was apparent, he accepted the necessity of cities. He rejected the reactionary views of Morris in favor of a frank acceptance of technological society. Indeed, Howard was something of a tinkerer himself, constantly engaged in inventing, and given to mechanical metaphors. He likened the town and country to opposing magnets and each person to a 'needle.' What was needed was a more powerful magnet than the existing city in order to redistribute the population in a 'spontaneous and healthy manner.' The garden-city was such a magnet, and Howard's book demonstrated how it could be constructed.

It was a curious and inconsistent mixture of Victorian traditions, put together by a mind of disarming naivety. And yet Howard's conception exhibited a remarkable vitality. It generated sufficient economic support to launch the garden-cities of Letchworth and Welwyn, and through its impact on the thought of Conservative and Labour party leaders it helped to shape the planning of the new towns constructed after World War II. In his naivety Howard had given a fresh and appealing expression to those impulses toward flight and reconciliation which ran so strongly through the Victorian middle-class sensibility.

These impulses, and the patterns of thought and behavior which gave form to them, were a relatively small part of the Victorian response to the city. That response came mainly, after all, from men and women who were neither in flight nor in a state requiring reconciliation, but who struggled throughout the Victorian period to come to terms with the immediate problems and possibilities of the urban situation. There were in all the Victorian cities self-correcting activities, or what Leon Marshall in his skillful survey of early nineteenth-century Manchester referred to as the 'integrative tendency of the industrial urban milieu.'[38] In the long run, developments inherent in the urban process itself have been far more decisive, however one may judge the outcome, than the efforts of the Victorian visionaries to alter the pattern of city growth.

Yet those who took the more drastic course of flight or envisioned radical alternatives to existing cities have a continuing significance, not only for students of Victorian society, but for a generation which has still failed to resolve many of the issues posed by the broader process of urbanization in the West. That process has continued to resist the growth of social policies sufficiently strong or enlightened to humanize the large cities of Europe and America. Meanwhile, the summons of the city to develop new conceptions of personal worth, new forms of human association, and new patterns of cultural life, has scarcely kept pace with the power of the city to dissolve traditional values and allegiances. To this summons the Victorians who rejected their cities were, however dimly, responding.

Notes

1 *The Writings of Ruskin*, ed. E. T. Cook and Alexander Wedderburn (1908), XXXIV, p. 205.

2 For a discussion of British anti-urbanism see Ruth Glass, 'Urban Sociology in England,' *Readings in Urban Sociology*, ed. R. E. Pahl (1968), pp. 63–73. Victorian attitudes toward the city are surveyed in Asa Briggs, *Victorian Cities* (1963), ch. 2.

3 The responses of some prominent Victorian writers to the machine are examined in Herbert L. Sussman, *Victorians and the Machine* (Cambridge, Mass., 1968).

4 Élie Reclus, 'The Evolution of Cities,' *Contemporary Review*, lxvii (1895), 276, and Lord Rosebery, quoted by Ebenezer Howard, *Garden Cities of Tomorrow* (1902), p. 42.

5 H. G. Wells, *Anticipations* (New York, 1902), pp. 55–6.

6 H. D. Traill, 'In Praise of the Country,' *Contemporary Review*, lii (1887), 479–81.

7 Élie Halévy, *The Growth of Philosophical Radicalism* (1934), p. 478.

8 Simmel's essay, 'Metropolis and Mental Life,' is reprinted in Kurt Wolff, *The Sociology of Georg Simmel* (Chicago, 1950). The Wirth essay, 'Urbanism as a Way of Life,' is reprinted in Louis Wirth, *On Cities and Social Life, Selected Papers*, ed. Albert J. Reiss, Jr (Chicago, 1964).

9 For a useful survey of the literature on Romanticism see René Wellek, 'Romanticism Re-examined,' in *Romanticism Reconsidered*, ed. Northrop Frye (New York, 1963).

10 See the essays in these volumes by G. Robert Stange and U. C. Knoepflmacher. Also see John Henry Raleigh, 'The Novel and the City: England and America in the Nineteenth Century,' *Victorian Studies*, xi (1968), 277–90, and Leo Marx, 'Pastoral Ideas and City Troubles,' in *The Fitness of Man's Environment*, Smithsonian Annual Symposium, ii (1968), 119–44.

11 See R. A. Forsyth, 'Nature and the Victorian City: The Ambivalent Attitude of Robert Buchanan,' *ELH*, xxxvi (1969), 382–415; 'The Victorian Self Image and the Emergent City Sensibility,' *University of Toronto Quarterly*, xxxiii (1963), 61–77; 'The Conserving Myth of William Barnes,' *Victorian Studies*, vi (1963), 325–54; 'Evolutionism and the Pessimism of James Thomson (BV),' *Essays in Criticism*, xii (1962), 148–66; 'The Myth of Nature and the Victorian Compromise of the Imagination,' *ELH*, xxxi (1964) 213–40.

12 Walter Ong, 'Evolution, Myth and Poetic Vision,' *Comparative Literature Studies*, iii (1966), 1–20. For a psychoanalytical approach to the regression of the Victorian literary imagination see Norman Holland, 'Psychological Depths and Dover Beach,' *Victorian Studies*, Supplement to ix (1965), 5–28.

13 James Anthony Froude, *Thomas Carlyle, The First Forty Years* (New York, 1910), II, pp. 195, 361.

14 *Writings of Ruskin*, XX, p. 113.

15 See the section on the 'rustic vision' in W. H. Armytage, *Heavens Below* (1961), pp. 289–440.

16 Quoted by Armytage, op. cit., p. 359.

17 Armytage, op. cit., provides the fullest account. I have drawn additional details from the movement's journal, *The New Order*.

18 See Nellie Shaw, *Whiteway* (1935).

19 *The New Order*, June 1898, August 1899.

20 See Armytage, op. cit., pp. 385–401.

21 Sidney Pollard, *The Genesis of Modern Management* (1955), pp. 197–208. Also see his article, 'The Factory Village in the Industrial Revolution,' *English Historical Review*, lxxix (1964), 513–31.

22 J. F. C. Harrison, *Quest for the New Moral World* (New York, 1969), pp. 56 ff.

23 See Armytage, op. cit., pp. 215–23. Also Harrison, op. cit., pp. 32–6, 57–9.

24 See the discussion of Buckingham in William Ashworth, *The Genesis of Modern British Town Planning* (1954), pp. 123–6. There is a diagram of Buckingham's city in Helen Rosenau, *The Ideal City, Its Architectural Evolution* (1959), pp. 137–9. Buckingham sets out his plan in *National Evils and Practical Remedies* (1849).

25 Walter Creese, *The Search for Environment* (New Haven, Conn., 1966), pp. 13–60. I have not had the benefit of the recent study by Colin and Rose Bell, *City Fathers, The Early History of Town Planning in Britain* (1970).

26 Akroyd, according to a contemporary account, 'is very desirous of keeping up the old English notion of a village—the squire and the parson, as the head and centre of all progress and good fellowship; then the tenant farmer; and lastly the working populations.' Quoted by Creese, op. cit., p. 43.

27 My account of Saltaire draws mainly on Robert K. Dewhirst, 'Saltaire,' *Town Planning Review*, xxxi (1960), 135–44.

28 Quoted by Creese, op. cit., p. 43.

29 James Hole, *The Homes of the Working Classes* (1866), provides a contemporary description of Akroydon and the West Hill Estate.

30 Quoted by Creese, op. cit., p. 52.

31 My discussion of Bournville and Port Sunlight draws mainly on Creese and Ashworth, op. cit.

32 Charles Kingsley, *Sanitary and Social Lectures and Essays* (1880), pp. 215–16.

33 Francis Newman, 'The Barbarisms of Civilization,' *Contemporary Review*, lx (1881), 476.

34 Wells, *Anticipations*, pp. 68–9.

35 Slightly revised, it was re-published in 1902 as *Garden Cities of Tomorrow*.

36 Ebenezer Howard, *Garden Cities of Tomorrow*, p. 48. For a discussion of Howard's work in relation to other modern urban visionaries see Leonard Reissman, *The Urban Process* (New York, 1964), pp. 39–68.

37 Ch. 10 of Howard's book is headed by a long quotation from Tolstoy's *The Kingdom of God is Within You*.

38 Leon S. Marshall, 'The Emergence of the First Industrial City: Manchester, 1780–1850,' *The Cultural Approach to History*, ed. Caroline Ware (New York, 1940), pp. 140–61.

VIII Epilogue

38   The Way We Live Now

H. J. Dyos and Michael Wolff

To all appearances the Victorian city is now virtually a thing of the past. The actual city, the physical monument, that pile of solemn but exuberant shapes that has been for so long and for so many people the very emblem of urbanity is at last melting away. Those massive realities that once commanded the ground in such numbers are being furiously singled out as trophies by conservationists or reduced to rubble by property developers. The urban past has never had a very secure future. The ponderous and ever-accumulating mass that no Victorian generation could perceive as complete has remained intact, it now seems, for only the first two post-Victorian generations. Only now therefore can we be conscious of the whole cycle. We can even sense the shape of some of the things to come. The technologies that underpinned these first cities of the industrial era are being superseded by others with quite different implications, and the processes that built up such high densities in those cities may even be going into reverse. For the urban mass no longer generates forces of attraction directly proportionate to its density. Density, though susceptible to almost limitless engineering possibilities, is no longer a necessary condition of urban intercourse. No human settlement in Britain lies beyond the city's range. The perspective we got of the Victorian city from the ground is therefore a finite, tentative, historical one. In such respects it seems no longer contemporary.

Yet, if we look harder, what we see is something rather different. Our evolving cities are still governed by the ways in which earlier occupants of the ground divided their fields or settled their estates, and the centres of commercial gravity if not their circumferences are commonly still fixed where earlier convenience required. Inertia is part of the dynamic of urban change: the structures outlast the people who put them there, and impose constraints on those who have to adapt them later to their own use. The fact is that the framework of growth, however hastily devised, tends to become the permanent structure, and to be held fast by property titles and convenient routines that can seldom be undone at a stroke. Even urban clearways are making surprisingly clean-cut slices through the elaborate residues of nineteenth-century growth. Within that arena the relative standing of neighbourhoods changes less than that of their salient as a whole, largely because housing produced in the mass must conform to standard specifications and be occupied by correspondingly uniform social groups. Then, as now, the social framework devised by developers, whether with eyes open or shut, becomes embodied in the structures themselves and is a bequest no less lightly given away than a more strictly entailed inheritance. Even when neighbourhoods decay such covenants remain, for houses built for the servant-keeping classes decline inexorably into whole districts of one-roomed dwellings. The configuration of the ground, the prevailing wind, the means of locomotion, the location of the gas-works, the precise whereabouts of cemeteries, golf-courses, schools, hospitals, parks, sewage works, factories, railway sidings, and shopping centres— all amenities whose distribution tended to be settled at an early stage of urban growth—are ineradicable influences on subsequent patterns of urban life. To that extent what happened in the nineteenth century plainly matters still.

There is nevertheless a more fundamental reason for regarding the Victorian city as belonging to the present. The growth of cities in the nineteenth century not only marked the beginning of a period in which so many of the aches and aspirations of modernity were first felt but the beginnings of processes which have had since to be seen in unified global terms. It was then that the urbanization of the world first gathered momentum and a framework for the contemporary history of man became perceptible. It was then that the inherent characteristics of our present social condition became actual in comprehensive terms: the city as the environment of the social mass could be seen taking shape and its ultimate possibilities visualized. Britain was the first to complete this modern transformation, just as she had been the first to undergo the industrialization of her economy, and represents therefore the prototype of all industrializing, urbanizing, modernizing societies. Here, indeed, was a foretaste of the way we live now.

What unifies these Victorian and latterday phases of urbanization as a universal experience is, above all, the sharp awareness of multiplying numbers, of man by the million, of whole systems of growth points, of a prospect of cities without end, and of a political arithmetic that must embrace them all. The obsession with numbers which characterized the social investigations of the Victorians themselves was almost congenitally determined and the inevitable prefix to so many of their judgments, as to ours. For the unprecedented acceleration in the growth of the population gave to cities for the first time in six thousand years a totally new role. No longer dominated by the numbers and capacities of those living off the land, these new aggregates could generate their own energies, impose their own demands on the countryside, and develop a new culture. Though they first grew more by taking people off the land than by breeding them, British cities were, by the end of the nineteenth century, coming within reach of maintaining their numbers for themselves. That transition, presently followed by other European countries and their overseas settlements, was within a century being made throughout the world, under constraints not basically different from those prevailing in Victorian Britain. Once again the control of death preceded the control of birth, though with much more dramatic effect in our own time. Urbanization among the emerging countries in the third quarter of the twentieth century has become in consequence a simple function of population growth and the cities the decanters for agrarian poverty. Perhaps one-third of the world's population already live in urban places of some description and even the most halting extrapolations would bring this urban concentration to something like that of Britain in mid-nineteenth century before the end of the twentieth. Britain alone could be described as predominantly urbanized by the end of the nineteenth century; already the most advanced countries are comparably so; the rest are following behind.

The Victorian city is part of our culture in a still more general sense. The promise of modernity, however distant, is abundance and equality, the material and ideological products of the dual revolution in England and France in the late-eighteenth century, and the city is its exponent, if not its redeemer. Here, new opportunities for communication intersected, new patterns of human relationships began to form, new institutions sprang up, new values, sensations, conventions, and problems were expressed; while older perceptions, behaviour, and limitations changed their pitch or disappeared altogether: everywhere a flickering failure of absolutes in ideas and attitudes, a stumbling advance towards free association between people, a more democratized urbanity. The humanization of mankind became for the first time a momentarily imaginable possibility, even if the petty realities of individual lives too often remained stubbornly gross and seemingly hopeless. In the modern world, we contend, the path of progress has been an urban one. The very existence of the city has been a demonstration of the capacity, however uneven, to lift human effort beyond subsistence and a preoccupation with the brute facts of mere existence; and the urbanization of the whole population is an index, however crude, of rising standards of material welfare. Here is a measure of our civilization.

What is so conspicuous in the city is the gathering of vast crowds of ordinary people for everyday purposes, something hitherto impossible. It has by the last quarter of the twentieth century become such a routine of urban life that deserted streets betoken something wrong. Perhaps nothing illustrates better than our joint numerosity the affinities we have with the first modern city-dwellers of Victorian Britain and the differences that exist between us both and the generations that went before. Modern man is essentially thick on the ground. On the lower and darker side of pre-Victorian respectability what we see is a vast ignorable pit of shadows from which few ever emerged to make any distinguishable mark of personal achievement.

The traditional urban mob was personified only by its ringleaders and remained essentially anonymous and undifferentiated. The modern aspect of the crowd militant as we see it developing early in the nineteenth century included implicit disciplining, the dawning of a new sense which the urban working classes began to have of themselves, and the heightened sensitivity felt by the ruling classes towards popular unrest. What also began to happen at the same time, though barely perceptibly, was something that can only be described as a process of faces appearing in the crowd.

In conditions of urbanization, a dominant culture is always faced by new groups of people previously thought of as beneath consideration. The close juxtaposition of rich and poor, of the mercantile and servile elements in urban society, which had persisted since ancient times, only began to break down in England during the eighteenth century and it was not until the nineteenth that this disintegration became at all marked. Before this time the allocation of social space was determined more than anything by the divisions between crafts and between townsmen and aliens, though the accumulation of private property, the award of public honours, and the expanding scope for conspicuous consumption had also helped to draw such groups apart. The analogue to this process was the suburb, at one time a no-man's-land for all that was disreputable—dungheaps, gallows, stinking trades, bloodsports, low taverns, prostitutes, thieves, and the mob—and at another the means for keeping such things at a safe distance. It represented at once a glint of mutual perception between the middle and working classes and a blindfolding of their social relations wherever it happened at least during the nineteenth century. This mutual recognition and distancing has supplied many of the images and realities probed in this book. To that extent they are symptoms of the Victorian city as a phenomenon of modernity, of the capacity for sustained awareness of other societies or cultures. What the Victorian city began to do by way of opening up the possibilities of the dual revolution was to permit this sustained awareness of differences in social conditions to take place. Here, almost for the first time, was some visible prospect of the advancement of whole classes but, more than that, a stirring consciousness among the lower ranks of society of the removable differences in the quality of human life. It was the city which enabled such things to be seen.

It was not an ennobling experience through and through. For the working classes had been thought of as sub-human for so long that it was almost natural for them to display, or for their superiors to see them as displaying, their reputation for animality—brute strength, brute instincts, brute deserts. The faces in the crowd were as often as not seen to be marked by strong drink, violent passions, degraded character. The great unwashed were socially unclean, too, and the typical attitudes first expressed to this emergent group by those above them were also stereotyped—a blend of contempt, fear, hate, and physical revulsion. Threaded into such attitudes was a mixture of awe and envy derived from general knowledge of the profligacy of the working classes, itself partly dependent on the common, if not first-hand, observation that prostitutes, like prize-fighters, ordinarily came from the lower orders. The pornography of the period assumed that all servants, shop girls, and

896

labourers were inexhaustibly libidinous. To the respectable classes such things spoke of an almost totally unregenerative condition redeemable in very few instances and then only by acts of grace and forgiveness. They remained deeply gloomy about the lower reaches of the Victorian city and conceived the notion of a residuum to cover the unknowable poor. Slum missionaries brought back their tales of horror and pathos from this nether world as if they had been journeying in darkest Africa. They were for the most part, as it seems now, both deaf and dumb, incapable of hearing the authentic tongue of the voiceless or of telling the prisoners how to escape. The poor man was in truth a long way from paradise and the rich man from longing for his touch, but the gulf between them was no longer fixed and the city itself was capable of closing it in other ways.

The Victorian city was essentially a great leveller, even though it began, like the railway, by hardening the categories of those using it and directing them into socially segregated compartments. To be sure, its population was distributed more explicitly in this regard by night than it was by day, and there were always incongruous pockets of privilege and understood affiliations. Urban society developed diversity, too, so that the range of its modes of behaviour and particular attributes became almost a function of size. Yet the city was above all the province of anonymity and the nondescript. In it the individual's identity tended to be smudged and made less distinguishable; he could lose himself in the crowd, become part of the common multiple, disappear. This is precisely what he could never do in village society. There, understood roles, systems of deference, and clear lines of demarcation designating ground to be covered or avoided, still expressed the animus of feudalism. The difference between the city and the village was not so well established everywhere, especially in the nascent industrial cities, where the lords of the loom and the mine were creating conditions in which individuals could be marked men and their lives could be moulded to new forms of serfdom. The general tendency was altogether less idiosyncratic and more organizational. The urban masses were in truth composed, not of social atoms, but of individual human beings. Yet for purposes of social action, as for mutual perception, it was the extra-familial grouping, the collective label, more generalized identification of ordinary needs, more abstract reference to people as such, that now began to pass into common parlance about the city. Inhospitable to the stranger, unyielding even to its own, the city was nevertheless a great force towards equalizing its inhabitants.

There we are bound to pause. The characteristics of urban life are still in far too great a flux to be quite sure what we are seeing. That the Victorian city leapt beyond the accepted human scale and imposed on its citizens new patterns of association does not mean that it was utterly inhumane. The inhumanities of the Victorian city derived largely from the crisis of numbers and of personal identity which it provoked, though the problems of coming to terms with the new environment itself were not all solved with human regard. Far from it, but it does seem clear that the curse of privatism, the headlong and egocentric pursuit of private wealth and power irrespective of the hurt done to others, was sufficiently inhibited in Britain to avoid complete havoc. Municipal responsibilities were shouldered sometimes with a casualness that was almost venal but in ways that headed off the worst aspects of what Tawney called the tyranny of functionless property. It is also not difficult to see that the loosening tissue of personal ties that bound up each pre-urban community implied release as well as insecurity. The blank wall that faced the newcomer to the city cannot obscure the fact that the whole civilizing process, of which the city is the most powerful agent, has involved a lengthening of the lines of human communication, not a constriction of them. Larger networks of social intercourse had already breached the city walls in feudal times; the city of the industrial era merely extends these possibilities to all and sundry.

The passage to urbanity which the Victorian city offered was not contrived exclusively within itself but evolved to a degree that is seldom acknowledged from rustic beginnings of various kinds. Modern industry began to a large extent outside the existing towns and moved into them only when water-power gave way to steam or the entrepreneurial advantages of an urban location outweighed those of an industrial colony. As it did so the whole economic matrix began to shift from country-dominated town to town-dominated country. In the context of a larger transition still, the city as a type was shifting in power and influence from the condition it had known under the Renaissance as a state literally of its own to that of an organ of the nation-state—the administrative, economic, and cultural hub of a much larger whole. Beyond this focus again lies the control mechanism of the metropolis and a system of world cities. The self-evident physical and social mass that we see in any one of them does little of itself, however, to distinguish its generic urbanity. The mere possession by a place of a given number of digits to denote size, density, or employment is not enough to clinch the matter, and the sociological hypothesis that urban life is characterized by impersonal, secondary, and contractual relationships has been submitted to surprisingly few historical tests. We know next to nothing even of kinship patterns in the Victorian city, let alone its more elaborate community structures and the sense of belonging or separation that permeated its various social layers. What we can perhaps perceive is that the Victorian city was a hybrid growth, drawing one strain from its commercial past, another from its rustic environment, a third from its own necessities. Its interpenetration by a rural culture, planted there by its country-bred citizens and kept alive by force of family upbringing and an apparently unquenchable longing for some semblance of pastoral bliss, is one of its fundamental, if elusive, aspects. The functional affinities of the city with villages and market towns remains a persistent, if sometimes surprising, one, even though we see in the seasonal movements of the wayfaring classes and their less nomadic counterparts, the landed squirearchy of London's West End, some evidence of how the life of the city and the village was periodically mediated.

In the nineteenth century no English city had severed itself from its rural connections. The largest of them still conducted extensive back-yard agriculture, not merely half-a-dozen hens in a coop of soap-boxes, but cow-stalls, sheep-folds, pig-sties above and below ground, in and out of dwellings, on and off the streets, wherever this rudimentary factory-farming could be made to work. The larger the city the more liable was it to contain these things in relative abundance, not simply because there was some kind of living to be made out of it but because the gobbling up of the countryside had meant swallowing villages whole. Their old way of life slowly eroded but its associations were often deliberately reinforced to generate a new kind of village atmosphere. Moreover, in back-streets of a certain formation or social composition, lived little communities that knew themselves so well, that shared their common identity with such jealous pride, that for all ordinary purposes of life they comprised a village of a sort that was not basically distinguishable from those surrounded by fields. The old face-to-face relationships more readily associated with the traditional village were implanted in the heart of the Victorian city in its slums. That kind of situation is palpable still, just as the transient and impersonal characteristics commonly attached to the city itself are to be seen nowadays transfixing so many suburbanized and urban-tenanted villages far from its doors. The recognized territorial and sociological distinctions between the city and village which held good, with certain exceptions, in the nineteenth century are in some sense now being turned inside out, and clear dividing lines between them are becoming even more difficult to draw.

The sense of community—at once enlivening and stifling—that was once carried in the very marrow of village society has never quite deserted the cities, even though it occurs only in small pockets, for poverty and injustice tend to bind those that share them, and the city tolerates both. It even succeeds in perpetuating uncharacteristically urban events, like the August bank holiday walk by thousands together out of Leeds onto the moor, which goes on under its own momentum and a desire by those taking part to declare a common identity. There are, too, latent capacities which are brought into the open only in an emergency, like that secret understanding between complete strangers that de Tocqueville recalled in his *Souvenir* when he wrote of a kind of morality peculiar to times of disorder, and a special code for days of rebellion. A city like Liverpool has its own language of the walls, not merely through its babble of posters or the forlorn *graffiti* of telephone kiosks and public lavatories, but in the rank subtleties inscribed with chalk or aerosol spray on its most public surfaces. This is city talk, not country: urban walls were endless, disowned almost, open invitations to fly-posting and sloganizing alike. In the village street virtually every brick was a personal belonging, every act public knowledge, all information by word of mouth.

So much of this sub-literary world of the city's streets must remain inscrutable. Of the millions of yards of street ballads hawked for sale before the last quarter of the nineteenth century only scraps survive, but they probe for us other ephemeralities, and give us a glimpse of the imaginative content of a million brief lives, a view from the gutter, and in terms of popular appeal an anticipation of the tabloids of our own time. The true verbal and graphic equivalent of urbanism is journalism proper, the best lens we have for a close-up of the Victorian city, of its disconnections, intimacies, conflicts, aberrations, incidents—of its whole symbiotic continuum and style. The concentration of people in such numbers created for the first time the readership on the required scale to launch newspapers and magazines in their thousands and to give vent to opinion and interests of almost every kind. Here is the earliest running commentary we have on what it felt like to have the city burgeoning out at such speed and throwing up issues of such novelty and discord. What is omitted from those pages and by whom is as important to the reading of them as it is to the reading of history itself, and what is pictured and how is as revealing of their readers' receptivity as the magazine advertisement of today. The hard social substance of the city was at first filtered by convention and only gradually was the distance interposed between readers and reality by such means foreshortened, chiefly by humour, and finally disposed of altogether. The city street and the city poor ultimately came into some kind of focus—the faces in the crowd even began to wear recognizable expressions—and the actual distance between them and the well-to-do was paced out, if only vicariously. It was an object-lesson patiently conducted though perhaps barely half-learned. Even a man as humane and concerned with the predicament of the poor as Mayhew could not, despite his own best feelings and judgments and the insuppressible empathy of his interviewing, prevent himself from setting the poor at a distance. This he did partly by confusing the poor in general with the most depressed and degraded of their number, and partly by stressing the discontinuities in the hierarchy of the urban working class. What the illustrated magazines and the products of the slum presses teach us is that there are attitudes toward the city and its mechanisms of amelioration that we have hardly begun to clarify, and that the contents of a whole uncatalogued archive of material are as yet unread.

A good deal of this book has been concerned with the art of reading the city. That art is architectonic and archaeological as well as literary. If we want simply to evoke the urban landscape that we have lost we must not only lift off the encrustations of the motor age but re-invest with their own coarse original grain the places which we have veneered over. There are severe limits to this, for so many of the incidental noises, smells, colours, sense of place have gone beyond recall: who, for instance, even now remembers the vivid litter of bus tickets on London pavements, the sulphurous flavour of a pea-souper, the horsy din and strain of Ludgate Hill? If we want to be more than mere resurrectionists and breathe some life and meaning into the language of the city we must expect to study it with all the senses. Engels is in this respect a surer guide than Augustus Hare simply because he had the imagination to search for an organizing principle behind the masquerade of the principal streets and to look for it, not among the historical relics that were dotted about, but in the conditions of contemporary life and work that bore testimony everywhere he looked. Behind the assertive commercial façade of Manchester he detected a deeper meaning than the simple proposition that it pays to set up shop where customers collect. The fuller message of these streets to him was that, without conscious design, the city had revealed its inherent structure in the organization of its own space. It was as if Mill's civilizing process, whereby pain and suffering are kept from the sight of rulers, had preserved Manchester's merchant princes from the spectacle of the means of their own enrichment. The workers' quarters were concentrated always round the back, and their presence expressed by mere allusion.

That is no longer such a startling discovery. The relationships between the slums and suburbs of other cities are now seen to have been equally expressive of their respective production functions, and the capacity of the upper classes to spin a web of communications that enabled them to commute to the centre without being encumbered by needless distractions no less developed. The precise topography of the paths along which they moved and the extent to which the separation of the classes was adjusted behind them as they pushed further afield can be read with little difficulty from any residue still left on the ground—the symbolic language of domestic architecture and the more explicit references in the lay-out, naming, and furnishing of the streets. In every place there is some such little tale to tell, of what it was that once meant so much to people living there, of how such things could never last, and why it all had to be repeated, more or less, just along the road. And if we could work down the social heap to its very bottom the stones would have much more to say, of how much had to be done just to keep going, of how the numbers grew and the room shrank, of how the ground eventually opened and swallowed everything up. Thankfully, we cannot read many of these hieroglyphs any longer for ourselves, for the sight of them eventually brought about their destruction, but we can see the urban decay organically following the urban growth, the wretchedness mirroring the contentment, the poverty subtending the riches, and recognize in it all a structure, not of chaos, but of logically related parts.

Behind these landmarks and structures lie private worlds of thought and feeling that we are conscious though not cognizant of, things that matter in any understanding of the Victorian city but which are buried too secretly to be explored by ordinary historical means. The quality of urban life which we seek cannot, except in a very limited sense, be quantified. It says something for the affective conditioning of large areas of Victorian life that the Victorians' chief sense of fact was numerical, that they should have felt compelled to quantify their qualitative statements about urban society above all. The city has always had an inexorable calculus. But numbers have no feelings and are at best mere explanatory agents. What satisfactions and hurts, what sense of community or deprivation, what consciousness of beauty or ugliness or merely of environment and actuality, stirred those very countable people we long to know. Our best informants are those imaginatively concerned with the contemporary scene, above all the novelists, who penetrate sometimes the very structure of feeling and prevailing values, and persuade us of the truths they utter, though without a shred of proof. What they have to tell us about the impact of urbanism as an all-enveloping experience is perhaps less direct and sure-handed. What they offer over all is simply evidence about the city in a new form.

In evaluating what the Victorian novel has to say about the city we have to keep reminding ourselves of its underlying predisposition to treat its subject as a hostile environment, and to recognize that this is an aspect of the tendency of the high culture of Victorian Britain to express a pre-urban system of values. There was, Jerome Schneewind pointed out some years ago, a fundamental Victorian debate that straddled formal philosophy, styles of consciousness, and imaginative expression— a debate that surfaced, for example, in the arguments between Intuitionists and Utilitarians about ethics. For the former, good behaviour was the result of sympathy and emotional understanding; for the latter, of wise calculation and the observation of agreed rules. Each had its appropriate setting. Intuitionism suited small groups, typically friendly and personal; Utilitarianism, large groups, typically strangers. We might say that the one was the ethic of the family and the village, and the other of the crowd and the city. The tradition that had been brought into life by the family and the village had in turn suffused Victorian literature and helped thereby to sharpen the concept of the city as its destroyer, the enemy of culture and moral values, the ally of anarchy, materialism, and the deadly sins. What the Victorian novel tried to do in fact was to redeem the city, to domesticate the unruly scene, to personalize the dreadful anonymity, to make a family of the crowd. The popular bardic literature of the great Victorian writers was committed to the task of drawing the whole literate nation into a kind of cousinship that embraced especially its newly awakening and wayward members. The great authors—a type of uncles and aunts reinforcing the parental roles of Queen, Church, and Ministerial Government— ventured dutifully into city streets where the squire and the justices no longer could and policemen seldom dared to go, to exhort and reassure, to embrace and admonish its unfamiliar types, and to offer the souls that might be saved an avenue of escape.

What we see in this whole literary enterprise—as in drawing and painting, too, though their social outlines are far less clear and much slower to form—is a gigantic effort by creative artists to adapt to the highly original scenes and experiences of the city without abandoning the categories set for them by the pre-urban generations that had gone before. They approached it from the outside, on the basis of intuitionist values, quintessentially humane, paternally structured, and pastoral—the counter-part to the painters' pre-occupation meanwhile with landscape and portraiture and of the dramatists with melodrama and urban stereotypes. The idea of an urban nature, so exultantly proclaimed by Lamb at the very beginning of the century in a famous letter to Wordsworth, was unthinkable among creative artists for a very long time. The standard of comparison implicitly invoked instead was the tamed nature of rural England. Some of the most revealing passages come at points where the transition from this supposedly earthly paradise to the city occurred—as, for example, in the initiation of the country-born into the shock city of Manchester in *Mary Barton*, or, in reverse, in the intrusion of the city-bred villainy of Mr Slope into the pastoral peace of Barchester. Sometimes such gaps were too wide to be bridged, even in the imagination. The emotional difficulty offered to sensitive newcomers to the city comes out with unexpected force in the tendency shown by the working-class poets of the shock city itself to increase their use of their beloved country dialects to echo their rural past rather than to portray the social realities on their own doorsteps.

By the end of the nineteenth century this choice of attitudes towards the city had become less invidious, and the city as an object for the expression of continuous art, unflawed by rustic associations, much more readily accepted. Dickens was the necessary pioneer. He had always been the great exception, not so much in his preference for any city-derived values (for he thought he was as anti-Utilitarian as anyone), but in his inability to forgo the city as a locale or to disguise his excitement at its vitality and diversity. He was as incapable of deserting it as Hardy was of developing any empathy with it. No one has been able to match his subtle and unerring command of the curious social topography of London, and the intensity of his love affair with his mass readership has about it a preview of modern encounters between popular artist and mass audience.

But there was no general readiness on the part of novelists, poets, and painters to make such materials as Dickens's so unaffectedly urban until the 1890s. Perhaps the city at that time occupied a place in the English imagination similar to that of sex and was similarly repressed. It was not something to celebrate with open joy but remained within the Puritan tradition a source of guilt and alarm. The fact of the city, as of manufacturing industry, was never accepted with any real trust, and both have been contested suspiciously ever since. The world's first nation of city-dwellers remains its most reluctant. The release of imaginative energies to interpret the city in the nineties was part of a general, albeit partial, adjustment to the facts of life— an adjustment which also included a somewhat more realistic attitude towards the mysteries of sex, a correlation which no English Baudelaire quite portrayed. Yet for the first time a whole generation of artists was growing up that was not afraid of the city, and could make it appear something less than a monster.

The very note of terror and obscurity that had been struck so insistently by some of the massed structures of the earlier part of the century was being subdued, their awful rhetoric stilled. Once the demands of commerce and industry could no longer be met by designs drawn exclusively from the ancient or the rural world the city became the theatre of opposing aesthetic forces, and the looming shapes of railway termini, viaducts, factories, and penitentiaries were deposited relentlessly among them. These vast structures owed rather more to eighteenth-century inspiration than to the modular possibilities of cast iron and reinforced concrete, but during the latter part of the nineteenth century the beginnings of a great rebuilding of business quarters, in London at least, helped to open the way for a more cosmopolitan explosion of architectural style than the city had ever known. Meanwhile, a more domestic theme wound persistently on—the declension of the villa of the country gentry into the suburban semi-detached. Here many things met. Among the railway suburbs of the largest cities the dominant influence by the end of the century was unquestionably the picturesque, a fitting architecture perhaps for an urban middle class still dreaming dreams of landed possessions and of a haven for the family. The suburb was a supremely ambivalent invention and therefore a key element in the history of the Victorian city. It was fitting that the architectural forms of the suburb should have diverged from the purely urban, for the suburb was, after all, a gesture of non-commitment to the city in everything but function. Even the functions might be abstracted in garden cities or model villages or communitarian colonies, and the cities abandoned to their shame. The final phase of the Victorian city was in several respects a fugitive one, not only for the middle classes retreating to their laburnum groves but for the masses following behind in workmen's trains or making for emigrant ships instead.

The whole of this long Victorian episode in the process of urbanization might well be thought of as a kind of training that society had to undergo. It was not a simple programme of adaptation to changed circumstances or a new environment, but a fundamental restructuring of attitudes, the acquiring of new social techniques, the acceptance of new codes of discipline, the pursuit of new opportunities. The sequence was neither settled in advance nor even known and it could never be considered complete. The adjustment proceeded at a different rate for different groups, and it involved the absorption of new knowledge not merely by the young but by whole classes. The process was literally that of acculturation to an urban way of life. We see symptoms of it on every level, not merely in the daily flows along commuter corridors or in the scrupulous calculations of site values, but in the cell-like accretion of municipal powers, the sectarian shepherding of the poor, the organization of charity, the rise of spectator sports, the widening scope for enjoyment and freer association. In this larger education the pub occupied a peculiar and versatile position, a place in which many roles were played and adaptations made, both in the institution itself and in those frequenting it. We do not even now recognize all the subtleties of this socialization. More generally, however, the most fundamental lesson that urban society had to learn was that it could no longer neglect to take account of the implications of its own actions, to remain ignorant of itself. It had on the contrary to undertake a continuous series of acts of self-knowledge, to adopt an empirical stance, and to develop, implicitly or explicitly, some kind of social policy.

Natural laws, which under divine authority had acquired benevolent force in the eighteenth century, no longer served. That God made the country and man the town did not immediately annul the proposition that Nature should flourish everywhere: that, for example, even the city slum was a natural phenomenon, the proper habitat of the ever-present poor, and that the nomads whom Mayhew found filtering through them could be seen as belonging to a lower natural order, ordained to their underworld. Yet the inclination to refuse to tamper with so-called natural forces was not in tune with technology and the encouragement it gave to rising expectations of life. The rash assault of the railways (to take Wordsworth's phrase) and the vastly more blatant interference with the natural landscape by industrialization itself developed the overriding notion that permanence was giving way to change and

904

helped to place cultural emphasis on functional achievement and human responsibility. The conscience of the new rich became an index of the relative deprivation of the urban poor. The sense of crisis that began to pervade the whole social condition was entirely man-made.

The concept of Nature as a cultural force was therefore inclined to become by the middle of the century tremendously confused and its moral and spiritual sanctions neutralized—though not, as we now know, extinguished. We see Victorian urban society wrestling with its lessons, to be or not to be natural, especially when it came to the drains. 'It might be worthwhile, sometimes, to inquire what Nature is,' remarks Dickens in a familiar passage in *Dombey and Son*, 'how men work to change her, and whether, in the enforced distortions so produced, it is not natural to be unnatural.' He then takes the reader into a slum and reflects on outraged Nature, ending thus: 'When we shall gather grapes from thorns, and figs from thistles; when fields of grain shall spring up from the offal in the bye-ways of our wicked cities, and roses bloom in the fat churchyards that they cherish; then we may look for natural humanity and find it growing from such seed.' The authority of a traditional concept is plainly giving way to a recognition of the primacy of human needs. The old idea that there was something natural about suffering, something to be tolerated, begins to yield to the new idea that men should use whatever political and technical skills they can command to raise the level, demeanour, and satisfactions of human life in the city—use it to lift the potential of its whole culture. The city, which was being spoken of in mid-Victorian England as the burial pit of the human species, was a promise that these things could be done—a promise that partly explains the Liberals' positive enthusiasm for the city, as it does the reformation of urban government they sought so zealously.

For the time being the city was a laboratory of public medicine. Discovering the pathological and psychological consequences of human density, and learning the fearful capacity of some of the most mortal diseases to bridge the widest social gaps, took a dreadful time—the etiology of typhus even was not fully known until the twentieth century. No emergent society ever proceeded so far in urbanizing itself with such little established fact about its implications, nor ever will: the rate of urbanization among the emergent countries of today rests substantially on the control of crude death-rates first demonstrated when the major advances in public health were being pioneered in the nineteenth century. At first sight, such progress was matched by what now seems to have been a shocking perversity in actually taking the first steps—taking due pains to collect drinking water where sewers did not discharge, to build sound homes, and to eat enough good food. Such lessons were in fact part of a much larger syllabus that included the training of a multiplying band of experts of every kind to make and run a machine fit for living in, and to adapt the human being to the machine—to make of him, conceivably, a sentient machine himself. In fact a more systematic and fundamental interference with the behaviour of the individual was required than any earlier society had known. Small wonder therefore that the political counterpart to the psychological challenge of delivering up full personal freedom of action which urban society required, namely centralization, should have been so bitterly fought over in mid-century. However, within another generation sanitary reform had been so completely accepted within the canon of municipal improvement that the only real issue was, not how much public money should be spent, nor what men should do to stay alive, but who should pay. Ridding the cities of their slums eventually meant rehousing their occupants below cost and taxing the country for most of the difference. The ultimate lesson of urbanization is that no one is left out.

That was also the ultimate message of the Church, framed as it still was by rural conventions, dispensing a pastoral role. For Nonconformists, who had never encountered in the towns the resistance to their teachings that they had found in the country, the cities were a larger opportunity, which they seized, and from which they proselytized with varying success the industrial valleys of Wales and the North of England. The Established Church was an older institution, bereft in the cities of its natural setting and of its single-handed job of saving the souls of people who had so little hope of bodily ministrations. It now found the emphasis given by urbanization to the relief of bodily suffering a chalice difficult to refuse. The settlement movement must have seemed to many at the time the noblest gesture engendered by the late-Victorian city, but its Christian purpose tended to be enlisted in practice more in the cause of bestowing middle-class attitudes on the poor than in enrolling them in the company of heaven. Whatever adamant of religious feeling of their own the urban working classes had, they did not seek their salvation in Protestantism. The forces that activated any such allegiances were inclined rather to be derived from deep cultural or ethnic roots which, in the circumstances of the city, meant in turn forming enclaves of streets and, in circumstances recognized widely in the cities of the twentieth century, providing bases for ghettoes or for urban guerilla warfare.

As we read over again the chapters in this book and stare at its pictures two things in particular stay in our minds. One is the ready familiarity one feels with the Victorian city—its people, its problems, the basic patterns of its life—almost as if it belonged to a long-remembered experience of one's own. In several senses, as we have been saying in these closing reflections, this is almost literally true. The camera, through which we perceive so much of our own world, has transmitted to us a whole gallery of likenesses and recognizable shapes that draws us and them involuntarily closer. At one end of the gallery these celluloid images actually spring into action or their living representatives tell us face to face how it all was, and the sense of identification and unbroken continuity becomes irresistible, sometimes movingly so. These impressions are not in themselves out of place, for the distinction our language draws between past and present is not so tidily sustained in our perception of the world about us, and standard intervals of chronological time are not the only way of structuring human experience. Yet we must beware of becoming involuntary ventriloquists and of mixing up the scenery, of failing to distinguish between the things that once were and no longer are, of creating fantasy. One of the main tasks of this book has been to clarify the sources of the images of contemporary life that were current in the Victorian city and to set them against the prevailing realities of the time. It is as well to remember that although their world is part of our own, ours was never part of theirs.

The second abiding impression we now have is not of having brought our subject to a finish but of having barely opened it up. There is a great deal yet to be said about the Victorian city itself, especially in regard to the definition and mutations of an urban culture in all parts of Britain and among British possessions overseas, not to mention those larger inter-cultural studies that are needed before we can take proper stock of the way the twentieth century has shaped, and been shaped by, the rise of the city. Despite its length, this book has scarcely done more than touch on these things, reminding us how incomplete our agenda have been. The list that might be compiled—more in the hope of stimulating others' researches than exculpating our own—of topics that might have augmented our picture of this process unfolding includes the formal and more general aspects of education itself, the penal system, philanthropy, the press, and the wider provincial aspects of almost everything. More than this, however, we have become more acutely aware than we were at the start of the innumerable intersections between the disciplines engaged in this work and of the extent to which the fields of Urban History and Victorian Studies are complementary to each other. The vast intercontinental transfers of population and power and the formation of large nation-states in the nineteenth century have made that period one of the hinges of history, and the enormous strides taken by industrialization and technology have made its cities the template for the whole structure of modern life. The city has set us the task of examining everything that has claimed to be permanent and essentially human in our heritage and systems of values. What we see therefore as urgent in the serious study of these things is some means of connecting the humanistic and the scientific traditions that are available. We shall then be able to interpret more subtly and richly the impact of urbanization on the minds and spirits of city-dwellers and learn more intimately the secrets both of the way we live now and of the way we might live.

Notes on Contributors

Mrs Sybil E. Baker, B.A., is Warden of University Hall and Lecturer in History at the University College of North Wales, Bangor. She is reading for a Ph.D. at Queen's University, Belfast on Edwardian Belfast and for a D.Phil. at Oxford University on ethnic violence in industrialized urban societies, particularly a comparison of Belfast with similar German and American cities.

J. A. Banks, M.A., is Professor of Sociology at the University of Leicester and chairman of its Victorian Studies Centre. He is also chairman of the British Sociological Association. His major writings include: *Prosperity and Parenthood* (1954), *Industrial Participation* (1963), *Marxist Sociology in Action* (1970), and *Feminism and Family Planning in Victorian England* [with Olive Banks] (1964). He is currently engaged in studies of trade unionism from a sociological point of view, and of the employment of British sociologists, 1952–70.

G. F. A. Best, M.A., Ph.D., is Sir Richard Lodge Professor of History in the University of Edinburgh. He was the British editor of *Victorian Studies* (1958–68), and among his writings are *Temporal Pillars* (1964), *Shaftesbury* (1964), and *Mid-Victorian Britain* (1971) in The History of British Society series edited by E. J. Hobsbawm. He is now writing a history of the international law and the national customs of war since the later Enlightenment.

Michael R. Booth, B.A., M.A., Ph.D., is Professor of English and Director of Drama in the University of Guelph, Ontario. His major publications include *English Melodrama* (1965) and the anthologies *Hiss the Villain* (1964), *Eighteenth Century Tragedy* (1965), and the five volumes of *English Plays of the Nineteenth Century* (1969–72). He is currently at work on a book to be entitled *The Victorian Spectacular Theatre.*

Asa Briggs, M.A., B.Sc.(Econ.), is Professor of History and Vice-Chancellor of the University of Sussex and sometime Visiting Professor in the National University of Australia and the University of Chicago; he has received a number of honorary degrees. He has served on numerous academic and public councils, including the Council of the Royal Economic Society and the Council of Industrial Design. He is Chairman of the Committee of Enquiry into the role of the Nurse, of the Standing Conference for Local History, and of the National Selection Panel for Film Festivals, and serves as Governor of the British Film Institute, President of the Sussex Archaeological Society, and member of the Council of the Royal Economic Society and of the Victorian Society. Among his many writings on social history are *Victorian People* (1954), *The Age of Improvement* (1959), *Victorian Cities* (1963), and three volumes in the History of Broadcasting in the United Kingdom (*The Birth of Broadcasting* (1961), *The Golden Age of Wireless* (1965), and *The War of Words* (1970)). He has edited a number of other works, including *Chartist Studies* (1959) and *The Nineteenth Century: The contradictions of progress* (1970), and is now engaged in a study of Victorian history with particular reference to the history of Victorian things. He continues to be occupied with the social history of the nineteenth and twentieth centuries.

G. F. Chadwick, B.Sc. Tech., M.A., Ph.D., F.R.T.P.I., F.I.L.A., is Professor of Town and Country Planning in the University of Newcastle upon Tyne. He spent seven years with various English planning authorities, and five years working on one of the London New Towns. His major writings include: *The Works of Sir Joseph Paxton, 1803–1865* (1961), *The Park and the Town: Public landscape in the nineteenth and twentieth centuries* (1966), and *A Systems View of Planning: Towards a theory of the urban and regional planning process* (1971). He is now studying dynamic simulation and other methods of modelling regional and ecological systems, especially in the developing countries of Africa.

Philip Collins, M.A., is Professor and Head of the Department of English in the University of Leicester and has held visiting professorships at University of California and Columbia University. His many writings include *Dickens and Crime* (1962), *Dickens and Education* (1963), and *The Impress of the Moving Age* (1965), and he has edited *Dickens: The Critical Heritage* (1971) and written an introduction to George Augustus Sala's *Twice Round the Clock* (1971) in The Victorian Library of Leicester University Press. Deeply interested in professional theatre, he is currently serving on the Arts Council of Great Britain Drama Panel, is the Secretary of the Leicester civic theatre, and has had a play produced in London (Mermaid Theatre, 1965). He is a member of the Advisory Council of the Victorian Society. He is at present studying Charles Dickens's journalism, and aspects of Victorian stage-performances.

H. J. Dyos, B.Sc.(Econ.), Ph.D., F.R.Hist.S., is Professor of Urban History in the University of Leicester. He has published numerous articles on the history of London, and has written *Victorian Suburb: A study of the growth of Camberwell* (1961), *The Study of Urban History* (ed.) (1968), and [with D. H. Aldcroft] *British Transport: An economic survey from the seventeenth century to the twentieth* (1969). He is the founder and editor (since 1963) of the *Urban History Newsletter*, and chairman of the editorial board of The Victorian Library of Leicester University Press. He is also on the editorial boards of *Victorian Studies* and the *Journal of Transport History*, and is general editor of the series Studies in Urban History. He is a member of the Council of the Economic History Society, the Executive Committee of the Victorian Society, the Council of the London Record Society, and the Urban Research Committee of the Council for British Archaeology. He is now working on a book to be entitled *London, 1870–1914: The world metropolis* for the History of London series, and is continuing his research on the social structure of Camberwell in the nineteenth century; he is also occupied with preparing the new *Urban History Yearbook*, due to appear at the beginning of 1974.

Celina Fox, B.A., is a graduate student at St Antony's College, Oxford, where she is reading for a D.Phil. She is currently engaged in a study of nineteenth-century graphic journalism.

David Francis, B.Sc.(Econ.), is Purchasing Assistant for BBC TV Purchased Programmes and is responsible for selecting foreign language feature films and documentaries. He previously served as the Deputy Curator of the National Film Archive, as Secretary of the Society for Film History Research, and as Television Acquisitions Officer at the British Film Institute. At present, he is engaged in a study of the social and technical history of the magic lantern, of which he has a substantial private collection, as well as many thousands of nineteenth-century slides and stereo cards.

Derek Fraser, B.A., M.A., Ph.D., is Lecturer in History in the University of Bradford. He has written *The Evolution of the British Welfare State* (1972) and numerous articles on urban history, especially in the journals of local historical societies. He is now working on an analysis of the political structure of Victorian cities for a book entitled *Urban Politics in Victorian England.*

Sheridan Gilley, B.A., Ph.D., is Tutor in Ecclesiastical History at St Mary's College in the University of St Andrews. He has published several articles on Irish immigrants in London during the nineteenth century and has contributed to the 1970 volume of *Studies in Church History*, and to a collection of essays on English attitudes towards race edited by Dr Colin Holmes for publication in 1973. He is now continuing his researches into the nineteenth-century Irish immigration into England, and is engaged in a study of religious attitudes to the Victorian city, and of the pro-Papal Irish riots in London.

Brian Harrison, M.A., D.Phil., F.R.Hist.S., is Fellow and Tutor in Modern History and Politics, Corpus Christi College, Oxford, and has held a visiting professorship at Michigan State University. He is the editor of *History at the Universities* [with George Barlow] (1966), and the author of *Drink and Sobriety in an Early Victorian Country Town* [with Barrie Trinder] (1969), and of *Drink and the Victorians* (1971). He has also published several articles on nineteenth-century English social and political history. He is currently studying aspects of recreational, religious, and working-class history in Britain during the nineteenth and twentieth centuries.

Gertrude Himmelfarb, Ph.D., is Professor of History in the City University of New York and has held a number of fellowships and awards. Among her publications are *Lord Acton: A study in conscience and politics* (1952), *Darwin and the Darwinian Revolution* (1959), *Victorian Minds* (1968), and editions of Acton, *Essays on Freedom and Power* (1948), Malthus, *On Population* (1960), and J. S. Mill, *Essays on Politics and Culture* (1962). She is now engaged in a study of changes in the conception of poverty and the identity of the poor.

E. D. H. Johnson, B.A., Ph.D., is Chairman and Professor of English at Princeton University. Among his publications are *The Alien Vision of Victorian Poetry* (1952), *Charles Dickens: An introduction to his novels* (1969), and the anthologies *The World of the Victorians* (1964), and *The Poetry of Earth: A collection of nature writings from Gilbert White of Selborne to Richard Jefferies* (1966). He is presently working on studies in the genre school of English painting.

P. J. Keating, B.A., D.Phil., is Lecturer in English in the University of Edinburgh. Among his publications are *The Working Classes in Victorian Fiction* (1971), *George Gissing: New Grub Street* (1968); and editions of *Matthew Arnold: Selected Prose* (1971), *Working Class Stories of the 1890s* (1971), and *A Child of the Jago,* in which he included a biographical study of its author, Arthur Morrison. He is now writing a social history of the English novel, 1875–1914.

John Kent, M.A., Ph.D., is Reader in Historical Theology in the University of Bristol, having previously entered the Methodist ministry and taught in theological colleges. Among his publications are *The Age of Disunity* (1966), *From Darwin to Blatchford* (1967), and the Pelican Guide, *Historical Theology* [with J. Danielou and A. H. Couratin] (1969). He is now engaged in a study of the relations between working-class religion and politics in the nineteenth century in the West of England.

U. C. Knoepflmacher, A.B., M.A., Ph.D., is Professor of English at the University of California at Berkeley. He has published *Religious Humanism and the Victorian Novel: George Eliot, Walter Pater, Samuel Butler* (1965), *George Eliot's Early Novels: The limits of realism* (1968), and *Laughter and Despair: Readings in ten novels of the Victorian era* (1971), and has written an introduction to F. W. Newman's *Phases of Faith* (1970) in The Victorian Library. He was written many articles on major Victorian writers, and is presently working on a book-length study of the relationships and differences that link Romantic poetry to Victorian poetry and fiction.

Eric E. Lampard, B.Sc.(Econ.), Ph.D., is Professor of History at the State University of New York at Stony Brook, formerly Professor of Economic History and Adjunct Professor of Urban and Regional Planning at the University of Wisconsin and sometime Visiting Professor at Stanford, Harvard, and Yale Universities. He is a member of the Social Science Research Council's Committee on Urbanization, of the National Research Council Advisory Panel to U.S. Department of Housing & Urban Development, and of the Committee on Urban Economics for Resources for the Future, Inc. Among his numerous publications are *Industrial Revolution: Interpretations and perspectives* (1957), *The Rise of the Dairy Industry* (1963), *Regions, Resources, and Economic Growth* [with Harvey S. Perloff] (1960). He is now engaged in the study of the economic and demographic aspects of urbanization in the U.S.A.

Lynn Lees, M.A., Ph.D., is Assistant Professor of History at Mount Holyoke College and formerly a Fellow at the Joint Center for Urban Studies of Harvard University and Massachusetts Institute of Technology. She is a member of the Urban Studies Committee of the Council for European Studies, and contributed a paper to *Nineteenth-Century Cities,*

912

eds Stephan Thernstrom and Richard Sennett (1969). She has recently completed a study of the June Days uprising of 1848 in Paris and is now writing a book on Irish migrants in London during the nineteenth century.

George Levine, B.A., M.A., Ph.D., is Professor and Chairman of English at Livingston College, Rutgers University, and has been Visiting Professor at the Victorian Studies Centre in the University of Leicester. He is the author of *The Boundaries of Fiction* (1968), and the editor of *The Art of Victorian Prose* [with William Madden] (1968), and of *The Emergence of Victorian Consciousness* (1967). He served as co-editor of *Victorian Studies* (1959–68). He is now engaged in a study of conventions of realism in the novel, with the focus on developments within the Victorian novel.

Steven Marcus, B.A., M.A., Ph.D., is Professor of English and Comparative Literature at Columbia University and sometime Visiting Professor to the Victorian Studies Centre at the University of Leicester. Among his numerous writings are *Dickens: From Pickwick to Dombey* (1965), *The Other Victorians* (1966), and *Engels, Manchester and the Working Class*, which is due in 1972. He has also edited *The World of Fiction* (1962) and, with Lionel Trilling, Ernest Jones's *Life and Work of Sigmund Freud* (1961). He is Associate Editor of the *Partisan Review*.

G. H. Martin, M.A., D.Phil., F.R.Hist.S., is Reader in History and Dean of the Faculty of Arts in the University of Leicester and has twice served as Visiting Professor of History at Carleton University, Ottawa. He is a member of the International Commission for the History of Towns and the Urban Research Committee of the Council for British Archaeology, and serves as a consultant on the conservation of historic towns. Among his publications are *Colchester from Roman Times to the Present Day* (1959); *The Town* (1961); *The Royal Charters of Grantham, 1463–1688* (1963); *The Early Court Rolls of Ipswich* (1964); and an edition of Gross's *Bibliography of British Municipal History* (1966). He has recently completed [with S. C. McIntyre] a *Bibliography of British and Irish Municipal History* (1972), and is developing studies of the administration of the medieval English borough and of urban property in the thirteenth and fourteenth centuries.

David E. H. Mole, M.A., Ph.D., is Chapel Warden of Legon Hall and Lecturer in Church History in the Department for the Study of Religions at the University of Ghana, Legon. He was previously Chaplain and Research Fellow of Peterhouse, Cambridge. He has published several articles on Victorian church history, and is now working on the history of the Church in West Africa. He is also continuing his studies of the churches in Victorian cities, particularly Birmingham.

Victor E. Neuburg, M.Ed., is Lecturer in Local History in the School of Librarianship, the Polytechnic of North London, and was Visiting Professor of Popular Literature at State College, Buffalo, in 1970–1. Among his publications are *Chapbooks: A bibliography* (1964), *The Penny Histories* (1968), and *Popular Education in England* (1971). He has recently completed *The Past We See Today*, and is currently continuing his research on popular literature and its relation to popular education. He is also occupied with a study of English radicalism, 1688–1791.

Donald J. Olsen, B.A., M.A., Ph.D., is Professor and Chairman of History at Vassar College and has been Visiting Professor in the Victorian Studies Centre in the University of Leicester. He has written *Town Planning in London: The eighteenth and nineteenth centuries* (1964). He is at present studying the Norfolk estate in Sheffield, 1770–1870, the Eton College estate in London in the nineteenth century, and more generally, the growth of Victorian London.

Stanley Pierson, B.A., A.M., Ph.D., is Professor of History at the University of Oregon. He has written *Marxism and the Origins of British Socialism: 1881–1900* (1972), and has published several articles on various aspects of British Socialism in the late nineteenth century. He is now writing a sequel to the earlier study of British Socialism, which will deal with the impact of the political process on Socialist ideology before 1914.

D. A. Reeder, B.Sc.(Econ.), M.A., Ph.D., is Head of the Department of Education at the Garnett College of Education. He is editor of the journal, *The Vocational Aspects of Education*. He has contributed to *The Study of Urban History*, ed. H. J. Dyos (1969) and to *A History of Fulham*, ed. P. D. Whitting (1970). He is now working on a comparative study of Victorian suburbs to be published as *The Genesis of Surburbia* in the Studies in Urban History series. He is also occupied with the history of middle-class and technical education in the nineteenth century.

George Rosen, B.Sc., M.D., Ph.D., M.P.H., is Professor of the History of Medicine, and Epidemiology and Public Health, at Yale University, and has received a number of distinguished awards. Since 1957 he has been the editor of the *American Journal of Public Health*. In 1946, he participated in founding the *Journal of the History of Medicine* and was its editor until 1952. He has written a great many papers on various aspects of medicine and medical history. Among his major writings are: *Die Aufnahme der Entdeckung William Beaumonts durch die europäische Medizin* (1935); *The History of Miners' Diseases* (1943); *The Specialization of Medicine* (1944); *Fees and Feebills: Some economic aspects of medical practice in 19th century America* (1946); *400 Years of a Doctor's Life* [with Beate Caspari-Rosen] (1947); *A History of Public Health* (1958); and *Madness in Society* (1968). He has also translated and edited a number of other works. He is an Honorary Fellow of the Royal College of Medicine and currently President of the Society of the Social History of Medicine and Vice President of the International Academy of the History of Medicine. He is continuing his studies in the relations between urban life and health problems, the history and sociology of psychology, the development of biomedical research in the United States, and the evolution of health institutions.

Raphael Samuel is Tutor in Social History, Ruskin College, Oxford, and editor of the History Workshop publications.

Richard L. Schoenwald, A.B., A.M., Ph.D., is Professor of History at Carnegie-Mellon University. He has written articles and reviews on Freud, and has published *Freud: The man and his mind* (1956), and an anthology *Nineteenth-Century Thought: The discovery of change* (1965). He is now working on a biography of Herbert Spencer, and is continuing his researches into the application of psychology to history.

914

Jack Simmons, M.A., F.R.S.L., F.R.Hist.S., is Professor of History in the University of Leicester and formerly Beit Lecturer in the History of the British Empire at Oxford University. He has written a large number of books and articles, chiefly on local and transport history, which include: *Southey* (1945), *Parish and Empire* (1952), *Livingstone and Africa* (1955), *New University* (1958), *The Railways of Britain* (1961), *Britain and the World* (1965), *St Pancras Station* (1968), *Transport Museums* (1970). He is President of the Leicestershire Archaeological and Historical Society, and a member of the Advisory Council of the Science Museum, London. He is now continuing his researches into the history of Leicester and into the development of the railway in England and Wales. He is editor and co-founder of the *Journal of Transport History*.

G. Robert Stange, Ph.D., is Professor and Chairman of English at Tufts University and has held a visiting professorship in the University of Chicago. He is the author of *Matthew Arnold; The poet as humanist* (1967), and the editor [with W. E. Houghton] of *Victorian Poetry and Poetics* (1959). He is now engaged in a study of the relations between literature and the visual arts in the nineteenth century.

Sir John Summerson, C.B.E., F.B.A., F.S.A., A.R.I.B.A., M.A., is Curator of Sir John Soane's Museum, London, and has held several academic appointments. He has served on various commissions and committees concerned with architecture and historic buildings, chiefly the Royal Commission on Historical Monuments, the Historical Manuscripts Commission, and the Listed Buildings Committee of the Ministry of Housing and Local Government, and was chairman of the National Council for Diplomas in Art and Design (1961–70). His major writings include *John Nash, Architect of George IV* (1935), *Georgian London* (1945), *Heavenly Mansions* (1949), *Sir John Soane* (1952), and *Architecture in Britain 1530–1830* (1953). His current subject of research is Victorian London.

Nicholas Taylor, M.A., is an architectural historian who has lectured on Victorian architecture at the Courtauld Institute of Art, the Cambridge University School of Architecture, the Architectural Association School of Architecture, and the Polytechnic of Central London. He has now been appointed to the staff of the Greater London Council's *Survey of London*. Also a freelance journalist and broadcaster, he served as the Environmental Correspondent of the *Sunday Times*, and is currently the compiler and introducer of the BBC Radio-4 programme 'This Island Now'. He is the founder-chairman of the Lewisham Society, and serves as a Labour councillor of the London Borough of Lewisham. Among his publications are *St. Peter's Bournemouth* (1962), *Cambridge New Architecture* (1964), *Monuments of Commerce* (1968), *Looking at Cathedrals* (1968), and *Roskill: A debate on values* (1971). He has published many articles in the technical and lay press, and has recently completed *The Village in the City* to be published shortly, and *Collins Guide to English Country Houses* to be published in 1973. He is presently working on a biography of Sir Edwin Lutyens, and is continuing his research on Hampstead and other garden suburbs.

Paul Thompson, M.A., D.Phil., is Reader in Sociology (Social History) in the University of Essex. His writings include *Socialists, Liberals and Labour: The struggle for London 1885–1914* (1967), *The Work of William Morris* (1967), and *William Butterfield* (1971). He is a member of the Executive Committee of the Victorian Society. He is at present writing *The Edwardians* in The History of British Society series edited by E. J. Hobsbawm.

Eric Trudgill, B.A., M.A., Ph.D., is Lecturer in Drama at Hatfield Polytechnic. He is now preparing his doctoral thesis, 'Madonnas and Magdalens: The origins and development of Victorian sexual attitudes in society and literature', for publication.

Martha Vicinus, B.A., M.A., Ph.D., is Assistant Professor of English at Indiana University. Since 1970 she has been editor of *Victorian Studies*. She has written on working-class literature in the nineteenth century, and has edited two anthologies which are now in the press: *Suffer and Be Still* and *Broadsides of the Industrial North*. She is now completing a book on the literature, songs, and music of the nineteenth-century working class, and is also engaged in a study of the image of women in Victorian pornography.

Anthony S. Wohl, B.A., Ph.D., is Associate Professor of History at Vassar College, and has been a visiting lecturer in the Victorian Studies Centre in the University of Leicester. He has published several articles on working-class housing in Victorian and Edwardian London and has edited *The Bitter Cry of Outcast London* (1970). He is presently completing a book on the housing of artisans and labourers in Victorian and Edwardian London for the Studies in Urban History series.

Michael Wolff, B.A., M.A., Ph.D., is Professor of English and Victorian Studies at the University of Massachusetts, Amherst, formerly of Indiana University, and sometime Fellow of the Center for the Humanities, Wesleyan University. He has been founding co-editor, editor, and chairman of the editorial board of *Victorian Studies*, and is the founding editor of the *Victorian Periodicals Newsletter*. He is also the founder and President of the Research Society for Victorian Periodicals. He is a member of the Advisory Council of the Victorian Society and an Advisory Editor of the *Wellesley Index to Victorian Periodicals, 1824–1900*. He has edited [with Philip Appleman and W. A. Madden] *1859: Entering An Age of Crisis* (1959), and [with John North and Dorothy Deering] the forthcoming *Waterloo Directory of Victorian Periodicals*. He is presently working on problems in the history of Victorian journalism and in the teaching of Victorian studies.

Index

Index

Figures in italic type indicate illustrations; those in bold type indicate principal entries. Superior figures refer to notes.

Index by **Marie Forsyth**